THE
ENDURING DEBATE

CLASSIC AND CONTEMPORARY READINGS
IN AMERICAN POLITICS

Ninth Edition

THE
ENDURING DEBATE

CLASSIC AND CONTEMPORARY READINGS
IN AMERICAN POLITICS

Ninth Edition

Edited by
David T. Canon
John J. Coleman
Kenneth R. Mayer

W. W. NORTON & COMPANY
Celebrating a Century of Independent Publishing

W. W. Norton & Company has been independent since its founding in 1923, when William Warder Norton and Mary D. Herter Norton first published lectures delivered at the People's Institute, the adult education division of New York City's Cooper Union. The firm soon expanded its program beyond the Institute, publishing books by celebrated academics from America and abroad. By midcentury, the two major pillars of Norton's publishing program—trade books and college texts—were firmly established. In the 1950s, the Norton family transferred control of the company to its employees, and today—with a staff of five hundred and hundreds of trade, college, and professional titles published each year—W. W. Norton & Company stands as the largest and oldest publishing house owned wholly by its employees.

Editor: Pete Lesser
Editorial Assistant: Tichina Sewell-Richards
Associate Project Editor: Selin Tekgurler
Production Manager: Brenda Manzanedo
Composition: Westchester Publishing Services
Manufacturing: Core Publishing Solutions

Permission to use copyrighted material is included at the back of the book.

ISBN: **978-0-393-42756-1** (pbk.)

W. W. Norton & Company Inc., 500 Fifth Avenue, New York, NY 10110
wwnorton.com
W. W. Norton & Company Ltd., 15 Carlisle Street, London W1D 3BS
1 2 3 4 5 6 7 8 9 0

Contents

PART II   Institutions

PART III   Political Behavior: Participation

CHAPTER 10   Elections and Voting   358

CHAPTER 11   Political Parties   390

Preface

We compiled this reader with two goals in mind. The first was to introduce students to some of the classic works in political science, so that they could see how these historic arguments connected to the broad themes generally covered in college-level introductory courses in American government. We also introduce students to classic primary-source documents. Combining these classic readings with more modern selections is a good way to show how the main themes in American politics endure. As the title suggests, many contemporary issues are similar to what earlier generations of Americans—and the framers themselves—had to work out through existing political institutions and processes, or by changing those institutions and processes when they proved inadequate.

Our second goal was to expose students to debates on important contemporary political controversies. These debates give students examples of high-level political argumentation, showing how scholars and other expert commentators probe, analyze, and confront competing arguments. In some of the debates, authors directly challenge each other in a point/counterpoint format. In most of the debates, the authors do not directly engage each other, but rather present a range of arguments on opposing sides of issues. For example, in this edition we have added new debates on the COVID-19 pandemic in a federal system, "cancel culture," the role of the United States in the world, and more. Our hope is that students will see the value of real argument and become discerning consumers of political information.

Finally, in addition to editing down selections to a manageable length while preserving the authors' central arguments, the book includes two pedagogical devices: the introduction to each article and debate, and discussion questions at the conclusion to each piece or cluster. The introductions provide students with the context of a given article or debate while briefly summarizing the arguments. The questions provide the basis for students to engage with some of the main ideas of an article.

About the Editors

David T. Canon is professor of political science at the University of Wisconsin, Madison. His teaching and research interests focus on American political institutions, especially Congress, and racial representation. He is the author of several books, including the introductory text *American Politics Today* (with William Bianco), now in its eighth edition; *Actors, Athletes, and Astronauts: Political Amateurs in the United States Congress; Race, Redistricting, and Representation: The Unintended Consequences of Black Majority Districts* (winner of the Richard F. Fenno, Jr. Prize); *The Dysfunctional Congress? The Individual Roots of an Institutional Dilemma* (with Kenneth Mayer); and various articles and book chapters. He served a term as the Congress editor of *Legislative Studies Quarterly*. He is an AP® consultant and has taught in the University of Wisconsin AP® Summer Institute for U.S. Government and Politics since 1997. Professor Canon is the recipient of a University of Wisconsin Chancellor's Distinguished Teaching Award.

John J. Coleman is dean of the College of Liberal Arts and professor of political science at the University of Minnesota. His teaching and research interests focus on political party coalitions, factions, and organizations; elections and campaign finance; legislative-executive relations; and the intersection of politics and economic policy across U.S. history. He is the author or editor of several books, including *Party Decline in America: Policy, Politics, and the Fiscal State*, and numerous articles. Professor Coleman is a past president of the Political Organizations and Parties section of the American Political Science Association. At the University of Wisconsin, he received a Chancellor's Distinguished Teaching Award, held a Glenn B. and Cleone Orr Hawkins Professorship, and was a Jeffrey and Susanne Lyons Family Faculty Fellow.

Kenneth R. Mayer is professor of political science at the University of Wisconsin, Madison, with research interests in the presidency, campaign finance, and election administration. He is the author of *With the Stroke of a Pen: Executive Orders and Presidential Power* (winner of the Richard E. Neustadt Award); *The Political Economy of Defense Contracting; The Dysfunctional Congress? The Individual Roots of an Institutional Dilemma* (with David Canon); and *Presidential Leadership: Politics and Policy Making* (with George C. Edwards, III and Stephen J. Wayne), now in its 12th edition. In 2006, he was the inaugural Fulbright-ANU Distinguished Chair in Political Science at the Australian National University and the recipient of a University of Wisconsin System teaching award.

THE
ENDURING DEBATE

CLASSIC AND CONTEMPORARY READINGS
IN AMERICAN POLITICS

Ninth Edition

PART I

The Constitutional System

CHAPTER 1

Political Culture

1

"Beyond Tocqueville, Myrdal, and Hartz: The Multiple Traditions in America"

Rogers M. Smith

Political culture refers to the orientation of citizens toward the political system and toward themselves as actors in it. This includes the basic values, beliefs, attitudes, predispositions, and expectations that citizens bring to political life. Given the great diversity of the American population, one might expect a similarly diverse array of thought within political culture, with rival sets of political values challenging each other. However, even amidst this diversity of population, many scholars have argued that American political culture centers around commonly held beliefs, in part because of the unique characteristics of the founding of the United States. One influential interpretation is that American political life has been guided by the "liberal tradition." The terms liberalism, liberal consensus, *and* American creed *have been used by other authors. Liberal here refers to its original meaning from eighteenth-century political and economic theory—a philosophy that focuses on the individual and minimizing government intervention in daily life. Within the liberal tradition, the beliefs in equality, private property, liberty, individualism, protection of religious freedom, and democracy are especially powerful. There is certainly debate over what these terms mean or how heavily to weigh one belief versus another when they are in conflict, and these clashes drive a wedge between Republicans and Democrats in the United States today. But in this interpretation, social and political movements in the United States, such as the civil rights and women's rights movements, have generally not directly challenged these beliefs. On the contrary, most movements seek to show how their beliefs are highly consistent with these basic American principles.*

Where liberalism points to notions of equality, political scientist Rogers M. Smith argues that there is another, very different, tradition in American political thought that has been influential. He does not deny the significance of liberalism in American political history, as described most prominently by political scientist Louis

Hartz. Smith, however, contends that an equally significant strand of thought, "ascriptive Americanism," has been important across U.S. history. In this way of thinking, society is a hierarchy, where some groups are on top and others are below. Those on top are deemed to be deserving of the rights and benefits that the liberal tradition can offer. Those below are not. The most glaring examples of this disturbing pattern throughout American history have been the treatment of racial and ethnic minorities, especially African Americans, and the structure of laws that denied women the same opportunities as men. Smith notes that those holding these illiberal views were not on the fringes of society but, rather, were probably the majority view at many times. We should not, Smith argues, minimize the impact of ascriptive Americanism or those who held these views. American public policy at the highest levels was influenced by its premises. Researchers at universities and other institutions aimed to show through science the inferiority of some races and groups to others. Moreover, the same individuals expended great intellectual energy to make these illiberal views seem acceptable and consistent with the liberal beliefs that they held simultaneously. American political culture, in Smith's view, combines multiple traditions of thought.

Since the nation's inception, analysts have described American political culture as the preeminent example of modern liberal democracy, of government by popular consent with respect for the equal rights of all. They have portrayed American political development as the working out of liberal democratic or republican principles, via both "liberalizing" and "democratizing" socioeconomic changes and political efforts to cope with tensions inherent in these principles. Illiberal, undemocratic beliefs and practices have usually been seen only as expressions of ignorance and prejudice, destined to marginality by their lack of rational defenses. * * *

[Alexis de] Tocqueville's thesis—that America has been most shaped by the unusually free and egalitarian ideas and material conditions that prevailed at its founding—captures important truths. Nonetheless, the purpose of this essay is to challenge that thesis by showing that its adherents fail to give due weight to inegalitarian ideologies and conditions that have shaped the participants and the substance of American politics just as deeply. For over 80% of U.S. history, its laws declared most of the world's population to be ineligible for full American citizenship solely because of their race, original nationality, or gender. For at least two-thirds of American history, the majority of the domestic adult population was also ineligible for full citizenship for the same reasons. * * *

The Tocquevillian story is thus deceptive because it is too narrow. It is centered on relationships among a minority of Americans (white men, largely of northern European ancestry) analyzed via reference to categories derived from the hierarchy of political and economic statuses men have held in Europe: monarchs and aristocrats, commercial burghers, farmers, industrial and rural laborers, and indigents. Because most European observers and British American men have regarded these categories as politically fundamental, it is understandable that they have always found the most striking fact about the new nation to be its lack of one type of ascriptive hierarchy. There was no hereditary monarchy or nobility native to British America, and the revolutionaries rejected both the authority of the British king and aristocracy and the creation of any new American substitutes. Those features of American political life made the United States appear remarkably egalitarian by comparison with Europe.

But the comparative moral, material, and political egalitarianism that prevailed at the founding among moderately propertied white men was surrounded by an array of other fixed, ascriptive systems of unequal status, all largely unchallenged by the American revolutionaries. Men were thought naturally suited to rule over women, within both the family and the polity. White northern Europeans were thought superior culturally— and probably biologically—to black Africans, bronze Native Americans, and indeed all other races and civilizations. Many British Americans also treated religion as an inherited condition and regarded Protestants as created by God to be morally and politically, as well as theologically, superior to Catholics, Jews, Muslims, and others.

These beliefs were not merely emotional prejudices or "attitudes." Over time, American intellectual and political elites elaborated distinctive justifications for these ascriptive systems, including inegalitarian scriptural readings, the scientific racism of the "American school" of ethnology, racial and sexual Darwinism, and the romantic cult of Anglo-Saxonism in American historiography. All these discourses identified the true meaning of *Americanism* with particular forms of cultural, religious, ethnic, and especially racial and gender hierarchies. Many adherents of ascriptive Americanist outlooks insisted that the nation's political and economic structures should formally reflect natural and cultural inequalities, even at the cost of violating doctrines of universal rights. Although these views never entirely prevailed, their impact has been wide and deep.

Thus to approach a truer picture of America's political culture and its characteristic conflicts, we must consider more than the familiar categories of (absent) feudalism and socialism and (pervasive) bourgeois liberalism and republicanism. The nation has also been deeply constituted by the ideologies and practices that defined the relationships of the white male minority with subordinate groups, and the relationships of these groups with each other. When these elements are kept in view, the flat plain of American egalitarianism mapped by Tocqueville and others suddenly looks quite different. We instead perceive America's initial conditions as exhibiting only a rather small, recently leveled valley of relative equality nestled amid steep mountains of hierarchy. And though we can see forces working to erode those mountains over time, broadening the valley, many of the peaks also prove to be volcanic, frequently responding to seismic pressures with outbursts that harden into substantial peaks once again.

To be sure, America's ascriptive, unequal statuses, and the ideologies by which they have been defended have always been heavily conditioned and constrained by the presence of liberal democratic values and institutions. The reverse, however, is also true. Although liberal democratic ideas and practices have been more potent in America than elsewhere, American politics is best seen as expressing the interaction of multiple political traditions, including *liberalism, republicanism,* and *ascriptive forms of Americanism,* which have collectively comprised American political culture, without any constituting it as a whole. Though Americans have often struggled over contradictions among these traditions, almost all have tried to embrace what they saw as the best features of each.

Ascriptive outlooks have had such a hold in America because they have provided something that neither liberalism nor republicanism has done so well. They have offered creditable intellectual and psychological reasons for many Americans to believe that their social roles and personal characteristics express an identity that has inherent and transcendant worth, thanks to nature, history, and God. Those rationales have obviously aided those who sat atop the nation's political, economic, and social hierarchies. But many Americans besides elites have felt that they have gained meaning, as well as material and political benefits, from their nation's traditional structures of ascribed places and destinies.

Conventional narratives, preoccupied with the absence of aristocracy and socialism, usually stress the liberal and democratic elements in the rhetoric of even America's dissenters. These accounts fail to explain how and why liberalizing efforts have frequently lost to forces favoring new forms of racial and gender hierarchy. Those forces have sometimes negated major liberal victories, especially in the half-century following Reconstruction; and the fate of that era may be finding echoes today.

My chief aim here is to persuade readers that many leading accounts of American political culture are inadequate. * * * This argument is relevant to contemporary politics in two ways. First, it raises the possibility that novel intellectual, political, and legal systems reinforcing racial, ethnic, and gender inequalities might be rebuilt in America in the years ahead. That prospect does not seem plausible if the United States has always been essentially liberal democratic, with all exceptions marginal and steadily eliminated. It seems quite real, however, if liberal democratic traditions have been but contested parts of American culture, with in-egalitarian ideologies and practices often resurging even after major enhancements of liberal democracy. Second, the political implications of the view that America has never been completely liberal, and that changes have come only through difficult struggles and then have often not been sustained, are very different from the complacency—sometimes despair—engendered by beliefs that liberal democracy has always been hegemonic.

* * *

The Multiple-Traditions Thesis of American Civic Identity

It seems prudent to stress what is not proposed here. This is not a call for analysts to minimize the significance of white male political actors or their conflicts with each other. Neither is it a call for accounts that assail "Eurocentric" white male oppressors on behalf of diverse but always heroic subjugated groups. The multiple-traditions thesis holds that Americans share a *common* culture but one more complexly and multiply constituted than is usually acknowledged. Most members of all groups have shared and often helped to shape all the ideologies and institutions that have structured American life, including ascriptive ones. A few have done so while resisting all subjugating practices. But members of every group have sometimes embraced "essentialist" ideologies valorizing their own ascriptive traits and denigrating those of others, to bleak effect. Cherokees enslaved blacks, champions of women's rights disparaged blacks and immigrants, and blacks have often been hostile toward Hispanics and other new immigrants. White men, in turn, have been prominent among those combating invidious exclusions, as well as those imposing them.

Above all, recognition of the strong attractions of restrictive Americanist ideas does not imply any denial that America's liberal and democratic traditions have had great normative and political potency, even if they have not been so hegemonic as some claim. Instead, it sheds a new—and, in some respects, more flattering—light on the constitutive role of liberal democratic values in American life. Although some Americans have been willing to repudiate notions of democracy and universal rights, most have not; and though many have tried to blend those commitments with exclusionary ascriptive views, the illogic of these mixes has repeatedly proven a major resource for successful reformers. But we obscure the difficulty of those reforms (and thereby diminish their significance) if we slight the ideological and political appeal of contrary ascriptive traditions by portraying them as merely the shadowy side of a hegemonic liberal republicanism.

At its heart, the multiple-traditions thesis holds that the definitive feature of American political culture has been not its liberal, republican, or "ascriptive Americanist" elements but, rather, this more complex pattern of apparently inconsistent combinations of the traditions, accompanied by recurring conflicts. Because standard accounts neglect this pattern, they do not explore how and why Americans have tried to uphold aspects of all three of these heterogeneous traditions in combinations that are longer on political and psychological appeal than on intellectual coherency.

A focus on these questions generates an understanding of American politics that differs from Tocquevillian ones in four major respects. First, on this view, purely liberal and republican conceptions of civic identity are seen as frequently unsatisfying to many Americans, because they contain elements that threaten, rather than affirm, sincere, reputable beliefs in the propriety of the privileged positions that whites, Christianity, Anglo-Saxon traditions, and patriarchy have had in the United States. At the same time, even Americans deeply attached to those inegalitarian arrangements have also had liberal democratic values. Second, it has therefore been typical, not aberrational, for Americans to embody strikingly opposed beliefs in their institutions, such as doctrines that blacks should and should not be full and equal citizens. But though American efforts to blend aspects of opposing views have often been remarkably stable, the resulting tensions have still been important sources of change. Third, when older types of ascriptive inequality, such as slavery, have been rejected as unduly illiberal, it has been normal, not anomalous, for many Americans to embrace new doctrines and institutions that reinvigorate the hierarchies they esteem in modified form. Changes toward greater inequality and exclusion, as well as toward greater equality and inclusiveness, thus can and do occur. Finally, the dynamics of American development cannot simply be seen as a rising tide of liberalizing forces progressively submerging contrary beliefs and practices. The national course has been more serpentine. The economic, political, and moral forces propelling the United States toward liberal democracy have often been heeded by American leaders, especially since World War II. But the currents pulling toward fuller expression of alleged natural and cultural inequalities have also always won victories. In some eras they have predominated, appearing to define not only the path of safety but that of progress. In all eras, including our own, many Americans have combined their allegiance to liberal democracy with beliefs that the presence of certain groups favored by history, nature, and God has made Americans an intrinsically "special" people. Their adherents have usually regarded such beliefs as benign and intellectually well founded; yet they also have always had more or less harsh discriminatory corollaries.

To test these multiple-traditions claims, consider the United States in 1870. By then the Civil War and Reconstruction had produced dramatic advances in the liberal and democratic character of America's laws. Slavery was abolished. All persons born in the United States and subject to its jurisdiction were deemed citizens of the United States and the states in which they resided, regardless of their race, creed or gender. None could be denied voting rights on racial grounds. The civil rights of all were newly protected through an array of national statutes. The 1790 ban on naturalizing Africans had been repealed, and expatriation declared a natural right. Over the past two decades women had become more politically engaged and had begun to gain respect as political actors.

* * *

[Neither liberal or republican analyses] would have had the intellectual resources to explain what in fact occurred. Over the next fifty years, Americans did not make blacks, women, and members of other races full and equal citizens, nor did racial and gender prejudices undergo major erosion. Neither, however, were minorities and women declared to be subhuman and outside the body politic. And although white Americans engaged in extensive violence against blacks and Native Americans, those groups grew in population, and no cataclysm loomed. Instead, intellectual and political elites worked out the most elaborate theories of racial and gender hierarchy in U.S. history and partially embodied them in a staggering array of new laws governing naturalization, immigration, deportation, voting rights, electoral institutions, judicial procedures, and economic rights—but only partially. The laws retained important liberal and democratic features, and some were strengthened. They had enough purchase on the moral and material interests of most Americans to compel advocates of inequality to adopt contrived, often clumsy means to achieve their ends.

The considerable success of the proponents of inegalitarian ideas reflects the power these traditions have long had in America. But after the Civil War, * * * evolutionary theories enormously strengthened the intellectual prestige of doctrines presenting the races and sexes as naturally arrayed into what historians have termed a "raciocultural hierarchy," as well as a "hierarchy of sex." Until the end of the nineteenth century, most evolutionists * * * thought acquired characteristics could be inherited. Thus beliefs in biological differences were easily merged with the * * * historians' views that peoples were the products of historical and cultural forces. Both outlooks usually presented the current traits of the races as fixed for the foreseeable future. Few intellectuals were shy about noting the implications of these views for public policy. Anthropologist Daniel G. Brinton made typical arguments in his 1895 presidential address to the American Association for the Advancement of Science. He contended that the "black, brown and red races" each had "a peculiar mental temperament which has become hereditary," leaving them constitutionally "recreant to the codes of civilization." Brinton believed that this fact had not been adequately appreciated by American lawmakers. Henceforth, conceptions of "race, nations, tribes" had to "supply the only sure foundations for legislation; not *a priori* notions of the rights of man."

As Brinton knew, many politicians and judges had already begun to seize on such suggestions. In 1882, for example, California senator John Miller drew on the Darwinian "law of the 'survival of the fittest'" to explain that "forty centuries of Chinese life" had "ground into" the Chinese race characteristics that made them unbeatable competitors against the free white man. They were "automatic engines of flesh and blood," of "obtuse nerve," marked by degradation and demoralization, and thus far below the Anglo-Saxon, but were still a threat to the latter's livelihood in a market economy. Hence, Miller argued, the immigration of Chinese laborers must be banned. His bill prevailed, many expressing concern that these Chinese would otherwise become American citizens. The Chinese Exclusion Act was not a vestige of the past but something new, the first repudiation of America's long history of open immigration; and it was justified in terms of the postwar era's revivified racial theories.

Yet although men like Miller not only sustained but expanded Chinese exclusions until they were made virtually total in 1917 (and tight restrictions survived until 1965), they never managed to deny American citizenship to all of the "Chinese race." Until 1917 there were no restrictions on the immigration of upper-class Chinese, and in 1898 the Supreme Court declared that children born on U.S. soil to Chinese parents were American citizens (*United States* v. *Wong Kim Ark* 1898). Birthplace citizenship was a doctrine enshrined in common law, reinforced by the Fourteenth Amendment, and vital to citizenship for the children of *all* immigrant aliens. Hence it had enough legal and political support to override the Court's recognition of Congress's exclusionary desires. Even so, in other cases the Court sustained bans on Chinese immigration while admitting the racial animosities behind them, as in the "Chinese Exclusion Case" (*Chae Chan Ping* v. *United States* 1889); upheld requirements for Chinese-Americans to have certificates of citizenship not required of whites (*Fong Yue Ting* v. *United States* 1893); and permitted officials to deport even Chinese persons who had later been judged by courts to be native-born U.S. citizens (*United States* v. *Ju Toy* 1905).

The upshot, then, was the sort of none-too-coherent mix that the multiple-traditions thesis holds likely. Chinese were excluded on racial grounds, but race did not bar citizenship to those born in the United States; yet Chinese ancestry could subject some American citizens to burdens, including deportation, that others did not face. The mix was not perfect from any ideological viewpoint, but it was politically popular. It maintained a valued inclusive feature of American law (birthplace citizenship) while sharply reducing the resident Chinese population. And it most fully satisfied the increasingly powerful champions of Anglo-Saxon supremacy.

From 1887 on, academic reformers and politicians sought to restrict immigration more generally by a means that paid lip service to liberal norms even as it aimed at racist results—the literacy test. On its face, this measure expressed concern only for the intellectual merits of immigrants. But the test's true aims were spelled out in 1896 by its sponsor, Senator Henry Cabot Lodge, a Harvard Ph.D. in history and politics. Committee research, he reported, showed that the test would exclude "the Italians, Russians, Poles, Hungarians, Greeks, and Asiatics," thereby preserving "the quality of our race and citizenship." Citing "modern history" and "modern science," Thomas Carlyle and Gustave le Bon, Lodge contended that the need for racial exclusion arose from "something deeper and more fundamental than anything which concerns the intellect." Race was above all constituted by moral characteristics, the "stock of ideas, traditions, sentiments, modes of thought" that a people possessed as an "accumulation of centuries of toil and conflict." These mental and moral qualities constituted the "soul of a race," an inheritance in which its members "blindly believe," and upon which learning had no effect. But these qualities could be degraded if "a lower race mixes with a higher"; thus, exclusion by race, not reading ability, was the nation's proper goal.

When the literacy test finally passed in 1917 but proved ineffective in keeping out "lower races," Congress moved to versions of an explicitly racist national-origins quota system. It banned virtually all Asians and permitted European immigration only in ratios preserving the northern European cast of the American citizenry. Congressman Albert Johnson, chief author of the most important quota act in 1924, proclaimed that through it, "the day of indiscriminate acceptance of all races, has definitely ended." The quota system, repealed only in 1965, was a novel, elaborate monument to ideologies holding that access to American citizenship should be subject to racial and ethnic limits. It also served as the prime model for similar systems in Europe and Latin America.

*   *   *

But despite the new prevalence of such attitudes on the part of northern and western elites in the late nineteenth century, the Reconstruction amendments and statutes were still on the books, and surviving liberal sentiments made repealing them politically difficult. Believers in racial inequality were, moreover, undecided on just what to do about blacks. * * * "Radical" racists * * * argued that blacks, like other lower races, should be excluded from American society and looked hopefully for evidence that they were dying out. Their position was consistent with Hartz's claim that Americans could not tolerate permanent unequal statuses; persons must either be equal citizens or outsiders. But * * * "Conservatives" believed * * * that blacks and other people of color might instead have a permanent "place" in America, so long as "placeness included hierarchy." Some still thought that blacks, like the other "lower races," might one day be led by whites to fully civilized status, but no one expected progress in the near future. Thus blacks should instead be segregated, largely disfranchised, and confined to menial occupations via inferior education and discriminatory hiring practices—but not expelled, tortured, or killed. A few talented blacks might even be allowed somewhat higher stations.

* * * The result was a system closest to Conservative desires, one that kept blacks in their place, although that place was structured more repressively than most Conservatives favored. And unlike the ineffective literacy test, here racial inegalitarians achieved much of what they wanted without explicitly violating liberal legal requirements. Complex registration systems, poll taxes, and civics tests appeared race-neutral but were designed and administered to disfranchise blacks. This intent was little masked. * * * These efforts succeeded. Most dramatically, in Louisiana 95.6% of blacks were registered in 1896, and over half (130,000) voted. After disfranchising measures, black registration dropped by 90% and by 1904 totaled only 1,342. The Supreme Court found convoluted ways to close its eyes to these tactics.

By similar devices, blacks were virtually eliminated from juries in the south, where 90% of American blacks lived, sharply limiting their ability to have their personal and economic rights protected by the courts. "Separate but equal" educational and business laws and practices also stifled the capacities of blacks to participate in the nation's economy as equals, severely curtailed the occupations they could train for, and marked them—unofficially but clearly—as an inferior caste. Thus here, as elsewhere, it was evident that the nation's laws and institutions were not meant to confer the equal civic status they proclaimed for all Americans; but neither did they conform fully to doctrines favoring overt racial hierarchy. They represented another asymmetrical compromise among the multiple ideologies vying to define American political culture.

So, too, did the policies governing two groups whose civic status formally improved during these years: Native Americans and women.

* * *

This period also highlights how the influence of inegalitarian doctrines has not been confined to white male intellectuals, legislators, and judges. The leading writer of the early twentieth-century women's movement, Charlotte Perkins Gilman, was a thoroughgoing Darwinian who accepted that evolution had made women inferior to men in certain respects, although she insisted that these differences were usually exaggerated and that altered social conditions could transform them. And even as he attacked Booker T. Washington for appearing to accept the "alleged inferiority of the Negro race," W. E. B. DuBois embraced the widespread Lamarckian view that racial characteristics were socially conditioned but then inherited as the "soul" of a race. He could thus accept that most blacks were "primitive folk" in need of tutelage. * * *

The acceptance of ascriptive inegalitarian beliefs by brilliant and politically dissident female and black male intellectuals strongly suggests that these ideas had broad appeal. Writers whose interests they did not easily serve still saw them as persuasive in light of contemporary scientific theories and empirical evidence of massive inequalities. It is likely, too, that for many the vision of a meaningful natural order that these doctrines provided had the psychological and philosophical appeal that such positions have always had for human beings, grounding their status and significance in something greater and more enduring than their own lives. * * *

In sum, if we accept that ideologies and institutions of ascriptive hierarchy have shaped America in interaction with its liberal and democratic features, we can make more sense of a wide range of inegalitarian policies newly contrived after 1870 and perpetuated through much of the twentieth century. Those policies were dismantled only through great struggles, aided by international pressures during World War II and the Cold War; and it is not clear that these struggles have ended. The novelties in the policies and scientific doctrines of the Gilded Age and Progressive Era should alert us to the possibility that new intellectual systems and political forces defending racial and gender inequalities may yet gain increased power in our own time.

* * *

The achievements of Americans in building a more inclusive democracy certainly provide reasons to believe that illiberal forces will not prevail. But just as we can better explain the nation's past by recognizing how and why liberal democratic principles have been contested with frequent success, we will better understand the present and future of American politics if we do not presume they are rooted in essentially liberal or democratic values and conditions. Instead, we must analyze America as the ongoing product of often conflicting multiple traditions.

DISCUSSION QUESTIONS

1. According to Smith, what are some examples of how Americans in the late nineteenth century simultaneously held liberal and ascriptive Americanist views?

2. How would you know if belief in ascriptive hierarchy was as widespread as Smith contends? What kind of evidence would you look for?

3. How might advocates of liberalism and ascriptive Americanism define "the public good"?

"Bowling Alone: America's Declining Social Capital"

Robert D. Putnam

One of the central questions in political culture is the nature of citizenship and the role of the citizen. What obligations does citizenship place upon government and the state, and what obligations does it place upon the individual? What, if any, is the obligation of the individual to participate in civic life, and what factors encourage or discourage such participation? What if a healthy democratic life depends on participation, but public participation declines? To political scientist Robert D. Putnam, participation in social and civic life is vital for a stable, vibrant, and thriving democracy. Writing in the early 1990s, Putnam is alarmed by signs of deterioration of participation in civic life. While noting that traditional measures of participation, such as voting, had shown declines, Putnam focuses his attention elsewhere. Building from Tocqueville's observations about the importance of civil society in America— participation in social groups, fraternal organizations, religious houses of worship, professional associations, and so on—Putnam identifies numerous indicators of a decline in Americans' connectedness with each other. This included, famously, the decline of participation in bowling leagues and the rise of "bowling alone," the title of this article and Putnam's highly influential book. Putnam's argument is that participation in such organizations and activities builds "social capital," meaning the skills of interaction, cooperation, and coordination that are built through this kind of involvement. These skills can build the prospects for one's individual success. As or more important to Putnam, they boost the potential for people to work together, advance shared values, and build and appreciate the importance of a well-functioning democratic system. When people become more isolated, Putnam argues that all of these virtues are threatened. In this article, Putnam reviews what he sees as worrisome trends toward individual isolation and the decline of civil society. He concludes by identifying some possible causes for these trends.

Many students of the new democracies that have emerged over the past decade and a half have emphasized the importance of a strong and active civil society to the consolidation of democracy. Especially with regard to the postcommunist countries, scholars and democratic activists alike have lamented the absence or obliteration of traditions of independent civic engagement and a widespread tendency toward passive reliance on the state. To those concerned with the weakness of civil societies in the developing or postcommunist world, the advanced Western democracies and above all the United States have typically been taken as models to be emulated. There is striking evidence, however, that the vibrancy of American civil society has notably declined over the past several decades.

Ever since the publication of Alexis de Tocqueville's *Democracy in America*, the United States has played a central role in systematic studies of the links between democracy and civil society. Although this is in part because trends in American life are often regarded as harbingers of social modernization, it is also because America has traditionally been considered unusually "civic" (a reputation that, as we shall later see, has not been entirely unjustified).

When Tocqueville visited the United States in the 1830s, it was the Americans' propensity for civic association that most impressed him as the key to their unprecedented ability to make democracy work. "Americans of all ages, all stations in life, and all types of disposition," he observed, "are forever forming associations. There are not only commercial and industrial associations in which all take part, but others of a thousand different types—religious, moral, serious, futile, very general and very limited, immensely large and very minute. . . . Nothing, in my view, deserves more attention than the intellectual and moral associations in America."

Recently, American social scientists of a neo-Tocquevillean bent have unearthed a wide range of empirical evidence that the quality of public life and the performance of social institutions (and not only in America) are indeed powerfully influenced by norms and networks of civic engagement. Researchers in such fields as education, urban poverty, unemployment, the control of crime and drug abuse, and even health have discovered that successful outcomes are more likely in civically engaged communities. Similarly, research on the varying economic attainments of different ethnic groups in the United States has demonstrated the importance of social bonds within each group. These results are consistent with research in a wide range of settings that demonstrates the vital importance of social networks for job placement and many other economic outcomes.

* * *

No doubt the mechanisms through which civic engagement and social connectedness produce such results—better schools, faster economic development, lower crime, and more effective government—are multiple and complex. While these briefly recounted findings require further confirmation and perhaps qualification, the parallels across hundreds of empirical studies in a dozen disparate disciplines and subfields are striking. Social scientists in several fields have recently suggested a common framework for understanding these phenomena, a framework that rests on the concept of *social capital*. By analogy with notions of physical capital and human capital—tools and training that enhance individual productivity— "social capital" refers to features of social organization such as networks, norms, and social trust that facilitate coordination and cooperation for mutual benefit.

* * *

Whatever Happened to Civic Engagement?

We begin with familiar evidence on changing patterns of political participation, not least because it is immediately relevant to issues of democracy in the narrow sense. Consider the well-known decline in turnout in national elections over the last three decades. From a relative high point in the early 1960s, voter turnout had by 1990 declined by nearly a quarter; tens of millions of Americans had forsaken their parents' habitual readiness to engage in the simplest act of citizenship. Broadly similar trends also characterize participation in state and local elections.

It is not just the voting booth that has been increasingly deserted by Americans. A series of identical questions posed by the Roper Organization to national samples ten times each year over the last two decades reveals that since 1973 the number of Americans who report that "in the past year" they have "attended a public meeting on town or school affairs" has fallen by more than a third (from 22 percent in 1973 to 13 percent in 1993). Similar (or even greater) relative declines are evident in responses to questions about attending a political rally or speech, serving on a committee of some local organization, and working for a political party. By almost every measure, Americans' direct engagement in politics and government has fallen steadily and sharply over the last generation, despite the fact that average levels of education—the best individual-level predictor of political participation—have risen sharply throughout this period. Every year over the last decade or two, millions more have withdrawn from the affairs of their communities.

Not coincidentally, Americans have also disengaged psychologically from politics and government over this era. The proportion of Americans who reply that they "trust the government in Washington" only "some of the time" or "almost never" has risen steadily from 30 percent in 1966 to 75 percent in 1992.

These trends are well known, of course, and taken by themselves would seem amenable to a strictly political explanation. Perhaps the long litany of political tragedies and scandals since the 1960s (assassinations, Vietnam, Watergate, Irangate, and so on) has triggered an understandable disgust for politics and government among Americans, and that in turn has motivated their withdrawal. I do not doubt that this common interpretation has some merit, but its limitations become plain when we examine trends in civic engagement of a wider sort.

Our survey of organizational membership among Americans can usefully begin with a glance at the aggregate results of the General Social Survey, a scientifically conducted, national-sample survey that has been repeated 14 times over the last two decades. Church-related groups constitute the most common type of organization joined by Americans; they are especially popular with women. Other types of organizations frequently joined by women include school-service groups (mostly parent-teacher associations), sports groups, professional societies, and literary societies. Among men, sports clubs, labor unions, professional societies, fraternal groups, veterans' groups, and service clubs are all relatively popular.

Religious affiliation is by far the most common associational membership among Americans. Indeed, by many measures America continues to be (even more than in Tocqueville's time) an astonishingly "churched" society. For example, the United States has more houses of worship per capita than any other nation on Earth. Yet religious sentiment in America seems to be becoming somewhat less tied to institutions and more self-defined.

How have these complex crosscurrents played out over the last three or four decades in terms of Americans' engagement with organized religion? The general pattern is clear: [t]he 1960s witnessed a significant drop in reported weekly churchgoing—from roughly 48 percent in the late 1950s to roughly 41 percent in the early 1970s. Since then, it has stagnated or (according to some surveys) declined still further. Meanwhile, data from the General Social Survey show a modest decline in membership in all "church-related groups" over the last 20 years. It would seem, then, that net participation by Americans, both in religious services and in church-related groups, has declined modestly (by perhaps a sixth) since the 1960s.

For many years, labor unions provided one of the most common organizational affiliations among American workers. Yet union membership has been falling for nearly four decades, with the steepest decline occurring between 1975 and 1985. Since the mid-1950s, when union membership peaked, the unionized portion of the nonagricultural work force in America has dropped by more than half, falling from 32.5 percent in 1953 to 15.8 percent in 1992. By now, virtually all of the explosive growth in union membership that was associated with the New Deal has been erased. The solidarity of union halls is now mostly a fading memory of aging men.

The parent-teacher association (PTA) has been an especially important form of civic engagement in twentieth-century America because parental involvement in the educational process represents a particularly productive form of social capital. It is, therefore, dismaying to discover that participation in parent-teacher organizations has dropped drastically over the last generation, from more than 12 million in 1964 to barely 5 million in 1982 before recovering to approximately 7 million now.

Next, we turn to evidence on membership in (and volunteering for) civic and fraternal organizations. These data show some striking patterns. First, membership in traditional women's groups has declined more or less steadily since the mid-1960s. For example, membership in the national Federation of Women's Clubs is down by more than half (59 percent) since

1964, while membership in the League of Women Voters (LWV) is off 42 percent since 1969.

Similar reductions are apparent in the numbers of volunteers for mainline civic organizations, such as the Boy Scouts (off by 26 percent since 1970) and the Red Cross (off by 61 percent since 1970). But what about the possibility that volunteers have simply switched their loyalties to other organizations? Evidence on "regular" (as opposed to occasional or "drop-by") volunteering is available from the Labor Department's Current Population Surveys of 1974 and 1989. These estimates suggest that serious volunteering declined by roughly one-sixth over these 15 years, from 24 percent of adults in 1974 to 20 percent in 1989. The multitudes of Red Cross aides and Boy Scout troop leaders now missing in action have apparently not been offset by equal numbers of new recruits elsewhere.

Fraternal organizations have also witnessed a substantial drop in membership during the 1980s and 1990s. Membership is down significantly in such groups as the Lions (off 12 percent since 1983), the Elks (off 18 percent since 1979), the Shriners (off 27 percent since 1979), the Jaycees (off 44 percent since 1979), and the Masons (down 39 percent since 1959). In sum, after expanding steadily throughout most of this century, many major civic organizations have experienced a sudden, substantial, and nearly simultaneous decline in membership over the last decade or two.

The most whimsical yet discomfiting bit of evidence of social disengagement in contemporary America that I have discovered is this: more Americans are bowling today than ever before, but bowling in organized leagues has plummeted in the last decade or so. Between 1980 and 1993 the total number of bowlers in America increased by 10 percent, while league bowling decreased by 40 percent. (Lest this be thought a wholly trivial example, I should note that nearly 80 million Americans went bowling at least once during 1993, *nearly a third more than voted in the 1994 congressional elections* and roughly the same number as claim to attend church regularly. Even after the 1980s' plunge in league bowling, nearly 3 percent of American adults regularly bowl in leagues.) The rise of solo bowling threatens the livelihood of bowling-lane proprietors because those who bowl as members of leagues consume three times as much beer and pizza as solo bowlers, and the money in bowling is in the beer and pizza, not the balls and shoes. The broader social significance, however, lies in the social interaction and even occasionally civic conversations over beer and pizza that solo bowlers forgo. Whether or not bowling beats balloting in the eyes of most Americans, bowling teams illustrate yet another vanishing form of social capital.

Countertrends

At this point, however, we must confront a serious counterargument. Perhaps the traditional forms of civic organization whose decay we have been tracing have been replaced by vibrant new organizations. For example, national environmental organizations (like the Sierra Club) and feminist groups (like the National Organization for Women) grew rapidly during the 1970s and 1980s and now count hundreds of thousands of dues-paying members. An even more dramatic example is the American Association of Retired Persons (AARP), which grew exponentially from 400,000 card-carrying members in 1960 to 33 million in 1993, becoming (after the Catholic Church) the largest private organization in the world. The national administrators of these organizations are among the most feared lobbyists in Washington, in large part because of their massive mailing lists of presumably loyal members.

These new mass-membership organizations are plainly of great political importance. From the point of view of social connectedness, however, they are sufficiently different from classic "secondary associations" that we need to invent a new label—perhaps "tertiary associations." For the vast majority of their members, the only act of membership consists in writing a check for dues or perhaps occasionally reading a newsletter. Few ever attend any meetings of such organizations, and most are unlikely ever (knowingly) to encounter any other member. The bond between any two members of the Sierra Club is less like the bond between any two members of a gardening club and more like the bond between any two Red Sox fans (or perhaps any two devoted Honda owners): they root for the same team and they share some of the same interests, but they are unaware of each other's existence. Their ties, in short, are to common symbols, common leaders, and perhaps common ideals, but not to one another. The theory of social capital argues that associational membership should, for example, increase social trust, but this prediction is much less straightforward with regard to membership in tertiary associations. From the point of view of social connectedness, the Environmental Defense Fund and a bowling league are just not in the same category.

* * *

Broken down by type of group, the downward trend is most marked for church-related groups, for labor unions, for fraternal and veterans' organizations, and for school-service groups. Conversely, membership in professional associations has risen over these years, although less than might have been predicted, given sharply rising educational and occupational levels. Essentially the same trends are evident for both men and women in the sample. In short, the available survey evidence confirms our earlier conclusion: American social capital in the form of civic associations has significantly eroded over the last generation.

Good Neighborliness and Social Trust

I noted earlier that most readily available quantitative evidence on trends in social connectedness involves formal settings, such as the voting booth, the union hall, or the PTA. One glaring exception is so widely discussed as to require little comment here: the most fundamental form of social capital is the family, and the massive evidence of the loosening of bonds within the family (both extended and nuclear) is well known. This trend, of course, is quite consistent with—and may help to explain—our theme of social decapitalization.

A second aspect of informal social capital on which we happen to have reasonably reliable time-series data involves neighborliness. In each General Social Survey since 1974 respondents have been asked, "How often do you spend a social evening with a neighbor?" The proportion of Americans who socialize with their neighbors more than once a year has slowly but steadily declined over the last two decades, from 72 percent in 1974 to 61 percent in 1993. (On the other hand, socializing with "friends who do not live in your neighborhood" appears to be on the increase, a trend that may reflect the growth of workplace-based social connections.)

Americans are also less trusting. The proportion of Americans saying that most people can be trusted fell by more than a third between 1960, when 58 percent chose that alternative, and 1993, when only 37 percent did. The same trend is apparent in all educational groups; indeed, because social trust is also correlated with education and because educational levels have risen sharply, the overall decrease in social trust is even more apparent if we control for education.

*   *   *

Why Is U.S. Social Capital Eroding?

As we have seen, something has happened in America in the last two or three decades to diminish civic engagement and social connectedness. What could that "something" be? Here are several possible explanations, along with some initial evidence on each.

The movement of women into the labor force. Over these same two or three decades, many millions of American women have moved out of the home into paid employment. This is the primary, though not the sole, reason why the weekly working hours of the average American have increased significantly during these years. It seems highly plausible that this social revolution should have reduced the time and energy available for building social capital. For certain organizations, such as the PTA, the League of Women Voters, the Federation of Women's Clubs, and the Red Cross, this is almost certainly an important part of the story. The sharpest decline in women's civic participation seems to have come in the 1970s; membership in such "women's" organizations as these has been virtually halved since the late 1960s. By contrast, most of the decline in participation in men's organizations occurred about ten years later; the total decline to date has been approximately 25 percent for the typical organization. On the other hand, the survey data imply that the aggregate declines for men are virtually as great as those for women. It is logically possible, of course, that the male declines might represent the knock-on effect of women's liberation, as dishwashing crowded out the lodge, but time-budget studies suggest that most husbands of working wives have assumed only a minor part of the housework. In short, something besides the women's revolution seems to lie behind the erosion of social capital.

Mobility: [t]he "re-potting" hypothesis. Numerous studies of organizational involvement have shown that residential stability and such related phenomena as homeownership are clearly associated with greater civic engagement. Mobility, like frequent re-potting of plants, tends to disrupt root systems, and it takes time for an uprooted individual to put down new roots. It seems plausible that the automobile, suburbanization, and the movement to the Sun Belt have reduced the social rootedness of the average American, but one fundamental difficulty with this hypothesis is apparent: the best evidence shows that residential stability and homeownership in America have risen modestly since 1965, and are surely higher now than during the 1950s, when civic engagement and social connectedness by our measures was definitely higher.

Other demographic transformations. A range of additional changes have transformed the American family since the 1960s—fewer marriages, more divorces, fewer children, lower real wages, and so on. Each of these changes might account for some of the slackening of civic engagement, since married, middle-class parents are generally more socially involved than other people. Moreover, the changes in scale that have swept over the American economy in these years—illustrated by the replacement of the corner grocery by the supermarket and now perhaps of the supermarket by electronic shopping at home, or the replacement of community-based enterprises by outposts of distant multinational firms—may perhaps have undermined the material and even physical basis for civic engagement.

The technological transformation of leisure. There is reason to believe that deep-seated technological trends are radically "privatizing" or "individualizing" our use of leisure time and thus disrupting many opportunities for social-capital formation. The most obvious and probably the most powerful instrument of this revolution is television. Time-budget studies in the 1960s showed that the growth in time spent watching television dwarfed all other changes in the way Americans passed their days and nights. Television has made our communities (or, rather, what we experience as our communities) wider and shallower. In the language of economics, electronic technology enables individual tastes to be satisfied more fully, but at the cost of the positive social externalities associated with more primitive forms of entertainment. The same logic applies to the replacement of vaudeville by the movies and now of movies by the VCR. The new "virtual reality" helmets that we will soon don to be entertained in total isolation are merely the latest extension of this trend. Is technology thus driving a wedge between our individual interests and our collective interests? It is a question that seems worth exploring more systematically.

What Is to Be Done?

*   *   *

The concept of "civil society" has played a central role in the recent global debate about the preconditions for democracy and democratization. In the newer democracies this phrase has properly focused attention on the need to foster a vibrant civic life in soils traditionally inhospitable to self-government. In the established democracies, ironically, growing numbers of citizens are questioning the effectiveness of their public institutions at the very moment when liberal democracy has swept the battlefield, both ideologically and geopolitically. In America, at least, there is reason to suspect that this democratic disarray may be linked to a broad and continuing erosion of civic engagement that began a quarter-century ago. High on our scholarly agenda should be the question of whether a comparable erosion of social capital may be under way in other advanced democracies, perhaps in different institutional and behavioral guises. High on America's agenda should be the question of how to reverse these adverse trends in social connectedness, thus restoring civic engagement and civic trust.

DISCUSSION QUESTIONS

1. Putnam's argument is based on the premise that as civil society declines, the quality of democratic life declines as well. Do you agree? If voting participation in elections is high, does it matter if people are less involved in social clubs and other forms of participation?

2. Putnam, writing in the early 1990s, has serious concerns about the fraying of the societal fabric that ties people together. Another 30 years have elapsed since Putnam wrote this article. Are there new forms of connection among people that have emerged and that provide the building of social capital? From today's vantage point, was Putnam right to worry about the impact of the technological transformation of leisure?

"The Three Political Cultures"

Daniel J. Elazar

Political scientist Daniel J. Elazar agrees with Rogers M. Smith that American political culture consists of competing political traditions. Elazar sees three types of value systems across the country: individualism, traditionalism, and moralism. Individualism focuses on individual rights and views governing as a set of transactions among various individuals and groups. Traditionalism attempts to use government to preserve existing social arrangements. Moralism is focused on the community and engaging in politics to do good, similar to a thread in American political thought known as classical republicanism. Reacting to the argument that American political culture was predominantly individualistic and liberal, some historians argued that classical republicanism also played an important role in American political life and, perhaps, the dominant role in the revolutionary era. One's individual liberty and freedom, which are paramount in the liberal tradition, might be more subject to societal and community limits in the classical republican view. In this view, defined as moralism by Elazar, politics is not primarily about achieving one's personal interest. Rather, the focus is on serving the community and society, and individuals are to be motivated not by self-interest but by morality and virtue. According to Elazar, these three approaches vary in their prevalence across the country, and even within states there may be variation as to which of the three predominates. Some regions have a mixture of two of these value systems, whereas other areas are more purely of one type. In large part, the uneven distribution of the three political belief systems across the country has to do with migration patterns. Once certain ethnic groups and nationalities predominated in a particular area, their political and cultural beliefs influenced government, other institutions, and the way politics was practiced. These habits of how institutions and politics operate have perpetuated over time because newcomers find that behaving in a manner consistent with local beliefs and culture increases one's chances of being politically successful.

The United States is a single land of great diversity inhabited by what is now a single people of great diversity. The singleness of the country as a whole is expressed through political, cultural, and geographic unity. Conversely, the country's diversity is expressed through its states, subcultures, and sections. In this section, we will focus on the political dimensions of that diversity-in-unity—on the country's overall political culture and its subculture.

Political culture is the summation of persistent patterns of underlying political attitudes and characteristic responses to political concerns that is manifest in a particular political order. Its existence is generally unperceived by those who are part of that order, and its origins date back to the very beginnings of the particular people who share it. Political culture is an intrinsically political phenomenon. As such, it makes its own demands on the political system. For example, the definition of what is "fair" in the political arena—a direct manifestation of political culture—is likely to be different from the definition of what is fair in family or business relationships. Moreover, different political cultures will define fairness in politics differently. Political culture also affects all other questions confronting the political system. For example, many factors go into shaping public expectations regarding government services, and political culture will be significant among them. Political systems, in turn, are in some measure the products of the political cultures they serve and must remain in harmony with their political cultures if they are to maintain themselves.

*   *   *

Political-culture factors stand out as particularly influential in shaping the operations of the national, state, and local political systems in three ways: (1) by molding the perceptions of the political community (the citizens, the politicians, and the public officials) as to the nature and purposes of politics and its expectations of government and the political process; (2) by influencing the recruitment of specific kinds of people to become active in government and politics—as holders of elective offices, members of the bureaucracy, and active political workers; and (3) by subtly directing the actual way in which the art of government is practiced by citizens, politicians, and public officials in the light of their perceptions. In turn, the cultural components of individual and group behavior are manifested in civic behavior as dictated by conscience and internalized ethical standards, in the forms of law-abidingness (or laxity in such matters) adhered to by citizens and officials, and in the character of the positive actions of government.

*   *   *

The national political culture of the United States is itself a synthesis of three major political subcultures. These subcultures jointly inhabit the country, existing side by side or sometimes overlapping one another. All three are of nationwide proportions, having spread, in the course of time, from coast to coast. Yet each subculture is strongly tied to specific sections of the country, reflecting the streams and currents of migration that have carried people of different origins and backgrounds across the continent in more or less orderly patterns.

Given the central characteristics that define each of the subcultures and their centers of emphasis, the three political subcultures may be called individualistic, moralistic, and traditionalistic. Each reflects its own particular synthesis of the marketplace and the commonwealth.

It is important, however, not only to examine this description and the following ones very carefully but also to abandon the preconceptions associated with such idea-words as individualistic, moralistic, marketplace, and so on. Thus, for example, nineteenth-century individualistic conceptions of minimum intervention were oriented toward *laissez-faire*, with the role of government conceived to be that of a policeman with powers to act in certain limited fields. And in the twentieth century, the notion of what constitutes minimum intervention has been drastically expanded to include such things as government regulation of utilities, unemployment compensation, and massive subventions to maintain a stable and growing economy—all within the framework of the same political culture. The demands of manufacturers for high tariffs in 1865 and the demands of labor unions for worker's compensation in 1965 may well be based on the same theoretical justification that they are aids to the maintenance of a working marketplace. Culture is not static. It must be viewed dynamically and defined so as to include cultural change in its very nature.

The Individualistic Political Culture

The *individualistic political culture* emphasizes the conception of the democratic order as a marketplace. It is rooted in the view that government is instituted for strictly utilitarian reasons, to handle those functions demanded by the people it serves. According to this view, government need not have any direct concern with questions of the "good society" (except insofar as the government may be used to advance some common conception of the good society formulated outside the political arena, just as it serves other functions). Emphasizing the centrality of private concerns, the individualistic political culture places a premium on limiting community intervention—whether governmental or nongovernmental—into private activities, to the minimum degree necessary to keep the marketplace in proper working order. In general, government action is to be restricted to those areas, primarily in the economic realm, that encourage private initiative and widespread access to the marketplace.

The character of political participation in systems dominated by the individualistic political culture reflects the view that politics is just another means by which individuals may improve themselves socially and economically. In this sense politics is a "business," like any other that competes for talent and offers rewards to those who take it up as a career. Those individuals who choose political careers may rise by providing the governmental services demanded of them and, in return, may expect to be adequately compensated for their efforts.

Interpretation of officeholders' obligations under the individualistic political culture vary among political systems and even among individuals within
a single political system. Where the standards are high, such people are
expected to provide high-quality government services for the general public
in the best possible manner in return for the status and economic rewards
considered their due. Some who choose political careers clearly commit
themselves to such norms; others believe that an office-holder's primary
responsibility is to serve him- or herself and those who have supported him
or her directly, favoring them at the expense of others. In some political systems, this view is accepted by the public as well as by politicians.

Political life within an individualistic political culture is based on a
system of mutual obligations rooted in personal relationships. Whereas
in a simple civil society those relationships can be direct ones, those with
individualistic political cultures in the United States are usually too complex to maintain face-to-face ties. So the system of mutual obligation is har-
nessed through political parties, which serve as "business corporations"
dedicated to providing the organization necessary to maintain that system.
Party regularity is indispensable in the individualistic political culture
because it is the means for coordinating individual enterprise in the political arena; it is also the one way of preventing individualism in politics
from running wild.

In such a system, an individual can succeed politically, not by dealing
with issues in some exceptional way or by accepting some concept of good
government and then by striving to implement it, but by maintaining his
or her place in the system of mutual obligations. A person can do this by
operating according to the norms of his or her particular party, to the exclusion of other political considerations. Such a political culture encourages
the maintenance of a party system that is competitive, but not overtly so,
in the pursuit of office. Its politicians are interested in office as a means of
controlling the distribution of the favors or rewards of government rather
than as a means of exercising governmental power for programmatic ends;
hence competition may prove less rewarding than accommodation in certain situations.

Since the individualistic political culture eschews ideological concerns
in its "business-like" conception of politics, both politicians and citizens
tend to look upon political activity as a specialized one—as essentially the
province of professionals, of minimum and passing concern to laypersons,
and with no place for amateurs to play an active role. Furthermore, there
is a strong tendency among the public to believe that politics is a dirty—
albeit necessary—business, better left to those who are willing to soil themselves by engaging in it. In practice, then, where the individualistic
political culture is dominant, there is likely to be an easy attitude toward
the limits of the professional's perquisites. Since a fair amount of corruption is expected in the normal course of things, there is relatively little
popular excitement when any is found, unless it is of an extraordinary

character. It is as if the public were willing to pay a surcharge for services rendered, rebelling only when the surcharge becomes too heavy. Of course, the judgments as to what is "normal" and what is "extraordinary" are themselves subjective and culturally conditioned.

Public officials, committed to "giving the public what it wants," are normally not willing to initiate new programs or open up new areas of government activity on their own initiative. They will do so when they perceive an overwhelming public demand for them to act, but only then. In a sense, their willingness to expand the functions of government is based on an extension of the *quid pro quo* "favors" system, which serves as the central core of their political relationships. New and better services are the reward they give the public for placing them in office. The value mix and legitimacy of change in the individualistic political culture are directly related to commercial concerns.

The individualistic political culture is ambivalent about the place of bureaucracy in the political order. In one sense, the bureaucratic method of operation flies in the face of the favor system that is central to the individualistic political process. At the same time, the virtues of organizational efficiency appear substantial to those seeking to master the market. In the end, bureaucratic organization is introduced within the framework of the favor system; large segments of the bureaucracy may be insulated from it through the merit system, but the entire organization is pulled into the political environment at crucial points through political appointment at the upper echelons and, very frequently, also through the bending of the merit system to meet political demands.

*   *   *

The Moralistic Political Culture

To the extent that American society is built on the principles of "commerce" (in the broadest sense) and that the marketplace provides the model for public relationships, all Americans share some of the attitudes that are of great importance in the individualistic political culture. At the same time, substantial segments of the American people operate politically within the framework of two political cultures—the moralistic and traditionalistic political cultures—whose theoretical structures and operational consequences depart significantly from the individualistic pattern at crucial points.

The *moralistic political culture* emphasizes the commonwealth conception as the basis for democratic government. Politics, to this political culture, is considered one of the great human activities: the search for the good society. True, it is a struggle for power, but it is also an effort to exercise power for the betterment of the commonwealth. Accordingly, in the moralistic political culture, both the general public and the politicians conceive of politics as a public activity centered on some notion of the public good and properly devoted to the advancement of the public interest. Good government, then, is measured by the degree to which it promotes the public good and in terms of the honesty, selflessness, and commitment to the public welfare of those who govern.

In the moralistic political culture, individualism is tempered by a general commitment to utilizing communal (preferably nongovernmental, but governmental if necessary) power to intervene in the sphere of "private" activities when it is considered necessary to do so for the public good or the well-being of the community. Accordingly, issues have an important place in the moralistic style of politics, functioning to set the tone for political concern. Government is considered a positive instrument with a responsibility to promote the general welfare, although definitions of what its positive role should be may vary considerably from era to era.

As in the case of the individualistic political culture, the change from nineteenth- to twentieth-century conceptions of what government's positive role should be has been great; for example, support for Prohibition has given way to support for wage and hour regulation. At the same time, care must be taken to distinguish between a predisposition toward communal activism and a desire for federal government activity. For example, many representatives of the moralistic political culture oppose federal aid for urban renewal without in any way opposing community responsibility for urban development. The distinction they make (implicitly, at least) is between what they consider legitimate community responsibility and what they believe to be central government encroachment; or between communitarianism, which they value, and "collectivism," which they abhor. Thus, on some public issues we find certain such representatives taking highly conservative positions despite their positive attitudes toward public activity generally. Such representatives may also prefer government intervention in the social realm—that is, censorship or screening of books and movies—over government intervention in the economy, holding that the former is necessary for the public good and the latter, harmful.

Since the moralistic political culture rests on the fundamental conception that politics exists primarily as a means for coming to grips with the issues and public concerns of civil society, it embraces the notion that politics is ideally a matter of concern for all citizens, not just those who are professionally committed to political careers. Indeed, this political culture considers it the duty of every citizen to participate in the political affairs of his or her commonwealth.

Accordingly, there is a general insistence within this political culture that government service is public service, which places moral obligations upon those who participate in government that are more demanding than the moral obligations of the marketplace. There is an equally general rejection of the notion that the field of politics is a legitimate realm for private economic enrichment. Of course, politicians may benefit economically because of their political careers, but they are not expected to *profit* from political activity; indeed, they are held suspect if they do.

Since the concept of serving the community is the core of the political relationship, politicians are expected to adhere to it even at the expense of individual loyalties and political friendships. Consequently, party regularity is not of prime importance. The political party is considered a useful political device, but it is not valued for its own sake. Regular party ties can be abandoned with relative impunity for third parties, special local parties, or nonpartisan systems if such changes are believed to be helpful in gaining larger political goals. People can even shift from party to party without sanctions if such change is justified by political belief.

In the moralistic political culture, rejection of firm party ties is not to be viewed as a rejection of politics as such. On the contrary, because politics is considered potentially good and healthy within the context of that culture, it is possible to have highly political nonpartisan systems. Certainly nonpartisanship is instituted not to eliminate politics but to improve it, by widening access to public office for those unwilling or unable to gain office through the regular party structure.

In practice, where the moralistic political culture is dominant today, there is considerably more amateur participation in politics. There is also much less of what Americans consider to be corruption in government and less tolerance of those actions considered to be corrupt. Hence politics does not have the taint it so often bears in the individualistic environment.

By virtue of its fundamental outlook, the moralistic political culture creates a greater commitment to active government intervention in the economic and social life of the community. At the same time, the strong commitment to *communitarianism* characteristic of that political culture tends to channel the interest in government intervention into highly localistic paths, such that a willingness to encourage local government intervention to set public standards does not necessarily reflect a concomitant willingness to allow outside governments equal opportunity to intervene. Not infrequently, public officials themselves will seek to initiate new government activities in an effort to come to grips with problems as yet unperceived by a majority of the citizenry. The moralistic political culture is not committed to either change or the status quo *per se* but, rather, will accept either depending upon the morally defined ends to be gained.

The major difficulty of this political culture in adjusting bureaucracy to the political order is tied to the potential conflict between communitarian principles and the necessity for large-scale organization to increase bureaucratic efficiency, a problem that could affect the attitudes of moralistic culture states toward federal activity of certain kinds. Otherwise, the notion of a politically neutral administrative system creates no problem within the moralistic value system and even offers many advantages. Where merit systems are instituted, they are rigidly maintained.

*   *   *

The Traditionalistic Political Culture

The *traditionalistic political culture* is rooted in an ambivalent attitude toward the marketplace coupled with a paternalistic and elitist conception of the commonwealth. It reflects an older, precommercial attitude that accepts a substantially hierarchical society as part of the ordered nature of things, authorizing and expecting those at the top of the social structure to take a special and dominant role in government. Like its moralistic counterpart, the traditionalistic political culture accepts government as an actor with a positive role in the community, but in a very limited sphere—mainly that of securing the continued maintenance of the existing social order. To do so, it functions to confine real political power to a relatively small and self-perpetuating group drawn from an established elite who often inherit their "right" to govern through family ties or social position. Accordingly, social and family ties are paramount in a traditionalistic political culture; in fact, their importance is greater than that of personal ties in the individualistic political culture, where, after all is said and done, a person's first responsibility is to him- or herself. At the same time, those who do not have a definite role to play in politics are not expected to be even minimally active as citizens. In many cases, they are not even expected to vote. In return, they are guaranteed that, outside of the limited sphere of politics, family rights (usually labeled "individual rights") are paramount, not to be taken lightly or ignored. As in the individualistic political culture, those active in politics are expected to benefit personally from their activity, though not necessarily through direct pecuniary gain.

Political parties are of minimal importance in a traditionalistic political culture, inasmuch as they encourage a degree of openness and competition that goes against the fundamental grain of an elite-oriented political order. Their major utility is to recruit people to fill the formal offices of government not desired by the established power-holders. Political competition in a traditionalistic political culture is usually conducted through factional alignments, as an extension of the personalistic politics that is characteristic of the system; hence political systems within the culture tend to have a loose one-party orientation if they have political parties at all.

Practically speaking, a traditionalistic political culture is found only in a society that retains some of the organic characteristics of the pre-industrial social order. "Good government" in the political culture involves the maintenance and encouragement of traditional patterns and, if necessary, their adjustment to changing conditions with the least possible upset. Where the traditionalistic political culture is dominant in the United States today, political leaders play conservative and custodial rather than initiatory roles unless pressed strongly from the outside.

Whereas the individualistic and moralistic political cultures may encourage the development of bureaucratic systems of organization on the grounds of "rationality" and "efficiency" in government (depending on their particular situations), traditionalistic political cultures tend to be instinctively anti-bureaucratic. The reason is that bureaucracy by its very nature interferes with the fine web of informal interpersonal relationships that lie at the root of the political system and have been developed by following traditional patterns over the years. Where bureaucracy is introduced, it is generally confined to ministerial functions under the aegis of the established power-holders.

The Distribution and Impact of Political Subcultures

Map 1 on pages 30–31 shows how migrational patterns have led to the concentration of specific political subcultures in particular states and localities. The basic patterns of political culture were set during the period of the rural-land frontier by three great streams of American migration that began on the East Coast and moved westward after the colonial period. Each stream moved from east to west along more or less fixed paths, following lines of least resistance that generally led them due west from the immediately previous area of settlement.

* * *

Political Culture: Some Caveats

By now the reader has no doubt formed his or her own value judgments as to the relative worth of the three political subcultures. For this reason a particular warning against *hasty* judgments must be added here. Each of the three political subcultures contributes something important to the configuration of the American political system, and each possesses certain characteristics that are inherently dangerous to the survival of that system.

The moralistic political culture, for example, is the primary source of the continuing American quest for the good society, yet there is a noticeable tendency toward inflexibility and narrow-mindedness among some of its representatives. The individualistic political culture is the most tolerant of out-and-out political corruption, yet it has also provided the framework for the integration of diverse groups into the mainstream of American life. When representatives of the moralistic political culture, in their striving for a better social order, try to limit individual freedom, they usually come up against representatives of the individualistic political culture, to whom individual freedom is the cornerstone of their pluralistic order, though not for any noble reasons. Conversely, of course, the moralistic political culture acts as a restraint against the tendencies of the individualistic political culture to tolerate anything as long as it is in the marketplace.

The traditionalistic political culture contributes to the search for continuity in a society whose major characteristic is change; yet in the name of continuity, its representatives have denied African Americans (as well as Native Americans and Latinos) their civil rights. When it is in proper working

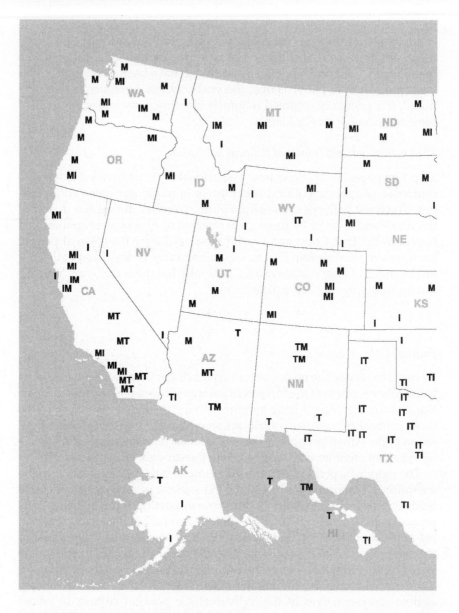

Map 1 The Regional Distribution of Political Cultures Within the States. *Source:* Daniel J. Elazar, *American Federalism: A View from the States,* 3rd ed. (New York: Harper and Row Publishers, 1984), pp. 124–25.

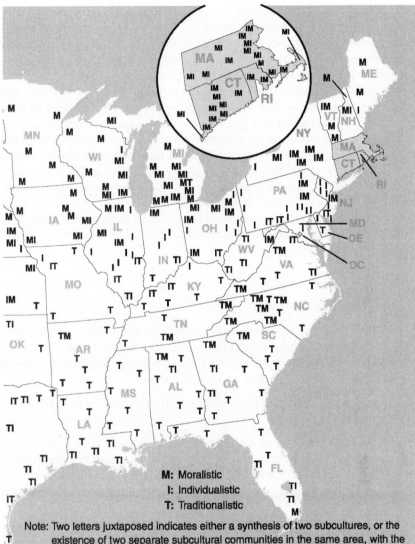

M: Moralistic
I: Individualistic
T: Traditionalistic

Note: Two letters juxtaposed indicates either a synthesis of two subcultures, or the existence of two separate subcultural communities in the same area, with the first dominant and the second secondary.

order, the traditionalistic culture has produced a unique group of first-rate national leaders from among its elites; but without a first-rate elite to draw upon, traditionalistic political-culture systems degenerate into oligarchies of the lowest level. Comparisons like these should induce caution in any evaluation of a subject that, by its very nature, evokes value judgments.

It is equally important to use caution in identifying individuals and groups as belonging to one cultural type or another on the basis of their public political behavior at a given moment in time. Immediate political responses to the issues of the day may reveal the political culture of the respondents, but not necessarily. Often, in fact, people will make what appear to be the same choices for different reasons—especially in public affairs, where the choices available at any given time are usually quite limited. Deeper analysis of what is behind those responses is usually needed. In other words, the names of the political cultures are not substitutes for the terms *conservative* and *liberal*, and should not be taken as such.

* * *

DISCUSSION QUESTIONS

1. Consider the definitions Elazar presents in his analysis. What would you say are the fundamental differences and similarities among the three approaches with regard to the proper scope of government involvement in economic and social matters?

2. How important is public participation in politics across the three philosophies?

3. Examine Elazar's map for the part of the country where you attend school or the area you consider home. In your view, how accurately do the labels describe the politics of that area? What kinds of evidence are you considering when answering the question?

Debating the Issues: What Does It Mean to Be an American?

What does it mean to be an American? This deceptively simple question is challenging to answer. Because the United States encompasses a vast array of races, ethnicities, religions, and cultures, it can be difficult to define "American" by reference to these criteria. The country's geography differs dramatically from region to region, and economic ways of life accordingly differ greatly as well. In many ways, diverse groups of Americans have experienced American history differently, so a common historical identity is not obviously the answer either. One popular argument is that the United States is united by a set of political ideals. As far back as the early nineteenth century, scholars have tried to identify the nature of American political culture: Is it a commitment to individualism? A belief in equality? A shared set of values about the appropriate role of government? Openness?

Public-opinion data today show the country embracing diversity and tolerance, but it is also divided along sharp political lines. Each of the authors in this debate suggests that these political differences may create problems beyond the inevitable tensions that emerge in a diverse and dynamic society. Each examines the tension between unity and disunity from a different perspective.

Alia E. Dastagir notes that there is significant agreement among Americans around some basic values. Treating people equally, being personally responsible, voting, paying taxes, and following the law rank high. Civic participation, such as serving on a jury or participating in the U.S. Census, is valued, as is respecting the opinions of those with whom you disagree. Nonetheless, Dastagir argues that Americans differ substantially along political lines on some values and behaviors, on what it means to be patriotic, on who is an American, and on whether the label "American" is meaningful to an individual. She notes in conclusion that young people's experience with a more diverse population may bode well for some of the prized values of American identity, including equality, inclusion, and opportunity.

To political scientist Steven B. Smith, patriotism is important and worthy, but it stands at a crossroads. It presupposes some degree of consensus, he argues, but we as Americans see many signs of division. He suggests that Americans may no longer "possess an agreed-upon narrative that could provide a foundation for national unity." In part, these difficulties are caused by two narratives that guide our thinking about the United States. The narrative of return tells us who we are by looking back to the nation's beginning, the founding. It sees the United States as a nation on a special mission, born in historically unique circumstances by a confluence of brilliant thinkers forging a new style and philosophy of governance and individual liberty. The narrative of progress does not venerate the past but instead emphasizes the possibility of progress opened by human exploration, experimentation, and expertise. Imperfect beginnings are improved, and that quest to improve is ongoing. The narrative of return sees patriotism as loyalty to an already established nation, while the narrative of progress sees patriotism as "an aspiration to a country still to be accomplished." Smith sees patriotism as a vital force, but neither of these narratives is sufficient. Patriotism, properly understood, is a way of understanding each other that helps us see where we share values as well as where we seek improvement. It "is tied to place and rooted in experience, in how we have been brought up, our rituals and habits, our customs and feelings. . . . Being a patriot is like possessing a language . . . the whole network of signs, informal codes, cultural references, gestures and inflections. . . . It is what makes us instantly recognizable to each other as ones who share a common background."

Jonathan Holloway, president of Rutgers University, worries that Americans are "caught in a vortex of intoxication," hearing messages that reinforce our views and thoughts rather than those that help us understand each other. Are we better off? he asks. Is America? Holloway proposes that Americans, before reaching the age of 25, be required to perform a year of national civilian or military service. Such a system, he believes, would build bridges between people with a wide range of differences as they work for a common purpose that serves an important public interest. It would help people see each other as Americans and build an understanding of what it means to be an American.

4

"Amid Protests and a Pandemic, What Does It Mean to Be American in 2020?"

ALIA E. DASTAGIR

It's a difficult time to celebrate America.

This Fourth of July, the coronavirus pandemic rages nationwide, and the 127,000-person death toll continues to climb. The resulting health and economic crises have left more than 80% of Americans stressed about the future of the country and 75% feeling the nation is "pretty seriously" off track. Civil unrest embroils the nation after the deaths of Black Americans at the hands of police. And while a majority of U.S. adults still say they are "extremely" or "very" proud to be American, both numbers are at a 20-year low, according to Gallup.

As we prepare to mark the birth of the nation, debate intensifies over what it means to be an American—who qualifies and how a good one behaves. Are protesters good Americans? The Black Lives Matter protesters or the anti-lockdown ones? Are you American if you were born here but don't know the history? Are you American if you've lived here nearly your whole life but don't have a piece of paper to prove it?

Experts say the heart of the debate is whether being American depends on who you are—such as being an English speaker—or on what you believe—such as valuing freedom or equality. This old debate is inflamed by protests over personal liberties amid the pandemic and severe racial disparities, all against the backdrop of increasingly diverse demographics.

"White Americans have defined the nation, its norms, what it means to be an American for decades. That means that, by definition, some individuals . . . have been on the outs," said Efrén Pérez, a professor of political science and psychology at UCLA. "Now things have changed demographically, politically, where some of those individuals are saying: '[h]old on a minute. If I'm excluded by that version of being American, which I view as very narrow, we're going to develop our own sense of what it means to be an American.'"

Experts say this isn't just a fight over who belongs. It's about one version of the United States versus another.

What Is American?

Despite the political polarization of the country, there are elements of American identity people generally agree on.

When it comes to being a "real American," 90% said it meant treating people equally and 88% said it meant being personally responsible in a 2018 Grinnell College National Poll of 1,000 U.S. adults. When it comes to being a good citizen, a Pew Research Center survey that year found 74% said voting, 71% said paying taxes and 69% said always following the law.

Republicans and Democrats closely agree on several other aspects of good citizenship, including serving on juries, participating in the Census and respecting the opinions of those with whom you disagree.

But political identity still influences how people feel about the country and how they believe devotion to the nation should be expressed.

Republicans are far more likely to say they are "extremely" proud of being an American than Democrats, according to Gallup. Half of Republicans say displaying the American flag is very important, compared with a quarter of Democrats. While 52% of Democrats say it's very important to protest when government actions are wrong, only 35% of Republicans say the same.

There are also perceptions not about behaviors but about qualities, for instance, how people believe a "real American" looks. Research shows Americans are much more likely to associate Kate Winslet, an English actress, with being American than they are Lucy Liu, an American actress. The Grinnell College poll found nearly a quarter of respondents said real Americans are born in the [United States] and are Christian, and 44% said real Americans speak English.

"That's why they ask someone who is Asian, 'Oh, what country do you come from?' without thinking 'Oh, this person could actually be an American citizen who's born here and maybe the parents are born here and the grandparents,'" said Leonie Huddy, a professor of political science at the State University of New York-Stony Brook and co-author of the study American Patriotism, National Identity, and Political Involvement.

For those who believe American identity is defined by values, there's potential for a larger tent.

"Some people think that being American means . . . I believe in equal opportunity. In that sense it doesn't matter if you're white, black, brown, green, purple. All that matters is that you endorse these bedrock principles," Pérez said.

Liz French, 32, of Severance, Colorado, says that while this is a volatile time for the nation, she's confident America's core values will see the country through.

"I think of Hurricane Harvey in Houston a few years back, and how many people came from all different sides of the country to really help rebuild that community. And that's what America means to me," French said. "We've seen over and over in our country's history, periods of strife and Americans coming back together and realizing we may not have the same ideologies, we may not live the same way, but we're all citizens of this country and we all want to make it better. That's why I'm so patriotic in this moment, regardless of what's happening."

Who Is a Patriot?

Four years ago, Colin Kaepernick took a knee and eventually lost his NFL career. His critics, including President Donald Trump, said he was unpatriotic.

His supporters and the athletes who joined his protest against racial injustice and police brutality said his actions intended to make the [United States] better.

Time and tragedy have many people rethinking their stances on Kaepernick.

NFL Commissioner Roger Goodell admitted after the George Floyd protests that the league did not handle the Kaepernick situation properly. He said he will "encourage" any team thinking of signing Kaepernick, adding that he's open to the former quarterback working with the league on social justice issues.

The way George Floyd's death catalyzed nationwide protests and tapped into rage and frustration centuries in the making shows that the [United States] is in a different place than it was just a few years ago.

"It's clear that we're divided, not just on racial lines, but there are splits within the white population. I think that's what is different," Huddy said. "Seeing solidarity across racial lines suggests it's a fight for the country itself, what it means and what its values are."

Johnna James, 42, was raised in Anadarko, Oklahoma, a predominately Native American community, and says she is proud of her country but doesn't ignore its history.

"As a member of the Chickasaw Nation and an Indigenous woman, I'm very proud to . . . (see) lots of people from diverse backgrounds coming together for the common goal of peace and even some correction in the original framework of this country that was no doubt built on systems of oppression," she said.

Public protests are protected by the First Amendment, and experts say they can be deeply patriotic. "Constructive patriotism" maintains it is appropriate to expose when the country does not live up to those values. It differs from "blind patriotism," which conveys that "my country does no wrong" and can bleed into nationalism.

"This country was founded on dissent. Think about who the founding fathers were. They were dissenting against British rule," said Christopher Parker, a University of Washington political science professor. "A real patriot is about criticizing the country when it needs to be criticized in order to bring the social practices in alignment with the values on which the country was founded."

There is strong agreement on founding American values, but there are important distinctions in how we interpret them. White Americans, for example, generally think of freedom as being free from the central government, Parker said. When people of color think about freedom, they think of it as freedom from discrimination and racism.

"Liberty can be a very capacious term depending on who you are," he said.

Who Is American?

Alycia Kamil, 19, is a Black activist in Chicago who recently co-organized an anti-racism protest in the city's Bronzeville neighborhood. Being "American," she said, is not a central part of her identity.

"As Black people, as people of color, it is incredibly hard to love a country that historically has oppressed us," she said. "When we're fighting for our rights, it's not even necessarily as an American. It's as a human."

For her to feel pride in America, she said, there would need to be widespread recognition that the systems upon which the country was built are inherently violent and racist, and that they have to be dismantled for Black people to feel safe.

Moises Rodriguez Cruz, 22, has also organized and protested racial injustice in several U.S. cities. Cruz's relationship to national identity is complicated.

Cruz—who identifies as queer, Latinx, "poor" and a [Deferred Action for Childhood Arrivals (DACA)] recipient—is a community organizer for Semillas, a social justice organization in Chattanooga, Tennessee.

"When you grow up undocumented, you grow up in a world that tells you that you're illegal. There's no way that you fit into the American narrative because you don't have this magical paper that validates your existence and your identity in the country," Cruz said.

And yet, Cruz's presence is well-documented. Cruz went to school, goes to work, has relationships, walks the same streets as white Americans, attends the same health clinics. Cruz wishes that when people talk about what it means to be an American, they would do more to acknowledge its diversity without whitewashing its past.

"When we talk about America and what it means to be American, what we really should celebrate is queer people, trans people, black people," Cruz said. "This country was founded on colonization. This country was people arriving on this land and stealing from Indigenous people, from Native Americans. Let's talk about the realities of the world."

Cruz said he doesn't feel pride in a "nationalistic project" but is often proud of the people who make up the United States.

What's Ahead?

Young people are more familiar with diversity, and many are using activism to edge the country closer toward a version of America they feel embraces different identities. Generation Z or the "post-millennial" generation is the most racially and ethnically diverse, according to Pew. Today's 6- to 21-year-olds are projected to become "majority nonwhite" in 2026, according to Census Bureau projections.

"People can understand, even if they don't articulate, that things have changed. Some Americans, some of them who happen to be white, will tell you, 'America doesn't feel like the America I knew,'" Pérez said. "Exactly. It isn't."

American identity is a powerful concept. It animates people's behavior and sets norms for what's expected. Some argue that in a culturally diverse nation, this identity is the glue that keeps people together. Without it, there's worry the country can't cohesively operate.

"Even those that have disagreed with a given policy or administration have been able to look at the United States and see an example of a country that is not homogeneous, full of different people from different backgrounds and countries, but that collectively makes democracy work," said Jack Petroskey, 29, of Royal Oak, Michigan. "It is such an incredible legacy, and I am personally so proud of it."

5

From *Reclaiming Patriotism in an Age of Extremes*

STEVEN B. SMITH

A T a recent Fourth of July picnic at the home of a colleague, the hostess asked the group if we all felt patriotic. This question created a moment of acute embarrassment; it seemed to have breached some unspoken rule of political correctness. Was it even appropriate to ask such a thing? Had any of us grown up in a house that flew the flag? (She was the only one who had.) We then read the Declaration of Independence before tucking into our hamburgers and hot dogs. This was hardly an unusual experience. We were celebrating our national founding, and yet for several around the table, the meaning of this celebration was cloudy. It is not that they were unpatriotic but that the language of patriotism had become strangely foreign to them. Many Americans have a vague feeling of patriotism yet would be unable to offer any articulate rationale for this feeling. The aim of this short book is to provide it.

Americans have become deeply divided over the meaning of patriotism. When the San Francisco 49ers quarterback Colin Kaepernick decided to take a knee during the national anthem to protest racism and police brutality, was he being unpatriotic? Many clearly thought so; many others did not. What of those who—as I write—are taking to the streets to protest the murder of George Floyd and calling for racial justice? Is their protest patriotic? How you answer will depend on what you believe patriotism involves.

Patriotism is above all a form of loyalty. We admire loyalty to family, friends, sports teams, even institutions—up to a point. I am deeply devoted to the New York Yankees; the team is a formative part of my identity. I am a loyal Jew who cares deeply for the land of Israel, warts and all. And I believe myself to be a loyal American. Yet loyalty often sits uneasily with other qualities that we equally admire, such as fairness, justice, mercy, equality, and open-mindedness. There seems something primitive, almost primordial, about patriotism. It seems like the mafia code of silence, or *omertà*, which protects members from outsiders. Does loyalty to my country require me to adopt a belligerent attitude toward other countries? Does it require me, in the jargon of our time, to put "America first"? Does loyalty to America mean that I overlook the nation's faults, or would this be a form of bad faith? These are some of the vexing questions I want to consider.

*   *   *

Like much else in our public lives, patriotism or loyalty to country has become politicized. It would be easy, as we witness the rise of ethno-nationalism in many parts of the world, to reject patriotism as tainted with xenophobia, racism, and other forms of religious and ethnic bigotry. But things are not so simple. Those are not expressions of patriotism but corruptions of it. I submit that nearly every person, even those who seem the most alienated or most cosmopolitan, feels some form of love of country. Certainly the guests at that Fourth of July picnic do: all of them have the option to live elsewhere, yet they choose to stay. So long as we remain political animals, we cannot avoid patriotism. The question is only what form it will take. Will it be harsh and barbarous, or humane and enlightened? There is no third option. It might be possible to wish for a world without patriotism, as many from Leo Tolstoy to Martha Nussbaum have done, but such a world would be a world without politics. Maybe it would be a more desirable world than the one we have now, but I find it hard to imagine what it would be like to live there.

Return or Progress

Today American patriotism finds itself at a crossroads. Patriotism presupposes some kind of national consensus around which citizens might coalesce. But at this time of intense partisan conflict, when we are deeply divided by class, race, education, and culture, even that minimal consensus seems to be lacking. Are the American framers to be celebrated for creating the first and most enduring experiment in self-government, or condemned for their complicity in the evils of slavery and their blindness to the fate of indigenous peoples? Is American hegemony in the postwar era a source of freedom and a beacon of light to other nations, or are we the agents of a new imperialism spreading a degrading commercial culture? Are companies like Amazon and Google a tribute to American creativity and entrepreneurial genius or products of an out-of-control business culture that has become an engine of inequality and corporate exploitation? Are the immigrants flooding our southern border aspiring participants in the great American experiment in freedom, or are they illegal aliens who would take our jobs while corroding our culture? We cannot agree even on the basic facts by which to debate these questions. We seem no longer to possess an agreed-upon narrative that could provide a foundation for national unity.

Part of our current discontent grows out of the bifurcated origins of American identity. Being an American has never been easy. Those of us who were born here take it for granted. America, we like to say, is an idea but it is not a single idea, more like a cluster or a family of ideas. There is a polarity at the heart of our identity. This is not simply a difference between liberals and conservatives, multiculturalists and nationalists, Democrats and Republicans; it gets to something more fundamental. At the core of our identity are two conflicting narratives—by which I do not mean stories or histories but the basic beliefs, cognitive values, affective dispositions, and prescriptions for action that constitute our shared way of life. These two competing accounts are the bifocal lenses through which we understand ourselves. I will call them the narrative of return and the narrative of progress.

The narrative of return is an origin story. It tells who we are by taking us back to our beginnings. In Hebrew, the term *Ba'al teshuva* is a person who has returned to God, driven by feelings of sin, guilt, and atonement, as well as by hope for redemption. The Hebrew origin story, based on the prophetic ideal of a chosen people that goes back to ancient Israel, connects faith with fidelity to tradition. In the American context, the narrative of return is usually associated with the founding. It suggests a golden moment that can never be recovered but to which we can and should remain faithful. This moment might be associated with the Pilgrims who landed on Plymouth Rock, George Washington at Valley Forge, or the founders who signed the Constitution in Independence Hall—all of whom are seen as more venerable, more worthy of honor and respect, than any present-day person could be.

The first people fully to espouse this narrative of return were the Puritans. "I see the entire destiny of America embodied in the first Puritan to land on its shores, just as the entire human race was embodied in the first man," Tocqueville wrote in *Democracy in America*. This is a bit of hyperbole. The legacy of Puritanism was peculiar to New England, not to the entire United States, and it is what made New England different. You might even call it New England Exceptionalism. Had Tocqueville spent more time in Virginia or South Carolina, he would have found a very different political culture. Still, he was on to something. America was and to some degree still is a Puritan republic. We continue to see ourselves through the old Puritan conception of a chosen people, the indispensable nation, the bearer of the torch of liberty. To be sure, Puritanism has never entirely lived down its reputation for hypocrisy and sexual repression, canonized in Nathaniel Hawthorne's *The Scarlet Letter*. "Puritanism," according to H. L. Mencken's famous quip, is "the haunting fear that someone, somewhere, may be happy." Nevertheless, its legacy has done as much as anything to shape the American character.

* * *

This idea of establishing a new community, untouched by history and the Old World, has its roots in these Puritan founders who came to this country to found "a city upon a hill" as John Winthrop declared in his 1630 sermon "A Model of Christian Charity," delivered on board the *Arabella*. America would be a new Jerusalem for a new chosen people, one that would serve as a light to nations around the world. These men and women saw themselves as a new community of saints who were on an "errand in the wilderness"; they would create towns and cities across New England with names like New Canaan, Bethel, Salem, and New Haven.

*   *   *

Winthrop's vision of the city on a hill, famously revived by Ronald Reagan, became the basis for the idea of America as an exceptional nation with a special mission, even while there has been much disagreement on what that mission is. Our modern idea of American exceptionalism is inseparable from this sense of mission. Winthrop's phrase has its source in the parable of Light and Salt from the Sermon on the Mount, where Jesus tells his listeners, "You are a light of the world. A city that is set on a hill cannot be hidden" (Matthew 5:14), although Jesus was himself echoing Isaiah: "we shall be as a city upon a hill; the eyes of all people are upon us" (Isaiah 42:6). Yet behind these aspirational words lay the perpetual fear of backsliding. "The eyes of all people are upon us," Winthrop warned, "so that if we shall deal falsely with our God in this work we have undertaken and so cause him to withdraw his present help from us, we shall be made a story and a by-word through the world."

The idea that the "eyes of all people" were watching the fate of this tiny band of religious dissidents departing for a largely uninhabited world— uninhabited, that is, by Europeans—testifies to the remarkable strength and confidence they drew from religious faith. The fear of dealing "falsely" with our founding principles remains a staple of present-day conservatism. For conservatives, American patriotism means a *return* to the "original intent" of the founders as expressed in the jurisprudence of Antonin Scalia and other icons of the right.

The second narrative we tell about ourselves is the narrative of progress. Progress is a secular idea, a product of the Enlightenment, that is less concerned with veneration of the past than with hope for the future. The belief in progress is rooted in the modern conception of science. Science, as everyone learns in school, is a cumulative activity capable of almost infinite improvement. Through trial and error, it builds on previous knowledge to improve and surpass what went before. We may not know where science is going, but we do know that the truths of today will be replaced tomorrow by higher truths. The central idea is that through the application of the scientific method, the human condition can be bettered; want, poverty, and ignorance can be abolished; and the future will be superior to the present, just as the present is superior to the past.

The progressive ideal stresses not perfect beginnings followed by backsliding and punctuated by periodic calls for moral renewal, but imperfect beginnings followed by cumulative efforts at correction, reform, and improvement. Progress, or what became known as progressivism, was based on the belief that history—dubbed the "historical process"—could be shaped and directed by human intelligence. In the past, progress was achieved piecemeal and haphazardly, but with new methods of scientific planning and expertise, it would be possible not only to know the direction of history but to get there more quickly as well. For progressives, history is the story of the collective self-improvement of humankind.

* * *

For progressives, patriotism is not so much loyalty to an already established nation, but an aspiration to a country still to be accomplished. It is not that progressives do not love their country; they have just become less certain about whose country it is. On their account, America is rooted in a flawed beginning tainted by slavery and other moral failings that require continual adjustment to the needs of the present. The recent dispute over the roles of Thomas Jefferson and Andrew Jackson, once considered democratic heroes, is a case in point. Jefferson's failure to free his slaves and Jackson's Indian policy have made them anathema to progressives.

Progressivism has become less concerned with improving on the past than with erasing it. The debate over national me-morialization has morphed from a demand to remove monuments to Confederate heroes—men who actually fought against the Union—to the removal of monuments to Christopher Columbus, George Washington, Ulysses S. Grant, Teddy Roosevelt, and Woodrow Wilson. For progressives, patriotism is best exemplified by protest movements like the abolitionists of the nineteenth century, the suffragettes and civil rights protesters of the early and mid-twentieth century, or the Stonewall riots of 1969 that set off the LGBT movement. They believe that "dissent is the highest form of patriotism," a phrase wrongly attributed to Thomas Jefferson that is still enshrined in our national discourse. America is regarded as a continual work in progress, and celebration of past accomplishments draws attention away from the considerable work still to be done.

* * *

If the narrative of return can become too exclusionary, the progressive narrative is insufficiently American. Here we should distinguish an older version of progressivism from its current form. The progressives of the early twentieth century, like Randolph Bourne and Walter Lippmann, were ardent patriots and nationalists. They sought to create a more robust national state in reaction to the doctrines of federalism and "states' rights," which they viewed as having led to civil war and the dominance of private interests over the public good. This strain of progressivism can still be found occupying the mainstream of the Democratic Party, but a different form has developed alongside it. New age progressives, as I call them, have adopted a form of multicultural politics increasingly focused on race and ethnicity as hallmarks of identity, but they reject any appeal to patriotism or national selfhood. Multiculturalism represents a fragmentation of the older progressive narrative that was centered around the patriotic idea of a single people engaged in a common enterprise.

Many on the new age left still support traditional progressive policies such as single-payer health care, extended parental leave, and college tuition forgiveness, but they regard any assertion of American patriotism as the problem, not the solution. They have nurtured a deep hostility to the nation-state and national institutions—even some who aspire to national political office—regarding them as the source of all political evil. Indeed, it is difficult to understand why so many call themselves progressives when their theory of history is often anything but. The earlier optimistic narratives of progress, from the Civil War to the New Deal and Great Society to the election of Barack Obama, described America on an upward trajectory toward greater justice and inclusion. While progressives once believed that "the arc of the moral universe is long but it bends toward justice," today's new age progressives view the prospect of piecemeal political reform as hopelessly naïve. The optimistic narrative of progress has been replaced by counter-narratives of victimization and irredeemability that have produced racism, climate catastrophe, and an impending fascism foreshadowed by the election of Donald Trump.

New age progressives, like their nationalist counterparts, have walled themselves off into self-reinforcing enclaves with little reason to communicate with the outside world or hear challenges to their certainties. They have fostered a kind of grievance politics that never misses an opportunity to take offense at a slight, either real or imagined. They may call themselves progressives and may celebrate certain universal values—democracy, human rights, freedom—but nothing as ostensibly parochial as God or country. New age progressives lack a core value of patriotism, a sense of loyalty to a particular tradition and way of life. Anyone can embrace the ideas of progress and rights, but only an American can be patriotic about America. The progressive patriot—like most of those in attendance at my colleague's Fourth of July picnic—is devoted not to the America that exists, but to the idea of America as it is yet to be. What remains of actual patriotism has become vanishingly thin.

Patriotism needs to be distinguished—and reclaimed—from these two competing dispositions. On the right, patriotism has become indistinguishable from nationalism, a quite different sentiment. * * * The nationalist mentality thrives on the language of "us" and "them" and cannot survive without it.

Patriotism speaks a different language, one of loyalty and respect. It suggests a home or an extended family. We love our families not because we think they are better than other families, but because they have nurtured and sustained us through good times and bad. * * * Patriotism is rooted in a rudimentary, even primordial love of one's own; the customs, habits, manners, and traditions that make us who and what we are.

On the left, patriotism is often contrasted unfavorably with cosmopolitanism. Cosmopolitanism has roots in the Western tradition that go back to the Roman Stoics, who thought of themselves as "citizens of the world" with no particular allegiances to state or nation. * * * This is in many ways a noble ideal. But too close an attachment to the idea of a global humanity runs the risk of ignoring the specific loyalties that bind people to their own countries. At the extreme, cosmopolitanism cuts people off from their national traditions, leaving them alienated from the culture in which they are embedded.

In contrast to both nationalism and cosmopolitanism, American patriotism has a dual structure that captures elements of both progress and return. * * * From the beginning, Americans have been a people of the book who have sought to ground national identity in higher principles like equality, rights, and freedom of religion. These ideas are embedded in our earliest national documents, from the Mayflower Compact, the Declaration of Independence, the Constitution, and the Bill of Rights to their later articulation by our leading jurists, political leaders, and public figures. American patriotism is a uniquely principled patriotism.

Yet American patriotism is based not solely on the high principles of self-government and civil rights, but also on the sentiments and dispositions that have shaped our common history, both good and bad. Patriotism is tied to place and rooted in experience, in how we have been brought up, our rituals and habits, our customs and feelings. It is not only a matter of the head, but also one of the heart. It is not entirely rational, but neither is it irrational. Being a patriot is like possessing a language—by which I do not mean simply written and spoken English or any national vernacular, but the whole network of signs, informal codes, cultural references, gestures and inflections that shape our perceptions, feelings, and beliefs, as well as our body language, facial expressions, posture, and accent. It is what makes us instantly recognizable to each other as ones who share a common background. * * *

* * *

"To Unite a Divided America, Make People Work for It"

Jonathan Holloway

If we Americans listened to one another, perhaps we would recognize how absurd our discourse has become. It is our own fault that political discussions today are hotheaded arguments over whether the hooligans storming the halls of the Capitol were taking a tour or fomenting an insurrection; if we broadened our audiences, perhaps we would see the fallacy of claims that all Republicans are committed to voter suppression and that all Democrats are committed to voter fraud.

It seems like an easy challenge to address, but we lack the incentives to change our behavior. We are all, regardless of where we sit on the political spectrum, caught in a vortex of intoxication. We have fooled ourselves into thinking that our followers on social media are our friends. They aren't. They are our mirrors, recordings of our own thoughts and images played back to us, by us and for us. We feel good about ourselves, sure, but do we feel good as citizens? Do we feel good as Americans? Are we better off? Is America?

There are many problems in America, but fundamental to so many of them is our unwillingness to learn from one another, to see and respect one another, to become familiar with people from different racial and ethnic backgrounds and who hold different political views. It will take work to repair this problem, but building blocks exist. A good foundation would be a one-year mandatory national service program.

Nearly 90 years ago, in response to the Great Depression, President Franklin Roosevelt created the Civilian Conservation Corps, what was then America's largest organized nationwide civilian service program. About 30 years later, President Lyndon Johnson brought to fruition President John Kennedy's "domestic Peace Corps" initiative, the Volunteers in Service to America program, known as VISTA. Today, domestic civilian service is dominated by AmeriCorps and nongovernmental programs like Teach for America.

Taken together, these programs have been enormously successful at putting people to work, broadening the reach of basic social services related to education, health, and welfare. Most important, they have helped citizens see the crucial role that they can play in strengthening our democracy. Given that we know service programs can be so effective in shoring up the nation in moments of crisis, the time has come for a broader initiative, with higher aspirations and goals. The time has come for compulsory national service for all young people—with no exceptions.

Universal national service would include one year of civilian service or military service for all adults to be completed before they reach the age of 25, with responsibilities met domestically or around the world. It would channel the conscience of the Civilian Conservation Corps and put young people in the wilderness repairing the ravages of environmental destruction. It would draw on the lessons of the Peace Corps and dispatch young Americans to distant lands where they would understand the challenges of poor countries and of people for whom basic health and nutrition are aspirational goals. It would draw on the success of our military programs that in the past created pathways toward financial stability and educational progress for those with limited resources, while also serving as great unifiers among America's races, religions, and social classes.

These are but three examples. A one-year universal national service program could take many other forms, but it is easy to imagine that it could be a vehicle to provide necessary support to underserved urban and rural communities, help eliminate food deserts, contribute to rebuilding the nation's infrastructure, enrich our arts and culture, and bolster our community health clinics, classrooms, and preschools.

Furthermore, because service would be mandatory, it would force all of our young people to better know one another, creating the opportunities to learn about and appreciate our differences. Speaking as an educator, I know that we get better answers to complex problems when we assemble teams from a wide range of backgrounds. Once these teams realize that they share a common purpose, their collective differences and diversity in race, gender, expertise, faith, sexual orientation, and political orientation start to emerge as a strength. If you look at the state of our civic culture, it is clear that we have a long way to go before we can claim that we are doing the best that we can. The kind of experiential education I am advocating could change a life, could open a mind, and could save a democracy.

A sensible system of compulsory national service would build bridges between people and turn them into citizens. It would shore up our fragile communities and strengthen us as individuals and as a nation. Compulsory national service would make us more self-reliant and at the same time more interdependent. It would help us to realize our remarkable individual strengths and would reveal the enormous collective possibilities when we pull together instead of rip apart.

At its core, we need to heed the call for citizenship. We need to take the natural inclination to help out our friends and families and turn it into a willingness to support strangers. We need to inspire people to answer the call to serve because in so doing they will discover ways to have their voices heard and their communities seen and respected.

This is neither a new nor a partisan idea. This call to serve and inspire is written into the preamble of the United States Constitution. When the founders sought to "form a more perfect union, establish justice, ensure domestic tranquility, provide for the common defense, promote the general welfare, and secure the blessings of liberty," they were talking about establishing an ethos of citizenship and participation.

Compulsory national service is not a panacea, but neither is it a mere placebo. It could be a very real solution to a very real problem that already has wrought havoc on our democracy and that threatens our future as a nation, our viability as a culture and our very worth as human beings. This nation and its democratic principles need our help. We can and must do better.

DISCUSSION QUESTIONS

1. Is it important for the United States to have a sense of shared values or not? What are the risks and benefits for individuals and the country of having a sense of shared values? Is a sense of patriotism valuable, as Smith argues?

2. Occasionally in political campaigns, a candidate's beliefs or actions will be described as "un-American." What do you think people mean when they use this term? Would you describe any of the views presented in the Dastagir article as "un-American"? Are there any beliefs that you would define as "un-American"?

3. What are your views about Holloway's proposal for a year of universal mandatory service? Would it have the outcomes he suggests? How might Smith respond to Holloway's proposal?

4. A visitor from another country asks you, "What does it mean to be an American?" What do you say?

CHAPTER 2

The Founding and the Constitution

7

"The Nature of American Constitutionalism," from *The Origins of the American Constitution*

MICHAEL KAMMEN

The Constitution is a remarkably simple document that has provided a framework of governance for the United States for more than 230 years. It establishes a shared sovereignty between the states and the federal government, a separation and checking of powers between three branches of government, qualifications for citizenship and holding office, and a delineation of the rights considered so fundamental that their restriction by the government requires extensive due process and a compelling national or state concern. Yet the Constitution's simple text produces constant controversy over its interpretation and efforts to bend, twist, and nudge its application to changing economic markets, technology, social trends, and family structures. The document's durability and flexibility amidst conflict and social change is a tribute not only to the men who drafted the Constitution in 1787, but to the American people and their willingness to embrace the challenges of self-governance at the time of the Revolution and today.

    In the following article, Michael Kammen argues that in order to begin to understand the Constitution and the continuous debate surrounding its interpretation, we must look to the history of American constitutionalism. Informed by John Locke's Second Treatise of Government, the British constitution, and a colonial experience deemed an affront to basic liberties and rights, Americans plunged into the writing of the Constitution as a means to delegate power from the sovereign people to their elected and appointed agents. It is, as Kammen notes, quite remarkable that, even before the drafting of the federal Constitution, the American states chose to draft state constitutions in the midst of a revolutionary battle for independence rather than establish provisional governments. It is similarly remarkable that these state constitutions have grown significantly in length over the years and are so readily amended and even rewritten, in contrast to the relatively short and difficult-to-amend Constitution of the United States. (More than 12,000 amendments to the Constitution have been proposed in Congress, but only 27 have been ratified.)

Kammen suggests that the Constitution's simplicity and durability lie in both the historic need for compromise between conflicting interests as well as the surprising common ground that nevertheless existed over basic principles: the need to protect personal liberty, the commitment to a republican form of government, and the importance of civic virtue for preserving citizen sovereignty. This embrace of basic governing principles could explain the deeper devotion to the U.S. Constitution, in contrast to the state documents, as well as the fear that an amended or completely altered Constitution might prove less malleable and accommodating for the governance of a diverse nation.

The Nature of American Constitutionalism

"Like the Bible, it ought to be read again and again." Franklin Delano Roosevelt made that remark about the U.S. Constitution in March 1937, during one of those cozy "fireside chats" that reached millions of Americans by radio. "It is an easy document to understand," he added. And six months later, speaking to his fellow citizens from the grounds of the Washington Monument on Constitution Day—a widely noted speech because 1937 marked the sesquicentennial of the Constitution, and because the President had provoked the nation with his controversial plan to add as many as six new justices to the Supreme Court—Roosevelt observed that the Constitution was "a layman's document, not a lawyer's contract," a theme that he reiterated several times in the course of this address.

It seems fair to say that Roosevelt's assertions were approximately half true. No one could disagree that the Constitution ought to be read and reread. Few would deny that it was meant to be comprehended by laymen, by ordinary American citizens and aspirants for citizenship. Nevertheless, we must ponder whether it is truly "an easy document to understand." Although the very language of the Constitution is neither technical nor difficult, and although it is notably succinct—one nineteenth-century expert called it "a great code in a small compass"—abundant evidence exists that vast numbers of Americans, ever since 1787, have not understood it as well as they might. Even the so-called experts (judges, lawyers, political leaders, and teachers of constitutional law) have been unable to agree in critical instances about the proper application of key provisions of the Constitution, or about the intentions of those who wrote and approved it. Moreover, we do acknowledge that the Constitution developed from a significant number of compromises, and that the document's ambiguities are, for the most part, not accidental.

Understanding the U.S. Constitution is essential for many reasons. One of the most urgent is that difficult issues are now being and will continue to be settled in accordance with past interpretations and with our jurists' sense of what the founders meant. In order to make such difficult determinations, we begin with the document itself. Quite often, however, we also seek guidance from closely related or contextual documents, such as the notes kept by participants in the Constitutional Convention held at Philadelphia in 1787, from the correspondence of delegates and other prominent leaders during the later 1780s, from *The Federalist* papers, and even from some of the Anti-Federalist tracts written in opposition to the Constitution. In doing so, we essentially scrutinize the origins of American constitutionalism.

If observers want to know what is meant by constitutionalism, they must uncover several layers of historical thought and experience in public affairs. Most obviously we look to the ideas that developed in the United States during the final quarter of the eighteenth century—unquestionably the most brilliant and creative era in the entire history of American political thought. We have in mind particularly, however, a new set of assumptions that developed after 1775 about the very nature of a constitution. Why, for example, when the colonists found themselves nearly in a political state of nature after 1775, did they promptly feel compelled to write state constitutions, many of which contained a bill of rights? The patriots were, after all, preoccupied with fighting a revolution. Why not simply set up provisional governments based upon those they already had and wait until Independence was achieved? If and when the revolution succeeded, there would be time enough to write permanent constitutions.

The revolutionaries did not regard the situation in such casual and pragmatic terms. They shared a strong interest in what they called the science of politics. They knew a reasonable amount about the history of political theory. They believed in the value of ideas applied to problematic developments, and they felt that their circumstances were possibly unique in all of human history. They knew with assurance that their circumstances were changing, and changing rapidly. They wanted self-government, obviously, but they also wanted legitimacy for their newborn governments. Hence a major reason for writing constitutions. They believed in the doctrine of the social contract (about which Jean-Jacques Rousseau had written in 1762) and they believed in government by the consent of the governed: two more reasons for devising written constitutions approved by the people or by their representatives.

The men responsible for composing and revising state constitutions in the decade following 1775 regarded constitutions as social compacts that delineated the fundamental principles upon which the newly formed polities were agreed and to which they pledged themselves. They frequently used the word "experiment" because they believed that they were making institutional innovations that were risky, for they seemed virtually unprecedented. They intended to create republican governments and assumed that to do so successfully required a fair amount of social homogeneity, a high degree of consensus regarding moral values, and a pervasive capacity for virtue, by which they meant unselfish, public-spirited behavior.

Even though they often spoke of liberty, they meant civil liberty rather than natural liberty. The latter implied unrestrained freedom—absolute liberty for the individual to do as he or she pleased. The former, by contrast, meant freedom of action so long as it was not detrimental to others and was beneficial to the common weal. When they spoke of *political* liberty they meant the freedom to be a participant, to vote and hold public office, responsible commitments that ought to be widely shared if republican institutions were to function successfully.

The colonists' experiences throughout the seventeenth and eighteenth centuries had helped to prepare them for this participatory and contractual view of the nature of government. Over and over again, as the circles of settlement expanded, colonists learned to improvise the rules by which they would be governed. They had received charters and had entered into covenants or compacts that may be described as protoconstitutional, i.e., cruder and less complete versions of the constitutional documents that would be formulated in 1776 and subsequently. These colonial charters not only described the structure of government, but frequently explained what officials (often called magistrates) could or could not do.

As a result, by the 1770s American attitudes toward constitutionalism were simultaneously derivative as well as original. On the one hand, they extravagantly admired the British constitution ("unwritten" in the sense that it was not contained in a single document) and declared it to be the ultimate achievement in the entire history of governmental development. On the other hand, as Oscar and Mary Handlin have explained, Americans no longer conceived of constitutions in general as the British had for centuries.

> In the New World the term, constitution, no longer referred to the actual organization of power developed through custom, prescription, and precedent. Instead it had come to mean a written frame of government setting fixed limits on the use of power. The American view was, of course, closely related to the rejection of the old conception that authority descended from the Crown to its officials. In the newer view—that authority was derived from the consent of the governed—the written constitution became the instrument by which the people entrusted power to their agents.

* * *

Issues, Aspirations, and Apprehensions in 1787–1788

The major problems that confronted the Constitution-makers, and the issues that separated them from their opponents, can be specified by the key words that recur so frequently in the documents that follow in this collection. The Federalists often refer to the need for much more energy, stability, and efficiency in the national government. They fear anarchy and seek a political system better suited to America's geographical expanse: "an extensive sphere" was Madison's phrase in a letter to Jefferson.

The Anti-Federalists were apprehensive about "unrestrained power" (George Mason's words), about the great risk of national "consolidation" rather than a true confederation, about the failure to include a bill of rights in the new Constitution, about the prospect of too much power in the federal judiciary, about the "tendency to aristocracy" (see the "Federal Farmer"*), about insufficient separation of powers, and a government unresponsive to the needs of diverse and widely scattered people.

Because the two sides disagreed so strongly about the nature of the proposed government—was it genuinely federal or really national?—it is all too easy to lose sight of the common ground that they shared, a common ground that made it possible for many Anti-Federalists to support the Constitution fully even before George Washington's first administration came to a close in 1793. Both sides felt an absolute commitment to republicanism and the protection of personal liberty, as we have already seen. Both sides acknowledged that a science of politics was possible and ought to be pursued, but that "our own experience" (Madison's view, though held by "Brutus"† also) ought to be heeded above all. A majority on both sides accepted the inevitable role that interests would play in public affairs and recognized that public opinion would be a powerful force. The phrase "public opinion" appears eleven times explicitly in *The Federalist* papers, and many other times implicitly or indirectly.

The desire for happiness was invoked constantly. Although admittedly a vague and elusive concept, it clearly meant much more than the safeguarding of property (though the protection of property belonged under the rubric of happiness in the minds of many). For some it simply meant personal contentment; but increasingly there were leaders, such as George Washington, who spoke of "social happiness," which referred to harmony among diverse groups. David Humphreys's "Poem on the Happiness of America" (1786) provides an indication that this notion had national as well as individual and societal connotations.

Although both sides believed that the preservation of liberty was one of the most essential ends of government, the continued existence of chattel slavery in a freedom-loving society created considerable awkwardness for the founders. In 1775–1776, when the revolutionaries had explained the reasons for their rebellion, they frequently referred to a British plot to "enslave" Americans. The constant invocation of that notion has puzzled many students because whatever the wisdom or unwisdom of imperial policy in general, there most certainly was no conspiracy in London to enslave America.

There really should be no mystery about the colonists' usage, however, because as good Lockeans they knew full well the argument in chapter four of John Locke's *Second Treatise of Government*, entitled "Of Slavery" (an

*The pen name of Richard Henry Lee of Virginia, a noted Anti-Federalist [*Editors*].
†The pen name of Robert Yates, an Anti-Federalist [*Editors*].

argument reiterated in Rousseau's *Social Contract*). "The liberty of man in society," Locke wrote, "is to be under no other legislative power but that established by consent in the commonwealth, nor under the dominion of any will or restraint of any law but what that legislative shall enact according to the trust put in it." The denial of *full* freedom quite simply meant "slavery."

Slavery and the international slave trade were discussed extensively in 1787 at the Constitutional Convention. By then, however, "slavery" was not often used as a theoretical and general synonym for unfreedom. It meant the permanent possession of one person (black) by another (white), usually for life, the slaveowner being entitled to own the children of his or her chattel as well. We must remember that the Convention met in secret session, and that the delegates agreed not to divulge information about their proceedings for fifty years. Consequently not very much was said publicly about slavery in 1787–1788 in connection with the Constitution. Not until 1840, when the U.S. government published James Madison's detailed notes on the Convention debates, did Americans learn just how much had been compromised at Philadelphia in order to placate South Carolina and Georgia. The Constitution essentially protected slavery where it existed, and remained mute about the legality of slavery in territories that might one day become additional states. Accommodation had prevailed in 1787, which meant, as it turned out, postponing for seventy-four years the moral and political crisis of the Union.

Legacies of American Constitutionalism

Although it is difficult for us fully to imagine the complexities of interest group politics, regional rivalries, and ideological differences in 1787, the instrumental achievement of that extraordinary Convention has generally been appreciated over the years. Even such a sardonic mind as H. L. Mencken's conceded as much. "The amazing thing about the Constitution," he wrote, "is that it is as good as it is—that so subtle and complete a document emerged from that long debate. Most of the Framers, obviously, were second-rate men; before and after their session they accomplished nothing in the world. Yet during that session they made an almost perfect job of the work in hand."

Their accomplishment was, indeed, remarkable. The distribution and separation of powers among three branches at the national level, and the development of federalism as a means of apportioning sovereignty between the nation and the states, have received broad recognition and the compliment of imitation by many other nations.

Equally appreciated is the fact that the U.S. Constitution is the oldest written national constitution in the world. (The Massachusetts Constitution of 1780, although amended and revised many times, is even older.) Its endurance is genuinely remarkable. We should therefore note that the framers deserve much of the credit for that endurance, not simply because they transcended their own limitations, * * * but because they contrived to restrict the ease with which the Constitution might be revised or reconsidered. There was considerable talk in 1787–1788 about holding a second convention in order to refine the product of the first. Anti-Federalists and many who were undecided wanted such a course of action. George Washington, however, regarded that idea as impractical. Hamilton, despite his dissatisfaction with many aspects of the Constitution, doubted whether a second convention could possibly be as successful as the first; and Madison feared a serious erosion of what had been accomplished in 1787.

It is easy to forget that the Philadelphia Convention vastly exceeded its authority, and that the men who met there undertook what amounted to a usurpation of legitimate authority. As [President] Franklin Delano Roosevelt pointed out on Constitution Day in 1937, contemporaries who opposed the newly drafted document "insisted that the Constitution itself was unconstitutional under the Articles of Confederation. But the ratifying conventions overruled them." The right of revolution had been explicitly invoked in 1776 and implicitly practiced in 1787. Having done their work, however, most of the delegates did not believe that it ought to be repealed or casually revised.

The complexity of changing or adding to the original document had profound implications for the subsequent history of American constitutionalism. First, it meant that in order to gain acceptance of their handiwork, the Federalists had to commit themselves, unofficially, to the formulation of a bill of rights when the first Congress met in 1789, even though many Federalists felt that such a list of protections was superfluous. They protested that a finite list of specified safeguards would imply that numerous other liberties might not be protected against encroachment by the government. The point, ultimately, is that promulgation of the U.S. Constitution required two sets of compromises rather than one: those that took place among the delegates to the Convention, and the subsequent sense that support for ratification would be rewarded by the explicit enumeration of broad civil liberties.

Next, the existence of various ambiguities in the Constitution meant that explication would subsequently be required by various authorities, such as the Supreme Court. The justices' interpretations would become part of the total "package" that we call American constitutionalism; but the justices did not always agree with one another, and the rest of the nation did not always agree with the justices. Those realities gave rise to an ongoing pattern that might be called conflict-within-consensus.

Some of those disputes and ambiguities involved very basic questions: What are the implications and limits of consent? Once we have participated in the creation of a polity and agreed to abide by its rules, then what? How are we to resolve the conflict that arises when the wishes or needs of a majority diminish the liberties or interests of a minority? This last question was the tough issue faced by the New England states in 1814, when they contemplated secession, and by South Carolina in 1828–1833 when a high tariff designed to protect northern manufacturing threatened economic distress to southern agricultural interests. And that, of course, was the thorny issue that precipitated southern secession and the greatest constitutional crisis of all in 1860–1861.

There is yet another ambiguity, or contradiction, in American constitutional thought—though it is less commonly noticed than the one described in the previous paragraph. As we have observed, the founders were not eager for a second convention, or for easy revisions or additions to their handiwork. They did provide for change; but they made the process complicated and slow. They did not believe that the fundamental law of a nation should be casually altered; and most Americans have accepted that constraint.

Nevertheless, on the *state* level Americans have amended, expanded, revised, and totally rewritten their constitutions with some frequency. A great deal of so-called positive law (i.e., legislative enactments) finds its way into state constitutions, with the result that many modern ones exceed one hundred pages in length. There is no clear explanation for this striking pattern of divergence between constitutionalism on the national and state levels. The curious pattern does suggest, however, that Americans have regarded the U.S. Constitution of 1787 as more nearly permanent than their state constitutions. Perhaps the pattern only tells us that achieving a national consensus for change in a large and diverse society is much more difficult than achieving a statewide consensus for change.

Whatever the explanation for this dualism in American constitutionalism, the paradox does not diminish the historical reality that writers of the federal as well as the first state constitutions all tried to establish charters clearly suited to the cultural assumptions and political realities of the American scene. Even though the founders explored the history of political thought in general and the history of republics in particular, they reached the commonsense conclusion that a constitution must be adapted to the character and customs of a people. Hence the debate in 1787–1788 over the relative merits of "consolidation" versus "confederation." Hence the concern about what sort of governmental system would work most effectively over a large geographical expanse. James Madison conveyed this sense of American exceptionalism several times in a letter to Thomas Jefferson (then U.S. minister to France) in 1788, when a bill of rights was under consideration.

On August 28, 1788, a month after New York became the eleventh state to ratify the Constitution, George Washington sent Alexander Hamilton a letter from his temporary retirement at Mount Vernon. The future president acknowledged that public affairs were proceeding more smoothly than he had expected. Consequently, he wrote, "I hope the political Machine may be put in motion, without much effort or hazard of miscarrying." As he soon discovered, to put the new constitutional machine in motion would require considerable effort. It did not miscarry because the "machine" had been so soundly designed. A concerted effort would be required, however, to keep the machine successfully in operation. That should not occasion surprise. The founders had assumed an involved citizenry; and the governmental system they created functions best when their assumption is validated. That is the very essence of democratic constitutionalism.

DISCUSSION QUESTIONS

1. In your view, what would Kammen think about recent efforts to amend the Constitution to ban abortion, require a two-thirds vote to raise the debt ceiling, lower the voting age to 16, and protect victims' rights?

2. Although the flexibility of the Constitution helps explain its longevity, that flexibility comes at a price: ambiguity and gaps in constitutional language. What are some examples of constitutional language that is ambiguous?

3. One reason that Kammen argues it is important to understand the origins of American constitutionalism is that many judges today use their understanding of the Founders' intentions to inform their decisions. To what extent should the Founders' intentions influence modern court decisions? What are the advantages and disadvantages of this "original intent" perspective on jurisprudence?

The Federalist, No. 15

ALEXANDER HAMILTON

Despite the deference given the Constitution today, it did not command instant respect in 1787. The fight for ratification was bitter between the Federalists (those who supported the Constitution) and the Anti-Federalists (those who feared that the Constitution would allow the new national government to become too powerful).

The Federalist Papers, originally written as a series of newspaper editorials intended to persuade New York to ratify the Constitution, remain the most valuable exposition of the political theory underlying the Constitution. In The Federalist, No. 15, *Alexander Hamilton is at his best, arguing for the necessity of a stronger central government than that established under the Articles of Confederation. He points out the practical impossibility of engaging in concerted action when each of the 13 states retains virtual sovereignty, and the need for a strong central government to hold the new country together politically and economically.*

In the course of the preceding papers I have endeavored, my fellow-citizens, to place before you in a clear and convincing light the importance of Union to your political safety and happiness. * * * [T]he point next in order to be examined is the "insufficiency of the present Confederation to the preservation of the Union." * * * There are material imperfections in our national system and * * * something is necessary to be done to rescue us from impending anarchy. The facts that support this opinion are no longer objects of speculation. They have forced themselves upon the sensibility of the people at large, and have at length extorted * * * a reluctant confession of the reality of those defects in the scheme of our federal government which have been long pointed out and regretted by the intelligent friends of the Union.

We may indeed with propriety be said to have reached almost the last stage of national humiliation. There is scarcely anything that can wound the pride or degrade the character of an independent nation which we do not experience. Are there engagements to the performance of which we are held by every tie respectable among men? These are the subjects of constant and unblushing violation. Do we owe debts to foreigners and to our own citizens contracted in a time of imminent peril for the preservation of our political existence? These remain without any proper or satisfactory provision for their discharge. * * * Are we in a condition to resent or to repel the aggression? We have neither troops, nor treasury, nor government. * * * Is public credit an indispensable resource in time of public danger? We seem to have abandoned its cause as desperate and irretrievable. Is commerce of importance to national wealth? Ours is at the lowest point of declension. Is respectability in the eyes of foreign powers a safeguard against foreign encroachments? The imbecility of our government even forbids them to treat with us. * * * Is private credit the friend and patron of industry? That most useful kind which relates to borrowing and lending is reduced within the narrowest limits, and this still more from an opinion of insecurity than from a scarcity of money. * * *

This is the melancholy situation to which we have been brought by those very maxims and counsels which would now deter us from adopting the proposed Constitution; and which, not content with having conducted us to the brink of a precipice, seem resolved to plunge us into the abyss that awaits us below. Here, my countrymen, impelled by every motive that ought to influence an enlightened people, let us make a firm stand for our safety, our tranquility, our dignity, our reputation. Let us at last break the fatal charm which has too long seduced us from the paths of felicity and prosperity.

* * * While [opponents of the Constitution] admit that the government of the United States is destitute of energy, they contend against conferring upon it those powers which are requisite to supply that energy. * * * This renders a full display of the principal defects of the Confederation necessary in order to show that the evils we experience do not proceed from minute or partial imperfections, but from fundamental errors in the structure of the building, which cannot be amended otherwise than by an alteration in the first principles and main pillars of the fabric.

The great and radical vice in the construction of the existing Confederation is in the principle of LEGISLATION FOR STATES OR GOVERNMENTS, in their CORPORATE OR COLLECTIVE CAPACITIES, and as contradistinguished from the INDIVIDUALS of whom they consist. Though this principle does not run through all the powers delegated to the Union, yet it pervades and governs those on which the efficacy of the rest depends. Except as to the rule of apportionment, the United States have an indefinite discretion to make requisitions for men and money; but they have no authority to raise either by regulations extending to the individual citizens of America. The consequence of this is that though in theory their resolutions concerning those objects are laws constitutionally binding on the members of the Union, yet in practice they are mere recommendations which the States observe or disregard at their option. * * *

There is nothing absurd or impracticable in the idea of a league or alliance between independent nations for certain defined purposes precisely stated in a treaty regulating all the details of time, place, circumstance, and quantity, leaving nothing to future discretion, and depending for its execution on the good faith of the parties. * * *

If the particular States in this country are disposed to stand in a similar relation to each other, and to drop the project of a general DISCRETIONARY SUPERINTENDENCE, the scheme would indeed be pernicious and would entail upon us all the mischiefs which have been enumerated under the first head; but it would have the merit of being, at least, consistent and practicable. Abandoning all views towards a confederate government, this would bring us to a simple alliance offensive and defensive; and would place us in a situation to be alternate friends and enemies of each other, as our mutual jealousies and rivalships, nourished by the intrigues of foreign nations, should prescribe to us.

But if we are unwilling to be placed in this perilous situation; if we still will adhere to the design of a national government, or, which is the same thing, of a superintending power under the direction of a common council, we must resolve to incorporate into our plan those ingredients which may be considered as forming the characteristic difference between a league and a government; we must extend the authority of the Union to the persons of the citizens—the only proper objects of government.

Government implies the power of making laws. It is essential to the idea of a law that it be attended with a sanction; or, in other words, a penalty or punishment for disobedience. If there be no penalty annexed to disobedience, the resolutions or commands which pretend to be laws will, in fact, amount to nothing more than advice or recommendation. This penalty, whatever it may be, can only be inflicted in two ways: by the agency of the courts and ministers of justice, or by military force; by the COERCION of the magistracy, or by the COERCION of arms. The first kind can evidently apply only to men; the last kind must of necessity be employed against bodies politic, or communities, or States. * * * In an association where the general authority is confined to the collective bodies of the communities that compose it, every breach of the laws must involve a state of war; and military execution must become the only instrument of civil obedience. Such a state of things can certainly not deserve the name of government, nor would any prudent man choose to commit his happiness to it.

There was a time when we were told that breaches by the States of the regulations of the federal authority were not to be expected; that a sense of common interest would preside over the conduct of the respective members, and would beget a full compliance with all the constitutional requisitions of the Union. This language, at the present day, would appear as wild as a great part of what we now hear from the same quarter will be thought, when we shall have received further lessons from that best oracle of wisdom, experience. It at all times betrayed an ignorance of the true springs by which human conduct is actuated, and belied the original inducements to the establishment of civil power. Why has government been instituted at all? Because the passions of men will not conform to the dictates of reason and justice without constraint. * * *

In addition to all this * * * it happens that in every political association which is formed upon the principle of uniting in a common interest a number of lesser sovereignties, there will be found a kind of eccentric tendency in the subordinate or inferior orbs by the operation of which there will be a perpetual effort in each to fly off from the common center. This tendency is not difficult to be accounted for. It has its origin in the love of power. Power controlled or abridged is almost always the rival and enemy of that power by which it is controlled or abridged. This simple proposition will teach us how little reason there is to expect that the persons intrusted with the administration of the affairs of the particular members of a confederacy will at all times be ready with perfect good humor and an unbiased regard to the public weal to execute the resolutions or decrees of the general authority. * * *

If, therefore, the measures of the Confederacy cannot be executed without the intervention of the particular administrations, there will be little prospect of their being executed at all. * * * [Each state will evaluate every federal measure in light of its own interests] and in a spirit of interested and suspicious scrutiny, without that knowledge of national circumstances and reasons of state, which is essential to a right judgment, and with that strong predilection in favor of local objects, which can hardly fail to mislead the decision. The same process must be repeated in every member of which the body is constituted; and the execution of the plans, framed by the councils of the whole, will always fluctuate on the discretion of the ill-informed and prejudiced opinion of every part. * * *

In our case the concurrence of thirteen distinct sovereign wills is requisite under the Confederation to the complete execution of every important measure that proceeds from the Union. It has happened as was to have been foreseen. The measures of the Union have not been executed; and the delinquencies of the States have step by step matured themselves to an extreme, which has, at length, arrested all the wheels of the national government and brought them to an awful stand. Congress at this time scarcely possess the means of keeping up the forms of administration, till the States can have time to agree upon a more substantial substitute for the present shadow of a federal government. * * * Each State yielding to the persuasive voice of immediate interest or convenience has successively withdrawn its support, till the frail and tottering edifice seems ready to fall upon our heads and to crush us beneath its ruins.

PUBLIUS

DISCUSSION QUESTIONS

1. Do you think the national government is sufficiently held in check as Hamilton argues? Or is the exercise of its authority so vast as to give credence to the Anti-Federalists' fears? To put it another way, would the framers be surprised or pleased with the balance between national and state powers today?

2. According to Hamilton, what are the weaknesses of a "league" compared to a government?

3. What is the significance of Hamilton's statement that "we must extend the authority of the Union to the persons of the citizens"?

9

From *An Economic Interpretation of the Constitution of the United States*

CHARLES A. BEARD

One of the longest-running debates over the Constitution focuses upon the motivation of the Founders in drafting the document. Was the motivation ideological, based upon beliefs of self-governance, the nature of a social contract, and the role of representation? Or was the motivation primarily economic, based upon a need to preserve economic interests that were threatened under the system of governance of the Articles of Confederation? And if the motivation was economic, what economic interests divided the Anti-Federalists from the Federalists in their opposition to or support for the Constitution?

One of the earliest and most controversial efforts to answer the question of motivation was written by Charles A. Beard in 1913. Beard argued that those who favored the Constitution and played the primary role in its drafting were motivated by the need to better protect their substantial "personality" interests—money, public securities, manufactures, and trade and shipping (or commerce)—in contrast to their opponents, who were primarily debtors and small farmers (with small real estate holdings). Not only was its motivation less than democratic, Beard argued, but the Constitution was ratified by only one-sixth of the male population because voting was limited to property owners.

Subsequent critiques of Beard have pointed out that there were far more economic interests than mercantilists versus farmers; that having a certain set of economic interests did not dictate the political views of the framers; and that ideas such as republicanism and liberty were more important in shaping the Constitution than the Founders' economic interests. Nonetheless, the idea that economic interests influence political outcomes resonates today.

The requirements for an economic interpretation of the formation and adoption of the Constitution may be stated in a hypothetical proposition which, although it cannot be verified absolutely from ascertainable data, will at once illustrate the problem and furnish a guide to research and generalization.

It will be admitted without controversy that the Constitution was the creation of a certain number of men, and it was opposed by a certain number of men. Now, if it were possible to have an economic biography of all those connected with its framing and adoption,—perhaps about 160,000 men altogether—the materials for scientific analysis and classification would be available. Such an economic biography would include a list of the real and personal property owned by all of these men and their families; lands and houses, with incumbrances, money at interest, slaves, capital invested in shipping and manufacturing, and in state and continental securities.

Suppose it could be shown from the classification of the men who supported and opposed the Constitution that there was no line of property division at all; that is, that men owning substantially the same amounts of the same kinds of property were equally divided on the matter of adoption or rejection—it would then become apparent that the Constitution had no ascertainable relation to economic groups or classes but was the product of some abstract causes remote from the chief business of life—gaining a livelihood.

Suppose, on the other hand, that substantially all of the merchants, money lenders, security holders, manufacturers, shippers, capitalists, and financiers and their professional associates are to be found on one side in support of the Constitution and that substantially all or the major portion of the opposition came from the non-slaveholding farmers and the debtors—would it not be pretty conclusively demonstrated that our fundamental law was not the product of an abstraction known as "the whole people," but of a group of economic interests which must have expected beneficial results from its adoption? Obviously all the facts here desired cannot be discovered, but the data presented in the following chapters bear out the latter hypothesis, and thus a reasonable presumption in favor of the theory is created.

* * *

The purpose of such an inquiry is not, of course, to show that the Constitution was made for the personal benefit of the members of the Convention. Far from it. Neither is it of any moment to discover how many hundred thousand dollars accrued to them as a result of the foundation of the new government. The only point here considered is: Did they represent distinct groups whose economic interests they understood and felt in concrete, definite form through their own personal experience with identical property rights, or were they working merely under the guidance of abstract principles of political science?

* * *

The Disfranchised

In an examination of the structure of American society in 1787, we first encounter four groups whose economic status had a definite legal expression: the slaves, the indentured servants, the mass of men who could not qualify for voting under the property tests imposed by the state constitutions and laws, and women, disfranchised and subjected to the discriminations of the common law. These groups were, therefore, not represented in the Convention which drafted the Constitution, except under the theory that representation has no relation to voting.

How extensive the disfranchisement really was cannot be determined. In some states, for instance, Pennsylvania and Georgia, propertyless mechanics in the towns could vote; but in other states the freehold qualifications certainly excluded a great number of the adult males.

In no state, apparently, had the working class developed a consciousness of a separate interest or an organization that commanded the attention of the politicians of the time. In turning over the hundreds of pages of writings left by eighteenth-century thinkers one cannot help being impressed with the fact that the existence and special problems of a working class, then already sufficiently numerous to form a considerable portion of society, were outside the realm of politics, except in so far as the future power of the proletariat was foreseen and feared.

When the question of the suffrage was before the Convention, Madison warned his colleagues against the coming industrial masses: "[v]iewing the subject in its merits alone, the freeholders of the Country would be the safest depositories of Republican liberty. In future times a great majority of the people will not only be without landed [property], but any other sort of property. These will either combine under the influence of their common situation; in which case, the rights of property and the public liberty will not be secure in their hands, or, which is more probable, they will become the tools of opulence and ambition; in which case there will be equal danger on another side."

* * *

It is apparent that a majority of the states placed direct property qualifications on the voters, and the other states eliminated practically all who were not taxpayers. Special safeguards for property were secured in the qualifications imposed on members of the legislatures in New Hampshire, Massachusetts, New York, New Jersey, Maryland, North Carolina, South Carolina, and Georgia. Further safeguards were added by the qualifications imposed in the case of senators in New Hampshire, Massachusetts, New Jersey, New York, Maryland, North Carolina, and South Carolina.

While these qualifications operated to exclude a large portion of the adult males from participating in elections, the wide distribution of real property created an extensive electorate and in most rural regions gave the legislatures a broad popular basis. Far from rendering to personal property that defence which was necessary to the full realization of its rights, these qualifications for electors admitted to the suffrage its most dangerous antagonists: the small farmers and many of the debtors who were the most active in all attempts to depreciate personalty [private property] by legislation. Madison with his usual acumen saw the inadequacy of such defence and pointed out in the Convention that the really serious assaults on property (having in mind of course, personalty) had come from the "freeholders."

Nevertheless, in the election of delegates to the Convention, the representatives of personalty in the legislatures were able by the sheer weight of their combined intelligence and economic power to secure delegates from the urban centres or allied with their interests. Happily for them, all the legislatures which they had to convince had not been elected on the issue of choosing delegates to a national Convention, and did not come from a populace stirred up on that question. The call for the Convention went forth on February 21, 1787, from Congress, and within a few months all the legislatures, except that of Rhode Island, had responded. Thus the heated popular discussion usually incident to such a momentous political undertaking was largely avoided, and an orderly and temperate procedure in the selection of delegates was rendered possible.

* * *

A survey of the economic interests of the members of the Convention presents certain conclusions:

A majority of the members were lawyers by profession.

Most of the members came from towns, on or near the coast, that is, from the regions in which personalty was largely concentrated.

Not one member represented in his immediate personal economic interests the small farming or mechanic classes.

The overwhelming majority of members, at least five-sixths, were immediately, directly, and personally interested in the outcome of their labors at Philadelphia, and were to a greater or less extent economic beneficiaries from the adoption of the Constitution.

1. Public security interests were extensively represented in the Convention. Of the fifty-five members who attended no less than forty appear on the Records of the Treasury Department for sums varying from a few dollars up to more than one hundred thousand dollars: * * *

It is interesting to note that, with the exception of New York, and possibly Delaware, each state had one or more prominent representatives in the Convention who held more than a negligible amount of securities, and who could therefore speak with feeling and authority on the question of providing in the new Constitution for the full discharge of the public debt: * * *

2. Personalty invested in lands for speculation was represented by at least fourteen members: * * *

3. Personalty in the form of money loaned at interest was represented by at least twenty-four members: * * *

4. Personalty in mercantile, manufacturing, and shipping lines was represented by at least eleven members: * * *

5. Personalty in slaves was represented by at least fifteen members: * * *

It cannot be said, therefore, that the members of the Convention were "disinterested." On the contrary, we are forced to accept the profoundly significant conclusion that they knew through their personal experiences in economic affairs the precise results which the new government that they were setting up was designed to attain. As a group of doctrinaires, like the Frankfurt assembly of 1848, they would have failed miserably; but as practical men they were able to build the new government upon the only foundations which could be stable: fundamental economic interests.

* * *

Conclusions

At the close of this long and arid survey—partaking of the nature of catalogue—it seems worthwhile to bring together the important conclusions for political science which the data presented appear to warrant.

[1.] The movement for the Constitution of the United States was originated and carried through principally by four groups of personalty interests which had been adversely affected under the Articles of Confederation: money, public securities, manufactures, and trade and shipping.

[2.] The first firm steps toward the formation of the Constitution were taken by a small and active group of men immediately interested through their personal possessions in the outcome of their labors.

[3.] No popular vote was taken directly or indirectly on the proposition to call the Convention which drafted the Constitution.

[4.] A large propertyless mass was, under the prevailing suffrage qualifications, excluded at the outset from participation (through representatives) in the work of framing the Constitution.

[5.] The members of the Philadelphia Convention which drafted the Constitution were, with a few exceptions, immediately, directly, and personally interested in, and derived economic advantages from, the establishment of the new system.

[6.] The Constitution was essentially an economic document based upon the concept that the fundamental private rights of property are anterior to government and morally beyond the reach of popular majorities.

[7.] The major portion of the members of the Convention are on record as recognizing the claim of property to a special and defensive position in the Constitution.

[8.] In the ratification of the Constitution, about three-fourths of the adult males failed to vote on the question, having abstained from the elections at which delegates to the state conventions were chosen, either on account of their indifference or their disfranchisement by property qualifications.

[9.] The Constitution was ratified by a vote of probably not more than one-sixth of the adult males.

[10.] It is questionable whether a majority of the voters participating in the elections for the state conventions in New York, Massachusetts, New

Hampshire, Virginia, and South Carolina, actually approved the ratification of the Constitution.

[11.] The leaders who supported the Constitution in the ratifying conventions represented the same economic groups as the members of the Philadelphia Convention; and in a large number of instances they were also directly and personally interested in the outcome of their efforts.

[12.] In the ratification, it became manifest that the line of cleavage for and against the Constitution was between substantial personalty interests on the one hand and the small farming and debtor interests on the other.

[13.] The Constitution was not created by "the whole people" as the jurists have said; neither was it created by "the states" as Southern nullifiers long contended; but it was the work of a consolidated group whose interests knew no state boundaries and were truly national in their scope.

DISCUSSION QUESTIONS

1. When they drafted the Constitution, do you think the framers were governed by self-interest or a commitment to principle, or some combination? Explain your answer.

2. What does Beard's argument say about the use of historical evidence to support one's argument? How can historical evidence be misused and how can historians, or even readers of history, sort out what "really" happened in any specific context?

3. Think of examples of wealthy people in politics, such as former president Donald Trump or Senator Rick Scott (R-Fla.), the wealthiest member of Congress. Do they tend to support positions that would enhance their own economic position? Can you think of examples of wealthy politicians who do not behave this way?

Debating the Issues: Should the Constitution Be Fundamentally Changed?

Veneration for the Constitution is a classic American value; indeed, it is often said that the essence of being an American is a set of shared values and commitments expressed within that document, most notably equality and liberty. The Constitution is the embodiment of those values, celebrated as the first, and most enduring, written constitution in human history. We celebrate the first words of the Preamble, "We the People," salute the framers as men of historic wisdom and judgment, and honor the structures and processes of government.

We also note the practical wisdom of the framers in their ability to reconcile competing tensions by creating a government powerful enough to function, but not at the risk of giving majorities the right to trample minority rights. Political theory at the time held that efforts to create democracies inevitably devolved into one of two end results: either mob rule, as majorities took control and used their power to oppress political minorities; or autocracy, as elites assumed control and did not give it up. The many carefully considered elements of constitutional structure—bicameralism, the balance between federal and state power, the equilibrium of checks and balances—have lasted for more than two centuries. And apart from one exceptional period of civil war, the structures have channeled political conflict peacefully.

Is that veneration truly warranted? Sanford Levinson, a professor at the University of Texas Law School, thinks not. He considers the Constitution to be a seriously flawed document in need of fundamental change. As originally written, the Constitution came nowhere near the aspirations of the Preamble, explicitly allowing slavery, and even after amendments retains several antidemocratic elements, including the electoral college (which elected another popular vote loser to the presidency in 2016); the vastly unequal representation in the Senate, in which Wyoming (population over 581,000) has the same voting power as California (population over 39 million, over 67 times as large); and lifetime tenure for judges. These features fail to live up to the Preamble, which Levinson considers to be the foundation of the rest of the Constitution—the whole point of the constitutional enterprise. Levinson points out that several key figures of the American Founding—Thomas Jefferson especially—believed that the Constitution would require frequent updating. This was the purpose of Article V, which sets out the process for amending the document. And, Levinson notes, many of the features of the Constitution that we venerate were not thought through but were instead the product of pure compromise, in which the framers took vastly inconsistent positions when necessary in order to secure sufficient support for ratification. So, far from being a philosophically perfect

document or system, the Constitution created a cumbersome and inequitable system, one that no other democratic system has chosen to copy
since.

The problem with amending the Constitution is that the features
Levinson considers most offensive are very difficult or, in the case of
unequal representation in the Senate, virtually impossible to change.
Article V specifies that no state can be deprived of its equal representation in the Senate without its consent (something that no state could ever
be expected to do). The only recourse is a constitutional convention, in
which delegates would consider fundamental reform. Levinson regards
this as essential in order to allow the national government to respond
to the challenge of modern economic and political times.

Travis Waldron and Greg Abbott weigh in on opposing sides of the
wisdom of calling a constitutional convention. Abbott, the governor of
Texas, hails a convention as a way to "restore the rule of law" and
counters fears about a "runaway convention." He points out that the
scope of a convention could be constrained by each state legislature that
endorses the idea, and even if the convention ends up "throwing the
entire Constitution in the trash can," anything the convention proposes
would still have to be ratified by three-fourths of the states. Abbott concludes that we cannot allow the "federal government to continue ignoring the very document that created it."

Travis Waldron argues that a constitutional convention comes with
potential risks. Waldron points out that there is disagreement on the
actual mechanism for triggering a convention: Does each state need to
agree on the same language of the topics to be discussed at the convention, such as term limits or requiring a balanced budget? Or is it sufficient to have two-thirds of the states call for a convention for any reason?
Waldron notes that while both the Left and the Right have called for a
convention in recent years (like Levinson and Olson), the current movement is dominated by the extreme right, which wants to severely limit the
power of the government. It is even possible that they could rewrite the
rules for ratifying amendments, which would remove one of the safeguards against a runaway convention.

"The Ratification Referendum: Sending the Constitution to a New Convention for Repair"

Sanford Levinson

The U.S. Constitution is radically defective in a number of important ways. Unfortunately, changing the Constitution is extremely difficult, for both political and constitutional reasons. But the difficulty of the task does not make it any less important that we first become aware of the magnitude of the deficiencies in the current Constitution and then turn our minds, as a community of concerned citizens, to figuring out potential solutions. This [reading] is organized around the conceit that Americans [should] have the opportunity to vote on the following proposal: "Shall Congress call a constitutional convention empowered to consider the adequacy of the Constitution, and, if thought necessary, to draft a new constitution that, upon completion, will be submitted to the electorate for its approval or disapproval by majority vote? Unless and until a new constitution gains popular approval, the current Constitution will continue in place."

Although such a referendum would be unprecedented with regard to the U.S. Constitution, there is certainly nothing "un-American" about such a procedure. As Professor John J. Dinan has noted in his recent comprehensive study of what he terms "the American state constitutional tradition," fourteen American states in their own constitutions explicitly give the people an opportunity "to periodically vote on whether a convention should be called." Article XIX of the New York Constitution, for example, provides that the state electorate be given the opportunity every twenty years to vote on the following question: "Shall there be a convention to revise the constitution and amend the same?" Should the majority answer in the affirmative, then the voters in each senate district will elect three delegates "at the next ensuring general election," while the statewide electorate "shall elect fifteen delegates-at-large." It should occasion no surprise that one author has described such a "mandatory referendum" as a means of "enforcing the people's right to reform their government."

It is no small matter to give people a choice with regard to the mechanisms—as well as the abstract principles—by which they are to be governed. The imagined referendum would allow "We the People of the United

States of America," in whose name the document is ostensibly "ordain[ed],"
to examine the fit between our national aspirations, set out in the Preamble to the Constitution, and the particular means chosen to realize those
goals.

I am assuming that those reading this * * * are fellow Americans united
by a deep and common concern about the future of our country. * * * I hope
to convince you that, as patriotic Americans truly committed to the deepest principles of the Constitution, we should vote yes and thus trigger a
new convention. My task is to persuade you that the Constitution we currently live under is grievously flawed, even in some ways a "clear and present danger" to achieving the laudable and inspiring goals to which this
country professes to be committed, including republican self-government.

I believe that the best way to grasp the goals of our common enterprise
is to ponder the inspiring words of the Preamble to the Constitution:

> We the People of the United States, in Order to form a more perfect Union, establish Justice, insure domestic tranquility, provide for the common defence, promote the general Welfare, and secure the Blessings of Liberty to ourselves and
> our Posterity, do ordain and establish this Constitution for the United States of
> America.

It is regrettable that law professors rarely teach and that courts rarely cite
the Preamble, for it is *the single most important part* of the Constitution. The
reason is simple: [i]t announces the *point* of the entire enterprise. The 4,500
or so words that followed the Preamble in the original, unamended Constitution were all in effect merely means that were thought to be useful to
achieving the great aims set out above. It is indeed the ends articulated in
the Preamble that justify the means of our political institutions. And to the
extent that the means turn out to be counterproductive, then we should
revise them.

It takes no great effort to find elements in the original Constitution that
run counter to the Preamble. It is impossible for us today to imagine how
its authors squared a commitment to the "Blessings of Liberty" with the
toleration and support of chattel slavery that is present in various articles
of the Constitution. The most obvious example is the bar placed on Congress's ability to forbid the participation by Americans in the international
slave trade until 1808. The most charitable interpretation of the framers,
articulated by Frederick Douglass, is that they viewed these compromises
with the acknowledged evil of slavery as temporary; the future would see
its eradication through peaceful constitutional processes.

One might believe that the Preamble is incomplete because, for example, it lacks a commitment to the notion of equality. Political scientist Mark
Graber has suggested that the reference to *"our* Posterity" suggests a potentially unattractive limitation of our concerns *only* to members of the
American political community, with no notice taken of the posterity of
other societies, whatever their plight. Even if one would prefer a more

explicitly cosmopolitan Preamble, I find it hard to imagine rejecting any of the overarching values enunciated there. In any event, I am happy to endorse the Preamble as the equivalent of our creedal summary of America's civil religion.

There are two basic responses to the discovery that ongoing institutional practices are counterproductive with regard to achieving one's announced goals. One is to adjust the practices in ways that would make achievement of the aims more likely. This is, often, when we mean by the very notion of rationality: [o]ne does not persist in behaviors that are acknowledged to make more difficult the realization of one's professed hopes. Still, a second response, which has its own rationality, is to adjust the goals to the practices. Sometimes, this makes very good sense if one comes to the justified conclusion that the goals may be utopian. In such cases, it is a sign of maturity to recognize that we will inevitably fall short in our aims and that "the best may be enemy of the good" if we are tempted to throw over quite adequate, albeit imperfect, institutions in an attempt to attain the ideal.

Perhaps one might even wish to defend the framers' compromises with slavery on the ground that they were absolutely necessary to the achievement of the political union of the thirteen states. One must believe that such a union, in turn, was preferable to the likely alternative, which would have been the creation of two or three separate countries along the Atlantic coast. Political scientist David Hendrickson has demonstrated that many of the framers—and many other theorists as well—viewed history as suggesting a high probability that such separate countries would have gone to war with one another and made impossible any significant measure of "domestic tranquility." Hendrickson well describes the Constitution as a "peace pact" designed to prevent the possibility of war. If there is one thing we know, it is that unhappy compromises must often be made when negotiating such pacts. Of course, American slaves—and their descendants— could scarcely be expected to be so complacently accepting of these compromises, nor, of course, should *any* American who takes seriously the proclamation of the Pledge of Allegiance that ours is a system that takes seriously the duty to provide "liberty and justice for all."

Not only must we restrain ourselves from expecting too much of any government; we must also recognize that the Preamble sets out potentially conflicting goals. It is impossible to maximize the achievement of all of the great ends of the Constitution. To take an obvious example, providing for the "common defence" may require on occasion certain incursions into the "Blessings of Liberty." One need only refer to the military draft, which was upheld in 1918 by the Supreme Court against an attack claiming that it constituted the "involuntary servitude"—that is, slavery—prohibited by the Thirteenth Amendment. We also properly accept certain limitations on the freedom of the press with regard, say, to publishing certain information— the standard example is troop movements within a battle zone—deemed to be vital to American defense interests. The year 2005 ended with the beginning of a great national debate about the propriety of warrantless interceptions of telephone calls and other incursions on traditional civil liberties in order, ostensibly, to protect ourselves against potential terrorists.

Even if one concedes the necessity of adjusting aims in light of practical realities, it should also be readily obvious that one can easily go overboard. At the very least, one should always be vigilant in assessing such adjustments lest one find, at the end of the day, that the aims have been reduced to hollow shells. It is also necessary to ask if a rationale supporting a given adjustment that might well have been convincing at time A necessarily continues to be present at time B. Practical exigencies that required certain political compromises in 1787 no longer obtain today. We have long since realized this about slavery. It is time that we apply the same critical eye to the compromise of 1787 that granted all states an equal vote in the Senate.

To criticize that particular compromise—or any of the other features of the Constitution that I shall examine below—is not necessarily to criticize the Founders themselves. My project—and, therefore, your own vote for a new convention, should you be persuaded by what follows—requires no denigration of the Founders. They were, with some inevitable exceptions, an extraordinary group of men who performed extraordinary deeds, including drafting a Constitution that started a brand-new governmental system. By and large, they deserve the monuments that have been erected in their honor. But they themselves emphasized the importance—indeed, necessity—of learning from experience.

They were, after all, a generation that charted new paths by overturning a centuries-long notion of the British constitutional order because it no longer conformed to their own sense of possibility (and fairness). They also, as it happened, proved ruthlessly willing to ignore the limitations of America's "first constitution," the Articles of Confederation. Although Article XIII of that founding document required unanimous approval by the thirteen state legislatures before any amendment could take effect, Article VII of the Constitution drafted in Philadelphia required the approval of only nine of the thirteen states, and the approval was to be given by state conventions rather than by the legislatures.

The most important legacies handed down by the founding generation were, first, a remarkable willingness to act in bold and daring ways when they believed that the situation demanded it, coupled with the noble visions first of the Declaration of Independence and then of the Preamble. Both are as inspiring—and potentially disruptive—today as when they were written more than two centuries ago. But we should also be inspired by the copious study that Madison and others made of every available history and analysis of political systems ranging from ancient Greece to the Dutch republic and the British constitutional order. We best honor the framers by taking the task of creating a republican political order as seriously as they did and being equally willing to learn from what the history of the past 225 years, both at home and abroad, can teach us about how best to achieve and maintain such an order. At the time of its creation, we could legitimately believe that we were the only country committed to democratic self-governance. That is surely no longer the case, and we might well have lessons to learn from our co-ventures in that enterprise. To the extent that experience teaches us that the Constitution in significant aspects demeans "the consent of the governed" and has become an impediment to achieving the goals of the Preamble, we honor rather than betray the founders by correcting their handiwork.

Overcoming Veneration

* * * I suspect * * * that at least some readers might find it difficult to accept even the possibility that our Constitution is seriously deficient because they venerate the Constitution and find the notion of seriously criticizing it almost sacrilegious.

In an earlier book, *Constitutional Faith*, I noted the tension between the desire of James Madison that Americans "venerate" their Constitution and the distinctly contrasting views of his good friend Thomas Jefferson that, instead, the citizenry regularly subject it to relentless examination. Thus, whatever may have been Jefferson's insistence on respecting what he called the "chains" of the Constitution, he also emphasized that the "Creator has made the earth for the living, not the dead." It should not be surprising, then, that he wrote to Madison in 1789, "No society can make a perpetual constitution, or even a perpetual law."

Jefferson and Madison might have been good friends and political associates, but they disagreed fundamentally with regard to the wisdom of subjecting the Constitution to critical analysis. Jefferson was fully capable of writing that "[w]e may consider each generation as a distinct nation, with a right, by the will of its majority, to bind themselves, but none to bind the succeeding generation, more than the inhabitants of another country." His ultimate optimism about the Constitution lay precisely in its potential for change: "[h]appily for us, that when we find our constitutions defective and insufficient to secure the happiness of our people, we can assemble with all the coolness of philosophers, and set it to rights, while every other nation on earth must have recourse to arms to amend or restore their constitutions." * * *

Madison, however, would have none of this. He treated 1787 almost as a miraculous and singular event. Had he been a devotee of astrology, he might have said that the stars were peculiarly and uniquely aligned to allow the drafting of the Constitution and then its ratification. Though Madison was surely too tactful to mention this, part of the alignment was the absence of the famously contentious Jefferson and John Adams. Both were 3,000 miles across the sea, where they were serving as the first ambassadors from the new United States to Paris and London, respectively. Moreover, it certainly did not hurt that Rhode Island had refused to send any delegates at all and therefore had no opportunity to make almost inevitable mischief, not to mention being unable to vote in an institutional structure where the vote of one state could make a big difference. And, if pressed, Madison would presumably have agreed that the Constitutional Convention—and the ratifying conventions thereafter—would never have succeeded had the delegates included American slaves, Native Americans, or women in the spirit of Abigail Adams. She had famously—and altogether unsuccessfully—told her husband that leaders of the new nation should "remember the ladies." One need not see the framers in Philadelphia as an entirely homogeneous group—they were not—in order to realize that the room was devoid of those groups in America that were viewed as merely the *objects,* and not the active *subjects,* of governance.

Madison sets out his views most clearly in the *Federalist,* No. 49, where he explicitly takes issue with Jefferson's proposal for rather frequent constitutional conventions that would consider whether "alter[ation]" of the constitution might be desirable. Madison acknowledges the apparent appeal, in a system where "the people are the only legitimate fountain of power," of "appeal[ing] to the people themselves." However, "there appear to be insuperable objections against the proposed recurrence to the people." Perhaps the key objection is that *"frequent appeal to the people would carry an implication of some defect in the government [and] deprive the government of that veneration which time bestows on every thing, and without which perhaps the wisest and freest governments would not possess the requisite stability."* Only "a nation of philosophers" can forgo this emotion of veneration—and, therefore, feel free of guilt-ridden anxiety about the idea of constitutional change. However, "a nation of philosophers is as little to be expected as the philosophical race of kings wished for by Plato."

Madison is thus fearful of "disturbing the public tranquillity by interesting too strongly the public passions." The success of Americans in replacing a defective Articles of Confederation with a better Constitution does not constitute a precedent for future action. We should "recollect," he says, "that all the existing constitutions were formed in the midst of a danger which repressed the passions most unfriendly to order and concord." Moreover, the people at large possessed "an enthusiastic confidence . . . in their patriotic leaders," which, he says, fortunately "stifled the ordinary diversity of opinions on great national questions." He is extremely skeptical that the "future situations in which we must expect to be usually placed" will "present any equivalent security against the danger" of an excess of public passion, disrespect for leaders, and the full play of diverse opinions. In case there is any doubt, he writes of his fear that the *"passions,* therefore, not the *reasons,* of the public would sit in judgment."

Madison's view of his fellow Americans was far closer to that of Alexander Hamilton, with whom he had coauthored the *Federalist.* One can doubt that Madison expressed any reservations when hearing Hamilton, addressing his fellow delegates to the Philadelphia convention on June 18,

1787, denounce the conceit that "the voice of the people" is "the voice of God." On the contrary, said Hamilton: "[t]he people are turbulent and changing; they seldom judge or determine right." Although Madison was not opposed to constitutional amendment as such, he clearly saw almost no role for a public that would engage in probing questions suggesting that there might be serious "defects" in the Constitution. Only philosophers (like himself?) or, perhaps, "patriotic leaders" could be trusted to engage in dispassionate political dialogue and reasoning. In contrast, the general public should be educated to feel only "veneration" for their Constitution rather than be encouraged to use their critical faculties and actually assess the relationship between the great ends set out in the Preamble and the instruments devised for their realization.

*   *   *

This is a mistake. To the extent that we continue thoughtlessly to venerate, and therefore not subject to truly critical examination, our Constitution, we are in the position of the battered wife who continues to profess the "essential goodness" of her abusive husband. To stick with the analogy for a moment, it may well be the case that the husband, when sober or not gambling, is a decent, even loving, partner. The problem is that such moments are more than counterbalanced by abusive ones, even if they are relatively rare. And he becomes especially abusive when she suggests the possibility of marital counseling and attendant change. Similarly, that there are good features of our Constitution should not be denied. But there are also significantly abusive ones, and it is time for us to face them rather than remain in a state of denial.

Trapped Inside the Article V Cage

The framers of the Constitution were under no illusion that they had created a perfect document. The best possible proof for this proposition comes from George Washington himself. As he wrote to his nephew Bushrod two months after the conclusion of the Philadelphia convention over which he had presided, *"The warmest friends and the best supporters the Constitution has do not contend that it is free from imperfections;* but they found them unavoidable and are sensible if evil is likely to arise there from, the remedy must come hereafter." Sounding a remarkably Jeffersonian note, Washington noted that the "People (for it is with them to Judge) can, as they will have the advantage of experience on their Side, decide with as much propriety on the alteration[s] and amendment[s] which are necessary." Indeed, wrote the man described as the Father of Our Country, "I do not think we are more inspired, have more wisdom, or possess more virtue, than those who will come after us."

Article V itself is evidence of the recognition of the possibility—and inevitable reality—of imperfection, else they would have adopted John

Locke's suggestion in a constitution that he drafted for the Carolina colonies that would have made the document unamendable. It is an unfortunate reality, though, that Article V, practically speaking, brings us all too close to the Lockean dream (or nightmare) of changeless stasis.

As University of Houston political scientist Donald Lutz has conclusively demonstrated, the U.S. Constitution is the most difficult to amend of any constitution currently existing in the world today. Formal amendment of the U.S. Constitution generally requires the approval of two-thirds of each of the two houses of our national Congress, followed by the approval of three-quarters of the states (which today means thirty-eight of the fifty states). Article V does allow the abstract possibility that amendments could be proposed through the aegis of a constitutional convention called by Congress upon the petition of two-thirds of the states; such proposals, though, would still presumably have to be ratified by the state legislatures or, in the alternative, as was done with regard to the Twenty-first Amendment repealing the prohibition of alcohol required by the Eighteenth Amendment, by conventions in each of the states. As a practical matter, though, Article V makes it next to impossible to amend the Constitution with regard to genuinely controversial issues, even if substantial—and intense—majorities advocate amendment.

As I have written elsewhere, some significant change functionally similar to "amendment" has occurred informally, outside of the procedures set out by Article V. One scholar has aptly described this as a process of "constitutional change off-the-books." Yale law professor Bruce Ackerman has written several brilliant books detailing the process of "non-Article V" amendment, and I warmly commend them to the reader. Yet it is difficult to argue that such informal amendment has occurred, or is likely to occur, with regard to the basic *structural* aspects of the American political system with which this book is primarily concerned.

It is one thing to argue, as Ackerman has done, that the New Deal worked as a functional amendment of the Constitution by giving Congress significant new powers to regulate the national economy. Similarly, one could easily argue that the president, for good or for ill, now possesses powers over the use of armed forces that would have been inconceivable to the generation of the framers. Whatever the text of the Constitution may say about the power of Congress to "declare war" or whatever the original understanding of this clause, it is hard to deny that many presidents throughout our history have successfully chosen to take the country to war without seeking a declaration of war (or, in some cases, even prior congressional approval of any kind). Ackerman and David Golove have also persuasively argued that the Treaty Clause, which requires that two-thirds of the Senate assent to any treaty, has been transformed through the use of "executive agreements." Although such agreements are unmentioned in the text of the Constitution, presidents have frequently avoided the strictures of the Treaty Clause by labeling an "agreement" what earlier would have been viewed as a "treaty." Thus, the North American Free Trade Agreement did not have to leap the hurdles erected by the Treaty Clause; instead, it was validated by majority votes of both the House of Representatives and the Senate.

These developments are undoubtedly important, and any complete analysis of our constitutional system should take account of such flexibility. But we should not overemphasize our system's capacity to change, and it is *constitutional stasis* rather than the potential for adaptation that is my focus.

* * *

One cannot, as a practical matter, litigate the obvious inequality attached to Wyoming's having the same voting power in the Senate as California. Nor can we imagine even President George W. Bush, who has certainly not been a shrinking violet with regard to claims of presidential power, announcing that Justice John Paul Stevens—appointed in 1976 and embarking on this fourth decade of service on the Supreme Court at the age of eighty-six—is simply "too old" or has served "long enough," and that he is therefore nominating, and asking the Senate to confirm, a successor to Justice Stevens in spite of the awkward fact that the justice has not submitted his resignation.

In any event, * * * the Constitution makes it unacceptably difficult to achieve the inspiring goals of the Preamble and, therefore, warrants our disapproval. * * *

Although I am asking you to take part in a hypothetical referendum and to vote no with regard to the present Constitution, I am *not* asking you to imagine simply tearing it up and leaping into the unknown of a fanciful "state of nature." All you must commit yourself to is the proposition that the Constitution is sufficiently flawed to justify calling a new convention authorized to scrutinize all aspects of the Constitution and to suggest such changes as are felt to be desirable. The new convention would be no more able to bring its handiwork into being by fiat than were the framers in Philadelphia. All proposals would require popular approval in a further national referendum. This leaves open the possibility that, even after voting to trigger the convention, you could ultimately decide that the "devil you know" (the present Constitution) is preferable to the "devil you don't" (the proposed replacement). But the important thing, from my perspective, is to recognize that there are indeed "devilish" aspects of our present Constitution that should be confronted and, if at all possible, exorcised. To complete this metaphor, one might also remember that "the devil is in the details." * * *

"A Radical Right-Wing Dream to Rewrite the Constitution Is Close to Coming True"

Travis Waldron

The project to overhaul the Constitution is much closer to fruition than most people realize.

Six weeks before Donald Trump won the 2016 presidential election, more than 100 state lawmakers gathered in Williamsburg, Virginia, for a week of Founding Fathers cosplay. Their task, over three days in the town that bills itself as a living museum to America's colonial period, was to approve a dramatic overhaul of the United States' foundational text.

The lawmakers, nearly all Republicans, ratified six new Constitutional amendments: [t]hey imposed term limits on members of Congress, abolished the federal income tax and placed severe limits on the federal government's ability to levy taxes, implement new regulations or spend money. While the rest of the country focused on the presidential election, the Virginia gathering partied like it was 1787.

"The events at Williamsburg will be remembered as a turning point in history," Michael Farris, a co-founder of the Convention of States Project, the conservative group that organized the event, said as the mock convention closed.

That may have been a comically grandiose statement at the time. But nobody should be laughing today. The project to overhaul the Constitution is much closer to fruition than most people realize.

Since 2014, the Convention of States Project and other conservative groups, including the American Legislative Exchange Council (ALEC) have helped persuade lawmakers in 15 states to pass resolutions that call for a new constitutional convention.

Led by a prominent right-wing activist—former Tea Party Patriots founder Mark Meckler, who is also the current acting CEO of Parler, a social media platform popular on the right—the Convention of States Project has spread the gospel of a convention to an increasingly radical audience. This year, lawmakers proposed 42 Convention of States resolutions in at least 24 new states, according to the Center for Media and Democracy, which has long monitored the convention push.

The passage of those resolutions would trigger the provision in Article V of the Constitution that allows a convention to be called if 34 states demand it. Backers of another resolution—one that calls for a Balanced Budget Amendment—have begun to argue that they have already reached that threshold. And last year, former Wisconsin Gov. Scott Walker (R) began pushing Republican officials to sue Congress in an effort to force a convention call.

"I think if [Republicans] win the midterm elections, if they take the House and Senate, they will try to call an Article V convention immediately," said David Super, a Georgetown University law professor who has closely followed the movement for a new convention. "It's not a foregone conclusion that the simple Republican majority would get there, but if they get big majorities, I think they'll try."

That has set off a furious tug-of-war between the groups and lawmakers that want a convention and those desperate to stop it. Almost as quickly as advocates have introduced new resolutions in key states that could tip the balance their way, opponents have mobilized to persuade other legislatures to repeal their existing calls, tipping it right back.

Primarily a conservative effort now, the prospect of a convention excites elements of both the right and left who see it as a useful way to improve a broken and dated founding document, check the powers of Congress, and work around the influence of special interest groups that have derailed popular policies, be they a limit on corporate campaign contributions or fiscal restraints on the feds.

Opponents, on the other hand, see a far more nefarious plot: a master class in astroturfing that could open the entire document up to a radical rewrite meant to serve the right-wing corporate interests that already dominate our politics, especially at the state level. The convention, they argue, could lead to the demolition of everything from the social safety net and environmental protections to civil rights laws. Or maybe even the Constitution itself.

"The First Amendment, the 14th Amendment, the 15th Amendment," said Jay Riestenberg of Common Cause, a liberal group that campaigns against the calling of a convention. "Any civil rights, any constitutional protection in the Constitution could be up for grabs in this constitutional convention."

For others, the fear is less about what the convention could accomplish than what might happen simply because it takes place. An untested process will likely face questions about its legitimacy from the start. And in a fractured nation where a substantial number of Republican voters falsely believe the last election was invalid, a messy or deadlocked convention could lead to an all-out constitutional crisis that would make the democratic catastrophe that occurred on Jan. 6 look tame in comparison.

"We shouldn't want to go down that road, especially now that we've just had an experience of how dangerous and unpleasant it is to get close to a constitutional legitimacy crisis," said Walter Olson, a senior fellow at the Cato Institute who has long warned against the convention effort.

Dangers of A "Runaway Convention"

Article V lays out two methods to amend the Constitution. The first, and most common, is for Congress to approve an amendment and send it to the states for ratification. The second allows states to petition for a convention to consider amendments, stipulating that a convention will occur once two-thirds of the states have done so.

States have filed various petitions seeking to amend the Constitution almost since the day it was ratified. But the modern push to use the second method, which proponents refer to as an Article V convention, traces its roots to 1957 when Indiana passed a resolution seeking to convene the states to consider the passage of an amendment that would require the federal government to balance its budget each year.

Wyoming joined four years later, but no other state picked up the baton until the 1970s, when conservatives widely adopted the cause. Between 1973 and 1979, 29 states called for a convention to consider a Balanced Budget Amendment, a proposal that economists have repeatedly warned would hamstring the federal government's tax-and-spend authorities, leave it unable to respond to economic crises and force it to gut popular programs like Social Security, Medicare, and Medicaid.

In theory, if 34 states approve resolutions solely related to a Balanced Budget Amendment, delegates wouldn't be allowed to propose or pass anything else for states to ratify. That's what proponents of a budget-related convention say, anyway.

But it's not clear they are right, nor that courts would agree. Since an Article V convention has never been called, the legal limits haven't yet been meaningfully tested. And critics have long argued that there is no language in Article V to ensure its limited scope, or that a convention would necessarily follow the contours advocates lay out in their supposedly limited convention calls.

A broad convention, Super has argued, could possibly write its own rules or even change the existing ratification process, and courts aren't likely to intervene. They may not even have the authority to do so. So there is an inherent risk of a "runaway convention" that goes beyond its purported aim and opens up the entire Constitution to an overhaul.

Those fears were especially strong early on among conservatives who worried that special interest groups had foul intentions and that a convention would go awry the minute it began.

"If I tell you I'm going home this afternoon to Illinois, but you look at my plane ticket and it reads to the Bahamas, I think you would deduce that I wasn't in any hurry to get home, and I was planning some fun and games along the way," conservative activist Phyllis Schlafly testified in the Oregon state Senate in 1989 in a successful attempt to persuade the legislature there to repeal its convention call.

"That is exactly what I think about the people who propose a 'ConCon' as a route to getting a Balanced Budget Amendment. There's no evidence that the one will lead to the other, and there is enormous evidence that it will lead to a lot of mischief," she said.

During that time, both liberals and hard-core conservatives like Schlafly teamed up to persuade more than a dozen states to rescind their calls for a convention and derailed the idea altogether—for a while.

In 2010, the idea experienced a resurgence among conservatives who weaponized racism and the national debt in an effort to thwart the biggest aims of Barack Obama's presidency, including the Affordable Care Act and efforts to kickstart the economy after the Great Recession.

Florida passed a resolution calling for a convention to consider a Balanced Budget Amendment in 2010; over the next decade, 21 other states joined (some of them already had existing convention calls on the books). Most counts place the total number states with of active resolutions at 28, while Robert Natelson, a conservative constitutional scholar who supports the idea of calling a convention, considers 27 of the petitions valid.

The Balanced Budget Amendment resolutions are still the closest to making a convention a reality, but unable to clearly get over the hump, proponents of the Balanced Budget Amendment convention last year proposed a different strategy: to sue Congress, which has the discretion to determine when the Article V threshold has been met, and force its hand.

Walker, the former Wisconsin governor, laid out that plan during an ALEC annual meeting last July as conservatives once again railed against extra-constitutional abuses of power related to the COVID-19 pandemic. The theory rests on the fact that, in addition to the states that have active Balanced Budget Amendment resolutions on the books, six states have passed calls for a plenary convention to consider general changes to the document.

Combine them, and the necessary two-thirds of states have filed petitions, meaning Congress has an obligation to call a convention. If Congress does not comply, a friendly state attorney general will sue in court, the *Associated Press* reported last year.

The plenary convention calls are not new and are largely, if not entirely, unrelated to the Balanced Budget Amendment petitions. New York's, for instance, dates to 1789, before the ratification of the Bill of Rights. Nevertheless, conservative legal scholars like Natelson have argued that, by law, they are likely valid when combined with the Balanced Budget Amendment resolutions.

That doesn't mean that Natelson thinks Walker's plan will work. Asked if he thought a legal order against Congress would succeed, he answered with a flat "no." Hesitant to project when a convention call might actually reach the necessary threshold, Natelson guessed that any legitimate push is at least a few election cycles away.

Common Cause and other groups have, over the last few years, focused their efforts on persuading states with longstanding convention resolutions to rescind them, with some success. Colorado's state legislature in April voted to rescind all of the previous convention resolutions its general assembly had passed in an effort to ensure the state did not play an unwitting role in the calling of a new convention.

Colorado's move could be a striking blow to the movement to call a convening of the states: [n]ow, combining the Balanced Budget Amendment and plenary resolutions doesn't add up to the necessary 34.

Still, that Walker and other conservatives may even be willing to try the legal route has aroused concern among convention opponents.

"They know their agenda is unpopular," Riestenberg said. "So they have to find a different way to push their agenda without getting legislators or voters to care about it."

A Sharp Right Turn

If the Balanced Budget Amendment convention is the closest one to fruition, it's Meckler's group that appears to have the most momentum and money behind it. Meckler launched the Convention of States Project in 2014 under the umbrella of another group he formed after splitting with Tea Party Patriots, the organization he co-founded to help foment protests in the earliest days of that "movement."

Meckler's proposal does not limit the ideal convention to a single idea like term limits—another popular focal point for convention advocate—or a Balanced Budget Amendment; rather, it broadens the scope of the gathering to include any amendments that will "impose fiscal restraints on the federal government, limit the power and jurisdiction of the federal government, and limit the terms of office for its officials and for members of Congress."

The effort quickly gained steam. Georgia, Alaska, and Florida passed Convention of States proposals in 2014, and five others—Alabama, Indiana, Louisiana, Oklahoma, and Tennessee—followed over the next two years.

Meckler signed a litany of prominent conservatives onto the effort. Florida Sen. Marco Rubio (R) was an early endorser, according to the organization's website. Members of the Republican establishment (like ex-Florida Gov. Jeb Bush), its right-wing conservative fringe (like former Florida Rep. Allen West), and its media echo chamber (Mark Levin and Ben Shapiro) have also given the idea their blessing.

Trump's victory in 2016 did not stall the push. Seven states—Arizona, Arkansas, Missouri, North Dakota, Texas, and Utah—joined the crusade between 2017 and 2019, bringing the total to 15. In at least a half-dozen other states, single legislative chambers passed resolutions that failed to fully advance.

The Convention of States Project goes to lengths to make itself look like a grassroots movement. It boasts that nearly 2 million people have signed its petition calling for an Article V convention, encourages visitors to send auto-generated letters to state lawmakers to urge them forward, and has insisted that the majority of its funding comes from small donors eager to support the cause.

Much of what it says it's after, meanwhile, is broadly popular: [t]he American public generally supports term limits, balanced budgets, and vague ideas like "fiscal responsibility" and "reducing the power of the federal government."

But everything else about it suggests rather clearly that, much like the tea party, the push for a convention is more of a priority for its wealthy, right-wing backers than it is for the conservative grassroots.

The Convention of States Project's source of funding is opaque, but its parent organization received more than $12 million from groups linked to brothers Charles and David Koch and other major conservative donors between 2010 and 2018, according to IRS filings reported by the Center for Media and Democracy and Splinter. The Mercer family, which through its foundation has showered tens of millions of dollars on right-wing causes over the last decade, has donated at least $500,000 to the group, CMD has reported.

ALEC, the Koch-funded membership organization of business-friendly and government-skeptical conservative state lawmakers, is among the biggest proponents of a new convention. It has pushed model legislation calling for a Balanced Budget Amendment convention for more than a decade, and in 2015 produced a model bill along the lines of what Meckler's group prefers. FreedomWorks, another corporate-backed right-wing group that helped foment the original tea party protests, also supports an Article V convention.

"I'm not convinced that the Convention of States Project really is a movement," said Super, who has testified against the organization's resolutions in multiple states. "It's a well-funded organization that passes itself off as a movement."

For its part, the Convention of States Project has never done much to combat the notion that it is a steroid-infused outgrowth of the tea party: [i]n 2017, when he signed on as an adviser, former South Carolina Sen. Jim DeMint—a tea party darling who left the Senate to work for the Heritage Foundation—called an Article V convention the tea party's "new mission."

"They realize that all the work they did in 2010 has not resulted in all the things they hoped for," DeMint told USA Today. "Many of them are turning to Article V."

Them, however, does not refer to the more lightly funded elements of the conservative movement, or rank-and-file Republican voters. Many local tea party groups oppose the plan. And although polling on the subject is limited, a majority of Americans and an even larger majority of Republicans oppose the idea of a new convention, according to a 2021 survey that Common Cause has touted.

The broad nature of Meckler's proposed convention makes the idea even more toxic for conservatives who've long feared what a convention might bring. Second Amendment activists, for instance, have in the past worried that a "runaway convention" could lead to the demise of their most cherished element of the Constitution, given that it does not inspire the religious devotion among the general public that it does among gun enthusiasts and Republican lawmakers.

Grassroots conservative opponents of the convention, meanwhile, fear as Schlafly once did that the convention call is a backhanded way for special interests to advance their own plans. As one conservative activist who opposes the idea put it: [m]any movement conservatives want the government and federal courts to more aggressively adhere to an originalist interpretation of *this Constitution*, not throw it out altogether. Andy Biggs, the Arizona Republican congressman who has faced allegations that he helped organize the Capitol insurrection, strikes a similar note in a book he published in 2015 that described the convention plan as "a con."

"Their approach is like overhauling an engine to fix a flat tire," Biggs wrote.

Natelson, the conservative constitutional expert who has advised the Convention of States Project and is a member of ALEC's board of scholars, dismissed concerns about a "runaway convention," saying that his research into past conventions has convinced him that it is "literally impossible" for one to spiral out of control.

Although there has never been a convention called under Article V, states have convened for both general and regional conventions to discuss single topics, or a limited number of topics, without branching off to other subjects. Article V, he argued, does not lay out specific rules because the rules are well understood.

Neither the First Amendment nor Second Amendment are under threat at a convention like the one Meckler's group favors, he insisted, because by definition, repealing or overhauling them would *expand* federal powers, rather than limit them. (That argument suffers from the fact that Republican state legislatures are currently pushing a rash of new bills that would curb First Amendment protest rights.)

"There never has been a convention that has run away," Natelson said. "This argument is totally fabricated. It was fabricated in the 20th century by conservatives and more recently has been used by liberals. It has no historical merit whatsoever."

"But," he added, "it scares people."

Meckler and the Convention of States Project did not respond to *Huff-Post*'s interview requests or questions about their effort. But Meckler has similarly dismissed fears of a "runaway convention" in recent interviews with other outlets. (Term limits, abolition of the Department of Education and a requirement that two-thirds of states agree to any change in immigration law top Meckler's priority list, he told *Newsweek*.) And over the last few years, his group has ramped up its efforts to alleviate those concerns and bolster support among newer constituencies, making its case to gun rights groups and individual gun owners during appearances at gun shows across the nation.

Last year, Meckler and the conservative groups pushing for a convention found another source of right-wing frustration to stoke: the COVID-19 pandemic. As governors used emergency executive powers to shut down businesses and impose mask requirements and other restrictions meant to slow the spread of the virus, a cadre of conservative groups—including ALEC and FreedomWorks—began to organize and foment protests outside state capitols. Meckler was one of the chief proponents of the so-called "reopen" movement, such that it was one.

Much as they had with the tea party movement, the groups wielded rhetoric about "liberty" and "freedom" to provoke small but angry gatherings, then translated that energy into a push for priorities they had always supported—in particular, restrictions on the executive powers of democratically elected governors, many of whom lost those powers as soon as conservative legislators wielding ALEC's model bills returned to state capitols.

Yet if they hoped the energy fueling those protests would generate similar momentum behind calls for a new convention, it hasn't yet materialized: [c]onservative state legislatures in Montana, New Hampshire, and South Dakota have already killed such resolutions this year, and the proposal went nowhere in Kentucky, one of several states Meckler's group has prioritized. Others face uncertain futures in legislative sessions crowded with other GOP priorities.

No such resolution has passed yet this year, but Wisconsin Republicans have advanced Convention of States Project resolutions out of committees in both chambers of the state legislature and could bring them up for floor votes soon. (Sixteen of the GOP lawmakers behind the resolutions have links to ALEC, the Center for Media and Democracy reported.) South Carolina's version of the resolution advanced out of a state House committee for the second straight year, but it's not clear whether it will receive a full vote. (The sponsor of that bill, state Rep. Bill Taylor, declined an interview request. Sponsors in four other states did not respond to *HuffPost*'s inquiries.)

The anti-lockdown protests became a haven for right-wing extremism that expressed itself in increasingly violent ways, under the guise of fighting "tyrants" who were abusing the Constitution. In Kentucky, a member of the Three Percenters, a white supremacist militia group, hanged the governor in effigy during one demonstration. In Michigan, men with ties to militias were arrested for plotting to kidnap Gov. Gretchen Whitmer; they had previously discussed "creating a society that followed the U.S. Bill of Rights and where they could be self-sufficient." Protests in Michigan and Oregon eventually led to armed demonstrators entering state capitols in an effort to intimidate lawmakers, episodes that became a trial run for the riot in Washington months later.

Longtime observers of the push for an Article V convention worry that it, too, is becoming a vehicle for extremists to express their disdain for the federal government, especially given the prevalence of conspiracy theories pushed by Trump and his supporters that the election was stolen and that the country itself is being purloined by liberals, "the Deep State" and other extraconstitutional actors.

Those fears deepened earlier this year when Meckler assumed the position as interim CEO of Parler, the right-wing social media platform that has served as an incubator for extremism and that along with other, similar services was used to plan the attack on the U.S. Capitol. Rebekah Mercer, the head of the Mercer Family Foundation, pushed Meckler—himself an extremist who has called Black Lives Matter an "evil" and "anti-American" movement—into the job, Bloomberg reported in March.

"Their strategy for years now has been to play hard to the right-wing," said Arn Pearson, the executive director of the Center for Media and Democracy. Meckler's job at Parler, he added, "is just their latest move to try to connect with right-wing extremists" and "energize that base around the Convention of States approach."

What a Convention Might Do

Fantasies of an Article V convention that will fix the United States' ills have also percolated on the left in the last decade, particularly among supporters of a constitutional amendment to overturn *Citizens United v. FEC*—the 2010 Supreme Court decision that tossed out most restrictions on corporate and special interest spending in federal elections.

In 2011, progressive television host Cenk Uygur launched WolfPAC, a group that supports such an amendment and cites an Article V convention as a potential path to get it. Other left-leaning groups that favor a similar amendment have also expressed some openness to a convention, even if it's not their preferred route. And at times, the right and left have joined forces: [a]s far back as 2011, Meckler and Lawrence Lessig—a Harvard professor who has advised WolfPAC and later waged a brief campaign for the 2016 Democratic presidential nomination on the sole issue of campaign finance reform—held a joint conference on the merits of an Article V convention.

"You can see how that appeals to people who have lost faith in conventional politics and see themselves as the new founding generation," Olson, of the Cato Institute, said. "I think it's a delusion, but I can see how a lot of people are attracted to it."

The vast majority of liberal and leftist energy focused on the issue, however, remains steadfastly opposed to any convention call, both out of fear over how it would work and about what its better-funded and organized proponents on the right would like it to accomplish.

The impact of a Balanced Budget Amendment alone is potentially massive: [e]conomists have warned that it could demolish any semblance of the country's social welfare state while imposing restrictions on federal spending that make it almost impossible for the government to respond to massive crises like the next Great Recession or global pandemic. In addition to a Balanced Budget Amendment and a repeal of the federal income tax, the 2016 mock convention sought to weaken the Commerce Clause—a major source of Congress' regulatory power on civil rights and other matters—and allowed states to nullify federal laws if three-fifths agreed to.

And it's not hard to guess what else the right would push hard to enshrine into the nation's new governing text, given the priorities of the groups that are out front about their support for the convention. Like, say, a total gutting of the federal government's ability to respond to crises like climate change or hold corporations accountable for environmental disasters. Super, the Georgetown professor, worries that it could even lead to the total opening of protected lands to mining, drilling, or extraction contracts.

"My fears are basically that the oil and gas industry makes sure that we can ever have cap-and-trade or a carbon tax, and makes it very easy for a single friendly administration to give them irrevocable rights to public lands that the Takings Clause would prevent anyone from ever taking from them," Super said. "So basically crippling environmental enforcement."

Others see the convention as a way the right can enshrine its ability to govern without ever winning a majority of votes at the federal level, especially as states redraw their congressional and state legislative maps over the next year, a process that is likely to result in heavy rounds of partisan gerrymandering.

"If the GOP is able to control its grasp on the states following the next round of redistricting, then adopting amendments via [constitutional convention] would enable them to dominate law and policy in a majority of states, even if they lose power in Washington or at the gubernatorial level," Pearson said.

The liberals who oppose the calling of a convention, in other words, largely believe that groups that support it on the left are blind to what would actually take place. Instead of improving the current Constitution, a convention would likely seek to overhaul it with a laundry list of priorities that the right-wing's corporate donor class has already sought through more typical legislative means, or alter the Constitution in a way that makes it easier to achieve those aims through more typical means down the road.

Natelson, the conservative scholar who supports the Article V convention, believes all of these arguments amount to hyperventilating nonsense. While no Article V convention has been held, there is sufficient precedent and constitutional understanding to determine how the founders intended such a convention to work, and to protect it from going off the rails, he argued.

The convention, he said, would almost certainly be closely monitored by the media and state lawmakers, keeping it from going beyond its scope.

States, he said, could recall delegates who went rogue, if they chose to. And the high threshold required for ratification of any amendment—38 state legislatures must eventually approve—means that only incredibly popular proposals would stand even the slightest chance of ratification.

"I would say term limits, if the amendment is drafted well, would have a high chance of being ratified," Natelson said. "Some kind of simple fiscal restraint that is well drafted and has exceptions for emergencies probably would be ratifiable. And my guess that some kind of campaign finance reform, if it got two-thirds of the states to propose it, would probably be ratifiable."

And fears that the convention would quickly be co-opted by special interest groups, lobbyists, and those big donors?

"Like Congress?" he laughed.

Olson is similarly skeptical that a convention would produce radical change, not in a polarized country that hasn't been able to alter its founding documents through more tried and true means. No amendment has been added to the Constitution since 1991, and that only happened because enough states finally ratified a proposal put forth 202 years prior. It's been half a century since an amendment was proposed and ratified in a timeframe typical of the majority of the other alterations.

"If the national consensus is missing for the retail, one-at-a-time amendments, then the national consensus is also absent for a big, radical change-lots-of-things-at-once national convention," Olson said of the Convention of States Project's plan. "People are deluding themselves if they think that kind of huge national consensus exists for either conservative or liberal views."

But he worries a convention could lead to an even bigger splintering of the country and an even deeper legitimacy crisis for its democracy. Without a clear mandate or obvious rules it should follow, any convention, Olson argued, would inherently be seen as illegitimate by a huge swath of a country.

The left, for good reason, isn't going to trust a convention that results from a Hail Mary legal challenge or a Republican Congress' decision to call it, especially not when the majority of delegates would be appointed by GOP state legislatures that are steadily radicalizing against the basic tenets of democracy—and "just a few months ago tried to throw out the results of a free and fair election," Riestenberg said. And especially not if a conservative-heavy Supreme Court eventually blesses the whole process.

The right, meanwhile, has spent the last decade wading deeper and deeper into the fever swamps, bathing itself in conspiracy theories and the increasingly extremist notion that the country has been stolen from them. An entire political party is now premised on and beholden to false beliefs so rampant that they generated an armed insurrection in the United States Capitol. What happens inside that movement—especially as Meckler and his allies continue to foment anger and court extremists—when a convention that has been sold as a cure-all fails to produce what they want?

Riestenberg fears another potential outcome of that scenario: a compromise amendment ostensibly meant to walk the country back from the sort of crisis the convention could potentially create. To stave off disaster, the convention delegates might agree to bar corporate election funding but also force the government to balance its budget each year. Comity, at the price of crippling the federal government's most basic functions.

Natelson isn't swayed by any of these concerns, or the idea that it's too dangerous a time to open the Constitution up to potentially massive changes. On the eve of the Civil War, he said, Virginia called for a convention of states in an attempt to lower the nation's temperature. In February 1861, delegates from the participating states met in Washington to discuss a compromise amendment to the Constitution that they hoped would stave off a war.

"The debates were bitter between South and North, beyond anything today," Natelson said. "And yet, when the dust is cleared, they had successfully negotiated and drafted a constitutional amendment, which if adopted might very well have averted a civil war."

The proposed amendment went nowhere. Had it been ratified, it might have helped avoid the war. But it also would have permanently barred Congress or a future constitutional amendment from outlawing slavery in the South, leaving any future decision to abolish the practice solely up to the states.

12

"Restoring the Rule of Law with States Leading the Way"

GREG ABBOTT

The Constitution is increasingly eroded with each passing year. That is a tragedy given the volume of blood spilled by patriots to win our country's freedom and repeatedly defend it over the last 240 years. Moreover, the declining relevance of our Nation's governing legal document is dangerous. Thomas Hobbes's observation more than 350 years ago remains applicable today: [t]he only thing that separates a nation from anarchy is its collective willingness to know and obey the law.

But today, most Americans have no idea what our Constitution says. According to a recent poll, one-third of Americans cannot name the three branches of government; one-third cannot name any branch; and one-third thinks that the President has the "final say" about the government's powers. Obviously, the American people cannot hold their government accountable if they do not know what the source of that accountability says.

The Constitution is not just abstract and immaterial to average Americans; it also is increasingly ignored by government officials. Members of Congress used to routinely quote the Constitution while debating whether a particular policy proposal could be squared with Congress's enumerated powers. Such debates rarely happen today. In fact, when asked to identify the source of constitutional authority for Obamacare's individual mandate, the Speaker of the House revealed all too much when she replied with anger and incredulity: *"Are you serious?"* And, while the Supreme Court continues to identify new rights protected by the Constitution's centuries-old text, it is telling that the justices frequently depart from what the document actually says and rely instead on words or concepts that are found nowhere in the document. That is why one scholar observed that "in this day and age, discussing the doctrine of enumerated powers is like discussing the redemption of Imperial Chinese bonds."

Abandoning, ignoring, and eroding the strictures of the Constitution cheapens the entire institution of law. One of the cornerstones of this country was that ours would be a Nation of laws and not of men. The Constitution is the highest such law and the font of all other laws. As long as all Americans uphold the Constitution's authority, the document will continue to provide the ultimate defense of our liberties. But once the Constitution loses its hold on American life, we also lose confidence in the ability of law to protect us. Without the rule of law the things we treasure can be taken away by an election, by whims of individual leaders, by impulsive social-media campaigns, or by collective apathy.

The Constitution provides a better way—if only we were willing to follow it. The Constitution imposes real limits on Congress and forces its members to do their jobs rather than pass the buck. The Constitution forces the President to work with Congress to accomplish his priorities rather than usurping its powers by circumventing the legislative process with executive orders and administrative fiats. And the Constitution forces the Supreme Court to confront the limits on its powers to transform the country. Although the Constitution provides no assurance that any branch of government will make policy choices you like, the Constitution offers *legitimacy* to those choices and legitimate pathways to override those choices. The people who make those choices would have to stand for election, they would have to work with others who stand for election, and crucially, they would have to play by rules that we all agree to beforehand rather than making them up as they go along.

Of course, the Constitution already does all of this. And thus it bears emphasis at the outset that *the Constitution itself is not broken*. What *is* broken is our Nation's willingness to obey the Constitution and to hold our leaders accountable to it. As explained in the following pages, all three branches of the federal government have wandered far from the roles that the Constitution sets out for them. For various reasons, "We the People" have allowed all three branches of government to get away with it. And with each power grab the next somehow seems less objectionable. When measured by how far we have strayed from the Constitution we originally agreed to, the government's flagrant and repeated violations of the rule of law amount to a wholesale abdication of the Constitution's design.

That constitutional problem calls for a constitutional solution, just as it did at our Nation's founding. Indeed, a constitutional crisis gave birth to the Constitution we have today. The Articles of Confederation, which we adopted after the Revolutionary War, proved insufficient to protect and defend our fledgling country. So the States assembled to devise what we now know as our Constitution. At that assembly, various States stepped up to offer their leadership visions for what the new Constitution should say. Virginia's delegates offered the "Virginia Plan," New Jersey's delegates offered the "New Jersey Plan," and Connecticut's delegates brokered a compromise called the "Connecticut Plan." Without those States' plans, there would be no Constitution and probably no United States of America at all.

Now it is Texas's turn. The Texas Plan is not so much a vision to alter the Constitution as it is a call to restore the rule of our current one. The problem is that we have forgotten what our Constitution means, and with that amnesia, we also have forgotten what it means to be governed by laws instead of men. The solution is to restore the rule of law by ensuring that our government abides by the Constitution's limits. Our courts are supposed to play that role, but today, we have judges who actively subvert the Constitution's original design rather than uphold it. Yet even though we can no longer rely on our Nation's leaders to enforce the Constitution that "We the People" agreed to, the Constitution provides another way forward. Acting through the States, the people can amend their Constitution to force their leaders in all three branches of government to recognize renewed limits on federal power. Without the consent of any politicians in Washington, D.C., "We the People" can rein in the federal government and restore the balance of power between the States and the United States. The Texas Plan accomplishes this by offering nine constitutional amendments:

    I. Prohibit Congress from regulating activity that occurs wholly within one State.

    II. Require Congress to balance its budget.

    III. Prohibit administrative agencies—and the unelected bureaucrats that staff them—from creating federal law.

    IV. Prohibit administrative agencies—and the unelected bureaucrats that staff them—from preempting state law.

    V. Allow a two-thirds majority of the States to override a U.S. Supreme Court decision.

    VI. Require a seven-justice super-majority vote for U.S. Supreme Court decisions that invalidate a democratically enacted law.

    VII. Restore the balance of power between the federal and state governments by limiting the former to the powers expressly delegated to it in the Constitution.

    VIII. Give state officials the power to sue in federal court when federal officials overstep their bounds.

    IX. Allow a two-thirds majority of the States to override a federal law or regulation.

*   *   *

Objections to an Article V Convention Lack Merit

The framers intended for States to call for conventions to propose constitutional amendments when, as now, the federal government has overstepped its bounds. And over the last 200 or so years, there have been hundreds of applications calling for such a convention spread out among virtually every state legislature. Yet no application has reached the critical two-thirds threshold to require the convention.

The States' previous failures to reach the two-thirds threshold for a convention could stem from the fact that, before now, circumstances did not demand it. But it is also possible that the States' efforts have been thwarted by counterarguments that surely will surface again in response to the Texas Plan. Whatever influence such counterarguments may have in previous contexts and other state legislatures' applications for constitutional conventions, they lack merit here.

*   *   *

Nor can critics credibly claim that a convention is "scary" or that it somehow threatens valuable tenets of the Constitution. That is so for at least two reasons. First, whatever happens at the convention, no amendments will be made to the Constitution unless and until they are approved by an overwhelming majority (three-fourths) of the States. That is an extraordinary super-majority requirement that ensures, in James Iredell's words, that "[i]t is highly probable that amendments agreed to in either of [Article V's] methods would be conducive to the public welfare, when so large a majority of the states consented to them." It takes only 13 States to block any measure from becoming a constitutional amendment.

* * * [It] is not as if the three-fourths approval requirement is the Constitution's only failsafe against imprudent amendments. The Constitution also leaves it to the States to limit the scope of the convention itself. In fact, four States already have applied for constitutional conventions that include some portion of the Texas Plan, and all of them limit their applications to specific issues. Likewise, the Texas Legislature can limit its application for a convention—or its participation in a convention—to the specific issues

included in the Texas Plan and discussed above. To the extent the convention strayed from those issues, Texas's consent to the convention's activities would automatically dissolve. State legislatures could even command in their laws authorizing participation in a convention that the state must vote against any constitutional convention provision not authorized by the state.

Some nonetheless argue that the Constitution does not allow state legislatures to limit the scope of a convention. The critics seize on this argument to raise the specter of a "runaway convention," in which the States propose a convention to debate limited amendments, but in which the delegates end up throwing the entire Constitution in the trashcan. Even if that happened, none of the delegates' efforts would become law without approval from three-fourths of the States. But even on its own terms, the criticism lacks merit.

The specter of a "runaway convention" goes like this. First, the critics argue, the Constitution says state legislatures "shall call a Convention for proposing Amendments," not for *confirming* a pre-written amendment that the state legislatures included in their applications for a convention. That means, the critics say, that States must call general, open-ended conventions; the convention delegates then perform the work of drafting the amendments; and the States' only option is to give a thumbs-up or thumbs-down at the end of the convention process. If the framers of Article V wanted to authorize conventions limited to particular issues, the critics conclude, they would have said so.

It is true that Article V does not expressly authorize States to limit conventions to particular issues—but the problem for would-be critics of the Texas Plan is that Article V *also* does not require general and open-ended conventions. Indeed, that is by design. As noted above, the whole point of the second path for proposing amendments was to *empower* States to propose amendments to the Constitution. In adopting that second path, the framers agreed with George Mason that the States should have constitutional redress when the federal government overstepped its bounds. And nothing that Mason (or his fellow framers) said would suggest that the States were somehow limited in *how* they exercised that power to defend their prerogatives against a federal government. To the contrary, James Madison specifically noted that the Constitution was silent on the issue, and he argued that that silence was good and necessary to preserve the States' flexibility. In Madison's words, "Constitutional regulations [of such matters] ought to be as much as possible avoided."

While the Constitution's text is silent on the topic, the framers themselves were not. To take just one example, George Nicholas pointed out during Virginia's ratification debates that conventions called by the States could—indeed, *would*—be limited to particular issues: "[t]he conventions which shall be so called will have their deliberations confined to a few points; no local interest to divert their attention; nothing but the necessary alterations." And because the States would limit their applications for conventions to particular issues, "[i]t is natural to conclude that those states who apply for calling the convention will concur in the ratification of the proposed amendments." Of course, it would not be natural to assume that the States would support the results of the convention they called if—as the critics argue—the States could have zero assurances regarding what the convention delegates would do at that convention.

The very thing that belies any allegation of radicalism in the Texas Plan—namely, the super-majority requirements for proposing and ratifying amendments—arguably undermines its efficacy as a check on federal overreach. The latter was the principal point of Patrick Henry, one of the greatest orators of the eighteenth century and a ferocious Anti-Federalist. He argued that the States' power to amend the Constitution did not go nearly far enough to protect the people from an overbearing federal government. In particular, he bemoaned Article V's super-majority requirements:

This, Sir, is the language of democracy; that a majority of the community have a right to alter their Government when found to be oppressive: [b]ut how different is the genius of your new Constitution from this! How different from the sentiments of freemen, that a contemptible minority can prevent the good of the majority! * * * If, Sir, amendments are left to the twentieth or tenth part of the people of America, your liberty is gone forever. * * * It will be easily contrived to procure the opposition of one tenth of the people to any alteration, however judicious. The Honorable Gentleman who presides, told us, that to prevent abuses in our Government, we will assemble in Convention, recall our delegated powers, and punish our servants for abusing the trust reposed in them. Oh, Sir, we should have fine times indeed, if to punish tyrants, it were only sufficient to assemble the people!

Patrick Henry might be right that even an assembly of the people will be insufficient to restore the rule of law and to bring the federal government to heel. And it is true that Article V allows a minority to oppose any amendment that the overwhelming majority of Americans support.

But far from dissuading the effort to amend our Constitution, Henry's words should encourage it. The benefits of the Texas Plan are many because any change effectuated by an assembly of the people will force the federal government—whether in big ways or small—to take the Constitution seriously again. And the downsides of such an assembly are virtually nonexistent, given that any change to our Constitution's text requires such overwhelming nationwide support. The only true downside comes from doing nothing and allowing the federal government to continue ignoring the very document that created it.

DISCUSSION QUESTIONS

1. Most of the time, people become critical of the Constitution when they don't get the policy results they want. When Congress fails to pass legislation because of the power of small-state senators, when the Supreme Court issues a ruling they oppose, or when the president makes a decision regarding the use of force that they oppose, the immediate impulse is to blame the system and call for change that would make their preferred policies more likely. Is this a valid reason for wanting to amend the Constitution?

2. The Constitution was written more than 230 years ago by a group of White men who had very "unmodern" views about democracy and equality. On what basis should we be bound by the decisions that they made? What would be the result if each generation were permitted to remake the rules, as Abbott suggests? Do you agree with Waldron's concerns about the constitutional convention?

3. Often, opinions about the Constitution divide along philosophical lines. On one side are people who believe that the most important purpose of a constitution is to limit government size and power. On the other are people who believe that the Constitution must protect rights and promote equality, which almost always involves expanding the size and power of government. Who has the better case? Why?

CHAPTER 3

Federalism

13

The Federalist, No. 46

JAMES MADISON

Some of the most divisive and bitter political battles in our nation's history have occurred over interpretations of the constitutional principle of federalism—the division of powers and functions between the state governments and the national government. The struggle for desegregation and the civil rights of minorities, the legalization of abortion, the selective incorporation of the Bill of Rights under the Fourteenth Amendment, slavery, and the Civil War all ultimately turned on the question, "Who has the authority to govern: the states, or the national government?" Our federal system is a delicate balance of power and shared responsibility between nation and states, each with constitutional authority to pass laws, levy taxes, and protect the interests and rights of citizens. It is a dynamic balance of power, easily destabilized by economic crises, political initiatives, and Supreme Court rulings, but often resolved in more recent years by the question, "Who will pay the price for implementing and enforcing government policy?"

The "double security" that James Madison discussed in The Federalist, *No. 51, did not satisfy those who feared that the national powers would encroach on state sovereignty. In* The Federalist, *No. 46, Madison went to great lengths to reassure the states that they would continue to wield a high degree of power, arguing that "the first and most natural attachment of the people will be to the governments of their respective states." While recognizing the potential for conflicts between state and federal governments, Madison concluded that the power retained by the states would be sufficient to resist arrogation by the newly established national government.*

I proceed to inquire whether the federal government or the State governments will have the advantage with regard to the predilection and support of the people. Notwithstanding the different modes in which they are appointed, we must consider both of them as substantially dependent on the great body of the citizens of the United States. * * * The federal and State governments are in fact but different agents and trustees of the people, constituted with different powers and designed for different purposes. The adversaries of the Constitution seem to have lost sight of the people altogether in their reasonings on this subject; and to have viewed these different establishments not only as mutual rivals and enemies, but as uncontrolled by any common superior in their efforts to usurp the authorities of each other. These gentlemen must here be reminded of their error. They must be told that the ultimate authority, wherever the derivative may be found, resides in the people alone, and that it will not depend merely on the comparative ambition or address of the different governments whether either, or which of them, will be able to enlarge its sphere of jurisdiction at the expense of the other. Truth, no less than decency, requires that the event in every case should be supposed to depend on the sentiments and sanction of their common constituents.

Many considerations * * * seem to place it beyond doubt that the first and most natural attachment of the people will be to the governments of their respective States. Into the administration of these a greater number of individuals will expect to rise. From the gift of these a greater number of offices and emoluments will flow. By the superintending care of these, all the more domestic and personal interests of the people will be regulated and provided for. With the affairs of these, the people will be more familiarly and minutely conversant. And with the members of these will a greater proportion of the people have the ties of personal acquaintance and friendship, and of family and party attachments; on the side of these, therefore, the popular bias may well be expected most strongly to incline.

The remaining points on which I propose to compare the federal and State governments are the disposition and the faculty they may respectively possess to resist and frustrate the measures of each other.

It has been already proved that the members of the federal will be more dependent on the members of the State governments than the latter will be on the former. It has appeared also that the prepossessions of the people, on whom both will depend, will be more on the side of the State governments than of the federal government. So far as the disposition of each towards the other may be influenced by these causes, the State governments must clearly have the advantage. But in a distinct and very important point of view, the advantage will lie on the same side. The prepossessions, which the members themselves will carry into the federal government, will generally be favorable to the States; whilst it will rarely happen that the members of the State governments will carry into the public councils a bias in favor of the general government. A local spirit will infallibly prevail much more in the members of Congress than a national spirit will prevail in the legislatures of the particular States.

* * * What is the spirit that has in general characterized the proceedings of Congress? A perusal of their journals, as well as the candid acknowledgments of such as have had a seat in that assembly, will inform us that the members have but too frequently displayed the character rather of partisans of their respective States than of impartial guardians of a common interest; that where on one occasion improper sacrifices have been made of local considerations to the aggrandizement of the federal government, the great interests of the nation have suffered on a hundred from an undue attention to the local prejudices, interests, and views of the particular States. I mean not by these reflections to insinuate that the new federal government will not embrace a more enlarged plan of policy than the existing government may have pursued; much less that its views will be as confined as those of the State legislatures; but only that it will partake sufficiently of the spirit of both to be disinclined to invade the rights of the individual States, or the prerogatives of their governments.

Were it admitted, however, that the federal government may feel an equal disposition with the State governments to extend its power beyond the due limits, the latter would still have the advantage in the means of defeating such encroachments. If an act of a particular State, though unfriendly to the national government, be generally popular in that State, and should not too grossly violate the oaths of the State officers, it is executed immediately and, of course, by means on the spot and depending on the State alone. The opposition of the federal government, or the interposition of federal officers, would but inflame the zeal of all parties on the side of the State, and the evil could not be prevented or repaired, if at all, without the employment of means which must always be resorted to with reluctance and difficulty. On the other hand, should an unwarrantable measure of the federal government be unpopular in particular States, which would seldom fail to be the case, or even a warrantable measure be so, which may sometimes be the case, the means of opposition to it are powerful and at hand. The disquietude of the people; their repugnance and, perhaps, refusal to co-operate with the officers of the Union; the frowns of the executive magistracy of the State; the embarrassments created by legislative devices, which would often be added on such occasions, would oppose, in any State, difficulties not to be despised; would form, in a large State, very serious impediments; and where the sentiments of several adjoining States happened to be in unison, would present obstructions which the federal government would hardly be willing to encounter.

But ambitious encroachments of the federal government on the authority of the State governments would not excite the opposition of a single State, or of a few States only. They would be signals of general alarm. Every government would espouse the common cause. A correspondence would be opened. Plans of resistance would be concerted. One spirit would animate and conduct the whole. The same combinations, in short, would result from an apprehension of the federal, as was produced by the dread of a foreign yoke; and unless the projected innovations should be voluntarily renounced, the same appeal to a trial of force would be made in the one case as was made in the other.

The only refuge left for those who prophesy the downfall of the State governments is the visionary supposition that the federal government may previously accumulate a military force for the projects of ambition. The reasonings contained in these papers must have been employed to little purpose indeed, if it could be necessary now to disprove the reality of this danger. That the people and the States should, for a sufficient period of time, elect an uninterrupted succession of men ready to betray both; that the traitors should, throughout this period, uniformly and systematically pursue some fixed plan for the extension of the military establishment; that the governments and the people of the States should silently and patiently behold the gathering storm and continue to supply the materials until it should be prepared to burst on their own heads must appear to everyone more like the incoherent dreams of a delirious jealousy, or the misjudged exaggerations of a counterfeit zeal, than like the sober apprehensions of genuine patriotism. Extravagant as the supposition is, let it, however, be made. Let a regular army, fully equal to the resources of the country, be formed; and let it be entirely at the devotion of the federal government: still it would not be going too far to say that the State governments with the people on their side would be able to repel the danger.

Besides the advantage of being armed, which the Americans possess over the people of almost every other nation, the existence of subordinate governments, to which the people are attached and by which the militia officers are appointed, forms a barrier against the enterprises of ambition, more insurmountable than any which a simple government of any form can admit of.

Let us not insult the free and gallant citizens of America with the suspicion that they would be less able to defend the rights of which they would be in actual possession than the debased subjects of arbitrary power would be to rescue theirs from the hands of their oppressors. Let us rather no longer insult them with the supposition that they can ever reduce themselves to the necessity of making the experiment by a blind and tame submission to the long train of insidious measures which must precede and produce it.

The argument under the present head may be put into a very concise form, which appears altogether conclusive. Either the mode in which the federal government is to be constructed will render it sufficiently dependent on the people, or it will not. On the first supposition, it will be restrained by that dependence from forming schemes obnoxious to their constituents. On the other supposition, it will not possess the confidence of the people, and its schemes of usurpation will be easily defeated by the State governments, who will be supported by the people.

On summing up the considerations stated in this and the last paper, they seem to amount to the most convincing evidence that the powers proposed to be lodged in the federal government are as little formidable to those reserved to the individual States as they are indispensably necessary to accomplish the purposes of the Union; and that all those alarms which have been sounded of a meditated and consequential annihilation of the State governments must, on the most favorable interpretation, be ascribed to the chimerical fears of the authors of them.

Publius

Discussion Questions

1. Is Madison right when he states that people are more attached to their state governments than to the national government? Why or why not? If not, would it better facilitate the democratic process if they were more attached to state governments?

2. Would your answer change at all during different political times? For example, are people more attached to the national government during times of war? Do people lose their faith in the national government during tough economic times? How about responses to the COVID-19 pandemic by the national and state governments?

From *The Price of Federalism*

Paul E. Peterson

In this concise overview of American federalism, Paul E. Peterson argues that both the early system and more modern system of shared sovereignty between the national government and the states have had their disadvantages. From the early period of "dual federalism" to today's system of a dominant national government, the battle over national and state government jurisdiction and power has led to bloodshed and war; the denial of political, social, and economic rights; and regional inequalities among the states.

Nevertheless, Peterson argues, there are advantages to federalism. Federalism has also facilitated capital growth and development, the creation of infrastructures, and social programs that greatly improved the quality of life for millions of Americans. Once the national government took responsibility for guaranteeing civil rights and civil liberties, the states "became the engines of economic development." Not all states are equally wealthy, but the national government has gradually diminished some of these differences by financing many social and economic programs. One battle over the proper form of federal relations involved welfare policy in the 1990s. Republicans in Congress wanted to give back to states the power to devise their own programs, whereas most Democrats and President Bill Clinton initially wanted to retain a larger degree of federal government control. However, President Clinton eventually agreed to end welfare as an entitlement and return substantial control over the program to the states. Debate continues over the proper balance between federal and state funding for the state-level welfare programs, and some states have pushed back against the expansion of federal power in health care.

These same debates have cropped up in more recent years in homeland security policy. Ideally, this policy would be run at the national level, and resources would be allocated to parts of the country that pose the greatest security risks. However, every state wants its share of the federal pie, so resources are not always allocated in the most efficient manner. Federalism also poses challenges for coordinating policy for "first responders" in a time of crisis: Who is responsible for coming to the aid of people in distress—local, state, or national agencies?

The Price of Early Federalism

As a principle of government, federalism has had a dubious history. It remains on the margins of political respectability even today. I was recently invited to give a presentation on metropolitan government before a United Nations [UN] conference. When I offered to discuss how the federal principle could be used to help metropolitan areas govern themselves more effectively, my sponsors politely advised me that this topic would be poorly received. The vast majority of UN members had a unified form of government, I was told, and they saw little of value in federalism. We reached a satisfactory compromise. I replaced "federal" with "two-tier form of government."

Thomas Hobbes, the founder of modern political thought, would have blessed the compromise, for he, too, had little room for federalism in his understanding of the best form of government. Hobbes said that people agreed to have a government over them only because they realized that in a state of nature, that is, when there is no government, life becomes a war of all against all. If no government exists to put malefactors in jail, everyone must become a criminal simply to avoid being a victim. Life becomes "nasty, brutish and short." To avoid the violent state of nature, people need and want rule by a single sovereign. Division of power among multiple sovereigns encourages bickering among them. Conflicts become inevitable, as each sovereign tries to expand its power (if for no other reason than to avoid becoming the prey of competing sovereigns). Government degenerates into anarchy and the world returns to the bitter state of nature from which government originally emerged.

The authors of *The Federalist* papers defended dual sovereignty by turning Hobbes's argument in favor of single sovereignty on its head. While Hobbes said that anything less than a single sovereign would lead to war of all against all, *The Federalist* argued that the best way of preserving liberty was to divide power. If power is concentrated in any one place, it can be used to crush individual liberty. Even in a democracy there can be the tyranny of the majority, the worst kind of tyranny because it is so stifling and complete. A division of power between the national and state governments reduces the possibility that any single majority will be able to control all centers of governmental power. The national government, by defending the country against foreign aggression, prevents external threats to liberty. The state governments, by denying power to any single dictator, reduce threats to liberty from within. As James Madison said in his defense of the Constitution, written on the eve of its ratification,

> The power surrendered by the people is first divided between two distinct governments, and then the portion allotted to each subdivided among distinct and separate departments. Hence a double security arises to the rights of the people. The different governments will control each other, at the same time that each will be controlled by itself. [*The Federalist*, No. 51]

Early federalism was built on the principle of dual sovereignty. The Constitution divided sovereignty between state and nation, each in control of its own sphere. Some even interpreted the Constitution to mean that state legislatures could nullify federal laws. Early federalism also gave both levels of government their own military capacity. Congress was given the power to raise an army and wage war, but states were allowed to maintain their own militia.

The major contribution of early federalism to American liberties took place within a dozen years after the signing of the Constitution. Liberty is never established in a new nation until those in authority have peacefully ceded power to a rival political faction. Those who wrote the Constitution and secured its ratification, known as the Federalists, initially captured control of the main institutions of the national government: Congress, the presidency, and the Supreme Court. Those opposed to the new constitutional order, the antifederalists, had to content themselves with an opposition role in Congress and control over a number of state governments, most notably Virginia's.

The political issues dividing the two parties were serious. The Federalist party favored a strong central government, a powerful central bank that could facilitate economic and industrial development, and a strong, independent executive branch. Federalists had also become increasingly disturbed by the direction the French Revolution had taken. They were alarmed by the execution of thousands, the confiscation of private property, and the movement of French troops across Europe. They called for the creation of a national army and reestablished close ties with Britain.

The antifederalists, who became known as Democratic-Republicans, favored keeping most governmental power in the hands of state governments. They were opposed to a national bank, a strong presidency, and industrial government. They thought the United States would remain a free country only if it remained a land of independent farmers. They bitterly opposed the creation of a national army for fear it would be used to repress political opposition. Impressed by the French Revolution's commitment to the rights of man, they excused its excesses. The greater danger, they thought, was the reassertion of British power, and they denounced the Federalists for seeming to acquiesce in the seizure of U.S. seamen by the British navy.

The conflict between the two sides intensified after George Washington retired to his home in Mount Vernon. In 1800 Thomas Jefferson, founder of the Democratic-Republican party, waged an all-out campaign to defeat Washington's Federalist successor, John Adams. In retrospect, the central issue of the election was democracy itself. Could an opposition party drive a government out of power? Would political leaders accept their defeat?

So bitter was the feud between the two parties that Representative Matthew Lyon, a Democratic-Republican, spit in the face of a Federalist on the floor of Congress. Outside the Congress, pro-French propagandists relentlessly criticized Adams. To silence the opposition, Congress, controlled by the Federalists, passed the Alien and Sedition Acts. One of the Alien Acts gave President Adams the power to deport any foreigners "concerned in any treasonable or secret machinations against the government." The Sedition

Act made it illegal to "write, print, utter, or publish . . . any false, scandalous and malicious writing . . . against . . . the Congress of the United States, or the President."

The targets of the Sedition Acts soon became clear. Newspaper editors supporting the Democratic-Republicans were quickly indicted, and ten were brought to trial and convicted by juries under the influence of Federalist judges. Matthew Lyon was sentenced to a four-month jail term for claiming, presumably falsely, that President Adams had an "unbounded thirst for ridiculous pomp, foolish adulation, and selfish avarice." Even George Washington lent his support to this political repression.

Federalism undoubtedly helped the fledgling American democracy survive this first constitutional test. When the Federalists passed the Alien and Sedition Acts, Democratic-Republicans in the Virginia and Kentucky state legislatures passed resolutions nullifying the laws. When it looked as if Jefferson's victory in the election of 1800 might be stripped away by a Federalist controlled House of Representatives, both sides realized that the Virginia state militia was at least as strong as the remnants of the Continental Army. Lacking the national army they had tried to establish, the Federalists chose not to fight. They acquiesced in their political defeat in part because their opponents had military as well as political power, and because they themselves could retreat to their own regional base of power, the state and local governments of New England and the mid-Atlantic states.

Jefferson claimed his victory was a revolution every bit as comprehensive as the one fought in 1776. The Alien and Sedition Acts were discarded, nullified not by a state legislature but by the results of a national election. President Adams returned to private life without suffering imprisonment or exile. Many years later, he and Jefferson reconciled their differences and developed through correspondence a close friendship. They died on the same day, the fiftieth anniversary of the Declaration of Independence. To both, federalism and liberty seemed closely intertwined.

The price to be paid for early federalism became more evident with the passage of time. To achieve the blessings of liberty, early federalism divided sovereign power. When Virginia and Kentucky nullified the Alien and Sedition Acts, they preserved liberties only by threatening national unity. With the election of Jefferson, the issue was temporarily rendered moot, but the doctrine remained available for use when southerners once again felt threatened by encroaching national power.

The doctrine of nullification was revived in 1830 by John C. Calhoun, sometime senator from South Carolina, who objected to high tariffs that protected northern industry at the expense of southern cotton producers. When Congress raised the tariff, South Carolina's legislature threatened to declare the law null and void. Calhoun, then serving as Andrew Jackson's vice president, argued that liberties could be trampled by national majorities unless states could nullify tyrannical acts. Andrew Jackson, though elected on a state's rights ticket, remained committed to national supremacy.

At the annual Democratic banquet honoring the memory of Thomas Jefferson, Calhoun supporters sought to trap Jackson into endorsing the doctrine. But Jackson, aware of the scheme, raised his glass in a dramatic toast to "[o]ur federal union: it must be preserved!" Not to be outdone, Calhoun replied in kind: "[t]he union, next to our liberty, most dear!"

A compromise was found to the overt issue, the tariff, but it was not so easy to resolve the underlying issue of slavery. In the infamous Dred Scott* decision, the Supreme Court interpreted federalism to mean that boundaries could not be placed on the movements of masters and slaves. Northern territories could not free slaves that came within their boundaries; to do so deprived masters of their Fifth Amendment right not to be deprived of their property without due process of law. The decision spurred northern states to elect Abraham Lincoln president, which convinced southern whites that their liberties, most dear, were more important than federal union.

To Lincoln, as to Jackson, the union was to be preserved at all costs. Secession meant war. War meant the loss of 1 million lives, the destruction of the southern economy, the emancipation of African Americans from slavery, the demise of the doctrine of nullification, and the end to early federalism. Early federalism, with its doctrine of dual sovereignty, may have initially helped to preserve liberty, but it did so at a terrible price. As Hobbes feared, the price of dual sovereignty was war.

Since the termination of the Civil War, Americans have concluded that they can no longer trust their liberties to federalism. Sovereignty must be concentrated in the hands of the national government. Quite apart from the dangers of civil war, the powers of state and local governments have been used too often by a tyrannical majority to trample the rights of religious, racial, and political minorities. The courts now seem a more reliable institutional shelter for the nation's liberties.

But if federalism is no longer necessary or even conducive to the preservation of liberty, then what is its purpose? Is it merely a relic of an outdated past? Are the majority of the members of the United Nations correct in objecting to the very use of the word?

The Rise of Modern Federalism

The answers to these questions have been gradually articulated in the 130 years following the end of the Civil War. Although the states lost their sovereignty, they remained integral to the workings of American government. Modern federalism no longer meant dual sovereignty and shared military capacity. Modern federalism instead meant only that each level of government had its own independently elected political leaders and its

---

*In *Dred Scott v. Sanford* (1857), the Supreme Court declared the antislavery provision of the Missouri Compromise of 1820 to be unconstitutional [*Editors*].

own separate taxing and spending capacity. Equipped with these tools of quasi-sovereignty, each level of government could take all but the most violent of steps to defend its turf.

Although sovereignty and military capacity now rested firmly in the hands of the national government, modern federalism became more complex rather than less so. Power was no longer simply divided between the nation and its states. Cities, counties, towns, school districts, special districts, and a host of additional governmental entities, each with its own elected leaders and taxing authority, assumed new burdens and responsibilities.

Just as the blessings bestowed by early federalism were evident from its inception, so the advantages of modern federalism were clear from the onset. If states and localities were no longer the guarantors of liberty, they became the engines of economic development. By giving state and local governments the autonomy to act independently, the federal system facilitated the rapid growth of an industrial economy that eventually surpassed its European competitors. Canals and railroads were constructed, highways and sewage systems built, schools opened, parks designed, and public safety protected by cities and villages eager to make their locality a boomtown.

The price to be paid for modern federalism did not become evident until government attempted to grapple with the adverse side effects of a burgeoning capitalist economy. Out of a respect for federalism's constitutional status and political durability, social reformers first worked with and through existing components of the federal system, concentrating much of their reform effort on state and local governments. Only gradually did it become clear that state and local governments, for all their ability to work with business leaders to enhance community prosperity, had difficulty meeting the needs of the poor and the needy.

It was ultimately up to the courts to find ways of keeping the price of modern federalism within bounds. Although dual sovereignty no longer meant nullification and secession, much remained to be determined about the respective areas of responsibility of the national and state governments. At first the courts retained remnants of the doctrine of dual sovereignty in order to protect processes of industrialization from governmental intrusion. But with the advent of the New Deal, the constitutional power of the national government expanded so dramatically that the doctrine of dual sovereignty virtually lost all meaning. Court interpretations of the constitutional clauses on commerce and spending have proved to be the most significant.

According to dual sovereignty theory, [Article I] of the Constitution gives Congress the power to regulate commerce "among the states," but the regulation of intrastate commerce was to be left to the states. So, for example, in 1895 the Supreme Court said that Congress could not break up a sugar monopoly that had a nationwide impact on the price of sugar, because the monopoly refined its sugar within the state of Pennsylvania.

The mere fact that the sugar was to be sold nationwide was only "incidental" to its production. As late as 1935, the Supreme Court, in a 6-to-3 decision, said that Congress could not regulate the sale of poultry because the regulation took effect after the chickens arrived within the state of Illinois, not while they were in transit.

Known as the "sick chicken" case, this decision was one of a series in which the Supreme Court declared unconstitutional legislation passed in the early days of President Franklin Roosevelt's efforts to establish his New Deal programs. Seven of the "nine old men" on the Court had been appointed by Roosevelt's conservative Republican predecessors. By declaring many New Deal programs in violation of the commerce clause, the Supreme Court seemed to be substituting its political views for those of elected officials. In a case denying the federal government the right to protect workers trying to organize a union in the coal industry, the Republican views of the Court seemed to lie just barely below the surface of a technical discussion of the commerce clause. Justice George Sutherland declared, "The relation of employer and employee is a local relation . . . over which the federal government has no legislative control."

The Roosevelt Democrats were furious at decisions that seemed to deny the country's elected officials the right to govern. Not since *Dred Scott* had judicial review been in such disrepute. Roosevelt decided to "pack the court" by adding six new judges over and above the nine already on the Court. Although Roosevelt's court-packing scheme did not survive the political uproar on Capitol Hill, its effect on the Supreme Court was noticeable. In the midst of the court-packing debate, Justices Charles Hughes and Owen Roberts, who had agreed with Sutherland's opinion in the coal case, changed their mind and voted to uphold the Wagner Act, a new law designed to facilitate the formation of unions. In his opinion, Hughes did not explicitly overturn the coal miner decision (for which he had voted), but he did say: "When industries organize themselves on a national scale, . . . how can it be maintained that their industrial labor relations constitute a forbidden field into which Congress may not enter?" Relations between employers and their workers, once said to be local, suddenly became part of interstate commerce.

The change of heart by Hughes and Roberts has been called "the switch in time that saved nine." The New Deal majority that emerged on the court was soon augmented by judges appointed by Roosevelt. Since the New Deal, the definition of interstate commerce has continued to expand. In 1942 a farmer raising twenty-three acres of wheat, all of which might be fed to his own livestock, was said to be in violation of the crop quotas imposed by the Agricultural Adjustment Act of 1938. Since he was feeding his cows himself, he was not buying grain on the open market, thereby depressing the worldwide price of grain. With such a definition of interstate commerce, nothing was local.

The expansion of the meaning of the commerce clause is a well-known part of American political history. The importance to federalism of court interpretations of the "spending clause" is less well known. The constitutional clause in question says that Congress has the power to collect taxes to "provide for the . . . general welfare." But how about Congress's power to collect taxes for the welfare of specific individuals or groups?

The question first arose in a 1923 case, when a childless woman said she could not be asked to pay taxes in order to finance federal grants to states for programs that helped pregnant women. Since she received no benefit from the program, she sued for return of the taxes she had paid to cover its costs. In a decision that has never been reversed, the Supreme Court said that she had suffered no measurable injury and therefore had no right to sue the government. Her taxes were being used for a wide variety of purposes. The amount being spent for this program was too small to be significant. The court's decision to leave spending issues to Congress was restated a decade later when the social security program was also challenged on the grounds that monies were being directed to the elderly, not for the general welfare. Said Justice Benjamin N. Cardozo for a court majority: "[t]he conception of the spending power . . . [must find a point somewhere] between particular and general. . . . There is a middle ground . . . in which discretion is large. The discretion, however, is not confided to the Court. The discretion belongs to Congress, unless the choice is clearly wrong."

The courts have ever since refused to review Congress's power to spend money. They have also conceded to Congress the right to attach any regulations to any aid Congress provides. In 1987, Congress provided a grant to state governments for the maintenance of their highways, but conditioned 5 percent of the funds on state willingness to raise the drinking age from eighteen to twenty-one. The connection between the appropriation and the regulation was based on the assumption that youths under the age of twenty-one are more likely to drive after drinking than those over twenty-one. Presumably, building more roads would only encourage more inebriated young people to drive on them. Despite the fact that the connection between the appropriation and the regulation was problematic, the Supreme Court ruled that Congress could attach any reasonable conditions to its grants to the states. State sovereignty was not violated, because any state could choose not to accept the money.

In short, the courts have virtually given up the doctrine of judicial review when it comes to matters on which Congress can spend money. As a consequence, most national efforts to influence state governments come in the form of federal grants. Federal aid can also be used to influence local governments, such as counties, cities, towns, villages, and school districts. These local governments, from a constitutional point of view, are mere creatures of the state of which they are part. They have no independent sovereignty.

The Contemporary Price of Federalism

If constitutional doctrine has evolved to the point that dual sovereign theory has been put to rest, this does not mean that federalism has come to an end. Although ultimate sovereignty resides with the national government, state and local governments still have certain characteristics and capabilities that make them constituent components of a federal system. * * * Two characteristics of federalism are fundamental. First, citizens elect officials of their choice for each level of government. Unless the authority of each level of government rests in the people, it will become the agent of the other. Second, each level of government raises money through taxation from the citizens residing in the area for which it is responsible. It is hard to see how a system could be regarded as federal unless each level of government can levy taxes on its residents. Unless each level of government can raise its own fiscal resources, it cannot act independently.

Although the constitutional authority of the national government has steadily expanded, state and local governments remain of great practical significance. Almost half of all government spending for domestic (as distinct from foreign and military) purposes is paid for out of taxes raised by state and local governments.

The sharing of control over domestic policy among levels of government has many benefits, but federalism still exacts its price. It can lead to great regional inequalities. Also, the need for establishing cooperative relationships among governments can contribute to great inefficiency in the administration of government programs.

DISCUSSION QUESTIONS

1. What is the constitutional basis for federalism?

2. How has the relationship between state governments and the national government changed since the early years of the Republic?

3. Does a federal system serve our needs today? Does the federal government have too much power relative to the states? What would be the advantages and disadvantages of a reduced federal presence in state matters?

15

"Will Federalism (and Conflicts of Law Doctrine) Deregulate Abortion?"

RICK HILLS

In 1973, Roe v. Wade *established a constitutional right to an abortion.* Planned Parenthood v. Casey *(1992) clarified that some state restrictions on abortions were acceptable, such as waiting periods or parental notification for minors, but it upheld the constitutional right to an abortion before viability. That all changed in June 2022, when the Supreme Court overturned* Roe *and* Casey *in* Dobbs v. Jackson Women's Health Organization. *By eliminating the constitutional right to an abortion, the Court turned abortion policy over to the states.*

Devolving power to the states has been a long-term trend in federalism over the last 30 years, with policies such as welfare, marijuana regulation, the right to die, federal aid to the states, and even health care reform, which carved out a role for the states through their health care exchanges and allowed states to reject the expansion of Medicaid (because of another Supreme Court decision). But as Rick Hills points out, the consequences of turning over abortion policy to the states are complicated. Hills predicts that pro-life advocates will be disappointed by the ultimate impact of federalism on how this plays out because of the "conflicts of law doctrine." That is, what happens when two state laws conflict? Some states will allow abortion, and some will outlaw it, but can a pro-life state prevent one of its residents from having an abortion in a different state? Hills says that while such restrictions would be constitutional (he gives the example of child custody laws that prevent a divorced parent from moving out of a state without the other parent's consent), they are unlikely to be enforced. Thus, he predicts that "foot voting" will mean that people who will not be able to get an abortion in Texas, for example, will go to New Mexico. He concludes that this result "should be comforting to pro-choice readers and sobering to those pro-life readers who thought reversing Roe/Casey *would practically advance their cause." Hills believes that while this outcome of nationalizing the pro-choice position through "foot voting" will be good for civic peace, it has some troubling implications for democratic pluralism.*

O ver the last three decades, commentators have provided both skeptical and optimistic assessments about whether and how federal decentralization might cope with abortion were *Roe-Casey* to be reversed. The optimistic view is that *Roe-Casey*'s reversal would promote pluralism by allowing each state to go its own way on a divisive topic, thereby reducing political polarization and gridlock at the national level. The pessimistic take comes mostly from law profs familiar with the train wreck known as conflicts of law "doctrine." In a post-*Roe/Casey* world, women in anti-abortion states would have to migrate to pro-choice jurisdictions in order to take advantage of less restrictive abortion laws, but conflicts of law doctrine does not define plainly which state law ought to govern such interstate transactions. State legislatures seeking to end abortion will attempt to extend their bans into pro-choice states, perhaps by penalizing those who facilitate interstate migration or by bringing criminal actions against women upon their departures from, or return to, their states of domicile. The resulting controversies over which state's laws should apply will simply reproduce the divisiveness of *Roe/Casey*, especially if judicial measurements of rival states' interest in regulating abortion turn on assessments of the value of fetal/unborn infant life. In the words of * * * Will Baude back in 2006, "[S]tate regulation will make a complex legal matter even more complicated, and the divisions over abortion that much wider." * * * In my view, both the optimistic and pessimistic predictions about a post-*Roe/Casey* world are likely mistaken. Federal decentralization will not produce a diversity of different states' responses to abortion but rather a fairly uniform policy of de-regulation. Put bluntly, in a world of federalism-based interstate migration, deregulatory states will always have the advantage. But the pessimists are also mistaken in thinking that, because conflicts of law doctrine is a mess, the question of which state's law to apply will be messy.

My prediction is that, to the contrary, state legislatures, courts, and Congress will all gravitate towards a fairly crude "territorial" rule that enforces the law of the place where the abortion was performed, a rule that insures nationwide victory for pro-choice states. My reasoning, explained in more detail [below], is rooted more in politics than doctrine—to be precise, the politics of case captions. No politician, even one clad in black robes, wants to put an abortion-seeking woman on one side of the "v." in a criminal case. The great political advantage that anti-abortion legislators have enjoyed since *Roe* was decided is that there have been few Roes as parties: [a]bortion clinics (often Planned Parenthood) have instead appeared in the captions. *Roe-Casey*'s reversal will end that political advantage, because the domicile of the migrating woman will be the most likely legally available basis for applying the restrictive abortion laws of a regulating state to an out-of-state transaction. Anti-abortion politicians will find it politically unpalatable, however, to drag women rather than abortion clinics into courtrooms, so they will shrink from using the only regulatory tools left open to them by interstate migration. The result will be that anti-abortion laws fall into practical desuetude [disuse] by foot-voting women escaping such restrictions with bus tickets rather than lawsuits. * * *

A Quick Summary of Conflicts of Law and Abortion

Start with the messiness of conflicts of law doctrine. Not only are such state-law doctrines chaotic but federal constitutional law also does little to make sense of the chaos. Under the half-dozen or so "conflicts theories" that jostle for predominance among state courts, the applicable law is defined by some "controlling contact" (to use Doug Laycock's phrase) that variously include the domicile of an actor, the location of an activity, or the location of the deciding forum. Due Process and Full Faith & Credit doctrine imposes only minimal limits on a state's extension of its own law to a dispute, just so long as the regulating state coincides with either the location of the disputed activity or the domicile of a disputant. Such domicile or physical location of an activity suffices if the connection suggests that the state has some sort of "interest" in the resolution of the dispute. * * * In theory, therefore, anti-abortion states would be free, insofar as the Constitution is concerned, to impose their abortion restrictions on women who migrate to other states seeking to take advantage of less restrictive rules. Yes, there is some language in *Bigelow v. Virginia* (1975) stating that "[a] State does not acquire power or supervision over the internal affairs of another State merely because the welfare and health of its own citizens may be affected when they travel to that State." But *Bigelow's* language, perhaps dicta, is probably superseded by the *Hague/Shutts* doctrine allowing states with an interest to impose their law on disputes arising out of activities taking place in other state's territory.

With *Roe-Casey's* demise, therefore, it would likely be constitutionally permissible for an anti-abortion state like, say, Texas to prohibit women from traveling to pro-choice states like New Mexico to terminate a pregnancy. The obvious precedents for imposing Texas law on transactions occurring in New Mexico would be cases dealing with child custody, where state courts have repeatedly upheld court orders limiting parents' rights to relocate without the permission of the other parent. If the state can protect the best interests of the child by barring a parent from traveling to another state, then the state can probably likewise protect the best interests of a fetus/unborn infant in the same manner. Of course, it remains theoretically open for SCOTUS to hold that states have no legitimate interest under *Hague/Shutts* in protecting the fetus/unborn child by so limiting the movement of mothers, because the former is not really a "person." But that sort of analysis would likely run up against the reversal of *Roe-Casey.* In any case, such a holding would reproduce all of the controversy created by *Roe-Casey* that federalism is supposed to defuse.

In sum, at least so long as the person seeking an abortion remains domiciled in the regulating state, that state has an interest in regulating that domiciliary's behavior, even if that behavior takes place in other states. As Don Regan observed 35 years ago, even if "one can . . . abandon one's state and its laws by changing one's citizenship," it does not follow that "one can take a holiday from the state's laws, while remaining a citizen, by sojourning elsewhere." It might be that women could place themselves beyond the constitutional reach of their home state's restrictive laws by changing their domicile, but changing domicile is extremely costly, especially for low-income persons dependent on networks of family, friends, and employers in their home state. "Abortion tourism," in short, is likely regulable by the home state of the "tourists." The old cases placing ex parte divorces in Nevada beyond the reach of the divorcee's home state are instructive here. Those cases required those divorcees to acquire Nevada domicile while they were getting their quickie divorce). As Justice Douglas observed back in *Williams v. North Carolina* (1945) in requiring parties to an ex parte divorce to acquire domicile in the state conferring the divorce, the regulating state "ought not to be foreclosed by the interested actions of others, especially not a State which is concerned with the vindication of its own social policy and has no means, certainly no effective means, to protect that interest against the selfish action of those outside its borders."

A Quick Assessment of the Politics of Case Captions

Does this doctrinal permissiveness, allowing aggressive extension of anti-abortion laws to interstate abortion transactions by enforcing those laws against migrating women, really mean that (in Will Baude's words) states will actually "use child custody laws to curtail the movements of pregnant women"? A Disclaimer: [i]n answering this question about political prediction, I concede I am on shakier ground than when I discuss legal doctrine. I am, after all, just a law [professor], not a political scientist.

Speaking purely as an informed lay observer, however, I am skeptical that Texas politicians will be eager to deploy cops waving ultrasound wands on the New Mexico border to interdict buses containing women headed for a clinic in Albuquerque. I also doubt that Texas prosecutors will relish arresting those women on their return and arraigning them on charges of evading Texas' anti-abortion laws. The optics of such enforcement actions simply do not fit with the preferred narrative of the pro-life movement, which has been focused on the alleged villainy of abortion clinics and the alleged victimhood for their clients. Pro-life rhetoric pitches itself in a pro-woman key, arguing that those women seeking abortions are victims exploited by "abortion mills" who later regret their decision to terminate their pregnancies. I humbly submit that nothing could be more devastating to this rhetorical stance than photos of women in orange jumpsuits, awaiting punishment for crossing state lines with the immoral purpose of ending a pregnancy.

In short, the only way that state politicians can interdict pro-choice migration is to sacrifice their most valued rhetorical posture of attacking the clinic rather than the woman who uses it. I predict, therefore, that the politics of case captions will deter anti-abortion DAs and attorneys general from bringing such cases or state legislators from allowing them to be brought.

Just to be clear, I am not suggesting that such cases will *never* be brought by the more diehard opponents of abortion: [w]e live in strange times where bad politics do not deter fanatics on either side of the aisle. I am certain, however, that the political strategists of the abortion movement will reasonably regard such prosecutions as a political liability. Undoubtedly, such politicians will strain to drag out-of-state abortion clinics into anti-abortion states' courts, perhaps by using on-line advertisements as the minimum contact sufficient to create personal jurisdiction. Unfortunately for them, the absence of the clinics' domicile or physical presence in, or any other "purposeful availment" of, the regulating state probably dooms such efforts under *Bristol-Myers Squibb*.

Or maybe *fortunately* for such politicians: [n]othing would provide them with better political cover than to enact grabby long-arm statutes purporting to drag abortion clinics into anti-abortion states' clutches only to have federal courts veto such prosecutions invoking boring personal jurisdiction doctrine. Such a post-*Roe/Casey* strategy protects both politicians and courts from the diehards while allowing the politicians to avoid the political suicide of prosecuting likely indigent women for crossing state lines to escape an unwanted pregnancy.

In sum, I predict that the theoretical availability of extra-territorial regulation based on domicile will yield to the political necessity of avoiding lawsuits and prosecutions against pregnant women. My prediction is worth what you paid for it: I repeat that I am not an expert here. The important point, however, is that, by decentralizing abortion law, the reversal of *Roe/Casey* changes abortion politics by changing the "localizing contacts" that trigger state law. Those contacts determine the caption, and the caption importantly affects the political optics of anti-abortion prosecutions. Concede me that much, and I am happy to yield on political odds-making.

Two Cheers for the Faux Decentralization of Federalism

The likely consequence of ending *Roe/Casey*, in short, is to nationalize the pro-choice states' deregulation of abortion through interstate migration. Yes, I am aware that such migration is not costless. Given the paucity of abortion clinics even under *Roe/Casey*, however, the *marginal increase* in migration costs from reversing *Roe/Casey* will be small, and it is the *marginal* increase in cost from that reversal, not the *absolute* cost of travel, that is relevant to predictions about how reversing *Roe/Casey* will affect behavior. Right now, a woman in Lubbock has to travel hundreds of miles *within* Texas to get an abortion: [t]raveling to Tucumcari or Albuquerque NM might be a pretty small *additional* increase in cost above the *Roe/Casey* status quo. Moreover, organizations like NARAL and Planned Parenthood will, post-*Roe/Casey* be able to devote the resources they now use for litigating "undue burden" to defraying those travel costs: [a]s they switch from hiring law firms to paying for hotel rooms and buses, they can also re-deploy besieged clinics within restrictive states to the frontiers of pro-choice states. That shift in strategy should reduce further the costs of interstate travel.

Should we applaud or deplore this deregulatory consequence? Obviously, the answer to this question will mostly depend on where you stand on abortion. My predictions, therefore, should be comforting to pro-choice readers and sobering to those pro-life readers who thought reversing *Roe/Casey* would practically advance their cause.

But what about those few who, like me, actually care about federalism as a system for handling divisive social questions? Should I applaud federal devolutions that lead to nationally uniform deregulatory outcomes? After all, federalism is often defended as a form of pluralistic tolerance. (I myself have made such a defense of federalism in both articles and blog posts.) It turns out, however, that, at least on the issue of abortion, formal federal decentralization is not likely to lead to a pluralistic diversity of state policies. Instead, such devolution leads (if I am correct in my prediction above) to nationally uniform deregulation via interstate migration. Some states' deregulatory policies will practically defeat other states' restrictive policies across the national board, because women will vote with their feet for less regulation, turning those restrictions into dead letters, on the law books but not actually stopping any abortions.

Should we regard this practical national deregulation through denationalization as a bug or a feature of federalism? I am of two minds on this question. There is both a problem with and a benefit from practical nationalization of policy through decentralized foot-voting. The benefit is that the nation gets to choose sides in a divisive fight in a covert and, therefore, less divisive way. The problem is that the mechanism by which this choice is made—interstate migration by those burdened by regulation—arguably does not give fair representation to regulation's beneficiaries. Nationalizing foot-voting, in short, might be politically advantageous for civil peace but nevertheless be illegitimate from the perspective of promoting pluralistic democracy.

Start with the benefits of nationalizing foot-voting in terms of civil peace. Unlike the national rule established by *Roe/Casey*, the nationalization achieved through footvoting is covert. There is no rule announced, no general principle based on legalistic concepts like trimesters and viability. There are only hundreds of thousands of individual choices that, in the end, amount to a pattern of deregulation without any single set of reasons justifying or explaining that pattern. Unlike *Roe/Casey*, such results without reasons do not contradict anyone's beliefs or criticize anyone's arguments. Mere results take no position on when life begins or what personhood consist of. They will be, I predict, much less divisive than judicial opinions that take loquacious stances on contentious issues. * * * As for political divisiveness, I have no doubt that anti-abortion activists will be frustrated (and pro-choice ones, elated) by caravans of buses crossing state lines. Those activists will, however, lose SCOTUS as a visible target for their frustration. They will have to content themselves with enacting anti-abortion restrictions that will gradually become as emptily symbolic as fault-based divorce laws did in the 1960s. Just as the latter lost all practical effect with the rise of ex parte divorces in Reno, the former will gradually become impractical relics that can be evaded with a bus ticket rather than a lawsuit.

In short, I predict that overruling *Roe/Casey* will promote civil peace. But will it provide pluralistic respect to both of the contending sides, by giving pro-choice and pro-life factions geographic enclaves in which their respective views can prevail through subnational democratic processes? I am doubtful. The decentralized uniformity produced by foot-voting is faux pluralism: [i]t shortchanges any constituencies that benefit from the regulations that foot-voters evade. For pro-life voters, those constituencies consist of footless fetuses/unborn infants whose interests the pro-life voters believe are ignored by foot-voting migrants who carry them. Pro-life voters might rightly argue, therefore, that the diversity of legal regimes produced by federal decentralization is a practical fraud. Federalism does not equally accommodate rival views on abortion, anymore than devolution of usury law has produced diverse regulation of credit cards. Instead, women seeking abortions will escape restrictive laws by visiting uniformly pro-choice states just as banks evade limits on credit card charges by sending their card operations to South Dakota.

My tentative view, therefore, is that the federal devolution of abortion scores higher on civil peace than on democratic pluralism. It is difficult to argue, however, that *Roe/Casey* performs better on either of these criteria. So two cheers for the Potemkin pluralism of federal devolution: [i]t will likely disappoint anti-abortion activists, but it will do so without endlessly miring our politics in the bitter struggle that *Roe/Casey* has provoked for almost a half-century.

DISCUSSION QUESTIONS

1. What problems can you see with Hills's argument about "foot voting" as a mechanism for producing a different outcome than pro-life advocates are hoping for? Do you think his "marginal cost" analysis helps address those concerns?

2. Do you think he is right about the impact of federalism on the outcome in terms of "civic peace"? As he points out, abortion politics has been very tumultuous in the *Roe/Casey* era. Will the politics of abortion become less intense?

3. What about his prediction that pro-life states will not enforce restrictions imposed on women who choose to have abortions in a different state?

Debating the Issues: The COVID-19 Pandemic in a Federal System

As the COVID-19 pandemic entered its third year, the United States continued to fare worse than most countries in the number of infections and deaths. In early 2022, according to the Johns Hopkins University Coronavirus Resource Center, 166 out of 187 countries had a lower death rate than the United States (for example, the United States had 265 deaths per 100,000 people, compared to 141 for Germany, 86 for Canada, and 15 for Japan). What is the impact of our federal system of government on our COVID-19 response?

Jennifer Selin thinks that federalism's impact on our ability to control the pandemic is more complex. She recognizes the division of power required by federalism but says that key constitutional issues "remain unresolved as we move forward in this crisis." First, the governors' executive powers have expanded to fight the pandemic to an extent that would have surprised many of the framers of our Constitution. Second, federalism makes the process of democratic accountability more difficult. States adapted to the pandemic in different ways when it came to running elections because election administration is so decentralized. Even more fundamentally, "[V]oters may not be able to discern whom to blame when things go poorly and [whom] to reward when things go well." If you are unhappy with the response to COVID-19, is it Washington's fault or your state government's? Selin also notes that national politicians often look to governors for "partisan wins" concerning COVID-19, a theme that is developed in the last selection.

Walter Olson touts the virtues of federalism when it comes to fighting a pandemic. Writing in the early days of the pandemic, Olson points out that the president and the national government don't have the power to tell the states what to do concerning stay-at-home lockdowns or mask mandates (or, as the Supreme Court ruled, requiring vaccinations for large businesses). Echoing James Madison's *Federalist*, No. 46, Olson says that state politicians are closer to the people and have a better understanding than the federal government of their state's resources and the specific problems in their state, have better knowledge of response priorities, and are quicker and more flexible in correcting mistakes.

John Kincaid and J. Wesley Leckrone examine the four models of federalism and conclude that while dual federalism is the dominant response, with states acting to fill the void created by federal inaction, partisanship undermined a more effective response. While Democratic states were hit hardest in the first year of the pandemic, resistance to vaccines in Republican states contributed to worse outcomes in those states in subsequent years (all 20 of the states with the highest vaccination rates in early 2022 were carried by Joe Biden in the 2020 election). The authors conclude, "Partisan divisions among state and local executives thwarted both cooperative federalism and a more widely coordinated dual federalist response among the states." But they also note that "federal inaction" is exactly what some states wanted.

16

"How the Constitution's Federalist Framework Is Being Tested by COVID-19"

Jennifer Selin

As all 50 states start to reopen their economies, government officials face questions about their response to the coronavirus pandemic. While a vast majority of discourse focuses on the important health consequences resulting from variation in state restrictions, conflicting policies across the country highlight some key constitutional issues that remain unresolved as we move forward in this crisis.

The COVID-19 pandemic brought increasing attention to our federalist form of government. The traditional story of federalism recognizes that the national government can make policy in some areas, while the states reserve the right to regulate in other areas. However, as the pandemic has highlighted, things are not always that clear-cut. The constitutional boundaries between state and federal authority are increasingly difficult to ascertain. As a result of political decisions by both state and federal elected officials, today's American government looks different than originally contemplated by the nation's founders. Here are four developments in our federal system of government illuminated by COVID-19.

Governors' Executive Powers Have Expanded

One of the Anti-Federalist critiques of the Constitution was that the presidency was a disguised monarchy that, in collaboration with the Senate, would rule the country tyrannically. The Federalists countered that, combined with separation of powers, the distribution of authority between the state and national governments would prevent executive power grabs.

However, over time, the executive branch at each level of government has grown in size and authority. National executive agencies now create policies that regulate Americans' economic, social, and political activities, prompting Chief Justice John Roberts to muse that the current executive branch would leave the Framers "rubbing their eyes." A similar expansion of executive power has occurred at the state level. A cycle of reform in state government has marked the past decades, prompted by a concerted effort to strengthen historically weak governorships.

This transfer of power to the executive is heightened in times of crisis. At the onset of an emergency, citizens look to executive officials to direct government action. Additionally, as a result of their deliberative nature, the legislative and judicial branches tend to play a more reactive role. We've seen this in both national and state responses to COVID-19. For example, while the Trump administration took its first actions in response to the pandemic in early February, Congress did not pass the CARES Act until late March. At the state level, only 29 state legislatures have passed legislation relating to the coronavirus, while every state governor has taken executive action.

National Politicians Look to Governors for Partisan Wins

Even with an expanded executive branch, the national government simply does not have the resources to do everything it wants. As a result, it increasingly turns to the states to carry out important governmental tasks. Such reliance further develops and strengthens executive branch actors at the state level. This is particularly true in healthcare, where lines between state and federal policy are quite blurred.

How politicians engage this complicated relationship between the state and federal government is strategic—federalism has become an important tool in political negotiations. National political figures enact vague policies that allow for variation in state implementation, claiming credit for acting on important issues while shifting the responsibility for figuring out the details to the states. Not only does this strategy allow for some states to take minimal efforts in implementing federal policy, but it can enhance partisan conflict. President Trump's actions * * * illustrate this point. When his administration began to respond to the crisis, issuing guidelines and emergency use authorizations, he used his relationships with various governors for partisan gain. In one of his more colorful statements on the issue, Trump tweeted, "Tell the Democrat Governors that 'Mutiny On The Bounty' was one of my all time favorite movies. A good old fashioned mutiny every now and then is an exciting and invigorating thing to watch, especially when the mutineers need so much from the Captain." Such comments suggest that political competition may no longer flow through the separation of powers or federalist system, but rather through political parties.

Thousands of Jurisdictions Administer Elections

Of course, elections provide citizens with a way to comment on the policies that the political parties adopt. However, elections represent a classic example of how federalism presents the nation with new challenges. The decentralized process provided by the Elections Clause of the U.S. Constitution ensures that the regulation and administration of elections occur at the state level. While designed to enhance geographically based representation, this decentralization results in tremendous variation in the legal frameworks that govern the electoral process. Because of how states delineate responsibility for elections, approximately 8,000 different jurisdictions administer American elections. This incredible number has led many to refer to election administration as "hyperfederalized."

Such a system not only makes governing the electoral process complex, but also has profound implications for how administrators will implement and citizens will experience that framework in the pandemic. We have already seen it play out * * *, with more than 20 states postponing elections due to coronavirus and federal and state litigation arising over several states' mail-in and absentee voting policies.

Accountability for Responding to COVID-19 Is Complicated

Even if all citizens have equal opportunity to vote under comparable electoral rules, one could question whom citizens should hold accountable for COVID-19 policy. When the states and national government act in the same policy space, voters may not be able to discern whom to blame when things go poorly and to reward when things go well.

This accountability problem only amplifies when unelected administrators are thrown into the mix. For example, what if the Food and Drug Administration moves too quickly in approving a coronavirus vaccine that has harmful side-effects? The president will undoubtedly blame faceless bureaucrats in the "deep state," state governors will blame the Trump administration (and likely the president himself) for fast-tracking dangerous drugs, and voters will be left wondering why government seems dysfunctional. As the 2020 presidential election approache[d] and voters beg[a]n to evaluate elected officials, the ability to hold politicians responsible for their actions [became] particularly important.

Ironically, the Framers anticipated that federalism would increase accountability and further the general welfare of American citizens. As we move forward * * *, whether our constitutional design furthers these goals remains to be seen.

17

"Federalism and the Coronavirus Lockdown"

Walter Olson

President Trump no longer hopes to see lockdown restrictions relaxed and many businesses reopened by Easter—April 30 now looks like the target date—but it isn't his call. Public-health merits aside, the president can't legally order the nation back to work. The lockdown and closure orders were issued by state governments, and the president doesn't have the power to order them to reverse their policies.

In America's constitutional design, while federal law is supreme, the national government is confined to enumerated powers. It has no general authority to dictate to state governments. Many of the powers government holds, in particular the "police power" invoked to counter epidemics, are exercised by state governments and the cities to which states delegate power. When yellow fever ravaged Philadelphia in 1793, it was the city of Albany, N.Y., that required the arriving Alexander Hamilton and his wife, Eliza, to wait out a quarantine at the Schuyler Mansion. To this day, U.S. states remain in charge of responding to epidemics.

Trump can't order the country back to normalcy by April 30 or any day. That's for states to decide.

Modernizers have long scoffed at America's federalist structure as inefficient and outdated, especially in handling emergencies. Only the mighty national government, they argue, can quickly assemble the best information, use it to design and adopt a consistent set of policies, and then get the word out clearly and persuasively to the entire country.

Today you won't find these critics scoffing at the states or overglamorizing Washington. One federal institution after another, including the Food and Drug Administration and Centers for Disease Control and Prevention, has been caught flat-footed by COVID-19. White House briefings have been contradictory, unfocused, and often at variance with actual policy, while Congress spent days bedecking a legislative Christmas tree of a relief bill, sagging under the weight of superfluous ornaments.

State governments, by contrast, with some exceptions here and there, have responded to the emergency more skillfully and in a way that has won more public confidence. States have had four key advantages:

- *Knowledge of resources.* States know far more than Washington about available local resources, such as closed hospitals, and how to activate them. Thus the quick plans to convert convention centers in New York,

Baltimore, and Santa Clara, Calif., into temporary hospitals, and Maryland Gov. Larry Hogan's idea of repurposing the state's vehicle-emissions inspection centers for drive-through medical testing.

- *Knowledge of hazards.* In some states, tourist crowds and late-night revelers pose the most urgent danger of spreading the virus, while in others it's church gatherings. States with dense, transit-dependent cities face one set of challenges; those at the hub of international air travel, another. States can tailor local policy emphasis and messages in ways that would elude or overcomplicate any federal plan.
- *Knowledge of response priorities.* After the federal government's fiasco in failing to approve COVID-19 tests, Gov. Andrew Cuomo of New York made sure his state took the lead in rolling out testing. His instincts were proved correct when that testing confirmed New York City's status as the hotspot of the U.S. outbreak.
- *Quicker, more flexible mistake correction.* Pennsylvania Gov. Tom Wolf drew fire when, after waiting longer than his neighbors to respond to the crisis, he instituted sweeping closures. Almost at once, local voices pointed out that many of the facilities being closed—from rest stops relied on by truckers to laundromats, forestry companies, and accounting firms—were either more vital to everyday life than the state had reckoned, less risky to operate, or both. Mr. Wolf heard them and promptly backed off on multiple categories. It's a lot easier for locals to reach someone in the governor's office than the president's.

Whether America begins returning to normalcy on April 30 or not, the coronavirus crisis will put the U.S. system of government to the test. The record of federal systems—some of the best known are in Canada, Germany, and Switzerland—suggests there's a lot of resilience packed into the model.

18

"Partisan Fractures in U.S. Federalism's COVID-19 Policy Responses"

JOHN KINCAID AND J. WESLEY LECKRONE

Introduction

Despite ranking first among 195 countries on the 2019 Global Health Security Index, the U.S. COVID-19 response is widely seen as a failure, with 16.3 million infections by December 15, 2020, and low public approvals of pandemic management by the federal (23 percent approval), state (44 percent), and local governments (48 percent) by August 2020. By November, a third COVID-19 wave brought the most cases and deaths. Among federal countries, only Belgium (158.1 COVID-19 deaths per 100,000 population), Spain (102.8), Bosnia and Herzegovina (102.0), and Argentina (92.2) performed worse than the United States (91.8).

Regarding states filling vacuums created by federal inaction, we examine U.S. pandemic responses through four prominent models of American federalism: coercive or regulatory federalism, which highlights federal rules imposed on states and localities; nationalist cooperative federalism, which values state compliance with federal directives; non-centralized cooperative federalism, which emphasizes reciprocal federal-state-local cooperation; and dual federalism, which denotes separate federal and state spheres of authority. The responses do not fit one model neatly. The federal government responded vigorously in some respects but, due to constitutional dualism, lacked authority to impose some policies, such as a national stay-at-home order (SAHO) or mask mandate.

Failures to act when federal action was possible were associated with party polarization and with President Donald Trump, who "undersold the virus risks and oversold his own achievements." Parties are central to the intergovernmental dynamics of federal systems, and research has consistently demonstrated the salience of partisan polarization in shaping the COVID-19 responses of U.S. public officials and citizens. Partisan divisions over COVID-19 were deeper in the United States than in twelve other advanced democracies. Among that study's other federal countries, federal and regional officials more frequently addressed COVID-19 across party lines.

Federal Government Responses

The federal government's responses were initially robust, although partisan sniping marked the start and, crucially, the Centers for Disease Control and Prevention (CDC) delayed its coronavirus test rollout by a month due to bungled production.

Presidential Responses

On January 29, 2020, Trump created the White House Coronavirus Task Force headed by Vice President Mike Pence. The World Health Organization (WHO) declared a global health emergency on January 30. The next day, Trump restricted travel from China and suspended entry by others deemed COVID-19 risks. Former Vice President Joseph Biden responded on January 31: "[t]his is no time for Donald Trump's record of . . . hysterical xenophobia." However, Trump was downplaying COVID-19's dangers, claiming the virus was under control even though he knew it was deadly and control would be uncertain.

The CDC issued guidelines for state and local governments, and many federal agencies interacted cooperatively with state and local officials. However, the president overshadowed agency accomplishments by engaging in combative rhetoric with governors and mayors, especially Democrats. He delivered inconsistent public-health messages, promoted unapproved medications, contradicted agency scientists, refused to model CDC-recommended behavior such as mask wearing, and appeared to put his political interests before the public good. Public approval of his pandemic management plummeted, and prices of his rhetoric included low compliance with public-health advisories by many citizens and public skepticism about a vaccine. In 2019, Trump had signed Executive Order 13887 to modernize flu-vaccine production. It was employed to speed production of a COVID-19 vaccine. Pfizer was the first to announce a vaccine on November 9.

Trump's insistence that state and local governments be the pandemic's first responders was consistent with past practices. However, the president did not generate robust federal support on matters outside the reach of state and local governments. Although Trump invoked the Defense Production Act on March 18, and his administration provided considerable material support to states and localities, the overall pattern was erratic, insufficient, and sometimes destructive, such as Trump's pitting the states against each other when he admonished governors on March 16 to "try getting" medical supplies themselves and claiming on March 19 that the federal government was not "a shipping clerk." By mid-April, the administration, believing it had done enough, executed a "state authority handoff." Although Trump lacked constitutional authority to close states' economies, he did not use his commanding media position to foster coherent, national leadership. Clear and consistent messaging is fundamental to effective pandemic management.

Burst of Congressional and Presidential Bipartisanship

Not until the first announced COVID-19 death on February 29 did the parties' leaders address domestic mitigation. Congress enacted, 96–1 and 415–2, an $8.3-billion emergency supplemental appropriation signed by Trump on March 6. WHO declared a global pandemic on March 11. Two days later, Trump declared a national emergency and issued fifty-seven simultaneous disaster declarations for all states, Washington, D.C., and U.S. territories—the first all-state declarations in U.S. history. The Families First Coronavirus Response Act (March 18), which passed by 90–8 Senate votes and 363–40 House votes, provided $95 billion. The March 27 Coronavirus Aid, Relief, and Economic Security Act (CARES), which passed by a 96–0 Senate vote and House voice vote, provided $2.2 trillion. The April 23

$484-billion Paycheck Protection Program and Health Care Enhancement Act passed the House by 388–5 and Senate by voice vote. On June 5, Trump signed the Paycheck Protection Program Flexibility Act, which passed the House by 417–1 and the Senate by voice vote. The Federal Reserve initiated stimulus programs, including a $2.3 trillion lending program for many economic sectors that included a Municipal Liquidity Facility for the state-local bond market.

CARES allocated about $150 billion in direct aid to state and local governments, $260 billion for unemployment, $100 billion for hospitals, $45 billion for disaster relief, $30 billion for education, $25 billion for public transportation, $8 billion for tribal governments, a 6.2 percentage-point increase in federal Medicaid funding, and up to $1,200 per adult to nearly 130 million Americans. Altogether, Congress provided state and local governments about $277 billion.

Return to Partisanship

However, Congress soon gridlocked. Democrats wanted more federal spending; Republicans resisted. On May 15, the Democratic House voted 208–199 for a $3 trillion Health and Economic Recovery Omnibus Emergency Solutions (HEROES) Act doomed in the Senate. On September 10, the Senate, by 52–47, failed to end a filibuster of a $650-billion relief bill that would have died in the House. Two major fault lines were COVID-19 liability protection for businesses, supported by Republicans, and aid to states and localities, supported by Democrats. The parties' positions were consistent with findings that Democrats more than Republicans benefit electorally from federal spending on constituents and that Republicans more than Democrats support risk protections for businesses.

State and local governments faced an estimated $74-billion shortfall in FY 2020, $268 billion in FY 2021, and $312 billion in FY 2022. Ending FY 2019, states had only $74.9 billion of rainy-day funds to compensate for revenue losses. A December National League of Cities (2020) survey reported an average 21 percent city-revenue decline since April, while COVID-related expenditures increased 17 percent. Also, 29 percent of municipalities received no CARES aid.

HEROES included about $1 trillion in state-local aid; the Senate bill contained none. HEROES also restored the full state and local tax deduction for two years, a move opposed by most Republicans. Democrats argued that more aid would stimulate the economy and save public-sector jobs. Many state and local officials and their national associations lobbied for more aid, and Federal Reserve officials endorsed another stimulus. Senate Majority Leader Mitch McConnell suggested on April 22 that states pursue bankruptcy. Most Republicans contended that aid would mainly benefit Democratic jurisdictions experiencing losses due to SAHOs and pre-COVID overspending, encourage prolonged SAHOs, discourage reform, and increase federal debt. Further, Illinois Senate President Don Harmon's April 14 letter to Illinois' congressional delegation requesting $10 billion for the state's pension fund angered many Republicans unwilling to aid public-sector unions.

Trump employed emergency powers on August 8 to provide a six-week $300 per week unemployment supplement to replace an expired $600 supplement and also allow individuals to defer student loan and Social Security tax payments until 2021. After prevaricating on another stimulus, Trump shocked congressional Republicans by endorsing a $1.5 trillion proposal on September 16.

Cross-party talks resumed after the presidential election, but despite a third pandemic wave, Trump did not engage Congress, and Congress did not enact more relief (about $920 billion) until December 21 when U.S. deaths reached 316,844. The measure included a $600 subsidy for most Americans but omitted direct state-local aid and business liability protection. After calling the bill a "disgrace" and urging a $2000 subsidy, Trump did not sign it until December 27.

State and Local Government Responses

Needs for dispatch during crises often trigger more executive than legislative or judicial action. Many governors, county officials, and mayors reacted by mid-March, usually without legislative approval. Party differences were evident immediately. From March 19 (187 U.S. deaths) when California issued the first SAHO to April 7 (13,000 deaths), forty-three governors issued SAHOs of varying stringency and geographic scope. Of the first ten governors issuing SAHOs, nine were Democrats, even though only twenty-four governors were Democrats. All seven states having no SAHO had Republican governors, although Republican Mike DeWine of Ohio was one of the first four governors to issue a SAHO.

San Francisco acted first by banning gatherings of more than 1,000 people on March 11. It joined five neighboring counties to issue the first SAHO on March 16. Between March 16 and April 1, 136 counties nationwide, accounting for 66.9 million people, imposed SAHOs before their state.

We focus on SAHOs because they were the most visible and onerous policies, and they affected all state or local residents. SAHOs required most residents to remain home, except for essential travel, and closed businesses governors deemed non-essential as well as some public functions, such as mass transit.

State SAHOs differed greatly, especially definitions of essential businesses and public services. For example, Pennsylvania's Democratic Governor Tom Wolf was the only governor to impose prohibition by closing all state-owned liquor stores (the only shops authorized to sell distilled liquors). About twelve Republican states tried to shutter abortion services as non-essential; Democratic states deemed them essential.

Like Trump, many Democratic leaders initially downplayed COVID-19. On February 13, New York City Mayor Bill de Blasio urged residents to visit Chinatown and, on March 2, to attend a movie theater. U.S. House Speaker Nancy Pelosi toured San Francisco's Chinatown on February 24 to counter coronavirus fears. During the five Democratic primary debates (January 14 to March 15), COVID-19 was not engaged until March 15 when Biden equivocated on a national SAHO.

In the pandemic's initial epicenter, Governor Andrew Cuomo and Mayor de Blasio, both Democrats, clashed frequently. When de Blasio advised residents on March 17 to prepare to shelter in place, Cuomo accused the mayor of "scaring people." Preempting de Blasio, Cuomo delayed a SAHO until March 22. He also ordered elderly COVID-19 hospital patients relocated to nursing homes. By April 22, New York, with 5.9 percent of the U.S. population, had 41.5 percent of U.S. deaths (which declined to 11.8 percent by December 15). Commuter-connected Connecticut (March 23 SAHO), New Jersey (March 21 SAHO), and New York, with 9.6 percent of the U.S. population, had 55.8 percent of U.S. deaths, which dropped to 19.6 percent by December 15. Earlier SAHOs in these epicenter states would have reduced U.S. cases and deaths. Of the three states larger than New York, Democratic California, with 12.1 percent of the national population, had 7.0 percent of all deaths by December 15. Republican-led Texas and Florida, with 8.9 and 6.7 percent of the country's population respectively, had 8.0 and 6.7 percent of the nation's deaths.

States' Party Patterns

Supplemental Table 1 [not included] arrays the states by party control of the governorship and one or both legislative houses. The [data suggest] no causal relationships; it illustrates only that the four groups of states experienced COVID-19 differently and reacted differently. Post-pandemic research will be needed to identify causal factors.

All Democratic trifectas and split states issued a SAHO; seven Republican trifectas did not. Democratic trifectas issued earlier and longer SAHOs than did Republican trifectas; the split states fell between the trifectas. On average, Democratic trifecta SAHOs lasted sixty-six days; Republican trifecta SAHOs lasted thirty-five days. Democratic trifectas issued a statewide mask mandate ninety-three days earlier, on average, than did Republican trifectas that issued a mask mandate. The split states fell between the trifectas. (Nine Republican trifectas and one split state with a Republican governor had issued no statewide mask mandate by December 15.)

Before COVID-19's third wave, Democratic trifectas had experienced 55.4 deaths per 100,000 population compared to 34.2 for Republican trifectas. The split states again fell between. However, convergence occurred by November 30 as the pandemic's third wave surged into Republican states.

The Democratic trifecta death rate was 79.3, and the Republican trifecta rate was 72.7, with the split states in the middle.

Unemployment in the four groups was not markedly different in March, but by April, the Democratic trifectas, which had earlier and longer SAHOs, had a 15.0 percent rate compared to 12.2 percent for the Republican trifectas, with the split states falling in between. Rates converged thereafter. Democratic trifectas had an average 8.9 percent unemployment rate during August–October compared to 6.0 percent for Republican trifectas, with the split states in between again. Public sector job losses were highest in states with a Republican governor and Democratic legislature and Democratic trifectas. Losses were smallest in Republican trifectas.

These data help explain the U.S. Senate's partisan split over federal aid. Democratic senators represented states that were hit hardest on the above measures and had the earliest and longest SAHOs and mask mandates; Republican senators represented states that were affected less severely and had no SAHO or mask mandate or had later and shorter SAHOs and mask mandates. As late as December 15, 18 Republican senators represented states with no statewide mask mandate.

Policy Responses and Models of Federalism

Many critics argue that a key U.S. failure was lack of a federally managed, presidentially led, national response. Given the emergency uncertainty accompanying the novel coronavirus, however, the best national policy response was not immediately evident. Further, the federal government lacks constitutional authority to command a national response. When Trump claimed "total" power to reopen states' economies on April 13, he retreated the next day under heavy criticism. Biden, citing "a constitutional issue," retreated from a mid-August call for a national mask mandate. In addressing federal inaction, it is important, therefore, to account for constitutional limits and consider whether breaching those limits to trigger national action during emergencies is desirable.

Coercive or Regulatory Federalism

Coercive or regulatory federalism did not bark in 2020. No branch of the federal government sought to use the COVID-19 crisis to increase federal power over the states with novel mandates, conditions of aid, preemptions, or court orders. The bipartisan legislation enacted during the spring channeled most relief through extant programs such as the unemployment compensation system, Medicaid/CHIP, and Community Development Block Grant. However, some Democrats, especially U.S. Senator Diane Feinstein (D-CA), proposed requiring states to institute mask mandates as a condition of receiving future federal-stimulus funds, a rule likely to be blocked if the Senate remains Republican. The Republicans' business-liability protection proposal assigned federal courts jurisdiction over coronavirus-exposure cases through 2024. This coheres with the party's support for removing certain business torts from state to federal courts.

Nationalist Cooperative Federalism

The nationalist federalism model comes closest to full national action by defining cooperative federalism as states' willingness to follow national directives. It "situates uniformity and finality for first-order norms at the national level, while allowing dialogue and plurality at the level of state implementation of those norms." State refusals to comply constitute "unco-operative federalism."

White House issuances of pandemic guidelines through the CDC ful-filled a first-order federal function, but state and local governments, often along partisan lines, responded differently to the guidelines (e.g., mask mandates), and President Trump damaged the CDC's credibility by con-tradicting the agency and pressuring it to conform guidelines to his mes-saging. Trump declined to criticize "uncooperative" Republican governors who ignored CDC guidelines while criticizing many Democratic gover-nors who cooperatively adhered to CDC guidelines and refused to lift SAHOs early. Deeming these Democrats uncooperative, Trump labeled them "mutineers" and dispatched such tweets as "LIBERATE VIRGINIA." In December, the CDC issued vaccination-priority recommendations but required states to report to the CDC personal data about vaccine recipi-ents. Some governors refused to comply due to patient-privacy concerns.

The nationalist cooperative model overlooks James Madison's warning that "[e]nlightened statesmen will not always be at the helm" and, thus, whether first order norms emanating from a Trump-led national response would have been desirable. The model is also vulnerable to executive aggrandizement as crises often precipitate centralization and executive overreach. There was little evidence of this, despite concerns about Trump's authoritarian proclivities, although Trump's directing the CDC in Septem-ber to issue a nationwide moratorium on tenant evictions to reduce infec-tion transmissions triggered alarms.

Centralization has shrunk state autonomy, making states, in many respects, administrative arms of the federal government, but COVID-19 showed that state sovereignty is not yet a vacuum.

Non-centralized Cooperative Federalism

A national response can also rest on reciprocal federal-state-local cooper-ation and coordination. In this model, the federal system is non-centralized rather than decentralized, and cooperation is rooted in federal-state-local partnerships.

Congressional enactment of five relief bills reflected cooperative support for state and local governments. This massive bipartisan response proved short-lived, however, because the president did not build on its comity, and congressional Democrats and Republicans split over next steps. Cooperation occurred in Germany where Chancellor Angela Merkel and the sixteen *Länder* heads negotiated common guidelines and maintained communications and in Australia where Prime Minister Scott Morrison formed a "national cabinet" that included the heads of the state and territorial governments. Cooperative federalism in the United States foundered on (1) partisan polarization, (2) Trump's "personal presidency," and (3) the coronavirus's arrival during a presidential election year, an impeachment trial of a president seeking reelection, and low public trust in the federal government and in fellow citizens.

Trump held more than ninety conference calls with state, local, and tribal leaders from late January through March 31 but did not negotiate a reciprocally cooperative relationship. He sought to shift blame for failures onto governors, and he dealt with them more bilaterally than multilaterally, especially feuding with Democratic governors. He treated federal aid as personal favors, such as insisting in mid-April that Democratic California Governor Gavin Newsom call him personally to request test swabs and thank him publicly for delivering them. He also battled with a few Republican governors, including Maryland's Larry Hogan, who chaired the National Governors Association (NGA) until August 2020. Many governors turned to Vice President Mike Pence for help.

The president did not conceptualize federalism as a partnership of shared powers aimed at achieving common objectives. The transgressive character of Trump's presidency breached customary intergovernmental norms, although many agencies, such as the CDC and Army Corps of Engineers largely maintained those norms, while some usually cooperative agencies, such as the Food and Drug Administration (FDA) and Federal Emergency Management Agency (FEMA) were hobbled by revolving-door leaders and White House interventions. The president further thwarted cooperation by refusing to wear a mask and deliver consistent public-health messages, thus undercutting governors' efforts to sustain public compliance with mitigation. Congress could not compensate for Trump's uncooperative federalism, in part because congressional Republicans feared alienating Trump's electoral base, which was hostile to SAHOs and masks.

The third branch was indirectly cooperative by not interfering with states' powers, except for a narrow U.S. Supreme Court ruling against Governor Cuomo in a November religion case (*Diocese of Brooklyn v. Cuomo*, 592 U. S. _____ 2020). On September 14, a federal district-court judge ruled that Pennsylvania Governor Wolf's March SAHO violated the U.S. Constitution (*County of Butler v. Wolf*, 2:20-cv-677 2020) but the case remained on appeal as of December 15.

Governors also played a role in failing to formulate a cooperative national response because of party divisions among them as compared, for example, to cross-party cooperation among the heads of Germany's *Länder*. Governors cooperated on some technical matters through NGA but pursued separate paths on such major policies as SAHOs and mask wearing. Most Democratic governors and mayors saw greater danger from COVID-19 than did most Republican executives and, thus, imposed earlier, longer, and stricter SAHOs than Republicans. Democrats prioritized virus suppression. Republicans saw the economy as equally or more important. This partisanship generated conflicts not only between the president and Democratic governors but also between governors of one party and county and municipal executives of the other party. There were also partisan divisions within electorates as Democrats reduced social activities and practiced social distancing more than independents, while Republicans engaged in more social activities and less social distancing than either group.

Interstate, state-local, and interlocal cooperation are other dimensions of cooperative federalism, although post-COVID research will be needed to gauge the extent and robustness of these forms of cooperation. Fifty-state cooperation was not evident on major policies, but states cooperated in some ways, especially along party and regional lines. State health officials and other specialized officials shared information and aid. Governor Cuomo, who said in March he needed 30,000 ventilators, was sending ventilators to other states by April 17. States loaned or donated equipment to each other. On April 12, the governors (six Democrats, one Republican) of Connecticut, Delaware, Massachusetts, New Jersey, New York, Pennsylvania, and Rhode Island agreed to cooperate on some pandemic actions. The Democratic governors of California, Oregon, and Washington had earlier agreed to cooperate. The Democratic governors of California, Oregon, Washington, Nevada, and Colorado formed the Western States Pact in April to coordinate SAHO liftings, although they ended their SAHOs on widely different dates. A number of states, including Colorado, Massachusetts, New York, and Washington waived licensing barriers to out-of-state health personnel.

While state-local cooperation appears to have been common during COVID-19's first two waves, Democratic and Republican governors clashed with some county and municipal officials of the opposite party. Some Democratic governors faced resistance from Republican localities and from sheriffs and police chiefs refusing to enforce gubernatorial orders. Republican governors faced resistance from Democratic localities that imposed more stringent SAHOs and other mandates. After major Texas cities with Democratic mayors followed Laredo in April in requiring masks, Governor Greg Abbott prohibited counties and cities from requiring face covers. When he relented, conservatives attacked him.

Governors sought to maintain control by threatening to withhold state and federal funds from recalcitrant counties and revoke licenses and permits from uncooperative businesses. A few also filed lawsuits against local officials, such as Georgia Governor Brian Kemp's eventually withdrawn August lawsuit seeking to overturn the Atlanta mayor's mask mandate.

In sum, after the spring burst of congressional bipartisanship, cooperative federalism did not shape the principal course of federal-state pandemic policy-making. Cooperation requires the willingness of political leaders to transcend party, geographic, and other differences in order to promote intergovernmental coordination. Instead, the polarized parties were more intergovernmentally disintegrative than integrative.

Dual Federalism

The predominant COVID-19 responses fit the dual federalism model of separate authority spheres. Dual federalism has been deemed dead by many scholars but path dependency and the system's dualist constitutional structure preserve important elements of dual federalism, and the U.S. Supreme Court recently reaffirmed dual sovereignty in *Gamble v. United States*.

The powers exercised independently by most governors, and many mayors and county executives, were unprecedented in U.S. history and marked extraordinary manifestations of dual federalism, demonstrating that the police power, which was not delegated to the United States, remains potent. The Tenth Amendment reiterates this non-delegation, and Chief Justice John Marshall affirmed it by including states' "quarantine laws" and "health laws of every description" in the "immense mass of legislation" falling under state sovereignty and outside the federal interstate commerce power. Consequently, even though state SAHOs and other measures shut down a considerable portion of the national economy and contributed to April's 14.7 percent unemployment rate, the president was powerless to compel states to reopen on his schedule.

The dual federalist response to COVID-19 coheres with past pandemic practices in which the federal government played small roles, usually confined to interstate and foreign commerce matters, such as port quarantines. Trump's international travel restrictions followed such precedents. President Woodrow Wilson remained aloof during the deadly 1918 pandemic. Gerald Ford was the first president to react quickly to a potential epidemic, but his 1976 vaccination program was dubbed election-year fearmongering. President Barack Obama quickly declared a public-health emergency after H1N1's discovery, but Biden's former vice-presidential chief of staff recalled: "[w]e did every possible thing wrong." It was "a fortuity that" H1N1 was not "one of the great mass casualty events in American history."

Trump's most significant achievement was financial ($11 billion) and regulatory support for development of a vaccine—a role feasible only for the federal government—but his politicization of COVID-19 contributed to only 47 percent of Americans expressing willingness in early December to get vaccinated. Trump was widely criticized for insufficiently fulfilling other federal roles such as providing enough medical supplies, expanding testing capacity, and delivering consistent messages.

Dual federalism enables states to act in the face of federal inaction, experiment with policies under conditions of uncertainty, and tailor policy responses to local conditions and constituent preferences. Dual federalism's disadvantages include disparate state responses, insufficient coordination, failures to learn from each other, negative externalities created by states with lax mitigation policies, divergent messages from officials in different states, and publicized cases of public officials violating their own pandemic rules. Such disadvantages were especially evident during COVID-19's third wave. A few Democratic governors reinstituted short-term SAHOs in early December, but most governors instituted more targeted measures in the face of public fatigue, business pressures, and the absence of a new federal stimulus to compensate for SAHO-induced economic losses.

Conclusion

After a burst of bipartisan legislation in response to COVID-19's first surge, the comparatively weak U.S. follow-through was not due to structural flaws in federalism but to partisan fractures and presidential and gubernatorial preferences that blocked a cooperative federalism response and diluted the second-best dual federalism response. Party differences over appropriate policy responses frustrated the federal system's capacity to respond more effectively, though it also stemmed more centralization and left the federal system largely unchanged by the end of 2020.

The need for dispatch is often said to justify executive action; however, even though the pandemic placed elected executives at the center of policymaking, both the Republican president and Democratic governors in the commuter-connected epicenter (New York, New Jersey, and Connecticut) of COVID-19's first wave acted slowly. The United States fell behind other developed federal countries early on. Partisan divisions among state and local executives thwarted both cooperative federalism and a more widely coordinated dual federalist response among the states. Many Democratic executives criticized President Trump for failing to pursue more cooperation and coordination, but many Republican executives welcomed Trump's hands-off policies.

Responses to the pandemic also highlighted a need to unpack the notion of "federal inaction" by distinguishing between constitutional and political limits on federal action and recognizing that inaction by one elected branch of the federal government does not necessarily mean inaction by the other branches or by bureaucrats. There also are phases of action and inaction, as with COVID-19. Further, there is a need to grapple with the normative judgment embedded in the concept of "federal inaction" because, as COVID-19 highlighted, what is deemed inaction by one party may be deemed appropriate action by another.

DISCUSSION QUESTIONS

1. What are the advantages and disadvantages of our federal system of government when it comes to responding to a pandemic?

2. Do you think that federal inaction was appropriate, in that it left more of the response up to the states, or did it contribute to our relative failure to adequately respond to COVID-19?

3. Would cooperative federalism have been a better model than dual federalism in responding to COVID-19?

CHAPTER 4

Civil Liberties and Civil Rights

19

"What to the Slave Is the Fourth of July?"

FREDERICK DOUGLASS

By the early 1850s, Frederick Douglass had become one of the most prominent abolitionists in the country, captivating audiences with public orations. He had become more militant and had split with William Lloyd Garrison (another prominent abolitionist) over how to end slavery. Garrison was convinced that the Constitution was a proslavery document and had gone so far as to urge the North to break away from the Union. Douglass, in contrast, insisted that the Constitution should be read as enshrining liberty for all people and that the injustices of slavery constituted a failure to live up to those principles.

By 1852, the country was roiled in controversies that would soon split the nation over slavery. The Fugitive Slave Act, enacted in 1850, meant that escaped enslaved people had no sanctuary anywhere in the country; they could be arrested and returned to their owners without trial or a meaningful judicial oversight of any kind, and local officials could be fined if they did not enforce the law. This was part of the Compromise of 1850, an attempt to split the difference between slave and free territories in newly acquired land. None of these efforts would last, and the Civil War would come within a decade.

The Rochester Ladies' Anti-Slavery Society invited Douglass to give a Fourth of July oration in 1852. Douglass insisted on giving the speech on July 5, as July 4 was not a commonly observed holiday among Black people (in part because auctions of enslaved people were held on the date throughout the South).

Douglass's speech is broken into several parts. In the first, he lauds the framers, calling them men of courage and vision—"statesmen, patriots, and heroes." It is consistent with Douglass's view that the founding documents are antislavery in their promises of natural rights and liberty. In the second, Douglass hammers the contradiction of the values of the nation's founding and the realities of slavery. The day is a celebration for the free, but for enslaved people it "reveals . . . the gross injustice and cruelty to which he is the constant victim." The hypocrisy, Douglass insists, makes "your celebration a sham; your boasted liberty, an unholy license . . . your shouts of liberty and equality, hollow." In the last part of the speech, Douglass presents a more hopeful picture, prophesizing that slavery will end and that the values of the Founding will become universally applied.

It was a speech that combined irony, praise, harsh criticism, and a path forward. One can imagine the effect on the audience after Douglass heaped praises on the Founders only to reverse course and excoriate Americans for failing to live up to their values, and then shine a light on a path out of slavery.

Historian David Blight, author of a Pulitzer Prize–winning biography of Douglass, called the speech "nothing less than the rhetorical masterpiece of American abolitionism."*

He who could address this audience without a quailing sensation, has stronger nerves than I have. I do not remember ever to have appeared as a speaker before any assembly more shrinkingly, nor with greater distrust of my ability, than I do this day. * * *

This, for the purpose of this celebration, is the Fourth of July. It is the birth day of your National Independence, and of your political freedom. * * *

On the 2nd of July, 1776, the old Continental Congress, to the dismay of the lovers of ease, and the worshipers of property, clothed that dreadful idea with all the authority of national sanction. They did so in the form of a resolution; and as we seldom hit upon resolutions, drawn up in our day, whose transparency is at all equal to this, it may refresh your minds and help my story if I read it.

> Resolved, That these united colonies are, and of right, ought to be free and Independent States; that they are absolved from all allegiance to the British Crown; and that all political connection between them and the State of Great Britain is, and ought to be, dissolved.

Citizens, your fathers made good that resolution. They succeeded; and today you reap the fruits of their success. The freedom gained is yours; and you, there fore, may properly celebrate this anniversary. The 4th of July is the first great fact in your nation's history—the very ringbolt in the chain of your yet undeveloped destiny. * * *

Fellow Citizens, I am not wanting in respect for the fathers of this republic. The signers of the Declaration of Independence were brave men. They were great men, too—great enough to give frame to a great age. It does not often happen to a nation to raise, at one time, such a number of truly great men. The point from which I am compelled to view them is not, certainly, the most favorable; and yet I cannot contemplate their great deeds

*David W. Blight, Frederick Douglass: Prophet of Freedom. New York: Simon & Schuster, 2018, p. 230.

with less than admiration. They were statesmen, patriots, and heroes, and for the good they did, and the principles they contended for, I will unite with you to honor their memory.

They loved their country better than their own private interests; and, though this is not the highest form of human excellence, all will concede that it is a rare virtue, and that when it is exhibited it ought to command respect. He who will, intelligently, lay down his life for his country is a man whom it is not in human nature to despise. Your fathers staked their lives, their fortunes, and their sacred honor, on the cause of their country. * * *

Of this fundamental work, this day is the anniversary. Our eyes are met with demonstrations of joyous enthusiasm. Banners and pennants wave exultingly on the breeze. The din of business, too, is hushed. Even mammon seems to have quitted his grasp on this day. The ear-piercing fife and the stirring drum unite their accents with the ascending peal of a thousand church bells. Prayers are made, hymns are sung, and sermons are preached in honor of this day; while the quick martial tramp of a great and multitudinous nation, echoed back by all the hills, valleys, and mountains of a vast continent, bespeak the occasion one of thrilling and universal interest-nation's jubilee. * * *

Fellow-citizens, pardon me, allow me to ask, why am I called upon to speak here to-day? What have I, or those I represent, to do with your national independence? Are the great principles of political freedom and of natural justice, embodied in that Declaration of Independence, extended to us? [A]nd am I, therefore, called upon to bring our humble offering to the national altar, and to confess the benefits and express devout gratitude for the blessings resulting from your independence to us?

Would to God, both for your sakes and ours, that an affirmative answer could be truthfully returned to these questions! Then would my task be light, and my burden easy and delightful. For who is there so cold, that a nation's sympathy could not warm him? Who so obdurate and dead to the claims of gratitude, that would not thankfully acknowledge such priceless benefits? Who so stolid and selfish, that would not give his voice to swell the hallelujahs of a nation's jubilee, when the chains of servitude had been torn from his limbs? I am not that man. In a case like that, the dumb might eloquently speak, and the "lame man leap as an hart." But such is not the state of the case. I say it with a sad sense of the disparity between us. I am not included within the pale of this glorious anniversary! Your high independence only reveals the immeasurable distance between us. The blessings in which you, this day, rejoice, are not enjoyed in common. The rich inheritance of justice, liberty, prosperity, and independence, bequeathed by your fathers, is shared by you, not by me. The sunlight that brought light and healing to you, has brought stripes and death to me. This Fourth July is yours, not mine. You may rejoice, I must mourn. To drag a man in fetters into the grand illuminated temple of liberty, and call upon him to join you in joyous anthems, were inhuman mockery and sacrilegious irony. Do you mean, citizens, to mock me, by asking me to speak to-day? If so, there is a parallel to your conduct. And let me warn you that it is dangerous to copy the example of a nation whose crimes, towering up to heaven, were thrown down by the breath of the Almighty, burying that nation in irrevocable ruin! I can to-day take up the plaintive lament of a peeled and woe-smitten people! * * *

Fellow-citizens, above your national, tumultuous joy, I hear the mournful wail of millions! [W]hose chains, heavy and grievous yesterday, are, to-day, rendered more intolerable by the jubilee shouts that reach them. If I do forget, if I do not faithfully remember those bleeding children of sorrow this day, "may my right hand forget her cunning, and may my tongue cleave to the roof of my mouth!" To forget them, to pass lightly over their wrongs, and to chime in with the popular theme, would be treason most scandalous and shocking, and would make me a reproach before God and the world. My subject, then, fellow-citizens, is American slavery. I shall see this day and its popular characteristics from the slave's point of view. Standing there identified with the American bondman, making his wrongs mine, I do not hesitate to declare, with all my soul, that the character and conduct of this nation never looked blacker to me than on this 4th of July! Whether we turn to the declarations of the past, or to the professions of the present, the conduct of the nation seems equally hideous and revolting. America is false to the past, false to the present, and solemnly binds herself to be false to the future. Standing with God and the crushed and bleeding slave on this occasion, I will, in the name of humanity which is outraged, in the name of liberty which is fettered, in the name of the constitution and the Bible which are disregarded and trampled upon, dare to call in question and to denounce, with all the emphasis I can command, everything that serves to perpetuate slavery—the great sin and shame of America! "I will not equivocate; I will not excuse"; I will use the severest language I can command. * * *

What, am I to argue that it is wrong to make men brutes, to rob them of their liberty, to work them without wages, to keep them ignorant of their relations to their fellow men, to beat them with sticks, to flay their flesh with the lash, to load their limbs with irons, to hunt them with dogs, to sell them at auction, to sunder their families, to knock out their teeth, to burn their flesh, to starve them into obedience and submission to their masters? Must I argue that a system thus marked with blood, and stained with pollution, is wrong? No! I will not. I have better employment for my time and strength than such arguments would imply. * * *

What, to the American slave, is your 4th of July? I answer; a day that reveals to him, more than all other days in the year, the gross injustice and cruelty to which he is the constant victim. To him, your celebration is a sham; your boasted liberty, an unholy license; your national greatness, swelling vanity; your sounds of rejoicing are empty and heartless; your denunciation of tyrants, brass fronted impudence; your shouts of liberty and equality, hollow mockery; your prayers and hymns, your sermons and thanksgivings, with all your religious parade and solemnity, are, to Him, mere bombast, fraud, deception, impiety, and hypocrisy—a thin veil to cover up crimes which would disgrace a nation of savages. There is not a nation on the earth guilty of practices more shocking and bloody than are the people of the United States, at this very hour. * * *

Americans! [Y]our republican politics, not less than your republican religion, are flagrantly inconsistent. You boast of your love of liberty, your superior civilization, and your pure Christianity, while the whole political power of the nation (as embodied in the two great political parties) is solemnly pledged to support and perpetuate the enslavement of three millions of your countrymen. You hurl your anathemas at the crowned headed tyrants of Russia and Austria and pride yourselves on your Democratic institutions, while you yourselves consent to be the mere tools and body-guards of the tyrants of Virginia and Carolina. You invite to your shores fugitives of oppression from abroad, honor them with banquets, greet them with ovations, cheer them, toast them, salute them, protect them, and pour out your money to them like water; but the fugitives from oppression in your own land you advertise, hunt, arrest, shoot, and kill. You glory in your refinement and your universal education; yet you maintain a system as barbarous and dreadful as ever stained the character of a nation—a system begun in avarice, supported in pride, and perpetuated in cruelty. * * *

Fellow-citizens, I will not enlarge further on your national inconsistencies. The existence of slavery in this country brands your republicanism as a sham, your humanity as a base pretense, and your Christianity as a lie. It destroys your moral power abroad: it corrupts your politicians at home. It saps the foundation of religion; it makes your name a hissing and a bye-word to a mocking earth. It is the antagonistic force in your government, the only thing that seriously disturbs and endangers your Union. it fetters your progress; it is the enemy of improvement; the deadly foe of education; it fosters pride; it breeds insolence; it promotes vice; it shelters crime; it is a curse to the earth that supports it; and yet you cling to it as if it were the sheet anchor of all your hopes. * * *

I have detained my audience entirely too long already. At some future period I will gladly avail myself of an opportunity to give this subject a full and fair discussion.

Allow me to say, in conclusion, notwithstanding the dark picture I have this day presented, of the state of the nation, I do not despair of this country. There are forces in operation which must inevitably work the downfall of slavery.

DISCUSSION QUESTIONS

1. Do you agree with Douglass that slavery was inconsistent with the principles set out in the Constitution? Or do you think it was more of a rhetorical stance that he took to make the speech more persuasive?

2. What did Douglass have to say about the framers? He does not directly mention that some of them—Jefferson, Madison, Washington—were slave owners. Does this change the meaning of the speech?

20

"The Religious Freedom Bomb May Be About to Detonate"

David Von Drehle

In the landmark 2015 Obergefell v. Hodges *case, the Supreme Court held that same-sex couples had a constitutional right to marry; all existing bans on recognizing same-sex marriage fell. Since then, state and federal courts have grappled multiple times with the question of what happens when people's religious beliefs run up against antidiscrimination law and the legality of same-sex marriage. Can county clerks refuse to issue marriage licenses to same-sex couples because doing so would violate their religious beliefs? Can bakers (or caterers, florists, or any other service providers) refuse to bake cakes for same-sex couples or transgender individuals? Can cities refuse to work with social service organizations that won't place foster children with same-sex couples? The answers to these specific questions, based on state or federal rules, are sometimes no and sometimes yes, and the precise boundaries of where religious belief gives way to generally applicable law remain blurry. Jack Phillips, the owner of Masterpiece Cakeshop, was fined by the Colorado Civil Rights Commission for refusing to bake a wedding cake for a same-sex couple. The Supreme Court ruled that he did not get a fair hearing and that the commissioners showed animus against religion. At a second hearing, the commission dismissed the complaint. However, in 2019, Phillips refused to bake a cake for a transgender woman celebrating her transition, and a state judge ruled that he had violated Colorado laws against discrimination and fined him $500. (As of early 2022, the case was under appeal.)*

This lack of clarity is a problem, writes David Von Drehle, in part because two important rights are in tension: the right of Americans "to be free of discrimination based on who they are" and the right that people "cannot be compelled by the government to express or reject any religious views or political opinions." The question becomes even more difficult when the choice is not simply between providing or refusing a service but between agreeing or refusing to express a specific view. If bakers can be forced against their wishes to write a pro-same-sex-marriage message on cakes, how is this different from forcing tailors or seamstresses to make robes for a Klan rally? Trying to specify a clear legal rule for such cases is extremely difficult in Drehle's view. Perhaps, he writes, "'I'll take my business elsewhere!' is preferable to 'I'll see you in court!'"

The 2015 Supreme Court decision extending the right to marry to same-sex adult couples contained a ticking time bomb. Six years later, the noise is getting loud.

The explosive material has to do with religious freedom. While polls clearly show that a growing majority of Americans support marriage equality, a significant number of religious people continue to believe that same-sex marriage and other evolving understandings of gender and sexuality are transgressions against God's law.

But how can their dissent be lawfully expressed? The five-vote majority in 2015 papered over this question by insisting that the ruling applied only to civil marriage—and thus posed no burden on the right of religions to choose which marriages to bless. As we've learned since, however, sanctifying marriages is not the only way religion enters this picture.

You may remember Jack Phillips, baker, and his Masterpiece Cakeshop in Lakewood, Colo. Phillips is a devout conservative Christian who sees his work as an expression of talents given to him by God. Therefore, he chooses not to sell products that he believes to be offensive to God. He doesn't do Halloween cakes, for example—and he doesn't do wedding cakes to celebrate same-sex unions.

The Colorado Civil Rights Commission found this to be a violation of anti-discrimination laws; the case went to the Supreme Court. In 2018, the justices dodged the question of the baker's rights by ruling that he had not received a fair hearing.

On Thursday [2021], the Supreme Court again dodged the problem of religious freedom vs. discrimination. This time, the question was whether the city of Philadelphia could force Catholic Social Services to include qualified same-sex couples as prospective foster parents. Seizing on the fact that Philadelphia's anti-discrimination law allows for certain exemptions, a unanimous Supreme Court ruled that fairness required an exemption be considered for CSS.

Beneath the unanimity, however, lay a splintered court, with a number of justices saying the bomb must finally detonate. Either religious freedom protects those who treat same-sex couples unequally in public life, or it doesn't.

Justice Neil M. Gorsuch, in a concurring opinion, counted the cost of dodging this uncomfortable question: "[i]ndividuals and groups across the country will pay the price" of endless litigation over the unsettled question, "in dollars, in time, and in continued uncertainty about their religious liberties."

Religious liberty or freedom from discrimination: [a]dvocates on both sides insist the question is simple. In fact, it is very difficult. Two bedrock principles of the Constitution are brought into direct conflict. Americans have a right in their public lives to be free from discrimination based on who they are. This right finds expression in laws requiring businesses and agencies that serve the public to do so without discrimination. Americans also have a protected freedom of belief and expression. They cannot be compelled by the government to express or reject any religious views or political opinions.

No case puts the matter more sharply in relief than the matter of the baker and his cakes, which may well be headed back to the Supreme Court for round two. A transgender individual has asked Phillips to create a celebratory cake. When Phillips refused, a state district judge levied a fine without any of the gratuitous commentary that previously gave the justices their wiggle room.

The fact that these bedrock principles have collided inside a bag of cake frosting does not make them frivolous. Either the baker's freedom of belief allows him to sell customized cakes only to those people whose identities and conduct comport with his religious beliefs, or the would-be cake buyers of Lakewood have a right to decide what Phillips will write on cakes as long as he operates a public business.

Underlying this dispute—the really explosive part—is a slippery slope. It seems monstrous to think that artisans have no control over the expressive content of their creations. Surely a seamstress who willingly provides choir robes and judicial robes should not be compelled to make robes for a Ku Klux Klan rally.

You and I might agree that a same-sex wedding is not remotely like a Klan rally. But some number of religious people would say that both are examples of sinful gatherings. I greatly prefer our view of the matter, but I'm not sure the government should—or rightfully can—put those who disagree out of business.

In a short but instructive concurring opinion to the Philadelphia ruling, Justice Amy Coney Barrett laid out difficult questions that will hit like shrapnel if and when this bomb goes off. Her insight reminds us that, of all the ways change can be made in a free society—by persuasion, by compromise, through boycotts and marches and social media campaigns—lawsuits can be the most destructive. "I'll take my business elsewhere!" may be preferable to "I'll see you in court!"

Discussion Questions

1. Can you articulate a general rule for when religious beliefs should give way to public interest (through nondiscrimination laws, public health, taxes, or other collective interests)? Can you identify difficult cases that can still arise under such a rule?

2. Can market forces—Drehle's "I'll take my business elsewhere!"—resolve these disputes? What happens if there is only one business available in a city or town?

DEBATING THE ISSUES: FREE SPEECH—IS CRITICISM "CANCEL CULTURE"?

Free speech—explicitly protected by the First Amendment—is fundamental to democratic governance. People must be able to speak freely in order to criticize government, advocate or oppose policy, and engage in artistic expression or protest. But this right is not absolute. Is there a line where my right to speak infringes on your wish not to hear what I have to say, particularly when my words are perceived as offensive, harmful, or prejudicial? Is it ever permissible to prevent people from speaking or imposing penalties (perhaps trying to get them fired from their jobs), or should the only remedy against offensive speech be counterspeech and criticism? It is easy to identify examples of writers, public figures, or even private individuals who face consequences for taking positions that are unpopular. Does the right to free speech mean that there can never be consequences for one's speech?

These two writings offer different perspectives on these questions. Jonathan Rauch adamantly opposes trying to curtail or discipline speech because people might find it offensive. Writing in 1995, he articulates themes that remain relevant today: workplaces, schools, and the media (to name a few) try to regulate speech in ways designed to eradicate prejudice. In his view, even trying to control speech in this way is foolish, because such efforts inevitably wind up imposing impossible rules. The only way to challenge and correct prejudiced views is through more speech, much of which we might not want to hear. Government, he concludes, is at its liberal best when it preserves rather than prevents the free flow of ideas, no matter how distasteful or hurtful they might be.

Susan J. Brison critiques the claim that free speech is an unfettered fundamental value in itself and critiques the validity of the argument that the only rightful response to harmful speech is more speech. What is the purpose of free speech? she asks, evaluating free speech as furthering the values of truth, self-realization, democracy, and tolerance. She also points to the "slippery slope" argument that efforts to restrict speech inevitably result in unwarranted government interference. False claims of stolen elections, speech that further marginalizes already disadvantaged groups, and extremist speech that threatens democratic institutions, she argues, should not be *automatically* defended under a free speech principle.

21

"In Defense of Prejudice"

Jonathan Rauch

The war on prejudice is now, in all likelihood, the most uncontroversial social movement in America. Opposition to "hate speech," formerly identified with the liberal left, has become a bipartisan piety. In the past year, groups and factions that agree on nothing else have agreed that the public expression of any and all prejudices must be forbidden. On the left, protesters and editorialists have insisted that Francis L. Lawrence resign as president of Rutgers University for describing blacks as "a disadvantaged population that doesn't have that genetic, hereditary background to have a higher average." On the other side of the ideological divide, Ralph Reed, the executive director of the Christian Coalition, responded to criticism of the religious right by calling a press conference to denounce a supposed outbreak of "name-calling, scapegoating, and religious bigotry." Craig Rogers, an evangelical Christian student at California State University, recently filed a $2.5-million sexual-harassment suit against a lesbian professor of psychology, claiming that anti-male bias in one of her lectures violated campus rules and left him feeling "raped and trapped."

In universities and on Capitol Hill, in workplaces and newsrooms, authorities are declaring that there is no place for racism, sexism, homophobia, Christian-bashing, and other forms of prejudice in public debate or even in private thought. "Only when racism and other forms of prejudice are expunged," say the crusaders for sweetness and light, "can minorities be safe and society be fair." So sweet, this dream of a world without prejudice. But the very last thing society should do is seek to utterly eradicate racism and other forms of prejudice.

I suppose I should say, in the customary I-hope-I-don't-sound-too-defensive tone, that I am not a racist and that this is not an article favoring racism or any other particular prejudice. It is an article favoring intellectual pluralism, which permits the expression of various forms of bigotry and always will. Although we like to hope that a time will come when no one will believe that people come in types and that each type belongs with its own kind, I doubt such a day will ever arrive. By all indications, *Homo sapiens* is a tribal species for whom "us versus them" comes naturally and must be continually pushed back. Where there is genuine freedom of expression, there will be racist expression. There will also be people who believe that homosexuals are sick or threaten children or—especially among teenagers—are rightful targets of manly savagery. Homosexuality will always be incomprehensible to most people, and what is incomprehensible is feared. As for anti-Semitism, it appears to be a hardier virus than influenza. If you want pluralism, then you get racism and sexism and homophobia, and communism and fascism and xenophobia and tribalism, and that is just for a start. If you want to believe in intellectual freedom and the progress of knowledge and the advancement of science and all those other good things, then you must swallow hard and accept this: for as thickheaded and wayward an animal as us, the realistic question is how to make the best of prejudice, not how to eradicate it.

Indeed, "eradicating prejudice" is so vague a proposition as to be meaningless. Distinguishing prejudice reliably and nonpolitically from nonprejudice, or even defining it crisply, is quite hopeless. We all feel we know prejudice when we see it. But do we? At the University of Michigan, a student said in a classroom discussion that he considered homosexuality a disease treatable with therapy. He was summoned to a formal disciplinary hearing for violating the school's policy against speech that "victimizes" people based on "sexual orientation." Now, the evidence is abundant that this particular hypothesis is wrong, and any American homosexual can attest to the harm that the student's hypothesis has inflicted on many real people. But was it a statement of prejudice or of misguided belief? Hate speech or hypothesis? Many Americans who do not regard themselves as bigots or haters believe that homosexuality is a treatable disease. They may be wrong, but are they all bigots? I am unwilling to say so, and if you are willing, beware. The line between a prejudiced belief and a merely controversial one is elusive, and the harder you look the more elusive it becomes. "God hates homosexuals" is a statement of fact, not of bias, to those who believe it; "American criminals are disproportionately black" is a statement of bias, not of fact, to those who disbelieve it.

Who is right? You may decide, and so may others, and there is no need to agree. That is the great innovation of intellectual pluralism (which is to say, of post-Enlightenment science, broadly defined). We cannot know in advance or for sure which belief is prejudice and which is truth, but to advance knowledge we don't need to know. The genius of intellectual pluralism lies not in doing away with prejudices and dogmas but in channeling them—making them socially productive by pitting prejudice against prejudice and dogma against dogma, exposing all to withering public criticism. What survives at the end of the day is our base of knowledge.

What they told us in high school about this process is very largely a lie. The Enlightenment tradition taught us that science is orderly, antiseptic, rational, the province of detached experimenters and high-minded logicians. In the popular view, science stands for reason against prejudice, open-mindedness against dogma, calm consideration against passionate attachment—all personified by pop-science icons like the magisterially deductive Sherlock Holmes, the coolly analytic Mr. Spock, the genially

authoritative Mr. Science (from our junior-high science films). Yet one of science's dirty secrets is that although science as a whole is as unbiased as
anything human can be, scientists are just as biased as anyone else, sometimes more so. "One of the strengths of science," writes the philosopher of
science David L. Hull, "is that it does not require that scientists be unbiased,
only that different scientists have different biases." Another dirty secret is
that, no less than the rest of us, scientists can be dogmatic and pigheaded.
"Although this pigheadedness often damages the careers of individual scientists," says Hull, "it is beneficial for the manifest goal of science," which
relies on people to invest years in their ideas and defend them passionately.
And the dirtiest secret of all, if you believe in the antiseptic popular view of
science, is that this most ostensibly rational of enterprises depends on the
most irrational of motives—ambition, narcissism, animus, even revenge.
"Scientists acknowledge that among their motivations are natural curiosity,
the love of truth, and the desire to help humanity, but other inducements
exist as well, and one of them is to 'get that son of a bitch,'" says Hull. "Time
and again, scientists whom I interviewed described the powerful spur that
'showing that son of a bitch' supplied to their own research."

Many people, I think, are bewildered by this unvarnished and all too
human view of science. They believe that for a system to be unprejudiced,
the people in it must also be unprejudiced. In fact, the opposite is true. Far
from eradicating ugly or stupid ideas and coarse or unpleasant motives,
intellectual pluralism relies upon them to excite intellectual passion and
redouble scientific effort. I know of no modern idea more ugly and stupid
than that the Holocaust never happened, nor any idea more viciously motivated. Yet the deniers' claims that the Auschwitz gas chambers could not
have worked led to closer study and, in 1993, research showing, at last, how
they actually did work. Thanks to prejudice and stupidity, another opening for doubt has been shut.

An enlightened and efficient intellectual regime lets a million prejudices
bloom, including many that you or I may regard as hateful or grotesque.
It avoids any attempt to stamp out prejudice, because stamping out prejudice really means forcing everyone to share the same prejudice, namely
that of whoever is in authority. The great American philosopher Charles
Sanders Peirce wrote in 1877: "[w]hen complete agreement could not
otherwise be reached, a general massacre of all who have not thought in a
certain way has proved a very effective means of settling opinion in a country." In speaking of "settling opinion," Peirce was writing about one of the
two or three most fundamental problems that any human society must
confront and solve. For most societies down through the centuries, this
problem was dealt with in the manner he described: errors were identified by the authorities—priests, politburos, dictators—or by mass opinion, and then the error-makers were eliminated along with their putative
mistakes. "Let all men who reject the established belief be terrified into
silence," wrote Peirce, describing this system. "This method has, from the

earliest times, been one of the chief means of upholding correct theological and political doctrines."

Intellectual pluralism substitutes a radically different doctrine: we kill our mistakes rather than each other. Here I draw on another great philosopher, the late Karl Popper, who pointed out that the critical method of science "consists in letting our hypotheses die in our stead." Those who are in error are not (or are not supposed to be) banished or excommunicated or forced to sign a renunciation or required to submit to "rehabilitation" or sent for psychological counseling. It is the error we punish, not the errant. By letting people make errors—even mischievous, spiteful errors (as, for instance, Galileo's insistence on Copernicanism was taken to be in 1633)—pluralism creates room to challenge orthodoxy, think imaginatively, experiment boldly. Brilliance and bigotry are empowered in the same stroke.

Pluralism is the principle that protects and makes a place in human company for that loneliest and most vulnerable of all minorities, the minority who is hounded and despised among blacks and whites, gays and straights, who is suspect or criminal among every tribe and in every nation of the world, and yet on whom progress depends: the dissident. I am not saying that dissent is always or even usually enlightened. Most of the time it is foolish and self-serving. No dissident has the right to be taken seriously, and the fact that Aryan Nation racists or Nation of Islam anti-Semites are unorthodox does not entitle them to respect. But what goes around comes around. As a supporter of gay marriage, for example, I reject the majority's view of family, and as a Jew I reject its view of God. I try to be civil, but the fact is that most Americans regard my views on marriage as a reckless assault on the most fundamental of all institutions, and many people are more than a little discomfited by the statement "Jesus Christ was no more divine than anybody else" (which is why so few people ever say it). Trap the racists and anti-Semites, and you lay a trap for me too. Hunt for them with eradication in your mind, and you have brought dissent itself within your sights.

The new crusade against prejudice waves aside such warnings. Like earlier crusades against antisocial ideas, the mission is fueled by good (if cocksure) intentions and a genuine sense of urgency. Some kinds of error are held to be intolerable, like pollutants that even in small traces poison the water for a whole town. Some errors are so pernicious as to damage real people's lives, so wrongheaded that no person of right mind or goodwill could support them. Like their forebears of other stripe—the Church in its campaigns against heretics, the McCarthyites in their campaigns against Communists—the modern anti-racist and anti-sexist and anti-homophobic campaigners are totalists, demanding not that misguided ideas and ugly expressions be corrected or criticized but that they be eradicated. They make war not on errors but on error, and like other totalists they act in the name of public safety—the safety, especially, of minorities.

The sweeping implications of this challenge to pluralism are not, I think, well enough understood by the public at large. Indeed, the new brand of totalism has yet even to be properly named. "Multiculturalism," for instance, is much too broad. "Political correctness" comes closer but is too trendy and snide. For lack of anything else, I will call the new anti-pluralism "purism," since its major tenet is that society cannot be just until the last traces of invidious prejudice have been scrubbed away. Whatever you call it, the purists' way of seeing things has spread through American intellectual life with remarkable speed, so much so that many people will blink at you uncomprehendingly or even call you a racist (or sexist or homophobe, etc.) if you suggest that expressions of racism should be tolerated or that prejudice has its part to play.

The new purism sets out, to begin with, on a campaign against words, for words are the currency of prejudice, and if prejudice is hurtful then so must be prejudiced words. "We are not safe when these violent words are among us," wrote Mari Matsuda, then a UCLA law professor. Here one imagines gangs of racist words swinging chains and smashing heads in back alleys. To suppress bigoted language seems, at first blush, reasonable, but it quickly leads to a curious result. A peculiar kind of verbal shamanism takes root, as though certain expressions, like curses or magical incantations, carry in themselves the power to hurt or heal—as though words were bigoted rather than people. "Context is everything," people have always said. The use of the word "nigger" in *Huckleberry Finn* does not make the book an "act" of hate speech—or does it? In the new view, this is no longer so clear. The very utterance of the word "nigger" (at least by a non-black) is a racist act. When a *Sacramento Bee* cartoonist put the word "nigger" mockingly in the mouth of a white supremacist, there were howls of protest and 1,400 canceled subscriptions and an editorial apology, even though the word was plainly being invoked against racists, not against blacks.

Faced with escalating demands of verbal absolutism, newspapers issue lists of forbidden words. The expressions "gyp" (derived from "Gypsy") and "Dutch treat" were among the dozens of terms stricken as "offensive" in a much-ridiculed (and later withdrawn) *Los Angeles Times* speech code. The University of Missouri journalism school issued a *Dictionary of Cautionary Words and Phrases*, which included *"Buxom*: [o]ffensive reference to a woman's chest. Do not use. See 'Woman.' *Codger*: [o]ffensive reference to a senior citizen."

As was bound to happen, purists soon discovered that chasing around after words like "gyp" or "buxom" hardly goes to the roots of the problem. As long as they remain bigoted, bigots will simply find other words. If they can't call you a kike then they will say Jewboy, Judas, or Hebe, and when all those are banned they will press words like "oven" and "lampshade" into their service. The vocabulary of hate is potentially as rich as your dictionary, and all you do by banning language used by cretins is to let them decide what the rest of us may say. The problem, some purists have concluded, must therefore go much deeper than laws: it must go to the deeper level of ideas. Racism, sexism, homophobia, and the rest must be built into the very structure of American society and American patterns of thought, so pervasive yet so insidious that, like water to a fish, they are both omnipresent and unseen. The mere existence of prejudice constructs a society whose very nature is prejudiced.

This line of thinking was pioneered by feminists, who argued that pornography, more than just being expressive, is an act by which men construct an oppressive society. Racial activists quickly picked up the argument. Racist expressions are themselves acts of oppression, they said. "All racist speech constructs the social reality that constrains the liberty of nonwhites because of their race," wrote Charles R. Lawrence III, then a law professor at Stanford. From the purist point of view, a society with even one racist is a racist society, because the idea itself threatens and demeans its targets. They cannot feel wholly safe or wholly welcome as long as racism is present. Pluralism says: [t]here will always be some racists. Marginalize them, ignore them, exploit them, ridicule them, take pains to make their policies illegal, but otherwise leave them alone. Purists say: [t]hat's not enough. Society cannot be just until these pervasive and oppressive ideas are searched out and eradicated.

And so what is now under way is a growing drive to eliminate prejudice from every corner of society. I doubt that many people have noticed how far-reaching this anti-pluralist movement is becoming.

In universities: [d]ozens of universities have adopted codes proscribing speech or other expression that (this is from Stanford's policy, which is more or less representative) "is intended to insult or stigmatize an individual or a small number of individuals on the basis of their sex, race, color, handicap, religion, sexual orientation or national and ethnic origin." Some codes punish only persistent harassment of a targeted individual, but many, following the purist doctrine that even one racist is too many, go much further. At Penn, an administrator declared: "[w]e at the University of Pennsylvania have guaranteed students and the community that they can live in a community free of sexism, racism, and homophobia." Here is the purism that gives "political correctness" its distinctive combination of puffy high-mindedness and authoritarian zeal.

In school curricula: "[m]ore fundamental than eliminating racial segregation has to be the removal of racist thinking, assumptions, symbols, and materials in the curriculum," writes theorist Molefi Kete Asante. In practice, the effort to "remove racist thinking" goes well beyond striking egregious references from textbooks. In many cases it becomes a kind of mental engineering in which students are encouraged to see prejudice everywhere; it includes teaching identity politics as an antidote to internalized racism; it rejects mainstream science as "white male" thinking; and it tampers with history, installing such dubious notions as that the ancient Greeks stole their culture from Africa or that an ancient carving of a bird is an example of "African experimental aeronautics."

In criminal law: [c]onsider two crimes. In each, I am beaten brutally; in each, my jaw is smashed and my skull is split in just the same way. However, in the first crime my assailant calls me an "asshole"; in the second he calls me a "queer." In most states, in many localities, and, as of September 1994, in federal cases, these two crimes are treated differently: the crime motivated by bias—or deemed to be so motivated by prosecutors and juries—gets a stiffer punishment. "Longer prison terms for bigots," shrilled Brooklyn Democratic Congressman Charles Schumer, who introduced the federal hate-crimes legislation, and those are what the law now provides. Evidence that the assailant holds prejudiced beliefs, even if he doesn't actually express them while committing an offense, can serve to elevate the crime. Defendants in hate-crimes cases may be grilled on how many black friends they have and whether they have told racist jokes. To increase a prison sentence only because of the defendant's "prejudice" (as gauged by prosecutor and jury) is, of course, to try minds and punish beliefs. Purists say, "Well, they are dangerous minds and poisonous beliefs."

In the workplace: [t]hough government cannot constitutionally suppress bigotry directly, it is now busy doing so indirectly by requiring employers to eliminate prejudice. Since the early 1980s, courts and the Equal Employment Opportunity Commission have moved to bar workplace speech deemed to create a hostile or abusive working environment for minorities. The law, held a federal court in 1988, "does require that an employer take prompt action to prevent . . . bigots from expressing their opinions in a way that abuses or offends their co-workers," so as to achieve "the goal of eliminating prejudices and biases from our society." So it was, as UCLA law professor Eugene Volokh notes, that the EEOC charged that a manufacturer's ads using admittedly accurate depictions of samurai, kabuki, and sumo were "racist" and "offensive to people of Japanese origin"; that a Pennsylvania court found that an employer's printing Bible verses on paychecks was religious harassment of Jewish employees; that an employer had to desist using gender-based job titles like "foreman" and "draftsman" after a female employee sued.

On and on the campaign goes, darting from one outbreak of prejudice to another like a cat chasing flies. In the American Bar Association, activists demand that lawyers who express "bias or prejudice" be penalized. In the Education Department, the civil-rights office presses for a ban on computer bulletin board comments that "show hostility toward a person or group based on sex, race or color, including slurs, negative stereotypes, jokes or pranks." In its security checks for government jobs, the FBI takes to asking whether applicants are "free of biases against any class of citizens," whether, for instance, they have told racist jokes or indicated other "prejudices." Joke police! George Orwell, grasping the close relationship of jokes to dissent, said that every joke is a tiny revolution. The purists will have no such rebellions.

The purist campaign reaches, in the end, into the mind itself. In a lecture at the University of New Hampshire, a professor compared writing to sex ("You and the subject become one"); he was suspended and required to apologize, but what was most insidious was the order to undergo university-approved counseling to have his mind straightened out. At the University of Pennsylvania, a law lecturer said, "We have ex-slaves here who should know about the Thirteenth Amendment"; he was banished from campus for a year and required to make a public apology, and he, too, was compelled to attend a "sensitivity and racial awareness" session. Mandatory re-education of alleged bigots is the natural consequence of intellectual purism. Prejudice must be eliminated!

Ah, but the task of scouring minds clean is Augean. "Nobody escapes," said a Rutgers University report on campus prejudice. Bias and prejudice, it found, cross every conceivable line, from sex to race to politics: "[n]o matter who you are, no matter what the color of your skin, no matter what your gender or sexual orientation, no matter what you believe, no matter how you behave, there is somebody out there who doesn't like people of your kind." Charles Lawrence writes: "[r]acism is ubiquitous. We are all racists." If he means that most of us think racist thoughts of some sort at one time or another, he is right. If we are going to "eliminate prejudices and biases from our society," then the work of the prejudice police is unending. They are doomed to hunt and hunt and hunt, scour and scour and scour.

What is especially dismaying is that the purists pursue prejudice in the name of protecting minorities. In order to protect people like me (homosexual), they must pursue people like me (dissident). In order to bolster minority self-esteem, they suppress minority opinion. There are, of course, all kinds of practical and legal problems with the purists' campaign: the incursions against the First Amendment; the inevitable abuses by prosecutors and activists who define as "hateful" or "violent" whatever speech they dislike or can score points off of; the lack of any evidence that repressing prejudice eliminates rather than inflames it. But minorities, of all people, ought to remember that by definition we cannot prevail by numbers, and we generally cannot prevail by force. Against the power of ignorant mass opinion and group prejudice and superstition, we have only our voices. If you doubt that minorities' voices are powerful weapons, think of the lengths to which Southern officials went to silence the Reverend Martin Luther King Jr. (Recall that the city commissioner of Montgomery, Alabama, won a $500,000 libel suit, later overturned in *New York Times v. Sullivan* [1964], regarding an advertisement in the *Times* placed by civil-rights leaders who denounced the Montgomery police.) Think of how much gay people have improved their lot over twenty-five years simply by refusing to remain silent. Recall the Michigan student who was prosecuted for saying that homosexuality is a treatable disease, and notice that he was black. Under that Michigan speech code, more than twenty blacks were charged with racist speech, while no instance of racist speech by whites was punished. In Florida, the hate-speech law was invoked against a black man who called a policeman a "white cracker"; not so surprisingly, in the first hate-crimes case to reach the Supreme Court, the victim was white and the defendant black.

In the escalating war against "prejudice," the right is already learning to play by the rules that were pioneered by the purist activists of the left. Last year [1994], leading Democrats, including the President, criticized the Republican Party for being increasingly in the thrall of the Christian right. Some of the rhetoric was harsh ("fire-breathing Christian radical right"), but it wasn't vicious or even clearly wrong. Never mind: when Democratic Representative Vic Fazio said Republicans were "being forced to the fringes by the aggressive political tactics of the religious right," the chairman of the Republican National Committee, Haley Barbour, said, "Christian-bashing" was "the left's preferred form of religious bigotry." Bigotry! Prejudice! "Christians active in politics are now on the receiving end of an extraordinary campaign of bias and prejudice," said the conservative leader William J. Bennett. One discerns, here, where the new purism leads. Eventually, any criticism of any group will be "prejudice."

Here is the ultimate irony of the new purism: words, which pluralists hope can be substituted for violence, are redefined by purists *as* violence. "The experience of being called 'nigger,' 'spic,' 'Jap,' or 'kike' is like receiving a slap in the face," Charles Lawrence wrote in 1990. "Psychic injury is no less an injury than being struck in the face, and it often is far more severe." This kind of talk is commonplace today. Epithets, insults, often even polite expressions of what's taken to be prejudice are called by purists "assaultive speech," "words that wound," "verbal violence." "To me, racial epithets are not speech," one University of Michigan law professor said. "They are bullets." In her speech accepting the 1993 Nobel Prize for Literature in Stockholm, Sweden, the author Toni Morrison said this: "[o]ppressive language does more than represent violence; it is violence."

It is not violence. I am thinking back to a moment on the subway in Washington, a little thing. I was riding home late one night and a squad of noisy kids, maybe seventeen or eighteen years old, noisily piled into the car. They yelled across the car and a girl said, "Where do we get off?"

A boy said, "Farragut North."

The girl, "*Faggot* North!"

The boy, "Yeah! Faggot North!"

General hilarity.

First, before the intellect resumes control, there is a moment of fear, an animal moment. Who are they? How many of them? How dangerous? Where is the way out? All of these things are noted preverbally and assessed by the gut. Then the brain begins an assessment: they are sober, this is probably too public a place for them to do it, there are more girls than boys, they were just talking, it is probably nothing.

They didn't notice me and there was no incident. The teenage babble flowed on, leaving me to think. I became interested in my own reaction: the jump of fear out of nowhere like an alert animal, the sense for a brief time that one is naked and alone and should hide or run away. For a time, one ceases to be a human being and becomes instead a faggot.

The fear engendered by these words is real. The remedy is as clear and as imperfect as ever: protect citizens against violence. This, I grant, is something that American society has never done very well and now does quite poorly. It is no solution to define words as violence or prejudice as oppression, and then by cracking down on words or thoughts pretend that we are doing something about violence and oppression. No doubt it is easier to pass a speech code or hate-crimes law and proclaim the streets safer than actually to make the streets safer, but the one must never be confused with the other. Every cop or prosecutor chasing words is one fewer chasing criminals. In a world rife with real violence and oppression, full of Rwandas and Bosnias and eleven-year-olds spraying bullets at children in Chicago and in turn being executed by gang lords, it is odious of Toni Morrison to say that words are violence.

Indeed, equating "verbal violence" with physical violence is a treacherous, mischievous business. Not long ago a writer was charged with viciously and gratuitously wounding the feelings and dignity of millions of people. He was charged, in effect, with exhibiting flagrant prejudice against Muslims and outrageously slandering their beliefs. "What is freedom of expression?" mused Salman Rushdie a year after the ayatollahs sentenced him to death and put a price on his head. "Without the freedom to offend, it ceases to exist." I can think of nothing sadder than that minority activists, in their haste to make the world better, should be the ones to forget the lesson of Rushdie's plight: for minorities, pluralism, not purism, is the answer. The campaigns to eradicate prejudice—all of them, the speech codes and workplace restrictions and mandatory therapy for accused bigots and all the rest—should stop, now. The whole objective of eradicating prejudice, as opposed to correcting and criticizing it, should be repudiated as a fool's errand. Salman Rushdie is right, Toni Morrison wrong, and minorities belong at his side, not hers.

22

"Free Speech Skepticism"

Susan J. Brison

Is There a Human Right to Free Speech?

Contemporary theorizing about free speech done by American scholars tends to take the free speech clause of the First Amendment of the
U.S. Constitution to be the articulation of a legal right grounded in a fundamental human right, rather than a piece of positive law which may or
may not be based on a moral imperative. U.S. legal theorists engaged in
debates about free speech controversies typically argue that the First
Amendment, when interpreted correctly, clearly supports their position.
Virtually no theorists question whether the First Amendment is morally
justified to begin with. But if the right to free speech is to be considered as
prior to and more fundamental than mere positive law, if it is the principle underlying the series of cases that the courts decided (or at least those
that were decided correctly), then the right to free speech must be grounded
in something *other* than the precedents of earlier cases. It must have a foundation of some sort.

I think there's reason to be skeptical that there is such a foundation. In
this article, I argue that, although there is, as a matter of contingent historical fact, a right to free speech embedded in the First Amendment, none
of the main arguments adduced in support of such a right succeeds in
showing why even harmful speech is deserving of special protection not
afforded non-speech conduct. Absent such a defense, the view that the First
Amendment, as interpreted by the U.S. Supreme Court, articulates a legal
right that is grounded in a moral imperative is an article of faith, not an
uncontroversial fact.

The question of whether there is some underlying moral justification for
a First Amendment right to free speech is currently a pressing one for two
reasons. The first is that we need to resolve the question of whether nongovernmental entities, such as Twitter and Facebook, can, and sometimes
do, violate people's right to free speech, even though their policies do not,
because they cannot, violate the First Amendment. Given the central role
of the internet in contemporary communications, we need to ask whether
those who own and operate social media platforms violate speakers' and
others' right to free speech by moderating content or deplatforming speakers. If the only free speech right in question is the one articulated in the

First Amendment, non-state actors, no matter how powerful, cannot violate anyone's right to free speech. However, given how much power they have to control not only what's on their platforms, but also who uses them, the actions of Jack Dorsey and Mark Zuckerberg can and do have drastic effects on people's abilities to speak and to access others' speech. If there is a universal moral right to free speech that underlies and justifies the First Amendment, then the question arises what, if any, moral obligation do companies such as Facebook and Twitter have to protect *that* right.

The second reason is that, in the digital age, the massive, worldwide, and instantaneous reach of the internet has made for inevitable clashes among diverse free speech regimes, creating an urgent need for new ways of understanding free speech that might aid in resolving such conflicts. Views about free speech on the internet originated, as did the internet itself, in the United States and so have been heavily influenced by First Amendment exceptionalism, but the United States is an outlier in the extent to which it protects speech. Whereas the right to freedom of expression, including the right to engage in hate speech, is widely considered in the United States to be a fundamental human right of virtually paramount value, in most other countries, free speech rights are constrained by other rights, such as the rights to dignity, respect, and equality; and laws restricting hate speech, such as speech inciting racial hatred and Holocaust denial, are relatively uncontroversial. There is today an international consensus that, however valuable the right to freedom of expression may be, it is overridden or irrelevant in the case of much of what gets labeled "hate speech." No other country has the strong constitutional protection of hate speech that First Amendment jurisprudence has led to in the United States.

* * *

The extraordinary protection of hate speech in the United States can be explained by the existence of the First Amendment of the U.S. Constitution, ratified in 1791, which states: "Congress shall make no law . . . abridging the freedom of speech, or of the press." (The Fourteenth Amendment due process guarantee applies this constraint to state and local legislatures as well.) No other country's legal system has such a longstanding and firmly entrenched protection of free speech.

The United States does, however, regulate some speech. The U.S. Supreme Court has not followed the absolutist interpretation of the First Amendment that one might have thought could be read off its straightforward wording. In spite of Justice Black's famous statement—"I read 'no law . . . abridging' to mean *no law abridging*"—the Court has considered many categories of speech to be unprotected. Examples include perjury, insider trading, defamation of private individuals, "fighting words," and "true threats." However, in the United States, racist hate speech is considered to be covered by the First Amendment, which is to say that restricting it requires a greater justification than would be required to restrict non-speech conduct that is equally harmful. The U.S. Supreme Court has not only considered racist hate speech to be *covered* by the First Amendment; it has also ruled that is *protected* by it, meaning that laws restricting it have failed to meet the higher standard of justification.

*   *   *

In contrast, in the United States, the right to free speech is taken to be so central that it functions rhetorically as the *sine qua non* of the right to *all* freedoms. This may have something to do with the fact that, in the United States, the constitutional protection of free speech came well before the commitment to equality of status, to a caste-free state, whereas most other Western democracies formally guaranteed free speech only after granting universal suffrage and only after witnessing the rise of anti-Semitism in Europe and the atrocity of the Holocaust.

What Is a Free Speech Principle?

If the free speech clause of the First Amendment is interpreted to mean that speech is to be granted special protection not accorded to other forms of conduct, then a free speech principle, distinct from a principle of general liberty, must be posited and must receive a distinct justification. Such a principle must hold that speech is special, in the following way, as articulated by Frederick Schauer: "[u]nder a Free Speech Principle, any governmental action to achieve a goal, whether that goal be positive or negative, must provide a stronger justification when the attainment of that goal requires the restriction of speech than when no limitations on speech are employed." Understood in this way, a free speech principle constrains state action, but not private action. The right to free speech protected by the First Amendment is a negative right to be free from governmental interference of a certain sort, not a right to be free from private interference, nor a positive right actually to be able to speak and to have the wherewithal to gain access to others' speech.

*   *   *

In order to know whether a free speech argument is even relevant to a particular case at hand, we need to know the rationale for the free speech principle. Once it's determined that the act in question raises free speech concerns, however, the matter isn't resolved. To be *covered* by a free speech principle is not the same thing as being *protected* by it. A free speech principle does not state that *everything* that counts as speech, no matter how harmful, must be protected. It states only that a stronger rationale for restricting it is required than would be required in the case of equally harmful non-speech conduct. In the United States this means the law or policy prohibiting the speech must pass the strict scrutiny test, since free speech is a liberty falling under the due process clause (in the Fifth and

Fourteenth Amendments). Even in the United States, some conduct that counts as speech, and is, thus, covered by an independent free speech principle, may be restricted, without running afoul of the First Amendment, if the law restricting that conduct passes strict scrutiny, that is, provided it serves a compelling state interest and does so in the least intrusive way possible.

Is a Free Speech Principle Justified?

Our constitutional democracy in the United States is based, apart from a few unfortunate aberrations, on the view, articulated by Mill, that the government may justifiably exercise power over individuals, against their will, only to prevent harm to others. Mill considered his harm principle to apply equally to governmental regulation and to "the moral coercion of public opinion." Mill does not, however, specify what counts as harm. Following Joel Feinberg (1984), I consider it to be a wrongful setback to one's significant interests, so it encompasses much more than the hit-on-the-head sort of physical harm. (The U.S. legal system already takes into account harms understood in this way. Even in the case of physical injury, it is not merely the extent of the hurt—that is, the physical pain or damage—that is addressed by the law, but also the harm, construed so as to include long-term financial and emotional damage.)

* * *

A defense of a free speech principle must explain why the harm principle either does not apply in the case of speech or applies with less force than in the case of all other forms of human conduct. Many theorists have argued that one thing or another—the desirability of arriving at truth in the long run, say, or the need for a well-functioning democracy, or the importance of self-realization—provides the foundation for a right to free speech. This kind of argument proceeds as follows: [w]e value x. The right to free speech is essential for (or at least instrumental in) the achievement of x. Therefore, we must posit the right to free speech and design social structures (constitutions, laws, public policies) to protect and possibly even foster it. Such consequentialist defenses of free speech purport to show that speech must be protected for the sake of some other value. I discuss below the most commonly invoked ones: 1. the argument from truth, 2. the argument from democracy, 3. the argument from self-realization, 4. the argument from tolerance, and 5. the argument from distrust of government. This fifth defense of free speech does not invoke a value so much as conjure up a threat of a disastrous result should the government be permitted to restrict speech. All of these have been offered as defenses of conceptions of free speech that, like the First Amendment, prohibit only government restriction of speech. The first four, if successful, could also be used to defend conceptions of free speech that prohibit non-governmental entities, such as Facebook and Twitter, from restricting speech.

Free Speech Values: Truth

* * *

* * * [T]his defense of free speech has been labeled a "marketplace of ideas" approach, as articulated in Oliver Wendell Holmes Jr.'s famous dissent in *Abrams v. United States*, in which he wrote that "when men have realized that time has upset many fighting faiths, they may come to believe even more than they believe the very foundations of their own conduct that the ultimate good desired is better reached by free trade in ideas—that the best test of truth is the power of the thought to get itself accepted in the competition of the market. . . . That, at any rate, is the theory of our Constitution. It is an experiment, as all life is an experiment."

* * *

In the case of harmful speech, one also needs to take into account the possibility of the silencing effect of the speech on those harmed by it. (I suppose the most extreme case would be the deathly silence of those duped by false or misleading advertising of potentially lethal products.) For example, if vulnerable minority members are targeted by hate speech, they may well become less, rather than more, likely to express their ideas, and, even if they do speak, they may not be taken as seriously as they would be in an environment that did not tolerate hate speech.

A further objection to the argument from truth is that, at some point, an increase in speech may become counterproductive if there is so much information (including redundancies and misinformation) to be examined that arriving at the truth becomes more difficult or takes much longer than it otherwise would. We are faced here with something like a violation of H. P. Grice's rule of quantity: saying too much, that is, allowing too many different opinions, including misleading and erroneous ones, to be aired, can get in the way of achieving truth by undermining the informativeness of what is said. Even more concerning, in the digital age, is the *intentional* dissemination of falsehoods via a medium that can reach billions of people instantaneously.

Free Speech Values: Self-Realization and Diversity

The argument from self-realization (or self-fulfillment or autonomy) and diversity holds that restrictions on speech impose a stifling uniformity on individuals' expression and prevent them from accessing the unrestricted speech of others, and that these things, in turn, limit the extent to which people can develop their own individual personalities.

* * *

In order to examine the plausibility of this claim we need to look at the context in which restrictions are being considered. If hate speech, such as cross-burning on the lawn of the only Black family in an otherwise all white neighborhood, not only intimidates and silences the immediate victims, but also deters other Blacks from moving into the neighborhood, that environment will suffer a diminishment of perspectives, and certain kinds of individual personalities (those celebrating their African-American heritage, for example) will be discouraged from flourishing, to put it mildly.

The above example of cross-burning points to another difficulty with this argument, which is that it does not explain why speech should be given special protection, since other actions can contribute at least as much to the development of individual personalities. The Black family—or at least the head(s) of the household who made the decision to move—who settled in the formerly all-white neighborhood expressed a great deal about themselves, their aspirations, their hopes for racial harmony, etc. by moving into their new house. The cross-burning on their lawn was an attempt to stifle that expression and, thus, lessen the diversity of views in that area. Likewise, if discriminatory harassment of minority students is permitted on college campuses, with the effect that the targeted students leave, silence themselves, or simply keep a lower profile on campus than they otherwise would, then, again, individual self-realization and diversity are diminished, rather than fostered, by unrestricted speech.

* * *

Free Speech Values: Democracy

The argument from democracy * * * defends a free speech principle by pointing out that citizens in a democracy need access to information in order to make well-informed political decisions. They also need to be free from obstruction in making their own views known and having an impact on the political process. If this argument is taken to defend a near-absolute right to free speech which would preclude restrictions even on harmful speech such as hate speech, however, it must presuppose a democratic system in which access to speech is distributed roughly equally and in which voters are interested in getting and can realistically get full access to others' speech. As we know, however, power is distributed unequally in this democracy and many have virtually no access to the enormous political advertising potential of the media. And voters are not prepared to take the time and trouble to wade through masses of political speech. (Processing information has its costs.) The argument must assume that letting the market regulate speech is fairer—and more conducive to representative democracy—than any governmental regulation would be, but this assumption requires further defense.

* * *

Given the extent to which false, misleading, and extremist speech on the internet has undermined fair, free elections in recent years and threatened to destroy the very foundations of our democracy, this defense of a free speech principle, if taken to prohibit government regulation of democracy-undermining speech, appears weaker than ever.

Free Speech Values: Tolerance

The argument from tolerance * * * emphasizes the educational effect of a principle of free speech and is premised on the assumptions that tolerance is a good that society ought to encourage, since our society suffers from too much intolerance, and that the best way to foster this good is to tolerate human conduct in some area, namely, the realm of speech. Although I agree * * * that our society is plagued by intolerance, it is not clear to me that intolerance of *speech* poses a special problem, since intolerance is also exhibited, with arguably more harmful effects, in discrimination in the workplace, in housing, and in education. The other empirical premise * * * that the best way to counter a general climate of intolerance is to pick one area, that of speech, in which to be especially vigilant about tolerating others' behavior, is even more questionable. Since * * * that speech can be as harmful as other forms of conduct, there seems to be no rationale for singling out speech as the domain in which to attempt to inculcate the virtue of tolerance. And in the case of hate speech, which disproportionately harms certain groups, no justification is given for imposing this extra burden on its targets.

* * *

This argument presupposes that the expression of hate speech serves to lessen or dissipate the racist (or other bigoted) attitudes of the speaker. It also, implicitly, assumes that such expressions mitigate or, at any rate, do not increase the racist tendencies of listeners, since, if expressing hate speech made the speaker less likely to engage in racially motivated violence, but made many listeners *more* likely to, it would not function as a safety valve. Both assumptions lack empirical support, however, and there are substantial, although perhaps not conclusive, grounds for supposing them to be false. For example, studies of bias-motivated violence against members of certain groups show that such violence is preceded and precipitated by a process of stereotyping and dehumanizing of the victims. Such stereotyping occurs by means of speech, and, when it targets an already stigmatized and marginalized group, it is more likely to stick and be resistant to correction by counter-speech. Speech is also the means by which stereotypes spread and become more, not less, dangerous.

Free Speech Values: Distrust of Government
and the Slippery Slope Threat

[Some authors] have given a free speech defense known as the argument from distrust of government, or, alternatively, the argument from governmental incompetence. This defense conjures up a threat of harm if the government is permitted to restrict speech more than it already does. It does not invoke a specific value fostered by free speech, unless that value is the avoidance of some harm worse than the harm caused by the speech in question. On this account, the government cannot be trusted to make the appropriate distinctions, to tell truth from falsity, or to act in the best interests of the electorate. Even if one agrees with this premise (and there is surely ample reason to), it, by itself, provides no reason why *speech* should be considered to be the *only* area the government cannot be trusted to meddle in. No explanation is given for why we should suppose that the government is any more competent to regulate us in other domains in which we do allow regulation. The libertarian R. H. Coase (1974) has argued that, to be consistent, we should be equally wary of governmental regulation in the market for goods and in the market for ideas. Coase argues from the inadmissibility of governmental interference in the area of speech to the unjustifiability of economic constraints, but one can also run this argument the other way. If the government is considered competent to regulate economic affairs—and, for example, to exact income tax—in the service of important governmental interests such as equality of opportunity, it should also be considered competent to regulate speech for the same purposes.

* * *

Slippery slope arguments are generally suspect, however. By means of them we can "prove" that there is no difference between an infant and an adult or an acorn and an oak tree, since there is no non-arbitrary way of determining when one turns into the other. In addition, the selective application of the slippery slope charge—to restrictions on speech, but not to other kinds of governmental regulation—is unmotivated. One can almost always conjure up the threat of a slippery slope in legal argument—in debates about affirmative action, for example, or race- or sex-discrimination. But many legal theorists who are bothered by slippery slopes in the area of hate speech are curiously unconcerned about them in these other areas of the law, including in other areas of speech regulation. Richard Delgado and Jean Stefancic note that there are indeed line-drawing problems faced by hate speech regulations, but that these "are no greater than those attending other, long-accepted doctrines that limit speech we do not like, such as libel, defamation, plagiarism, copyright [infringement], threat[s], and so on." As they note, "Everyone knows what a clear-cut case of plagiarism looks like; at the margin we are less sure. Hate-speech rules should be no different." Or, as Justice Holmes put it, in a case concerning, not free speech, but tax law, "where to draw the line . . . is the question in pretty much everything worth arguing in the law."

*   *   *

When subjected to rigorous scrutiny, however, the belief that there is a justified independent free speech principle turns out to be an article of faith. Recall that when Holmes wrote, in his dissent in *Abrams*, that "the ultimate good desired"—truth—"is better reached by free trade in ideas" than by any restrictions on speech, he added, "That, at any rate, is the theory of our Constitution. It is an experiment, as all life is an experiment." Now may be a good time to ask how that experiment is working out. For, as Holmes also observed in that dissent, "[T]ime has upset many fighting faiths." Perhaps our faith in the justifiability of an independent free speech principle will turn out to be one of them.

DISCUSSION QUESTIONS

1. Do you agree that some groups—especially marginalized groups—warrant protection against offensive or hurtful ideas and speech? How do you define "offensive"? (And who gets to decide?) Where is the First Amendment in this dispute?

2. Is there a difference between the government punishing speech—imposing fines, for example—and private entities imposing consequences? Can a corporation discipline an employee, cancel a television show, or impose some other consequence for an employee's public speech?

3. Would a campus newspaper be justified in rejecting a paid ad from someone (1) denying that climate change is occurring, (2) advocating for the end of affirmative action in college admissions, or (3) urging students to shut down campus to protest university investments in fossil fuel companies?

PART II

Institutions

CHAPTER 5

Congress: The First Branch

23

From *Congress: The Electoral Connection*

David R. Mayhew

Most people would like to believe that members of Congress are motivated by the desire to make good public policy that will best serve the public and national interest. Some would even support the idea that members of Congress should be willing to go against their constituents' opinions when they think that it is the right thing to do. The political scientist David R. Mayhew argues that politicians' motivations are not so idealistic or complex. Members of Congress simply want to be re-elected, and most of their behavior—advertising, credit claiming, and position taking—is designed to make re-election easier. Further, Mayhew argues that the structure of Congress is ideally suited to facilitate the re-election pursuit. Congressional offices and staff advertise member accomplishments; committees allow for the specialization necessary to claim credit for particularistic benefits provided to the district; and the political parties in Congress do not demand loyalty when constituent interests run counter to the party line.

Mayhew's argument is not universally accepted. Many political scientists accept his underlying premise as a given: elected officials are self-interested, and this is manifest in their constant pursuit of re-election. But others disagree with the premise. Motivations, they argue, are far more complex than allowed for by such a simple statement or theory. People often act unselfishly, and members of Congress have been known to vote with their conscience even if it means losing an election. Others have pointed out that parties now put stronger constraints on congressional behavior than they did when Mayhew was writing in the early 1970s.

The organization of Congress meets remarkably well the electoral needs of its members. To put it another way, if a group of planners sat down and tried to design a pair of American national assemblies with the goal of serving members' electoral needs year in and year out, they would be hard pressed to improve on what exists. * * * Satisfaction of electoral needs requires remarkably little zero-sum conflict among members. That is, one member's gain is not another member's loss; to a remarkable degree members can successfully engage in electorally useful activities without denying other members the opportunity successfully to engage in them. In regard to credit claiming, this second point requires elaboration further on. Its application to advertising is perhaps obvious. The members all have different markets, so that what any one member does is not an inconvenience to any other. There are exceptions here—House members are sometimes thrown into districts together, senators have to watch the advertising of ambitious House members within their states, and senators from the same state have to keep up with each other—but the case generally holds. With position taking the point is also reasonably clear. As long as congressmen do not attack each other—and they rarely do—any member can champion the most extraordinary causes without inconveniencing any of his colleagues.

*   *   *

A scrutiny of the basic structural units of Congress will yield evidence to support both these * * * points. First, there are the 535 Capitol Hill *offices*, the small personal empires of the members. * * * The Hill office is a vitally important political unit, part campaign management firm and part political machine. The availability of its staff members for election work in and out of season gives it some of the properties of the former; its casework capabilities, some of the properties of the latter. And there is the franking privilege for use on office emanations. * * * A final comment on congressional offices is perhaps the most important one: office resources are given to all members regardless of party, seniority, or any other qualification. They come with the job.

Second among the structural units are the *committees*. * * * Committee membership can be electorally useful in a number of different ways. Some committees supply good platforms for position taking. The best example over the years is probably the House Un-American Activities Committee (now the Internal Security Committee), whose members have displayed hardly a trace of an interest in legislation. [Theodore] Lowi has a chart showing numbers of days devoted to HUAC public hearings in Congresses from the Eightieth through the Eighty-ninth. It can be read as a supply chart, showing biennial volume of position taking on subversion and related matters; by inference it can also be read as a measure of popular demand (the peak years were 1949–56). Senator Joseph McCarthy used the Senate Government Operations Committee as his investigative base in the Eighty-third Congress; later on in the 1960s Senators Abraham Ribicoff (D., Conn.) and William Proxmire (D., Wis.) used subcommittees of this same unit in catching public attention respectively on auto safety and defense waste. With membership on the Senate Foreign Relations Committee goes a license to make speeches on foreign policy. Some committees perhaps deserve to be designated "cause committees"; membership on them can confer an ostentatious identification with salient public causes. An example is the House Education and Labor Committee, whose members, in Fenno's analysis, have two "strategic premises": "to prosecute policy partisanship" and "to pursue one's individual policy preferences regardless of party." Committee members do a good deal of churning about on education, poverty, and similar matters. In recent years Education and Labor has attracted media-conscious members such as Shirley Chisholm (D., N.Y.), Herman Badillo (D., N.Y.), and Louise Day Hicks (D., Mass.).

Some committees traffic in particularized benefits. * * * Specifically, in giving out particularized benefits where the costs are diffuse (falling on taxpayer or consumer) and where in the long run to reward one congressman is not obviously to deprive others, the members follow a policy of universalism. That is, every member, regardless of party or seniority, has a right to his share of benefits. There is evidence of universalism in the distribution of projects on House Public Works, projects on House Interior, projects on Senate Interior, project money on House Appropriations, project money on Senate Appropriations, tax benefits on House Ways and Means, tax benefits on Senate Finance, and (by inference from the reported data) urban renewal projects on House Banking and Currency. The House Interior Committee, in Fenno's account, "takes as its major decision rule a determination to process and pass *all* requests and to do so in such a way as to maximize the chances of passage in the House. Succinctly, then, Interior's major strategic premise is: *to secure House passage of all constituency-supported, Member-sponsored bills."*

* * *

Particularism also has its position-taking side. On occasion members capture public attention by denouncing the allocation process itself; thus in 1972 a number of liberals held up some Ways and Means "members' bills" on the House floor. But such efforts have little or no effect. Senator Douglas used to offer floor amendments to excise projects from public works appropriations bills, but he had a hard time even getting the Senate to vote on them.

Finally, and very importantly, the committee system aids congressmen simply by allowing a division of labor among members. The parceling out of legislation among small groups of congressmen by subject area has two effects. First, it creates small voting bodies in which membership may be valuable. An attentive interest group will prize more highly the favorable issue positions of members of committees pondering its fortunes than the favorable positions of the general run of congressmen. Second, it creates specialized small-group settings in which individual congressmen can make things happen and be perceived to make things happen. "I put that bill through committee." "That was my amendment." "I talked them around on that." This is the language of credit claiming. It comes easily in the committee setting and also when "expert" committee members handle bills on the floor. To attentive audiences it can be believable. Some political actors follow committee activities closely and mobilize electoral resources to support deserving members.

* * *

The other basic structural units in Congress are the *parties*. The case here will be that the parties, like the offices and committees, are tailored to suit members' electoral needs. They are more useful for what they are not than for what they are.

* * *

What is important to each congressman, and vitally so, is that he be free to take positions that serve his advantage. There is no member of either house who would not be politically injured—or at least who would not think he would be injured—by being made to toe a party line on all policies (unless of course he could determine the line). There is no congressional bloc whose members have identical position needs across all issues. Thus on the school busing issue in the Ninety-second Congress, it was vital to Detroit white liberal Democratic House members that they be free to vote one way and to Detroit black liberal Democrats that they be free to vote the other. In regard to these member needs the best service a party can supply to its congressmen is a negative one; it can leave them alone. And this in general is what the congressional parties do. Party leaders are chosen not to be program salesmen or vote mobilizers, but to be brokers, favor-doers, agenda-setters, and protectors of established institutional routines. Party "pressure" to vote one way or another is minimal. Party "whipping" hardly deserves the name. Leaders in both houses have a habit of counseling members to "vote their constituencies."

DISCUSSION QUESTIONS

1. If members are motivated by the desire to be re-elected, is this such a bad thing? After all, shouldn't members of Congress do things that will keep the voters happy? Does the constant quest for re-election have a positive or negative impact on "representation"?

2. How could the institutions of Congress (members' offices, committees, and parties) be changed so that the collective needs of the institution would take precedence over the needs of individual members? Would there be any negative consequences for making these changes?

3. Some have argued that term limits are needed to break the never-ending quest for re-election. Do you think that term limits for members of Congress are a good idea?

24

"U.S. House Members in Their Constituencies: An Exploration"

Richard F. Fenno, Jr.

Through much of the 1970s, political scientist Richard F. Fenno, Jr. traveled with House members in their districts, "looking over their shoulders" as the politicians met with their constituents. Fenno was interested in answering the questions, "What do elected representatives see when they see a constituency? And, as a natural follow-up, what consequences do these perceptions have for their behavior?" This approach to research, which Fenno called "soaking and poking," gave us new insight into how House members represent their constituents.

In this excerpt from his classic book Home Style: House Members in their Districts, *Fenno argues that members perceive their districts as a set of concentric circles: the geographic, re-election, primary, and personal constituencies. The outer part of the circle is the geographic constituency, which is the entire district. At the center of the circle is the personal constituency—the inner group of advisers who are central to the member's campaign and governing operations (with the re-election and primary constituencies in between). Fenno describes how each part of the constituency has a different representational relationship with the member.*

Fenno also discusses how members develop a distinctive "home style" in dealing with their constituency, which determines the components of district representation: the allocation of resources, the presentation of self, and the explaining of Washington activity. Fenno concludes by pointing out that we have an incomplete picture of how Congress operates if we only focus on what happens in Washington. He says, "The more one focuses on the home activities of its members, the more one comes to appreciate the representative strengths and possibilities of Congress. Congress is the most representative of our national political institutions."

Despite a voluminous literature on the subject of representative-constituency relationships, one question central to that relationship remains underdeveloped. It is: What does an elected representative see when he or she sees a constituency? And, as a natural follow-up, what consequences do these perceptions have for his or her behavior? The key problem is that of perception. And the key assumption is that the constituency a representative reacts to is the constituency he or she sees. The corollary assumption is that the rest of us cannot understand the representative-constituency relationship until we can see the constituency through the eyes of the representative. These ideas are not new. They were first articulated for students of the United States Congress by Lewis Dexter. Their importance has been widely acknowledged and frequently repeated ever since. But despite the acceptance and reiteration of Dexter's insights, we still have not developed much coherent knowledge about the perceptions members of Congress have of their constituencies.

A major reason for this neglect is that most of our research on the representative-constituency linkage gets conducted at the wrong end of that linkage. Our interest in the constituency relations of U.S. senators and representatives has typically been a derivative interest, pursued for the light it sheds on some behavior—like roll call voting—in Washington. When we talk with our national legislators about their constituencies, we typically talk to them *in Washington* and, perforce, in the Washington context. But that is a context far removed from the one in which their constituency relationships are created, nurtured, and changed. And it is a context equally far removed from the one in which we might expect their perceptions of their constituencies to be shaped, sharpened or altered. Asking constituency-related questions on Capitol Hill, when the House member is far from the constituency itself, could well produce a distortion of perspective. Researchers might tend to conceive of a separation between the representative "here in Washington" and his or her constituency "back home," whereas the representative may picture himself or herself as a part of the constituency—me *in* the constituency, rather than me *and* the constituency. As a research strategy, therefore, it makes some sense to study our representatives' perceptions of their constituencies while they are actually in their constituencies—at the constituency end of the linkage.

Since the fall of 1970, I have been traveling with some members of the House of Representatives while they were in their districts, to see if I could figure out—by looking over their shoulders—what it is they see there. These expeditions, designed to continue through the 1976 elections, have been totally open-ended and exploratory. I have tried to observe and inquire into anything and everything the members do. Rather than assume that I already know what is interesting or what questions to ask, I have been prepared to find interesting questions emerging in the course of the experience. The same with data. The research method has been largely one of soaking and poking—or, just hanging around. This paper, therefore, conveys mostly an impressionistic feel for the subject—as befits the earliest stages of exploration and mapping.

*   *   *

Perceptions of the Constituency

The District: The Geographical Constituency

What then do House members see when they see a constituency? One way they perceive it—the way most helpful to me so far—is as a nest of concentric circles. The largest of these circles represents the congressman's broadest view of his constituency. This is "the district" or "my district." It is the entity to which, from which, and in which he travels. It is the entity whose boundaries have been fixed by state legislative enactment or by court decision. It includes the entire population within those boundaries. Because it is a legal entity, we could refer to it as the legal constituency. It captures more of what the congressman has in mind when he conjures up "my district," however, if we label it the *geographical constituency*. We retain the idea that the district is a legally bounded space and emphasize that it is located in a particular place.

The Washington community is often described as a group of people all of whom come from somewhere else. The House of Representatives, by design, epitomizes this characteristic; and its members function with a heightened sense of their ties to place. There are, of course, constant reminders. The member's district is, after all, "the Tenth District of *California*." Inside the chamber, he is "the gentleman from *California*"; outside the chamber he is Representative X (D. *California*). So, it is not surprising that when you ask a congressman, "What kind of district do you have?", the answer often begins with, and always includes, a geographical, space-and-place, perception. Thus, the district is seen as "the largest in the state, twenty-eight counties in the southeastern corner" or "three layers of suburbs to the west of the city, a square with the northwest corner cut out." If the boundaries have been changed by a recent redistricting, the geography of "the new district" will be compared to that of "the old district."

If one essential aspect of "the geographical constituency" is seen as its location and boundaries, another is its particular internal makeup. And House members describe their districts' internal makeup using political science's most familiar demographic and political variables—socioeconomic structure, ideology, ethnicity, residential patterns, religion, partisanship, stability, diversity, etc. Every congressman, in his mind's eye, sees his geographical constituency in terms of some special configuration of such variables. For example,

> Geographically, it covers the northern one-third of the state, from the border of (state X) to the border of (state Y), along the Z river—twenty-two counties. The basic industry is agriculture—but it's a diverse district. The city makes up one-third of the population. It is dominated by the state government and education. It's an independent-minded constituency, with a strong attachment to the work ethic. A good percentage is composed of people whose families emmigrated from Germany, Scandinavia, and Czechoslovakia. I don't exactly know the figures, but over one-half the district is German. And this goes back to the

work ethic. They are a hardworking, independent people. They have a strong thought of 'keeping the government off my back, we'll do all right here.' That's especially true of my out-counties.

Some internal configurations are more complex than others. But, even at the broadest level, no congressman sees, within his district's boundaries, an undifferentiated glob. And we cannot talk about his relations with his "constituency" as if he did.

All of the demographic characteristics of the geographical constituency carry political implications. But as most Representatives make their first perceptual cut into "the district," political matters are usually left implicit. Sometimes, the question, "What kind of district do you have?" turns up the answer, "It's a Democratic district." But much more often, that comes later. It is as if they first want to sketch a prepolitical background against which they can later paint in the political refinements. We, of course, know—for many of the variables—just what those political refinements are likely to be. (Most political scientists would guess that the district just described is probably more Republican than Democratic—which it is.) There is no point to dwelling on the general political relevance of each variable. But one summary characterization does seem to have special usefulness as a background against which to understand political perceptions and their consequences. And that characteristic is the relative homogeneity or heterogeneity of the district.

As the following examples suggest, members of Congress do think in terms of the homogeneity or heterogeneity of their districts—though they may not always use the words.

> It's geographically compact. It's all suburban—no big city in the accepted sense of the word and no rural area. It's all white. There are very few blacks, maybe 2 per cent. Spanish surnamed make up about 10 per cent. Traditionally, it's been a district with a high percentage of home ownership. . . . Economically, it's above the national average in employment . . . the people of the district are employed. It's not that it's very high income. Oh, I suppose there are a few places of some wealth, but nothing very wealthy. And no great pockets of poverty either. And it's not dominated by any one industry. The X County segment has a lot of small, clean, technical industries. I consider it very homogeneous. By almost any standard, it's homogeneous.
>
> This district is a microcosm of the nation. We are geographically southern and politically northern. We have agriculture—mostly soy beans and corn. We have big business—like Union Carbide and General Electric. And we have unions. We have a city and we have small towns. We have some of the worst poverty in the country in A County. And we have some very wealthy sections, though not large. We have wealth in the city and some wealthy towns. We have urban poverty and rural poverty. Just about the only thing we don't have is a good-sized ghetto. Otherwise, everything you can have, we've got it right here.

Because it is a summary variable, the perceived homogeneity-heterogeneity characteristic is particularly hard to measure; and no metric is proposed here. Intuitively, both the number and the compatibility of significant interests within the district would seem to be involved. The greater the number of significant interests—as opposed to one dominant interest—the more likely it is that the district will be seen as heterogeneous. But if the several significant interests were viewed as having a single lowest common denominator and, therefore, quite compatible, the district might still be viewed as homogeneous. One indicator, therefore, might be the ease with which the congressman finds a lowest common denominator of interests for some large proportion of his geographical constituency. The basis for the denominator could be any of the prepolitical variables. We do not think of it, however, as a political characteristic—as the equivalent, for instance, of party registration or political safeness. The proportion of people in the district who have to be included would be a subjective judgment—"enough" so that the congressman saw his geographical constituency as more homogeneous than heterogeneous, or vice versa. All we can say is that the less actual or potential conflict he sees among district interests, the more likely he is to see his district as homogeneous. Another indicator might be the extent to which the geographical constituency is congruent with a natural community. Districts that are purely artificial (sometimes purely political) creations of districting practices, and which pay no attention to pre-existing communities of interest are more likely to be heterogeneous. Pre-existing communities or natural communities are more likely to have such homogenizing ties as common sources of communication, common organizations, and common traditions.

The Supporters: The Re-election Constituency

Within his geographical constituency, each congressman perceives a smaller, explicitly political constituency. It is composed of the people he thinks vote for him. And we shall refer to it as his *re-election constituency*. As he moves about the district, a House member continually draws the distinction between those who vote for him and those who do not. "I do well here"; "I run poorly here." "This group supports me"; "this group does not." By distinguishing supporters from nonsupporters, he articulates his baseline political perception.

House members seem to use two starting points—one cross-sectional and the other longitudinal—in shaping this perception. First, by a process of inclusion and exclusion, they come to a rough approximation of the upper and lower ranges of the re-election constituency. That is to say, there are some votes a member believes he almost always gets; there are other votes he believes he almost never gets. One of the core elements of any such distinction is the perceived partisan component of the vote—party identification as revealed in registration or poll figures and party voting. "My district registers only 37 per cent Republican. They have no place else to go. My problem is, how can I get enough Democratic votes to win the general election?" Another element is the political tendencies of various demographic groupings.

> My supporters are Democrats, farmers, labor—a DFL operation—with some academic types. . . . My opposition tends to be the main street hardware dealer. I look at that kind of guy in a stable town, where the newspaper runs the community—the typical school board member in the rural part of the district— that's the kind of guy I'll never get. At the opposite end of the scale is the country club set. I'll sure as hell never get them, either.

Starting with people he sees, very generally, as his supporters, and leaving aside people he sees, equally generally, as his nonsupporters, each congressman fashions a view of the people who give him his victories at the polls.

The second starting point for thinking about the re-election constituency is the congressman's idea of who voted for him "last time." Starting with that perception, he adds or subtracts incrementally on the basis of changes that will have taken place (or could be made by him to take place) between "last time" and "next time." It helps him to think about his re-election constituency this way because that is about the only certainty he operates with—he won last time. And the process by which his desire for re-election gets translated into his perception of a re-election constituency is filled with uncertainty. At least that is my strong impression. House members see re-election uncertainty where political scientists would fail to unearth a single objective indicator of it. For one thing, their perceptions of their supporters and nonsupporters are quite diffuse. They rarely feel certain just who did vote for them last time. And even if they do feel fairly sure about that, they may perceive population shifts that threaten established calculations. In the years of my travels, moreover, the threat of redistricting has added enormous uncertainty to the make-up of some re-election constituencies. In every district, too, there is the uncertainty which follows an unforeseen external event—recession, inflation, Watergate.

Of all the many sources of uncertainty, the most constant—and usually the greatest—involves the electoral challenger. For it is the challenger who holds the most potential for altering any calculation involving those who voted for the congressman "last time." "This time's" challenger may have very different sources of political strength from "last time's" challenger. Often, one of the major off-year uncertainties is whether or not the last challenger will try again. While it is true that House members campaign all the time, "the campaign" can be said to start only when the challenger is known. At that point, a redefinition of the re-election constituency may have to take place. If the challenger is chosen by primary, for example, the congressman may inherit support from the loser. A conservative southern Republican, waiting for the Democratic primary to determine whether his challenger would be a black or a white (both liberal), wondered about the shape of his re-election constituency:

It depends on my opponent. Last time, my opponent (a white moderate) and I split many groups. Many business people who might have supported me, split up. If I have a liberal opponent, all the business community will support me. . . . If the black man is my opponent, I should get more Democratic votes than I got before. He can't do any better there than the man I beat before. Except for a smattering of liberals and radicals around the colleges, I will do better than last time with the whites. . . . The black vote is 20 per cent and they vote right down the line Democratic. I have to concede the black vote. There's nothing I can do about it. . . . [But] against a white liberal, I would get some of the black vote.

The shaping of perceptions proceeds under conditions of considerable uncertainty.

The Strongest Supporters: The Primary Constituency

In thinking about their political condition, House members make distinctions within their re-election constituency—thus giving us a third, still smaller concentric circle. Having distinguished between their nonsupporters and their supporters, they further distinguish between their routine or temporary supporters and their very strongest supporters. Routine supporters only vote for them, often merely following party identification; but others will support them with a special degree of intensity. Temporary supporters back them as the best available alternative; but others will support them regardless of who the challenger may be. Within each re-election constituency are nested these "others"—a constituency perceived as "my strongest supporters," "my hard core support," "my loyalists," "my true believers," "my political base." We shall think of these people as the ones each congressman believes would provide his best line of electoral defense in a primary contest, and label them *the primary constituency*. It will probably include the earliest of his supporters—those who recruited him and those who tendered identifiably strong support in his first campaign—thus, providing another reason for calculating on the basis of "last time." From its ranks will most likely come the bulk of his financial help and his volunteer workers. From its ranks will least likely come an electoral challenger.

A protected congressional seat is as much one protected from primary defeat as from general election defeat. And a primary constituency is something every congressman must have.

Everybody needs some group which is strongly for him—especially in a primary. You can win a primary with 25,000 zealots. . . . The most exquisite case I can give you was in the very early war years. I had very strong support from the anti-war people. They were my strongest supporters and they made up about 5 per cent of the district.

The primary constituency, I would guess, draws a special measure of a congressman's interest; and it should, therefore, draw a special measure of ours. But it is not easy to delineate—for us or for them. Asked to describe his "very strongest supporters," one member replied, "That's the hardest question anyone has to answer." The primary constituency is more subtly shaded than the re-election constituency, where voting provides an objective membership test. Loyalty is not the most predictable of political qualities. And all politicians resist drawing invidious distinctions among their various supporters, as if it were borrowing trouble to begin classifying people according to fidelity. House members who have worried about or fought a primary recently may find it somewhat easier. So too may those with heterogeneous districts whose diverse elements invite differentiation. Despite some difficulty, most members—because it is politically prudent to do so—make some such distinction, in speech or in action or both. By talking to them and watching them, we can begin to understand what those distinctions are.

Here are two answers to the question, "Who are your very strongest supporters?"

> My strongest supporters are the working class—the blacks and labor, organized labor. And the people who were in my state legislative district, of course. The fifth ward is low-income, working class and is my base of support. I grew up there; I have my law office there; and I still live there. The white businessmen who are supporting me now are late converts—very late. They support me as the least of two evils. They are not a strong base of support. They know it and I know it.

> I have a circle of strong labor supporters and another circle of strong business supporters. . . . They will 'fight, bleed and die' for me, but in different ways. Labor gives you the manpower and the workers up front. You need them just as much as you need the guy with the two-acre yard to hold a lawn party to raise money. The labor guy loses a day's pay on election day. The business guy gets his nice lawn tramped over and chewed up. Each makes a commitment to you in his own way. You need them both.

Each description reveals the working politician's penchant for inclusive thinking. Each tells us something about a primary constituency, but each leaves plenty of room for added refinements.

The best way to make such refinements is to observe the congressman as he comes in contact with the various elements of his re-election constituency. Both he and they act in ways that help delineate the "very strongest supporters." For example, the author of the second comment above drew a standing ovation when he was introduced at the Labor Temple. During his speech, he spoke directly to individuals in the audience. "Kenny, it's good to see you here. Ben, you be sure and keep in touch." Afterward, he lingered for an hour drinking beer and eating salami. At a businessman's annual Christmas luncheon the next day, he received neither an introduction nor applause when the main speaker acknowledged his presence, saying, "I see our congressman is here; and I use the term 'our' loosely." This congressman's "circle of strong labor supporters" appears to be larger than his "circle of strong business supporters." And the congressman, for his part, seemed much more at home with the first group than he did with the second.

Like other observers of American politics, I have found this idea of "at homeness" a useful one in helping me to map the relationship between politicians and constituents—in this case the perception of a primary constituency. House members sometimes talk in this language about the groups they encounter:

> I was born on the flat plains, and I feel a lot better in the plains area than in the mountain country. I don't know why it is. As much as I like Al [whom we had just lunched with in a mountain town], I'm still not comfortable with him. I'm no cowboy. But when I'm out there on that flat land with those ranchers and wheat farmers, standing around trading insults and jibes and telling stories, I feel better. That's the place where I click.

It is also the place where he wins elections—his primary constituency. "That's my strong area. I won by a big margin and offset my losses. If I win next time, that's where I'll win it—on the plains." Obviously, there is no one-to-one relationship between the groups with whom a congressman acts and feels most at home and his primary constituency. But it does provide a pretty good unobtrusive clue. So I found myself fashioning a highly subjective "at homeness index" to rank the degree to which each congressman seems to have support from and rapport with each group.

I recall, for example, watching a man whose constituency is dominantly Jewish participating in an afternoon installation-of-officers ceremony at a Young Men's Hebrew Association attended by about forty civic leaders of the local community. He drank some spiked punch, began the festivities by saying, "I'm probably the first tipsy installation officer you ever had," told an emotional story about his own dependence on the Jewish "Y," and traded banter with his friends in the audience throughout the proceedings. That evening as we prepared to meet with yet another and much larger (Democratic party) group, I asked where we were going. He said, "We're going to a shitty restaurant to have a shitty meal with a shitty organization and have a shitty time." And he did—from high to low on the "at homeness index." On the way home, after the meal, he talked about the group.

> Ethnically, most of them are with me. But I don't always support the party candidate, and they can't stand that. . . . This group and half the other party groups in the district are against me. But they don't want to be against me too strongly for fear I might go into a primary and beat them. So self-preservation wins out. . . . They know they can't beat me.

Both groups are Jewish. The evening group was a part of his re-election constituency, but not his primary constituency. The afternoon group was a part of both.

The Intimates: The Personal Constituency

Within the primary constituency, each member perceives still a fourth, and final, concentric circle. These are the few individuals whose relationship with him is so personal and so intimate that their relevance to him cannot be captured by their inclusion in any description of "very strongest supporters."

In some cases they are his closest political advisers and confidants. In other cases, they are people from whom he draws emotional sustenance for his political work. We shall think of these people as his *personal constituency*.

One Sunday afternoon, I sat in the living room of a congressman's chief district staff assistant watching an NFL football game—with the congressman, the district aide, the state assemblyman from the congressman's home county, and the district attorney of the same county. Between plays, at halftime and over beer and cheese, the four friends discussed every aspect of the congressman's campaign, listened to and commented on his taped radio spots, analyzed several newspaper reports, discussed local and national personalities, relived old political campaigns and hijinks, discussed their respective political ambitions. Ostensibly they were watching the football game; actually the congressman was exchanging political advice, information, and perspectives with three of his six or seven oldest and closest political associates.

Another congressman begins his weekends at home by having a Saturday morning 7:30 coffee and doughnut breakfast in a cafe on the main street of his home town with a small group of old friends from the Rotary Club. The morning I was there, the congressman, a retired bank manager, a hardware store owner, a high school science teacher, a retired judge, and a past president of the city council gossiped and joked about local matters—the county historian, the library, the board of education, the churches and their lawns—for an hour. "I guess you can see what an institution this is," he said as we left. "You have no idea how invaluable these meetings are for me. They keep me in touch with my home base. If you don't keep your home base, you don't have anything."

The personal constituency is, doubtless, the most idiosyncratic of the several constituencies. Not all members will open it up to the outside observer. Nine of the seventeen did, however; and in doing so, he usually revealed a side of his personality not seen by the rest of his constituencies. "I'm really very reserved, and I don't feel at home with most groups—only with five or six friends," said the congressman after the football game. The relationship probably has both political and emotional dimensions. But beyond that, it is hard to generalize, except to say that the personal constituency needs to be identified if our understanding of the congressman's view of his constituency is to be complete.

In sum, my impression is that House members perceive four constituencies—geographical, re-election, primary, and personal—each one nesting within the previous one.

Political Support and Home Style

What, then, do these perceptions have to do with a House member's behavior? Our conventional paraphrase of this question would read: [W]hat do these perceptions have to do with behavior at the other end of the line—in Washington? But the concern that disciplines the perceptions we have been talking about is neither first nor foremost a Washington-oriented concern. It is a concern for political support at home. It is a concern for the scope of that support—which decreases as one moves from the geographical to the personal constituency. It is a concern for the stability of that support—which increases as one moves from the geographical to the personal constituency. And it ultimately issues in a concern for manipulating scopes and intensities in order to win and hold a sufficient amount of support to win elections. Representatives, and prospective representatives, think about their constituencies because they seek support there. They want to get nominated and elected, then renominated and re-elected. For most members of Congress most of the time, this electoral goal is primary. It is the prerequisite for a congressional career and, hence, for the pursuit of other goals. And the electoral goal is achieved—first and last—not in Washington but at home.

Of course, House members do many things in Washington that affect their electoral support at home. Political scientists interpret a great deal of their behavior in Washington in exactly that way—particularly their roll-call votes. Obviously, a congressman's perception of his several constituencies will affect such things as his roll-call voting, and we could, if we wished, study the effect. Indeed, that is the very direction in which our conditioned research reflexes would normally carry this investigation. But my experience has turned me in another—though not, as we shall see an unrelated—direction. I have been watching House members work to maintain or enlarge their political support at home, by going to the district and doing things there.

Our Washington-centered research has caused us systematically to underestimate the proportion of their working time House members spend in their districts. As a result, we have also underestimated its perceived importance to them. In all our studies of congressional time allocation, time spent outside of Washington is left out of the analysis. So, we end up analyzing "the average work week of a congressman" by comparing the amounts of time he spends in committee work, on the floor, doing research, handling constituent problems—but all of it in Washington. Nine of my members whose appointment and travel records I have checked carefully for the year 1973—a nonelection year—averaged 28 trips to the district and spent an average of 101 working (not traveling) days in their districts that year. A survey conducted in 419 House offices covering 1973, indicates that the average number of trips home (not counting recesses) was 35 and the number of days spent in the district during 1973 (counting recesses) was 138. No fewer than 131, nearly one-third, of the 419 members went home to their districts *every single weekend*. Obviously, the direct personal cultivation of their various constituencies takes a great deal of their time; and they must think it is worth it in terms of winning and holding political support. If it is worth *their* time to go home so much, it is worth *our* time to take a commensurate degree of interest in what they do there and why.

As they cultivate their constituencies, House members display what I shall call their *home style*. When they discuss the importance of what they are doing, they are discussing the importance of *home style* to the achievement of their electoral goal. At this stage of the research, the surest generalization one can make about home style is that there are as many varieties as there are members of Congress. "Each of us has his own formula—a truth that is true for him," said one. It will take a good deal more immersion and cogitation before I can improve upon that summary comment. At this point, however, three ingredients of home style appear to be worth looking at. They are: first, the congressman's allocation of his personal resources and those of his office; second, the congressman's presentation of self; and third, the congressman's explanation of his Washington activity. Every congressman allocates, presents, and explains. The amalgam of these three activities for any given representative constitutes (for now, at least) his home style. His home style, we expect, will be affected by his perception of his four constituencies.

* * *

It may be, that the congressman's effectiveness in Washington is vitally influenced by the pattern of support he has developed at home and by the allocational, presentational, and explanatory styles he displays there. To put the point most strongly, perhaps we cannot understand his Washington activity without first understanding his perception of his constituencies and the home style he uses to cultivate their support.

No matter how supportive of one another their Washington and home activities may be, House members still face constant tension between them. Members cannot be in two places at once. They cannot achieve legislative competence and maintain constituency contact, both to an optimal degree. The tension is not likely to abate. The legislative workload and the demand for legislative expertise are growing. And the problems of maintaining meaningful contact with their several constituencies— which may make different demands upon them—are also growing. Years ago, House members returned home for months at a time to live with their supportive constituencies, soak up the home atmosphere, absorb local problems at first hand. Today, they race home for a day, a weekend, a week at a time. The citizen demand for access, for communication, for the establishment of trust is as great as ever. The political necessity and the representational desirability of going home is as great as ever. So members of Congress go home. But the quality of their contact has deteriorated. It is harder to sustain a genuine two-way relationship—of a policy or an extra-policy sort—than it once was. They worry about it and as they do, the strain and frustration of the job increases. Many cope; others retire.

* * *

Our professional neglect of the home relationship has probably contributed to a more general neglect of the representational side of Congress's institutional capabilities. At least it does seem to be the case that the more one focuses on the home activities of its members, the more one comes to appreciate the representative strengths and possibilities of Congress. Congress *is* the most representative of our national political institutions. It mirrors much of our national diversity, and its members maintain contact with a variety of constituencies at home. While its representative strengths surely contribute to its deserved reputation as our slow institution, the same representative strengths give it the potential for acquiring a reputation as our fair institution. In a period of our national life when citizen sacrifice will be called for, what we shall be needing from our political institutions are not quick decisions, but fair decisions. * * *

Members should participate in consensus building in Washington; they should accept some responsibility for the collective performance of Congress; and they should explain to their constituents what an institution that is both collective and fair requires of its individual members.

*   *   *

DISCUSSION QUESTIONS

1. Do you agree with Fenno that Congress is the most representative of our national political institutions? If so, does Fenno's argument help address Hibbing and Theiss-Morse's conclusion that Congress may be too responsive (see next article)?

2. Think about your own member of Congress. Does he or she have a strong presence in the district, or does your member seem more like a Washington politician?

3. What do you see as the relationship between how members operate in Washington and what they do in their districts? Should the two be closely tied together (as in Fenno's account of "explaining Washington activity"), or should they be more separate (as with an extensive district-based constituency service operation)?

25

"Too Much of a Good Thing: More Representative Is Not Necessarily Better"

John R. Hibbing and Elizabeth Theiss-Morse

David R. Mayhew describes an institution that should be highly responsive to voters. If members of Congress want to get re-elected, they need to do what their constituents want them to do. However, John R. Hibbing and Elizabeth Theiss-Morse argue that having institutions that are too representative may be "too much of a good thing." That is, it may not be in the nation's interest to always do what the public wants, especially when it comes to issues of institutional reform. On questions of reform, the public is usually convinced that the only thing preventing ideal policies is that the "people in power" are serving their own interests rather than the public's interests. According to this view, the obvious—but wrong, according to Hibbing and Theiss-Morse—solution is to weaken political institutions through "reforms" such as term limits, reducing the salaries of members of Congress, and requiring Congress to balance the federal budget every year. Hibbing and Theiss-Morse argue that these reforms might make people even more disillusioned when they discover that weakening Congress will not solve our nation's problems.

The authors also argue that the public generally does not have a very realistic understanding of the inherent nature of conflict in the political process. The public believes that there is substantial consensus on most issues and that only small "fringe" groups disagree on a broad range of issues. If this were true, frustration with Congress would certainly be understandable. But in reality, as the authors point out, the nation is deeply divided about the proper course of action. This makes conflict and compromise an inherent part of the legislative process and, at the same time, dims the prospects for simple reforms.

Reform sentiments are much in evidence on the American political scene as we approach the end of the [twentieth] century, and improving the way public opinion is represented in political institutions is often the major motivation of reformers. This is clear * * * from the activities of contemporary political elites, and from the mood of ordinary people. Gross dissatisfaction exists with the nature of representation perceived to be offered by the modern political system. People believe the political process has been commandeered by narrow special interests and by political parties

whose sole aim is to contradict the other political party. Given the centrality of representation in the U.S. polity, the organizers and contributors to
this symposium are to be commended. It is laudable to want to consider
ways of improving the system and, thereby, making people happier with
their government. Many of the ideas described in the accompanying essays
have considerable merit.

We do, however, wish to raise two important cautions: one briefly and the
second in greater detail. Perhaps these cautions are not needed; the authors
of the accompanying pieces are almost certainly aware of them. Still, general
debate often neglects these two points. Therefore, quite apart from whether
it is a good idea or a bad idea, say, to reform campaign finance, enact term
limits, or move toward proportional representation and away from single-
member districts, it is important * * * to keep in mind that 1) "because the
people want them" is not a good justification for adopting procedural
reforms and 2) actual enactment of the reforms craved by the people will not
necessarily leave us with a system that is more liked even by the people who
asked for the reforms in the first place. We take each point in turn.

Ignoring the People's Voice on Process Matters Is Not Evil

It would be easy at this point to slip into a discussion of the political acumen possessed by the American public and, relatedly, of the extent to which
elected officials and political institutions should listen to the people. But
such a discussion has been going on at least since the time of Plato and it
is unlikely we would add much to it here. Instead, we merely wish to point
out that, whatever the overall talents of the rank and file, political change
in the realm of process should *not* be as sensitive to the public's wishes as
political change in the realm of policy.

It is one thing to maintain that in a democracy the people should get
welfare reform if they want it. It is quite another to maintain that those
same people should get term limits if they want them. Process needs to
have some relative permanence, some "stickiness." This is the *definiens* of
institutional processes. Without this trait, policy legitimacy would be compromised. The U.S. Constitution (like all constitutions) drives home this
contention by including much on process (vetoes, impeachments, representational arrangements, terms of officials, minimum qualifications for
holding particular offices, etc.) and precious little about policy. What policy proclamations *are* to be found in the Constitution have faced a strong
likelihood of being reversed in subsequent actions (slavery and the Thirteenth Amendment; tax policy and the Sixteenth Amendment; Prohibition
and the Twenty-First Amendment). Constitutions are written not to
enshrine policy but to enshrine a system that will then make policy. These
systemic structures should not be subjected lightly to popular whimsy.

The framers took great efforts to insulate processes from the momentary
fancies of the people; specifically, they made amending the Constitution

difficult. It is not unusual for reformers, therefore, to run up against the Constitution and its main interpreters—the courts. Witness recent decisions undermining the ability of citizens to impose legislative term limits on members of Congress save by constitutional amendment. This uphill battle to enact procedural reform is precisely what the Founders intended—and they were wise to do so.

It may be that the people's will should be reflected directly in public policy, perhaps through initiatives or, less drastically, through the actions of citizen-legislators who act as delegates rather than Burkean trustees. But this does not mean that the rules of the system themselves should change with public preferences in the same way health care policy should change with public preferences.

There may be many good reasons to change the processes of government—possibly by making government more representative—but a persuasive defense of process reforms is *not* embedded in the claim that the people are desirous of such reform. Just as the Bill of Rights does not permit a simple majority of the people to make decisions that will restrict basic rights, so the rest of the Constitution does not permit a simple majority of the people to alter willy-nilly the processes of government. There are good reasons for such arrangements.

Be Careful What You Wish For

One important reason we should be glad ordinary people are not in a position to leave their every mark on questions of political process and institutional design is the very good possibility that people will not be happy with the reforms they themselves advocate. The people generally clamor for reforms that would weaken institutions and strengthen the role of the people themselves in policy decisions. They advocate people's courts, an increased number of popular initiatives and referenda, devolution of authority to institutions "closer" to the people, term limits, staff cuts, emaciating the bureaucracy, elimination of committees, cessation of contact between interest groups and elected officials, and a weakening of political parties. These changes would clear the way for people to have greater influence on decisions, and this is what the people want, right?

Actually, our research suggests this is *not* what the people really want. The public does not desire direct democracy; it is not even clear that people desire democracy at all, although they are quite convinced they do. People want no part of a national direct democracy in which they would be asked to register their preferences, probably electronically, on important issues of the day. Proposals for such procedures are received warmly by a very small minority of citizens. Observers who notice the public's enthusiasm for virtually every populist notion sometimes go the next step of assuming the public wants direct democracy. This is simply an inaccurate assumption.

However, the public *does* want institutions to be transformed into something much closer to the people. The public sees a big disconnect between how they want representation to work and how they believe it is working. Strong support of populist government (not direct democracy) has been detected in innumerable polls conducted during the last couple of decades. That the public looks favorably upon this process agenda is beyond dispute. A national survey we conducted in 1992 found strong support for reforms that would limit the impact of the Washington scene on members of Congress. For example, seven out of 10 respondents supported a reduction in congressional salaries, eight out of 10 supported term limitations, and nine out of 10 supported a balanced-budget amendment. What ties these reforms together is the public's desire to make elected officials more like ordinary people. In focus groups we conducted at the same time as the survey, participants stated many times that elected officials in Washington had lost touch with the people. They supported reforms believed to encourage officials to start keeping in touch. Elected officials should balance the budget just like the people back home. Elected officials should live off modest salaries just like the people back home. And elected officials should face the prospect of getting a real job back home rather than staying in Washington for years and years. These reforms would force elected officials to understand the needs of their constituents rather than get swept up in the money and power that run Washington.

If these reforms were put into place, would the public suddenly love Congress? We do not think so. Certain reforms, such as campaign finance reform, may help, since they would diminish the perception that money rules politics in Washington. But the main reason the public is disgruntled with Congress and with politics in Washington is because they are dissatisfied with the processes intrinsic to the operation of a democratic political system—debates, compromises, conflicting information, inefficiency, and slowness. This argument may seem odd on its face, so in the next few paragraphs we provide our interpretation of why the public questions the need for democratic processes.

The public operates under the erroneous assumption that the majority of the American people agrees on policy matters. In focus groups we conducted in 1997, participants adamantly stated that "80 percent of the American people agree on what needs to be done [about serious societal problems], but it's the other 20 percent who have the power." This pervasive and persistent belief in the existence of popular consensus on tough policy issues is, of course, grossly mistaken. Virtually every well-worded survey question dealing with salient policy issues of the day reveals deep divisions in the American public. From welfare reform to health care; from remaining in Bosnia to the taxes-services trade-off; from a constitutional amendment on flag desecration to the situations in which abortion is believed to be properly permitted, the people are at odds with each other.

This level of popular disagreement would be quite unremarkable except for the fact that the people will not admit that the disagreement actually exists. Instead, people project their own particular views, however ill-formed, onto a clear majority of other "real" people. Those (allegedly) few people who allow it to be known that they do not hold these views are dismissed as radical and noisy fringe elements that are accorded far too much influence by polemical parties, self-serving special interests, and spineless, out-of-touch elected officials. Thus, the desire to move the locus of decision making closer to the people is based on a faulty assumption right off the bat. Many believe that if decisions emanated from the people themselves, we would get a welcome break from the fractious politics created by politicians and institutions. Pastoral, common-sensical solutions will instead quietly begin to find their way into the statute books. The artificial conflict to which we have unfortunately become accustomed will be no more and we can then begin to solve problems.

Given people's widespread belief in popular consensus, it is no wonder they despise the existing structure of governmental institutions. All that these institutions—and the people filling them—do is obscure the will of the people by making it look as though there is a great deal of divisiveness afoot. Who then can condone debate and compromise among elected officials if these processes only give disproportionate weight to nefarious fringe elements that are intent upon subverting the desires of healthy, red-blooded Americans? Who then can condone inefficiency and slowness when we all agree on what needs to be done and politicians ought just to do it? Democratic processes merely get in the way. People react positively to the idea that we ought to run government like a business—it would be efficient, frugal, and quick to respond to problems. Of course, what people tend not to realize is that it would also be undemocratic.

Too many people do not understand political conflict: they have not been taught to deal with it; they have not come to realize it is a natural part of a culture such as ours. When they are confronted with it, they conclude it is an indication something is woefully amiss and in need of correction. They jump at any solution perceived to have the potential of reducing conflict; solutions such as giving authority over to potentially autocratic and hierarchical business-like arrangements or to mythically consensual ordinary people.

Our fear is that, if the people were actually given what they want, they might soon be even more disillusioned with the political system than ever. Suppose people *were* made to feel more represented than they are now; suppose authority *were* really pushed toward the common person. The first thing people would learn is that these changes will have done nothing to eliminate political conflict. The deep policy divisions that polls now reveal among the citizenry would be of more consequence since these very views would now be more determinative of public policy. Conflict would still be pervasive. Popular discontent would not have been ameliorated. Quite likely, people would quickly grow ever more cynical about the potential for reform to accomplish what they want it to accomplish.

Instead of allowing the people to strive for the impossible—an open and inclusive democracy that is devoid of conflict—we need to educate the people about the unrealistic nature of their desires. Instead of giving the people every reform for which they agitate, we need to get them to see where their wishes, if granted, are likely to lead them. The people pay lip service to democracy but that is the extent of it. They claim to love democracy more than life itself, but they only love the concept. They do not love the actual practice of democracy because it suggests differences, because it is ponderous, because it revolves around debate (bickering) and compromise (selling out) and divisions (gridlock).

Conclusion

We hasten to point out that we are not opposed to reforms. For what it is worth, we believe the United States polity could certainly benefit from selective modifications to current institutional arrangements. But we *are* opposed to the tendency of many ordinary people to try to enact reforms intended to weaken political institutions even though these same people evince no real plan describing where that power should be transferred. It is often assumed that the people are populists and that they therefore want power in their own hands. As we have indicated, they do not in actuality want power. They only want to know that they could have this power if they wanted it. They only want to know that this power is not being exercised by those who are in a position to use it to their own advantage. They only want decisions to be made nonconflictually. And they are willing to entertain a variety of possible structures (some far from democratic) if those reforms appear to offer hope of bringing about all these somewhat contradictory desires.

Altering representational arrangements should be considered. The current system can and must be improved. The campaign finance system is an embarrassment and the dispute over drawing oddly-shaped districts for the purpose of obtaining majority-minority districts lays bare the very real problems of single member districts. But we should not jump to enact all reforms simply because people think they want them. No one said that in a democracy the people would get to shape processes however they wanted. It is not inconsistent to have democratic governmental structures that are themselves rather impervious to popular sentiments for change in those procedures. What makes the system democratic is the ability of people to influence policy, not the ability of people to influence process.

This is fortunate because the people's ideas about process are fundamentally flawed. People (understandably) think well of the American public writ large, and people (understandably) dislike conflict, so people (nonsensically) assume the two cannot go together in spite of the impressive array of factual evidence indicating that conflict and the American people—indeed any free people, as Madison so eloquently related in *Federalist 10*—go hand in hand. As a result of their misconception, the people will undoubtedly be quite dissatisfied with the actual consequences of most attempts to expand representation via campaign finance reform, term limits, or proportional representation. There may be good reasons to enact such reforms, but, we submit, neither a public likely to be suddenly pleased with the post-reform political system nor a public that is somehow deserving of a direct voice in process reform is one of them.

DISCUSSION QUESTIONS

1. In one of the more provocative claims in their article, Hibbing and Theiss-Morse say, "The public does not desire direct democracy; it is not even clear that people desire democracy at all, although they are quite convinced they do." Do you agree? What evidence do they provide to support this claim?

2. If the public had a more complex understanding of the political process, what types of reforms would it favor?

3. Is it possible to have a political system that is too responsive?

DEBATING THE ISSUES: HOW CAN CONGRESS BE REFORMED?

Congress is held in very low regard by the American public. For most of the past decade, polls show that less than 20 percent of the country approved of the job that Congress is doing (the brief exceptions were in President Trump's last year, when Congress passed COVID-19 relief, and in President Biden's first six months). Large majorities of Americans think that Congress is not serving their interests.

What can be done to fix Congress? All of the authors here believe that Congress must be reformed, but they have different takes on what should be done. Matt Ford is the most pessimistic, writing, "There is no single fix that could remedy all legislative woes nor is there a straightforward path to enacting them. Some problems are beyond the ability of any rule or law to change. Others may well be permanent." Ford discusses a range of reform proposals from groups such as Former Members of Congress, the American Political Science Association, and the FreedomWorks Foundation. He notes that common ground across the proposals includes a focus on the internal workings of Congress: how to improve the legislative process by returning more power to committees and individual members instead of leaving it with party leadership. Other more controversial ideas include reasserting power from the executive branch and restoring earmarks (often called pork-barrel spending). But Ford notes that none of this would do anything about the influence of the media, social media, and polarization on the politics in Washington.

Susan Davis reports on the recommendations of the House Select Committee on the Modernization of Congress (see the end of the reading for the full list). She is impressed that the House was able to come up with a comprehensive list of 97 recommendations that was unanimously approved by the bipartisan committee in the middle of deeply partisan conflict over the budget, the pandemic, and President Trump's impeachment. Some of the recommendations are very modest, such as modernizing House technology and improving constituency communication. Others are more ambitious (and align with the recommendations discussed by Matt Ford), such as strengthening Congress's powers relative to the president and the courts, as well as reforming the budget and appropriation process. Some are pie in the sky, such as "encouraging civility and bipartisanship in Congress." Interestingly, one controversial reform, bringing back earmarks, was not referred to by name but couched in more general language (item 85). Congress restored earmarks in the last session. The committee submitted a second round of recommendations in 2022, with a focus on staff, internships, accessibility, support agencies, and civility and collaboration.

One reform that critics of Congress have talked about for years is changing or getting rid of the filibuster in the Senate. Since the "filibuster track" was created in 1970, senators no longer need to hold the floor by talking when they want to stop a bill. They just announce their intent to filibuster, and a bill is taken off the agenda unless 60 senators vote to invoke cloture and bring the bill back to life. The filibuster was used to stop some of President Biden's agenda, such as voting rights reforms that would have provided more access to voting. The filibuster is viewed either as a tool of obstruction and gridlock or as an essential tool to protect the views of the minority party. However, Frances E. Lee and James M. Curry argue that the filibuster is rarely the source of gridlock—it is much more common that internal divisions within the majority party explain why legislation fails.

26

"How to Save Congress from Itself"

MATT FORD

The Republican-led Senate flew home without passing a bill to renew or extend its stimulus measure, raising the prospect that millions of Americans will face more economic hardship in the weeks and months ahead. Democrats in the House of Representatives passed their own version of a second stimulus bill in May. But Senate Majority Leader Mitch McConnell, President Donald Trump, and leading GOP senators have yet to coalesce to craft a counterproposal for further negotiation. Lawmakers have flatly failed in America's hour of need.

Part of the problem is that Senate Republicans appear to be ideologically incapable of doing their jobs. GOP discussions on another wave of economic stimulus have largely focused on shrinking the federal $600 unemployment supplement and narrowing other benefits, even as the economy shows signs of further collapse. "A strategy for the economy?" Indiana Senator Todd Young, a Republican, told the *New York Times* earlier this week. "That's not how economies work. [Trump] is not the Wizard of Oz, who controls the economy. Growth is created by innovators and entrepreneurs and rank and file workers, based on supply and demand."

Against this backdrop, I read through a new report released this week by the Association of Former Members of Congress, or FMC. Titled "Congress at a Crossroads," it takes a look at the forces that have bedeviled and hamstrung the legislative branch over the past few decades. The report, appropriately enough for the organization that drafted it, draws upon interviews with former members of Congress to give an insider's perspective of what's gone wrong. It broadly concludes that congressional leadership wields too much power, that fundraising and contributions have too much influence, and that lawmakers spend too little time building relationships with one another.

"The cumulative voice of these interviews portrays a Congress defined by earnest and hard-working representatives from across the political spectrum who are united by a shared dedication to serve both their communities and the national interest—but who are hamstrung by polarization, partisan distrust, political calculation, leadership pressure, institutional dysfunction, and too little encouragement to address it," the report said. "As the words of these former members detail, it is a complex and often conflicted institution—and one in need of significant change."

It's hard to imagine a more urgent moment than now for Congress to reassert itself as an active, representative force in American governance. But the FMC report, as well as two other reports on congressional reform released by Washington, D.C., think tanks earlier this year, also underscore how difficult it will be to rebuild Congress as a functional institution. There is no single fix that could remedy all legislative woes nor is there a straightforward path to enacting them. Some problems are beyond the ability of any rule or law to change. Others may well be permanent.

Perhaps the most feasible reforms are those that reshape the legislative process itself—not the constitutional path by which a bill becomes a law, of course, but the internal mechanisms of each legislative chamber as they write bills and hammer out compromises. In theory, Congress is supposed to fund the government each year through a series of bills crafted by the House and Senate Appropriations Committees. In practice, however, lawmakers have increasingly used "must-pass" continuing resolutions to keep the government open, essentially turning the budgetary process into a series of ticking clock stand-offs. Sometimes, the bomb goes off.

In a report on congressional reform released in January, a task force of the American Political Science Association, or APSA, partly blamed power shifts within each chamber for the dysfunction. "Relative power has shifted from committees to parties, as party leaders have centralized authority over the spending process at the expense of Appropriations committee and subcommittee chairs and rank-and-file members," the report noted. "Legislative compromises now tend to be orchestrated by leadership and their staff, limiting the influence of rank-and-file members in the legislative process." The result is a coercive process where most lawmakers must either vote for a bill where they had no influence or vote to partially shut down the government.

The APSA's task force avoided making recommendations where they could not reach a consensus on how to fix something, which makes the report somewhat more diagnostic than surgical. In January, however, the conservative FreedomWorks Foundation also released a report on congressional reform that delved into some of the possible solutions. It focuses more broadly on how legislators "ceded many of its constitutionally delegated powers to the executive branch and concentrated most of the rest in the hands of congressional leadership." Some of their proposals for regulatory reform and changes to the budgetary process will be met with skepticism from the left, as will their dismissal of the federal bureaucracy in general as an "unconstitutional fourth branch of government."

Despite these differences, there is some room for common ground. The FreedomWorks report's authors call for the repeal of the 2001 Authorization of Use of Military Force, or AUMF, as well as the War Powers Resolution reform that moves away from "mere consultation" when presidents carry out military strikes and instead imposes hard limits on a president's war-making authority without Congress's assent. They also call for Congress to claw back some of its authority over trade policy, reversing delegations to the executive branch that Trump used to wage a costly trade war with China and the European Union.

Perhaps the report's most ambitious proposals for reform are aimed at Congress's inner workings. Like the other two reports, the FreedomWorks report also expresses frustration about congressional leadership's tight grip over rank-and-file members, which it maintains through control over committee assignments, party fundraising efforts, and more subtle means of influence. The report called for the House to strictly enforce the rule that lawmakers get three days to read a bill before voting on it, reopening the amendment process for major legislation, giving minority parties an opportunity to amend the rules, and more. (Though it unfortunately opposes filibuster reform, the FreedomWorks report also supports a more open amendment process for Senate bills as well.)

These changes, the report concludes, would help restore the House to its proper constitutional role. "Ultimately, the House of Representatives by its nature will always behave as more of a populist, majoritarian body, but that should not mean that the entire power of legislating rests in the hands of just a few of its 435 elected representatives," the report said. "Restoring the ability of individual members to participate in the process and actually represent their constituents with their own local interests is of paramount importance for Congress to regain relevance. If instead we make all issues national and insist [on] monolithic party action, there is really no need for 435 local representatives."

Some of the best congressional reforms would actually overturn previous efforts at reform. Banning earmarks, for example, helped make Congress less effective by eliminating a means by which lawmakers could forge coalitions. "I would have done a lot for Obama if I got $30 million [for a local road]," one Republican ex-lawmaker told FMC, according to their report. The APSA report also recommended bringing back earmarks, citing the potential legislative benefits and the broad anecdotal support among members. The ban, they noted, only changed who decides which projects get funded. "Supporters [of ending the ban] note that eliminating earmarks has neither reduced overall spending nor eliminated political decision making," the APSA report noted. "Instead, the ban has only shifted power to the executive branch, since project-level decisions now get made by agency bureaucrats rather than by legislators."

After Republicans took the House in the 1994 midterms, Newt Gingrich and his allies enacted a wave of "reforms" that instead undermined Congress as an institution. Gingrich shortened the legislative week so that lawmakers could spend more time running for reelection in their home districts, which left far less time for actual lawmaking and legislative work. He oversaw deep cuts in member and committee staff budgets and closed Congress's Office of Technology Assessment, leaving lawmakers reliant on the executive branch and think tanks for policy development and analysis. Even the FreedomWorks report recognized that these changes, billed as part of an effort to fix Washington, only made things worse.

Perhaps Gingrich's worst contribution to Congress was the deep cultural shift he represented. He helped inaugurate an era where legislative battles became zero-sum fights between the two parties, where performative antics replaced substantive achievements as a means for political success, and where the base urge to hold power eclipsed all other considerations. In the FMC report, ex-lawmakers complained that the constant pressure to hold campaign events and solicit contributions from donors left little time for actual legislative work. "You are always raising money, and you're always dialing for dollars," said one. "It's a constant thing." The need to raise money, said another, limits time members have for socializing. It also takes away time and energy from what members can do "for their district, or their own community." Added another, "You're working on fundraising when you go home a lot. You're working over here, you go across the street, you make phone calls, you do whatever you gotta do."

One even argued that a reason why leadership frowns upon open rules—allowing amendments on the floor—is it would limit "time to go across the street" to call centers where they raise money. "The closed rule accommodates the money in politics" by giving members time to fundraise. "You have all these members of Congress sitting over there in these call centers like a bunch of middle-level telemarketers dialing for dollars instead of doing the work of the Congress."

Gingrich can't be blamed for all of these woes, of course. Twenty-four-hour cable networks, as well as the rise of the internet and social media, helped transform Congress from a legislative body into a theatrical stage for firing up the base and catching donors' attention. Hyperpolarization left lawmakers with little incentive to compromise with one another and even less ground upon which they could cooperate at all. The GOP's zeal for voter suppression and partisan gerrymandering over the past decade left its legislators more beholden to a small primary electorate instead of their constituents as a whole. And the Roberts Court's gutting of campaign-finance laws fueled an arms race in donations among lawmakers, leaving them even more beholden to wealthy and well-connected contributors.

All of that brings us to the central problem with congressional reform. Members of Congress could hire more staff, allow more bill amendments, spend more time in Washington, and get to know each other better. Deeper structural reforms—abolishing gerrymandering, for example, or passing sweeping campaign-finance reform—are theoretically feasible but incredibly difficult to enact in practice. And while individual lawmakers could try to take personal steps to improve Capitol Hill's culture, Congress can't actually abolish Fox News or Twitter, and no legislation or rule change could reverse the broader shifts in American politics that brought the country to this point.

It's hard to not feel despondent about the future of the American experiment after taking stock of its self-inflicted wounds. But that doesn't make the task of repairing it any less vital. The status quo, where billionaire-backed lawmakers complain about the national debt while millions of Americans prepare to be evicted, is no longer sustainable. A half-functioning Congress may not be enough to prevent or alleviate what America is about to go through. But it's hard to imagine that it will do a worse job than the Congress we already have.

27

"A Tale of Bipartisanship in Congress—No, Seriously"

Susan Davis

Last year, when House Minority Leader Kevin McCarthy asked Rep. Tom Graves, R-Ga., to help lead a new committee charged with investigating how to modernize the U.S. House, Graves cynically turned him down.

"I had declined it with the—I guess it's a sad acceptance that this was just going to be another failed attempt by Congress to say they're going to do something that they ultimately don't do," said Graves, who retired from Congress in early October. "And boy, was I pleasantly surprised by the outcome and the work of this committee."

He relented and, along with Rep. Derek Kilmer, D-Wash., set out with a joint mandate to examine ways to make the House more modern, more efficient, and more bipartisan. Kilmer knew it would not be easy.

"The fact that Congress, according to recent polling, is held in lower regard than head lice, colonoscopies and the band Nickelback is some indication that the public doesn't hold Congress in high regard," he said.

Graves and Kilmer spoke to NPR in a joint Zoom interview shortly before Christmas.

The Recommendations

After nearly two years, the six Democrats and six Republicans on the Select Committee on the Modernization of Congress put out a final report in October with 97 unanimous recommendations on how to change the House.

A lot of them involve logistics, like how to better schedule committee hearings. Others are more controversial, like bringing back some form of earmark spending. And some might elicit eye rolls, like designating bipartisan space in the Capitol where lawmakers can just hang out.

Graves said the committee's work was all the more notable because they were able to find broad agreement during these hyperpartisan times. "It all occurred during the longest government shutdown in the history of our country. It occurred during impeachment. It occurred during a pandemic," he said.

It has already had some impact. House Majority Leader Steny Hoyer's 2021 work calendar reflected the committee's recommendations for a more balanced schedule, and new member orientation last month included a new bipartisan session on decorum. House Democrats are also seriously considering bringing back a form of earmarks, which allowed legislators to designate funding for specific projects, in the new Congress.

Playing Nice

Two years studying how Congress works has given both men some perspective—and hope—for the new Congress, in which both chambers will be narrowly divided. "Tighter majorities could produce better results. It's a forced requirement to have to work together," Graves said.

House Democrats, Kilmer said, will have to be kinder to the Republican minority. "To some degree, Congress is not dissimilar to having a new puppy," he explained. "If you are not able to constructively engage members, particularly the minority, they chew the furniture."

Republicans, Graves said, need to negotiate in good faith with President-elect Joe Biden—something, he acknowledges, his party doesn't always do. "My hope is that members from my party will embrace that and will look for that as an opportunity to do something that, quite frankly, we didn't do as well as we could have when Barack Obama was president," he said.

Kilmer said good faith won't come easy, especially after over half of House Republicans supported a failed lawsuit to get the Supreme Court to overturn the presidential election results. "That's not to say that Congress can't get past that, but it would be dishonest of me to say that that's not something that people are concerned about," he said.

Both men readily agree that there's no House rules change or law that will suddenly make Congress work better. Kilmer said the hardest thing to change is how members treat one another and the institution.

"We did something very unusual on this committee, and that is we tried to change norms. Everything we recommended that committees do to encourage more bipartisan collaboration to be more productive, we actually modeled ourselves," he said. For example, Republicans and Democrats sat intermingled in committee hearings for this committee. In other committees, Republicans and Democrats sit on opposite sides.

The committee was set to expire at the end of this Congress' term, but Kilmer asked House Speaker Nancy Pelosi, D-Calif., to keep it going. She agreed right before Christmas in a statement stating the panel "will continue to champion the best ideas that ensure that the People's House can carry on its vital work now and for years to come."

Pelosi has tapped Kilmer to continue to chair the committee. Graves retired this year, so McCarthy will have to appoint someone else, but Graves told NPR he supports the committee continuing. The work of fixing Congress is never done.

Recommendations of the Select Committee on Modernization of Congress

Make Congress More Effective, Efficient, and Transparent

1. Streamline the bill-writing process to save time and reduce mistakes.
2. Finalize a new system that allows the American people to easily track how amendments change legislation and the impact of proposed legislation to current law.
3. Make it easier to know who is lobbying Congress and what they're lobbying for.
4. One-click access to a list of agencies and programs that have expired and need Congressional attention.
5. One-click access to see how Members of Congress vote in committees.

Streamline and Reorganize House Human Resources

6. Create a one-stop shop Human Resources HUB for Member, committee, and leadership staff.
7. Make permanent the Office of Diversity and Inclusion.
8. Examine and update the staff payroll system from monthly to semimonthly.
9. Raise the cap on the number of staff in Member offices.
10. Regularly survey staff on improving pay and benefits.

Overhaul the Onboarding Process and Provide Continuing Education for Members

11. Allow newly elected Members to hire and pay one transition staff member.
12. Offer new-Member orientation in a nonpartisan way.
13. Make new-Member orientation more comprehensive.
14. Promote civility during new-Member orientation.
15. Create a Congressional Leadership Academy to offer training for Members.
16. Make cybersecurity training mandatory for Members.

Modernize and Revitalize House Technology

17. Reestablish and restructure an improved Office of Technology Assessment.
18. Improve IT services in the House by reforming House Information Resources (HIR).
19. Require House Information Resources (HIR) to prioritize certain technological improvements.
20. Require House Information Resources (HIR) to reform the approval process for outside technology vendors.
21. Require House Information Resources (HIR) to allow Member offices to test new technologies.
22. Create one point of contact for technology services for each Member office.
23. Create a customer service portal to improve technology services in the House.
24. Leverage bulk purchasing of the House by removing technology costs out of Member offices' budgets and moving into a centralized account.
25. Prioritize a "rapid response" program at the Congressional Research Service for nonpartisan fact sheets on key issues.
26. Develop a constituent engagement and services best practices HUB for Members.

Make the House Accessible to All Americans

27. Improve access to congressional websites for individuals with disabilities.
28. Require all broadcasts of House proceedings to provide closed caption service.
29. Require a review of the Capitol complex to determine accessibility challenges for individuals with disabilities.

Encourage Civility and Bipartisanship in Congress

30. Create a bipartisan Members-only space in the Capitol to encourage more collaboration across party lines.
31. Institute biennial bipartisan retreats for Members and their families at the start of each Congress.
32. Update committee policies to increase bipartisan learning opportunities for staff.
33. Establish bipartisan committee staff briefings and agenda-setting retreats to encourage better policy making and collaboration among Members.

Streamline Processes and Save Taxpayer Dollars

34. Update House procedures to allow members to electronically add or remove their name as a bill cosponsor.
35. Require Members to undergo emergency preparedness training to ensure our government is fully prepared in the event of a crisis.
36. Identify ways the House and Senate can streamline purchases and save taxpayer dollars.
37. Encourage House-wide bulk purchasing of goods and services to cut back on waste and inefficiency.
38. Update travel expenditure policies to improve efficiencies, and boost accountability and transparency.

Increase the Quality of Constituent Communication

39. Consolidate the regulations governing Member office communications, including digital communications, into one easy to find place.
40. Rename the House Commission on Mailing Standards, also known as the Franking Commission, the House Communications Standards Commission to reflect 21st Century communications.
41. Increase opportunities for constituents to communicate with their Representatives.
42. Increase accountability and tracking for all Member-sponsored communications mail.
43. Allow for faster correspondence between Representatives and their constituents.
44. Update House social media rules to allow for better communication online between Members of Congress and their followers.
45. Allow the public to better access and view the types of communication sent by Members of Congress to their constituents.

Maintain Continuity of Operations

46. Each office should have a continuity of operations plan, including minimum safety requirements and an emergency communications plan, that is made available to all staff so offices continue functioning for the public.
47. Ensure that staff have the most up-to-date technology and equipment to continue effectively working on behalf of constituents in the event of a disruption or emergency.
48. Establish regular maintenance plans for office technology, so the equipment and technology needed during remote operations and telework is functional.
49. Crisis communications guidelines for constituent communication, including outreach plans for extended telework periods, should be approved and shared with all Member offices.
50. To help streamline casework requests and help constituents better access federal agencies and resources, the House should implement a secure document management system, and provide digital forms and templates for public access.
51. The House should prioritize the approval of platforms that staff need for effective telework, and each individual staff member should have licensed access to the approved technology.
52. Committees should establish telework policies on a bipartisan basis.
53. The House should make permanent the option to electronically submit committee reports.
54. Expand the use of digital signatures for a majority of House business, including constituent communications.
55. Committees should develop bipartisan plans on how technology and innovative platforms can be best incorporated into daily work.
56. A bipartisan, bicameral task force should identify lessons learned during the COVID-19 pandemic and recommend continuity of Congress improvements.
57. Continuity, telework and cybersecurity training should be given to all new Members of Congress.

Improve the Congressional Schedule and Calendar

58. Establish specific committee-only meeting times when Congress is in session.
59. Create a common committee calendar portal to help with scheduling and reduce conflicts.
60. Establish specific days—or weeks—where committee work takes priority.
61. Ensure there are more work days spent working than traveling.

62. The congressional calendar should accommodate a bipartisan member retreat.

Boost Congressional Capacity

63. Offer staff certifications, in additions to trainings, through the nonpartisan Congressional Staff Academy.
64. Provide institution-wide, standard onboarding training for new employees, including required training.
65. Remove constituent communications costs from Member office budgets and create a share account for communications.
66. Revaluate the funding formula and increase the funds allocated to each Member office.
67. Establish a nonbinding, voluntary pay band system for House staff that includes a salary floor and average salary for each position in Member offices. Regular services should be done to ensure the most up-to-date salary information.
68. Expand access to health insurance for congressional staff.
69. Provide more financial stability for congressional staff enrolled in the federal student loan program.
70. Staff pay should be delinked from Member pay and a new cap specific to staff should be established.
71. Allow Congressional Member Organizations to access benefits, and hire one intern to help support their work.
72. Publish a list of active Congressional Member Organizations annually to ensure transparency in the policy making and caucus creation process.

Reclaim Article One Responsibilities

73. Incentivize committees to experiment with alternative hearing formats to encourage more bipartisan participation.
74. Committees should hire bipartisan staff approved by both the Chair and Ranking Member to promote strong institutional knowledge, evidence-based policy making, and a less partisan oversight agenda.
75. Committees should hold bipartisan pre-hearing committee meetings.
76. Encourage subcommittees to pilot rules changes that could have a positive effect committee-wide.
77. Bipartisan Member retreats should encourage committee agenda-setting and civil decorum.
78. Establish committee-based domestic policy CODELs.
79. To encourage thoughtful debate and deliberation, establish a pilot for weekly Oxford-style debates on the House floor.

80. Provide Members and staff with training for debate and deliberation skills.
81. Identify how increased regulatory and legal resources could help strengthen the role of the legislative branch.
82. Facilitate a true system of checks and balances by ensuring the legislative branch is sufficiently represented in the courts.
83. Establish a district exchange program to allow Members to use the Members' Representational Allowance for traveling to other Members' districts.
84. Increase capacity for policy staff, especially for Committees, policy support organizations and a restored Office of Technology Assessment.
85. Reduce dysfunction in the annual budgeting process through the establishment of a congressionally-directed program that calls for transparency and accountability, and that supports meaningful and transformative investments in local communities across the United States. The program will harness the authority of Congress under Article One of the Constitution to appropriate federal dollars.

Reform the Budget and Appropriations Process

86. Require an annual Fiscal State of the Nation.
87. Require a biennial budget resolution.
88. Implement a deadline for Congress to complete action on a biennial budget.
89. Enhance the budget submission process from the executive branch.
90. Evaluate the effects of the biennial budget process to expediting congressional work.
91. Strengthen budget enforcement through the reconciliation process.
92. Allow more information to be included in the budget resolution.

Identify Administrative Inefficiencies

93. Identify areas in the U.S. Capitol Complex that could benefit from architectural modernization.
94. Develop a practice of negotiating House district office leases to lower costs, improve consistency of rental rates and save taxpayer dollars.

Improve Technology and Continuity in Congress

95. Establish a Congressional Digital Services Task Force to examine the need for and role of a specialized group of technologists, designers, and others to support the House's internal and public facing operations.

96. Make permanent the Bulk Data Task Force and rename it the Congressional Data Task Force.
97. Identify changes made to House operations due to the COVID-19 pandemic and determine what—if any—additional changes should be made.

28

"What's Really Holding the Democrats Back"

FRANCES E. LEE AND JAMES M. CURRY

Joe Manchin, West Virginia's Democratic senator, has put everyone on notice: [u]nder no circumstances will he vote to eliminate the Senate filibuster. If the support of at least 10 Republicans is needed to pass legislation, progressives have little hope for their agenda. At least that's what many seem to think. But eliminating the filibuster probably wouldn't matter as much as they believe it would. The bigger obstacle to any party's agenda is its members' inability to agree among themselves.

We compiled the stated policy goals of every congressional majority party from 1985 through 2018. We identified the parties' agendas by looking to the bills designated as leadership priorities and the issues flagged by the speaker of the House and the Senate majority leader in their opening speech to Congress, yielding a list on average of 15 top priorities per congressional term. Tracking each proposal, 265 in total, we found that the parties failed outright on their agenda priorities about half the time, meaning that no legislation on the issue was enacted.

We then analyzed when, how, and why each failed, and also whether the majority party faced a unified or divided government when it did. Naturally, when a party controlled the House, Senate, and presidency, it fared somewhat better in enacting its agenda than when it didn't, but not markedly so. Parties failed on 43 percent of their agenda priorities in unified government as compared with 49 percent in divided government. This failure rate varies from Congress to Congress, but has remained fairly consistent even in recent years. When Democrats most recently held all three branches of government (in 2009–10), they failed on 50 percent of their agenda items. When Republicans most recently held all three (in 2017–18), they failed on 36 percent.

When a party has unified control of government, the filibuster provides the Senate's minority party (if it has at least 41 senators) with the ability to stop the majority's legislative efforts. This is why partisans focus so much on the filibuster, and why progressive activists are so concerned over it right now. But the filibuster accounted for only about one-third of the majority party's failures during the periods of unified government we studied. In the two most recent instances of unified government—the Democrats in 2009–10 and the Republicans in 2017–18—agenda failures caused by the filibuster were even less common. The Democrats had just one of their priorities, immigration reform, fail because of the filibuster. The Republicans had none. Filibuster reform, then, may enable Democrats to achieve particular policy goals opposed by Republicans, and those would certainly be victories. But most failures, about two-thirds overall during years of unified government and 90 percent during the past two instances of unified government, stemmed from disagreements within the majority party rather than the minority party's ability to block legislation via the filibuster.

In fact, every party that has had unified control of government in the post-Reagan era, as the Democrats do now, has failed on at least one of its highest policy priorities because of the party's inability to reach internal consensus.

Newly returned to unified government for the first time since 1980, Democrats under President Bill Clinton collapsed on health-care reform, their top agenda item. The party deadlocked between moderates and liberals who could not agree on fundamentals, including an employer mandate and premium caps. Health-care reform never received a vote in either the House or the Senate in 1993–94. In 2003–04, Republicans could not agree among themselves to make the Bush tax cuts permanent; conservatives insisted that tax cuts pay for themselves, and moderates were concerned about deficits. In 2005–06, Republicans tried to add individual investment accounts to Social Security. But neither House nor Senate Republicans ever got a bill out of committee.

During the Obama administration, which had periods of unified and divided government, Senate Republican Leader Mitch McConnell used the filibuster aggressively to block the president's nominations. But filibusters of nominees do not tell us about the filibuster's impact on lawmaking. Other analysts have shown that the number of filed cloture petitions (a motion that precedes "cloture," or ending debate, requiring 60 senators in support) increased exponentially during McConnell's years as Republican leader. They point to this number as evidence of the power of the filibuster. But the act of filing for cloture does not mean that a bill is actively being filibustered, only that the Senate's majority leader wants to be ready, just in case it is.

For our analysis, we looked into the parties' legislative efforts on their agenda priorities, drawing on journalistic coverage and several interviews with key players to ascertain why failures occurred. We found that filibusters were the cause of failure on only about one-third of the Democrats' failed agenda items during the Obama years, and on just one of six failed items when the Democrats controlled both the House and Senate in 2009–10. This tally even includes instances in which news reporting indicated that the Democrats dropped a legislative drive in anticipation of a Senate filibuster. By contrast, almost 60 percent of failures during the Obama years were attributable to disagreements within the party.

For instance, in 2009–10, Senate Democrats never came close to passing a climate-change bill. Because of internal disagreements, the 2009 cap-and-trade bill passed the House of Representatives only with the help of a few Republican votes. But differences among Democrats then doomed the bill in the Senate, as lawmakers from oil-drilling and coal-mining states never got on board. Likewise, Democrats were unable to coalesce to repeal the "midnight regulations" adopted in the waning months of the Bush presidency. Democrats also failed to unify around a new direction in the Iraq and Afghanistan wars, and, after internal dissention, wound up passing military appropriations with overwhelming support from Republicans that continued operations with no significant change.

Republicans in recent years have also seen many of their party's legislative ambitions fail, but rarely because of the filibuster. In the most recent case of Republican unified control (2017–18), during the first two years of President Donald Trump's term, every case of failure in our data was due to disagreements within the GOP. Republicans could not agree on how to repeal and replace the Affordable Care Act [ACA]. Despite devoting nine months to the effort, Republicans were unable to overcome their differences, even on the "skinny repeal" bill, which three moderate Republican senators—Susan Collins of Maine, Lisa Murkowski of Alaska, and John McCain of Arizona—decisively rejected.

Although both parties have grown more cohesive in roll-call voting since the 1970s, they continue to struggle with intra-party disunity when it really counts. For instance, Republicans could agree on dozens of symbolic votes to repeal the ACA, but they were unable to do so when their votes would have had consequences in the real world. Turning vague campaign promises into actual legislative language is much harder than agreeing on messaging bills and other symbolic exercises.

Filibuster-reform proponents should therefore not assume that any proposal for which a Senate party previously mustered 51 votes would have passed if the filibuster had not existed. Many of these past votes and stances should not be taken at face value. Members of the majority are free to support policy proposals they have misgivings about when they know the minority will block them. In doing so, they can take positions appealing to their party's base without worrying about true consequences.

The Democratic Party in Congress today is less ideologically diverse than the Democratic Party of the Obama years. But it is also far smaller. A tiny number of dissenting votes is enough right now to deny the party its ability to pass anything by majority vote. In the Senate, Democrats can't afford even one "no" vote, and we are already seeing signs of disunity. Consider the Biden administration's $2 trillion infrastructure proposal, which has met opposition, not just from Republicans but also from moderate and progressive Democrats. Progressives have called the proposal "not nearly enough," urging the Biden administration to "go BIG" and backing a $10 trillion plan called the THRIVE Act. Moderate Democrats are either concerned that the proposal is too big or oppose the full extent of the corporate tax hike—or both. Eliminating the filibuster will not bridge these divides.

Majority parties need to be large and highly cohesive to deliver on a partisan agenda—and these two conditions seldom coincide. For many reasons beyond the filibuster, including disagreements within each party caucus, differences between House members and senators of the same party, and the frequency of divided government, bills rarely become law on the strength of only one party's votes. According to our calculations, since 2011, 90 percent of all new laws clearing the House, and 75 percent clearing the Senate, have initially passed the chamber with positive votes from at least a majority of minority-party members. Many of the bills that have gone on to become law have been written in a bipartisan manner from the start, even in the very majoritarian House of Representatives. Bills are often shaped in ways to get to at least 60 votes. Such efforts may involve painful compromises that can fracture intra-party consensus. But purposeful bipartisanship stems not from the filibuster alone. It is rooted in a constitutional policy-making system that obstructs party power in numerous ways.

Overall, we've seen that bipartisan accomplishments are still possible, even in recent, polarized years. The 116th Congress (2019–20) passed the CARES Act. Adopted in March 2020 in response to the coronavirus pandemic, it was the most effective antipoverty law passed in the United States in more than a generation. Combined with the other four COVID-related stimulus bills last year, Congress enacted almost $4 trillion in pandemic relief. All of this legislation had broad, in some cases universal, bipartisan support.

In fact, recent Congresses have been considerably more productive and bipartisan than is generally appreciated. In 2020 Congress passed legislation protecting 1.3 million new acres of wilderness and enacted a $35-billion energy package that a senior policy adviser at the Natural Resources Defense Council called "perhaps the most significant climate legislation Congress has ever passed." Since 2017, Congress has passed bipartisan legislation overhauling federal criminal-justice policy, revamping trade policy with Mexico and Canada, updating copyright law for the digital-streaming age, permanently extending the September 11th Victim Compensation Fund, and mandating paid maternity leave for more than 2 million federal civilian workers.

During President Barack Obama's tenure, Democrats and Republicans also accomplished some major policy making together, including an expansion of the Violence Against Women Act, a revamp of federal K–12 education policy, the 21st Century Cures Act (which, among other things, streamlined drug-approval processes in ways that may have helped speed up the release of the COVID-19 vaccines), and the USA Freedom Act, which rolled back many of the unpopular surveillance policies put in place under the PATRIOT Act.

Congress does not need to get rid of the filibuster to do big things, nor will its elimination clear the way for a sweeping progressive agenda. Filibuster reform may make the opposition to the majority party's agenda less potent, but it would do nothing to resolve the party's continuing, significant internal disagreements. Internal diversity in two continent-wide political parties makes it very difficult for either to legislate its activists' dreams into realities, filibuster or no.

Discussion Questions

1. If you could wave your magic wand and make three changes to how the House and Senate work, what would you do?

2. Now consider the proposals presented by the various authors. Which of those changes do you support? Which do you think are most likely to be implemented?

3. Are you convinced by Lee and Curry's evidence that the Senate filibuster doesn't contribute as much to gridlock as is commonly believed? Do you support the filibuster or think that it should be changed or eliminated?

CHAPTER 6

The Presidency

29

"The Power to Persuade," from *Presidential Power*

RICHARD NEUSTADT

An enduring theme in analyses of the presidency is the gap between what the public expects of the office and the president's actual powers. Richard Neustadt, who wrote the first edition of Presidential Power *in 1960, offered a new way of looking at the office. His main point is that formal powers (the constitutional powers set out in Article II and the statutory powers that Congress grants) are not the president's most important resource. The president cannot, Neustadt concluded, expect to get his way by command—issuing orders to subordinates and other government officials with the expectation of immediate and unquestioning compliance. In a system of "separate institutions sharing power," other political actors have their own independent sources of power and therefore can refuse to comply with presidential orders. Nobody, Neustadt argues, sees things from the president's perspective (or "vantage point"). Legislators, judges, and cabinet secretaries all have their own responsibilities, constituencies, demands of office, and resources, and their interests and the president's will often differ. The key to presidential power is the power to persuade—to convince others that they should comply with the president's wishes because doing so is in their interest. Presidents persuade by bargaining: making deals and reaching compromise positions; in other words, the give-and-take that is part of politics.*

The limits on command suggest the structure of our government. The constitutional convention of 1787 is supposed to have created a government of "separated powers." It did nothing of the sort. Rather, it created a government of separated institutions *sharing* powers. "I am part of the legislative process," Eisenhower often said in 1959 as a reminder of his veto.

Congress, the dispenser of authority and funds, is no less part of the administrative process. Federalism adds another set of separated institutions. The Bill of Rights adds others. Many public purposes can only be achieved by voluntary acts of private institutions; the press, for one, in Douglass Cater's phrase, is a "fourth branch of government." And with the coming of alliances abroad, the separate institutions of a London, or a Bonn, share in the making of American public policy.

What the Constitution separates our political parties do not combine. The parties are themselves composed of separated organizations sharing public authority. The authority consists of nominating powers. Our national parties are confederations of state and local party institutions, with a headquarters that represents the White House, more or less, if the party has a President in office. These confederacies manage presidential nominations. All other public offices depend upon electorates confined within the states. All other nominations are controlled within the states. The President and congressmen who bear one party's label are divided by dependence upon different sets of voters. The differences are sharpest at the stage of nomination. The White House has too small a share in nominating congressmen, and Congress has too little weight in nominating Presidents for party to erase their constitutional separation. Party links are stronger than is frequently supposed, but nominating processes assure the separation.

The separateness of institutions and the sharing of authority prescribe the terms on which a President persuades. When one man shares authority with another, but does not gain or lose his job upon the other's whim, his willingness to act upon the urging of the other turns on whether he conceives the action right for him. The essence of a President's persuasive task is to convince such men that what the White House wants of them is what they ought to do for their sake and on their authority.

Persuasive power, thus defined, amounts to more than charm or reasoned argument. These have their uses for a president, but these are not the whole of his resources. For the men he would induce to do what he wants done on their own responsibility will need or fear some acts by him on his responsibility. If they share his authority, he has some share in theirs. Presidential "powers" may be inconclusive when a President commands, but always remain relevant as he persuades. The status and authority inherent in his office reinforce his logic and his charm.

*   *   *

A president's authority and status give him great advantages in dealing with the men he would persuade. Each "power" is a vantage point for him in the degree that other men have use for his authority. From the veto to appointments, from publicity to budgeting, and so down a long list, the White House now controls the most encompassing array of vantage points in the American political system. With hardly an exception, the men who share in governing this country are aware that at some time, in some degree, the doing of *their* jobs, the furthering of *their* ambitions, may depend upon the president of the United States. Their need for presidential action, or their fear of it, is bound to be recurrent if not actually continuous. Their need or fear is his advantage.

A president's advantages are greater than mere listing of his "powers" might suggest. The men with whom he deals must deal with him until the last day of his term. Because they have continuing relationships with him, his future, while it lasts, supports his present influence. Even though there is no need or fear of him today, what he could do tomorrow may supply today's advantage. Continuing relationships may convert any "power," any aspect of his status, into vantage points in almost any case. When he induces other men to do what he wants done, a president can trade on their dependence now *and* later.

The president's advantages are checked by the advantages of others. Continuing relationships will pull in both directions. These are relationships of mutual dependence. A president depends upon the men he would persuade; he has to reckon with his need or fear of them. They too will possess status, or authority, or both, else they would be of little use to him. Their vantage points confront his own; their power tempers his.

* * *

The power to persuade is the power to bargain. Status and authority yield bargaining advantages. But in a government of "separated institutions sharing powers," they yield them to all sides. With the array of vantage points at his disposal, a President may be far more persuasive than his logic or his charm could make him. But outcomes are not guaranteed by his advantages. There remain the counter pressures those whom he would influence can bring to bear on him from vantage points at their disposal. Command has limited utility; persuasion becomes give-and-take. It is well that the White House holds the vantage points it does. In such a business any president may need them all—and more.

* * *

This view of power as akin to bargaining is one we commonly accept in the sphere of congressional relations. Every textbook states and every legislative session demonstrates that save in times like the extraordinary Hundred Days of 1933—times virtually ruled out by definition at mid-century—a president will often be unable to obtain congressional action on his terms or even to halt action he opposes. The reverse is equally accepted: Congress often is frustrated by the president. Their formal powers are so intertwined that neither will accomplish very much, for very long, without the acquiescence of the other. By the same token, though, what one demands the other can resist. The stage is set for that great game, much like collective bargaining, in which each seeks to profit from the other's needs and fears. It is a game played catch-as-catch-can, case by case. And everybody knows the game, observers and participants alike.

* * *

Like our governmental structure as a whole, the executive establishment consists of separated institutions sharing powers. The president heads one of these; Cabinet officers, agency administrators, and military commanders head others. Below the departmental level, virtually independent bureau chiefs head many more. Under mid-century conditions, Federal operations spill across dividing lines on organization charts; almost every policy entangles many agencies; almost every program calls for interagency collaboration. Everything somehow involves the president. But operating agencies owe their existence least of all to one another—and only in some part to him. Each has a separate statutory base; each has its statutes to administer; each deals with a different set of subcommittees at the Capitol. Each has its own peculiar set of clients, friends, and enemies outside the formal government. Each has a different set of specialized careerists inside its own bailiwick. Our Constitution gives the president the "take-care" clause and the appointive power. Our statutes give him central budgeting and a degree of personnel control. All agency administrators are responsible to him. But they *also* are responsible to Congress, to their clients, to their staffs, and to themselves. In short, they have five masters. Only after all of those do they owe any loyalty to each other.

"The members of the Cabinet," Charles G. Dawes used to remark, "are a President's natural enemies." Dawes had been Harding's Budget Director, Coolidge's Vice-President, and Hoover's Ambassador to London; he also had been General Pershing's chief assistant for supply in the First World War. The words are highly colored, but Dawes knew whereof he spoke. The men who have to serve so many masters cannot help but be somewhat the "enemy" of any one of them. By the same token, any master wanting service is in some degree the "enemy" of such a servant. A President is likely to want loyal support but not to relish trouble on his doorstep. Yet the more his Cabinet members cleave to him, the more they may need help from him in fending off the wrath of rival masters. Help, though, is synonymous with trouble. Many a Cabinet officer, with loyalty ill-rewarded by his lights and help withheld, has come to view the White House as innately hostile to department heads. Dawes's dictum can be turned around.

* * *

The more an officeholder's status and his "powers" stem from sources independent of the president, the stronger will be his potential pressure *on* the President. Department heads in general have more bargaining power than do most members of the White House staff; but bureau chiefs may have still more, and specialists at upper levels of established career services may have almost unlimited reserves of the enormous power which consists of sitting still. As Franklin Roosevelt once remarked:

> The Treasury is so large and far-flung and ingrained in its practices that I find it almost impossible to get the action and results I want—even with Henry [Morgenthau] there. But the Treasury is not to be compared with the State Department. You should go through the experience of trying to get any changes in the thinking, policy, and action of the career diplomats and then you'd know what a real problem was. But the Treasury and the State Department put together are nothing compared with the Na-a-vy. The admirals are really something to cope with—and I should know. To change anything in the Na-a-vy is like punching a feather bed. You punch it with your right and you punch it with your left until you are finally exhausted, and then you find the damn bed just as it was before you started punching.

* * *

There is a widely held belief in the United States that were it not for folly or for knavery, a reasonable president would need no power other than the logic of his argument. No less a personage than Eisenhower has subscribed to that belief in many a campaign speech and press conference remark. But faulty reasoning and bad intentions do not cause all quarrels with presidents. The best of reasoning and of intent cannot compose them all. For in the first place, what the president wants will rarely seem a trifle to the men he wants it from. And in the second place, they will be bound to judge it by the standard of their own responsibilities, not his. However logical his argument according to his lights, their judgment may not bring them to his view.

The men who share in governing this country frequently appear to act as though they were in business for themselves. So, in a real though not entire sense, they are and have to be. When Truman and MacArthur fell to quarreling, for example, the stakes were no less than the substance of American foreign policy, the risks of greater war or military stalemate, the prerogatives of presidents and field commanders, the pride of a proconsul and his place in history. Intertwined, inevitably, were other stakes, as well: political stakes for men and factions of both parties; power stakes for interest groups with which they were or wished to be affiliated. And every stake was raised by the apparent discontent in the American public mood. There is no reason to suppose that in such circumstances men of large but differing responsibilities will see all things through the same glasses. On the contrary, it is to be expected that their views of what ought to be done and what they then should do will vary with the differing perspectives their particular responsibilities evoke. Since their duties are not vested in a "team" or a "collegium" but in themselves, as individuals, one must expect that they will see things *for* themselves. Moreover, when they are responsible to many masters and when an event or policy turns loyalty against loyalty—a day-by-day occurrence in the nature of the case—one must assume that those who have the duties to perform will choose the terms of reconciliation. This is the essence of their personal responsibility.

When their own duties pull in opposite directions, who else but they can choose what they will do?

* * *

Outside the Executive Branch the situation is the same, except that loyalty to the President may often matter *less*. . . . And when one comes to congressmen who can do nothing for themselves (or their constituents) save as they are elected, term by term, in districts and through party structures *differing* from those on which a president depends, the case is very clear. An able Eisenhower aide with long congressional experience remarked to me in 1958: "[t]he people on the Hill don't do what they might *like* to do, they do what they think they *have* to do in their own interest as *they* see it. . . ." This states the case precisely.

The essence of a president's persuasive task with congressmen and everybody else, *is to induce them to believe that what he wants of them is what their own appraisal of their own responsibilities requires them to do in their interest, not his.* Because men may differ in their views on public policy, because differences in outlook stem from differences in duty—duty to one's office, one's constituents, oneself—that task is bound to be more like collective bargaining than like a reasoned argument among philosopher kings. Overtly or implicitly, hard bargaining has characterized all illustrations offered up to now. This is the reason why: persuasion deals in the coin of self-interest with men who have some freedom to reject what they find counterfeit.

Let me introduce a case * * *: the European Recovery Program of 1948, the so-called Marshall Plan. This is perhaps the greatest exercise in policy *agreement* since the Cold War began. When the then Secretary of State, George Catlett Marshall, spoke at the Harvard commencement in June of 1947, he launched one of the most creative, most imaginative ventures in the history of American foreign relations. What makes this policy most notable for present purposes, however, is that it became effective upon action by the 80th Congress, at the behest of Harry Truman, in the election year of 1948.

Eight months before Marshall spoke at Harvard, the Democrats had lost control of both Houses of Congress for the first time in fourteen years. Truman, whom the Secretary represented, had just finished his second troubled year as president-by-succession. Truman was regarded with so little warmth in his own party that in 1946 he had been urged *not* to participate in the congressional campaign. At the opening of Congress in January 1947, Senator Robert A. Taft, "Mr. Republican," had somewhat the attitude of a president-elect. This was a vision widely shared in Washington, with Truman relegated, thereby, to the role of caretaker-on-term. Moreover, within just two weeks of Marshall's commencement address, Truman was to veto two prized accomplishments of Taft's congressional majority: the Taft-Hartley Act and tax reduction. Yet scarcely ten months later the Marshall

Plan was under way on terms to satisfy its sponsors, its authorization completed, its first-year funds in sight, its administering agency in being: all managed by as thorough a display of executive-congressional cooperation as any we have seen since the Second World War. For any president at any time this would have been a great accomplishment. In years before mid-century it would have been enough to make the future reputation of his term. And for a Truman, at this time, enactment of the Marshall Plan appears almost miraculous.

How was the miracle accomplished? How did a President so situated bring it off? In answer, the first thing to note is that he did not do it by himself. Truman had help of a sort no less extraordinary than the outcome. Although each stands for something more complex, the names of Marshall, Vandenberg, * * * Bevin, Stalin, tell the story of that help.

In 1947, two years after V-J Day, General Marshall was something more than Secretary of State. He was a man venerated by the president as "the greatest living American," literally an embodiment of Truman's ideals. He was honored at the Pentagon as an architect of victory. He was thoroughly respected by the Secretary of the Navy, James V. Forrestal, who that year became the first Secretary of Defense. On Capitol Hill Marshall had an enormous fund of respect stemming from his war record as Army Chief of Staff, and in the country generally no officer had come out of the war with a higher reputation for judgment, intellect, and probity. Besides, as Secretary of State, he had behind him the first generation of matured foreign service officers produced by the reforms of the 1920s, and mingled with them, in the departmental service, were some of the ablest of the men drawn by the war from private life to Washington.

*   *   *

Taken together, these are exceptional resources for a Secretary of State. In the circumstances, they were quite as necessary as they obviously are relevant. The Marshall Plan was launched by a "lame duck" administration "scheduled" to leave office in eighteen months. Marshall's program faced a congressional leadership traditionally isolationist and currently intent upon economy. European aid was viewed with envy by a Pentagon distressed and virtually disarmed through budget cuts, and by domestic agencies intent on enlarged welfare programs. It was not viewed with liking by a Treasury intent on budget surpluses. The plan had need of every asset that could be extracted from the personal position of its nominal author and from the skills of his assistants.

Without the equally remarkable position of the senior Senator from Michigan, Arthur H. Vandenberg, it is hard to see how Marshall's assets could have been enough. Vandenberg was chairman of the Senate Foreign Relations Committee. Actually, he was much more than that. Twenty years a senator, he was the senior member of his party in the Chamber. Assiduously cultivated by F.D.R. and Truman, he was a chief Republican proponent of "bipartisanship" in foreign policy, and consciously conceived himself its living symbol to his party, to the country, and abroad. Moreover, by informal but entirely operative agreement with his colleague Taft, Vandenberg held the acknowledged lead among Senate Republicans in the whole field of international affairs. This acknowledgment meant more in 1947 than it might have meant at any other time. With confidence in the advent of a Republican administration two years hence, most of the gentlemen were in a mood to be responsive and responsible. The war was over, Roosevelt dead, Truman a caretaker, theirs the trust. That the Senator from Michigan saw matters in this light, his diaries make clear. And this was not the outlook from the Senate side alone; the attitudes of House Republicans associated with the Herter Committee and its tours abroad suggest the same mood of responsibility. Vandenberg was not the only source of help on Capitol Hill. But relatively speaking, his position there was as exceptional as Marshall's was downtown.

* * *

At Harvard, Marshall had voiced an idea in general terms. That this was turned into a hard program susceptible of presentation and support is due, in major part, to Ernest Bevin, the British Foreign Secretary. He well deserves the credit he has sometimes been assigned as, in effect, co-author of the Marshall Plan. For Bevin seized on Marshall's Harvard speech and organized a European response with promptness and concreteness beyond the State Department's expectations. What had been virtually a trial balloon to test reactions on both sides of the Atlantic was hailed in London as an invitation to the Europeans to send Washington a bill of particulars. This they promptly organized to do, and the American Administration then organized in turn for its reception without further argument internally about the pros and cons of issuing the "invitation" in the first place. But for Bevin there might have been trouble from the Secretary of the Treasury and others besides.

If Bevin's help was useful at that early stage, Stalin's was vital from first to last. In a mood of self-deprecation Truman once remarked that without Moscow's "crazy" moves "we would never have had our foreign policy . . . we never could have got a thing from Congress." George Kennan, among others, had deplored the anti-Soviet overtone of the case made for the Marshall Plan in Congress and the country, but there is no doubt that this clinched the argument for many segments of American opinion. There also is no doubt that Moscow made the crucial contributions to the case.

* * *

The crucial thing to note about this case is that despite compatibility of views on public policy, Truman got no help he did not pay for (except Stalin's). Bevin scarcely could have seized on Marshall's words had Marshall not been plainly backed by Truman. Marshall's interest would not have comported with the exploitation of his prestige by a president who under-cut him openly, or subtly, or even inadvertently, at any point. Vandenberg, presumably, could not have backed proposals by a White House which begrudged him deference and access gratifying to his fellow-partisans (and satisfying to himself). Prominent Republicans in private life would not have found it easy to promote a cause identified with Truman's claims on 1948—and neither would the prominent New Dealers then engaged in searching for a substitute.

Truman paid the price required for their services. So far as the record shows, the White House did not falter once in firm support for Marshall and the Marshall Plan. Truman backed his Secretary's gamble on an invitation to all Europe. He made the plan his own in a well-timed address to the Canadians. He lost no opportunity to widen the involvements of his own official family in the cause. Averell Harriman the Secretary of Commerce, Julius Krug the Secretary of the Interior, Edwin Nourse the Economic Council Chairman, James Webb the Director of the Budget—all were made responsible for studies and reports contributing directly to the legislative presentation. Thus these men were committed in advance. Besides, the president continually emphasized to everyone in reach that he did not have doubts, did not desire complications and would foreclose all he could. Reportedly, his emphasis was felt at the Treasury, with good effect. And Truman was at special pains to smooth the way for Vandenberg. The Senator insisted on "no politics" from the Administration side; there was none. He thought a survey of American resources and capacity essential; he got it in the Krug and Harriman reports. Vandenberg expected advance consultation; he received it, step by step, in frequent meetings with the president and weekly conferences with Marshall. He asked for an effective liaison between Congress and agencies concerned; Lovett and others gave him what he wanted. When the Senator decided on the need to change financing and administrative features of the legislation, Truman disregarded Budget Bureau grumbling and acquiesced with grace. When, finally, Vandenberg desired a Republican to head the new administering agency, his candidate, Paul Hoffman, was appointed despite the president's own preference for another. In all of these ways Truman employed the sparse advantages his "powers" and his status then accorded him to gain the sort of help he had to have.

* * *

Had Truman lacked the personal advantages his "powers" and his status gave him, or if he had been maladroit in using them, there probably would not have been a massive European aid program in 1948. * * * The President's own share in this accomplishment was vital. He made his contribution by exploiting his advantages. Truman, in effect, lent Marshall and the rest the perquisites and status of his office. In return they lent him their prestige and their own influence. The transfer multiplied *his* influence despite his limited authority in form and lack of strength politically. Without the wherewithal to make this bargain, Truman could not have contributed to European aid.

* * *

Discussion Questions

1. Considering recent presidents—George W. Bush, Barack Obama, Donald Trump, and Joe Biden—identify cases in which they had to bargain or persuade to get what they want, rather than use command.

2. Can you think of any recent examples when a president was able to get what he wanted by giving a command (that is, to someone not in the military)?

3. Does the president have any capacity to *force* a member of Congress to vote for legislation that the president wants? Why or why not?

30

"Reconstructing the Presidency," from *After Trump*

Bob Bauer and Jack Goldsmith

Whether you supported him or not, no one could argue that Donald Trump was not a "typical" president. From his open rejection of presidential norms, attacks on the press, authoritarian language and claims of a "right to do whatever I want as president," transparent lies, and financial conflicts of interest to his refusal to recognize that he lost the 2020 election (culminating in the violent insurrection at the U.S. Capitol that forced Congress to suspend its certification of the 2020 results), he was unlike any other. While his supporters applauded his defiance of expectations of how presidents should behave, his opponents saw him as the sort of demagogue that Alexander Hamilton warned about in The Federalist *Papers.*

The guardrails of democracy—the rule of law—held, but barely. Trump exposed the weaknesses of institutions and processes that had been assumed to be robust. The very things that make the president powerful, and which present opportunities for leadership in the mold of a Washington, Lincoln, or Roosevelt, also pose the risk that a president could wield those powers illegitimately.

Bob Bauer (a longtime Democratic lawyer) and Jack Goldsmith (an assistant attorney general under George W. Bush) consider the question of whether the presidential office should be reformed. They propose, among other reforms, prohibiting presidents from active involvement in any business and requiring them to seek congressional approval of any income from foreign state–controlled businesses; prohibiting presidents from appointing recent campaign officials to positions in the Department of Justice; prohibiting presidential campaigns from receiving information or data (such as opposition research) from foreign governments; requiring presidents to disclose their tax returns; prohibiting presidents from issuing self-pardons or issuing pardons to obstruct justice; tightening restrictions on declaring national emergencies for more than one year; and expediting judicial consideration of congressional subpoenas.

The Need for Reform

Trump is not the first president to spark questions about the legitimacy of presidential power. But his characteristic excesses have not been those of his predecessors. The George W. Bush administration often invoked Article II powers to disregard congressional statutes in important contexts. Trump has not done so to the same degree. The Obama administration engaged in presidential action that often rested on aggressive interpretations of congressional statutory delegations. Trump has done some of that, especially during the conflict with Congress over pandemic relief, but not as much. Despite his targeted killing of Iranian Gen. Qassem Soleimani, Trump has not been as aggressive as his two predecessors in expanding available unilateral presidential war powers. Nor did Trump follow through on his campaign pronouncements that indicated a readiness to break the law by, for example, reinstating waterboarding, censoring the internet, using the military for indiscriminate attacks on civilians, throwing his opponents in jail, and the like.

Trump did proudly claim a "right to do whatever I want as president," and he has shown little patience for the idea that law meaningfully constrains his freedom of action. But the argument for reform of the presidency does not rest primarily on Trump's defiance of the law. Trump's law-breaking bark—though undoubtedly corrosive, as we explain below—has often been worse than his bite. And many of his efforts to break the law have been checked by courts and executive branch officials. The case for reform rests less on Trump's law-breaking tendencies and more on how his conception of the office of the presidency and his actions in it have exposed gaps and ambiguities in the law and norms governing the office, and broader weaknesses in presidential accountability. These concerns flow from four related elements of Trump's conduct of the presidency.

First, as has been noted widely, Trump is indifferent to the nonlegal norms of presidential behavior that have been established since Watergate to constrain presidential power and ensure presidential accountability. The examples are too legion to list but include his refusal to release his tax returns; his frequent public comment on and threats to intervene in law enforcement actions; his abandonment of routine White House press briefings and presidential press conferences; and his vicious personal attacks on judges, governors, executive branch officials, and even private citizens.

Second, Trump has merged the institution of the presidency with his personal interests and has used the former to serve the latter like no previous occupant of the office. To give just a few examples, many of which are norms violations as well: [h]e repeatedly sought to intervene in the special counsel's investigation of himself and his associates, and declined to cooperate with the special counsel where his own conduct was at issue. He has often publicly urged the Justice Department to investigate and prosecute his political opponents. He has used the presidency to make money off his businesses. He has used his control over diplomacy to seek the assistance of foreign powers to win an election. He has used the bully pulpit at the height of the coronavirus public health crisis to glorify his television ratings and attack his political opponents. He has tried to direct law enforcement to protect friends, family, and himself, and he has threatened to use the pardon power to do the same.

Third, Trump has aggressively and often mendaciously attacked core institutions of American democracy—especially the press, the judiciary, Congress, state and local governments, and many elements of his own executive branch, including the Justice Department and the intelligence agencies. Trump's institution-bashing usually goes hand in hand with his brand of populist anti-elitism and his resistance to limits on the assertion of his personal will. "The populist tends to believe that institutions are inherently corrupt because they are so easily captured by 'elites,'" notes Eric Posner. Trump routinely makes these claims, and he clearly sees in institutions and institutional process impediments to the achievement of his purposes. Trump's attacks on institutions differ dramatically from the truth-shading and institution-criticizing that occurs in ordinary politics. Trump frequently tells big, verifiable lies in the course of condemning these institutions and persons in harsh, vicious, and demeaning ways. And he does so with the apparent intent and clear effect of weakening public confidence in these institutions. These institutions and related norms have often held up well to Trump's onslaught. But Trump has done a lot of damage, and he has paved the way for worse.

Fourth, Trump deploys authoritarian rhetoric and threatens authoritarian action, often before large crowds, even if he typically does not follow through. He has implied that he is not bound by law, or that he wants to break free of it, even though in the end he usually stops just shy of what would, by general agreement, be clear violations of the law. He threatens to crack down on the press with lawsuits but does not actually do so. He incites citizens to law-defiant behavior—for example, in his tweets urging citizens to disregard stay-at-home orders in some of the states during the coronavirus pandemic. He is harshly critical of leaders of democratic allies and allied institutions like NATO, and he expresses admiration for foreign authoritarian leaders like Vladimir Putin, though his administration has maintained traditional NATO policies and relationships and has heavily sanctioned Putin's Russia. In all of these contexts, and more, Trump's rhetoric matters even when it does not result in action or policy change. Especially when combined with Trump's indifference to norms, this rhetoric understandably disturbs many people, including many in the institutions under attack. And, of course, it weakens confidence in those institutions.

Taken together, the cluster of Trump's behaviors—the disregard for norms and attacks on institutions, the elevation of the personal over the public, the ceaseless lies, the vilification of and all-out assault on his opposition, and his authoritarian and law-defiant impulses and rhetoric—constitute classic *demagogic* behavior. Posner has defined a "demagogue" as "a charismatic, amoral person who obtains the support of the people through dishonesty, emotional manipulation, and the exploitation of social divisions; who targets the political elites, blaming them for everything that has gone wrong; and who tries to destroy institutions—legal, political,

religious, social—and other sources of power that stand in their way."
This fits Trump to a T.

Against this background, the case for reform of the presidency is straightforward. Trump has shown that the current array of laws and norms governing the presidency is inadequate to protect institutions vital to the American constitutional democracy and to ensure that the president is, and appears to be, constrained by law. Not every reform proposed in this book is a response to Trump's demagogic political and governing style. Some of Trump's excesses, and some flaws in presidential regulation, had been emerging in prior presidencies. But Trump's particular brand of executive action has added significantly to past problems in ways that now demand comprehensive treatment.

It is possible that the threats posed by Trump to the presidency and other American institutions will end when he leaves the scene, and that the next president will attend more closely to the norms, institutional practices, and rhetorical constraints of Trump's predecessors. On this view, the problems presented by Trump are personal to him and are not structural or pervasive ones that demand reform.

We do not share this view, for four reasons.

First, the experience with Trump has made clear that many of the laws and norms governing the presidency are defective. Some norms—such as the ones concerning release of public information about taxes, wealth, and business operations—proved ineffective and should not be left to the happenstance of who is president or a presidential candidate. * * * These norms should be embodied in binding statutes rather than in norms that the president and candidates can ignore should they wish to incur the political costs (or should they decide that trashing the norms is politically advantageous). Other norms should be fortified for any future presidency. As we explain * * *, Robert Mueller's investigation was the nation's first significant experience with the 1999 special counsel regulations, and many problems emerged from their use. For constitutional and practical reasons, Congress cannot comprehensively legislate on this topic, which must remain subject to a large degree to norms and executive branch regulation, albeit more powerful ones.

Second, [our argument] is not limited to reforms of only the president and the White House. The experience with Trump has revealed that other elements of the executive branch suffer from inadequate guidance and accountability, and sometimes excessive zeal or poor judgment, in important contexts. Consider three controversies over the past several years about FBI investigations of the president or presidential campaigns: the Hillary Clinton email investigation, the Trump campaign investigation, and the counterintelligence and obstruction of justice investigations of President Trump that began in 2017. One of the reasons that these investigations were so controversial is that the law and other guidance on how to handle such investigations were underdeveloped or unclear. Another reason is that officials conducting these investigations sometimes did not adhere to relevant norms. These types of investigations will always be politically controversial, but better, clearer, and firmer rules can help a lot going forward.

Third, even before Trump became president, our deeply polarized politics were leading presidents and their congressional allies to sweep past or give less weight to institutional practices that stood in the way of achieving short-term political aims. The bitter battles over nominations to the judiciary are one example. But they reflect a wider collapse of comity within Congress concerning the basic ground rules for partisan contestation that has undermined its capacity to enact major legislation or even to reach timely agreements on funding government operations. On the issues that most divide the parties, the norms that have guided and checked their interactions have been under pressure for a while and have become characterized by a downward spiralling tit-for-tat of norm-busting actions. Trump's norm-busting is a part of this pattern, and indeed, many people think that Trump is as much an effect of these larger pressures as a cause. But whatever the cause and effect may be * * *, norms regulating government institutions are under threat everywhere and must be attended to.

Fourth, and relatedly, while presidents after Trump might be more respectful of norms, the American people also may continue to elect presidents who distrust elites or profess to do so, who reject expertise and create "alternative facts," who attack and circumvent formal governing institutions, and who disrespect traditional principles of governance. The presidential selection process is now thoroughly democratized and lacks its traditional "vetting" function that, to some extent, the parties once performed. The two political parties, and the polity, are deeply polarized. And the perceived failures of elite institutions along a number of dimensions may continue to fuel populist sentiment on both the right and the left, especially in presidential elections. These presidencies may not be predictably Trumpist in their policies. A populist demagogue in the Oval Office purporting to embody the true will of the people against the elites can be a Democrat or a Republican, on the left or well to the right. And that future president might have a better command of the governance tools of the presidency than Trump, and be defter in circumventing legal and norms-based limits. In many ways, Trump, despite his destructiveness, has often been incompetent at operating the levers of the presidency to achieve his ends; a future president might not be so incompetent.

Discussion Questions

1. Bauer and Goldsmith stopped short of recommending significant changes to the president's constitutional powers. Do you think Article II should be amended? What changes—additions or subtractions of presidential or constitutional power—would you support?

2. Do you think that "norms" are strong enough to protect against abuses of power? Can you think of examples from past presidents where norms were sufficient? Insufficient?

Debating the Issues: Should We Abolish the Electoral College?

Donald Trump's 2016 victory was the fifth time a president won the election while losing the popular vote (1824, 1876, 1888, and 2000 were the others) and the second since 2000. Trump received about 2.9 million fewer votes than Hillary Clinton, the largest vote deficit for any elected president.

Is the electoral college a carefully calibrated process that balances state and popular interests in a way that creates an effective national mandate for a president? Or is it an antidemocratic relic that undermines political legitimacy? The question is more pointed because the electoral college gives more weight to small states relative to large states, undercutting the voting power of larger states (and even cities), which tend to be more demographically diverse than smaller states. The "winner take all" character also gives far more influence to swing states: presidential candidates in 2020 spent more time and money in New Hampshire (with 1.4 million people, four electoral college votes, four candidate events, and $5 million in ad spending) than they did in New York, California, Texas, and Illinois combined (with 101 million people and 142 electoral college votes, but with only three candidate events and $0 in campaign ad spending). In practice, this gives Republican candidates an advantage in the electoral college, in which they likely win the presidency even if they lose the popular vote by 4 percent.

Christina Villegas disputes the idea that the framers were afraid of voters and takes the unorthodox position that the framers designed the electoral college with the goal of furthering popular legitimacy and majority voice. Far from reflecting their distrust of the public, the framers designed the electoral college to reinforce the president's dependence on the people. The state-based and absolute majority requirements, moreover, help ensure that the president is supported across a wide geographic range. The process—unwieldy as it can be—was designed as "a prudential means of stimulating national majority support for the winning candidate." She is agnostic about reforms but suggests that people would be more supportive of the electoral college if they had a better understanding of its purpose.

Darrell M. West calls for the elimination of the electoral college, arguing that it is antidemocratic by design, reflecting the framers' distrust of popular opinion. Besides the obvious problem in which the popular vote loser can become president, West points to the problem of the vast overrepresentation of small, homogeneous areas in a diverse nation of 330 million people (and where 15 percent of counties, almost all on the coasts or around large cities, generate nearly two-thirds of the nation's gross domestic product, or GDP), as well as the problem of faithless electors, whereby the appointed electors might defect from the state results. West proposes either a direct popular vote or the National Popular Vote Interstate Compact, in which states commit their state electors to the national popular vote winner.

31

"Electing the People's President: The Popular Origins of the Electoral College"

CHRISTINA VILLEGAS

"It was desirable that the sense of the people should operate in the choice of the person to whom so important a trust was to be confided. This end will be answered by committing the right of making it, not to any pre-established body, but to men chosen by the people for the special purpose, and at a particular conjuncture."—Alexander Hamilton, *Federalist 68*

Introduction

The Electoral College is currently one of the least understood and most unpopular aspects of American constitutional democracy. Civic knowledge surveys reveal that a large percentage of the American public is unfamiliar with the process and how it operates, yet a majority of registered members of both major parties overtly favor eliminating the system. Indeed, transforming the system is the most frequently proposed constitutional reform, and statutory proposals to alter the process, such as the National Popular Vote Compact, have gained substantial support in recent years.

Most critiques of the Electoral College are based on the assumption that the system is undemocratic and outmoded and that electing the president by a straight popular vote or allocating electoral votes proportionally would make the system more representative of the public will. Thus, dissatisfaction with the process generally stems from the belief that the selection system was never intended to facilitate majority rule. Proponents of the Electoral College generally do not challenge this supposition but instead argue that the system serves other important ends, such as balancing the electoral interests of small and large states, maintaining the two-party system, and minimizing the possibility of fraud. Hence, the dominant view among critics and advocates of the Electoral College alike is that the system was never intended to directly represent the popular will.

In contrast to those who charge that the Electoral College was designed by men who "were deeply mistrustful of popular opinion" and "did not want the election of the president to be left to the people," a small number of scholars, including the late Martin Diamond and more recently Gary Glenn, have pointed out that "[a]nyone who takes the trouble to actually read the debates in the Constitutional Convention will see that what was behind the Electoral College was not a hostility to popular election of the president."

* * *

Federalism and Original Intent?

Contemporary proponents of the Electoral College commonly promulgate the view that preserving federalism and the prerogative and influence of the states, especially the small states, has always been and continues to be the system's leading objective. Law professor Robert Hardaway, for example, refers to the system's design, which includes a weighted influence in favor of the small states, as the "bulwark and foundation stone of [the] new federal system." Likewise, conservative political analyst Phyllis Schafly contends, "Our Founding Fathers understood that America is a nation of both 'we the people' and a federal system of states, so it allows all states, regardless of size, to be players in electing our President." Another supporter writes, "The Electoral College was originally designed by the Founding Fathers as a *federal hedge against the domination of the absolute national majority over the individual states*. Without the College, the delicate balance between national unity and regional distinctiveness would be lost and the various states would lose much of their power over the Executive Branch."

Critics of the Electoral College, who seek to adopt a more "democratic" selection process such as a nationwide popular vote, tend to agree that the core justification for the system's allocation of electoral votes to states is that it "forces candidates to pay attention to state-based interests in general and to the interests of the small states in particular." Some scholars have even contended that because of the transformation of the process that has occurred since the founding, the federalism justification for the system is the only original defense that remains relevant. Thus, the system's strongest adversaries attempt to demonstrate through empirical data that a move to adoption of direct election would have virtually no effect on federalism. George Edwards, for example, directly confronts the assumption that states, as states, currently "embody coherent, unified interests and communities" in need of special consideration or protection. Pointing out the substantial diversity of interests within individual states, such as Illinois, California, Virginia, and New York, Edwards cites historian Jack Rakove, who concludes, "States have no interest, as states, in the election of the president; only citizens do." In other words, even within smaller states that receive special consideration in the Electoral College, citizens do not have common interests in need of protection any more than large states because states have common interests. Those who defend the Electoral College on such grounds, Edwards contends, confuse the interests that may unite local communities or groups of individuals with the interests of states as a whole. Furthermore, Edwards and others have pointed out, that there is little empirical evidence that the Electoral College forces presidential candidates to be any more oriented to states or the interests within them than they would be under a system of direct popular vote. Thus, as another scholar maintains, while preserving a decisive role for the states may have been necessary for the new, fledgling government in 1787, it is no longer a relevant justification for violating the democratic principle of "one man, one vote."

Despite its widespread adoption by modern scholars, the belief that the chief aim of the Electoral College is the protection of state interests in the selection of the nation's chief executive is not rooted in specific statements of those who initially designed and defended the system. Rather, it is an outgrowth of the original rules and operation of the system. The process for selecting a president was initially laid out in Article II, Section 1 of the U.S. Constitution, which vests the power to elect the president in special electors chosen for that purpose. According to the Constitution, each state is designated a number of electors equal to its combined number of senators and representatives in Congress. These electors are chosen in each state and cast their votes in a manner prescribed by the state legislatures. As originally adopted, the constitutional electoral system, allowed each elector to vote for two persons, at least one of whom had to inhabit a different state than the elector. The person who received a majority of the states' combined electoral votes would be elected president, and the person who finished second would become vice president. Following the election of 1800, in which Thomas Jefferson and Aaron Burr received an equal number of electoral votes, this aspect of the college was fine-tuned by the Twelfth Amendment so that each elector would cast one vote for president and one for vice president. In the case when no candidate receives a majority of electoral votes, the Constitution specifies that the House of Representatives will choose the winner from the three highest vote recipients, with each state delegation in the House casting one vote, regardless of population.

Contemporary scholars of the Electoral College frequently reference the system's allocation of electoral votes to states (which slightly boosts the voting power of smaller states to a greater degree than their populations would merit) and the auxiliary mode of election by state in the House as evidence of the Framers' intent to promote federalism and the influence of the states in the selection of the chief executive.

* * *

It should be noted, however, that neither the main defenders of the original selection system nor the chief architects who devised the system in its original form while serving on the Committee of Eleven ever explicitly mentioned the preservation of federalism or the prerogatives of the state governments as a primary purpose for the system. In fact, leading constitutional architects, including James Madison, James Wilson, Alexander Hamilton, and Gouverneur Morris, only spoke of the components of the system that favored states as states as necessary and prudential compromises based on the unique political situation of the new nation—a situation in which sovereign states were assenting to yield a portion of their sovereignty to a central government that would be drawn directly from the people and would have the authority to operate on citizens as citizens. In the *Federalist Papers*, Madison, referring to the equal allocation of votes in the Senate (which became a partial component of the Electoral College system) asserts, "It is superfluous to try, by the standard of theory, a part of the Constitution which is allowed on all hands to be the result, not of theory, but of a spirit of amity, and that mutual deference and concessions which the peculiarity of our political situation rendered indispensable." In other words, the principle that, in a government drawn directly from the people, each district should have "a PROPORTIONAL share in the government," would not have been politically possible given the objections of the smaller states. As Madison points out in a letter on the Convention proceedings, "The little States [initially] insisted on retaining their equality in both branches [of Congress]." This demand, according to Madison, "created more embarrassment and a greater alarm" for the Convention than all other demands made by individual states. Consequently, Madison concludes in the *Federalist Papers*, "Under this alternative, the advice of prudence must be to embrace the lesser evil; and instead of indulging a fruitless anticipation of the possible mischiefs which may ensure, to contemplate rather the advantageous consequences which may qualify the sacrifice."

* * *

Popular Origins of the Selection System

Constitutional scholars frequently allege that the Framers of the Electoral College were seeking to set up a system that would not only shore up federalism but also minimize the influence of majoritarianism. * * * While such scholars are correct to point out the Framers' belief that unfettered majoritarianism would be inconsistent with social stability, the public good, and private rights, this fact is often used to give credence to the false claim that the Framers favored an aristocratic system in which majority opinion would have little influence over the operation of government—a claim regularly disseminated in commentary on the Electoral College system.

* * *

Although the Constitution limits the scope and character of power and channels the functions of government with a view to protecting the public good and private rights from unjust majorities and their representatives, the leading Framers were far from hostile to public opinion expressed through majority action. Throughout the *Federalist Papers*, Publius emphasizes the importance of a rational dependence on the people and identifies such a dependence as "the primary control on the government." Even in *Federalist 10*, where Madison famously emphasizes the threat of majority faction to republican government, Madison hopes to mitigate such threat while still "preserv[ing] the spirit and form of popular government." Madison implies that an extended republic will achieve this objective by necessitating that a national majority be a coalition of various interests. Representative democracy in such a republic, Madison believes, would be more in line with the true spirit of the nation and less susceptible to "men of factious tempers, local prejudices, and sinister designs," who would "first obtain the suffrages, and then betray the interests of the people."

The Constitutional Framers particularly sought the emergence of a non-parochial majority in the selection of the nation's president (the one representative whose constituency extends to the nation as whole). Far from seeking to minimize the influence of the majority in the selection of the chief executive, defenders of the Electoral College maintained that it would be the best means of facilitating such a majority. In fact, while the argument that the Electoral College was designed to protect federalism is based on individual components of the system, the principled arguments and expressed intent of the system's chief architects focused not on preserving the prerogatives of the states but on preserving popular influence among the citizenry as a whole.

Like other aspects of the Constitution, the Electoral College was shaped in part by the concessions demanded by the small and southern states. Despite these necessary concessions, however, two basic theoretical goals dominated the debate proceedings over presidential selection. The first was to facilitate the selection of the president by a truly national majority. The second was to promote the selection of a candidate with the proper qualifications and character for high office. As Madison summarized some years after the Convention, "Next to the propriety of having a President the real choice of a majority of his Constituents, it is desirable that he should inspire respect and acquiescence by qualifications not suffering too much by comparison."

The station of independent electors, adopted in place of direct popular election, was first introduced as a means of achieving these goals. At the outset both the Virginia and New Jersey Plans (the foundational documents of the Constitution) provided for the election of the chief executive by the national legislature. The initial defense in favor of legislative selection was that national legislators would be better suited than the people themselves to identify distinguished, continental characters who would represent a majority of the nation rather than a single region or state. The proposal for legislative selection, however, was immediately met with insurmountable skepticism on the grounds that it would threaten the independence of the branches by making the president overly dependent on the will of Congress. With few exceptions, the Convention's participants believed the nation's chief executive should function as an auxiliary guardian of the people's rights against legislative encroachment. Experience showed that legislators, despite their electoral dependence on the people, were often persuaded by corrupt or pernicious measures. One object of the National Executive, in so far as it was lodged with the veto power, was to control this propensity. Legislative selection, however, would negate this check by making the executive subservient to the predominant faction in Congress. Several delegates additionally expressed fear that legislative selection would give foreign powers undo opportunity to influence the election. Thus, South Carolina delegate Pierce Butler concluded, "The two great evils to be avoided [in the selection of the president] are cabal at home and influence from abroad. It will be difficult to avoid either if the Election be made by the Natl Legislature."

Consequently, a large portion of the debate centered on what method would replace legislative selection. The con-federalists at the Convention (those who favored retaining much of the state sovereignty that had existed under the Articles of Confederation) initially supported the election of the president by either the state legislatures or state governors. This plan gained little traction at the Convention, however, because most of the delegates were concerned that state legislative or executive selection would make the president overly beholden to the state governments in the same way that congressional election would make the president dependent on Congress. Constitutionally, this would be problematic because the president, as chief executive of the federal government, "is to act for *the people* not for the *States*."

The belief that "the ultimate authority," of both the state and national governments, "resides in the people alone," led several prominent members of the Convention, including James Wilson, James Madison, Gouverneur Morris, and others, to initially endorse direct popular election of the president. James Wilson was first at the convention to declare that he at least "in theory" favored "an election by the people" or by electors chosen by the people according to district "without the intervention of the states." Wilson's proposals were met with both intrigue and cynicism. George Mason favored the idea of direct election but thought it would be "impracticable." John Dickinson likewise regarded "an election by the people . . . as the best and purest source" but recognized that the partiality of citizens toward candidates from their own state would be problematic. Others were concerned that the states' righters would vehemently oppose either direct or indirect popular election without the intervention of states. Charles Pinckney expressed the widespread fear among the small states that the most populous states would always select the president under such a system. Eldbridge Gerry liked the idea of electors chosen directly by the people but feared that "it would alarm . . . the State partizans, as tending to supersede altogether the State authorities." Madison pointed out that although direct election by the people was "the fittest in itself," the southern states would never assent to such a plan because "[t]he right of suffrage was much more diffusive in the Northern than the Southern states; and the latter could have no influence in the election on the scores of the Negroes." In other words, although the southern states received representation in the House for three-fifths of their slave population, the eligible voting population in the southern states that could influence a presidential election in the case of a direct popular vote was small. Hence, Madison recognized that until slavery and suffrage discrepancies were eliminated in the South, the substitution of electors for a direct popular vote would "obviat[e] this difficulty" and would therefore be "liable to the fewest objections."

* * *

The substitution of electors for a direct popular vote was not only viewed as a necessary concession to the states to minimize, as much as possible, the role of state politicians in the selection of the president, it was also defended on the grounds that it would effectively facilitate the formation of a national majority behind a qualified, meritorious candidate. Contrary to the common claim that the leading Framers feared direct election because they did not trust the voters, Madison, Morris, and Wilson had expressed on separate occasions that the people themselves would be the best judge of candidates "whose merits had rendered [them] an object of general attention and esteem" and that direct election would be as likely as any other method proposed to "produce an Executive Magistrate of distinguished character." In fact, the Constitutional Framers had wholeheartedly embraced the idea of direct election for members of the House of Representatives based on the same belief that "the great body of the people of the United States" should be trusted to select for public office those citizens "whose merit may recommend [them] to the esteem and confidence of [their] country." The application of representative democracy to the entire nation in the selection of president, however, posed challenges nonexistent in the direct election of members of the House. As George Mason observed, "The extent of the Country renders it impossible that the people can have the requisite capacity to judge of the respective pretensions of the Candidates." For this reason, Mason—though a renowned champion of democratic causes—warned that granting the people at large the responsibility of choosing "a proper character for chief Magistrate" would be like "refer[ring] a trial of colours to a blind man." Even James Wilson, the Convention's strongest proponent of direct election, later acknowledged that direct election would be problematic in an electoral district the size of the whole union.

Throughout the proceedings, various apprehensions were raised concerning the effectiveness of representative democracy on a national scale. Several of the delegates openly feared that, in a country the size of the United States, it would be unlikely for a majority of the people to concur in favor of any one candidate. Individual voters would not always have sufficient information to make intelligent choices about the merits and qualifications of candidates outside of their state or region. Thus, they would naturally vote for a local "favorite son." This would make it nearly impossible for one candidate to emerge with the support of a national popular majority. Consequently, the president would frequently be chosen solely by votes of the more populous states or regions of the country. In such a situation, there would be a greater incentive for demagogic, nefarious characters to obtain the suffrages of the people by appealing to their parochial prejudices and geographical interests only to betray the true interests of the national electorate in the end. Under these circumstances, Shlomo Slonim observes, "[T]he popular election would have the trappings of representative democracy, but not the essence."

The leading defenders of a scheme of statewide electors defended the system on the grounds that it would remedy these concerns and thereby give a more accurate expression to the national public will. As Hamilton explains in *Federalist 68* the right of selecting the nation's chief executive would be vested in electors chosen directly by the people for that purpose alone. Hamilton continues that a small number of electors "selected by their fellow citizens" would be more likely than the general mass of citizens to possess the knowledge and discernment to choose "characters pre-eminent for ability and virtue." Thus, electors would be charged with the duty of making a wise choice that their constituents would support. Hamilton also points out that electors acting on behalf of their constituents will be required to operate under circumstances "favorable to deliberation." He explains that because the electors meeting in each state would be temporary bodies of men, not serving in any other office under the United States and chosen for the sole purpose of selecting the president, it would be difficult to tamper with them or bribe them "to prostitute their votes in advance." Thus, presidential electors would be less susceptible "to the cable, intrigue and corruption" that so often causes representatives of the people to betray their trust.

To increase the likelihood that a majority of electors would choose a continental character, each elector was given two votes, one of which had to be cast for a non-home state candidate. The intention of this extra vote, which was ultimately negated by the Twelfth Amendment, was to force the people's electors to cast at least one vote for an acceptable national figure. The rationale was that the first vote could be given to a favorite fellow citizen, while the second could be cast for a continental character supported by electors from multiple states. On the basis of these factors, Martin Diamond concludes, "Clearly, then, what the Framers were seeking was not an undemocratic way to substitute elite electors for the popular will; rather, as they claimed, they were trying to find a practicable way to extract from the popular will a non-parochial choice for the President."

Following the conclusion of the Constitutional Convention, the presidential selection process faced little opposition. Hamilton observed in the *Federalist* that "[t]he mode of appointment of the Chief Magistrate of the United States is almost the only part of the system, of any consequence, which has escaped censure, or which has received the slightest mark of approbation from its opponents." Because of this widespread support during the ratification period, the selection process was rarely mentioned in debate. Nevertheless, the conviction that the Electoral College would facilitate popular control over the presidency continued to be propagated. George Mason of Virginia was the only delegate to openly oppose the presidential selection process before his state ratifying convention. He worried that a majority of electors would rarely agree on a single candidate and that the auxiliary process would enable the House of Representatives to elect a candidate with a very small percentage of the popular vote. He argued that limiting House choice to the two highest vote recipients would give the people greater influence over the final choice.

Nearly all further discussion of the selection process in the state conventions merely affirmed the president's dependence on the people and his corresponding duty to guard their rights and interests. Several delegates in their respective states echoed James Madison and James Wilson's charge that electors would ultimately be chosen directly by the people. Rev. Peter Thacher of Massachusetts, for instance, defended the democratic nature of the proposed Constitution in comparison to the British government by stating that "[t]he President is chosen by electors, who are appointed by the people." In the North Carolina debate James Iredell likewise emphasized, "By the proposed Constitution, the President is of a very different nature from a monarch. He is to be chosen by electors appointed by the people." Governor Edmund Randolph of Virginia additionally reiterated, "How is the President elected? By the people—on the same day throughout the United States—by those whom the people please."

The selection process was also occasionally mentioned to assuage fears concerning other aspects of the presidency and its powers. For instance, Virginia's George Nicholas responded to George Mason's concerns that the president and the Senate might impose treaties without a majority of national support by arguing that the president had "no local views" but "depended on the people [at large] for his political existence" and therefore would be unlikely to "sacrifice the interest of the eight largest states, to accommodate the five smallest." In Pennsylvania James Wilson defended the president's qualified veto power by concluding, "The President will not be a stranger to our country, to our laws, or to our wishes. He will, under this Constitution, be placed in office as the President of the whole Union, and will be chosen in such a manner that he may be justly styled the *man of the people."*

Conclusion

The Electoral College is one of the most controversial aspects of American constitutional democracy. Support for the system among the public remains low in part because of a lack of understanding of how the system operates and in part because of the belief that the system is both archaic and undemocratic. In fact, the widely held conviction that the system was intentionally designed to frustrate the expression of the public will and minimize majoritarianism in the selection of the nation's chief executive has largely gone unchallenged. Even many of the system's defenders ignore its inherently democratic roots and instead focus on its various current advantages, the chief one being the system's role in preserving federalism and the prerogative of the states. This defense, however, is somewhat misleading because the leading architects of the system never defended the selection process based on its inherent federalism. On the contrary, the system's primary architects purely viewed the components of the process that favored states as states as necessary concessions to the con-federalists that should be mitigated as much as possible in so far as they would interfere with the popular will.

Moreover, in contrast with those who argue that the system was meant to "temper or limit the power of majority will," the Convention proceedings reveal that the leading architects of the system were not seeking to frustrate the public will. Rather, they sought to discover a prudential means of stimulating national majority support for the winning candidate—thereby maintaining popular influence over the selection of the president. As Martin Diamond points out, "[A]ny fair and full reading of the evidence demands the conclusion [that] the majority of the Convention, and especially the leading architects of the Constitution, conceived the Electoral College simply as the most practical means by which to secure a free, democratic choice of an independent and effective chief executive." Furthermore, although the system experienced significant changes in the early years of its operation—most notably resulting from the development of the party system—an understanding of the overtly popular intentions of the system provides a more accurate foundation for analyzing whether such structural changes have helped fulfill the original goal of minimizing the likelihood of an undemocratic House contingency election or the selection of a geographically or ideologically narrow candidate.

32

"It's Time to Abolish the Electoral College"

Darrell M. West

For years when I taught campaigns and elections at Brown University, I defended the Electoral College as an important part of American democracy. I said the founders created the institution to make sure that large states did not dominate small ones in presidential elections, that power between Congress and state legislatures was balanced, and that there would be checks and balances in the constitutional system.

In recent years, though, I have changed my view and concluded it is time to get rid of the Electoral College. In this paper, I explain the history of the Electoral College, why it no longer is a constructive force in American politics, and why it is time to move to the direct popular election of presidents. Several developments have led me to alter my opinion on this institution: income inequality, geographic disparities, and how discrepancies between the popular vote and Electoral College are likely to become more commonplace given economic and geographic inequities. The remainder of this essay outlines why it is crucial to abolish the Electoral College.

The Original Rationale for the Electoral College

The framers of the Constitution set up the Electoral College for a number of different reasons. According to Alexander Hamilton in *The Federalist Papers*, No. 68, the body was a compromise at the Constitutional Convention in Philadelphia between large and small states. Many of the latter worried that states such as Massachusetts, New York, Pennsylvania, and Virginia would dominate the presidency so they devised an institution where each state had Electoral College votes in proportion to the number of its senators and House members. The former advantaged small states since each state had two senators regardless of its size, while the latter aided large states because the number of House members was based on the state's population.

In addition, there was considerable discussion regarding whether Congress or state legislatures should choose the chief executive. Those wanting a stronger national government tended to favor Congress, while states' rights adherents preferred state legislatures. In the end, there was a compromise establishing an independent group chosen by the states with the power to choose the president.

But delegates also had an anti-majoritarian concern in mind. At a time when many people were not well-educated, they wanted a body of wise men (women lacked the franchise) who would deliberate over leading contenders and choose the best man for the presidency. They explicitly rejected a popular vote for president because they did not trust voters to make a wise choice.

How It Has Functioned in Practice

In most elections, the Electoral College has operated smoothly. State voters have cast their ballots and the presidential candidate with the most votes in a particular state has received all the Electoral College votes of that state, except for Maine and Nebraska which allocate votes at the congressional district level within their states.

But there have been several contested elections. The 1800 election deadlocked because presidential candidate Thomas Jefferson received the same number of Electoral College votes as his vice presidential candidate Aaron Burr. At that time, the ballot did not distinguish between Electoral College votes for president and vice president. On the 36th ballot, the House chose Jefferson as the new president. Congress later amended the Constitution to prevent that ballot confusion from happening again.

Just over two decades later, Congress had an opportunity to test the newly established 12th Amendment. All four 1824 presidential aspirants belonged to the same party, the Democratic-Republicans, and although each had local and regional popularity, none of them attained the majority of their party's Electoral College votes. Andrew Jackson came the closest, with 99 Electoral College votes, followed by John Quincy Adams with 84 votes, William Crawford with 41, and Henry Clay with 37.

Because no candidate received the necessary 131 votes to attain the Electoral College majority, the election was thrown into the House of Representatives. As dictated by the 12th Amendment, each state delegation cast one vote among the top three candidates. Since Clay no longer was in the running, he made a deal with Adams to become his secretary of state in return for encouraging congressional support for Adams' candidacy. Even though Jackson had received the largest number of popular votes, he lost the presidency through what he called a "corrupt bargain" between Clay and Adams.

America was still recovering from the Civil War when Republican Rutherford Hayes ran against Democrat Samuel Tilden in the 1876 presidential election. The race was so close that the electoral votes of just four states would determine the presidency. On Election Day, Tilden picked up the popular vote plurality and 184 electoral votes, but fell one vote short of an Electoral College majority. However, Hayes claimed that his party would have won Florida, Louisiana, and South Carolina if not for voter intimidation against African American voters; and in Oregon, one of Hayes' three electoral votes was in dispute.

Instead of allowing the House to decide the presidential winner, as prescribed by the 12th Amendment, Congress passed a new law to create a bipartisan Electoral Commission. Through this commission, five members each from the House, Senate, and Supreme Court would assign the 20 contested electoral votes from Louisiana, Florida, South Carolina, and Oregon to either Hayes or Tilden. Hayes became president when this Electoral Commission ultimately gave the votes of the four contested states to him. The decision would have far-reaching consequences because in return for securing the votes of the Southern states, Hayes agreed to withdraw federal troops from the South, thereby paving the way for vigilante violence against African Americans and the denial of their civil rights.

Allegations of election unfairness also clouded the 2000 race. The contest between Republican George Bush and Democrat Al Gore was extremely close, ultimately resting on the fate of Florida's 25 electoral votes. Ballot controversies in Palm Beach County complicated vote tabulation. It used the "butterfly ballot" design, which some decried as visually confusing. Additionally, other Florida counties that required voters to punch perforated paper ballots had difficulty discerning the voters' choices if they did not fully detach the appropriate section of the perforated paper.

Accordingly, on December 8, 2000, the Florida Supreme Court ordered manual recounts in counties that reported statistically significant numbers of undervotes. The Bush campaign immediately filed suit, and in response, the U.S. Supreme Court paused manual recounts to hear oral arguments from candidates. On December 10, in a landmark 7–2 decision, the Supreme Court struck down the Florida Supreme Court's recount decision, ruling that a manual recount would violate the 14th Amendment's Equal Protection Clause. Bush won Florida's Electoral College votes and thus the presidency even though Gore had won the popular vote by almost half a million votes.

The latest controversy arose when Donald Trump lost the popular vote by almost three million ballots yet won the Electoral College by 74 votes. That made him the fifth U.S. chief executive to become president without winning the popular vote. This discrepancy between the Electoral College and the popular vote created considerable contentiousness about the electoral system. It set the Trump presidency off on a rough start and generated a critical tone regarding his administration.

The Faithless Elector Problem

In addition to the problems noted above, the Electoral College suffers from another difficulty known as the "faithless elector" issue in which that body's electors cast their ballot in opposition to the dictates of their state's popular vote. Samuel Miles, a Federalist from Pennsylvania, was the first of this genre as for unknown reasons, he cast his vote in 1796 for the Democratic-Republican candidate, Thomas Jefferson, even though his own Federalist party candidate John Adams had won Pennsylvania's popular vote.

Miles turned out to be the first of many. Throughout American history, 157 electors have voted contrary to their state's chosen winner. Some of these individuals dissented for idiosyncratic reasons, but others did so because they preferred the losing party's candidate. The precedent set by these people creates uncertainty about how future Electoral College votes could proceed.

This possibility became even more likely after a recent court decision. In the 2016 election, seven electors defected from the dictates of their state's popular vote. This was the highest number in any modern election. A Colorado lawsuit challenged the legality of state requirements that electors follow the vote of their states, something which is on the books in 29 states plus the District of Columbia. In the *Baca v. Hickenlooper* case, a federal court ruled that states cannot penalize faithless electors, no matter the intent of the elector or the outcome of the state vote.

Bret Chiafalo and plaintiff Michael Baca were state electors who began the self-named "Hamilton Electors" movement in which they announced their desire to stop Trump from winning the presidency. Deriving their name from Founding Father Alexander Hamilton, they convinced a few members of the Electoral College to cast their votes for other Republican candidates, such as John Kasich or Mitt Romney. When Colorado decided to nullify Baca's vote, he sued. A three-judge panel on the U.S. Court of Appeals for the Tenth Circuit ruled that Colorado's decision to remove Baca's vote was unconstitutional since the founders were explicit about the constitutional rights of electors to vote independently. Based on this legal ruling and in a highly polarized political environment where people have strong feelings about various candidates, it is possible that future faithless electors could tip the presidency one way or another, thereby nullifying the popular vote.

Why the Electoral College Is Poorly Suited for an Era of High Income Inequality and Widespread Geographic Disparities

The problems outlined above illustrate the serious issues facing the Electoral College. Having a president who loses the popular vote undermines electoral legitimacy. Putting an election into the House of Representatives where each state delegation has one vote increases the odds of insider dealings and corrupt decisions. Allegations of balloting irregularities that require an Electoral Commission to decide the votes of contested states do not make the general public feel very confident about the integrity of the process. And faithless electors could render the popular vote moot in particular states.

Yet there is a far more fundamental threat facing the Electoral College. At a time of high income inequality and substantial geographical disparities across states, there is a risk that the Electoral College will systematically overrepresent the views of relatively small numbers of people due to the structure of the Electoral College. As currently constituted, each state has two Electoral College votes regardless of population size, plus additional votes to match its number of House members. That format overrepresents small- and medium-sized states at the expense of large states.

That formula is problematic at a time when a Brookings Metropolitan Policy Program study found that 15 percent of American counties generate 64 percent of America's gross domestic product. Most of the country's economic activity is on the East Coast, West Coast, and a few metropolitan areas in between. The prosperous parts of America include about 15 states having 30 senators while the less prosperous areas encapsulate 35 states having 70 senators.

Those numbers demonstrate the fundamental mismatch between economic vitality and political power. Through the Electoral College (and the U.S. Senate), the 35 states with smaller economic activity have disproportionate power to choose presidents and dictate public policy. This institutional relic from two centuries ago likely will fuel continued populism and regular discrepancies between the popular and Electoral College votes. Rather than being a historic aberration, presidents who lose the popular vote could become the norm and thereby usher in an anti-majoritarian era where small numbers of voters in a few states use their institutional clout in "left-behind" states to block candidates and legislation desired by large numbers of people.

Support for Direct Popular Election

For years, a majority of Americans have opposed the Electoral College. For example, in 1967, 58 percent favored its abolition, while in 1981, 75 percent of Americans did so. More recent polling, however, has highlighted a dangerous development in public opinion. Americans by and large still want to do away with the Electoral College, but there now is a partisan divide in views, with Republicans favoring it while Democrats oppose it.

For instance, POLITICO and Morning Consult conducted a poll in March 2019 that found that 50 percent of respondents wanted a direct popular vote, 34 percent did not, and 16 percent did not demonstrate a preference. Two months later, NBC News and the *Wall Street Journal* reported polling that 53 percent of Americans wanted a direct popular vote, while 43 percent wanted to keep the status quo. These sentiments undoubtably have been reinforced by the fact that in two of the last five presidential elections, the candidate winning the popular vote lost the Electoral College.

Yet there are clear partisan divisions in these sentiments. In 2000, while the presidential election outcome was still being litigated, a Gallup survey reported that 73 percent of Democratic respondents supported a constitutional amendment to abolish the Electoral College and move to direct popular voting, but only 46 percent of Republican respondents supported that view. This gap has since widened as after the 2016 election, 81 percent of Democrats and 19 percent of Republicans affirmatively answered the same question.

The March POLITICO and Morning Consult poll also found that 72 percent of Democratic respondents and 30 percent of Republican respondents endorsed a direct popular vote. Likewise, the NBC News and *Wall Street Journal* poll found that 78 percent of Hillary Clinton voters supported a national popular vote, while 74 percent of Trump voters preferred the Electoral College.

Ways to Abolish the Electoral College

The U.S. Constitution created the Electoral College but did not spell out how the votes get awarded to presidential candidates. That vagueness has allowed some states such as Maine and Nebraska to reject "winner-take-all" at the state level and instead allocate votes at the congressional district level. However, the Constitution's lack of specificity also presents the opportunity that states could allocate their Electoral College votes through some other means.

One such mechanism that a number of states already support is an interstate pact that honors the national popular vote. Since 2008, 15 states and the District of Columbia have passed laws to adopt the National Popular Vote Interstate Compact (NPVIC), which is an multi-state agreement to commit electors to vote for candidates who win the nationwide popular vote, even if that candidate loses the popular vote within their state. The NPVIC would become effective only if states ratify it to reach an electoral majority of 270 votes.

Right now, the NPVIC is well short of that goal and would require an additional 74 electoral votes to take effect. It also faces some particular challenges. First, it is unclear how voters would respond if their state electors collectively vote against the popular vote of their state. Second, there are no binding legal repercussions if a state elector decides to defect from the national popular vote. Third, given the Tenth Circuit decision in the *Baca v. Hickenlooper* case described above, the NPVIC is almost certain to face constitutional challenges should it ever gain enough electoral votes to go into effect.

A more permanent solution would be to amend the Constitution itself. That is a laborious process and a constitutional amendment to abolish the Electoral College would require significant consensus—at least two-thirds affirmation from both the House and Senate, and approval from at least 38 out of 50 states. But Congress has nearly reached this threshold in the past. Congress nearly eradicated the Electoral College in 1934, falling just two Senate votes short of passage.

However, the conversation did not end after the unsuccessful vote; legislators have continued to debate ending or reforming the Electoral College since. In 1979, another Senate vote to establish a direct popular vote failed, this time by just three votes. Nonetheless, conversation continued: the 95th Congress proposed a total of 41 relevant amendments in 1977 and 1978, and the 116th Congress has already introduced three amendments to end the Electoral College. In total, over the last two centuries, there have been over 700 proposals to either eradicate or seriously modify the Electoral College. It is time to move ahead with abolishing the Electoral College before its clear failures undermine public confidence in American democracy, distort the popular will, and create a genuine constitutional crisis.

Discussion Questions

1. Is there a way to determine the national popular vote winner, as West supports, besides just summing the statewide vote totals? In an election decided by 7 million votes, this would (probably) be noncontroversial. But what if an election is close—within a few tens of thousands of votes, for example? What would the process of determining the winner look like? Is this a reason to preserve the electoral college, even in the face of a popular vote loser winning office?

2. In the previous reading, Villegas argues that the framers were concerned about democratic legitimacy. Does it make a difference that they were, quite clearly, concerned only about the legitimacy of *some* voters (chiefly, propertied White men)?

3. Does the electoral college guarantee that a president has support across a wide geographic region? Does it matter that these regions might be geographically large but have small populations compared to places where larger populations are more concentrated?

CHAPTER 7

Bureaucracy

33

From *Bureaucracy: What Government Agencies Do and Why They Do It*

JAMES Q. WILSON

For decades, critics have insisted that government would be more efficient if it ran like a business. Perhaps a more "businesslike" government would issue our income tax refunds more promptly, protect the environment at a lower cost, and impose fewer burdens on citizens. The catch is, we want all this at low cost and minimal intrusiveness in our lives, yet we want government bureaucracies to be held strictly accountable for the authority they exercise.

James Q. Wilson argues that government will never operate like a business, nor should we expect it to. His comparison of the Watertown (Massachusetts) Registry of Motor Vehicles (representing any government bureaucracy) with a nearby McDonald's (representing any private profit-seeking organization) shows that the former will most likely never service its clientele as well as the latter. The problem is not bureaucratic laziness, or any of the conventional criticisms of government agencies, but is instead due to the very different characteristics of public versus private enterprises. In order to understand "what government agencies do and why they do it," Wilson argues we must first understand that government bureaucracies operate in a political marketplace, rather than an economic one. The annual revenues and personnel resources of a government agency are determined by elected officials, not by the agency's ability to meet the demands of its customers in a cost-efficient manner. The government agency's internal structure and decision-making procedures are defined by legislation, regulation, and executive orders, whereas similar decisions in a private business are made by executive officers and management within the organization. And, perhaps most critical, a government agency's goals are often vague, difficult if not impossible to measure, and even contradictory. In business, by contrast, the task is clearer. The basic goal of a private business has always been to maximize the bottom line: profit. Although suggesting we should not approach the reform of government agencies the way we might a private bureaucracy, Wilson notes in this 1980s analysis that we should nevertheless try to make government bureaucracies operate more effectively and efficiently.

By the time the office opens at 8:45 A.M., the line of people waiting to do business at the Registry of Motor Vehicles in Watertown, Massachusetts, often will be twenty-five deep. By midday, especially if it is near the end of the month, the line may extend clear around the building. Inside, motorists wait in slow-moving rows before poorly marked windows to get a driver's license or to register an automobile. When someone gets to the head of the line, he or she is often told by the clerk that it is the wrong line: "[g]et an application over there and then come back," or "[t]his is only for people getting a new license; if you want to replace one you lost, you have to go to the next window." The customers grumble impatiently. The clerks act harried and sometimes speak brusquely, even rudely. What seems to be a simple transaction may take 45 minutes or even longer. By the time people are photographed for their driver's licenses, they are often scowling. The photographer valiantly tries to get people to smile, but only occasionally succeeds.

Not far away, people also wait in line at a McDonald's fast-food restaurant. There are several lines; each is short, each moves quickly. The menu is clearly displayed on attractive signs. The workers behind the counter are invariably polite. If someone's order cannot be filled immediately, he or she is asked to step aside for a moment while the food is prepared and then is brought back to the head of the line to receive the order. The atmosphere is friendly and good-natured. The room is immaculately clean.

Many people have noticed the difference between getting a driver's license and ordering a Big Mac. Most will explain it by saying that bureaucracies are different from businesses. "Bureaucracies" behave as they do because they are run by unqualified "bureaucrats" and are enmeshed in "rules" and "red tape."

But business firms are also bureaucracies, and McDonald's is a bureaucracy that regulates virtually every detail of its employees' behavior by a complex and all-encompassing set of rules. Its operations manual is six hundred pages long and weighs four pounds. In it one learns that french fries are to be nine-thirty-seconds of an inch thick and that grill workers are to place hamburger patties on the grill from left to right, six to a row for six rows. They are then to flip the third row first, followed by the fourth, fifth, and sixth rows, and finally the first and second. The amount of sauce placed on each bun is precisely specified. Every window must be washed every day. Workers must get down on their hands and knees and pick up litter as soon as it appears. These and countless other rules designed to reduce the workers to interchangeable automata were inculcated in franchise managers at Hamburger University located in a $40-million facility. There are plenty of rules governing the Registry, but they are only a small fraction of the rules that govern every detail of every operation at McDonald's. Indeed, if the DMV manager tried to impose on his employees as demanding a set of rules as those that govern the McDonald's staff, they would probably rebel and he would lose his job.

It is just as hard to explain the differences between the two organizations by reference to the quality or compensation of their employees. The Registry workers are all adults, most with at least a high-school education; the McDonald's employees are mostly teenagers, many still in school. The Registry staff is well paid compared to the McDonald's workers, most of whom receive only the minimum wage. When labor shortages developed in Massachusetts during the mid-1980s, many McDonald's stores began hiring older people (typically housewives) of the same sort who had long worked for the Registry. They behaved just like the teenagers they replaced.

Not only are the differences between the two organizations not to be explained by reference to "rules" or "red tape" or "incompetent workers," the differences call into question many of the most frequently mentioned complaints about how government agencies are supposed to behave. For example: "[g]overnment agencies are big spenders." The Watertown office of the Registry is in a modest building that can barely handle its clientele. The teletype machine used to check information submitted by people requesting a replacement license was antiquated and prone to errors. Three or four clerks often had to wait in line to use equipment described by the office manager as "personally signed by Thomas Edison." No computers or word processors were available to handle the preparation of licenses and registrations; any error made by a clerk while manually typing a form meant starting over again on another form.

Or: "[g]overnment agencies hire people regardless of whether they are really needed." Despite the fact that the citizens of Massachusetts probably have more contact with the Registry than with any other state agency, and despite the fact that these citizens complain more about Registry service than about that of any other bureau, the Watertown branch, like all Registry offices, was seriously understaffed. In 1981, the agency lost 400 workers—about 25 percent of its work force—despite the fact that its workload was rising.

Or: "[g]overnment agencies are imperialistic, always grasping for new functions." But there is no record of the Registry doing much grasping, even though one could imagine a case being made that the state government could usefully create at Registry offices "one-stop" multi-service centers where people could not only get drivers' licenses but also pay taxes and parking fines, obtain information, and transact other official business. The Registry seemed content to provide one service.

In short, many of the popular stereotypes about government agencies and their members are either questionable or incomplete. To explain why government agencies behave as they do, it is not enough to know that they are "bureaucracies"—that is, it is not enough to know that they are big, or complex, or have rules. What is crucial is that they are *government* bureaucracies. * * * [N]ot all government bureaucracies behave the same way or suffer from the same problems. There may even be registries of motor vehicles in other states that do a better job than the one in Massachusetts. But all government agencies have in common certain characteristics that tend to make their management far more difficult than managing a McDonald's. These common characteristics are the constraints of public agencies.

The key constraints are three in number. To a much greater extent than is true of private bureaucracies, government agencies (1) cannot lawfully retain and devote to the private benefit of their members the earnings of the organization, (2) cannot allocate the factors of production in accordance with the preferences of the organization's administrators, and (3) must serve goals not of the organization's own choosing. Control over revenues, productive factors, and agency goals is all vested to an important degree in entities external to the organization—legislatures, courts, politicians, and interest groups. Given this, agency managers must attend to the demands of these external entities. As a result, government management tends to be driven by the *constraints* on the organization, not the *tasks* of the organization. To say the same thing in other words, whereas business management focuses on the "bottom line" (that is, profits), government management focuses on the "top line" (that is, constraints). Because government managers are not as strongly motivated as private ones to define the tasks of their subordinates, these tasks are often shaped by [other] factors.

* * *

Revenues and Incentives

In the days leading up to September 30, the federal government is Cinderella, courted by legions of individuals and organizations eager to get grants and contracts from the unexpended funds still at the disposal of each agency. At midnight on September 30, the government's coach turns into a pumpkin. That is the moment—the end of the fiscal year—at which every agency, with a few exceptions, must return all unexpended funds to the Treasury Department.

Except for certain quasi-independent government corporations, such as the Tennessee Valley Authority, no agency may keep any surplus revenues (that is, the difference between the funds it received from a congressional appropriation and those it needed to operate during the year). By the same token, any agency that runs out of money before the end of the fiscal year may ask Congress for more (a "supplemental appropriation") instead of being forced to deduct the deficit from any accumulated cash reserves.

Because of these fiscal rules agencies do not have a material incentive to economize: Why scrimp and save if you cannot keep the results of your frugality?

Nor can individual bureaucrats lawfully capture for their personal use any revenue surpluses. When a private firm has a good year, many of its officers and workers may receive bonuses. Even if no bonus is paid, these employees may buy stock in the firm so that they can profit from any growth in earnings (and, if they sell the stock in a timely manner, profit from a drop in earnings). Should a public bureaucrat be discovered trying to do what private bureaucrats routinely do, he or she would be charged with corruption.

We take it for granted that bureaucrats should not profit from their offices and nod approvingly when a bureaucrat who has so benefited is indicted and put on trial. But why should we take this view? Once a very different view prevailed. In the seventeenth century, a French colonel would buy his commission from the king, take the king's money to run his regiment, and pocket the profit. At one time a European tax collector was paid by keeping a percentage of the taxes he collected. In this country, some prisons were once managed by giving the warden a sum of money based on how many prisoners were under his control and letting him keep the difference between what he received and what it cost him to feed the prisoners. Such behavior today would be grounds for criminal prosecution. Why? What has changed?

Mostly we the citizenry have changed. We are creatures of the Enlightenment: [w]e believe that the nation ought not to be the property of the sovereign; that laws are intended to rationalize society and (if possible) perfect mankind; and that public service ought to be neutral and disinterested. We worry that a prison warden paid in the old way would have a strong incentive to starve his prisoners in order to maximize his income; that a regiment supported by a greedy colonel would not be properly equipped; and that a tax collector paid on a commission basis would extort excessive taxes from us. These changes reflect our desire to eliminate moral hazards—namely, creating incentives for people to act wrongly. But why should this desire rule out more carefully designed compensation plans that would pay government managers for achieving officially approved goals and would allow efficient agencies to keep any unspent part of their budget for use next year?

Part of the answer is obvious. Often we do not know whether a manager or an agency has achieved the goals we want because either the goals are vague or inconsistent, or their attainment cannot be observed, or both. Bureau chiefs in the Department of State would have to go on welfare if their pay depended on their ability to demonstrate convincingly that they had attained their bureaus' objectives.

But many government agencies have reasonably clear goals toward which progress can be measured. The Social Security Administration, the

Postal Service, and the General Services Administration all come to mind. Why not let earnings depend importantly on performance? Why not let agencies keep excess revenues?

* * *

But in part it is because we know that even government agencies with clear goals and readily observable behavior only can be evaluated by making political (and thus conflict-ridden) judgments. If the Welfare Department delivers every benefit check within 24 hours after the application is received, Senator Smith may be pleased but Senator Jones will be irritated because this speedy delivery almost surely would require that the standards of eligibility be relaxed so that many ineligible clients would get money. There is no objective standard by which the trade-off between speed and accuracy in the Welfare Department can be evaluated. Thus we have been unwilling to allow welfare employees to earn large bonuses for achieving either speed or accuracy.

The inability of public managers to capture surplus revenues for their own use alters the pattern of incentives at work in government agencies. Beyond a certain point additional effort does not produce additional earnings. (In this country, Congress from time to time has authorized higher salaries for senior bureaucrats but then put a cap on actual payments to them so that the pay increases were never received. This was done to insure that no bureaucrat would earn more than members of Congress at a time when those members were unwilling to accept the political costs of raising their own salaries. As a result, the pay differential between the top bureaucratic rank and those just below it nearly vanished.) If political constraints reduce the marginal effect of money incentives, then the relative importance of other, nonmonetary incentives will increase. * * *

That bureaucratic performance in most government agencies cannot be linked to monetary benefits is not the whole explanation for the difference between public and private management. There are many examples of private organizations whose members cannot appropriate money surpluses for their own benefit. Private schools ordinarily are run on a nonprofit basis. Neither the headmaster nor the teachers share in the profit of these schools; indeed, most such schools earn no profit at all and instead struggle to keep afloat by soliciting contributions from friends and alumni. Nevertheless, the evidence is quite clear that on the average, private schools, both secular and denominational, do a better job than public ones in educating children. Moreover, as political scientists John Chubb and Terry Moe have pointed out, they do a better job while employing fewer managers. Some other factors are at work. One is the freedom an organization has to acquire and use labor and capital.

Acquiring and Using the Factors of Production

A business firm acquires capital by retaining earnings, borrowing money, or selling shares of ownership; a government agency (with some exceptions) acquires capital by persuading a legislature to appropriate it. A business firm hires, promotes, demotes, and fires personnel with considerable though not perfect freedom; a federal government agency is told by Congress how many persons it can hire and at what rate of pay, by the Office of Personnel Management (OPM) what rules it must follow in selecting and assigning personnel, by the Office of Management and Budget (OMB) how many persons of each rank it may employ, by the Merit Systems Protection Board (MSPB) what procedures it must follow in demoting or discharging personnel, and by the courts whether it has faithfully followed the rules of Congress, OPM, OMB, and MSPB. A business firm purchases goods and services by internally defined procedures (including those that allow it to buy from someone other than the lowest bidder if a more expensive vendor seems more reliable), or to skip the bidding procedure altogether in favor of direct negotiations; a government agency must purchase much of what it uses by formally advertising for bids, accepting the lowest, and keeping the vendor at arm's length. When a business firm develops a good working relationship with a contractor, it often uses that vendor repeatedly without looking for a new one; when a government agency has a satisfactory relationship with a contractor, ordinarily it cannot use the vendor again without putting a new project out for a fresh set of bids. When a business firm finds that certain offices or factories are no longer economical it will close or combine them; when a government agency wishes to shut down a local office or military base often it must get the permission of the legislature (even when formal permission is not necessary, informal consultation is). When a business firm draws up its annual budget each expenditure item can be reviewed as a discretionary amount (except for legally mandated payments of taxes to government and interest to banks and bondholders); when a government agency makes up its budget many of the detailed expenditure items are mandated by the legislature.

All these complexities of doing business in or with the government are well known to citizens and firms. These complexities in hiring, purchasing, contracting, and budgeting often are said to be the result of the "bureaucracy's love of red tape." But few, if any, of the rules producing this complexity would have been generated by the bureaucracy if left to its own devices, and many are as cordially disliked by the bureaucrats as by their clients. These rules have been imposed on the agencies by external actors, chiefly the legislature. They are not bureaucratic rules but *political* ones. In principle the legislature could allow the Social Security Administration, the Defense Department, or the New York City public

school system to follow the same rules as IBM, General Electric, or Harvard University. In practice they could not. The reason is politics, or more
precisely, democratic politics.

*   *   *

Public versus Private Management

What distinguishes public from private organizations is neither their size nor
their desire to "plan" (that is, control) their environments but rather the rules
under which they acquire and use capital and labor. General Motors [GM]
acquires capital by selling shares, issuing bonds, or retaining earnings; the
Department of Defense [DOD] acquires it from an annual appropriation by
Congress. GM opens and closes plants, subject to certain government regulations, at its own discretion; DOD opens and closes military bases under the
watchful guidance of Congress. GM pays its managers with salaries it sets
and bonuses tied to its earnings; DOD pays its managers with salaries set by
Congress and bonuses (if any) that have no connection with organizational
performance. The number of workers in GM is determined by its level of
production; the number in DOD by legislation and civil-service rules.

   What all this means can be seen by returning to the Registry of Motor
Vehicles and McDonald's. Suppose you were just appointed head of the
Watertown office of the Registry and you wanted to improve service there
so that it more nearly approximated the service at McDonald's. Better service might well require spending more money (on clerks, equipment, and
buildings). Why should your political superiors give you that money? It is
a cost to them if it requires either higher taxes or taking funds from another
agency; offsetting these real and immediate costs are dubious and post-
poned benefits. If lines become shorter and clients become happier, no legislator will benefit. There may be fewer complaints, but complaints are
episodic and have little effect on the career of any given legislator. By contrast, shorter lines and faster service at McDonald's means more customers
can be served per hour and thus more money can be earned per hour. A
McDonald's manager can estimate the marginal product of the last dollar
he or she spends on improving service; the Registry manager can generate
no tangible return on any expenditure he or she makes and thus cannot
easily justify the expenditure.

   Improving service at the Registry may require replacing slow or surly
workers with quick and pleasant ones. But you, the manager, can neither
hire nor fire them at will. You look enviously at the McDonald's manager
who regularly and with little notice replaces poor workers with better ones.
Alternatively, you may wish to mount an extensive training program (perhaps creating a Registration University to match McDonald's Hamburger
University) that would imbue a culture of service in your employees. But
unless the Registry were so large an agency that the legislature would

neither notice nor care about funds spent for this purpose—and it is not that large—you would have a tough time convincing anybody that this was not a wasteful expenditure on a frill project.

If somehow your efforts succeed in making Registry clients happier, you can take vicarious pleasure in it; in the unlikely event a client seeks you out to thank you for those efforts, you can bask in a moment's worth of glory. Your colleague at McDonald's who manages to make customers happier may also derive some vicarious satisfaction from the improvement but in addition he or she will earn more money owing to an increase in sales.

In time it will dawn on you that if you improve service too much, clients will start coming to the Watertown office instead of going to the Boston office. As a result, the lines you succeeded in shortening will become longer again. If you wish to keep complaints down, you will have to spend even more on the Watertown office. But if it was hard to persuade the legislature to do that in the past, it is impossible now. Why should the taxpayer be asked to spend more on Watertown when the Boston office, fully staffed (naturally, no one was laid off when the clients disappeared), has no lines at all? From the legislature's point of view the correct level of expenditure is not that which makes one office better than another but that which produces an equal amount of discontent in all offices.

Finally, you remember that your clients have no choice: [t]he Registry offers a monopoly service. It and only it supplies drivers' licenses. In the long run all that matters is that there are not "too many" complaints to the legislature about service. Unlike McDonald's, the Registry need not fear that its clients will take their business to Burger King or to Wendy's. Perhaps you should just relax.

If this were all there is to public management it would be an activity that quickly and inevitably produces cynicism among its practitioners. But this is not the whole story. For one thing, public agencies differ in the kinds of problems they face. For another, many public managers try hard to do a good job even though they face these difficult constraints.

DISCUSSION QUESTIONS

1. Wilson argues that McDonald's and the Registry of Motor Vehicles operate differently because of the inherent differences between public and private organizations. Apply his reasoning to other cases, for instance, the U.S. Postal Service and FedEx, or any other area where the government and the private sector compete for business. Think about the goals of the organizations, who controls them, how you distinguish success from failure, and the consequences of failure.

2. What are the advantages and disadvantages of trying to run the government more like a business? How would you define the basic par-

ameters of a "businesslike" government—for instance, who are the "customers"?

3. Some critics of government inefficiency argue that nearly every domestic government function—from schools to road building—could be run more efficiently if it were "privatized"—turned over to private contractors. Do you agree? Are there any government functions that do not lend themselves to privatization?

34

From *Introduction to the Study of Public Administration*

Leonard White

The study of public administration—how public policies are actually implemented, who performs the tasks, how individuals perform the tasks, and how to carry out these tasks efficiently—became more important and more systematic as government grew in size and its functions became more complex. By the end of World War I, scholars turned to the question of how to manage the implementation of complicated and technical policies.

This selection, from one of the most important scholars of early public administration, depicts the administrative problem as a logical one: a major theory from the time is that efficiency should be achieved through good management, application of scientific principles, and technical expertise. This task, White argues, is quite different from the larger political functions of the "protection of private rights, the development of civic capacity, the due recognition of the manifold phases of public opinion, the maintenance of order, [and] the provision of a national minimum of welfare." The old ad hoc practices of the early nineteenth century were no longer adequate to modern government. Consistent with the accepted theory of the time, White considered public administration to be politically neutral, carried out by "permanent officials with suitable professional and technical training" and managed by officials who can mediate between politically neutral administrative personnel, politicians, and the public.

The Scope and Nature of Public Administration

* * *

Public administration is the management of men and materials in the accomplishment of the purposes of the state. This definition emphasizes the managerial phase of administration and minimizes its legalistic and formal aspect. It relates the conduct of government business to the conduct of the affairs of any other social organization, commercial, philanthropic, religious, or educational, in all of which good management is recognized as an element essential to success. It leaves open the question to what extent the administration itself participates in formulating the purposes of the state, and avoids any controversy as to the precise nature of administrative action.

The objective of public administration is the most efficient utilization of the resources at the disposal of officials and employees. These resources include not only current appropriations and material equipment in the form of public buildings, machinery, highways and canals, but also the human resources bound up in the hundreds of thousands of men and women who work for the state. In every direction good administration seeks the elimination of waste, the conservation of material and energy, and the most rapid and complete achievement of public purposes consistent with economy and the welfare of the workers.

*   *   *

Public administration is, then, the execution of the public business; the goal of administrative activity the most expeditious, economical, and complete achievement of public programs. This obviously is not the sole objective of the state as an organized unit; the protection of private rights, the development of civic capacity and sense of civic responsibility, the due recognition of the manifold phases of public opinion, the maintenance of order, the provision of a national minimum of welfare, all bespeak the constant solicitude of the state. Administration must be correlated with other branches of government, as well as adjusted to the immense amount of private effort which in America far more than elsewhere supplements public enterprise.

*   *   *

Students of public affairs are gradually discerning, in fact, that administration has become the heart of the modern problem of government. In an earlier and simpler age, legislative bodies had the time to deal with the major issues, the character of which was suited to the deliberations of the lay mind; they were primarily problems involving judgments on important questions of political ethics, such as the enfranchisement of citizens by abolishing property qualifications, the disposition of the public land, the disestablishment of the Anglican Church, or the liberalization of a monarchist state. The problems which crowd upon legislative bodies today are often entangled with, or become exclusively technical questions which the layman can handle only by utilizing the services of the expert. The control of local government, the regulation of utilities, the enforcement of the prohibition amendment, the appropriation for a navy, the organization of a health department, the maintenance of a national service of agricultural research, are all matters which can be put upon the statute book only with the assistance of men who know the operating details in each case. So we discover in the administrative service one official who knows all that can be known about the control of waterborne diseases, another who has at his fingertips the substance of all available information on wheat rust, and another who cannot be "stumped" on appropriations for the national park service. These men are not merely useful to legislators overwhelmed by the increasing flood of bills; they are simply indispensable. They are the government. One may indeed suggest that the traditional assignment of the legislature as the pivotal agency in the governmental triumvirate is destined at no distant date to be replaced by a more realistic analysis which will establish government as the task of administration, operating within such areas as may be circumscribed by legislatures and courts.

* * *

In every direction * * * the task of the modern state is enlarging. In every direction likewise the range of public administration is being extended, for every phase of the new program of the state is reflected in additional administrative activity.

* * *

The enormous improvements which have been made by scientific management in some industries have raised the question whether or not equally striking improvements are feasible in government. Whatever answer be given to this question, there can be no doubt that the achievements of scientific management have aroused a vast amount of dissatisfaction with the antiquated methods which have characterized many public offices. More and more clearly it is being understood that the promise of American life will never be realized until American administration has been lifted out of the ruts in which it has been left by a century of neglect.

Science and Administration

* * * The unexampled development of science and technology in the last half century has transformed not only the equipment but the tasks of administration as well. Science has revealed the objects to be achieved and also furnished the tools with which the state operates. Could one make a careful comparison of the actual work performed and methods used by an American commonwealth or municipality in 1825 with its work and methods in 1925, the contrast would be startling. Then highways were dirt roads, built with shovels, picks, horses, and human labor, on the "scientific" basis of the common sense of the town selectman. Schools were the province of the local "school-marm" and the town or county board of education, specializing in the three R's and plenty of "applied discipline." Public sanitation was nobody's business; the country doctor treated the sick and the undertaker disposed of those who fell before the onslaughts of uncontrolled epidemics. Agriculture, the chief occupation of the population, was completely innocent of any traffic with science. The care of the poor and the feebleminded, the custody of the criminal and the insane were all given over to the "overseers of the poor" in the rural districts, with no thought of classification, remedial treatment, scientific study or preventive action. And so one might go on; all the elaborate paraphernalia of

technology, investigation, and scientific procedure was absent from the social technique of a short hundred years ago.

To what extent the modern state now depends upon science is not easily described, for the whole technical equipment of present-day administration rests upon scientific achievement. More than that, the modern administrator has in many cases become not only a scientist, but a research scientist. Few of the major tasks of modern administration can be carried on without the constant support of the technician; education, sanitation, construction (highways, reclamation, public buildings), regulation, conservation, public welfare administration, criminology, the management of funds, the management of personnel, control of the administrative process, all these and many more demand the services of the specialist and of his unique body of knowledge.

* * *

Although we are entitled to certain reserve in the use of the phrase "the science of management," we are wholly justified in asserting that a science of management appears to be immediately before us. In some respects indeed it is now fairly well established. * * * [T]he measurement of efficiency has produced certain interesting and significant procedures which have some claim to the term scientific. Mechanical problems connected with routing, equipment, ventilation, lighting and the like have been dealt with on a strictly scientific basis. We may suppose that eventually more subtle and complicated problems will be attacked with the aid of scientific methods.

The growth of science and technology and their application to the business side of government has already created a new environment in which old theories need to be readjusted. It is manifestly impossible * * * to continue on the Jacksonian notion that "the duties of all public officers are, or at least admit of being made, so plain and simple that men of intelligence may readily qualify themselves for their performance." The duties of public office are complicated, highly specialized, professional, and immensely important. They can be adequately performed only by permanent officials, with suitable professional and technical training, acting under the direction of department heads of the broadest vision who are able by their personal leadership to mediate between the technician, the politician, and the public.

* * *

Public and Non-official Administration

The antecedents of American public administration are profoundly different from those of American business. For over a half century the spoils system held undisputed sway in government affairs, and for a century its influence has been great. The gigantic struggle to loosen the grip of the politician has inevitably left its marks upon the body of the civil service. Many of the conditions which seem to lessen the efficiency of government offices are the product of the legal protection evolved to guarantee even a moderate level of efficiency and integrity. These cannot be relaxed to any considerable degree without encouraging an immediate return to the evils of an age now happily waning. But in the city manager cities can be observed the relaxation of legal safeguards as they are replaced by a new ideal of the public service.

Business has not been scarred by a similar struggle to free itself from incompetence, although it has had other almost equally difficult conditions to meet. Business, too, has been more strongly armed, for the incentive of profit and the spur of competition have compelled constant improvement. Profits also furnished business an intelligible test of success, but they are of no help whatever in assessing the achievements of government. Government has not the profit incentive, either as a collectivity or viewed from the standpoint of the individual employee, nor is it deeply affected in America by any sort of competition, whereas in Europe international rivalry has done much to strengthen both the civil and military establishments. The sustaining incentives for high productivity in government must in fact be sought elsewhere, and the search constitutes at once the most delicate and the most important task of the student of administration.

Government is constrained to a rigid observance of the principle of consistency, which may be ignored by business. * * * The principle of consistency must be applied as between successive cases, over the whole of the area concerned, for the complete period of time involved.

But business (excluding public utilities), philanthropy, religion, endowed education, are under no such compulsion. A state university must throw open its resources to all qualified applicants alike, but a privately endowed institution may impose an arbitrary limit on the gross numbers, or draw racial lines, or vary its entrance requirements at will, so far as its governing authorities deem wise. The Federal Trade Commission is gradually building up certain standards of consistency in the conduct of business as it defines unfair practices, but business is still free to vary its service and prices in ways forbidden to government. * * *

Government affairs differ in another respect from private affairs; their conduct is subject to a degree of accountability which is far more minute and pervasive than business. Appropriation acts are much more specific and rigid than allotments of commercial funds; auditors are insistent upon exact compliance with the terms of the law; Congressmen are always alert to discover any violation of the statute book. * * * One may readily imagine the fate of an American business firm conducted on such a basis.

* * *

Public administration offers an opportunity for constructive leadership in America which is hardly paralleled in unofficial circles. The large scale of the operations, the variety of the tasks, their immediate relation to the commonweal, all strike the imagination through a combination of appeals which industry and commerce do not ordinarily achieve. The city manager is more than an engineer, and his profession as manager is likely to strike deeper than his profession as engineer.

The state need not attempt to compete with business on a financial basis for its administrative leadership. It needs as fine administrative capacity as business, but must attract it by means of other considerations. It must of course provide an adequate scale of salaries and proper provision for retirement, but it will hold its own in the competition with industry by capitalizing the prestige value which attaches to a "big" organization, to a "big" opportunity, and to the honor of public position. The state can and presumably will provide in constantly more generous measure a career which will call for and receive, so far as needed, the best brains of each decade.

Discussion Questions

1. Is it really possible for public administration to be truly "neutral"? Does this require that all administrative steps be spelled out in explicit and exhaustive detail so that the people carrying out the actual tasks have no discretion at all in deciding how to carry out the administrative function? What are the implications if discretion is inherent in the process?

2. The government is now many times larger and more complex than it was when White was writing about public administration during the 1920s. Do you think he would take the same stance if he were writing today?

Debating the Issues: Should Bureaucracies Be More Accountable to the President?

How responsive should government agencies be to elected officials (and, by inference, to the public)? A bureaucracy that does not have to consider public opinion or voters can become unaccountable (imagine an agency that won't implement a law because senior officials simply refuse to do so, and there is no recourse). At the same time, a bureaucracy that must be immediately responsive to short-term political demands will sacrifice competence and neutrality if the bureaucracy has to do anything that a governor or president orders it to do. Imagine an agency being forced to do something—approve a treatment or medication, award a lucrative contract to a friend of the governor's, implement an unproven air traffic control system, or prosecute someone—just because a president, governor, or powerful legislator demands it.

Concerns about balancing accountability with neutrality took a sharper edge over critics (including former president Donald Trump) who alleged that a "deep state" was corruptly interfering with and even sabotaging efforts to change government policy.

Rebecca Ingber contests the underlying charge of bureaucratic obstruction. Bureaucrats can serve as a vital constraint on presidential lawlessness, alerting both the public and Congress to abuses of power as whistle-blowers (such as Alexander Vindman, the National Security Council staffer who revealed Trump's efforts to condition U.S. military assistance to Ukraine on the country's willingness to dig up dirt on Joe Biden). Bureaucratic friction serves an important function, insulating policy from the whims (or tweets) of elected leaders. The real danger, she concludes, is presidential abuse of power, against which the bureaucracy can, quite properly, resist.

Jon D. Michaels argues that the federal bureaucracy is actually responsive to political leaders, balancing accountability with a professional ethos of neutrality and competence. The "deep state" myth, he concludes, is only the latest in a long history of attempts to discredit government agencies.

35

"Bureaucratic Resistance and the Deep State Myth"

Rebecca Ingber

The last three years have been a time of great crisis for the U.S. executive branch bureaucracy, and for the U.S. presidency. Career officials have fled their agencies in record numbers, taking their lifetime of expertise and institutional memory with them. Political positions are hard to fill with qualified candidates, and even the highest levels of the President's own political appointees have seen unusually high turnover, including those advisors—like the President's first Secretary of Defense—who have resigned in protest. Fanning the flames further, leaking has been rampant in this administration, often from within the President's own inner circle itself. And what of the President? For his part, the President has alternatively sought to weaponize, to delegitimize, or to dismiss the work of the public servants who keep the many offices and agencies of the modern-day administrative state running. The President's abuse of the human beings populating the executive branch bureaucracy has become inextricably linked with his abuse of the power of his office and, furthermore, his defense to it. His response to charges of malfeasance is an approach he has honed through crisis after crisis and will continue to use again, one that threatens the continued functions of good government: the claim that any threat to or constraint on his power is the working of a "deep state" seeking to undermine the will of the people.

The reports of the Ukraine affair, the riveted focus by many on a secret "whistleblower" inside the deep reaches of the intelligence community, and the tussling between career foreign services officers and political appointees at the State Department and Office of Management and Budget certainly give the President much to work with.

The involvement of career officials inside the government possibly working at cross purposes to the President's desires, seeking to disclose information about the President's activities to his political foes in Congress, and ultimately sparking an impeachment inquiry that could threaten his entire Presidency is the stuff of the President's greatest fever dreams. And right on cue, the President and his supporters have sought to paint the Ukraine whistleblower as a "deep state operative" working to effectuate a "coup," and will likely levy similar accusations as details emerge regarding the work of foreign service officers and others in the White House who appear to have questioned the withholding of security assistance to Ukraine in exchange for investigating the President's opponents.

This part of the saga is a reprise of the President's playbook during the Mueller investigation: paint any constraint on the President—whether it be legal, bureaucratic, or political—as not only disloyal, suspect, even treacherous, but also part of a broader "deep state" conspiracy to overturn the will of the people.

We can also expect a reprise of the reaction we saw to the Mueller investigation from those seeking to hold the President accountable. Throughout that saga, the President's political opponents and veterans of the executive branch came together—in some cases the oddest of bedfellows—to hail bureaucratic constraints on the President and independence of law enforcement as critical to presidential legitimacy. Some academics and pundits took that support to another level, fanning the "deep state" paranoia by calling (rightly or wrongly) for the bureaucracy to rise up and resist the President. These calls to resist became such a salient topic that the U.S. Office of Special Counsel produced guidance for civil servants forbidding discussion of "#Resistance" as a violation of the Hatch Act's prohibition on political activity. So how are we to think about these fears of bureaucrats as well as the calls for their resistance?

The Right Questions to Ask about the Existence of the "Deep State"

These events and perceptions raise countless questions both practical and theoretical, both for observers of the executive branch and for those holding or considering careers in government. Does the "deep state" exist, and can it save the country from the President? Is resistance inside the bureaucracy a subversion of the democratic system? And what power do bureaucrats actually have—legal, moral, practical—to defy the President's will?

I explore these questions in a recent article, "Bureaucratic Resistance and the National Security State," in which I argue that while the bureaucracy can be a force for continuity and a real constraint, it is neither the threat some fear, nor a cure to a President who poses such a threat. Nor should we wish for or seek to engender a bureaucracy that itself is capable of "saving" us from our electoral decisions.

Anatomy of the Administrative Bureaucracy and Resistance Within

The executive branch bureaucracy is not a "deep state"—in part because it does not have the organizational capacity or motivation to hold the reins of the state. It is both more functionally constrained, and more formally tethered to accountable sources of power, than either the deep state or the #Resistance approach generally conceives. It is also far more multilithic—and resistance within it more multidirectional. Unlike the stark image created by both deep state and #Resistance rhetoric, the bureaucracy is not a polarized dichotomy between a sharply defined civil service on one hand and the President on the other. And that divide is certainly not the focal point at which most bureaucrats tend to experience regular conflict.

Consider, in addition to the divide between the career and political bureaucracies, an axis along which to classify executive branch officials according to their expected taint from partisan politics. Where would you place the President's own, politically appointed Attorney General on that spectrum, and other political appointees throughout the law enforcement bureaucracy? Jeff Sessions, Rod Rosenstein, Chris Wray, Geoffrey Berman (the U.S. Attorney for the SDNY), even James Comey—many officials who have wielded real power to enforce a buffer between the President and his law enforcement agencies have been political appointees, not civil servants. The shock by many government watchers in Attorney General Bill Barr's embrace of the erosion of DOJ independence itself demonstrates how emphatically that norm has long been revered.

The normal, daily experience of most bureaucrats does involve conflict, not with the President, nor even necessarily with the politically appointed boss, but rather with other bureaucratic actors across the administrative state. These disputes are generally longstanding and survive from presidency to presidency. In fact, despite perceptions of the significant power that is wielded by "unelected bureaucrats" on the "front lines"—and despite the ambitions of Presidents during campaigns where they promise to bring swift change to government—most actors at every level of the federal bureaucracy, from the line officer to the President, have reason to feel quite hemmed in from all sides, much of the time.

Resistance, too, generally takes more nuanced forms than the mythical power wielded by either the "deep state" or the #Resistance. The fact that the entire architecture of the state does not reverse course on a tweet does not mean that the public servants dispersed throughout the government have conspired to undermine the President. I define resistance broadly, steeped in the empirical (if more mundane) reality of bureaucratic service. Resistance includes asking questions, insisting on normal process, voicing dissent to superiors, and trying to convince others of one's view. "I think it's crazy to withhold security assistance for help with a political campaign," is a fine example. All of these actions can slow down the works. They may even result in a change of course; but rather than evidence of mutiny, this is the bread and butter of bureaucratic life—though the scenarios in which they arise these days appear to have unusually dramatic facts.

And what of more aggressive pushback: refusal to change facts, refusal to violate laws, insistence on documenting directions or acts of malfeasance, using statutory whistleblower mechanisms to raise concerns internally, such as with one's inspector general, or externally, to Congress? The deep state decriers view such acts as undemocratic attempts to undermine the elected President. This view fails to take into account that the mechanisms and protections permitting—or even requiring—bureaucrats to take such actions are themselves created by an elected Congress. To the extent they are regulated further by elected Presidents and their appointees, Presidents can change those regulations, tweak the guidelines, and reshuffle internal players to suit their own agendas.

Leaks are a dicier matter than other acts of resistance, and I devote significant discussion to their consideration in "Bureaucratic Resistance." I conclude that unlike the weaponization of information via blackmail, in which the purpose was to influence action *without* releasing the information, and which *should* sound "deep state" alarms, as it did during the Hoover era, actual leaks derive their power from transparency and public engagement. While not without their own problems and repercussions, the leaks we see today, made for the purpose of disclosing information, even if made to sway a debate, are not generally indicative of a deep state, which is characterized by unaccountability to the public, and empowered by secrecy, not disclosure.

Formal and Functional Power to Resist

Whatever one's view on "deep state" rhetoric, many accounts of bureaucratic action tend to imbue bureaucratic actors with significant practical power to act to resist the President, despite not necessarily having the formal authority to do so. In other words, under these accounts, the bureaucrat *can* just drop that set of orders from her boss in the waste basket (or, as the case may be, snatch it off the President's desk) even if she *may* not disregard such commands. My article turns this orthodoxy on its head. I conclude that bureaucrats at every level have significant *formal* authority to engage in many kinds of resistance, and that this authority stems directly from traditional sources of power—Congress, the Executive itself, and also the courts. But, unlike the views of both deep state decriers and those who are hoping for a more mutinous #Resistance, the practical power of bureaucrats to steer the ship is heavily circumscribed.

Misplaced Faith and Fear: Lessons from the Mueller Saga for This Moment and Beyond

Ultimately, widespread embrace of either view of the bureaucracy—the "deep state" version or that of the #Resistance—may, at least in their extreme forms, create problems for the balance of power between the branches of government, and specifically, for a constrained President. In stoking fears of the bureaucracy, those pushing deep state rhetoric may encourage lawmakers and judges to erode protections of civil servants, to punish those who report abuse, to relax or cease reliance on bureaucratic fact-finding authority, or to undervalue the norms of independence and professional ethics among executive branch technocrats and national security officials. With those protections eroded or suspended, the bureaucracy will turn into precisely the partisan weapon that this President both seeks and accuses it of being. And Congress will lose the ability to extend its oversight into the vast reaches of the executive branch by empowering nonpartisans and technocrats to question their superiors, to follow the laws in the face of orders to the contrary, and to report malfeasance.

On the other side, over-reliance on bureaucratic constraints in the belief that some #Resistance—or even just normal government attorneys—will save the country from a tyrannical President can lead to abdication of authority by actors like the courts and Congress, who perform an essential check in the separation of powers that cannot be replaced by intra-executive constraints.

We have been watching this balancing act play out in real time during this Administration. The Mueller investigation and the reactions to it by supporters and foes of the President was one glaring example. Throughout the investigation, the President stoked old fears of the national security bureaucracy, painting it as a cabal of all-powerful actors working in the shadows to undermine the elected government, and weaponized those fears for his political gain. His outrage at the investigation into his campaign's connections to Russian election interference, his demands that the investigation end, and his accusations of politicization of the law enforcement agencies, not to mention his own calls for investigation of his political opponents—which we now see have turned into actual investigations in the hands of his Attorney General, and attempted compulsion of foreign states to do so as well—have all served to undermine faith in the ability of executive branch officials to conduct impartial investigations divorced from politics. And these actions have emboldened actors within Congress and elsewhere to seek to formalize that erosion through, for example, calls on the DOJ to investigate political opponents, attempts to undermine civil service protections, and accusations of treachery aimed at executive branch actors who implement the constraints on the President created by Congress or the Executive itself, including Mueller and the unknown whistleblowers.

On the other side, the two-year saga of the Mueller investigation allowed members of Congress to evade their responsibility for ensuring the security of the country and our elections in the face of a possible threat. Members of the President's party who might otherwise have felt some pressure—as a simple matter of good government if not politics—to consider evidence of foreign interference in our elections, were instead able to wave off questions by pointing to the Mueller investigation. The investigation was a useful lightening rod for which politicians could profess vague, substantively neutral support—"let the process continue"—without the political costs they might have incurred from challenging the President more directly. Ultimately, by painting the matter in legal terms, the investigation allowed Congress to abdicate their responsibility of presidential oversight to the courts and to executive branch actors themselves, actors who cannot alone constrain an unwilling President without congressional help.

Over-reliance on the bureaucracy's ability to resist presidential over-reach, however, can be as much a threat to the bureaucracy as is fear. Without external support, its strength will eventually give out. At the end of the day, there are few hard mechanisms to rein in the President. Those remaining include political costs imposed by the public and pushback from Congress, which actors within the President's circle have historically factored into their constraining advice. The President is fully capable, as we have seen, of removing officials who constrain him, including his Attorney General. The belief that there would be political repercussions to doing so is what ultimately held the President back from ending the Mueller investigation. But over time the lack of external consequences for his rampant norm breaking has evidently weakened the force of those within the executive who might seek to rein him in. And thus there are few internal hurdles that now stand between the President and the abuse of his power, including politicized prosecution of his enemies, whether through personal demands of our own Department of Justice, or of foreign states, as the Ukraine saga highlights.

As for the constraints posed by career bureaucrats, these are significant features of continuity inside the executive, even in entirely mundane times. And in the face of abuse, career bureaucrats can be canaries in the coal mine, possibly alerting Congress, the courts, and the public that something is awry, but they aren't going to "take down the President" in some vigilante dream of the hashtag Resistance. Bureaucratic constraints are important and legitimizing *precisely because* they will not do that. Career bureaucrats will ask questions, they may even write memos to the boss or to the file, a few (but note how very few!) brave souls may take advantageous of statutory means of disclosure of abuse to Congress, and some lone wolves may even leak information, thus multiplying their force but still leaving the ultimate power in the hands of the people. And, of course, some individuals may act corruptly, as human beings sometimes do in every profession. But career bureaucrats in the U.S. executive branch bureaucracy are neither sufficiently organized nor powerful nor constitutionally inclined to take over the reins of the state for themselves.

Politicians and the public taking these internal constraints on the President for granted while simultaneously abiding attacks on the legitimacy of the bureaucracy may ultimately find that the internal constraints have been eroded or washed away entirely. The relationship between external checks on the President and the internal checks from within the bureaucracy is a symbiotic one and a delicate balance. This does not mean Congress and the public should offer the bureaucracy their blind faith. On the contrary, the balance requires healthy inquiry, oversight, and support—not myths about bureaucratic power or abuse. Both fear of and over-reliance on bureaucratic resistance each risk upsetting that balance. The result of either may be an insufficiently checked President.

Presidential Power—Not the "Deep State"—Is a Genuine Threat

To the extent fears among the public of a "deep state" are in fact based in concern that the U.S. Executive as a whole has accumulated significant power at the expense of Congress, the courts, and perhaps even the public itself—this is a real and present danger. To the extent the "deep state" is just a symbol for the idea that the rich and powerful wield significant influence in Washington and elsewhere, I won't argue with that, though I cannot say it applies to most career bureaucrats, whom the deep state myth purports to describe. And to the extent people are concerned with the government's surveillance powers, or ability to use force, or overreliance on secrecy: yes, these are genuine issues that demand our vigilance. All of these concern the President's potential infringement on the rights of individuals, not the other way around. Individuals, and in particular the most vulnerable among us, are the potential victim of the state's abuses, not the President, who sits at its helm.

The term "deep state" is intended to describe regimes in which the elected government does not wield the actual power of the state, which is instead run by a body whom the public cannot see and has no power to control. Let us hold up the Ukraine saga to this lens. In this case one or more whistleblowers, as well as other actors inside the executive branch, have been trying to disclose to us, the people, in accordance with laws our elected Congress has passed, information about what our government is doing in our name. And it is our President, not some unelected, faceless bureaucrats, who is trying to keep this information from us, the people, who need it so that it can inform our decisions about whom to support, both in Congress and in the White House. Our elected President, wielding the enormous power of the executive branch, powers that our elected officials in Congress have over the years delegated to it, is the threat that should concern us. The deep state bogeyman is not. But it is not going to save us, either.

36

"The American Deep State"

JON D. MICHAELS

Whether cast as insidious or cast aside as fictitious, the American "deep state" is an increasingly compelling concept in the Age of Trump. In a year's time, a label that had practically no domestic resonance has been elevated to the status of public enemy number one. Indeed, when things have gone badly for the Trump administration—as they often have—the President, his allies, and White House surrogates have been quick to blame the deep state. Such a deep state, characterized by Team Trump as disloyal and undemocratic forces within and around government, has served as an all-purpose scapegoat. * * *

New to the United States, the concept of a deep state has considerable transnational purchase. Usually any mention of a deep state conjures up images of shadowy and powerful antidemocratic cabals that threaten popular rule. For good reason, one may look at some precariously (or simply nominally) democratic countries' militaries, key ministries, and state-owned industries with trepidation. Close observers of places like Egypt, Turkey, Pakistan, and Iran have witnessed enough crackdowns on free speech and assembly, electoral subversions, and rollbacks of good governance reforms to know how that movie ends.

* * * I argue that the American deep state has very little in common with those regimes usually understood to harbor deep states; that, far from being shadowy or elitist, the American bureaucracy is very much a demotic institution, demographically diverse, highly accountable, and lacking financial incentives or caste proclivities to subvert popular will; that demotic bureaucratic depth of the American variety should be celebrated, not feared; and that, going forward, we need greater, not lesser, depth insofar as the American bureaucracy serves an important, salutary, and quite possibly necessary role in safeguarding our constitutional commitments and enriching our public policies.

* * *

Broadly speaking, prior to 2017 our deep state has simply been referred to as our state. At its center—and at the center of the instant political maelstrom—is the vast expanse of federal administrative agencies. These entities are responsible for making and enforcing regulations, designing and running welfare programs, combating crime and corruption, and providing for the national defense. Our deep state also includes the personnel entrusted with the day-to-day operations of those agencies. Principal among them are federal employees—though we ought not forget the legions of private government contractors, state and local officials, and members of civil society who play any number of key, supporting, and contrarian roles when it comes to matters of administrative design, implementation, and oversight.

Drawing on their own sources of legal authority, professional credibility, and, occasionally, populist bona fides, and regularly functioning at some distance from the elected leaders in the White House and Congress, federal bureaucrats are a force to be reckoned with. This is particularly true in a modern, complex political economy such as ours, which is seemingly far more dependent on the hundreds of thousands of expert administrators and field agents than on a few hundred lay legislators and a single chief executive.

Much has been made of contemporary bureaucratic *resistance,* which some frame as subversive. Yet federal bureaucrats generally can be counted on to support and advance the President's programmatic goals. They do so out of deference, not docility, with the practical effect that Presidents enjoy considerable but not unbounded leeway. In those rare instances when Presidents (and their hand-chosen agency heads) go beyond the proverbial pale, those in the civil service are particularly well positioned to challenge, and even resist, directives lacking a scientific, legal, or commonsense foundation.

For instance, the career workforce in regulatory agencies can continue—defiantly, but lawfully—to enforce civil rights laws and health and safety regulations, leak information, drag their feet on the implementation of new but tendentious or insupportable orders, and produce reports useful to any number of audiences, including Congress, judges, the media, and civil society. Likewise, career diplomats and military and intelligence officials can point to longstanding treaties, bilateral agreements, international law, the laws of war, foreign aid appropriations, and extant, long-term projects to justify ongoing cooperation and to provide assurances of continuing support and engagement even during times of jarring political transition and programmatic upheaval at home. Lastly, any number of agency officials may use the authorities granted to them as whistleblowers, inspectors general, and the like to investigate, document, and publicize instances of high-level government malfeasance, suggestive of either venality or run-of-the-mill incompetence.

To be clear, these bureaucratic officials are emboldened to speak truth to power because most of them are civil servants, insulated by law and custom from politics and owed what in effect amounts to job tenure. They are further emboldened to speak truth to power because that is what's expected of them, both as professionals—lawyers, economists, scientists, and the like—and as loyal and faithful stewards of the laws, regulations, and conventions of the United States.

*   *   *

Not Elitist

U.S. domestic and national security bureaucracies are hardly bastions of privilege. American bureaucrats are, after all, drawn from a far greater set of schools and family backgrounds than is generally the case in Western Europe, where Oxbridge and École Nationale d'Administration graduates have historically predominated—let alone in Asia or the Middle East, with its clannish, cliquish ministries and state-owned enterprises, control of which may be a family affair and a remunerative one at that. Instead, American bureaucrats, even those serving in such prestigious redoubts as the State Department, are decidedly middle or upper-middle class, lacking the cultural or caste proclivities or financial incentives to deviate particularly far from median voter sentiments or statutory obligations.

One can push this claim further: the American bureaucracy is arguably even more demotic—and more in tune with median voters—than are our elected legislatures, which are increasingly populated by economic, educational, and dynastic elites.

* * *

American agencies by law and custom are overwhelmingly transparent and accessible, far more than are many Middle Eastern, Asian, and European ministries and, again, often more so than Congress and the White House, too. Indeed, unlike most conventionally invoked deep states that function best in the shadows, ours is *phototrophic*, gaining strength and legitimacy by operating in the sunlight and with full and extensive participation from the public at large.

American deep state photophilia is perhaps best evidenced by the fact that purportedly "rogue" bureaucratic muscle-flexing today regularly takes the forms described above—that is, tweets, leaks, investigations, and widely distributed (and carefully annotated) reports supporting or discrediting a particular economic, scientific, or legal claim. Even in the oft-secretive world of diplomacy, we see career foreign service personnel availing themselves of the State Department's "dissent channel," publishing objections to the President and Secretary's policies for all the world to see. Recent dissents have been written in opposition to positions taken by both John Kerry and Rex Tillerson. Occasionally, career officials may go so far as to sue the President or agency heads, as career immigration officials did during the Obama presidency when they challenged the then-President's "deferred action" programs as inconsistent with statutory law; and as an active duty Army captain did when he challenged President Obama's allegedly unauthorized military campaign against the Islamic State.

In short, in those rare instances when the American bureaucracy takes sides against the elected leadership, it tends to show its work, laying bare the justifications for any apparent affront to the White House. What's more, bureaucrats tend to bring others—judges, members of Congress, and the public at large—into the policymaking and policy-scrutinizing fold. Obviously, such transparency and inclusiveness is all the easier when deep state participants enjoy job tenure and are acting in a clearly non-self-serving fashion.

Not Monolithic

Not only is the American deep state accessible and knowable, it is also internally diverse and fragmented. Consider first the geographic sprawl within and among the federal agencies, with offices and bureaus dotting the vast American landscape. A sizable majority—close to 85% of civilian, nonpostal federal employees—work well outside the Beltway, and about half of all civilian, nonpostal federal employees work (and live) in so-called "red states," that is, politically conservative states that in 2016 voted for President Trump. This sprawl suggests that federal bureaucrats are not, as commonly thought, fully enveloped in the D.C. bubble; if anything, they may feel the centrifugal forces of their sometimes far-flung communities more strongly than the centripetal pull of headquarters. After all, these employees live, raise families, and develop personal and professional ties in places geographically and culturally different from Washington—and from one another. As David Fontana has recently observed in his work on a "decentralized" federal government, geographic dispersal is an essential component of limited government—as officials "in places distant and therefore different from Washington compete with and constrain one another."

* * *

And, lastly, consider the siloing of administrative responsibilities by subject matter, as exemplified by our having separate departments of education, labor, transportation, and health and human services, not to mention separate departments of defense, intelligence, homeland security, and justice. The limited jurisdictional scope of each agency coupled with the inevitable turf wars between each agency and its neighbors in adjacent regulatory fiefdoms serve to cabin the influence wielded by any small set of administrative officials. Though there are prominent examples of multiagency collaboration (and corresponding calls for more), the truth is that much of the federal government's work remains relatively compartmentalized.

Given such geographic, partisan, and subject-matter fragmentation, the American deep state is (like Congress) best described as a they, not an it. And this is important because our fragmented deep state has few of the interlocking features that characterize powerful clans' ready control over multiple ministries and state enterprises, as we find in nations with conventionally labeled deep states. Indeed, our fragmentation makes any type of coordinated, systematic attack on the political branches (or democracy itself) all but impossible and, in any event, implausible. Climate change experts are singularly focused on, well, climate change. Labor inspectors, in turn, zero in on wage theft or unsafe working conditions. And, cybersecurity officials are, for their part, concentrating their attention on data breaches, malware, and digital attacks. None of these groups is likely particularly interested in (or has any legal authority over) any of the others' casus belli, let alone in joining forces to categorically subvert Congress or the presidency.

* * *

A Bulwark, Not a Battering Ram

When clashes arise with the political leadership, the relevant contingent of civil servants typically assumes a defensive posture, challenging a problematic initiative rather than hurtling forward with an initiative of its own. The defensive posture reflects their limited legal powers—civil servants, almost by definition, are circumscribed in terms of the authority they wield and the discretion they possess. The legal fact that there's only so much that civil servants can do is buttressed by the political reality that civil servants are well aware of the dangers associated with overreaching. As unelected "mandarins," they are—or at least very much ought to be— cognizant of their own, even more acute version of the federal judiciary's "countermajoritarian difficulty," and thus must proceed cautiously and transparently. That is to say, they are—or, again, very much ought to be— well aware of the distrust and skepticism surrounding American bureaucracy (which surely antedates and transcends the Trump insurgency) and thus take pains to intervene carefully, modestly, and sparingly.

While one ought not make too much out of any act/inaction distinction, it is safe to say that foot dragging, report writing, leaking, and overall obstinacy all tend to be less dangerous, presumptuous, and liberty threatening than would be efforts to accelerate the workings of the State.

Not an Extraconstitutional Force

The defensive posture of American bureaucracy matters for two reasons. First, recognition that bureaucratic resistance is principally defensive in nature should serve to tamp down fears of a deep state putsch. Second, and of far greater importance to those who aren't actually fearful of a deep state takeover but are nevertheless discomforted by the notion of mandarin insubordination, bureaucratic resistance is entirely in keeping with one of our principal constitutional defaults—namely, the separating and checking of state power. Our constitutional order is one of multidimensional separations of power, not just the singular tripartite division among Congress, the President, and the judiciary. The American Republic obtains its constitutional structure and, by some lights, its legitimacy from pervasive and, again, multidimensional conflict—conflict between the sometimes, but not always, rivalrous political branches, the feds and the several states, and the public and private sectors. Since the New Deal, when Congress began delegating heaps of its own lawmaking power to a rapidly growing administrative state captained by the President, the instantiation of a strong, politically independent bureaucracy constituted a suddenly necessary internal counterweight to that otherwise unfettered, even imperial, President.

This strong, independent bureaucracy—again protected by duly enacted civil service laws and rendered credible and formidable by virtue of its reasoned, pragmatic, and impartial service to the State—redeemed and enlarged the Framers' commitment to checks and balances even as Congress faded into the background, as it has in many policy domains. With so much power already transferred from legislators (and judges) to agencies, it is the bureaucracy—not Congress (or even the courts)—that often serves as the last, if not best, check on presidential or agency-head overreach. And it is to this bureaucracy that those aggrieved by imperious presidential and cabinet-level directives increasingly turn.

For this reason, if no other, deep state resistance to the President should be seen as an evolutionary and ameliorative feature, not a bug, in our modern constitutional system that has drifted far from its original blueprint. Robust, even feisty, bureaucracy, however unsettling that concept may be to those who insist on thinking of the American Republic in its pre–New Deal bloom, should therefore elicit support rather than distrust.

* * *

Of course, any such endorsement of a bureaucratic counterweight hinges on the American deep state remaining true to form—that is, transparent, accessible, fragmented, and democratically pluralistic. Though we cannot take those defining characteristics of the American administrative state for granted—especially when confronted with evidence of the bureaucracy's warts, shortcomings, and vulnerabilities—we can take some solace in the fact that each of those signature attributes of the federal bureaucracy is a logical outgrowth of our laws, conventions, and cultural and political commitments. Specifically, transparency rules and laws providing for full and open public participation, a merit-based (yet still solidly middle class) bureaucracy, and a fragmented (ideologically diverse, programmatically siloed, and geographically dispersed) infrastructure all reflect considered public policy choices—and, not coincidentally, guard against elite domination. Surely, unprincipled or immoderate pushback may occur from time to time, but nowhere to the extent we are apt to see in fledgling democracies lacking much by way of a thick, vibrant civil society, an ethos of public service, and a law-drenched administrative state. (Note that civil society—a key contributor to administrative governance—constitutes an independent rival to the bureaucrats as well as to the President and her agency heads, and thus nonprofit groups, journalists, captains of industry, and random gadflies serve to keep both of those administrative rivals in check.) What's more, American bureaucracy is, in important respects, seemingly more resistant to systematic domination by special interests than is Congress, where the realities of permissive campaign finance laws, liberal lobbying rules, a revolving door culture, and generally tight party discipline conspire to enable readier capture.

* * *

A Deeper Deep State

Casting the American bureaucracy as a shadowy, unrepresentative superstructure serves to discredit the administrative state and, no doubt, cow its personnel into meek compliance, lest the civil service be further demonized. It is, for instance, a revealing sign of the times that federal civil servants feel compelled to reaffirm their oath of loyalty to the United States, as if their original avowal and years of heretofore unquestioned service were suddenly insufficient. It is also a revealing sign of the times when a cabinet secretary declares, without a hint of substantiation (or fear of backlash), that a third of his department's employees are disloyal; when the President blithely maligns FBI agents; and when a member of Congress (and former U.S. Ambassador) calls for a purge of the Justice Department.

* * *

In any event, the very fact that bureaucratic scapegoating can so easily pervade contemporary political discourse underscores the present weakness of our deep state. For decades—well before the Trump administration announced its intention to "drain the swamp"—the American bureaucracy has been under siege. Privatizing, political layering atop agencies, and converting civil servants into at-will employees—often in the name of "running government like a business"—have damaged the administrative architecture, demoralized agency personnel, and limited the bureaucracy's capacity to be meaningfully rivalrous.

In recognizing the full value of a vibrant, forceful bureaucracy, particularly in times of presidential instability and congressional dysfunction, perhaps the moment is ripe not simply to own the deep state terminology but also to fortify the clearly vulnerable and *insufficiently deep* deep state itself.

* * *

Support for the deep state thus requires an unflinching commitment to a strong and independent bureaucracy, ensuring our government personnel and the public authorized to participate in regulatory affairs have the legal and institutional platform to speak truth to power. It is this deep state that helped usher us through the Great Depression, World War II, the Cold War, Watergate, and the more recent travails of 9/11 and the Great Recession. Now, in this moment of great political, economic, and geostrategic upheaval, we will need to rely on the steadying hand of this deep state more than ever.

DISCUSSION QUESTIONS

1. Is there a way to fundamentally reconcile the tension between bureaucratic accountability and political neutrality? Or is it a balance that has to be continually renegotiated?

2. What would be the disadvantages of, say, allowing a president to fire any executive branch employee—including people now protected by civil service rules—for any reason? Or to replace large numbers of civil servants with party loyalists?

3. Is the "deep state" argument merely a way to discredit the basic functions of government agencies? Is it a tactical argument, or does it identify an actual problem with accountability?

CHAPTER 8

The Judiciary

37

The Federalist, No. 78

ALEXANDER HAMILTON

The judiciary, Hamilton wrote in The Federalist, No. 78, *"will always be the least dangerous to the political rights of the Constitution; because it will be least in a capacity to annoy or injure them." The lack of danger Hamilton spoke of stems from the courts' lack of enforcement or policy power. Or as Hamilton more eloquently put it, the judiciary has "no influence over either the sword or the purse": it must rely on the executive branch and state governments to enforce its rulings, and it depends on the legislature for its appropriations and rules governing its structure. Critics of "judicial activism" would likely disagree about the weakness of the judiciary relative to the other branches of government. But Hamilton saw an independent judiciary as an important check on the other branches' ability to assume too much power (the "bulwarks of a limited Constitution against legislative encroachments"). He also argued that the federal judiciary, as interpreter of the Constitution, would gain its power from the force of its judgments, which were rooted in the will of the people.*

To the People of the State of New York:

We proceed now to an examination of the judiciary department of the proposed government.

In unfolding the defects of the existing Confederation, the utility and necessity of a federal judicature have been clearly pointed out. It is the less necessary to recapitulate the considerations there urged, as the propriety of the institution in the abstract is not disputed; the only questions which have been raised being relative to the manner of constituting it, and to its extent. To these points, therefore, our observations shall be confined.

The manner of constituting it seems to embrace these several objects: 1ST. The mode of appointing the judges. 2D. The tenure by which they are to hold their places. 3D. The partition of the judiciary authority between different courts, and their relations to each other.

First. As to the mode of appointing the judges; this is the same with that of appointing the officers of the Union in general, and has been so fully discussed in the two last numbers, that nothing can be said here which would not be useless repetition.

Second. As to the tenure by which the judges are to hold their places: this chiefly concerns their duration in office; the provisions for their support; the precautions for their responsibility.

According to the plan of the convention, all judges who may be appointed by the United States are to hold their offices *during good behavior*; which is conformable to the most approved of the State constitutions, and among the rest, to that of this State. Its propriety having been drawn into question by the adversaries of that plan, is no light symptom of the rage for objection, which disorders their imaginations and judgments. The standard of good behavior for the continuance in office of the judicial magistracy is certainly one of the most valuable of the modern improvements in the practice of government. In a monarchy it is an excellent barrier to the despotism of the prince; in a republic it is a no less excellent barrier to the encroachments and oppressions of the representative body. And it is the best expedient which can be devised in any government to secure a steady, upright, and impartial administration of the laws.

Whoever attentively considers the different departments of power must perceive, that, in a government in which they are separated from each other, the judiciary, from the nature of its functions, will always be the least dangerous to the political rights of the Constitution; because it will be least in a capacity to annoy or injure them. The Executive not only dispenses the honors, but holds the sword of the community. The legislature not only commands the purse, but prescribes the rules by which the duties and rights of every citizen are to be regulated. The judiciary, on the contrary, has no influence over either the sword or the purse; no direction either of the strength or of the wealth of the society; and can take no active resolution whatever. It may truly be said to have neither FORCE NOR WILL, but merely judgment; and must ultimately depend upon the aid of the executive arm even for the efficacy of its judgments.

This simple view of the matter suggests several important consequences. It proves incontestably that the judiciary is beyond comparison the weakest of the three departments of power that it can never attack with success either of the other two; and that all possible care is requisite to enable it to defend itself against their attacks. It equally proves that though individual oppression may now and then proceed from the courts of justice, the general liberty of the people can never be endangered from that quarter; I mean so long as the judiciary remains truly distinct from both the legislature and the Executive. For I agree, that "there is no liberty, if the power of judging be not separated from the legislative and executive powers." And it proves, in the last place, that as liberty can have nothing to fear from the judiciary alone, but would have every thing to fear from its union with either of the other departments; that as all the effects of such a union must ensue from a dependence of the former on the latter, notwithstanding a nominal and apparent separation; that as, from the natural feebleness of the judiciary it is in continual jeopardy of being overpowered, awed, or influenced by its coordinate branches; and that as nothing can contribute so much to its firmness and independence as permanency in office, this quality may therefore be justly regarded as an indispensable ingredient in its constitution, and, in a great measure, as the citadel of the public justice and the public security.

The complete independence of the courts of justice is peculiarly essential in a limited Constitution. By a limited Constitution, I understand one which contains certain specified exceptions to the legislative authority; such, for instance, as that it shall pass no bills of attainder, no *ex-post-facto* laws, and the like. Limitations of this kind can be preserved in practice no other way than through the medium of courts of justice, whose duty it must be to declare all acts contrary to the manifest tenor of the Constitution void. Without this, all the reservations of particular rights or privileges would amount to nothing.

Some perplexity respecting the rights of the courts to pronounce legislative acts void, because contrary to the constitution, has arisen from an imagination that the doctrine would imply a superiority of the judiciary to the legislative power. It is urged that the authority which can declare the acts of another void must necessarily be superior to the one whose acts may be declared void. As this doctrine is of great importance in all the American constitutions, a brief discussion of the ground on which it rests cannot be unacceptable.

There is no position which depends on clearer principles than that every act of a delegated authority, contrary to the tenor of the commission under which it is exercised, is void. No legislative act, therefore, contrary to the Constitution, can be valid. To deny this would be to affirm that the deputy is greater than his principal; that the servant is above his master; that the representatives of the people are superior to the people themselves; that men acting by virtue of powers may do not only what their powers do not authorize, but what they forbid.

If it be said that the legislative body are themselves the constitutional judges of their own powers, and that the construction they put upon them is conclusive upon the other departments, it may be answered that this cannot be the natural presumption where it is not to be collected from any particular provisions in the Constitution. It is not otherwise to be supposed that the Constitution could intend to enable the representatives of the people to substitute their *will* to that of their constituents. It is far more rational to suppose that the courts were designed to be an intermediate body between the people and the legislature, in order, among other things, to keep the latter within the limits assigned to their authority. The interpretation of the laws is the proper and peculiar province of the courts. A constitution is, in fact, and must be regarded by the judges, as a fundamental law. It therefore belongs to them to ascertain its meaning, as well as the meaning of any particular act proceeding from the legislative body. If there should happen to be an irreconcilable variance between the two, that which has the superior obligation and validity ought, of course, to be preferred; or, in other words, the Constitution ought to be preferred to the statute, the intention of the people to the intention of their agents.

Nor does this conclusion by any means suppose a superiority of the judicial to the legislative power. It only supposes that the power of the people is superior to both; and that where the will of the legislature, declared in its statutes, stands in opposition to that of the people, declared in the Constitution, the judges ought to be governed by the latter rather than the former. They ought to regulate their decisions by the fundamental laws, rather than by those which are not fundamental.

This exercise of judicial discretion, in determining between two contradictory laws, is exemplified in a familiar instance. It not uncommonly happens that there are two statutes existing at one time, clashing in whole or in part with each other, and neither of them containing any repealing clause or expression. In such a case, it is the province of the courts to liquidate and fix their meaning and operation. So far as they can, by any fair construction, be reconciled to each other, reason and law conspire to dictate that this should be done; where this is impracticable, it becomes a matter of necessity to give effect to one in exclusion of the other. The rule which has obtained in the courts for determining their relative validity is, that the last in order of time shall be preferred to the first. But this is a mere rule of construction, not derived from any positive law but from the nature and reason of the thing. It is a rule not enjoined upon the courts by legislative provision but adopted by themselves, as consonant to truth and propriety for the direction of their conduct as interpreters of the law. They thought it reasonable, that between the interfering acts of an *equal* authority, that which was the last indication of its will should have the preference.

But in regard to the interfering acts of a superior and subordinate authority, of an original and derivative power, the nature and reason of the thing indicate the converse of that rule as proper to be followed. They teach us that the prior act of a superior ought to be preferred to the subsequent act of an inferior and subordinate authority; and that accordingly, whenever a particular statute contravenes the Constitution, it will be the duty of the judicial tribunals to adhere to the latter and disregard the former.

It can be of no weight to say that the courts, on the pretence of a repugnancy, may substitute their own pleasure to the constitutional intentions of the legislature. This might as well happen in the case of two contradictory statutes; or it might as well happen in every adjudication upon any single statute. The courts must declare the sense of the law; and if they should be disposed to exercise WILL instead of JUDGMENT, the consequence would equally be the substitution of their pleasure to that of the legislative body. The observation, if it prove any thing, would prove that there ought to be no judges distinct from that body.

If, then, the courts of justice are to be considered as the bulwarks of a limited Constitution against legislative encroachments, this consideration will afford a strong argument for the permanent tenure of judicial offices, since nothing will contribute so much as this to that independent spirit in the judges which must be essential to the faithful performance of so arduous a duty.

This independence of the judges is equally requisite to guard the Constitution and the rights of individuals from the effects of those ill humors, which the arts of designing men or the influence of particular conjunctures sometimes disseminate among the people themselves; and which, though they speedily give place to better information and more deliberate reflection, have a tendency, in the meantime, to occasion dangerous innovations in the government, and serious oppressions of the minor party in the community. Though I trust the friends of the proposed Constitution will never concur with its enemies in questioning that fundamental principle of republican government, which admits the right of the people to alter or abolish the established Constitution whenever they find it inconsistent with their happiness; yet it is not to be inferred from this principle that the representatives of the people, whenever a momentary inclination happens to lay hold of a majority of their constituents, incompatible with the provisions in the existing Constitution, would, on that account, be justifiable in a violation of those provisions; or that the courts would be under a greater obligation to connive at infractions in this shape, than when they had proceeded wholly from the cabals of the representative body. Until the people have by some solemn and authoritative act annulled or changed the established form, it is binding upon themselves collectively, as well as individually; and no presumption, or even knowledge, of their sentiments, can warrant their representatives in a departure from it, prior to such an act. But it is easy to see that it would require an uncommon portion of fortitude in the judges to do their duty as faithful guardians of the Constitution, where legislative invasions of it had been instigated by the major voice of the community.

But it is not with a view to infractions of the Constitution only that the independence of the judges may be an essential safeguard against the effects of occasional ill humors in the society. These sometimes extend no farther than to the injury of the private rights of particular classes of citizens by unjust and partial laws. Here also the firmness of the judicial magistracy is of vast importance in mitigating the severity and confining the operation of such laws. It not only serves to moderate the immediate mischiefs of those which may have been passed, but it operates as a check upon the legislative body in passing them; who, perceiving that obstacles to the success of iniquitous intention are to be expected from the scruples of the courts, are in a manner compelled by the very motives of the injustice they meditate to qualify their attempts. This is a circumstance calculated to have more influence upon the character of our governments, than but few may be aware of. The benefits of the integrity and moderation of the judiciary have already been felt in more States than one; and though they may have displeased those whose sinister expectations they may have disappointed, they must have commanded the esteem and applause of all the virtuous and disinterested. Considerate men of every description ought to prize whatever will tend to beget or fortify that temper in the courts; as no man can be sure that he may not be tomorrow the victim of a spirit of injustice by which he may be a gainer today. And every man must now feel that the inevitable tendency of such a spirit is to sap the foundations of public and private confidence, and to introduce in its stead universal distrust and distress.

That inflexible and uniform adherence to the rights of the Constitution and of individuals, which we perceive to be indispensable in the courts of justice, can certainly not be expected from judges who hold their offices by a temporary commission. Periodical appointments, however regulated or by whomsoever made, would, in some way or other, be fatal to their necessary independence. If the power of making them was committed either to the Executive or legislature, there would be danger of an improper complaisance to the branch which possessed it; if to both, there would be an unwillingness to hazard the displeasure of either; if to the people or to persons chosen by them for the special purpose, there would be too great a disposition to consult popularity, to justify a reliance that nothing would be consulted but the Constitution and the laws.

There is yet a further and a weightier reason for the permanency of the judicial offices, which is deducible from the nature of the qualifications they require. It has been frequently remarked, with great propriety, that a voluminous code of laws is one of the inconveniences necessarily connected with the advantages of a free government. To avoid an arbitrary discretion in the courts, it is indispensable that they should be bound down by strict rules and precedents, which serve to define and point out their duty in every particular case that comes before them; and it will readily be conceived from the variety of controversies which grow out of the folly and wickedness of mankind, that the records of those precedents must unavoidably swell to a very considerable bulk, and must demand long and laborious study to acquire a competent knowledge of them. Hence it is, that there can be but few men in the society who will have sufficient skill in the laws to qualify them for the stations of judges. And making the proper deductions for the ordinary depravity of human nature, the number must be still smaller of those who unite the requisite integrity with the requisite knowledge. These considerations apprise us that the government can have no great option between fit character; and that a temporary duration in office, which would naturally discourage such characters from quitting a lucrative line of practice to accept a seat on the bench, would have a tendency to throw the administration of justice into hands less able, and less well qualified, to conduct it with utility and dignity. In the present circumstances of this country and in those in which it is likely to be for a long time to come, the disadvantages on this score would be greater than they may at first sight appear; but it must be confessed that they are far inferior to those which present themselves under the other aspects of the subject.

Upon the whole, there can be no room to doubt that the convention acted wisely in copying from the models of those constitutions which have established *good behavior* as the tenure of their judicial offices, in point of duration; and that so far from being blamable on this account, their plan would have been inexcusably defective if it had wanted this important feature of good government. The experience of Great Britain affords an illustrious comment on the excellence of the institution.

PUBLIUS

DISCUSSION QUESTIONS

1. Was Hamilton correct in arguing that the judiciary is the least dangerous branch of government?

2. Critics of the Supreme Court often charge that it rules on issues that should be properly decided in the legislature, while supporters claim that the Court is often the last check against the tyranny of the majority. Who has the stronger case? Can both sides be correct?

3. Hamilton argues that the "power of the people is superior to both" the legislature and the judiciary, and that judges uphold the power of the people when they support the Constitution over a statute that runs counter to the Constitution. He asserts that the people's will is reflected in the Constitution but refers to statutes as reflecting the will of the legislators. Is it legitimate to argue that the Supreme Court is supporting the will of the people, given that it is an unelected body?

38

"The Court and American Life," from *Storm Center: The Supreme Court in American Politics*

David M. O'Brien

The "textbook" view of the federal judiciary is one in which judges sit in dispassionate review of complex legal questions, render decisions based on a careful reading of constitutional or statutory language, and expect their rulings to be adhered to strictly; the law is the law. This selection shows how unrealistic that picture is. David M. O'Brien notes that the Supreme Court is very much a political institution, whose members pay more attention to the political cycle and public opinion than one might expect. O'Brien reviews the decision-making process in the famous case of Brown v. Board of Education of Topeka, Kansas, *in which the Court invalidated segregated public schools, as an example of how the Court fits itself into the political process. Throughout the case, justices delayed their decision, consolidated cases from around the country, and refused to set a firm timetable for implementation, relying instead on the ambiguous standard "with all deliberate speed." Far from being a purely objective arbiter of legal questions, the Court must pay close attention to its own legitimacy and, by extension, the likelihood of compliance: it does no good to issue decisions that will be ignored.*

"Why does the Supreme Court pass the school desegregation case?" asked one of Chief Justice Vinson's law clerks in 1952. *Brown v. Board of Education of Topeka, Kansas* had arrived on the Court's docket in 1951, but it was carried over for oral argument the next term and then consolidated with four other cases and reargued in December 1953. The landmark ruling did not come down until May 17, 1954. "Well," Justice Frankfurter explained, "we're holding it for the election"—1952 was a presidential election year. "You're holding it for the election?" The clerk persisted in disbelief. "I thought the Supreme Court was supposed to decide cases without regard to elections." "When you have a major social political issue of this magnitude," timing and public reactions are important considerations, and, Frankfurter continued, "we do not think this is the time to decide it." Similarly, Tom Clark recalled that the Court awaited, over Douglas's dissent, additional cases from the District of Columbia and other regions, so as "to get a national coverage, rather than a sectional one." Such political considerations are by no means unique. "We often delay adjudication. It's not a question of evading at all," Clark concluded. "It's just the practicalities of life—common sense."

Denied the power of the sword or the purse, the Court must cultivate its institutional prestige. The power of the Court lies in the persuasiveness of its rulings and ultimately rests with other political institutions and public opinion. As an independent force, the Court has no chance to resolve great issues of public policy. *Dred Scott v. Sandford* (1857) and *Brown v. Board of Education* (1954) illustrate the limitations of Supreme Court policymaking. The "great folly," as Senator Henry Cabot Lodge characterized *Dred Scott*, was not the Court's interpretation of the Constitution or the unpersuasive moral position that blacks were not persons under the Constitution. Rather, "[T]he attempt of the Court to settle the slavery question by judicial decision was simple madness." As Lodge explained:

> Slavery involved not only the great moral issue of the right of one man to hold another in bondage and to buy and sell him but it involved also the foundations of a social fabric covering half the country and caused men to feel so deeply that it finally brought them beyond the question of nullification to a point where the life of the Union was at stake and a decision could only be reached by war.

A hundred years later, political struggles within the country and, notably, presidential and congressional leadership in enforcing the Court's school desegregation ruling saved the moral appeal of *Brown* from becoming another "great folly."

Because the Court's decisions are not self-executing, public reactions inevitably weigh on the minds of the justices. Justice Stone, for one, was furious at Chief Justice Hughes's rush to hand down *Powell v. Alabama* (1932). Picketers protested the Scottsboro boys' conviction and death sentence. Stone attributed the Court's rush to judgment to Hughes's "wish to put a stop to the [public] demonstrations around the Court." Opposition to the school desegregation ruling in *Brown* led to bitter, sometimes violent confrontations. In Little Rock, Arkansas, Governor Orval Faubus encouraged disobedience by southern segregationists. The federal National Guard had to be called out to maintain order. The school board in Little Rock unsuccessfully pleaded, in *Cooper v. Aaron* (1958), for the Court's postponement of the implementation of *Brown's* mandate. In the midst of the controversy, Frankfurter worried that Chief Justice Warren's attitude had become "more like that of a fighting politician than that of a judicial statesman." In such confrontations between the Court and the country, "the transcending issue," Frankfurter reminded the brethren, remains that of preserving "the Supreme Court as the authoritative organ of what the Constitution requires." When the justices move too far or too fast in their interpretation of the Constitution, they threaten public acceptance of the Court's legitimacy.

*   *   *

When deciding major issues of public law and policy, justices must consider strategies for getting public acceptance of their rulings. When striking down the doctrine of "separate but equal" facilities in 1954 in *Brown v. Board of Education (Brown I)*, for instance, the Warren Court waited a year before issuing, in *Brown II*, its mandate for "all deliberate speed" in ending racial segregation in public education.

Resistance to the social policy announced in *Brown I* was expected. A rigid timetable for desegregation would only intensify opposition. During oral arguments on *Brown II*, devoted to the question of what kind of decree the Court should issue to enforce *Brown*, Warren confronted the hard fact of southern resistance. The attorney for South Carolina, S. Emory Rogers, pressed for an open-ended decree—one that would not specify when and how desegregation should take place. He boldly proclaimed:

> Mr. Chief Justice, to say we will conform depends on the decree handed down. I am frank to tell you, right now [in] our district I do not think that we will send—[that] the white people of the district will send their children to the Negro schools. It would be unfair to tell the Court that we are going to do that. I do not think it is. But I do think that something can be worked out. We hope so.

"It is not a question of attitude," Warren shot back, "it is a question of conforming to the decree." Their heated exchange continued as follows:

> CHIEF JUSTICE WARREN: But you are not willing to say here that there would be an honest attempt to conform to this decree, if we did leave it to the district court [to implement]?
> MR. ROGERS: No, I am not. Let us get the word "honest" out of there.
> CHIEF JUSTICE WARREN: No, leave it in.
> MR. ROGERS: No, because I would have to tell you that right now we would not conform—we would not send our white children to the Negro schools.

The exchange reinforced Warren's view "that reasonable attempts to start the integration process is [sic] all the court can expect in view of the scope of the problem, and that an order to immediately admit all negroes in white schools would be an absurdity because impossible to obey in many areas. Thus, while total immediate integration might be a reasonable order for Kansas, it would be unreasonable for Virginia, and the district judge might decide that a grade a year or three grades a year is [sic] reasonable compliance in Virginia." Six law clerks were assigned to prepare a segregation research report. They summarized available studies, discussed how school districts in different regions could be desegregated, and projected the effects and reactions to various desegregation plans.

The Court's problem, as one of Reed's law clerks put it, was to frame a decree "so as to allow such divergent results without making it so broad that evasion is encouraged." The clerks agreed that there should be a simple decree but disagreed on whether there should be guidelines for its implementation. One clerk opposed any guidelines. The others thought that their absence "smacks of indecisiveness, and gives the extremists more time to operate." The problem was how precise a guideline should be established. What would constitute "good-faith" compliance? "Although we think a 12-year gradual desegregation plan permissible," they confessed, "we are not certain that the opinion should explicitly sanction it."

At conference, Warren repeated these concerns. Black and Minton thought that a simple decree, without an opinion, was enough. As Black explained, "[T]he less we say the better off we are." The others disagreed. A short, simple opinion seemed advisable for reaffirming *Brown I* and providing guidance for dealing with the inevitable problems of compliance. Harlan wanted *Brown II* expressly to recognize that school desegregation was a local problem to be solved by local authorities. The others also insisted on making clear that school boards and lower courts had flexibility in ending segregation. In Burton's view, "[N]either this Court nor district courts should act as a school board or formulate the program" for desegregation.

Agreement emerged that the Court should issue a short opinion-decree. In a memorandum, Warren summarized the main points of agreement. The opinion should simply state that *Brown I* held racially segregated public schools to be unconstitutional. *Brown II* should acknowledge that the ruling created various administrative problems, but emphasize that "local school authorities have the primary responsibility for assessing and solving these problems; [and] the courts will have to consider these problems in determining whether the efforts of local school authorities" are in good-faith compliance. The cases, he concluded, should be remanded to the lower courts "for such proceedings and decree necessary and proper to carry out this Court's decision." The justices agreed, and along these lines Warren drafted the Court's short opinion-decree.

The phrase "all deliberate speed" was borrowed from Holmes's opinion in *Virginia v. West Virginia* (1911), a case dealing with how much of the state's public debt, and when, Virginia ought to receive at the time West Virginia broke off and became a state. It was inserted in the final opinion at the suggestion of Frankfurter. Forced integration might lead to a lowering of educational standards. Immediate, court-ordered desegregation, Frankfurter warned, "would make a mockery of the Constitutional adjudication designed to vindicate a claim to equal treatment to achieve 'integrated' but lower educational standards." The Court, he insisted, "does its duty if it gets effectively under way the righting of a wrong. When the wrong is deeply rooted state policy the court does its duty if it decrees measures that reverse the direction of the unconstitutional policy so as to uproot it 'with all deliberate speed.'" As much an apology for not setting precise guidelines as a recognition of the limitations of judicial power, the phrase symbolized the Court's bold moral appeal to the country.

Ten years later, after school closings, massive resistance, and continuing litigation, Black complained. "There has been entirely too much deliberation and not enough speed" in complying with *Brown*. "The time for mere 'deliberate speed' has run out." *Brown*'s moral appeal amounted to little more than an invitation for delay.

* * *

Twenty years after *Brown*, some schools remained segregated. David Mathews, secretary of the Department of Health, Education, and Welfare, reported to President Ford the results of a survey of half of the nation's primary and secondary public schools, enrolling 91 percent of all students: of these, 42 percent had an "appreciable percentage" of minority students, 16 percent had undertaken desegregation plans, while 26 percent had not, and 7 percent of the school districts remained racially segregated.

For over three decades, problems of implementing and achieving compliance with *Brown* persisted. Litigation by civil rights groups forced change, but it was piecemeal, costly, and modest. The judiciary alone could not achieve desegregation. Evasion and resistance were encouraged by the reluctance of presidents and Congress to enforce the mandate. Refusing publicly to endorse *Brown*, Eisenhower would not take steps to enforce the decision until violence erupted in Little Rock, Arkansas. He then did so "*not* to enforce integration but to prevent opposition by violence to orders of a court." Later the Kennedy and Johnson administrations lacked congressional authorization and resources to take major initiatives in enforcing school desegregation. Not until 1964, when Congress passed the Civil Rights Act, did the executive branch have such authorization.

Enforcement and implementation required the cooperation and coordination of all three branches. Little progress could be made, as Assistant Attorney General Stephen Pollock has explained, "where historically there had been slavery and a long tradition of discrimination [until] all three branches of the federal government [could] be lined up in support of a movement forward or a requirement for change." The election of Nixon in 1968 then brought changes both in the policies of the executive branch and in the composition of the Court. The simplicity and flexibility of *Brown*, moreover, invited evasion. It produced a continuing struggle over measures, such as gerrymandering school district lines and busing in the 1970s and 1980s, because the mandate itself had evolved from one of ending segregation to one of securing integration in public schools. Republican and Democratic administrations in turn differed on the means and ends of their enforcement policies in promoting integration.

Almost forty years after *Brown*, over 500 school desegregation cases remained in the lower federal courts. At issue in most was whether schools had achieved integration and become free of the vestiges of past segregation. Although lower courts split over how much proof school boards had to show to demonstrate that present *de facto* racial isolation was unrelated to past *de jure* segregation, the Court declined to review major desegregation cases from the mid-1970s to the end of the 1980s. During that time the dynamics of segregation in the country changed, as did the composition and direction of the Court.

* * *

"By itself," the political scientist Robert Dahl observed, "the Court is almost powerless to affect the course of national policy." Another political scientist, Gerald Rosenberg, goes much further in claiming that "courts can *almost never* be effective producers of significant social reform." *Brown's* failure to achieve immediate and widespread desegregation is instructive, Rosenberg contends, in developing a model of judicial policy-making on the basis of two opposing theories of judicial power. On the theory of a "Constrained Court" three institutional factors limit judicial policy-making: "[t]he limited nature of constitutional rights"; "[t]he lack of judicial independence"; and "[t]he judiciary's lack of powers of implementation." On the other hand, a "Dynamic Court" theory emphasizes the judiciary's freedom "from electoral constraints and [other] institutional arrangements that stymie change," and thus enable the courts to take on issues that other political institutions might not or cannot. But neither theory is completely satisfactory, according to Rosenberg, because occasionally courts do bring about social change. The Court may do so when the three institutional restraints identified with the "Constrained Court" theory are absent and at least one of the following conditions exist to support judicial policy-making: when other political institutions and actors offer either (a) incentives or (b) costs to induce compliance; (c) "when judicial decisions can be implemented by the market"; or (d) when the Court's ruling serves as "a shield, cover, or excuse, for persons crucial to implementation who are *willing to act.*" On the historical basis of resistance and forced compliance with *Brown's* mandate, Rosenberg concludes that "*Brown* and its progeny stand for the proposition that courts are impotent to produce significant social reform."

Brown, nonetheless, dramatically and undeniably altered the course of American life in ways and for reasons that Rosenberg underestimates. Neither Congress nor President Eisenhower would have moved to end segregated schools in the 1950s, as their reluctance for a decade to enforce *Brown* underscores. The Court lent moral force and legitimacy to the civil rights movement and to the eventual move by Congress and President Johnson to enforce compliance with *Brown.* More importantly, to argue that the Court is impotent to bring about social change overstates the case. Neither Congress nor the president, any more than the Court, could have single-handedly dismantled racially segregated public schools. As political scientist Richard Neustadt has argued, presidential power ultimately turns on a president's power of persuasion, the Court's power depends on the persuasiveness of its rulings and the magnitude of change in social behavior mandated. The Court raises the ante in its bid for compliance when it appeals for massive social change through a prescribed course of action, in contrast to when it simply says "no" when striking down a law. The unanimous but ambiguous ruling in *Brown* reflects the justices' awareness that their decisions are not self-enforcing, especially when they deal with highly controversial issues and their rulings depend heavily on other institutions for implementation. Moreover, the ambiguity of *Brown*'s remedial decree was the price of achieving unanimity. Unanimity appeared necessary if the Court was to preserve its institutional prestige while pursuing revolutionary change in social policy. The justices sacrificed their own policy preferences for more precise guidelines, while the Court tolerated lengthy delays in recognition of the costs of open defiance, building consensus, and gaining public acceptance. But in the ensuing decades *Brown*'s mandate was also transformed from that of a simple decree for putting an end to state-imposed segregation into the more vexing one of achieving integrated public schools. With that transformation of *Brown*'s mandate the political dynamics of the desegregation controversy evolved, along with a changing Court and country.

DISCUSSION QUESTIONS

1. In what ways does the Supreme Court take politics and public opinion into account in making decisions? Is this appropriate? What would the alternative be?

2. How does the process of appointment to the Supreme Court shape Court decisions? Should presidents make nominations based on the political views of potential justices?

3. Does O'Brien's argument confirm Hamilton's observations about the power of the Court?

4. In its 2015 decision *Obergefell v. Hodges*, the Supreme Court ruled that same-sex marriage was protected by the Constitution. Did this ruling damage the Court's public standing by ignoring the political context (a majority of the public opposed same-sex marriage in many states that had laws or constitutional amendments prohibiting same-sex marriage), or did the Court do the correct thing by supporting the basic rights of historically marginalized groups? How about the Court's abortion decisions in 2022—to what extent were they influenced by public opinion? Is there some way the Court could have finessed these issues, the way it did in *Brown*? Should it have?

39

From *The Hollow Hope: Can Courts Bring About Social Change?*

Gerald N. Rosenberg

Despite Alexander Hamilton's argument that the Supreme Court would be the "least dangerous branch" because it could not accomplish much without the assistance of Congress and the president, most political observers have viewed the Court as an important agent of social change. That is, in many instances when Congress and the president have not been inclined to act, the Court has pushed the nation to change important policies. In areas such as civil rights, environmental policy, women's and reproductive rights, and political reform, the standard view is of a "dynamic court" that is a "powerful, vigorous, and potent proponent of change." Proponents of this perspective see it as almost self-evident, pointing to decisions such as Brown v. Board of Education *on school desegregation;* Roe v. Wade *on abortion (at least for 49 years until the Court overturned it in 2022);* Baker v. Carr *on "one-person, one-vote"; and* Obergefell v. Hodges *on same-sex marriage as examples of the Supreme Court producing important social change.*

Gerald N. Rosenberg says this view of the Court is simply wrong. In contrast, he presents a view of a "constrained court" that is "weak, ineffective, and powerless." Echoing Hamilton, Rosenberg points out that courts depend on political support to produce reform; that they are unlikely to produce change if they face any serious resistance because of their lack of implementation powers; and that if they lack established legal precedents, they are unlikely to break new ground in a way that promotes social change. For example, following Brown v. Board of Education, *there was massive resistance from southern states to implementing the ruling, so real change did not occur until Congress acted ten years later. He also argues that courts are in a weak position to change public opinion because most Americans are only vaguely aware of most landmark Supreme Court decisions.*

Rosenberg concludes that courts can only help produce significant social change when the "institutional, structural, and ideological barriers to change are weak. A court's contribution, then, is akin to officially recognizing the evolving state of affairs, more like the cutting of the ribbon on a new project than its construction."

In the last several decades movements and groups advocating what I will shortly define as significant social reform have turned increasingly to the courts. Starting with the famous cases brought by the civil rights movement and spreading to issues raised by women's groups, environmental groups, political reformers, and others, American courts seemingly have become important producers of political and social change. Cases such as *Brown* (school desegregation) and *Roe* (abortion) are heralded as having produced major change. Further, such litigation has often occurred, and appears to have been most successful, when the other branches of government have failed to act. While officious government officials and rigid, unchanging institutions represent a real social force which may frustrate popular opinion, this litigation activity suggests that courts can produce significant social reform even when the other branches of government are inactive or opposed. Indeed, for many, part of what makes American democracy exceptional is that it includes the world's most powerful court system, protecting minorities and defending liberty, in the face of opposition from the democratically elected branches. Americans look to activist courts, then, as fulfilling an important role in the American scheme. This view of the courts, although informed by recent historical experience, is essentially functional. It sees courts as powerful, vigorous, and potent proponents of change. I refer to this view of the role of the courts as the "Dynamic Court" view.

As attractive as the Dynamic Court view may be, one must guard against uncritical acceptance. Indeed, in a political system that gives sovereignty to the popular will and makes economic decisions through the market, it is not obvious why courts should have the effects it asserts. Maybe its attractiveness is based on something more than effects? Could it be that the self-understanding of the judiciary and legal profession leads to an overstatement of the role of the courts, a "mystification" of the judiciary? If judges see themselves as powerful; if the Bar views itself as influential, and insulated; if professional training in law schools inculcates students with such beliefs, might these factors inflate the self-importance of the judiciary? The Dynamic Court view may be supported, then, because it offers psychological payoffs to key actors by confirming self-images, not because it is correct. And when this "mystification" is added to a normative belief in the courts as the guardian of fundamental rights and liberties—what Scheingold (1974) calls the "myth of rights"—the allure of the Dynamic Court view may grow.

Further, for all its "obviousness," the Dynamic Court view has a well-established functional and historical competitor. In fact, there is a long tradition of legal scholarship that views the federal judiciary, in Alexander Hamilton's famous language, as the "least dangerous" branch of government. Here, too, there is something of a truism about this claim. Courts, we know, lack both budgetary and physical powers. Because, in Hamilton's words, they lack power over either the "sword or the purse," their ability to produce political and social change is limited. In contrast to the first view, the "least dangerous" branch can do little more than point out how actions have fallen short of constitutional or legislative requirements and hope that appropriate action is taken. The strength of this view, of course, is that it leaves Americans free to govern themselves without interference from non-elected officials. I refer to this view of the courts as weak, ineffective, and powerless as the "Constrained Court" view.

The Constrained Court view fully acknowledges the role of popular preferences and social and economic resources in shaping outcomes. Yet it seems to rely excessively on a formal-process understanding of how change occurs in American politics. But the formal process doesn't always work, for social and political forces may be overly responsive to unevenly distributed resources. Bureaucratic inertia, too, can derail orderly, processional change. There is room, then, for courts to effectively correct the pathologies of the political process. Perhaps accurate at the founding of the political system, the Constrained Court view may miss growth and change in the American political system.

Clearly, these two views, and the aspirations they represent, are in conflict on a number of different dimensions. They differ not only on both the desirability and the effectiveness of court action, but also on the nature of American democracy. The Dynamic Court view gives courts an important place in the American political system while the older view sees courts as much less powerful than other more "political" branches and activities. The conflict is more than one of mere definition, for each view captures a very different part of American democracy. We Americans want courts to protect minorities and defend liberties, *and* to defer to elected officials. We want a robust political life *and* one that is just. Most of the time, these two visions do not clash. American legislatures do not habitually threaten liberties, and courts do not regularly invalidate the acts of elected officials or require certain actions to be taken. But the most interesting and relevant cases, such as *Brown* and *Roe*, occur when activist courts overrule and invalidate the actions of elected officials, or order actions beyond what elected officials are willing to do. What happens then? Are courts effective producers of change, as the Dynamic Court view suggests, or do their decisions do little more than point the way to a brighter, but perhaps unobtainable future? Once again, this conflict between two deeply held views about the role of the courts in the American political system has an obvious normative dimension that is worth debating. But this book has a different aim. Relying heavily on empirical data, I ask under what conditions can courts produce political and social change? When does it make sense for individuals and groups pressing for such change to litigate? What do the answers mean about the nature of the American regime?

* * *

The findings show that, with the addition of the four conditions, the constraints derived from the Constrained Court view best capture the capacity of the courts to produce significant social reform. This is the case because, on the most fundamental level, courts depend on political support to produce such reform (Constraint II). For example, since the success of civil rights in fields such as voting and education depended on political action, political hostility doomed court contributions. With women's rights, lack of enforcement of existing laws, in addition to an unwillingness to extend legal protection, had a similar dampening effect. And with abortion and the environment, hostility from many political leaders created barriers to implementation. This finding appears clearly applicable to other fields.

Courts will also be ineffective in producing change, given any serious resistance because of their lack of implementation powers (Constraint III). The structural constraints of the Constrained Court view, built into the American judicial system, make courts virtually powerless to produce change. They must depend on the actions of others for their decisions to be implemented. With civil rights, little changed until the federal government became involved. With women's rights, we still lack a serious government effort, and stereotypes that constrain women's opportunities remain powerful. Similarly, the uneven availability of access to legal abortion demonstrates the point. Where there is local hostility to change, court orders will be ignored. Community pressure, violence or threats of violence, and lack of market response all serve to curtail actions to implement court decisions. This finding, too, appears applicable across fields.

Despite these constraints on change, in at least several of the movements examined major legal cases were won. The chief reason is that the remaining constraint, the lack of established legal precedents, was weak (Constraint I). That is, there were precedents for change and supportive movements within the broader legal culture. In civil rights, litigation in the 1930s and 1940s progressively battered the separate-but-equal standard, setting up the argument and decision in *Brown*. In women's rights, the progress of civil rights litigation, particularly in the expansion of the Fourteenth Amendment, laid the groundwork. In the area of abortion, notions of a sphere of privacy in sexual matters were first developed by the Supreme Court in 1965, broadened in 1972, and forcefully presented in several widely read law-review articles. And, by the date of the Supreme Court's abortion decisions, numerous lower courts had invalidated state abortion statutes on grounds that the Supreme Court came to enunciate. Without these precedents, which took decades to develop, it would have been years before even a legal victory could have been obtained. But legal victories do not automatically or even necessarily produce the desired change.

A quick comparison between civil rights and abortion illustrates these points. While both had legal precedents on which to construct a winning legal argument, little else was similar. With civil rights, there was a great deal of white hostility to blacks, especially in the South. On the whole, political leaders, particularly Southerners, were either supportive of segregation or unwilling to confront it as an important issue. In addition, court decisions required individuals and institutions hostile to civil rights to implement the changes. Until Congress acted a decade later, these two constraints remained and none of the conditions necessary for change were present. After congressional and executive actions were taken, the constraints were overcome and conditions for change were created, including the creation of incentives, costs, and the context in which courts could be used as cover. Only then did change occur. In contrast, at the time of the abortion decisions there was much public and elite support for abortion. There was an active reform movement in the states, and Congress was quiet, with no indication of the opposition that many of its members would later provide. Also, the presence of the market condition partially overcame the implementation constraint. To the extent that the abortion decisions had judicial effects, it is precisely because the constraints were weak and a condition necessary for change was present. Civil rights and abortion litigation, then, highlight the existence and force of the constraints and conditions.

Turning to the question of extra-judicial or indirect effects, courts are in a weak position to produce change. Only a minority of Americans know what the courts have done on important issues. Fewer still combine that knowledge with the belief in the Supreme Court's constitutional role, a combination that would enable the Court, and the lower courts, to legitimate behavior. This makes courts a particularly poor tool for changing opinions or for mobilization. As Peltason puts it, "[L]itigation, by its complexity and technical nature and by its lack of dramatic moments, furnishes an ineffective peg around which to build a mass movement." Rally round the flag is one thing but rally round the brief (or opinion) is quite another! The evidence from the movements examined makes dubious any claim for important extra-judicial effects of court action. It strikes at the heart of the Dynamic Court view.

The cases examined show that when the constraints are overcome, and one of the four conditions is present, courts can help produce significant social reform. However, this means, by definition, that institutional, structural, and ideological barriers to change are weak. A court's contribution, then, is akin to officially recognizing the evolving state of affairs, more like the cutting of the ribbon on a new project than its construction. Without such change, the constraints reign. When Justice Jackson commented during oral argument in *Brown*, "I suppose that realistically this case is here for the reason that action couldn't be obtained from Congress," he identified a fundamental reason why the Court's action in the case would have little effect.

Given the constraints and the conditions, the Constrained Court view is the more accurate: U.S. courts can *almost never* be effective producers of significant social reform. At best, they can second the social reform acts of the other branches of government. Problems that are unsolvable in the political context can rarely be solved by courts. As Scheingold puts it, the "law can hardly transcend the conflicts of the political system in which it is embedded." Turning to courts to produce significant social reform substitutes the myth of America for its reality. It credits courts and judicial decisions with a power that they do not have.

*   *   *

This conclusion does not deny that courts can sometimes help social reform movements. Occasionally, though rarely, when the constraints are overcome, and one of the conditions is present, courts can make a difference. Sometimes, too, litigation can remove minor but lingering obstacles. But here litigation is often a mopping-up operation, and it is often defensive. In civil rights, for example, when opponents of the 1964 and 1965 acts went to court to invalidate them, the courts' refusal to do so allowed change to proceed. Similarly, if there had never been a *Brown* decision, a Southern school board or state wanting to avoid a federal fund cut-off in the late 1960s might have challenged its state law requiring segregation. An obliging court decision would have removed the obstacle without causing much of a stir, or wasting the scarce resources of civil rights groups. This is a very different approach to the courts than one based on using them to produce significant social reform.

Litigation can also help reform movements by providing defense services to keep the movement afloat. In civil rights, the NAACP Legal Defense and Educational Fund, Inc. (Inc. Fund) provided crucial legal service that prevented the repressive legal structures of the Southern states from totally incapacitating the movement. In springing demonstrators from jail, providing bail money, and forcing at least a semblance of due process, Inc. Fund lawyers performed crucial tasks. But again, this is a far cry from a litigation strategy for significant social reform.

* * *

American courts are not all-powerful institutions. They were designed with severe limitations and placed in a political system of divided powers. To ask them to produce significant social reform is to forget their history and ignore their constraints. It is to cloud our vision with a naive and romantic belief in the triumph of rights over politics. And while romance and even naiveté have their charms, they are not best exhibited in courtrooms.

DISCUSSION QUESTIONS

1. Can you think of any examples of important Supreme Court decisions that may support the view that the Court can be an important agent of social change?

2. If Rosenberg is correct, does that mean that Hamilton's argument that the Court is the "least dangerous branch" is also correct? Or are there other ways that the Court exerts influence in the political system other than promoting social change?

3. If you don't find Rosenberg's argument convincing, what evidence would persuade you that he's correct?

Debating the Issues: Interpreting the Constitution— Originalism or a Living Constitution?

Debates over the federal judiciary's role in the political process often focus on the question of how judges should interpret the Constitution. Should judges apply the document's original meaning as stated by the framers, or should they use a framework that incorporates shifting interpretations across time? This debate intensified during Earl Warren's tenure as Chief Justice (1953–69) because of Court decisions that expanded the scope of civil liberties and criminal rights far beyond what "originalists" thought the Constitution's language authorized. The debate continues in the current, more conservative Court. The two readings in this section offer contrasting viewpoints from Justice Antonin Scalia, who died in 2016, and one retired Supreme Court justice (Stephen Breyer).

Scalia was the intellectual force behind the conservative wing of the Court and argued that justices must be bound by the original meaning of the document, because that is the only neutral principle that allows the judiciary to function as a legal body instead of a political one. The alternative is to embrace an evolving or "Living Constitution," which Scalia criticized as allowing judges to decide cases on the basis of what seems right at the moment. He said that this "evolutionary" approach does not have any overall guiding principle and therefore "is simply not a practicable constitutional philosophy." He provided several examples of how the Living Constitution approach had produced decisions that stray from the meaning of the Constitution in the areas of abortion rights, gay rights, the right to counsel, and the right to confront one's accuser. This last example is especially provocative, given that it concerned the right of an accused child molester to confront the child who accused him of the crime. Scalia argues that there is no coherent alternative to originalism and forcefully concludes, "The worst thing about the Living Constitution is that it will destroy the Constitution."

Stephen Breyer argues for the Living Constitution approach and places it within a broader constitutional and theoretical framework. He argues for a "consequentialist" approach that is rooted in basic constitutional purposes, the most important of which is "active liberty," which he defines as "an active and constant participation in collective power." Breyer applies this framework to a range of difficult constitutional issues, including freedom of speech in the context of campaign finance and privacy rights in the context of rapidly evolving technology. He argues that the plain language of the Constitution does not provide enough guidance to answer these difficult questions. He turns the tables on Scalia, arguing that it is the literalist or originalist position that will, ironically, lead justices to rely too heavily on their own personal views, whereas his consequentialist position is actually the view that is more likely to produce judicial restraint. Breyer goes on to criticize the originalist position as fraught with inconsistencies. It is inherently subjective, despite its attempt to emphasize the "objective" words of the Constitution. By relying on the consequentialist perspective, which emphasizes democratic participation and active liberty, justices are more likely to reach limited conclusions that apply to the facts at hand, while maximizing the positive implications for democracy.

Linda Greenhouse, an observer of the Supreme Court, summarized the debate between Scalia and Breyer in these terms: "[i]t is a debate over text versus context. For Justice Scalia, who focuses on text, language is supreme, and the court's job is to derive and apply rules from the words chosen by the Constitution's framers or a statute's drafters. For Justice Breyer, who looks to context, language is only a starting point to an inquiry in which a law's purpose and a decision's likely consequences are the more important elements."

40

"Constitutional Interpretation the Old-Fashioned Way"

Antonin Scalia

It's a pizzazzy topic: Constitutional Interpretation. It is, however, an important one. I was vividly reminded how important it was last week when the Court came out with a controversial decision in the *Roper* case. And I watched one television commentary on the case in which the host had one person defending the opinion on the ground that people should not be subjected to capital punishment for crimes they commit when they are younger than eighteen, and the other person attacked the opinion on the ground that a jury should be able to decide that a person, despite the fact he was under eighteen, given the crime, given the person involved, should be subjected to capital punishment. And it struck me how irrelevant it was, how much the point had been missed. The question wasn't whether the call was right or wrong. The important question was who should make the call. And that is essentially what I am addressing today.

I am one of a small number of judges, small number of anybody—judges, professors, lawyers—who are known as originalists. Our manner of interpreting the Constitution is to begin with the text, and to give that text the meaning that it bore when it was adopted by the people. I'm not a "strict constructionist," despite the introduction. I don't like the term "strict construction." I do not think the Constitution, or any text, should be interpreted either strictly or sloppily; it should be interpreted reasonably. Many of my interpretations do not deserve the description "strict." I do believe, however, that you give the text the meaning it had when it was adopted.

This is such a minority position in modern academia and in modern legal circles that on occasion I'm asked when I've given a talk like this a question from the back of the room—"Justice Scalia, when did you first become an originalist?"—as though it is some kind of weird affliction that seizes some people—"When did you first start eating human flesh?"

Although it is a minority view now, the reality is that, not very long ago, originalism was orthodoxy. Everybody at least *purported* to be an originalist. If you go back and read the commentaries on the Constitution by Joseph Story, he didn't think the Constitution evolved or changed. He said it means and will always mean what it meant when it was adopted.

Or consider the opinions of John Marshall in the Federal Bank case, where he says, we must not, we must always remember it is a constitution we are expounding. And since it's a constitution, he says, you have to give its provisions expansive meaning so that they will accommodate events that you do not know of which will happen in the future.

Well, if it is a constitution that changes, you wouldn't have to give it an expansive meaning. You can give it whatever meaning you want and, when future necessity arises, you simply change the meaning. But anyway, that is no longer the orthodoxy.

Oh, one other example about how not just the judges and scholars believed in originalism, but even the American people. Consider the 19th Amendment, which is the amendment that gave women the vote. It was adopted by the American people in 1920. Why did we adopt a constitutional amendment for that purpose? The Equal Protection Clause existed in 1920; it was adopted right after the Civil War. And you know that if the issue of the franchise for women came up today, we would not have to have a constitutional amendment. Someone would come to the Supreme Court and say, "Your Honors, in a democracy, what could be a greater denial of equal protection than denial of the franchise?" And the Court would say, "Yes! Even though it never meant it before, the Equal Protection Clause means that women have to have the vote." But that's not how the American people thought in 1920. In 1920, they looked at the Equal Protection Clause and said, "What does it mean?" Well, it clearly doesn't mean that you can't discriminate in the franchise—not only on the basis of sex, but on the basis of property ownership, on the basis of literacy. None of that is unconstitutional. And therefore, since it wasn't unconstitutional, and we wanted it to be, we did things the good old-fashioned way and adopted an amendment.

Now, in asserting that originalism used to be orthodoxy, I do not mean to imply that judges did not distort the Constitution now and then; of course they did. We had willful judges then, and we will have willful judges until the end of time. But the difference is that prior to the last fifty years or so, prior to the advent of the "Living Constitution," judges did their distortions the good old-fashioned way, the honest way—they lied about it. They said the Constitution means such and such, when it never meant such and such.

It's a big difference that you now no longer have to lie about it, because we are in the era of the evolving Constitution. And the judge can simply say, "Oh yes, the Constitution didn't used to mean that, but it does now." We are in the age in which not only judges, not only lawyers, but even school children have come to learn the Constitution changes. I have grammar school students come into the Court now and then, and they recite very proudly what they have been taught: "[t]he Constitution is a living document." You know, it morphs.

Well, let me first tell you how we got to the "Living Constitution." You don't have to be a lawyer to understand it. The road is not that complicated. Initially, the Court began giving terms in the text of the Constitution a meaning they didn't have when they were adopted. For example, the First Amendment, which forbids Congress to abridge the freedom of speech. What does the freedom of speech mean? Well, it clearly did not mean that Congress or government could not impose any restrictions upon speech. Libel laws, for example, were clearly constitutional. Nobody thought the First Amendment was *carte blanche* to libel someone. But in the famous case of *New York Times v. Sullivan*, the Supreme Court said, "But the First Amendment does prevent you from suing for libel if you are a public figure and if the libel was not malicious"—that is, the person, a member of the press or otherwise, thought that what the person said was true. Well, that had never been the law. I mean, it might be a good law. And some states could amend their libel law.

It's one thing for a state to amend its libel law and say, "We think that public figures shouldn't be able to sue." That's fine. But the courts have said that the First Amendment, which never meant this before, now means that if you are a public figure, that you can't sue for libel unless it's intentional, malicious. So that's one way to do it.

Another example is the Constitution guarantees the right to be represented by counsel. That never meant the state had to pay for your counsel. But you can reinterpret it to mean that.

That was step one. Step two, I mean, that will only get you so far. There is no text in the Constitution that you could reinterpret to create a right to abortion, for example. So you need something else. The something else is called the doctrine of "Substantive Due Process." Only lawyers can walk around talking about substantive process, inasmuch as it's a contradiction in terms. If you referred to substantive process or procedural substance at a cocktail party, people would look at you funny. But, lawyers talk this way all the time.

What substantive due process is is quite simple—the Constitution has a Due Process Clause, which says that no person shall be deprived of life, liberty, or property without due process of law. Now, what does this guarantee? Does it guarantee life, liberty, or property? No, indeed! All three can be taken away. You can be fined, you can be incarcerated, you can even be executed, but not without due process of law. It's a procedural guarantee. But the Court said, and this goes way back, in the 1920s at least—in fact the first case to do it was *Dred Scott*. But it became more popular in the 1920s. The Court said there are some liberties that are so important, that no process will suffice to take them away. Hence, substantive due process.

Now, what liberties are they? The Court will tell you. Be patient. When the doctrine of substantive due process was initially announced, it was limited in this way: the Court said it embraces only those liberties that are fundamental to a democratic society and rooted in the traditions of the American people.

Then we come to step three. Step three: that limitation is eliminated. Within the last twenty years, we have found to be covered by due process the right to abortion, which was so little rooted in the traditions of the American people that it was criminal for 200 years; the right to homosexual sodomy, which was so little rooted in the traditions of the American people that it was criminal for 200 years. So it is literally true, and I don't think this is an exaggeration, that the Court has essentially liberated itself from the text of the Constitution, from the text and even from the traditions of the American people. It is up to the Court to say what is covered by substantive due process.

What are the arguments usually made in favor of the Living Constitution? As the name of it suggests, it is a very attractive philosophy, and it's hard to talk people out of it—the notion that the Constitution grows. The major argument is the Constitution is a living organism; it has to grow with the society that it governs or it will become brittle and snap.

This is the equivalent of, an anthropomorphism equivalent to, what you hear from your stockbroker, when he tells you that the stock market is resting for an assault on the 11,000 level. The stock market panting at some base camp. The stock market is not a mountain climber and the Constitution is not a living organism, for Pete's sake; it's a legal document, and like all legal documents, it says some things, and it doesn't say other things. And if you think that the aficionados of the Living Constitution want to bring you flexibility, think again.

My Constitution is a very flexible Constitution. You think the death penalty is a good idea—persuade your fellow citizens and adopt it. You think it's a bad idea—persuade them the other way and eliminate it. You want a right to abortion—create it the way most rights are created in a democratic society: persuade your fellow citizens it's a good idea and enact it. You want the opposite—persuade them the other way. That's flexibility. But to read either result into the Constitution is not to produce flexibility, it is to produce what a constitution is designed to produce—rigidity. Abortion, for example, is offstage, it is off the democratic stage; it is no use debating it; it is unconstitutional. I mean prohibiting it is unconstitutional; I mean it's no use debating it anymore—now and forever, coast to coast, I guess until we amend the Constitution, which is a difficult thing. So, for whatever reason you might like the Living Constitution, don't like it because it provides flexibility.

That's not the name of the game. Some people also seem to like it because they think it's a good liberal thing—that somehow this is a conservative/liberal battle, and conservatives like the old-fashioned originalist Constitution and liberals ought to like the Living Constitution. That's not true either. The dividing line between those who believe in the Living Constitution and those who don't is not the dividing line between conservatives and liberals.

Conservatives are willing to grow the Constitution to cover their favorite causes just as liberals are, and the best example of that is two cases we announced some years ago on the same day, the same morning. One case was *Romer v. Evans*, in which the people of Colorado had enacted an amendment to the state constitution by plebiscite, which said that neither the state nor any subdivision of the state would add to the protected statuses against which private individuals cannot discriminate. The usual ones are race, religion, age, sex, disability and so forth. Would not add sexual preference—somebody thought that was a terrible idea, and, since it was a terrible idea, it must be unconstitutional. Brought a lawsuit, it came to the Supreme Court. And the Supreme Court said, "Yes, it is unconstitutional." On the basis of—I don't know. The Sexual Preference Clause of the Bill of Rights, presumably. And the liberals loved it, and the conservatives gnashed their teeth.

The very next case we announced is a case called *BMW v. Gore.* Not the Gore you think; this is another Gore. Mr. Gore had bought a BMW, which is a car supposedly advertised at least as having a superb finish, baked seven times in ovens deep in the Alps, by dwarfs. And his BMW apparently had gotten scratched on the way over. They did not send it back to the Alps; they took a can of spray paint and fixed it. And he found out about this and was furious, and he brought a lawsuit. He got his compensatory damages, a couple of hundred dollars—the difference between a car with a better paint job and a worse paint job—plus $2 million against BMW for punitive damages for being a bad actor, which is absurd of course, so it must be unconstitutional. BMW appealed to my Court, and my Court said, "Yes, it's unconstitutional." In violation of, I assume, the Excessive Damages Clause of the Bill of Rights. And if excessive punitive damages are unconstitutional, why aren't excessive compensatory damages unconstitutional? So you have a federal question whenever you get a judgment in a civil case. Well, that one the conservatives liked, because conservatives don't like punitive damages, and the liberals gnashed their teeth.

I dissented in both cases because I say, "A pox on both their houses." It has nothing to do with what your policy preferences are; it has to do with what you think the Constitution is.

Some people are in favor of the Living Constitution because they think it always leads to greater freedom—there's just nothing to lose, the evolving Constitution will always provide greater and greater freedom, more and more rights. Why would you think that? It's a two-way street. And indeed, under the aegis of the Living Constitution, some freedoms have been taken away.

Recently, last term, we reversed a 15-year-old decision of the Court, which had held that the Confrontation Clause—which couldn't be clearer, it says, "In all criminal prosecutions, the accused shall enjoy the right . . . to be confronted with the witness against him." But a Living Constitution Court held that all that was necessary to comply with the Confrontation Clause was that the hearsay evidence which is introduced—hearsay evidence means you can't cross-examine the person who said it because he's not in the court—the hearsay evidence has to bear indicia of reliability. I'm happy to say that we reversed it last term with the votes of the two originalists on the Court. And the opinion said that the only indicium of reliability that the Confrontation Clause acknowledges is confrontation. You bring the witness in to testify and to be cross-examined. That's just one example; there are others, of eliminating liberties.

So, I think another example is the right to jury trial. In a series of cases, the Court had seemingly acknowledged that you didn't have to have trial by jury of the facts that increase your sentence. You can make the increased sentence a "sentencing factor"—you get thirty years for burglary, but if the burglary is committed with a gun, as a sentencing factor the judge can give you another ten years. And the judge will decide whether you used a gun. And he will decide it, not beyond a reasonable doubt, but whether it's more likely than not. Well, we held recently, I'm happy to say, that this violates the right to a trial by jury. The Living Constitution would not have produced that result. The Living Constitution, like the legislatures that enacted these laws, would have allowed sentencing factors to be determined by the judge because all the Living Constitution assures you is that what will happen is what the majority wants to happen. And that's not the purpose of constitutional guarantees.

Well, I've talked about some of the false virtues of the Living Constitution; let me tell you what I consider its principle vices are. Surely the greatest—you should always begin with principle—its greatest vice is its illegitimacy. The only reason federal courts sit in judgment of the constitutionality of federal legislation is not because they are explicitly authorized to do so in the Constitution. Some modern constitutions give the constitutional court explicit authority to review German legislation or French legislation for its constitutionality; our Constitution doesn't say anything like that. But John Marshall says in *Marbury v. Madison:* [l]ook, this is lawyers' work. What you have here is an apparent conflict between the Constitution and the statute. And, all the time, lawyers and judges have to reconcile these conflicts—they try to read the two to comport with each other. If they can't, it's judges' work to decide which ones prevail. When there are two statutes, the more recent one prevails. It implicitly repeals the older one. But when the Constitution is at issue, the Constitution prevails because it is a "superstatute." I mean, that's what Marshall says: [i]t's judges' work.

If you believe, however, that the Constitution is not a legal text, like the texts involved when judges reconcile or decide which of two statutes prevail; if you think the Constitution is some exhortation to give effect to the most fundamental values of the society as those values change from year to year; if you think that it is meant to reflect, as some of the Supreme Court cases say, particularly those involving the Eighth Amendment, if you think it is simply meant to reflect the evolving standards of decency that mark the progress of a maturing society—if that is what you think it is, then why in the world would you have it interpreted by nine lawyers? What do I know about the evolving standards of decency of American society? I'm afraid to ask.

If that is what you think the Constitution is, then *Marbury v. Madison* is wrong. It shouldn't be up to the judges, it should be up to the legislature. We should have a system like the English—whatever the legislature thinks is constitutional is constitutional. They know the evolving standards of American society, I don't. So in principle, it's incompatible with the legal regime that America has established.

Secondly, and this is the killer argument—I mean, it's the best debaters' argument—they say in politics you can't beat somebody with nobody. It's the same thing with principles of legal interpretation. If you don't believe in originalism, then you need some other principle of interpretation. Being a non-originalist is not enough. You see, I have my rules that confine me. I know what I'm looking for. When I find it—the original meaning of the Constitution—I am handcuffed. If I believe that the First Amendment meant when it was adopted that you are entitled to burn the American flag, I have to come out that way even though I don't like to come out that way. When I find that the original meaning of the jury trial guarantee is that any additional time you spend in prison which depends upon a fact must depend upon a fact found by a jury—once I find that's what the jury trial guarantee means, I am handcuffed. Though I'm a law-and-order type, I cannot do all the mean conservative things I would like to do to this society. You got me.

Now, if you're not going to control your judges that way, what other criterion are you going to place before them? What is the criterion that governs the Living Constitutional judge? What can you possibly use, besides original meaning? Think about that. Natural law? We all agree on that, don't we? The philosophy of John Rawls? That's easy. There really is nothing else. You either tell your judges, "Look, this is a law, like all laws; give it the meaning it had when it was adopted." Or, you tell your judges, "Govern us. You tell us whether people under eighteen, who committed their crimes when they were under eighteen, should be executed. You tell us whether there ought to be an unlimited right to abortion or a partial right to abortion. You make these decisions for us." I have put this question— you know I speak at law schools with some frequency just to make trouble—and I put this question to the faculty all the time, or incite the students to ask their Living Constitutional professors: "[o]kay professor, you are not an originalist, what is your criterion?" There is none other.

And finally, this is what I will conclude with although it is not on a happy note. The worst thing about the Living Constitution is that it will destroy the Constitution. You heard in the introduction that I was confirmed, close to nineteen years ago now, by a vote of ninety-eight to nothing. The two missing were Barry Goldwater and Jake Games, so make it one hundred. I was known at that time to be, in my political and social views, fairly conservative. But still, I was known to be a good lawyer, an honest man— somebody who could read a text and give it its fair meaning—had judicial impartiality and so forth. And so I was unanimously confirmed. Today, barely twenty years later, it is difficult to get someone confirmed to the Court of Appeals. What has happened? The American people have figured out what is going on. If we are selecting lawyers, if we are selecting people to read a text and give it the fair meaning it had when it was adopted, yes, the most important thing to do is to get a good lawyer. If on the other hand, we're picking people to draw out of their own conscience and experience a new constitution with all sorts of new values to govern our society, then we should not look principally for good lawyers. We should look principally for people who agree with us, the majority, as to whether there ought to be this right, that right and the other right. We want to pick people that would write the new constitution that we would want.

And that is why you hear in the discourse on this subject, people talking about moderate—we want moderate judges. What is a moderate interpretation of the text? Halfway between what it really means and what you'd like it to mean? There is no such thing as a moderate interpretation of the text. Would you ask a lawyer, "Draw me a moderate contract?" The only way the word has any meaning is if you are looking for someone to write a law, to write a constitution, rather than to interpret one. The moderate judge is the one who will devise the new constitution that most people would approve of. So, for example, we had a suicide case some terms ago, and the Court refused to hold that there is a constitutional right to assisted suicide. We said, "We're not yet ready to say that. Stay tuned, in a few years, the time may come, but we're not yet ready." And that was a moderate decision, because I think most people would not want—if we had gone, looked into that and created a national right to assisted suicide—that would nave been an immoderate and extremist decision.

I think the very terminology suggests where we have arrived—at the point of selecting people to write a constitution, rather than people to give us the fair meaning of one that has been democratically adopted. And when that happens, when the Senate interrogates nominees to the Supreme Court, or to the lower courts—you know, "Judge so-and-so, do you think there is a right to this in the Constitution? You don't? Well, my constituents think there ought to be, and I'm not going to appoint to the court someone who is not going to find that"—when we are in that mode, you realize, we have rendered the Constitution useless, because the Constitution will mean what the majority wants it to mean. The senators are representing the majority, and they will be selecting justices who will devise a constitution that the majority wants. And that, of course, deprives the Constitution of its principle utility. The Bill of Rights is devised to protect you and me against, who do you think? The majority. My most important function on the Supreme Court is to tell the majority to take a walk. And the notion that the justices ought to be selected because of the positions that they will take, that are favored by the majority, is a recipe for destruction of what we have had for 200 years.

To come back to the beginning, this is new—fifty years old or so—the Living Constitution stuff. We have not yet seen what the end of the road is. I think we are beginning to see. And what it is should really be troublesome to Americans who care about a Constitution that can provide protections against majoritarian rule. Thank you.

41

"Our Democratic Constitution"

STEPHEN BREYER

I shall focus upon several contemporary problems that call for governmental action and potential judicial reaction. In each instance I shall argue that, when judges interpret the Constitution, they should place greater emphasis upon the "ancient liberty," i.e., the people's right to "an active and constant participation in collective power." I believe that increased emphasis upon this active liberty will lead to better constitutional law, a law that will promote governmental solutions consistent with individual dignity and community need.

At the same time, my discussion will illustrate an approach to constitutional interpretation that places considerable weight upon consequences—consequences valued in terms of basic constitutional purposes. It disavows a contrary constitutional approach, a more "legalistic" approach that places too much weight upon language, history, tradition, and precedent alone while understating the importance of consequences. If the discussion helps to convince you that the more "consequential" approach has virtue, so much the better.

Three basic views underlie my discussion. First, the Constitution, considered as a whole, creates a framework for a certain kind of government. Its general objectives can be described abstractly as including (1) democratic self-government, (2) dispersion of power (avoiding concentration of too much power in too few hands), (3) individual dignity (through protection of individual liberties), (4) equality before the law (through equal protection of the law), and (5) the rule of law itself.

The Constitution embodies these general objectives in particular provisions. In respect to self-government, for example, Article IV guarantees a "republican Form of Government"; Article I insists that Congress meet at least once a year, that elections take place every two (or six) years, that a census take place every decade; the Fifteenth, Nineteenth, Twenty-fourth, and Twenty-sixth Amendments secure a virtually universal adult suffrage. But a general constitutional objective such as self-government plays a constitutional role beyond the interpretation of an individual provision that refers to it directly. That is because constitutional courts must consider the relation of one phrase to another. They must consider the document as a whole. And consequently the document's handful of general purposes will inform judicial interpretation of many individual provisions that do not refer directly to the general objective in question. My examples seek to show how that is so. And, as I have said, they will suggest a need for judges to pay greater attention to one of those general objectives, namely participatory democratic self-government.

Second, the Court, while always respecting language, tradition, and precedent, nonetheless has emphasized different general constitutional objectives at different periods in its history. Thus one can characterize the early nineteenth century as a period during which the Court helped to establish the authority of the federal government, including the federal judiciary. During the late nineteenth and early twentieth centuries, the Court underemphasized the Constitution's efforts to secure participation by black citizens in representative government—efforts related to the participatory "active" liberty of the ancients. At the same time, it overemphasized protection of property rights, such as an individual's freedom to contract without government interference, to the point where President Franklin Roosevelt commented that the Court's Lochner-era decisions had created a legal "no-man's land" that neither state nor federal regulatory authority had the power to enter.

The New Deal Court and the Warren Court in part reemphasized "active liberty." The former did so by dismantling various Lochner-era distinctions, thereby expanding the scope of democratic self-government. The latter did so by interpreting the Civil War Amendments in light of their purposes and to mean what they say, thereby helping African-Americans become members of the nation's community of self-governing citizens—a community that the Court expanded further in its "one person, one vote" decisions.

More recently, in my view, the Court has again underemphasized the importance of the citizen's active liberty. I will argue for a contemporary reemphasis that better combines "the liberty of the ancients" with that "freedom of governmental restraint" that Constant called "modern."

Third, the real-world consequences of a particular interpretive decision, valued in terms of basic constitutional purposes, play an important role in constitutional decision-making. To that extent, my approach differs from that of judges who would place nearly exclusive interpretive weight upon language, history, tradition, and precedent. In truth, the difference is one of degree. Virtually all judges, when interpreting a constitution or a statute, refer at one time or another to language, to history, to tradition, to precedent, to purpose, and to consequences. Even those who take a more literal approach to constitutional interpretation sometimes find consequences and general purposes relevant. But the more "literalist" judge tends to ask those who cannot find an interpretive answer in language, history, tradition, and precedent alone to rethink the problem several times, before making consequences determinative. The more literal judges may hope to find in language, history, tradition, and precedent objective interpretive standards; they may seek to avoid an interpretive subjectivity that could confuse a judge's personal idea of what is good for that which the Constitution demands; and they may believe that these more "original" sources will more readily yield rules that can guide other institutions, including lower courts. These objectives are desirable, but I do not think the literal approach will achieve them, and, in any event, the constitutional price is too high. I hope that my examples will help to show you why that is so, as well as to persuade some of you why it is important to place greater weight upon constitutionally valued consequences, my consequential focus in this lecture being the effect of a court's decisions upon active liberty.

To recall the fate of Socrates is to understand that the "liberty of the ancients" is not a sufficient condition for human liberty. Nor can (or should) we replicate today the ideal represented by the Athenian agora or the New England town meeting. Nonetheless, today's citizen does participate in democratic self-governing processes. And the "active" liberty to which I refer consists of the Constitution's efforts to secure the citizen's right to do so.

To focus upon that active liberty, to understand it as one of the Constitution's handful of general objectives, will lead judges to consider the constitutionality of statutes with a certain modesty. That modesty embodies an understanding of the judges' own expertise compared, for example, with that of a legislature. It reflects the concern that a judiciary too ready to "correct" legislative error may deprive "the people" of "the political experience and the moral education that come from . . . correcting their own errors." It encompasses that doubt, caution, prudence, and concern—that state of not being "too sure" of oneself—that Learned Hand described as the "spirit of liberty." In a word, it argues for traditional "judicial restraint."

But active liberty argues for more than that. I shall suggest that increased recognition of the Constitution's general democratic participatory objectives can help courts deal more effectively with a range of specific constitutional issues. To show this I shall use examples drawn from the areas of free speech, federalism, privacy, equal protection, and statutory interpretation. In each instance, I shall refer to an important modern problem of government that calls for a democratic response. I shall then describe related constitutional implications. I want to draw a picture of some of the different ways that increased judicial focus upon the Constitution's participatory objectives can have a positive effect.

* * *

I begin with free speech and campaign finance reform. The campaign finance problem arises out of the recent explosion in campaign costs along with a vast disparity among potential givers. * * * The upshot is a concern by some that the matter is out of hand—that too few individuals contribute too much money and that, even though money is not the only way to obtain influence, those who give large amounts of money do obtain, or appear to obtain, too much influence. The end result is a marked inequality of participation. That is one important reason why legislatures have sought to regulate the size of campaign contributions.

The basic constitutional question, as you all know, is not the desirability of reform legislation but whether, how, or the extent to which, the First Amendment permits the legislature to impose limitations or ceilings on the amounts individuals or organizations or parties can contribute to a campaign or the kinds of contributions they can make. * * *

One cannot (or, at least, I cannot) find an easy answer to the constitutional questions in language, history, or tradition. The First Amendment's language says that Congress shall not abridge "the freedom of speech." But it does not define "the freedom of speech" in any detail. The nation's Founders did not speak directly about campaign contributions. Madison, who decried faction, thought that members of Congress would fairly represent all their constituents, in part because the "electors" would not be the "rich" any "more than the poor." But this kind of statement, while modestly helpful to the campaign reform cause, is hardly determinative.

Neither can I find answers in purely conceptual arguments. Some argue, for example, that "money is speech"; others say "money is not speech." But neither contention helps much. Money is not speech, it is money. But the expenditure of money enables speech; and that expenditure is often necessary to communicate a message, particularly in a political context. A law that forbids the expenditure of money to convey a message could effectively suppress that communication.

Nor does it resolve the matter simply to point out that campaign contribution limits inhibit the political "speech opportunities" of those who wish to contribute more. Indeed, that is so. But the question is whether, in context, such a limitation abridges "the freedom of speech." And to announce that this kind of harm could never prove justified in a political context is simply to state an ultimate constitutional conclusion; it is not to explain the underlying reasons.

To refer to the Constitution's general participatory self-government objective, its protection of "active liberty" is far more helpful. That is because that constitutional goal indicates that the First Amendment's constitutional role is not simply one of protecting the individual's "negative" freedom from governmental restraint. The Amendment in context also forms a necessary part of a constitutional system designed to sustain that democratic self-government. The Amendment helps to sustain the democratic process both by encouraging the exchange of ideas needed to make sound electoral decisions and by encouraging an exchange of views among ordinary citizens necessary to encourage their informed participation in the electoral process. It thereby helps to maintain a form of government open to participation (in Constant's words "by all citizens without exception").

The relevance of this conceptual view lies in the fact that the campaign finance laws also seek to further the latter objective. They hope to democratize the influence that money can bring to bear upon the electoral process, thereby building public confidence in that process, broadening the base of a candidate's meaningful financial support, and encouraging greater public participation. They consequently seek to maintain the integrity of the political process—a process that itself translates political speech into governmental action. Seen in this way, campaign finance laws, despite the limits they impose, help to further the kind of open public political discussion that the First Amendment also seeks to encourage, not simply as an end, but also as a means to achieve a workable democracy.

For this reason, I have argued that a court should approach most campaign finance questions with the understanding that important First Amendment-related interests lie on both sides of the constitutional equation and that a First Amendment presumption hostile to government regulation, such as "strict scrutiny" is consequently out of place. Rather, the Court considering the matter without benefit of presumptions, must look realistically at the legislation's impact, both its negative impact on the ability of some to engage in as much communication as they wish and the positive impact upon the public's confidence, and consequent ability to communicate through (and participate in) the electoral process.

The basic question the Court should ask is one of proportionality. Do the statutes strike a reasonable balance between their electoral speech-restricting and speech-enhancing consequences? Or do you instead impose restrictions on that speech that are disproportionate when measured against their corresponding electoral and speech-related benefits, taking into account the kind, the importance, and the extent of those benefits, as well as the need for the restrictions in order to secure them?

The judicial modesty discussed earlier suggests that, in answering these questions, courts should defer to the legislatures' own answers insofar as those answers reflect empirical matters about which the legislature is comparatively expert, for example, the extent of the campaign finance problem, a matter that directly concerns the realities of political life. But courts cannot defer when evaluating the risk that reform legislation will defeat the very objective of participatory self-government itself, for example, where laws would set limits so low that, by elevating the reputation-related or media-related advantages of incumbency to the point where they would insulate incumbents from effective challenge.

I am not saying that focus upon active liberty will automatically answer the constitutional question in particular campaign finance cases. I argue only that such focus will help courts find a proper route for arriving at an answer. The positive constitutional goal implies a systemic role for the First Amendment; and that role, in turn, suggests a legal framework, i.e., a more particular set of questions for the Court to ask. Modesty suggests where, and how, courts should defer to legislatures in doing so. The suggested inquiry is complex. But courts both here and abroad have engaged in similarly complex inquiries where the constitutionality of electoral laws is at issue. That complexity is demanded by a Constitution that provides for judicial review of the constitutionality of electoral rules while granting Congress the effective power to secure a fair electoral system.

I next turn to a different kind of example. It focuses upon current threats to the protection of privacy, defined as "the power to control what others can come to know about you." It seeks to illustrate what active liberty is like in modern America, when we seek to arrive democratically at solutions to important technologically based problems. And it suggests a need for judicial caution and humility when certain privacy matters, such as the balance between free speech and privacy, are at issue.

First, I must describe the "privacy" problem. That problem is unusually complex. It has clearly become even more so since the terrorist attacks. For one thing, those who agree that privacy is important disagree about why. Some emphasize the need to be left alone, not bothered by others, or that privacy is important because it prevents people from being judged out of context. Some emphasize the way in which relationships of love and friendship depend upon trust, which implies a sharing of information not available to all. Others find connections between privacy and individualism, in that privacy encourages non-conformity. Still others find connections between privacy and equality, in that limitations upon the availability of individualized information lead private businesses to treat all customers alike. For some, or all, of these reasons, legal rules protecting privacy help to assure an individual's dignity.

For another thing, the law protects privacy only because of the way in which technology interacts with different laws. Some laws, such as trespass, wiretapping, eavesdropping, and search-and-seizure laws, protect particular places or sites, such as homes or telephones, from searches and monitoring. Other laws protect not places, but kinds of information, for example laws that forbid the publication of certain personal information even by a person who obtained that information legally. Taken together these laws protect privacy to different degrees depending upon place, individual status, kind of intrusion, and type of information.

Further, technological advances have changed the extent to which present laws can protect privacy. Video cameras now can monitor shopping malls, schools, parks, office buildings, city streets, and other places that present law left unprotected. Scanners and interceptors can overhear virtually any electronic conversation. Thermal imaging devices can detect activities taking place within the home. Computers can record and collate information obtained in any of these ways, or others. This technology means an ability to observe, collate, and permanently record a vast amount of information about individuals that the law previously may have made available for collection but which, in practice, could not easily have been recorded and collected. The nature of the current or future privacy threat depends upon how this technological/legal fact will affect differently situated individuals.

These circumstances mean that efforts to revise privacy law to take account of the new technology will involve, in different areas of human activity, the balancing of values in light of prediction about the technological future. If, for example, businesses obtain detailed consumer purchasing information, they may create individualized customer profiles. Those profiles may invade the customer's privacy. But they may also help firms provide publicly desired products at lower cost. If, for example, medical records are placed online, patient privacy may be compromised. But the ready availability of those records may lower insurance costs or help a patient carried unconscious into an operating room. If, for example, all information about an individual's genetic make-up is completely confidential, that individual's privacy is protected, but suppose a close relative, a nephew or cousin, needs the information to assess his own cancer risk?

Nor does a "consent" requirement automatically answer the dilemmas suggested, for consent forms may be signed without understanding and, in any event, a decision by one individual to release or to deny information can affect others as well.

Legal solutions to these problems will be shaped by what is technologically possible. Should video cameras be programmed to turn off? Recorded images to self-destruct? Computers instructed to delete certain kinds of information? Should cell phones be encrypted? Should web technology, making use of an individual's privacy preferences, automatically negotiate privacy rules with distant web sites as a condition of access?

The complex nature of these problems calls for resolution through a form of participatory democracy. Ideally, that participatory process does not involve legislators, administrators, or judges imposing law from above. Rather, it involves law revision that bubbles up from below. Serious complex changes in law are often made in the context of a national conversation involving, among others, scientists, engineers, businessmen and -women, the media, along with legislators, judges, and many ordinary citizens whose lives the new technology will affect. That conversation takes place through many meetings, symposia, and discussions, through journal articles and media reports, through legislative hearings and court cases. Lawyers participate fully in this discussion, translating specialized knowledge into ordinary English, defining issues, creating consensus. Typically, administrators and legislators then make decisions, with courts later resolving any constitutional issues that those decisions raise. This "conversation" is the participatory democratic process itself.

The presence of this kind of problem and this kind of democratic process helps to explain, because it suggests a need for, judicial caution or modesty. That is why, for example, the Court's decisions so far have hesitated to preempt that process. In one recent case the Court considered a cell phone conversation that an unknown private individual had intercepted with a scanner and delivered to a radio station. A statute forbid the broadcast of that conversation, even though the radio station itself had not planned or participated in the intercept. The Court had to determine the scope of the station's First Amendment right to broadcast given the privacy interests that the statute sought to protect. The Court held that the First Amendment trumped the statute, permitting the radio station to broadcast the information. But the holding was narrow. It focused upon the particular circumstances present, explicitly leaving open broadcaster liability in other, less innocent, circumstances.

The narrowness of the holding itself serves a constitutional purpose. The privacy "conversation" is ongoing. Congress could well rewrite the statute, tailoring it more finely to current technological facts, such as the widespread availability of scanners and the possibility of protecting conversations through encryption. A broader constitutional rule might itself limit legislative options in ways now unforeseeable. And doing so is particularly dangerous where statutory protection of an important personal liberty is at issue.

By way of contrast, the Court held unconstitutional police efforts to use, without a warrant, a thermal imaging device placed on a public sidewalk. The device permitted police to identify activities taking place within a private house. The case required the Court simply to ask whether the residents had a reasonable expectation that their activities within the house would not be disclosed to the public in this way—a well established Fourth Amendment principle. Hence the case asked the Court to pour new technological wine into old bottles; it did not suggest that doing so would significantly interfere with an ongoing democratic policy conversation.

The privacy example suggests more by way of caution. It warns against adopting an overly rigid method of interpreting the constitution—placing weight upon eighteenth-century details to the point where it becomes difficult for a twenty-first-century court to apply the document's underlying values. At a minimum it suggests that courts, in determining the breadth of a constitutional holding, should look to the effect of a holding on the ongoing policy process, distinguishing, as I have suggested, between the "eavesdropping" and the "thermal heat" types of cases. And it makes clear that judicial caution in such matters does not reflect the fact that judges are mitigating their legal concerns with practical considerations. Rather, the Constitution itself is a practical document—a document that authorizes the Court to proceed practically when it examines new laws in light of the Constitution's enduring, underlying values.

My fourth example concerns equal protection and voting rights, an area that has led to considerable constitutional controversy. Some believe that the Constitution prohibits virtually any legislative effort to use race as a basis for drawing electoral district boundaries—unless, for example, the effort seeks to undo earlier invidious race-based discrimination. Others believe that the Constitution does not so severely limit the instances in which a legislature can use race to create majority-minority districts. Without describing in detail the basic argument between the two positions, I wish to point out the relevance to that argument of the Constitution's democratic objective.

That objective suggests a simple, but potentially important, constitutional difference in the electoral area between invidious discrimination, penalizing members of a racial minority, and positive discrimination, assisting members of racial minorities. The Constitution's Fifteenth Amendment prohibits the former, not simply because it violates a basic Fourteenth Amendment principle, namely that the government must treat all citizens with equal respect, but also because it denies minority citizens the opportunity to participate in the self-governing democracy that the Constitution creates. By way of contrast, affirmative discrimination ordinarily seeks to enlarge minority participation in that self-governing democracy. To that extent it is consistent with, indeed furthers, the Constitution's basic democratic objective. That consistency, along with its more benign purposes, helps to mitigate whatever lack of equal respect any such discrimination might show to any disadvantaged member of a majority group.

I am not saying that the mitigation will automatically render any particular discriminatory scheme constitutional. But the presence of this mitigating difference supports the view that courts should not apply the strong presumptions of unconstitutionality that are appropriate where invidious discrimination is at issue. My basic purpose, again, is to suggest that reference to the Constitution's "democratic" objective can help us apply a different basic objective, here that of equal protection. And in the electoral context, the reference suggests increased legislative authority to deal with multiracial issues.

The instances I have discussed encompass different areas of law—speech, federalism, privacy, equal protection, and statutory interpretation. In each instance, the discussion has focused upon a contemporary social problem—campaign finance, workplace regulation, environmental regulation, information-based technological change, race-based electoral districting, and legislative politics. In each instance, the discussion illustrates how increased focus upon the Constitution's basic democratic objective might make a difference—in refining doctrinal rules, in evaluating consequences, in applying practical cautionary principles, in interacting with other constitutional objectives, and in explicating statutory silences. In each instance, the discussion suggests how that increased focus might mean better law. And "better" in this context means both (a) better able to satisfy the Constitution's purposes and (b) better able to cope with contemporary problems. The discussion, while not proving its point purely through logic or empirical demonstration, uses example to create a pattern. The pattern suggests a need for increased judicial emphasis upon the Constitution's democratic objective.

My discussion emphasizes values underlying specific constitutional phrases, sees the Constitution itself as a single document with certain basic related objectives, and assumes that the latter can inform a judge's understanding of the former. Might that discussion persuade those who prefer to believe that the keys to constitutional interpretation instead lie in specific language, history, tradition, and precedent and who fear that a contrary approach would permit judges too often to act too subjectively?

Perhaps so, for several reasons. First, the area of interpretive disagreement is more limited than many believe. Judges can, and should, decide most cases, including constitutional cases, through the use of language, history, tradition, and precedent. Judges will often agree as to how these factors determine a provision's basic purpose and the result in a particular case. And where they differ, their differences are often differences of modest degree. Only a handful of constitutional issues—though an important handful—are as open in respect to language, history, and basic purpose as those that I have described. And even in respect to those issues, judges must find answers within the limits set by the Constitution's language. Moreover, history, tradition, and precedent remain helpful, even if not determinative.

Second, those more literalist judges who emphasize language, history, tradition, and precedent cannot justify their practices by claiming that is what the framers wanted, for the framers did not say specifically what factors judges should emphasize when seeking to interpret the Constitution's open language. Nor is it plausible to believe that those who argued about the Bill of Rights, and made clear that it did not contain an exclusive detailed list, had agreed about what school of interpretive thought should prove dominant in the centuries to come. Indeed, the Constitution itself says that the "enumeration" in the Constitution of some rights "shall not be construed to deny or disparage others retained by the people." Professor Bailyn concludes that the Framers added this language to make clear that "rights, like law itself, should never be fixed, frozen, that new dangers and needs will emerge, and that to respond to these dangers and needs, rights must be newly specified to protect the individual's integrity and inherent dignity." Instead, justification for the literalist's practice itself tends to rest upon consequences. Literalist arguments often seek to show that such an approach will have favorable results, for example, controlling judicial subjectivity.

Third, judges who reject a literalist approach deny that their decisions are subjective and point to important safeguards of objectivity. A decision that emphasizes values, no less than any other, is open to criticism based upon (1) the decision's relation to the other legal principles (precedents, rules, standards, practices, institutional understandings) that it modifies and (2) the decision's consequences, i.e., the way in which the entire bloc of decision-affected legal principles subsequently affects the world. The relevant values, by limiting interpretive possibilities and guiding interpretation, themselves constrain subjectivity, indeed the democratic values that I have emphasized themselves suggest the importance of judicial restraint. An individual constitutional judge's need for consistency over time also constrains subjectivity. That is why Justice O'Connor has explained that need in terms of a constitutional judge's initial decisions creating "footprints" that later decisions almost inevitably will follow.

Fourth, the literalist does not escape subjectivity, for his tools, language, history, and tradition, can provide little objective guidance in the comparatively small set of cases about which I have spoken. In such cases, the Constitution's language is almost always nonspecific. History and tradition are open to competing claims and rival interpretations. Nor does an emphasis upon rules embodied in precedent necessarily produce clarity, particularly in borderline areas or where rules are stated abstractly. Indeed, an emphasis upon language, history, tradition, or prior rules in such cases may simply channel subjectivity into a choice about: Which history? Which tradition? Which rules? It will then produce a decision that is no less subjective but which is far less transparent than a decision that directly addresses consequences in constitutional terms.

Finally, my examples point to offsetting consequences—at least if "literalism" tends to produce the legal doctrines (related to the First Amendment, to federalism, to statutory interpretation, to equal protection) that I have criticized. Those doctrines lead to consequences at least as harmful, from a constitutional perspective, as any increased risk of subjectivity. In the ways that I have set out, they undermine the Constitution's efforts to create a framework for democratic government—a government that, while protecting basic individual liberties, permits individual citizens to govern themselves.

To reemphasize the constitutional importance of democratic self-government may carry with it a practical bonus. We are all aware of figures that show that the public knows ever less about, and is ever less interested in, the processes of government. Foundation reports criticize the lack of high school civics education. Comedians claim that more students know the names of the Three Stooges than the three branches of government. Even law school graduates are ever less inclined to work for government—with the percentage of those entering government (or non-government public interest) work declining at one major law school from 12% to 3% over a generation. Indeed, polls show that, over that same period of time, the percentage of the public trusting the government declined at a similar rate.

This trend, however, is not irreversible. Indeed, trust in government has shown a remarkable rebound in response to last month's terrible tragedy [September 11]. Courts cannot maintain this upward momentum by themselves. But courts, as highly trusted government institutions, can help some, in part by explaining in terms the public can understand just what the Constitution is about. It is important that the public, trying to cope with the problems of nation, state, and local community, understand that the Constitution does not resolve, and was not intended to resolve, society's problems. Rather, the Constitution provides a framework for the creation of democratically determined solutions, which protect each individual's basic liberties and assures that individual equal respect by government, while securing a democratic form of government. We judges cannot insist that Americans participate in that government, but we can make clear that our Constitution depends upon it. Indeed, participation reinforces that "positive passion for the public good," that John Adams, like so many others, felt a necessary condition for "Republican Government" and any "real Liberty."

That is the democratic ideal. It is as relevant today as it was 200 or 2,000 years ago. Today it is embodied in our Constitution. Two thousand years ago, Thucydides, quoting Pericles, set forth a related ideal—relevant in his own time and, with some modifications, still appropriate to recall today. "We Athenians," said Pericles, "do not say that the man who fails to participate in politics is a man who minds his own business. We say that he is a man who has no business here."

DISCUSSION QUESTIONS

1. Critics of the originalist perspective often point to ambiguities in the language of the Constitution. Justice Breyer outlines several of them in his speech. What are some other examples of ambiguous language in the Constitution? (Look at the Bill of Rights as a start.) What alternative interpretations can you develop?

2. Critics of the Living Constitution, such as Justice Scalia, often argue that judges substitute their own reading of what they think the law should be for what the law is. Do you think it is possible for justices to avoid having their own views shape their decisions? How could they protect against this happening?

3. Should judges take public opinion or changing societal standards into account when ruling on the constitutionality of a statute or practice? If so, what evidence of public opinion or societal standards should matter? Surveys? Laws enacted in states? If not, what are the risks in doing so?

4. Consider Scalia's examples of when the Court has employed a Living Constitution approach. How would Breyer's approach of active liberty decide these cases? Which approach do you think leads to the better outcomes: Scalia's textualist approach or Breyer's active liberty?

PART III

Political Behavior:
Participation

CHAPTER 9

Public Opinion and the Media

42

"Polling the Public,"
from *Public Opinion in a Democracy*

George Gallup

Assessing public opinion in a democracy of over 330 million people is no easy task. George Gallup, who is largely responsible for the development of modern opin-ion polling, argued in his 1939 book that public-opinion polls enhance the demo-cratic process by providing elected officials with a picture of what Americans think about current events. Despite Gallup's vigorous defense of his polling techniques and the contribution of polling to democracy, the public-opinion poll remains con-troversial. Some critics charge that public officials pay too much attention to polls, making decisions based on fluctuations in public opinion rather than on informed, independent judgment. Others say that by urging respondents to give an opin-ion, even if they initially respond that they have no opinion on a question, polls may exaggerate the amount of division in American society. And some critics worry that election-related polls may affect public behavior: if a potential voter hears that her candidate is trailing in the polls, perhaps she becomes demoralized and does not vote, and the poll becomes a self-fulfilling prophecy. In effect, rather than reporting on election news, the poll itself becomes the news.

We have a national election every two years only. In a world which moves as rapidly as the modern world does, it is often desirable to know the people's will on basic policies at more frequent intervals. We can-not put issues off and say "let them be decided at the next election." World events do not wait on elections. We need to know the will of the people at all times.

If we know the collective will of the people at all times the efficiency of democracy can be increased, because we can substitute specific knowledge of public opinion for blind groping and guesswork. Statesmen who know the true state of public opinion can then formulate plans with a sure knowledge of what the voting public is thinking. They can know what degree of opposition to any proposed plan exists, and what efforts are necessary to gain public acceptance for it. The responsibility for initiating action should, as always, rest with the political leaders of the country. But the collective will or attitude of the people needs to be learned without delay.

The Will of the People

How is the will of the people to be known at all times?

Before I offer an answer to this question, I would like to examine some of the principal channels by which, at the present time, public opinion is expressed.

The most important is of course a national election. An election is the only official and binding expression of the people's judgment. But, as viewed from a strictly objective point of view, elections are a confusing and imperfect way of registering national opinion. In the first place, they come only at infrequent intervals. In the second place, as [James] Bryce pointed out in *The American Commonwealth*, it is virtually impossible to separate issues from candidates. How can we tell whether the public is voting for the man or for his platform? How can we tell whether all the candidate's views are endorsed, or whether some are favored and others opposed by the voters? Because society grows more and more complex, the tendency is to have more and more issues in an election. Some may be discussed; others not. Suppose a candidate for office takes a position on a great many public issues during the campaign. If elected, he inevitably assumes that the public has endorsed all his planks, whereas this may actually not be the case.

* * *

The Role of the Elected Representative

A second method by which public opinion now expresses itself is through elected representatives. The legislator is, technically speaking, supposed to represent the interests of all voters in his constituency. But under the two-party system there is a strong temptation for him to represent, and be influenced by, only the voters of his own party. He is subject to the pressure of party discipline and of wishes of party leaders back home. His very continuance in office may depend on giving way to such pressure. Under these circumstances his behavior in Congress is likely to be governed not by what he thinks the voters of his state want, but by what he thinks the leaders of his own party in that state want.

* * *

Even in the event that an elected representative does try to perform his duty of representing the whole people, he is confronted with the problem: What is the will of the people? Shall he judge their views by the letters they write him or the telegrams they send him? Too often such expressions of opinion come only from an articulate minority. Shall the congressman judge their views by the visitors or delegations that come to him from his home district?

Pressure Groups and the Whole Nation

Legislators are constantly subject to the influence of organized lobbies and pressure groups. * * * These include labor, agriculture, veterans, pension plan advocates, chambers of commerce, racial organizations, isolationists and internationalists, high-tariff and low-tariff groups, preparedness and disarmament groups, budget balancers and spending advocates, soft-money associations and hard-money associations, transportation groups, and states righters and centralizationists.

The legislator obviously owes a duty to his home district to legislate in its best interests. But he also owes a duty to legislate in the best interests of the whole nation. In order, however, to carry out this second duty he must *know* what the nation thinks. Since he doesn't always know what the voters in his own district think, it is just that much more difficult for him to learn the views of the nation. Yet if he could know those views at all times he could legislate more often in the interest of the whole country.

* * *

The Cross-Section Survey

This effort to discover public opinion has been largely responsible for the introduction of a new instrument for determining public opinion—the cross-section or sampling survey. By means of nationwide studies taken at frequent intervals, research workers are today attempting to measure and give voice to the sentiments of the whole people on vital issues of the day.

Where does this new technique fit into the scheme of things under our form of government? Is it a useful instrument of democracy? Will it prove to be vicious and harmful, or will it contribute to the efficiency of the democratic process?

The sampling referendum is simply a procedure for sounding the opinions of a relatively small number of persons, selected in such manner as to reflect with a high degree of accuracy the views of the whole voting population. In effect such surveys canvass the opinions of a miniature electorate.

Cross-section surveys do not place their chief reliance upon numbers. The technique is based on the fact that a few thousand voters correctly selected will faithfully reflect the views of an electorate of millions of voters. The key to success in this work is the cross section—the proper selection of voters included in the sample. Elaborate precautions must be taken to secure the views of members of all political parties—of rich and poor, old and young, of men and women, farmers and city dwellers, persons of all religious faiths—in short, voters of all types living in every State in the land. And all must be included in correct proportion.

*   *   *

Reliability of Opinion Surveys

Whether opinion surveys will prove to be a useful contribution to democracy depends largely on their reliability in measuring opinion. During the last four years [1935–39] the sampling procedure, as used in measuring public opinion, has been subjected to many tests. In general these tests indicate that present techniques can attain a high degree of accuracy, and it seems reasonable to assume that with the development of this infant science, the accuracy of its measurements will be constantly improved.

The most practical way at present to measure the accuracy of the sampling referendum is to compare forecasts of elections with election results. Such a test is by no means perfect, because a preelection survey must not only measure opinion in respect to candidates but must also predict just what groups of people will actually take the trouble to cast their ballots. Add to this the problem of measuring the effect of weather on turnout, also the activities of corrupt political machines, and it can easily be seen that election results are by no means a perfect test of the accuracy of this new technique.

*   *   *

Cloture on Debate?

It is sometimes argued that public opinion surveys impose a cloture on debate. When the advocates of one side of an issue are shown to be in the majority, so the argument runs, the other side will lose hope and abandon their cause believing that further efforts are futile.

Again let me say that there is little evidence to support this view. Every election necessarily produces a minority. In 1936 the Republicans polled less than 40 percent of the vote. Yet the fact that the Republicans were defeated badly wasn't enough to lead them to quit the battle. They continued to fight against the New Deal with as much vigor as before. An even better example is afforded by the Socialist Party. For years the Socialist candidate for President has received but a small fraction of the total popular vote, and could count on sure defeat. Yet the Socialist Party continues as a party, and continues to poll about the same number of votes.

Sampling surveys will never impose a cloture on debate so long as it is the nature of public opinion to change. The will of the people is dynamic; opinions are constantly changing. A year ago an overwhelming majority of voters were skeptical of the prospects of the Republican Party in 1940. Today, half the voters think the GOP will win. If elections themselves do not impose cloture on debate, is it likely that opinion surveys will?

Possible Effect on Representative Government

The form of government we live under is a representative form of government. What will be the effect on representative government if the will of the people is known at all times? Will legislators become mere rubber stamps, mere puppets, and the function of representation be lost?

Under a system of frequent opinion measurement, the function of representation is not lost, for two reasons. First, it is well understood that the people have not the time or the inclination to pass on all the problems that confront their leaders. They cannot be expected to express judgment on technical questions of administration and government. They can pass judgment only on basic general policies. As society grows more complex there is a greater and greater need for experts. Once the voters have indicated their approval of a general policy or plan of action, experts are required to carry it out.

Second, it is not the province of the people to initiate legislation, but to decide which of the programs offered they like best. National policies do not spring full-blown from the common people. Leaders, knowing the general will of the people, must take the initiative in forming policies that will carry out the general will and must put them into effect.

Before the advent of the sampling referendum, legislators were not isolated from their constituencies. They read the local newspapers; they toured their districts and talked with voters; they received letters from their home State; they entertained delegations who claimed to speak for large and important blocs of voters. The change that is brought about by sampling referenda is merely one which provides these legislators with a truer measure of opinion in their districts and in the nation.

* * *

How Wise Are the Common People?

The sampling surveys of recent years have provided much evidence concerning the wisdom of the common people. Anyone is free to examine this evidence. And I think that the person who does examine it will come away believing as I do that, collectively, the American people have a remarkably high degree of common sense. These people may not be brilliant or intellectual or particularly well read, but they possess a quality of good sense which is manifested time and again in their expressions of opinion on present-day issues.

*   *   *

It is not difficult to understand why the conception of the stupidity of the masses has so many adherents. Talk to the first hundred persons whom you happen to meet in the street about many important issues of the day, and the chances are great that you will be struck by their lack of accurate or complete knowledge on these issues. Few of them will likely have sufficient information in this particular field to express a well founded judgment.

But fortunately a democracy does not require that every voter be well informed on every issue. In fact a democracy does not depend so much on the enlightenment of each individual, as upon the quality of the collective judgment or intelligence of thousands of individuals.

*   *   *

It would of course be foolish to argue that the collective views of the common people always represent the most intelligent and most accurate answer to any question. But results of sampling referenda on hundreds of issues do indicate, in my opinion, that we can place great faith in the collective judgment or intelligence of the people.

The New England Town Meeting Restored

One of the earliest and purest forms of democracy in this country was the New England town meeting. The people gathered in one room to discuss and to vote on the questions of the community. There was a free exchange of opinions in the presence of all the members. The town meeting was a simple and effective way of articulating public opinion, and the decisions made by the meeting kept close to the public will. When a democracy thus operates on a small scale it is able to express itself swiftly and with certainty.

But as communities grew, the town meeting became unwieldy. As a result the common people became less articulate, less able to debate the vital issues in the manner of their New England forefathers. Interest in politics lagged. Opinion had to express itself by the slow and cumbersome method of election, no longer facilitated by the town meeting with its frequent give and take of ideas. The indifference and apathy of voters made it possible for vicious and corrupt political machines to take over the administration of government in many states and cities.

The New England town meeting was valuable because it provided a forum for the exchange of views among all citizens of the community and for a vote on these views. Today, the New England town meeting idea has, in a sense, been restored. The wide distribution of daily newspapers reporting the views of statesmen on issues of the day, the almost universal ownership of radios which bring the whole nation within the hearing of any voice, and now the advent of the sampling referendum which provides a means of determining quickly the response of the public to debate on issues of the day, have in effect created a town meeting on a national scale.

How nearly the goal has been achieved is indicated in the following data recently gathered by the American Institute of Public Opinion. Of the 45,000,000 persons who voted in the last presidential election [1936], approximately 40,000,000 read a daily newspaper, 40,000,000 have radios, and only 2,250,000 of the entire group of voters in the nation neither have a radio nor take a daily newspaper.

This means that the nation is literally in one great room. The newspapers and the radio conduct the debate on national issues, presenting both information and argument on both sides, just as the townsfolk did in person in the old town meeting. And finally, through the process of the sampling referendum, the people, having heard the debate on both sides of every issue, can express their will. After one hundred and fifty years we return to the town meeting. This time the whole nation is within the doors.

DISCUSSION QUESTIONS

1. What are the advantages and disadvantages of modern public-opinion polling for policy making and elections?

2. Setting aside the constitutional status of such a move, how would the American political system change if polls were banned?

3. Imagine you are an elected official. How would you determine when to pay attention to public-opinion polls and when to ignore them? In a representative democracy, should you, as an elected official, *ever* ignore public opinion as revealed in polls?

43

"News vs. Entertainment: How Increasing Media Choice Widens Gaps in Political Knowledge and Turnout"

MARKUS PRIOR

Although everyone has contact with the government nearly every day—attending a public school, driving on public roads, using government-regulated electricity, and so on—few citizens have direct contact with the policy-making process. Because of this distance between the public and policy makers, the behavior of intermediaries between the government and the governed is a significant issue in a democratic polity. The media, in particular the news media, are among the most significant of these intermediaries that tell the people what the government is doing and tell the government what the people want.

Political scientist Markus Prior notes that in today's media environment, information is more abundant than ever, yet participation and knowledge levels have remained stagnant. Rather than enhancing participatory democracy, as advocates of new media suggest is the norm, the onset of cable television and the Internet has worsened information and participation gaps between those individuals who like to follow the news and those who are more interested in entertainment. Prior argues that the spread of additional news choices, which sounds democratic, has had nondemocratic effects. Newshounds can dig ever deeper into the news, but other members of the public are increasingly able to ignore the news. Other critics have made a similar argument that new media tend to exacerbate public polarization because readers, viewers, and listeners gravitate to outlets presenting opinions they agree with and ignore those sources that would challenge their views.

The rise of new media has brought the question of audience fragmentation and selective exposure to the forefront of scholarly and popular debate. In one of the most widely discussed contributions to this debate, Sunstein has proposed that people's increasing ability to customize their political information will have a polarizing impact on democracy as media users become less likely to encounter information that challenges their partisan viewpoints. While this debate is far from settled, the issue which precedes it is equally important and often sidestepped: [A]s choice between different media content increases, who continues to access *any type* of political information? Cable television and the Internet have increased media choice so much in recent decades that many Americans now live in a high-choice media environment. As media choice increases, the likelihood of "chance encounters" *with any political content* declines significantly for many people. Greater choice allows politically interested people to access more information and increase their political knowledge. Yet those who prefer nonpolitical content can more easily escape the news and therefore pick up less political information than they used to. In a high-choice environment, lack of motivation, not lack of skills or resources, poses the main obstacle to a widely informed electorate.

As media choice increases, content preferences thus become the key to understanding political learning and participation. In a high-choice environment, politics constantly competes with entertainment. Until recently, the impact of content preferences was limited because media users did not enjoy much choice between different content. Television quickly became the most popular mass medium in history, but for decades the networks' scheduling ruled out situations in which viewers had to choose between entertainment and news. Largely unexposed to entertainment competition, news had its place in the early evening and again before the late-night shows. Today, as both entertainment and news are available around the clock on numerous cable channels and web sites, people's content preferences determine more of what those with cable or Internet access watch, read, and hear.

Distinguishing between people who like news and take advantage of additional information and people who prefer other media content explains a puzzling empirical finding: despite the spectacular rise in available political information, mean levels of political knowledge in the population have essentially remained constant. Yet the fact that average knowledge levels did not change hides important trends: political knowledge has risen in some segments of the electorate, but declined in others. Greater media choice thus widens the "knowledge gap." [N]umerous studies have examined the diffusion of information in the population and the differences that emerge between more and less informed individuals. According to some of these studies, television works as a "knowledge leveler" because it presents information in less cognitively demanding ways. To reconcile this effect with the hypothesis that more television widens the knowledge gap, it is necessary to distinguish the effect of news exposure from the effect of the medium itself. In the low-choice broadcast environment, access to the medium and exposure to news were practically one and the same, as less politically interested television viewers had no choice but to watch the news from time to time. As media choice increases, exposure to the news may continue to work as a "knowledge leveler," but the distribution of news exposure itself has become more unequal. Access to the medium no longer implies exposure to the news. Television news narrows the knowledge gap *among its viewers.* For the population as a whole, more channels widen the gap.

The consequences of increasing media choice reach beyond a less equal distribution of political knowledge. Since political knowledge is an impor-

tant predictor of turnout and since exposure to political information moti-
vates turnout, the shift from a low-choice to a high-choice media environment
implies changes in electoral participation as well. Those with a preference
for news not only become more knowledgeable, but also vote at higher rates.
Those with a stronger interest in other media content vote less.

This study casts doubt on the view that the socioeconomic dimension
of the digital divide is the greatest obstacle to an informed and participating electorate. Many casual observers emphasize the great promise new
technologies hold for democracy. They deplore current socioeconomic
inequalities in access to new media, but predict increasing political knowledge and participation among currently disadvantaged people once these
inequalities have been overcome. This ignores that greater media choice
leads to greater *voluntary* segmentation of the electorate. The present study
suggests that gaps based on socioeconomic status will be eclipsed by
preference-based gaps once access to new media becomes cheaper and
more widely available. Gaps created by unequal distribution of resources
and skills often emerged due to circumstances outside of people's control.
The preference-based gaps documented in this article are self-imposed as
many people abandon the news for entertainment simply because they like
it better. Inequality in political knowledge and turnout increases as a result
of voluntary, not circumstantial, consumption decisions.

*   *   *

Theory

The basic premise of this analysis is that people's media environment determines the extent to which their media use is governed by content preferences. According to theories of program choice, viewers have preferences
over program characteristics or program types and select the program that
promises to best satisfy these preferences. The simplest models distinguish
between preferences for information and entertainment. In the low-choice
broadcast environment, most people watched news and learned about politics because they were reluctant to turn off the set even if the programs
offered at the time did not match their preferences. One study conducted
in the early 1970s showed that 40% of the respondents reported watching
programs because they appeared on the channel they were already watching or because someone else wanted to see them. Audience research has
proposed a two-stage model according to which people first decide to
watch television and then pick the available program they like best. Klein
aptly called this model the "Theory of Least Objectionable Program." If
television viewers are routinely "glued to the box" and select the best available program, we can explain why so many Americans watched television
news in the 1960s and 70s despite modest political interest. Most television
viewing in the broadcast era did not stem from a deliberate choice of a
program, but rather was determined by convenience, availability of spare

time, and the decision to spend that time in front of the TV set. And since broadcast channels offered a solid block of news at the dinner hour and again after primetime, many viewers were routinely exposed to news even though they watched television primarily to be entertained.

Once exposed to television news, people learn about politics. Although a captive news audience does not exhibit the same political interest as a self-selected one and therefore may not learn as much, research on passive learning suggests that even unmotivated exposure can produce learning. Hence, even broadcast viewers who prefer entertainment programs absorb at least basic political knowledge when they happen to tune in when only news is on.

I propose that such accidental exposure should become less likely in a high-choice environment because greater horizontal diversity (the number of genres available at any particular point in time) increases the chance that viewers will find content that matches their preferences. The impact of one's preferences increases, and "indiscriminate viewing" becomes less likely. Cable subscribers' channel repertoire (the number of frequently viewed channels) is not dramatically higher than that of non-subscribers, but their repertoire reflects a set of channels that are more closely related to their genre preferences. Two-stage viewing behavior thus predicts that news audiences should decrease as more alternatives are offered on other channels. Indeed, local news audiences tend to be smaller when competing entertainment programming is scheduled. Baum and Kernell show that cable subscribers, especially the less informed among them, are less likely to watch the presidential debates than otherwise similar individuals who receive only broadcast television. According to my first hypothesis, the advent of cable TV increased the knowledge gap between people with a preference for news and people with a preference for other media content.

Internet access should contribute to an increasing knowledge gap as well. Although the two media are undoubtedly different in many respects, access to the Internet, like cable, makes media choice more efficient. Yet, while they both increase media users' content choice, cable TV and the Internet are not perfect substitutes for each other. Compared at least to dial-up Internet service, cable offers greater immediacy and more visuals. The web offers more detailed information and can be customized to a greater extent. Both media, in other words, have unique features, and access to both of them offers users the greatest flexibility. For instance, people with access to both media can watch a campaign speech on cable and then compare online how different newspapers cover the event. Depending on their needs or the issue that interests them, they can actively search a wealth of political information online or passively consume cable politics. Hence, the effects of cable TV and Internet access should be additive and the knowledge gap largest among people with access to both new media.

There are several reasons why exposure to political information increases the likelihood that an individual will cast a vote on election day. Exposure increases political knowledge, which in turn increases turnout because people know where, how, and for whom to vote. Furthermore, knowledgeable people are more likely to perceive differences between candidates and thus less likely to abstain due to indifference. Independent of learning effects, exposure to political information on cable news and political web sites is likely to increase people's campaign interest. Interest, in turn, affects turnout even when one controls for political knowledge. Entertainment fans with a cable box or Internet connection, on the other hand, will miss both the interest- and the information-based effect of broadcast news on turnout. My second hypothesis thus predicts a widening turnout gap in the current environment, as people who prefer news vote at higher rates and those with other preferences increasingly stay home from the polls.

* * *

Conclusion

When speculating about the political implications of new media, pundits and scholars tend to either praise the likely benefits for democracy in the digital age or dwell on the dangers. The optimists claim that the greater availability of political information will lead more people to learn more about politics and increase their involvement in the political process. The pessimists fear that new media will make people apolitical and provide mind-numbing entertainment that keeps citizens from fulfilling their democratic responsibilities. These two predictions are often presented as mutually exclusive. Things will either spiral upwards or spiral downwards; the circle is either virtuous or vicious. The analyses presented here show that both are true. New media do indeed increase political knowledge and involvement in the electoral process among some people, just as the optimists predict. Yet, the evidence supports the pessimists' scenario as well. Other people take advantage of greater choice and tune out of politics completely. Those with a preference for entertainment, once they gain access to new media, become less knowledgeable about politics and less likely to vote. People's media content preferences become the key to understanding the political implications of new media.

* * *

Ironically, we might have to pin our hopes of creating a reasonably evenly informed electorate on that reviled form of communication, political advertising. Large segments of the electorate in a high-choice environment do not voluntarily watch, read, or listen to political information. Their greatest chance for encounters with the political world occurs when commercials are inserted into their regular entertainment diet. And exposure to political ads can increase viewers' political knowledge. At least for the time being, before recording services like TiVo, which automatically skip the commercial breaks, or subscriber-financed premium cable channels without advertising become more widespread, political advertising is more likely than news coverage to reach these viewers.

It might seem counterintuitive that political knowledge has decreased for a substantial portion of the electorate even though the amount of political information has multiplied and is more readily available than ever before. The share of politically uninformed people has risen since we entered the so-called "information age." Television as a medium has often been denigrated as "dumb," but, helped by the features of the broadcast environment, it may have been more successful in reaching less interested segments of the population than the "encyclopedic" Internet. In contrast to the view that politics is simply too difficult and complex to understand, this study shows that motivation, not ability, is the main obstacle that stands between an abundance of political information and a well- and evenly informed public.

When differences in political knowledge and turnout arise from inequality in the distribution of resources and skills, recommendations for how to help the information have-nots are generally uncontroversial. To the extent that knowledge and turnout gaps in the new media environment arise from voluntary consumption decisions, recommendations for how to narrow them, or whether to narrow them at all, become more contestable on normative grounds. As [Anthony] Downs remarked a long time ago, "The loss of freedom involved in forcing people to acquire information would probably far outweigh the benefits to be gained from a better-informed electorate." Even if a consensus emerged to reduce media choice for the public good, it would still be technically impossible, even temporarily, to put the genie back in the bottle. Avoiding politics will never again be as difficult as it was in the "golden age" of television.

* * *

Discussion Questions

1. Are you concerned by the findings in Prior's study? If not, why not? If you are, can you think of any way to overcome the problem he has identified?

2. What lessons should public officials take from Prior's study? Should they pay less attention to public opinion because of the gaps in information and interest among members of the public?

3. Do you think the sharing of news and information through social media exacerbates or diminishes the trends identified by Prior?

44

"Reconceptualizing Political Knowledge: Race, Ethnicity, and Carceral Violence"

Cathy J. Cohen and Matthew D. Luttig

What is political knowledge? A standard practice is for a public-opinion researcher to ask questions about general policy matters, perhaps concerning the environment, health care, education, or a wide number of other topics. Or the researcher might ask a set of questions about American governmental institutions. Political scientists Cathy J. Cohen and Matthew D. Luttig argue that the traditional measures of political knowledge that emerge from these studies are valuable but limited. These studies of political knowledge look at one face of the state, the one that provides services, educates children, and raises revenue through taxation. What they miss, say Cohen and Luttig, is the carceral face of the state. Carceral refers to those aspects of governmental activity around its policing, incarceration, monitoring, and surveillance functions. These, too, are important aspects of political knowledge, the authors argue, and are aspects especially relevant to marginalized communities. Including carceral violence in measures of political knowledge in their study of survey respondents ages 15–29 reverses the pattern of White Americans having higher levels of political knowledge than Black Americans, with Black Americans knowing more facts and information concerning the carceral state. Adding an intersectional lens, Cohen and Luttig do not find differences in knowledge levels between women and men among Black and Latino survey respondents. The authors conclude that it is important to know how different communities define relevant and important political knowledge, especially when comparing knowledge levels across groups.

The concept of political knowledge—most often defined as "the range of factual information about politics that is stored in long-term memory"—is central to research in public opinion and political behavior. Numerous studies find differences in political belief systems, the ability to hold elected officials accountable, and political participation rates between low- and high-knowledge respondents. Furthermore, the extent to which the public possesses political knowledge is often used as an evaluative criterion for general claims of civic competence. Specifically, those who possess more knowledge about national institutional politics, or what is often called general political knowledge, are presumed to be more informed, and therefore more politically competent than those who know less. Given the importance of the idea of general political knowledge, one worrying finding to emerge from past research is that there are large group differences in knowledge levels. Of central concern to us is the finding of differences across race and ethnicity in general political knowledge levels, and specifically that whites are thought to possess greater political knowledge than African Americans and Latinos.

We argue that race and ethnicity-based differences in political knowledge are biased by the types of political facts researchers ask in the measurement of the concept. Scholars have too often labeled a set of five to seven recall questions about national political offices and democratic processes general political knowledge. We want to be clear; we do not contest the definition of political knowledge as "the range of factual information about politics that is stored in long-term memory." Moreover, we believe there is insight to be gained from the use of scales that measure static general political knowledge of the national government, especially when researchers are interested in examining and predicting liberal-democratic process such as voting.

However, like other scholars we find such an approach to be limited in its understanding of the information that different communities need to be active participants in the political domain. Specifically, we believe that general political knowledge questions get at how *some people*, some of the time, interact, engage with, and understand politics and government. But such questions do not do a good job of capturing the experiences of often marginalized communities who routinely interact with what scholars have called the carceral state or that face of the state focused on surveillance, criminalization, control and punishment.

We therefore depart from previous research on political knowledge by arguing that past scholarship too often focuses on what Soss and Weaver describe as one "face" of the American state, the "liberal-democratic" face that emphasizes electoral-representative processes and conceives of the relationship between government and citizen as one in which citizens have extensive power and control. Most of this research assumes a political landscape where increases in either general or domain-specific knowledge lead to better political judgement that can be easily exercised in an open democratic process. Instead, we argue that the varied experiences with the state of marginal communities has generated a "range of factual information about politics" and governance that are significantly different than what is measured with general or domain-specific measures of the liberal arm of politics.

As has been documented elsewhere, the experiences and socialization that poor communities of color have of and with government are fundamentally different. Significant numbers of people of color experience the government as a force that is "out to get them," not to represent them. For these communities, the state is too often perceived as an agent that actively exercises control through means of coercion and violence. And in this domain of state power, police and criminal justice institutions are front and center. This lived experience with the carceral state is all the more apparent today following the harrowing images that have spread—aided by social media—of police violence against African Americans in places like Ferguson, Baltimore, Chicago, and New York, and organizations and movements like the Black Lives Matter, BYP100, and the Movement for Black Lives that arose in the wake of such violence.

Consequently, we find that when looking at state violence against citizens, especially African Americans—or what we call carceral violence—African Americans possess greater political knowledge of such acts than whites and therefore are not necessarily less politically knowledgeable overall, as the existing literature would suggest. Instead, we show that African Americans and whites possess different *kinds* of political knowledge. Furthermore, we show that knowledge of carceral violence has explanatory power on a variety of important political outcome variables such as political efficacy and engagement in protest activity over and above the traditional political knowledge scale for young Americans.

So if, as James David Barber argues, "citizens need to know what the government is and does," and if Delli Carpini and Keeter are correct when they write that "much of what citizens are expected to do requires an understanding of the rules," then scholars need to understand that what the government *does* as well as *the rules* it plays by often vary by community. Moreover, if we as researchers are to fully understand how informed Americans are about politics or explain political engagement beyond voting (particularly for African Americans and Latinos), we need to include different measures of relevant political knowledge that get at the multiple ways in which citizens encounter, experience, and learn about the state and government.

Political Knowledge and the Carceral State

* * *

We believe that a focus on the carceral state changes the assumed relationship between political knowledge and political participation. Specifically, gaining greater expertise or political knowledge about the carceral state may work to depress engagement instead of encourage it. Most scholarship on domain-specific knowledge suggests that increased knowledge in any one area should lead to greater expertise and engagement in that area. For example, Ondercin and Jones-White, in their study of gender differences in political knowledge, found that "across all the acts of political participation we examined, more knowledgeable individuals were more likely to participate, regardless of sex." However, we expect, as others have shown, that knowing about the repressive arm of the state may discourage people from engaging in politics, especially those forms of participation such as protest where one is more likely to directly encounter the police. Similarly, knowledge of carceral violence may decrease respondents' sense of external efficacy. Thus, given the heavy police presence in many marginalized communities of color, especially African American communities, and the often-negative interactions between officers and those same community members, we hypothesize that African Americans will have greater knowledge of carceral violence than whites and possibly Latinos; and that such knowledge will lower rates of political participation such as protest where one is more likely to encounter agents of the carceral state.

*   *   *

Data and Variables

To measure and examine knowledge of carceral violence—and to compare this construct to the traditional conception of general political knowledge—we draw on data collected in Wave 3 of the Youth and Participatory Politics study commissioned in 2015. The survey is a nationally representative survey of young people, ages 15–29, and includes oversamples of both African Americans and Latinos.

The survey included a 5-item measure of *traditional or general knowledge* based on the types of questions suggested by Delli Carpini and Keeter. The questions are (1) Which party has a majority of seats in the U.S. House of Representatives?; (2) What majority is needed in the House and Senate to override a presidential veto?; (3) Which party is more conservative?; (4) Whose responsibility is judicial review?; and (5) What office is currently held by Joe Biden?

To measure *knowledge of carceral violence*, we included 6 questions asking respondents to identify individuals who were either victims of police and state violence or entangled in what has been framed as discriminatory legal battles driven by the state. * * *

Our carceral violence questions were introduced with the following statement: "[t]here have been a number of stories these days about confrontations between the police and citizens. Please match the name with the description of the person below." Respondents then received a list of six recent victims of carceral violence: Eric Garner, Michael Brown, Marissa Alexander, CeCe McDonald, John Crawford III, and Renisha McBride. We then provided respondents with * * * brief descriptions and asked them to match the description to the correct individual. * * *

*   *   *

Group Differences in Political Knowledge Depend
on Which Political Facts Are Measured

* * * Whites score higher on measures of traditional knowledge * * * than both African Americans * * * and Latinos. * * * African Americans are more knowledgeable about carceral violence * * * than whites * * * and Latinos

* * *. Given that carceral violence is something experienced most by African Americans, we anticipated African American young people would be more interested in, receive more information, and possess more knowledge about victims of police and state violence than young whites or young Latinos. These results are robust in a model that includes potentially confounding demographic characteristics and differences in survey sample, such as education, age, sex, language of interview (English versus Spanish), marital status, employment status, region (South versus non-South), and sampling frame. In short, African Americans possess the greatest factual knowledge of the carceral state as measured in terms of victims of carceral violence while whites know most about the liberal state using the traditional general political knowledge questionnaire.

* * *

Correlates of Different Types of Political Knowledge

* * *

A number of results * * * are worth highlighting. First, education has a consistent and very large effect on the traditional political knowledge battery for all racial and ethnic groups. However, when it comes to knowledge of carceral violence, we find that education is not predictive for Latinos and has a weaker relationship to this domain of knowledge among African Americans and is slightly weaker for whites. Consistent with other research on political knowledge, we find that the relationship between education and knowledge is stronger for general knowledge than for domain-specific facts including knowledge about carceral violence, especially among young people of color.

Another notable finding is the effect of sex on political knowledge. Specifically, while we find evidence consistent with the well-established "gender gap" in political knowledge among whites in both domains of knowledge, the results are quite different among African American and Latino young people. First, there are no differences between men and women in traditional knowledge or knowledge of carceral violence among African Americans. Second, for Latinos, there are no differences between men and women in knowledge of carceral violence. These findings indicate that, (a) differences between men and women in political knowledge levels vary across race and ethnicity and (b) that knowledge of the carceral state (carceral violence) is less "gendered" (that is, there are no differences between men and women) for African Americans and Latinos.

A consistent and large predictor of political knowledge (both traditional knowledge and knowledge of police and court violence) is frequency of Internet access. Specifically, while we expected to find that young people who were regularly online would have greater knowledge of carceral violence, what we found was that young people who are online every day are much more likely to possess knowledge of both domains of politics compared to young people who use the Internet with less frequency. Notably, the effect of Internet usage on knowledge of carceral violence is limited to African Americans * * * and Latinos * * *. Whites' knowledge of carceral violence does not vary as a function of Internet use. These findings provide suggestive evidence consistent with our expectation that the social media landscape promotes knowledge of carceral violence as visceral images spread online and through social networks, especially social networks among young people of color.

* * *

Political Correlates of Two Kinds of Political Knowledge

Our final analysis examines the correlates of these two types of knowledge on political attitudes and behavior. We focus in particular on five variables modeled as dependent variables: (1) linked fate; (2) internal and (3) external efficacy; (4) voting; and (5) taking part in a protest, demonstration, or sit-in.

* * *

Overall, these findings suggest that knowledge of carceral violence has different relationships with political attitudes and behaviors across racial and ethnic groups: for young people of color, knowledge about instances of state violence against people like them is associated with increased skepticism towards government and decreased engagement in protest activity. Young African Americans with this knowledge also have a stronger sense of linked fate with other African Americans as a group. However, young whites who possess knowledge of state violence against people of color do not differ from whites without this information in their beliefs about the efficacy of government or protest activity; instead, for whites this knowledge is associated with greater voting participation perhaps by raising awareness about racism and racial injustice. We also did the analysis with an eye toward how the findings might differ by sex for the categories of men and women and, in general, there were no differences.

Overall, the findings suggest that different forms of knowledge are correlated with different forms of activity. Like in previous research, we find that measures of traditional knowledge are correlates of voting behavior across race and ethnicity. Thus, if scholars want to understanding the voting behavior of young people, they would do well to include measures of traditional political knowledge in their models. If, however, they are interested in a range of political attitudes and behaviors, in particular of communities of color, including those that are more likely to result in direct and sometimes confrontational interactions with the state, such as protest, then measures of the carceral face of the state should be a part of their analysis.

Conclusion

What is political knowledge? At the outset, we introduced a definition from Delli Carpini and Keeter of political knowledge as political facts stored in long term memory. We think this definition is appropriate, but that we need to broaden the conception of what politics is, and for whom. The American state is broader than just the formal "rules of the game, . . . people and parties" as Delli Carpini and Keeter put it. These are important elements of American politics, no doubt, but they do not fully encapsulate the mechanisms of state power and influence. Yet these are the types of facts that most scholars, of both general and domain-specific knowledge, have largely considered in their models of political knowledge. We show that, particularly if we want to understand the political experiences, beliefs, and engagement of groups that often experience the state as a threat—which is too often the case for African American youth in particular—we need to expand the set of facts we ask about to include the coercive side of the state, which includes knowledge about victims of carceral violence.

Through a unique battery of questions about the victims of carceral violence, we begin to uncover knowledge about the carceral state. We show, first, that group-differences in levels of political knowledge are reversed when measuring knowledge of carceral violence: African Americans know more about victims of carceral violence than whites and Latinos. By contrast, our data on traditional knowledge was consistent with past findings: Whites know more about the rules, people and institutions, i.e., the liberal-democratic face of the state, than African Americans and Latinos. Second, people who can identify victims of carceral violence are not necessarily experts on other facts of institutional American politics; similarly, those with high levels of so-called "general" political knowledge are not especially effective at identifying victims of the carceral state. * * * Third, we showed that the social media landscape is correlated with increased knowledge of carceral violence, particularly for African Americans. * * * Finally, we found that knowledge of carceral violence has unique relationships with political attitudes and behavior: associated with reduced feelings of external efficacy and lower engagement in protest activity among African Americans and Latinos, a heightened sense of linked fate among African Americans, and greater self-reported voter turnout among whites.

* * *

Given both the growing diversity of the American population and the continued salience of carceral violence as a political issue, our findings suggest that previous measures of political knowledge will lead to incorrect and biased assessments about overall levels of political knowledge and group-differences in knowledge levels. In particular, a focus only on traditional or general knowledge questions would lead to the erroneous conclusion that African Americans youths and young adults are less informed than young whites. Our findings suggest that is not the case; young whites and African Americans are not differentially informed, but instead they possess different *types* of information. Furthermore, given the correlation we found between knowledge of carceral violence and political outcomes, the increasing spread of this information online has the potential to shape young adults' views of government, their sense of identity, and their level of political engagement. These findings indicate that knowledge of carceral violence is and will continue to be a fundamental feature of young Americans'—particularly young black Americans'—political socialization and experience. Thus, to fully understand public opinion and political behavior, especially the public opinion and political behavior of people of color, scholars need to be cognizant of the ways interactions with and knowledge of the state varies by race and ethnicity.

DISCUSSION QUESTIONS

1. What other kinds of political knowledge might you think would vary by group, whether they're along the lines of race, ethnicity, Indigenousness, sexual orientation, religion, or some other identity?

2. Cohen and Luttig argue that it is important to consider aspects of political knowledge that might vary by group depending on group members' lived experience. Are there types of political knowledge on which young people might score more highly than those who are middle-aged or older?

3. Usually, higher levels of knowledge correlate with higher levels of participation and perceived efficacy. However, in the case of knowledge of carceral violence, the authors report that these patterns do not hold for people of color. Are you surprised by this finding? Why or why not?

Debating the Issues: Is Partisan Media Exposure Bad for Democracy?

From the 1960s through the 1980s, when people thought of media and news, they thought of newspapers and the broadcast television networks (ABC, CBS, NBC). Cable news soon emerged to provide an alternative (CNN, Fox, MSNBC), but one that for the most part followed the same style in their major nightly newscasts as the big networks. In the late 1980s, talk radio, which had been around for some time, boomed in popularity, and hosts such as Rush Limbaugh became household names. Hosts gleefully tweaked the mainstream media and embraced a much more aggressive, hard-hitting style that was explicitly ideological and partisan. There was, in this new forum, no pretense to being objective, but, talk-radio fans would argue, the mainstream media were also not objective—they just pretended to be. News-oriented talk shows on CNN, Fox, and MSNBC followed the same pattern, as did politically oriented humor such as that offered by Stephen Colbert, John Oliver, and Trevor Noah. The rise of the Internet in the 1990s was the most recent dramatic change in communications technology. Today, Twitter receives much of the attention for breaking stories; blogs remain prominent in presenting wide-ranging opinion and analysis; and numerous social media platforms provide an easy way for individuals to voice their opinions on the news.

Is it a problem for democracy if the media outlets consumed by the public are explicitly partisan and ideological? One side of this debate says that selective exposure to partisan media is good for democracy: it enhances participation in politics, influences the flow of ideas in public discourse, and potentially portrays American politics with more accuracy than the conventional "balanced" press. From another perspective, one-sided media exposure is harmful: it encourages extreme political beliefs, polarizes the electorate, creates an "echo chamber" that diminishes the ability to learn from opposing views, and leads to stalemate and gridlock in Washington.

This chapter's debate provides three perspectives on the nature of partisan media exposure. Journalist Jihii Jolly describes a "filter bubble"—driven by new media platforms where prior searches and reading behavior influence what articles are presented to readers in the future—that makes it easy for individuals to expose themselves selectively to one particular point of view without even knowing it. Should we worry about filter bubbles? Quoting one analyst, Jolly suggests we should, noting that even individuals visiting the same site will have a different experience and "not have a baseline to compare what is real and what is not." Mark Jurkowitz and his coauthors show how polarized the information environment has become. Republicans are distrustful of, and less likely to use, a large number of media outlets, while

Democrats are more trustful. This gap has expanded in recent years, in large part due to growing distrust among Republicans. And among conservative Republicans and liberal Democrats, the gap is wider still. These patterns of use and trust affect the overall audience for a media outlet, which can encourage the outlet to become more partisan and ideological to attract and retain its partisan users. Political scientist Matt Grossmann focuses on how scholars have attempted to measure media bias. He observes that research on the possibility of partisan or ideological bias in news coverage is mixed. He also notes that it has been easier to study outright partisan bias rather than ideological bias, which can affect reporting in more subtle ways. No matter what the research may be able to say definitively, Grossmann notes that the public's growing distrust of traditional media due to perceptions of bias has driven news consumers to spend more time with explicitly partisan and ideological news outlets. The net effect is that the American news diet is growing more biased, in part due to the perception of bias in mainstream news.

45

"How Algorithms Decide the News You See"

Jihii Jolly

Homepage traffic for news sites continues to decrease. This trend is the result of an "if the news is important, it will find me" mentality that developed with the rise of social media, when people began to read links that their friends and others in their networks recommended. Thus, readers are increasingly discovering news through social media, email, and reading apps.

Publishers are well aware of this, and have tweaked their infrastructure accordingly, building algorithms that change the site experience depending on where a reader enters from.

While publishers view optimizing sites for the reading and sharing preferences of specific online audiences as a good thing, because it gets users to content they are likely to care about quickly and efficiently, that kind of catering may not be good for readers.

"We can actually act on the psychological predisposition to just expose ourselves to things that we agree with," explains Nick Diakopoulos, research fellow at the Tow Center for Digital Journalism, where he recently published a report on algorithmic accountability reporting. "And what the algorithms do is they throw gasoline on the fire."

Visitors who enter BuzzFeed via Pinterest, for instance, see a larger "Pin It" button, no Twitter share button, and a "hot on Pinterest" module. Medium, launched less than two years ago by Twitter co-founder Evan Williams, recommends content to readers via an intelligent algorithm primarily based on how long users spend reading articles. Recommended content sidebars on any news site are calculated via algorithm, and Facebook has a recommended news content block that takes into account previous clicks and offers similar links.

Diakopoulos categorizes algorithms into several categories based on the types of decisions they make. *Prioritization*, for example, ranks content to bring attention to one thing at the expense of another. *Association* marks relationships between entities, such as articles or videos that share subject matter of features. *Filtering* involves the inclusion or exclusion of certain information based on a set of criteria.

"Algorithms make it much easier not just for you to find the content that you're interested in, but for the content to find you that the algorithm thinks you're interested in," Diakopoulos says. That is, they maximize for clicks by excluding other kinds of content, helping reinforce an existing worldview by diminishing a reader's chance of encountering content outside of what they already know and believe.

This type of exclusion on the internet has become known as the filter bubble, after a 2011 book by Eli Pariser. As [Columbia Journalism Review]'s Alexis Fitts explains in a recent feature about Pariser's viral site, Upworthy:

> In Pariser's conception, the filter bubble is the world created by the shift from "human gatekeepers," such as newspaper editors who curate importance by what makes the front page, to the algorithmic ones employed by Facebook and Google, which present the content they believe a user is most likely to click on. This new digital universe is "a cozy place," Pariser writes, "populated by our favorite people and things and ideas." But it's ultimately a dangerous one. These unique universes "alter the way we'd encounter ideas and information," preventing the kind of spontaneous encounters with ideas that promote creativity and, perhaps more importantly, encouraging us to throw our attention to matters of irrelevance.
>
> "It's easy to push 'Like' and increase the visibility of a friend's post about finishing a marathon or an instructional article about how to make onion soup," writes Pariser. "It's harder to push the 'Like' button on an article titled, 'Darfur sees bloodiest month in two years.'"

These types of algorithms create a news literacy issue because if readers don't know they are influencing content, they cannot make critical decisions about what they choose to read. In the print world, partisan media was transparent about its biases, and readers could therefore select which bias they preferred. Today, readers don't necessarily know how algorithms are biased and and how nuanced the filters they receive content through really are.

"Newspapers have always been able to have an editorial voice and to possibly even affect voting patterns based on that editorial voice," says Diakopoulos. "But what we're seeing [now] is the ability to scale across a population in a much more powerful way." Facebook recently did a study that found that simply showing more news in the newsfeed affects voting decisions.

Furthermore, the algorithms that social sites use to promote content don't evaluate the validity of the content, which can and has spread misinformation.

Beyond the filter bubble, algorithmic bias extends to search engine manipulation, which refers to the process undertaken by many companies, celebrities, and public figures to ensure that favorable content rises to the top of search engine results in particular regions. Though not intuitive to the average Web user, it's actually a form of soft censorship, explains Wenke Lee, Director of the Georgia Tech Information Security Center.

After reading Pariser's book, Lee and his research team set out to test the effect of personalized search results on Google and built a tool called Bobble, a browser plug-in that runs simultaneous Google searches from different locations around the globe so users can see the difference between Google search returns for different people. They found that results differ based on several factors: [w]eb content at any given time, the region from which a search is performed, recent search history, and how much search engine manipulation has occurred to favor a given result. Though Bobble has largely been confined to research purposes, it has been downloaded close to 10,000 times and has tremendous potential as a news literacy teaching tool.

"When we do this kind of work, there is always some pushback from people who say 'Why should people care? Why should people care about the filter bubble or biased news?'" says Lee. "But in the print media age, if somebody was to give me a manipulated version of [the] *New York Times*, I would be able to put my newspaper next to yours and find out that mine is different. But now? You and I can very likely see different front pages of newspapers online because they are customized for individuals, and that's pretty dangerous. Because that means I don't have a baseline to compare what is real and what is not."

For these reasons, the Center for News Literacy at Stony Brook University dedicates a portion of its curriculum to the filter bubble, covering issues of search engine manipulation and teaching how to search incognito on a Web browser—that is, without it storing your information.

Other efforts to mitigate media bias from algorithmic personalization include NewsCube, a Web service which automatically provides readers with multiple viewpoints on a given news item, and Balance, a research project at the University of Michigan that seeks to diversify the result sets provided by news aggregators (such as Google News).

Meanwhile, Diakopoulous is working on a framework for how to be transparent about algorithms, as well as processes for how they can be investigated, be it through reverse engineering by users (for which he offers methods in his report) or policy regulations on an institutional level.

"Transparency is important for the same reason why we want our newspaper editors to be transparent," he says. "If the purveyor of this very powerful media tool is honest with us about how they are using it, then at least we can be a little bit more trusting of them."

And it's also a way to give people the choice to be more media savvy—to exit the filter bubble, if they wish. "If I know your search engine works that way and I know someone else's search engine works a different way, then I can choose which one I would prefer to use."

46

"U.S. Media Polarization and the 2020 Election: A Nation Divided"

MARK JURKOWITZ, AMY MITCHELL, ELISA SHEARER, AND MASON WALKER

As the [United States] enters a heated 2020 presidential election year, a new Pew Research Center report finds that Republicans and Democrats place their trust in two nearly inverse news media environments.

Overall, Republicans and Republican-leaning independents view many heavily relied on sources across a range of platforms as untrustworthy. At the same time, Democrats and independents who lean Democratic see most of those sources as credible and rely on them to a far greater degree, according to the survey of 12,043 U.S. adults conducted Oct. 29–Nov. 11, 2019, on Pew Research Center's American Trends Panel.

These divides are even more pronounced between conservative Republicans and liberal Democrats.

Moreover, evidence suggests that partisan polarization in the use and trust of media sources has widened in the past five years. A comparison to a similar study by the Center of web-using U.S. adults in 2014 finds that Republicans have grown increasingly alienated from most of the more established sources, while Democrats' confidence in them remains stable, and in some cases, has strengthened.

The study asked about use of, trust in, and distrust of 30 different news sources for political and election news. While it is impossible to represent the entire crowded media space, the outlets, which range from network television news to Rush Limbaugh to the *New York Times* to the *Washington Examiner* to *HuffPost*, were selected to represent popular media brands across a range of platforms.

Greater portions of Republicans express distrust than express trust of 20 of the 30 sources asked about. Only seven outlets generate more trust than distrust among Republicans—including Fox News and the talk radio programs of hosts Sean Hannity and Rush Limbaugh.

For Democrats, the numbers are almost reversed. Greater portions of Democrats express trust than express distrust in 22 of the 30 sources asked about. Only eight generate more distrust than trust—including Fox News, Sean Hannity, and Rush Limbaugh.

Another way to look at the diverging partisan views of media credibility: [a]lmost half of the sources included in this report (13) are trusted by at least 33% of Democrats, but only two are trusted by at least 33% of Republicans.

Republicans' lower trust in a variety of measured news sources coincides with their infrequent use. Overall, only one source, Fox News, was used by at least one-third of Republicans for political and election news in the past week. There are five different sources from which at least one-third of Democrats received political or election news in the last week (CNN, NBC News, ABC News, CBS News, and MSNBC).

And in what epitomizes this era of polarized news, none of the 30 sources is trusted by more than 50% of all U.S. adults.

The Fox News Phenomenon

In the more compact Republican media ecosystem, one outlet towers above all others: Fox News. It would be hard to overstate its connection as a trusted go-to source of political news for Republicans.

About two-thirds (65%) of Republicans and Republican leaners say they trust Fox News as a source. Additionally, 60% say they got political or election news there in the past week.

Among Democrats and Democratic leaners, CNN (67%) is about as trusted a source of information as Fox News is among Republicans. The cable network is also Democrats' most commonly turned to source for political and election news, with about half (53%) saying they got news there in the past week.

The big difference is that while no other source comes close to rivaling Fox News' appeal to Republicans, a number of sources other than CNN are also highly trusted and frequently used by Democrats.

The Impact of Political Ideology on Americans' Trust in News Outlets

The partisan gaps become even more dramatic when looking at the parties' ideological poles—conservative Republicans and liberal Democrats. About two-thirds of liberal Democrats (66%) trust the *New York Times*, for example. In comparison, just 10% of conservative Republicans trust the Times, while 50% outright distrust it. Rush Limbaugh, meanwhile, is the third-most trusted source among conservative Republicans (38%) but tied for the second-most distrusted source among liberal Democrats (55%).

At the same time, the gap is less pronounced among the more moderate segments in each party. For example, three-quarters of conservative Republicans trust Fox News, while just about half (51%) of moderate or liberal Republicans do. Conversely, moderate and conservative Democrats are more than twice as likely as liberal Democrats to trust Fox News (32% vs. 12%).

The Divide Widens over Time

There is also evidence that suggests that these partisan divides have grown over the past five years, particularly with more Republicans voicing distrust in a number of sources. A comparison to a similar study of web-using U.S. adults conducted by the Center in 2014 finds that Republicans' distrust increased for 15 of the 20 sources asked about in both years—with notable growth in Republicans' distrust of CNN, the *Washington Post*, and the *New York Times*.

Democrats' levels of trust and distrust in media sources have changed considerably less than Republicans' during this time span. Even accounting for the modest methodological differences between the two studies, these differences hold. (Details about the two studies can be found in the methodology.)

All in all, it's not that partisans live in entirely separate media bubbles when it comes to political news. There is some overlap in news sources, but determining the full extent of that overlap can be difficult to gauge. One factor is that getting news from a source does not always mean trusting that source. Indeed, the data reveals that while 24% of Republicans got news from CNN in the past week, roughly four-in-ten who did (39%) say they distrust the outlet. And of the 23% of Democrats who got political news from Fox News in the past week, nearly three-in-ten (27%) distrust it.

Americans Are Divided by Party in the Sources They Turn to for Political News

To a large degree, the pattern of partisan polarization that emerges in attitudes about the credibility of news sources is also evident in the sources that Republicans and Democrats rely on for news about politics and the election.

Overall, Republicans (and independents who lean Republican) get political and election news from a smaller group of sources than Democrats, with an overwhelming reliance on one source—Fox News. Democrats (including independents who lean Democratic), on the other hand, use a wider range of sources.

Six-in-ten Republicans say they got news from the Fox News cable network in the past week. After Fox News, there is a huge gap before the next most turned-to sources—ABC News, NBC News, and CBS News, all at similar levels (30%, 28%, and 26% respectively).

Despite Republicans' deep distrust of CNN, it is among the more commonly used sources among Republicans, with 24% who got political news there in the past week. Next come the radio shows of Sean Hannity (19%) and Rush Limbaugh (17%). No other source tops 15% among Republicans.

On the Democratic side, CNN is turned to by the greatest portion, with 53% saying they got political news there in the past week. As is the case with Republicans, the three major commercial broadcast networks are the next most turned to sources of political news for Democrats, albeit in bigger doses—NBC (40%), ABC (37%), and CBS (33%).

One-third of Democrats also got news from cable channel MSNBC (33%) in the past week. A similar share got political news from the *New York Times* (31%) and NPR (30%). About a quarter got news from the *Washington Post* (26%) and Fox News (23%).

Amid these divides, there are some in each party who turn to the most relied-on sources of the other party: [r]oughly a quarter of Republicans (24%) got political news from CNN in the past week, which virtually matches the percentage of Democrats (23%) who say the same of Fox News. In other words, even amid the tendency of partisans to seek political news from different sources, there is still some overlap in what partisans see.

Partisan Divides Lead to One-Sided Audiences for Many News Outlets

The preference for news sources based on party identification and ideology affects the partisan makeup of the audience of each outlet. * * *

For example, the average audience member of the *New York Post* sits very close to the party and ideology of the average U.S. adult. The average audience member of Breitbart, the Sean Hannity radio show, and Rush Limbaugh's radio program sit further to the right, as they tend to be more conservative and Republican. Fox News, even as it is turned to by large portions of conservatives Republicans, also has substantial numbers of more moderate Republicans and Democrats who get some news from it. Thus, Fox News sits closer to the middle than Breitbart and some others. It is worth noting that most of these outlets have an audience that falls at least slightly to the left of the average U.S. adult.

Furthermore, some adults only got political news in the past week from outlets whose audiences mostly share their political views. Roughly two-in-ten Republicans (18%) got political and election news in the past week only from outlets whose audiences lean disproportionately to the right— that is, there are two-thirds more conservative Republicans in their audience base than liberal Democrats. Similarly, 20% of Democrats got news only from outlets whose audiences lean disproportionately to the left (two-thirds more liberal Democrats than conservative Republicans).

* * *

47

"Media Bias (Real and Perceived) and the Rise of Partisan Media"

MATT GROSSMANN

In the age of Fox News Channel, talk radio, and MSNBC, it is tempting to think we have entered an unprecedented age of biased media. But partisan bias is actually the norm in media history. As Jonathan Ladd argues, "The existence of an independent, powerful, widely respected news media establishment is an historical anomaly. Prior to the twentieth century, such an institution had never existed in American history."

In the nineteenth century, overtly partisan newspapers were the norm. Independent journalism was a successful countervailing movement that brought with it standards of unbiased political coverage. Joseph Pulitzer, the Democratic politician and newspaperman, helped establish the Columbia School of Journalism in 1912 and the Pulitzer Prizes in 1917. The American Society of Newspaper Editors codified an impartiality principle in its 1923 code of ethics: "[n]ews reports should be free from opinion or bias of any kind."

But Republicans have long been skeptical of the ability of an independent press to equally represent their views. Donald Trump's declaration of any contrary coverage as "fake news" is a more extreme version of a long-standing complaint. As Ladd finds, "[C]riticism of the institutional news media was a defining characteristic" of the conservative movement and Barry Goldwater's nomination campaign. His supporters later founded the Committee to Combat Bias in Broadcasting and Accuracy in Media to monitor the news for bias. Complaints about media bias were common in subsequent Republican administrations and eventually came to dominate Republican campaigns. One study found that 92% of claims of media bias in the 1988, 1992, and 1996 elections came from Republicans alleging liberal bias.

These complaints were directly tied to the rise of explicitly conservative media as alternatives to mainstream news. Kathleen Hall Jamieson and Joseph Capella, who studied the Rush Limbaugh show for a full year, found that he mentioned media bias every single day. Fox News Channel was created to counter perceived liberal bias, calling itself "fair and balanced" with the motto "we report, you decide."

Conservative skepticism of the ability of an independent press to be unbiased was a reaction to the basic demographics of journalism. Reporters have been and remain disproportionately Democrats and liberals (compared to the general public). Lars Willnat and David Weaver found that the proportion of Republican reporters dropped from an already-low 26% in 1971 to 7% in 2013. Republicans and conservatives are more common in local television news, but are rarely seen at national mainstream news outlets.

Are the Mainstream Media Biased in Favor of Democrats and Liberalism?

Even if reporters are disproportionately Democrats and liberals, they may be able to produce unbiased news by pursuing objective evidence or balanced coverage. Do they succeed?

Overall, studies examining the content of news coverage have not found consistent evidence of bias favoring Democrats or Republicans across many different elections. There are studies finding Republican bias and studies finding Democratic bias. Others find only media bias toward the frontrunner, regardless of party. Dave D'Alessio examines 99 prior studies of presidential election coverage bias and finds no consistent partisan bias.

In an analysis of 95 Senate elections, Adam Schiffer finds that factors like incumbency, finances, poll standing, competitiveness, the state of the economy, and scandals explain the bulk of variation. But he does find a remaining slight advantage for Democrats in newspaper tone, even accounting for these factors.

Even where careful researchers do find bias, they tend not to find that it favors the same party all the time. Kim Fridkin Kahn and Patrick Kenney examined the positive or negative tone of each article and its coverage of issues and candidate traits and counted the number of criticisms of each candidate. They found that newspaper coverage favors incumbent candidates that the newspaper endorsed on its editorial page. But systematic studies of this kind depend on research choices that affect the results. If one candidate is quoted attacking another candidate, that shows up as a criticism, but it could reflect either an accurate portrayal of the opposing candidate's message or a choice by the reporter to emphasize the criticism. If a reporter mentions that one candidate has raised more money than another, it reflects both a reality about the race and a choice to mention fundraising over another indicator of support.

One might think that cataloging only the clearest instances of media bias is a solution to this problem, but media bias could be subtle. One study found, for example, that candidates endorsed by a newspaper get better-looking photographs in that newspaper.

The most famous study of media bias, by Tim Groseclose and Jeffrey Milyo, compared citations of interest groups and think tanks by media outlets with citations by members of Congress. They reasoned that an unbiased media outlet would cite material equally from sources favored by legislators in each party and from each ideological perspective. They found that most media outlets disproportionately cited sources favored by Democratic and more liberal members. Their measure of media bias allowed them to compare media outlets with members of Congress on the same ideological dimension.

But another study found that Groseclose and Milyo's methodology did not produce stable estimates over time. All outlets they studied appeared to be more moderate or conservative in later years. Brendan Nyhan leveled a different critique of Groseclose and Milyo: Democratic office holders and media organizations both cited more neutral experts, rather than favoring liberal perspectives. "Technocratic centrist to liberal organizations like Brookings and the Center on Budget and Policy Priorities tend to have more credentialed experts with peer-reviewed publications than their conservative counterparts." But conservatives also tend to doubt the ability of academic experts to maintain neutrality for the same reason that they are skeptical of the media: academics are also disproportionately Democrats and liberals. So the media bias debate reflects a broader conflict over whether technocratic expertise can be seen as neutral.

Despite these difficulties, studies of the relative treatment of Democratic and Republican candidates and their affiliated interest groups are relatively easy to conduct because there is a straightforward comparative baseline: balanced coverage of each candidate or each group. But that means the focus has been mostly on partisan biases, especially in election coverage, rather than broader ideological biases in the selection or description of political issues and events.

It may be easier, however, for reporters to treat two general election candidates or two parties in a congressional debate equally than it is to avoid ideological influences on coverage that stem from the reporters' underlying values. There is no evidence of a reporters' conspiracy to help the Democrats, but reporters with liberal viewpoints might (even inadvertently) choose different news to cover or frame it differently than does the much smaller number of conservative reporters.

The Promise of New Measures of Media Bias

State-of-the-art measures of media bias build on Groseclose and Milyo's strategy of comparing media outlets with members of Congress, but use "big data" approaches geared toward analyzing large sets of texts. This approach tries to capture more subtle biases in the use of language or the discussion of issues, which it might be more difficult for reporters to control.

In 2010, Matthew Gentzkow and Jesse Shapiro used the full 2005 *Congressional Record* to generate phrases disproportionately used by more liberal or conservative members of Congress and then compare the usage of those phrases across newspapers. This approach sidesteps some of the objections to Groseclose and Milyo's methodology by going beyond group citations, but it is still dependent on the idea that liberal and conservative legislators both use equivalently biased phrases and that, to be unbiased, reporters should tend to use them in roughly equal measure.

The approach still raises perennial difficulties in interpretation. The phrases disproportionately used by Democrats, according to Grentzkow and Shapiro, include some partisan messaging tropes—such as "workers' rights," "nuclear option," "sniper rifles," and "privatize Social Security"—but also nonpartisan, generic terms such as "trade agreement," "American people," "budget deficit," and "war in Iraq." Other Democratic phrases, such as "veterans' health care," "Congressional Black Caucus," and "minimum wage" reflect real partisan differences, but these are differences in issue agenda rather than message. Republican phrases similarly include poll-tested partisan language such as "death tax," "illegal aliens," "oil for food scandal," and "personal retirement accounts," but also neutral language referring to the names of courts and justices. Again, there are phrases that reflect issue priorities but not biased analysis, such as "stem cell" and "government spending." When reporters use these phrases, it may reflect anything from the neutral language in a paper's style guide to biased choices of what issues to cover to unfairly repeating one side's message more often. It is also difficult to distinguish between a reporter echoing liberal or conservative talking points and one side just being more "on message" in their communications with reporters.

Gregory Martin and Ali Yurukoglu recently used the same method to look for biased phrase usage on CNN, Fox News, and MSNBC in 2000, 2004, and 2008. They turned up significant but unsurprising Republican bias on Fox News and Democratic bias on MSNBC. Yet once again, the word lists found to be biased (based on congressional communications) alternatively instill confidence and raise questions. The most "Democratic" phrases included neutral language like "African American," "Republican leadership," and "Bush administration," along with more partisan phrases like "social justice" and "working families." The most "Republican" phrases included neutral phrases like "federal government" and "new refinery," alongside such ideologically tinged language as "death tax," "illegal aliens," and "limited government."

In a thoughtful appendix, the authors use several alternative measures to find similar trends. They analyze each year independently and all years together, they use different estimators of ideological position based on the same texts, and they produce an alternative measure: the time given to Democratic and Republican guests on each network. All measures produce the same basic contrast: Fox News is to the right of CNN and MSNBC and Fox News and MSNBC are getting more polarized over time. There is no reason to doubt these basic findings.

The improvement in measurement is quite welcome. But scholars should not lose sight of qualitative differences among media outlets. Regardless of word usage patterns, we should still categorically distinguish between CNN, which goes out of its way to find balanced panels of commentators even if it does not always succeed, and Fox and MSNBC. Similarly, we should be able to separate the journalism displayed on such Fox programs as Special Report with Bret Baier and Fox News Sunday from clearly biased programming such as the Sean Hannity Show. Even if the front page of a nonpartisan newspaper is subtly biased, this is qualitatively different from the bias openly displayed on the editorial page. Losing sight of that difference downplays the change wrought by the rise of openly partisan and ideological media.

*   *   *

*Perceptions of Bias Are Reducing Trust in News
and Empowering Partisan Media*

Regardless of the academic research, the public, and political professionals, are responding to their own perceptions of bias. William Eveland and Dhavan Shah found that even when Republicans and Democrats watch the same coverage, Democrats believe that it is more favorable for the Republican candidates and vice versa. Another study found that even presenting the same information but varying the label of where it came from (CNN or Fox) also changes the perceptions of bias.

Not surprisingly, then, faith in the news media has been in decline across the board. Yet mainstream media outlets get especially poor trust ratings from conservatives. Because Republicans regularly cite political bias in the mainstream media, their electorate only trusts explicitly conservative alternatives.

Given the strength of partisanship in contemporary political life, it is understandable that Republicans would be more likely to suspect and react to perceived biases among (disproportionately liberal) reporters. It would be surprising if the political views of reporters did not in any way affect their selection of news stories or their portrayal of events.

Only two out of the hundred-largest newspapers endorsed Trump in 2016, so there is no reason to believe that perceptions of bias will be diminishing any time soon. Trump's constant attacks on the media and invocations of "fake news" mean that the Republican electorate is likely to further reduce its trust in mainstream media and rely even more on explicitly conservative media. Fox News and talk radio have large effects on their audiences, and even on the friends of viewers and listeners who do not themselves watch or listen. They have also changed the behavior of legislators, instilling fears of primary challenges and base backlashes.

Even if Republican skepticism of mainstream media impartiality is justified, the rise of explicitly ideological media as the central information sources for Republicans is still alarming. It is as if Republicans reacted to perceived biases on the front page of the *New York Times* by deciding to only read the editorial page of the *Wall Street Journal*.

The die may therefore be cast for increasingly replacing traditional journalism with partisan media. Even as Democrats are more accepting of the mainstream news media, the recent doubling of MSNBC viewership suggests that liberals may eventually succeed at copying the conservative media model. The dominance of independent, trusted, putatively impartial media is not a natural state of affairs. It is a twentieth-century phenomenon that is not guaranteed to survive.

Be careful what you call biased news; complaints about mainstream journalism are empowering outlets that are not even trying to be even-handed.

DISCUSSION QUESTIONS

1. Which part or parts of the news media—newspapers, television, websites, aggregators like Google News, radio, podcasts, Facebook, Twitter—do you rely on most? Which would you say you trust the most? What makes these sources the most trustworthy?

2. Considering the evidence presented in these three articles, how pervasive is exposure to news coverage that is implicitly or explicitly partisan or ideological? On balance, is this exposure good or bad for American democracy? What are the strongest areas of concern? What might be the chief benefits?

3. How do you know partisan or ideological bias when you see it? Define three criteria you would use to determine whether a media outlet is catering to readers' or viewers' partisan or ideological bias.

CHAPTER 10

Elections and Voting

48

"The Voice of the People: An Echo," from *The Responsible Electorate*

V. O. Key, Jr.

The votes are cast, the tallies are in, the winning candidate claims victory and a mandate to govern—the people have spoken! But what exactly have the people said when they cast a plurality of the votes for one candidate? The political scientist V. O. Key, Jr., argues that the voice of the people is an echo of the cacophony and hubbub of candidates and parties scrambling for popular support. "Even the most discriminating popular judgment," wrote Key, "can reflect only ambiguity, uncertainty, or even foolishness if those are the qualities of the input into the echo chamber."

So what is the logic of the voting decision? Key argues that the effort among social scientists to develop theories for understanding the voting decision is important because of the ways political candidates and political leaders will respond to them. If research demonstrates that voters are influenced by "images and cultivation of style," rather than the "substance of politics," then that is what candidates will offer the voters. If the people receive only images and style as the input to the echo chamber, then eventually that is all they will come to expect. However, Key argues that contrary to the picture of voters held by many politicians and some academic researchers of his day, the "voters are not fools" who are easily manipulated by campaign tactics or who vote predictably according to the social groups they are in. Individual voters may behave oddly, he concedes, but "in the large, the electorate behaves about as rationally and responsibly as we should expect." His analysis of past presidential elections convinced him that the electorate made sensible decisions based upon a concern for public policy, the performance of government, and the personalities of the candidates.

In his reflective moments even the most experienced politician senses a nagging curiosity about why people vote as they do. His power and his position depend upon the outcome of the mysterious rites we perform as opposing candidates harangue the multitudes who finally march to the polls to prolong the rule of their champion, to thrust him, ungratefully, back into the void of private life, or to raise to eminence a new tribune of the people. What kinds of appeals enable a candidate to win the favor of the great god, The People? What circumstances move voters to shift their preferences in this direction or that? What clever propaganda tactic or slogan led to this result? What mannerism of oratory or style of rhetoric produced another outcome? What band of electors rallied to this candidate to save the day for him? What policy of state attracted the devotion of another bloc of voters? What action repelled a third sector of the electorate?

The victorious candidate may claim with assurance that he has the answers to all such questions. He may regard his success as vindication of his beliefs about why voters vote as they do. And he may regard the swing of the vote to him as indubitably a response to the campaign positions he took, as an indication of the acuteness of his intuitive estimates of the mood of the people, and as a ringing manifestation of the esteem in which he is held by a discriminating public. This narcissism assumes its most repulsive form among election winners who have championed intolerance, who have stirred the passions and hatreds of people, or who have advocated causes known by decent men to be outrageous or dangerous in their long-run consequences. No functionary is more repugnant or more arrogant than the unjust man who asserts, with a color of truth, that he speaks from a pedestal of popular approbation.

It thus can be a mischievous error to assume, because a candidate wins, that a majority of the electorate shares his views on public questions, approves his past actions, or has specific expectations about his future conduct. Nor does victory establish that the candidate's campaign strategy, his image, his television style, or his fearless stand against cancer and polio turned the trick. The election returns establish only that the winner attracted a majority of the votes—assuming the existence of a modicum of rectitude in election administration. They tell us precious little about why the plurality was his.

For a glaringly obvious reason, electoral victory cannot be regarded as necessarily a popular ratification of a candidate's outlook. The voice of the people is but an echo. The output of an echo chamber bears an inevitable and invariable relation to the input. As candidates and parties clamor for attention and vie for popular support, the people's verdict can be no more than a selective reflection from among the alternatives and outlooks presented to them. Even the most discriminating popular judgment can reflect only ambiguity, uncertainty, or even foolishness if those are the qualities of the input into the echo chamber. A candidate may win despite his tactics and appeals rather than because of them. If the people can choose only from among rascals, they are certain to choose a rascal.

*   *   *

The studies of electoral behavior by survey methods cumulate into an imposing body of knowledge which conveys a vivid impression of the variety and subtlety of factors that enter into individual voting decisions. In their first stages in the 1930s the new electoral studies chiefly lent precision and verification to the working maxims of practicing politicians and to some of the crude theories of political speculators. Thus, sample surveys established that people did, indeed, appear to vote their pocketbooks. Yet the demonstration created its embarrassments because it also established that exceptions to the rule were numerous. Not all factory workers, for example, voted alike. How was the behavior of the deviants from "group interest" to be explained? Refinement after refinement of theory and analysis added complexity to the original simple explanation. By introducing a bit of psychological theory it could be demonstrated that factory workers with optimistic expectations tended less to be governed by pocketbook considerations than did those whose outlook was gloomy. When a little social psychology was stirred into the analysis, it could be established that identifications formed early in life, such as attachments to political parties, also reinforced or resisted the pull of the interest of the moment. A sociologist, bringing to play the conceptual tools of his trade, then could show that those factory workers who associate intimately with like-minded persons on the average vote with greater solidarity than do social isolates. Inquiries conducted with great ingenuity along many such lines have enormously broadened our knowledge of the factors associated with the responses of people to the stimuli presented to them by political campaigns.

Yet, by and large, the picture of the voter that emerges from a combination of the folklore of practical politics and the findings of the new electoral studies is not a pretty one. It is not a portrait of citizens moving to considered decision as they play their solemn role of making and unmaking governments. The older tradition from practical politics may regard the voter as an erratic and irrational fellow susceptible to manipulation by skilled humbugs. One need not live through many campaigns to observe politicians, even successful politicians, who act as though they regarded the people as manageable fools. Nor does a heroic conception of the voter emerge from the new analyses of electoral behavior. They can be added up to a conception of voting not as a civic decision but as an almost purely deterministic act. Given knowledge of certain characteristics of a voter—his occupation, his residence, his religion, his national origin, and perhaps certain of his attitudes—one can predict with a high probability the direction of his vote. The actions of persons are made to appear to be only predictable and automatic responses to campaign stimuli.

*   *   *

Conceptions and theories of the way voters behave do not raise solely arcane problems to be disputed among the democratic and antidemocratic theorists or questions to be settled by the elegant techniques of the analysts of electoral behavior. Rather, they touch upon profound issues at the heart of the problem of the nature and workability of systems of popular government. Obviously the perceptions of the behavior of the electorate held by political leaders, agitators, and activists condition, if they do not fix, the types of appeals politicians employ as they seek popular support. These perceptions—or theories—affect the nature of the input to the echo chamber, if we may revert to our earlier figure, and thereby control its output. They may govern, too, the kinds of actions that governments take as they look forward to the next election. If politicians perceive the electorate as responsive to father images, they will give it father images. If they see voters as most certainly responsive to nonsense, they will give them nonsense. If they see voters as susceptible to delusion, they will delude them. If they see an electorate receptive to the cold, hard realities, they will give it the cold, hard realities.

In short, theories of how voters behave acquire importance not because of their effects on voters, who may proceed blithely unaware of them. They gain significance because of their effects, both potentially and in reality, on candidates and other political leaders. If leaders believe the route to victory is by projection of images and cultivation of styles rather than by advocacy of policies to cope with the problems of the country, they will project images and cultivate styles to the neglect of the substance of politics. They will abdicate their prime function in a democratic system, which amounts, in essence, to the assumption of the risk of trying to persuade us to lift ourselves by our bootstraps.

Among the literary experts on politics there are those who contend that, because of the development of tricks for the manipulation of the masses, practices of political leadership in the management of voters have moved far toward the conversion of election campaigns into obscene parodies of the models set up by democratic idealists. They point to the good old days when politicians were deep thinkers, eloquent orators, and farsighted statesmen. Such estimates of the course of change in social institutions must be regarded with reserve. They may be only manifestations of the inverted optimism of aged and melancholy men who, estopped from hope for the future, see in the past a satisfaction of their yearning for greatness in our political life.

Whatever the trends may have been, the perceptions that leadership elements of democracies hold of the modes of response of the electorate must always be a matter of fundamental significance. Those perceptions determine the nature of the voice of the people, for they determine the character of the input into the echo chamber. While the output may be governed by the nature of the input, over the longer run the properties of the echo chamber may themselves be altered. Fed a steady diet of buncombe [bunkum], the people may come to expect and to respond with highest predictability to buncombe. And those leaders most skilled in the propagation of buncombe may gain lasting advantage in the recurring struggles for popular favor.

The perverse and unorthodox argument of this little book is that voters are not fools. To be sure, many individual voters act in odd ways indeed; yet in the large the electorate behaves about as rationally and responsibly as we should expect, given the clarity of the alternatives presented to it and the character of the information available to it. In American presidential campaigns of recent decades the portrait of the American electorate that develops from the data is not one of an electorate straitjacketed by social determinants or moved by subconscious urges triggered by devilishly skillful propagandists. It is rather one of an electorate moved by concern about central and relevant questions of public policy, of governmental performance, and of executive personality. Propositions so uncompromisingly stated inevitably represent overstatements. Yet to the extent that they can be shown to resemble the reality, they are propositions of basic importance for both the theory and the practice of democracy.

To check the validity of this broad interpretation of the behavior of voters, attention will center on the movements of voters across party lines as they reacted to the issues, events, and candidates of presidential campaigns between 1936 and 1960. Some Democratic voters of one election turned Republican at the next; others stood pat. Some Republicans of one presidential season voted Democratic four years later; others remained loyal Republicans. What motivated these shifts, sometimes large and sometimes small, in voter affection? * * * Were these actions governed by images, moods, and other irrelevancies; or were they expressions of judgments about the sorts of questions that, hopefully, voters will weigh as they responsibly cast their ballots? * * * If one perseveres through the analysis of this extensive body of information, the proposition that the voter is not so irrational a fellow after all may become credible.

DISCUSSION QUESTIONS

1. When you cast your vote, how do you decide whom to vote for? Is your decision process affected by the nature of the political campaign that has just been completed, or does the campaign have little effect on your decision?

2. Does the 2020 presidential election support Key's view of the electoral process? What kinds of information would you want to have in order to answer this question?

49

"Democratic Ideals and Realities"

CHRISTOPHER ACHEN AND LARRY BARTELS

*Political scientists Christopher Achen and Larry Bartels make a less positive assess-
ment than V. O. Key, Jr. They posit as an appealing "folk theory" the idea that voters
influence the actions of their governments. Instead, Achen and Bartels report that
most citizens pay little attention to politics; they are swayed by "the nature of the
times"; and they lean on political and partisan attachments adopted in their childhood to make their voting choices. The "folk theory" of elections and democracy,
they report, is more fantasy than reality. Achen and Bartels elaborate on this idea
and explain that there are two main models of how democracy works. The populist
account has the people's preferences upheld through their election of representatives
or through direct democracy, such as voting on initiatives and referendums on the
ballot. A second model, more common among scholars, sees elections primarily as a
means to choose leaders rather than as a means for "the people," in a meaningful
sense, to control and direct the actions of government. One prominent form of this
second model says that voters may not be choosing among issue stances but rather
rendering judgments of their perception of the performance of public officials over
the preceding years. Achen and Bartels see Key as an advocate of that approach.
However, they argue that this model does not stand up to empirical scrutiny. In
their view, elections are much more about voters expressing their social identity
rather than making policy or issue choices. Why does this matter? "If voting behavior primarily reflects and reinforces voters' social loyalties," they write, "it is a
mistake to suppose that elections result in popular control of public policy."*

In the conventional view, democracy begins with the voters. Ordinary
people have preferences about what their government should do. They
choose leaders who will do those things, or they enact their preferences
directly in referendums. In either case, what the majority wants becomes
government policy—a highly attractive prospect in light of most human
experience with governments. Democracy makes the people the rulers, and
legitimacy derives from their consent. In Abraham Lincoln's stirring words
from the Gettysburg Address, democratic government is "of the people,
by the people, and for the people." That way of thinking about democracy
has passed into everyday wisdom, not just in the United States but in a
great many other countries around the globe. It constitutes a kind of "folk
theory" of democracy, a set of accessible, appealing ideas assuring people

that they live under an ethically defensible form of government that has their interests at heart.

Unfortunately, while the folk theory of democracy has flourished as an ideal, its credibility has been severely undercut by a growing body of scientific evidence presenting a different and considerably darker view of democratic politics. That evidence demonstrates that the great majority of citizens pay little attention to politics. At election time, they are swayed by how they feel about "the nature of the times," especially the current state of the economy, and by political loyalties typically acquired in childhood. Those loyalties, not the facts of political life and government policy, are the primary drivers of political behavior. Election outcomes turn out to be largely random events from the viewpoint of contemporary democratic theory. That is, elections are well determined by powerful forces, but those forces are not the ones that current theories of democracy believe should determine how elections come out. Hence the old frameworks will no longer do.

We want to persuade the reader to think about democracy in a fundamentally different way. We are not in the business of encouraging liberals to become conservatives or vice versa. Books of that kind are plentiful enough. Rather we show both liberals and conservatives that the mental framework they bring to democratic life, while it may once have seemed defensible, can now be maintained only by willful denial of a great deal of credible evidence. However disheartening the task, intellectual honesty requires all of us to grapple with the corrosive implications of that evidence for our understanding of democracy. * * *

Two Contemporary Approaches to Democracy

What are the conventional notions of democracy that we argue have outlived their time? We consider two main types of theory, one popular with broad swatches of democratic society and a second whose appeal is largely confined to scholars specializing in the study of elections.

The first model, which we refer to as the *populist* ideal of democracy, emphasizes the role of ordinary citizens in "determining the policies" of democratic communities. As we will see, this populist notion of popular sovereignty has inspired a good deal of sophisticated academic thinking derived from Enlightenment concepts of human nature and the political views of 19th-century British liberalism. In its less rarified forms it has also undergirded the folk theory of democracy celebrated in much Fourth of July rhetoric. As the homespun poet of democracy Carl Sandburg proclaimed, "The People, Yes."

But *how* precisely shall the people govern according to the populist theory? * * * We shall examine two different accounts of how populist democracy might work. In one, the public "decide[s] issues through the election of individuals who are to assemble in order to carry out its will," as an unsympathetic critic of this account put it. In the other, the people rule through "direct democracy," choosing policies themselves via initiative and referendum procedures. Both representative democracy and direct democracy loom large in popular understanding of democratic self-government. But as we shall see, the assumptions undergirding both versions of populist democracy are highly unrealistic.

The second contemporary model in defense of democracy is less widely popular, though more persuasive to most political scientists. This model focuses on elections as mechanisms for *leadership selection*. In contrast to the populist model, which he characterized as "the classical doctrine of democracy," Joseph Schumpeter famously defined the democratic method as "that institutional arrangement for arriving at political decisions in which individuals acquire the power to decide by means of a competitive struggle for the people's vote." Dispensing with the notion that "the people itself decide issues" by electing those who will "carry out its will," Schumpeter insisted that "democracy does not mean and cannot mean that the people actually rule in any obvious sense of the terms 'people' and 'rule.' Democracy means only that the people have the opportunity of accepting or refusing the men who are to rule them."

Schumpeter gave little attention to the criteria by which voters would—or *should*—choose among potential rulers. However, subsequent scholars have fleshed out his account. The most influential model of democratic selection in contemporary political science is the *retrospective theory of voting*, which portrays "the electorate in its great, and perhaps principal, role as an appraiser of past events, past performance, and past actions." In this view, election outcomes hinge not on ideas, but on public approval or disapproval of the actual performance of incumbent political leaders. This model of democratic accountability appeals to skeptical scholars because it puts much less pressure on the voters to have elaborate, well-informed policy views. Ordinary citizens are allowed to drive the automobile of state simply by looking in the rearview mirror. Alas, we find that this works about as well in government as it would on the highway. Thus, we will argue that this second model of democracy, like the first, crumbles upon empirical inspection.

Hence we must think again. * * * A dramatically different framework is needed to make sense of how democracy actually works. We will argue that voters, even the most informed voters, typically make choices not on the basis of policy preferences or ideology, but on the basis of who they are—their social identities. In turn, those social identities shape how they think, what they think, and where they belong in the party system. But if voting behavior primarily reflects and reinforces voters' social loyalties, it is a mistake to suppose that elections result in popular control of public policy. Thus, our approach makes a sharp break with conventional thinking. The result may not be very comfortable or comforting. Nonetheless, we believe that a democratic theory worthy of serious social influence must engage with the findings of modern social science. * * *

But Isn't Democracy Doing Just Fine?

At this point, the reader may be wondering whether all this is just some arcane academic dispute of no consequence to the health of actual democracies. After all, the very idea of democratic government carries enormous prestige in contemporary political discourse. For example, the World Values Survey asked ordinary people in dozens of countries around the world, "How important is it to you to live in a country that is governed democratically?" Majorities in many countries said "absolutely important"—a score of ten on a one-to-ten scale. * * * Americans may be surprised to see that the United States (with an average rating of 8.4) is unremarkable in its enthusiasm for democracy. Adherence to the ideal is nearly universal.

Perhaps for this reason, nearly all contemporary political regimes, no matter how repressive, claim to be democracies of some sort. What is more surprising is that their citizens mostly believe them. Respondents in the World Values Survey were also asked, "And how democratically is this country being governed today?" * * * In every country there was a gap between attachment to democracy as an ideal and perceptions of democratic reality. Nevertheless, perceptions of democratic reality were surprisingly robust in such unlikely places as Rwanda, Malaysia, and Kazakhstan. Even the Chinese respondents were virtually indistinguishable from Americans, not only in their enthusiasm for democracy as an ideal but also in their assessment of how democratically their own country is currently being governed. However various the conceptions of democracy, most people almost everywhere accept the proposition that their own political system is (somehow) democratic—and even more accept the proposition that democracy is (somehow) a good thing.

In the face of this universal acclaim, why tamper with conventional thinking about democracy? If it ain't broke, the reader may think, don't fix it. The problem is that the universal agreement does not extend much beyond the use of the word "democracy" itself. *What* makes a country democratic and *why* that is a good thing have generated much less agreement. The meanings that Western, communist, fascist, and tinhorn dictatorial governments have attached to democracy have very little in common. * * *

Even in Western scholarly treatments, the criteria for qualifying as a democracy vary markedly from one author to the next, and may extend to half a dozen or more items. At one point in his long career, Dahl emphasized "the continued responsiveness of the government to the preferences of its citizens, considered as political equals." Decades later, he elaborated by specifying criteria for a democratic process—"effective participation," "voting equality," "enlightened understanding," "control of the agenda," and "inclusion of adults"—arguing that "each is necessary" if citizens are to be "politically equal in determining the policies of the association."

Unfortunately for democratic theory, how all this is to be achieved remains frustratingly vague. No existing government comes close to meeting all of Dahl's criteria; in our view, no possible government could. What then is the value of such an unattainable definition? Dahl himself acknowledged that "no state has ever possessed a government that fully measured up to the criteria of a democratic process"—and, indeed, "none is likely to." But he went on to write * * * the criteria provide highly serviceable standards for measuring the achievements and possibilities of democratic government. * * * They do provide standards against which to measure the performance of actual associations that claim to be democratic. They can serve as guides for shaping and reshaping concrete arrangements, constitutions, practices, and political institutions. For all those who aspire to democracy, they can also generate relevant questions and help in the search for answers." Other democratic theorists routinely follow Dahl on this point. Even if reality necessarily fails to correspond to the ideals, they argue, the ideals are valuable and should serve as the basis for modifying or reconstructing the reality. But for this argument to make sense, it must at least be the case that the ideals are not *too* unrealistic. * * *

If conventional democratic ideals amount to fairy tales, then we are left with no assurance that all the scholarly definitions and all the popular endorsements are of any use in making government contribute to human welfare. Hopelessly naive theories are a poor guide to policy, often distracting reformers from attainable incremental improvements along entirely different lines.

* * *

The Critical Tradition

The folk theory of democracy celebrates the wisdom of popular judgments by informed and engaged citizens. The reality is quite different. Human beings are busy with their lives. Most have school or a job consuming many hours of the day. They also have meals to prepare, homes to clean, and bills to pay. They may have children to raise or elderly parents to care for. They may also be coping with unemployment, business reverses, illness, addictions, divorce, or other personal and family troubles. For most, leisure time is at a premium. Sorting out which presidential candidate has the right foreign policy toward Asia is not a high priority for them. Without shirking more immediate and more important obligations, people cannot engage in much well-informed, thoughtful political deliberation, nor should they.

* * *

The pioneering survey research of Paul Lazarsfeld and his colleagues at Columbia University, of Angus Campbell and his colleagues at the University of Michigan, and of other early analysts of electoral choice produced a rather bleak portrait of habitual, socially determined political behavior, once again calling into question whether citizens could perform the role that the folk theory of democracy seemed to require of them.

Philip Converse extended this seminal work, building a new, more formidable case for skepticism regarding the idealized image of democratic citizens. * * * Converse's essay set off a vibrant decades-long critical discussion of his methodology and the inferences he drew from his findings, but few public opinion scholars disputed the central point he made—that judged by the standards of the folk theory, the political "belief systems" of ordinary citizens are generally thin, disorganized, and ideologically incoherent.

* * * Converse's argument is, if anything, even better supported a half century later than it was when he wrote. A vast amount of supporting evidence has been added to his dispiriting comparison of actual human political cognition with the expectations derived from the folk theory of democracy. Well-informed citizens, too, have come in for their share of criticism, since their well-organized "ideological" thinking often turns out to be just a rather mechanical reflection of what their favorite group and party leaders have instructed them to think. Faced with this evidence, many scholars in the final chapters of their books continue to express idealistic hope that institutional reform, civic education, improved mass media, more effective mobilization of the poor, or stronger moral exhortation might bring public opinion into closer correspondence with the standards of the folk theory. But in sober moments most acknowledge the repeated failures of all those prescriptions.

Thus, scholars, too, persist uneasily in their schizophrenia, recognizing the power of the critical arguments but hoping against hope that those arguments can somehow be discredited or evaded, allowing the lackluster reality of democratic practice to be squared with conventional idealistic democratic thinking. Often, their attempts to bolster the tattered theoretical status quo bring them back to Winston Churchill's claim that "democracy is the worst form of government except all those others that have been tried from time to time." But that is a distinctly un-idealistic defense of democracy—and no defense at all of the folk theory of democracy.

* * *

Our view is that conventional thinking about democracy has collapsed in the face of modern social-scientific research.

* * *

We survey a substantial body of scholarly work demonstrating that most democratic citizens are uninterested in politics, poorly informed, and unwilling or unable to convey coherent policy preferences through "issue voting." How, then, are elections supposed to ensure ideological responsiveness to the popular will? In our view, they do not. The populist ideal of electoral democracy, for all its elegance and attractiveness, is largely irrelevant in practice, leaving elected officials mostly free to pursue their own notions of the public good or to respond to party and interest group pressures.

* * *

Now it may be thought that, for all the apparent defects of the folk theory, when one listens to ordinary citizens they often sound quite coherent. Democrats generally espouse judgments and policy views supporting their preferred candidates; so do Republicans. Maybe all is well somehow. * * * We take up this possibility. We show that citizens' perceptions of parties' policy stands and their own policy views are significantly colored by their party preferences. Even on purely factual questions with clear right answers, citizens are sometimes willing to believe the opposite if it makes them feel better about their partisanship and vote choices. * * *

* * *

We conclude that group and partisan loyalties, not policy preferences or ideologies, are fundamental in democratic politics.

The Challenge: Taking on the Divine Right of the People

* * *

In our view, the ideal of popular sovereignty plays much the same role in contemporary democratic ideology that the divine right of kings played in the monarchical era. It is "a quasi-religious commitment," in Stimson's terms, a fiction providing legitimacy and stability to political systems whose actual workings are manifestly—and inevitably—rather less than divine. The fiction feels natural within the Enlightenment mind-set of rationality and human perfectibility. Thoughtful people and important scholars believe it. And its credibility is bolstered by the undeniable practical successes of many of the political systems that invoke it.

* * *

Conventional thought has avoided the painful task of grappling seriously with all the evidence undermining the standard versions of democratic theory. "Well, yes, there are problems," we say, and then we turn back to the impossible dream. In consequence, cheerful illusions and wish fulfillment have dominated both popular and scholarly thought about democracy for two centuries. Democratic theory has sailed along as if no iceberg had struck and the engine room were not taking on water. But the damage to the intellectual structure is very real.

* * *

The history of democratic thought—including much contemporary political science—is marked by an addiction to romantic theories. As with any addiction, the first step toward recovery is to admit that we have a problem.

* * *

Discussion Questions

1. Achen and Bartels discuss different ways of thinking about the nature of elections in American politics. In your view, what difference does it make for your assessment of the health and success of the political system if voting is driven by issue stances, retrospective evaluations, or social identities?

2. The authors contend that group loyalties and social identity much more powerfully determine voting patterns than most Americans typically acknowledge. Do you think it is harder for people to vote differently from others who are like them in one or more key social identity characteristics, or is it harder to express a point of view on an issue that differs from the group? Explain why you see one as harder than the other or why you see them both as about the same.

50

"Girls Just Wanna Not Run: The Gender Gap in Young Americans' Political Ambition"

Jennifer L. Lawless and Richard L. Fox

It is important to know what might be influencing voters' decisions and why they prefer the candidates they do. It is also important to know who appears on the ballot as a candidate. Political scientists Jennifer L. Lawless and Richard L. Fox tackle that question by noting that there is a gender gap in those who hold office and those who run for office. Despite much progress in women's growing presence in the "feeder industries" of law, education, and business, women express less interest in considering elective office than men do. Also concerning, in the authors' view, is that this gap starts early. They survey over 2,000 college students between the ages of 18 and 25 and conclude that the gender gap in political ambition already appears at this life stage. They also find that the size of the political ambition gap is similar to the one found among older cohorts. Young women and young men are both interested in engaging in the world to bring about societal change; men are more likely than women to identify elective office as a means to that end, while women are more likely than men to see involvement in a charitable organization as key. The authors offer five possible explanations for this gap and some measures that might reduce it.

Studies of women and men who are well-situated to run for office uncover a persistent gender gap in political ambition. Among "potential candidates"—lawyers, business leaders, educators, and political activists—women are less likely than men to express interest in a political career. Given the emergence over the past ten years of high-profile women in politics, such as Hillary Clinton, Nancy Pelosi, Sarah Palin, and Michele Bachmann, though, the landscape of U.S. politics looks to be changing. Perhaps young women are now just as motivated as young men to enter the electoral arena. Maybe young women envision future candidacies at similar rates as their male counterparts. Until now, no research has provided an analysis—let alone an in-depth investigation—of these topics.

This report fills that void. Based on the results of a new survey of more than 2,100 college students between the ages of 18 and 25, we offer the first assessment of political ambition early in life. And our results are troubling. Young women are less likely than young men ever to have considered running for office, to express interest in a candidacy at some point in the future, or to consider elective office a desirable profession. Moreover, the size of the gender gap in political ambition we uncover among 18–25 year olds is comparable to the size of the gap we previously uncovered in studies of potential candidates already working in the feeder professions to politics. Our data suggest, therefore, that the gender gap in ambition is already well in place by the time women and men enter their first careers.

Why? We identify five factors that contribute to the gender gap in political ambition among college students:

1. Young men are more likely than young women to be socialized by their parents to think about politics as a career path.
2. From their school experiences to their peer associations to their media habits, young women tend to be exposed to less political information and discussion than do young men.
3. Young men are more likely than young women to have played organized sports and care about winning.
4. Young women are less likely than young men to receive encouragement to run for office—from anyone.
5. Young women are less likely than young men to think they will be qualified to run for office, even once they are established in their careers.

Given this persistent gender gap in political ambition, we are a long way from a political reality in which young women and men are equally likely to aspire to seek and hold elective office in the future. Certainly, recruitment efforts by women's organizations—nationally and on college campuses—can chip away at the gender imbalance in interest in running for office. Encouraging parents, family members, teachers, and coaches to urge young women to think about a political career can mitigate the gender gap in ambition, too. And spurring young women to immerse themselves in competitive environments, such as organized sports, can go a long way in reinforcing the competitive spirit associated with interest in a future candidacy. But women's under-representation in elective office is likely to extend well into the future. In short, this report documents how far from gender parity we remain and the deeply embedded nature of the obstacles we must still overcome to achieve it.

The Gender Gap in Young Americans' Political Ambition

Why do so few women hold positions of political power in the United States? For the last few decades, researchers have provided compelling evidence that when women run for office—regardless of the position they seek—they are just as likely as men to win their races. The large gender disparities in U.S. political institutions, therefore, do not result from systematic discrimination against female candidates. Rather, the fundamental reason for women's under-representation is that women do not run for office. There is a substantial and persistent gender gap in political ambition; men tend to have it, and women don't.

But if we glance at the television screen, peruse the newspaper, listen to the radio, or scan the Internet, it looks like women have made remarkable political gains. Nancy Pelosi currently serves as the Minority Leader in the U.S. House of Representatives. In 2011, polls consistently placed former vice presidential candidate Sarah Palin in the top tier of potential candidates for the Republican presidential nomination. Michele Bachmann garnered serious and sustained attention as a candidate for the GOP nomination for president in 2012. And former Secretary of State (and former U.S. Senator) Hillary Clinton not only received 18 million votes when she sought the Democratic nomination for president in 2008, but also achieved the highest favorability ratings of any member of the Obama Administration. Indeed, Clinton is considered the frontrunner should she seek the Democratic nomination for president in 2016.

These high-profile faces suggest that the landscape of U.S. politics has changed and that male dominance has waned. We might be tempted to conclude that women today are just as likely as men to aspire to run for office and that, in the future, women will be eager to seize the reins of political power. Clearly, whether the United States will move toward gender parity in political leadership depends heavily on the extent to which young women envision themselves as candidates and are open to the idea of entering the electoral arena. Yet, until now, no research has provided an analysis—let alone an in-depth investigation—of these topics.

This report offers the first assessment of political ambition among the next generation of potential candidates. Our findings are based on the results of a survey we conducted through GfK Custom Research LLC (formerly *Knowledge Networks*) from September 27–October 16, 2012. We surveyed a national random sample of 1,020 male and 1,097 female college students (ages 18–25), which makes for an ideal snapshot of future candidates because the vast majority of office-holders, especially at the federal level, hold a college degree.

* * *

The Persistent Gender Gap in Political Ambition

Put simply, our research reveals that young women and men are not equally politically ambitious. When we asked our sample of more than 2,100 college students whether they ever thought that, someday, when they were older, they might want to run for political office, nearly half the respondents (47 percent) stated that the idea of running for an elective position had at least "crossed their mind." The data, however, highlight a significant gender gap: men were twice as likely as women to have thought about running for office "many times," whereas women were 20 percentage points more likely than men never to have considered it.

When we turn to the question of college students' future plans to run for office, the prospects for women's full inclusion in electoral politics are just as bleak. Men were twice as likely as women to report that they "definitely" plan to run for office at some point in the future (14 percent of men, compared to 7 percent of women). Women, on the other hand, were more than 50 percent more likely than men to assert that they would never run (36 percent of women, compared to 23 percent of men, articulated "absolutely no interest" in a future candidacy).

To put these gender gaps in perspective, we can compare them to those we previously uncovered among adults in the "candidate eligibility pool." In 2001 and 2011, we surveyed thousands of male and female "potential candidates"—lawyers, business leaders, educators, and political activists, all of whom were well-situated to pursue a political candidacy. We found that women were less likely than men ever to have considered running for office; and even when they had considered a candidacy, women were less likely than men actually to seek an elected position.

* * * The 2001 and 2011 data show identical gender gaps: men were 16 percentage points more likely than women ever to have considered running for office at both points in time. Notably, these gender gaps persisted across political party, income level, age, race, profession, and region. Most striking, however, is * * * the gender gap in ambition among college students today. Our survey results make clear that gender differences are well in place before women and men enter the professions from which most candidates emerge. Moreover, the gender gap in ambition is as large among the next generation of potential candidates as it is among adult samples of the candidate eligibility pool.

* * *

Where Do We Go from Here?

* * *

In analyzing and summarizing the report's key findings, we emphasize several points:

• We uncovered a substantial gender gap in political ambition among college students. Women were less likely than men ever to have considered running for office, to express interest in a candidacy at some point in the future, and to consider elective office a desirable profession.

• The size of the gender gap in political ambition among college students is comparable to the size of the gap we previously uncovered in studies of "potential candidates"—lawyers, business leaders, educators, and political activists. Our data suggest, therefore, that the gender gap in ambition is already well in place among college students.

- Family, school, peers, and media habits work in concert to trigger and sustain young men's political interest and ambition. Young women, on the other hand, are less exposed to environments that would push them to consider running for office later in life. Further, women are less likely than men to receive encouragement to run for office and are more likely to doubt their political qualifications.

The findings from our study suggest that the gender gap in political ambition, as well as the consequences for women's numeric representation, will likely persist into the foreseeable future. But this is not because women have a lesser sense of civic duty or different aspirations for the future than do men. In fact, * * * women and men reported very similar life goals; they were equally likely to want children, earn a lot of money, and achieve career success. The main difference is that women were more likely than men to aspire to volunteer to improve their communities.

Yet despite their similar life goals, women and men reported very different views when asked about the most effective way to bring about societal change. Female respondents were 50 percent more likely than male respondents to say that working for a charity is the best way to bring about change. Men, on the other hand, were nearly twice as likely as women to see running for elective office as the best way to bring about change. Women and men both aspire to work to improve the world around them. But women are much less likely than men to see political leadership as a means to that end. Our findings, in essence, highlight the importance of deepening our understanding of the manner in which young women and men in contemporary society are still socialized about politics, the acquisition of political power, and the characteristics that qualify individuals to seek it.

At a practical level, though, our findings offer some direction for those interested in increasing the number of young women aspiring to seek and hold elective office.

- First, the data reveal that, although young women are less likely than young men ever to have considered running for office, they are just as likely as men to respond positively to encouragement to run. Early parental support for a political career, therefore, is a vital ingredient for closing the gender gap in political ambition. Yet parents are not equally likely to encourage their college sons and daughters to consider running for office later in life. Because mothers and fathers are just as likely to speak to their daughters as they are their sons about politics, though, urging parents to expand their political discussions to include careers in politics could close the gender gap.
- Second, a substantial barrier to thinking about a political career for many female college students is less exposure to organized sports and the

competitive spirit they foster and/or reinforce. Encouraging young women to play sports from an early age might generate a greater sense of competition and, ultimately, political ambition among young women.

- Finally, organizational efforts to engage young women politically can only help close the gender gap in political ambition. Because female college students are less likely than men to take political science classes, discuss politics with their friends, and seek out political information through the media, there are substantial opportunities for interventions by women's organizations—on college campuses and nationally—to make a difference. Exposing young women to female candidates and elected officials and providing examples of how pursuing electoral office can bring about societal change cannot be underestimated in closing the gap. These activities can also go a long way in combating women's tendency to self-assess as unqualified to run for office.

This report makes clear that we still have a long way to go before women and men express equal interest in and comfort with the idea of running for office. But our results suggest that focusing on the premier agents of political socialization—family, peers, school, and media—and being attentive to the manner in which they facilitate men's interest in a future candidacy, but detract from women's, can help narrow the gender gap in political ambition. Certainly, these are daunting challenges and involve complex change, but concerns about democratic legitimacy and political accountability necessitate that we continue to examine and work to ameliorate gender disparities in political ambition.

Discussion Questions

1. Lawless and Fox identify five potential factors to explain the gender gap in political ambition. Which of them would you consider to be the most powerful influence? Can you think of other possible factors?

2. The authors identify boosting parental encouragement, increasing young girls' involvement in sports, and enhanced activities by organizations as key to reducing the gender gap in running for office. How effective do you think these strategies would be? Are there other strategies you would suggest?

Debating the Issues: Electoral Reform—Improving Integrity or Suppressing Votes?

Recent national elections have raised concerns about the voting system and the standards for administering elections in the United States. Charges of impropriety in voting procedures and vote counting, as well as complaints that certain voting technologies were systematically likely to produce more voter error or not accurately record voter choices, were legion. Massive voter mobilization campaigns on both the political left and right registered millions of new voters. Huge sums were poured into campaign advertising, further stoking the interest of these newly registered voters and the public in general. In such a charged political environment, concerns about the integrity of the voting process have taken on a particular urgency. These issues reached a boiling point in 2020 due to the changes in voting regulations that states implemented because of the COVID-19 pandemic and President Donald Trump's charges that he had been denied re-election due to electoral fraud. Numerous states subsequently considered or made changes to their election and voting regulations in 2021 and 2022. The debate over voting rules and election administration in Georgia received a particularly high degree of national attention. In part, this attention was due to the crucial role that the state played in the outcome of the 2020 presidential election and in flipping control of the U.S. Senate to the Democratic Party. Although this debate focuses on the situation in Georgia, similar arguments were being made elsewhere around the nation. To supporters, Georgia's election reforms were revising procedures designed for the pandemic emergency of 2020 or returning to pre-2020 procedures to ensure election integrity; providing more consistency in election administration within a particular state; and overall expanding voter access compared to the recent past. To opponents, the election revisions were being designed to make it harder to vote for constituencies that leaned toward the Democratic Party, especially for people of color, and to add more partisanship to the counting of votes after the election. Major League Baseball moved its 2021 summer All-Star Game out of Atlanta in protest of the law.

The authors in this debate present different perspectives on the Georgia battle. While arguing that some of the most extreme statements about the law were hyperbolic (President Joe Biden compared it to segregationist Jim Crow laws), Derek Thompson believes that the law makes it more difficult and complicated to vote. This complication is especially acute, he argues, for absentee votes, which exploded in number in 2020 when people were hesitant to vote in person. Thompson also worries about changes to the leadership of the State Election Board, which verifies election outcomes. Jonah Goldberg faults politicians and activists on both sides for what he terms the "debacle" in Georgia. They could, he states, focus on good public policy and election rules that would inspire public confidence. Instead, Goldberg charges, neither side can let go of its charges of suppression and fraud because these charges energize the party faithful. Ilya Shapiro presents the legislation as expanding voter access and ensuring consistent application of voting procedures across the state. He also argues that with the Georgia law, voter access in Georgia would exceed that of many heavily Democratic-voting states.

51

"The Truth about Georgia's Voter Law"

DEREK THOMPSON

What can we honestly say about the new Georgia voting-rights law? The legislation is based on a craven conspiracy theory about 2020 voter fraud. It has drawn a barrage of criticism from Democrats, including the president, that toes the line between moral indignation and unhelpful hyperbole. And it has triggered a spasm of corporate activism that seems ethical but is, the closer you look at it, scattershot.

If that paragraph feels a bit incoherent, it's because the fiasco surrounding the Georgia law is enveloped in incoherence.

It starts with the law's reason for being. After the November election, Donald Trump insisted that he lost Georgia (among other states) because of widespread voter fraud, an accusation that melted on contact with reality before it dissolved in the legal system. Still, many Republican legislators seemed to agree with the former president—or at least seemed to sense that their voters agreed with him—and directed their ire toward absentee ballots used by 1.3 million Georgians. This year, the Georgia General Assembly passed a law meant to address this harmful conspiracy theory.

Democracy is complicated, but voting should be simple. You register; you get a ballot by mail or at a polling station; you check a box and deliver the ballot; your vote is counted. While the Georgia law isn't all bad, it complicates almost every step in the voting process, especially for absentee voters.

Under the new law, registration is harder: [a]n ID rule requires absentee voters to provide the number of their driver's license or an equivalent state-issued ID. Formerly, they could just sign their name on the application. Requesting a ballot is harder too: Georgians had six months to request an absentee ballot in 2020; with the new law, they have only about three months. And delivering a ballot is harder: [t]he law slashes the number of drop boxes in several urban and suburban areas; metro Atlanta, for instance, had 94 in 2020 but will have only 23 going forward. (Conservatives argue that the law *requires* drop boxes for the first time, and Democratic counties in Georgia will likely have more drop boxes than they did in 2016. But Georgia Republicans are straightforwardly making it harder to vote absentee just months after Trump falsely accused these ballots of being the source of a voter-fraud fantasy.)

For in-person voters, the Georgia law isn't as restrictive. Most important, it expands early-voting periods. But the law does little else to reduce Georgia's infamous long queues, and it even has a strange provision that outlaws offering water to a voter within 25 feet of the line or 150 feet from the polling station. Altogether, the law makes absentee voting harder, funneling citizens toward in-person voting that, on Election Day, may be a bit more parched and a bit more painful.

The most ominous provision of the law affects the final step in the voting process: the official count. The new law removes the Georgia secretary of state as chair of the State Election Board and allows the GOP-controlled legislature to handpick his replacement. "This issue is potentially pernicious," Richard Hasen, a law and political-science professor at UC Irvine, told me. "The reason you didn't have a total meltdown in Georgia last year is because you had a heroic secretary of state and a group of election administrators behind him who were not willing to mess with the fair counting of the vote. If this law had passed, there would have been other decision makers who would have had power to mess with the vote."

I asked several experts if this provision would have made it easier for Trump to steal the state in 2020. "I don't think we have any way of knowing," Hasen said. "It's an imponderable," agreed the University of Georgia political scientist Charles S. Bullock III. "Could the GOP-selected chair throw out ballots that have already been tabulated, or turn away people from the polls? I don't know how it would play out, but it would be very difficult to do, and there would be a court case."

The uncertainty itself is a troubling thing. Across the country, Republican-controlled state legislatures are politicizing the process of voting administration in the aftermath of a close election in which the GOP loser convinced a majority of his supporters that it was stolen by Democratic fraud. That's plenty eerie.

Does any of this actually matter? Some analysts have argued that the outrage is much ado about nothing. An analysis of voter-ID laws since 2000 found that these provisions have "no negative effect on registration or turnout" overall, or for any race, gender, or age group. The *New York Times* has reported that "making voting convenient doesn't necessarily translate into more votes, research shows." This may be, in part, because voter suppression triggers voter-mobilization efforts that overcome that suppression.

Before I bring in some liberal analysis for criticism, I want to plant a flag here. I am against voting restrictions like Georgia's, no matter what research says about the past effects of similar laws. Consider this analogy: [i]magine if every week, I put on a mask and steal an item from somebody leaving the Trader Joe's by my building in Washington, D.C. (Bear with me here.) The grocery staff, recognizing its bandit problem, responds with a policy that allows my victims to grab a replacement item from the store for free. One year later, a sociologist studying the "D.C. bandit effect" finds, on net, no effect, since all my stolen bananas and frozen pizzas were replaced by the store. The *New York Times* writes it up: "[n]eighborhood theft doesn't necessarily translate into social harm, research shows." Technically accurate? Sure. But a thief is a thief, and theft is worth discouraging no matter what an econometrics paper has to say.

This is perhaps a long-winded way of making a simple point: [l]imitations on voting rights in a democracy, especially those based on a conspiracy theory, are just plain wrong.

But [D]emocrats are accusing this unethical law of graver sins than plain wrongness. They're accusing Georgia Republicans of bringing back the Jim Crow era. To bolster their case, they're misrepresenting the truth.

President Joe Biden has called the law "Jim Crow on steroids" and has falsely suggested that it mandates ending voting hours early. White House Press Secretary Jen Psaki has seemed to double down on these misleading accusations. (During the expanded early-voting period, the law requires that polling stations are open, at a minimum, from 9 a.m. to 5 p.m. Biden claimed that these minimums were actually maximums that outlawed casting a ballot after 5 p.m.) Comparisons to Jim Crow have become commonplace among liberal critics, who are drawing historical connections between the law's restrictions and America's history of violently segregating Black Americans and systematically denying their suffrage.

Political hyperbole is neither sin nor modern invention. But suggesting that the Georgia provisions are a *steroidal* version of poll taxes, literacy tests, whites-only primaries, armed sheriffs patrolling voting lines, and outright domestic terrorism is not helpful. "There's no doubt about it: [t]his new law does not make it easier to vote," Bullock said. "But I hear it being billed as Jim Crow 2.0, and it's really not anywhere near that. This law does not compare to the cataclysms of the white primary or poll taxes."

As Delaware's former senator, Biden would be on firmer ground excoriating Georgia for "Jim Crow 2.0" if he could hold up his home state as a model for voting rights. But Delaware has been a laggard on early voting, and its legislature is still trying to legalize no-excuse absentee voting, which allows any voter to request a mail-in ballot. Georgia, by contrast, permits many weeks of early voting and has allowed no-excuse absentee voting since 2005. Voting-rights activists may justifiably focus their outrage on a swing state like Georgia that, unlike Delaware, actually determines the balance of power. But "Jim Crow" rhetoric from northeastern politicians and media figures loses some bite when we consider that Georgia's voting rights have long been more accommodating than those of deep-blue states including not only Delaware, but also Connecticut, Massachusetts, New Hampshire, and New York.

Voting-rights activism, hyperbolic or not, has been effective so far. Several large companies have publicly criticized the law, including Delta Air Lines, Georgia's largest employer; Coca-Cola; and others. Major League Baseball announced that it would move its All-Star Game and draft out of Atlanta, possibly to spare its players several months of having to answer post-game questions about absentee-voter restrictions.

As a matter of punishing states for moving in the wrong direction on election law, or of deterring states from passing rules with discriminatory intent, these corporate decisions are commendable. As a broader matter of identifying and punishing bad election rules wherever they may be, they're inconsistent. Baseball's headquarters and Hall of Fame are in New York, which has "abysmal election administration," Hasen said. He added that if New York "were a southern Republican state, there would be protests and calls for businesses to boycott [the state], because it's that terrible. But it's a blue state, so you don't see that." Granted, the difference in reception may also arise from the fact that New York's shortcomings tend to flow from mere incompetence and neglect rather than a direct reaction to Trumpist conspiracy.

Extreme and inconsistent rhetoric hasn't been limited to the Democratic side of the aisle. Senator Mitch McConnell, for instance, has threatened "consequences" for companies like Delta and Coca-Cola that punish states like Georgia. This is ridiculous too. With *Citizens United v. FEC* and similar cases, conservatives fought for the rights of companies to speak with their money. Now they're objecting to the rights of businesses to speak with their business. The fundamental facts of modern capitalism haven't changed in the age of so-called woke capital: [c]ompanies responding to social-justice campaigns are just acting, as they always will, to accommodate employees and maximize long-term cash flow. Fluctuating currencies, fluctuating tax rates, fluctuating outrage cycles—these are all mere appearances in corporate consciousness. Activists have learned this lesson, and it's taught them to harness the attention spans of chief executives when they have to. Just as politicians know they can entice companies with tax subsidies to move business *into* a state, activists know they can entice companies with moral suasion to move business *out* of a state. We are staring at a novel nexus of politics and capitalism, and everybody should probably just get used to it.

This is what we've learned from the Georgia voting-rights fiasco: [c]orporations are still corporations, the White House's metaphors are overheated, and the Georgia legislation is far worse. Democrats' rhetorical embellishments pale in comparison to both the voting-fraud conspiracy theory that inspired Georgia Republicans and the needless provisions of the law itself. Lurking beneath all this confusion and incoherence is a basic partisan difference: GOP activism is about making it harder to vote; Democratic activism is about *making it harder* to make it harder to vote. If that is the choice before us, I for one know which box I'm prepared to check.

52

"The Fallout in Georgia Shows What Endless Political War Gets You"

Jonah Goldberg

The Georgia debacle is a perfect example of the rolling collective action problem of our democracy. A collective action problem, simply put, is when there is a goal that would benefit everyone—in this case, confidence in our machinery of democracy—but the incentive structure for the individual players makes it impossible to cooperate to reach the goal.

The Georgia electoral mess goes back to the 2018 Georgia governor's race—and every faction in that state has made it worse over the last three years.

Former state Rep. Stacey Abrams ran for governor against then-Secretary of State Brian Kemp. Kemp oversaw the legal, but aggressive, updating—critics say "purging"—of the voter rolls. Abrams claimed this was a racist attempt to disenfranchise Black voters.

When she lost, she refused to formally concede, claiming Kemp had won the election because of "voter suppression." The charge is almost surely false. It was a huge turnout year, including among Black voters. Even if all of Abrams' specific claims were true, most experts think it wouldn't have come close to overcoming her losing margin of 55,000 votes. But her claim became gospel among Democrats and liberal pundits.

In 2020, Georgia—run by Republicans—carried out COVID-safe electoral measures, including easier absentee and early voting. In the lead-up to the election, former President Trump repeatedly let it be known that if he lost, he would blame such measures as evidence of widespread "fraud."

He was true to his word. He convinced large numbers of Republicans and right-wing media commentators that the election was stolen. This has come to be "the big lie."

Georgia was ground zero for the big lie, in part because Trump, and the GOP generally, feel Georgia is their rightful domain, even though it has been trending "purple" for a long time. Kemp, now governor, and Secretary of State Brad Raffensperger were singled out as traitors who were in on "the steal." This buffoonery undoubtedly cost the GOP two runoff Senate races and control of the U.S. Senate.

With the pandemic fading, Georgia Republicans moved to update their election laws. And because so many Republican officials needed to get right with their voters who still believe the big lie, the Legislature toyed with some bad ideas—like actually getting rid of no-excuse absentee voting entirely—that never made it into the bill. However, they did pass a troubling measure that allows the appointed and Republican-controlled State Election Board to overrule local election officials when it deems it necessary.

Overall, though, the "Election Integrity Act of 2021" is far more modest than its detractors claim. Its rules on absentee and early voting are more generous than many Democrat-controlled states, including President Biden's home state of Delaware. It's hardly immune to criticism, but it's certainly not "Jim Crow in the 21st century," as Biden called it.

But none of this matters. First, both political parties seem to have forgotten that there was a pandemic that required reasonable changes from the norm. The Trumpists want to pretend none of that was really necessary—or even the point. They claim it was all done to steal the election. And Democrats want to pretend that those extraordinary pandemic measures were ordinary and any attempt to roll them back even a little amounts to a Republican effort to steal future elections, too.

But the real problem is the incentive structure. Democrats are eagerly pushing the Jim Crow narrative, no doubt in part because many believe it to be true, but also because it is useful for turning out their base. Republicans, meanwhile, cling to Trump's stolen election lie because he remains popular with their base. And much of the media just follows along.

This political situation is the opposite of the "bootleggers and the Baptists" incentive model at work. In the early 20th century, bootleggers supported Baptist prohibitions against selling booze on Sundays because that policy drove up demand and prices for their product. Though the two groups had divergent moral views, they had parallel pragmatic interests.

The 2020 election was hugely successful by any conventional metric. There was precious little fraud and more people voted than ever before. But Democrats can't let go of the idea that their voters, especially Black voters, are being suppressed and Republicans can't let go of the idea the election was stolen. And when either side acts on these assumptions, legislatively or simply rhetorically, it confirms the darkest suspicions of the other side and undermines faith in the machinery of democracy even more.

53

"The Voter Suppression Lie"

Ilya Shapiro

The voting wars have flared up again, though they've never really been far from the national political debate since Donald Trump was elected in 2016, or the Supreme Court decided *Shelby County v. Holder* in 2013—or really *Bush v. Gore* in 2000. This time, a massive new Georgia law, the Election Integrity Act of 2021, also known as Senate Bill 202 (or SB 202), has triggered national apoplexy, with Democrats, including President Joe Biden, declaring it the new Jim Crow. Such comparisons are insulting to those who fought for civil rights in the 1960s, incendiary to a public discourse already hampered by low institutional confidence, and at base disingenuous.

Sorting out fact from fiction is not only important for this particular law, the fallout from which has already reached Major League Baseball and some Hollywood productions, but to understand the general debate over election regulation in America.

The Georgia law limits ballot drop boxes to places they can't be tampered with (such as early voting sites), standardizes weekend voting hours, and asks people to write a driver's license or Social Security number on absentee ballot envelopes.

Jim Crow was "literacy tests" and poll taxes, having to guess how many bubbles are in a bar of soap, and battling billy clubs and police dogs on the way to the voting precinct.

The *Washington Post* gave Biden "four Pinocchios" for his claim that SB 202 was "Jim Crow in the 21st century" for limiting voting hours and otherwise "deny[ing] the right to vote to countless voters." That paper, not exactly a right-wing house organ, reported that "experts say the net effect was to expand the opportunities to vote for most Georgians, not limit them." MIT elections expert Charles Stewart III found that "it indicated an expansion of hours, especially in rural counties."

SB 202 does indeed improve voting access for most Georgians, entrenching the new opportunities to vote early and absentee (by mail and drop-off) introduced during the pandemic. For example, during a generous, at least compared to blue states such as New York and the president's own home state of Delaware, 17 days of in-person early voting, voting locations have to be open *at least* eight hours, with county officials given leeway to adjust the times to suit their constituents. Election Day voting hours are even longer. The window for requesting absentee ballots, which can be done online, is reduced to a "mere" 67 days, starting 11 weeks and closing 11 days before an election, to allow time for the ballot to be mailed out and returned.

More restrictive proposals were floated early in the drafting process, such as eliminating no-excuse absentee voting entirely—the current policy of 16 states, including such retrogrades as Connecticut and New Hampshire—and prohibiting early voting on Sundays (criticized as targeting "souls to the polls" programs at black churches). But these sorts of measures never made it into the enacted law, even if some Democrats still claim that they did.

Gabriel Sterling, a Republican election official who came to prominence for countering Trump's election disinformation last fall, explained that some provisions "were phantoms that the leadership in both the Senate and the House told their guys, 'Hey, introduce whatever you need to to cover yourself with your people.'" In other words, given the level of distrust and anger in the electorate, state legislators had to show that they were "tough on fraud" even if they knew certain things weren't going to be part of the reform package.

That said, these "phantom" provisions certainly hobbled the reception of the final law. Democrats could hardly be blamed for seeing ill intent behind the legislation if the crafting process included winks and nods to fictitious fraud claims.

Donald Trump's insistence that he lost Georgia, among other states, due to widespread and systemic fraud has led about two-thirds of Republican voters not to believe that Biden was legitimately elected. So, it's no surprise that election reform has become a priority for GOP-controlled legislatures. But "ballot integrity" isn't synonymous with "voter suppression," even if this fact was undermined by the legislature itself.

SB 202 removes Georgia Secretary of State Brad Raffensperger, the main target of Trump's ire for not "finding the votes" to flip the state, from the state election board. Nevertheless, Raffensperger issued a statement that "Democrats and national media outlets asserting that Georgia's election reform will 'restrict access' to voting are just [repeating] partisan talking points, not facts." Sterling echoed that assessment in a tweet that sums up the larger state of affairs: "[t]he claim of voter suppression has the same level of truth as the claims of voter fraud in the last election."

Still, public pressure from activists outside the state, up through the president himself, resulted in Major League Baseball's decision to move the All-Star Game out of Atlanta in retaliation. This, after Democratic state and local officials practically begged them not to do so, warning it punished minority-owned businesses and black workers in the area the most. Georgia voting-rights activist Stacey Abrams saw her own misleading criticism of the new law backfire when her pleas to MLB Commissioner Rob Manfred went ignored. Will Smith then announced he was moving the production of his forthcoming Civil War film out of Georgia.

Hyperbolic attacks on ballot integrity thus not only decrease trust in the system nationally but can have sharp consequences locally. And comparing Georgia to other states also adds crucial context that undermines the "Jim Crow" narrative.

When New Jersey recently passed a law limiting early voting to nine days, requiring only some polling locations to be open during that process, and limiting mandatory Sunday hours, there was no groundswell of social media opposition or corporate hand-wringing. Abrams even lauded the move because "our democracy is made stronger when we make it easier for the people's voices to be heard." Neither are there calls to boycott New York, which had no early voting *at all* until last fall, when new rules created nine days of in-person early voting. Or Delaware, whose new early voting legislation doesn't take effect until next year. Six states still have no provision whatsoever for in-person early voting; I dare you to find some common thread among Connecticut, Kentucky, Mississippi, Missouri, New Hampshire, and South Carolina.

And yet, after Manfred announced that he was moving baseball's midsummer classic, he didn't clean out his Manhattan office. Baseball's Hall of Fame is also in New York, which has "abysmal election administration," the progressive UC–Irvine election law scholar Richard Hasen told the *Atlantic's* Derek Thompson. Hasen added that if New York "were a southern Republican state, there would be protests and calls for businesses to boycott [the state], because it's that terrible. But it's a blue state, so you don't see that." In fall 2018, before a recent legislative change, two scholars at New York University's Brennan Center for Justice called the state's voting system the "worst in the country."

Granted, New York's shortcomings tend to flow from incompetence, neglect, and corruption rather than as a reaction to Trumpist conspiracy, let alone racism, but two wrongs don't make a right. Still, the voting rights debate remains focused on the Peach State, whose election legislation, after an exceedingly close presidential race and two Senate runoffs marred by competing charges of fraud and suppression, aims to improve voter access while strengthening ballot integrity. It's hardly "Jim Crow on steroids," as Biden told ESPN.

Attempts by progressive groups and Democratic politicians to tie SB 202 to the era of segregation and systemic racial disenfranchisement are thus remarkably dishonest. Even the bizarre attack on the provision purportedly limiting the distribution of water to voters waiting in line is all wet. Many states have similar anti-electioneering (or anti-vote-buying) rules, which, as colorfully detailed by Dan McLaughlin in *National Review,* make it illegal to send "people in National Rifle Association t-shirts and MAGA hats to hand out free Koch-brothers-financed, Federalist Society-branded pizza to voters." To again pick on the Empire State, New York explicitly prohibits giving voters "meat, drink, tobacco, refreshment or provision" unless the sustenance is worth less than a dollar *and* the person providing it isn't identified. To be perfectly clear, under the new Georgia law, poll workers can still provide water to voters, *and anyone can donate food and drink for election workers to set out for those waiting in line.*

As for voter ID, SB 202 simply adds a requirement that voters provide the number of their driver's license or (free) state identification card to apply for a ballot, the same as California, New Jersey, and Virginia, and one of those (or the last four digits of a Social Security number) when returning it. Surely, applying a numerical voter-verification requirement to absentee or mailed ballots is better than the inexact science (to say the least) of signature-matching. Colorado, now a solidly blue state that votes entirely by mail. rejected 29,000 ballots last fall (about 1 in 112) because the mailed signatures didn't match those on file. That doesn't count the 11,000 who were allowed to "cure" the issue by texting in a picture of a—*gasp*—photo ID. Illustrating the point further, the *Tampa Bay Times* just came out with an amusing article about how Florida Gov. Ron DeSantis's signature has changed over the years, apparently leading to his ballot being tossed in a 2016 primary.

Voter ID more generally is hugely popular, including among Democrats (56% in a recent *Associated Press* poll) and African Americans (69% in a recent Rasmussen poll), despite in-person voter fraud being exceedingly rare. And majorities of all racial groups—64% of whites, 59% of blacks, and 58% of other minorities—reject the claim that voter ID laws discriminate against certain voters. Indeed, many democratic countries require voter ID of some form, including Canada, France, Germany, India, Israel, Italy, and Sweden. As do most states with professional baseball teams, not to mention airlines and many of the other corporations now virtue-signaling about Georgia.

To top it off, the bipartisan 2005 Commission on Federal Election Reform, led by Jimmy Carter and James Baker, recommended voter ID as one of many common-sense reforms to promote election integrity. As the Supreme Court explained in *Crawford v. Marion County Election Board* (2008), a 6–3 decision written by the liberal Justice John Paul Stevens, such requirements are constitutional so long as the state doesn't unduly burden the ability to get an ID. And anyway, a recent National Bureau of Economic Research study found that these provisions have "no negative effect on registration or turnout," either overall or for any race, gender, or age group.

Even as it's hard to believe that a single Georgia voter will be stopped from casting a ballot, Sen. Elizabeth Warren (a Democrat from Massachusetts, another state without no-excuse absentee voting) tweeted, "The Republican who is sitting in Stacey Abrams' chair just signed a despicable voter suppression bill into law to take Georgia back to Jim Crow." Thus Warren not only furthered misinformation about SB 202 but resurrected the toxic myth that Gov. Brian Kemp stole his 2018 election from Abrams. That's an evidence-challenged allegation that Kemp's 55,000-vote margin came from more than 100,000 people being improperly removed from the rolls.

*   *   *

Of course, the reason we're seeing new election legislation now, in both red and blue states, isn't just the latest iteration in the politicization of voting, or even a reaction and counterreaction to Trump's post-election shenanigans, culminating on Jan. 6. It's that the COVID-19 pandemic forced a chaotic process of ad hoc voting changes, including an overwhelming number of mailed ballots that local officials simply didn't have the capacity to process. And not just absentee and mail voting was expanded; ballot-harvesting (collecting ballots from unrelated voters) and the automatic mailing of ballots to all registered voters (at their last known address) led to an electoral process unique in our history.

Then, local officials and state courts changed rules on the fly, including those regarding the validity of ballots arriving after Election Day or without confirmable voter identification. This free-for-all was a recipe not just for chaos in election administration but for a further lessening of political trust and increase in perceptions of both fraud and suppression at a time when that trust was already in short supply. And so, states moved to rein in some of the looseness, to codify the regulations that would apply to absentee, early, and mailed ballots under normal circumstances.

Different states can rightly take different approaches to achieving the common goal of making it easy to vote but hard to cheat, just as they take differing approaches to administering other government programs. There's no Platonic number of early voting days and hours, for example, so I'm not really criticizing Delaware, New Jersey, or New York for coming late and cautiously to that game. Where you draw the various lines is a technocratic policy debate that can go differently in urban versus rural areas and also depends on other aspects of the overall election law. But Democratic criticism of Iowa for reducing early voting from 29 to 20 days is disingenuous when the District of Columbia, Delaware, Hawaii, Maryland, New York, and 16 other states all have shorter in-person voting periods. And slamming the Hawkeye State for closing poll locations at 8 p.m. (after opening at 7 a.m.) is rich given that California, D.C., Delaware, Massachusetts, and Rhode Island have the exact same hours.

Even from a progressive perspective, the outrage is much ado about nothing because, as the *New York Times* has reported, "making voting convenient doesn't necessarily translate into more votes." And convenience isn't the only criterion for voting rules. The ultimate goal is to preserve our orderly system of democratic decision-making and therefore the legitimacy of the governance it produces.

Democracy is complicated, but voting should be simple. And it largely is, at least when there's no pandemic—so simple that majorities of all races (59% of whites, 56% of blacks, and 63% of other minorities) say it's more important to prevent fraud than to make it easier to vote.

This isn't rocket science. You register; you get a ballot; you mark a box; you deliver the ballot; your vote is counted. But lurking behind that ideal is the need to maintain accurate voter rolls, have enough polling places so voters don't wait an unreasonable amount of time, and ensure speed and transparency in vote tabulation. The 2020 election failed on all those counts in many states, without anything nefarious necessarily going on.

Calling laws that attempt to create better electoral mechanisms post-pandemic "Jim Crow 2.0" is just as dangerous to citizens' confidence in their political institutions as spreading myths about illegitimate voting. "If American democracy is in peril," my Cato Institute colleague Walter Olson concluded earlier this month, "laws of this sort are not very good evidence for that proposition." Indeed, suggesting that the laws being passed in 2021 are updated versions of poll taxes, literacy tests, fire hoses, night riders, and white-only primaries isn't helpful.

Discussion Questions

1. Would you approve of a proposal that all voters be required to show photo identification at polling places? Do you think it would decrease turnout? If so, is this a reasonable cost to pay to ensure that people cannot vote using another person's name or cannot vote without proving that they live in the voting district? Or should turnout be prioritized and the risk that some people will vote inappropriately be accepted as a reasonable risk?

2. Consider the possibility of early voting. Is there a right number of days? Of available hours? Voting locations? What standards would you recommend to evaluate whether a registration or voting procedure like early voting is appropriate?

3. On which aspects of the Georgia law do Shapiro and Thompson most disagree? Who do you think has the better argument? Why?

4. Having read the accounts by Shapiro and Thompson, how would you assess Goldberg's argument that partisans on both sides are using debates over election reform to promote their own political interests rather than promoting public confidence in election processes?

CHAPTER 11

Political Parties

54

"The Decline of Collective Responsibility in American Politics"

MORRIS P. FIORINA

Political scientists have long studied the changing status of American political parties. Morris P. Fiorina suggests that political parties provide many benefits for American democracy, in particular by clarifying policy alternatives and letting citizens know whom to hold accountable when they are dissatisfied with government performance. Writing in the early 1980s, he sees decline in all the key areas of political-party activity: in the electorate, in government, and in party organizations. He argues that the decline eliminates the motivation for elected members of the parties to define broad policy objectives, leading to diminished political participation and a rise in alienation. Policies are aimed at serving the narrow interests of the various single-issue groups that dominate politics rather than the broad constituencies represented by parties. Without strong political parties to provide electoral accountability, American politics has suffered a "decline in collective responsibility" in Fiorina's view. In the effort to reform the often-corrupt political parties of the late 1800s—commonly referred to as "machines" led by "bosses"— Fiorina asks us to consider whether Americans have overly weakened the best institutional device available to hold elected officials accountable at the ballot box.

Though the Founding Fathers believed in the necessity of establishing a genuinely national government, they took great pains to design one that could not lightly do things *to* its citizens; what government might do *for* its citizens was to be limited to the functions of what we know now as the "watchman state."

* * *

Given the historical record faced by the Founders, their emphasis on constraining government is understandable. But we face a later historical record, one that shows two hundred years of increasing demands for government to act positively. Moreover, developments unforeseen by the Founders increasingly raise the likelihood that the uncoordinated actions of individuals and groups will inflict serious damage on the nation as a whole. The by-products of the industrial and technological revolutions impose physical risks not only on us, but on future generations as well. Resource shortages and international cartels raise the spectre of economic ruin. And the simple proliferation of special interests with their intense, particularistic demands threatens to render us politically incapable of taking actions that might either advance the state of society or prevent foreseeable deteriorations in that state. None of this is to suggest that we should forget about what government can do *to* us—the contemporary concern with the proper scope and methods of government intervention in the social and economic orders is long overdue. But the modern age demands as well that we worry about our ability to make government work *for* us. The problem is that we are gradually losing that ability, and a principal reason for this loss is the steady erosion of *responsibility* in American politics.

* * *

Unfortunately, the importance of responsibility in a democracy is matched by the difficulty of attaining it. In an autocracy, individual responsibility suffices; the location of power in a single individual locates responsibility in that individual as well. But individual responsibility is insufficient whenever more than one person shares governmental authority. We can hold a particular congressman individually responsible for a personal transgression such as bribe-taking. We can even hold a president individually responsible for military moves where he presents Congress and the citizenry with a *fait accompli*. But on most national issues individual responsibility is difficult to assess. If one were to go to Washington, randomly accost a Democratic congressman, and berate him about a 20 percent rate of inflation, imagine the response. More than likely it would run, "Don't blame me. If 'they' had done what I've advocated for *x* years, things would be fine today."

* * *

American institutional structure makes this kind of game-playing all too easy. In order to overcome it we must lay the credit or blame for national conditions on all those who had any hand in bringing them about: some form of *collective responsibility* is essential.

The only way collective responsibility has ever existed, and can exist given our institutions, is through the agency of the political party; in American politics, responsibility requires cohesive parties. This is an old claim to be sure, but its age does not detract from its present relevance. In fact, the continuing decline in public esteem for the parties and continuing efforts to "reform" them out of the political process suggest that old arguments for party responsibility have not been made often enough or, at least, convincingly enough, so I will make these arguments once again in this essay.

A strong political party can generate collective responsibility by creating incentive for leaders, followers, and popular supporters to think and act in collective terms. First, by providing party leaders with the capability (e.g., control of institutional patronage, nominations, and so on) to discipline party members, genuine leadership becomes possible. Legislative output is less likely to be a least common denominator—a residue of myriad conflicting proposals—and more likely to consist of a program actually intended to solve a problem or move the nation in a particular direction. Second, the subordination of individual officeholders to the party lessens their ability to separate themselves from party actions. Like it or not, their performance becomes identified with the performance of the collectivity to which they belong. Third, with individual candidate variation greatly reduced, voters have less incentive to support individuals and more incentive to support or oppose the party as a whole. And fourth, the circle closes as party-line voting in the electorate provides party leaders with the incentive to propose policies that will earn the support of a national majority, and party backbenchers* with the personal incentive to cooperate with leaders in the attempt to compile a good record for the party as a whole.

In the American context, strong parties have traditionally clarified politics in two ways. First, they allow citizens to assess responsibility easily, at least when the government is unified, which it more often was in earlier eras when party meant more than it does today. Citizens need only evaluate the social, economic, and international conditions they observe and make a simple decision for or against change. They do not need to decide whether the energy, inflation, urban, and defense policies advocated by their congressman would be superior to those advocated by [the president]—were any of them to be enacted!

The second way in which strong parties clarify American politics follows from the first. When citizens assess responsibility on the party as a whole, party members have personal incentives to see the party evaluated favorably. They have little to gain from gutting their president's program one day and attacking him for lack of leadership the next, since they share in the president's fate when voters do not differentiate within the party. Put simply, party responsibility provides party members with a personal stake in their collective performance.

Admittedly, party responsibility is a blunt instrument. The objection immediately arises that party responsibility condemns junior Democratic

---

*Back-benchers are junior members of the British Parliament, who sit in the rear benches of the House of Commons. Here, the term refers to junior members of political parties [*Editors*].

representatives to suffer electorally for an inflation they could do little to affect. An unhappy situation, true, but unless we accept it, Congress as a whole escapes electoral retribution for an inflation they *could* have done something to affect. Responsibility requires acceptance of both conditions. The choice is between a blunt instrument or none at all.

* * *

In earlier times, when citizens voted for the party, not the person, parties had incentives to nominate good candidates, because poor ones could have harmful fallout on the ticket as a whole. In particular, the existence of presidential coattails (positive and negative) provided an inducement to avoid the nomination of narrowly based candidates, no matter how committed their supporters. And, once in office, the existence of party voting in the electorate provided party members with the incentive to compile a good *party* record. In particular, the tendency of national midterm elections to serve as referenda on the performance of the president provided a clear inducement for congressmen to do what they could to see that their president was perceived as a solid performer. By stimulating electoral phenomena such as coattail effects and mid-term referenda, party transformed some degree of personal ambition into concern with collective performance.

* * *

The Continuing Decline of Party in the United States

Party Organizations

In the United States, party organization has traditionally meant state and local party organization. The national party generally has been a loose confederacy of subnational units that swings into action for a brief period every four years. This characterization remains true today, despite the somewhat greater influence and augmented functions of the national organizations. Though such things are difficult to measure precisely, there is general agreement that the formal party organizations have undergone a secular decline since their peak at the end of the nineteenth century. The prototype of the old-style organization was the urban machine, a form approximated today only in Chicago.

* * *

[*Fiorina discusses the reforms of the late nineteenth and early twentieth century.*] In the 1970s two series of reforms further weakened the influence of organized parties in American national politics. The first was a series of legal changes deliberately intended to lessen organized party influence in the presidential nominating process. In the Democratic party, "New Politics" activists captured the national party apparatus and imposed a series of rules changes designed to "open up" the politics of presidential nominations. The Republican party—long more amateur and open than the Democratic party—adopted weaker versions of the Democratic rules changes. In addition, modifications of state electoral laws to conform to the Democratic rules changes (enforced by the federal courts) stimulated Republican rules changes as well.

* * *

A second series of 1970s reforms lessened the role of formal party organizations in the conduct of political campaigns. These are financing regulations growing out of the Federal Election Campaign Act of 1971 as amended in 1974 and 1976. In this case the reforms were aimed at cleaning up corruption in the financing of campaigns; their effects on the parties were a by-product, though many individuals accurately predicted its nature. Serious presidential candidates are now publicly financed. Though the law permits the national party to spend two cents per eligible voter on behalf of the nominee, it also obliges the candidate to set up a finance committee separate from the national party. Between this legally mandated separation and fear of violating spending limits or accounting regulations, for example, the law has the effect of encouraging the candidate to keep his party at arm's length.

* * *

The ultimate results of such reforms are easy to predict. A lesser party role in the nominating and financing of candidates encourages candidates to organize and conduct independent campaigns, which further weakens the role of parties. * * * If parties do not grant nominations, fund their choices, and work for them, why should those choices feel any commitment to their party?

Party in the Electorate

In the citizenry at large, party takes the form of a psychological attachment. The typical American traditionally has been likely to identify with one or the other of the two major parties. Such identifications are transmitted across generations to some degree, and within the individual they tend to be fairly stable. But there is mounting evidence that the basis of identification lies in the individual's experiences (direct and vicarious, through family and social groups) with the parties in the past. Our current party system, of course, is based on the dislocations of the Depression period and the New Deal attempts to alleviate them. Though only a small proportion of those who experienced the Depression directly are active voters today, the general outlines of citizen party identifications much resemble those established at that time.

Again, there is reason to believe that the extent of citizen attachments to parties has undergone a long-term decline from a nineteenth-century high. And again, the New Deal appears to have been a period during which the decline was arrested, even temporarily reversed. But again, the decline of party has reasserted itself in the 1970s.

* * *

As the 1960s wore on, the heretofore stable distribution of citizen party identifications began to change in the general direction of weakened attachments to the parties. Between 1960 and 1976, independents, broadly defined, increased from less than a quarter to more than a third of the voting-age population. Strong identifiers declined from slightly more than a third to about a quarter of the population.

* * *

Indisputably, party in the electorate has declined in recent years. Why? To some extent the electoral decline results from the organizational decline. Few party organizations any longer have the tangible incentives to turn out the faithful and assure their loyalty. Candidates run independent campaigns and deemphasize their partisan ties whenever they see any short-term electoral gain in doing so. If party is increasingly less important in the nomination and election of candidates, it is not surprising that such diminished importance is reflected in the attitudes and behavior of the voter.

Certain long-term sociological and technological trends also appear to work against party in the electorate. The population is younger, and younger citizens traditionally are less attached to the parties than their elders. The population is more highly educated; fewer voters need some means of simplifying the choices they face in the political arena, and party, of course, has been the principal means of simplification. And the media revolution has vastly expanded the amount of information easily available to the citizenry. Candidates would have little incentive to operate campaigns independent of the parties if there were no means to apprise the citizenry of their independence. The media provide the means.

Finally, our present party system is an old one. For increasing numbers of citizens, party attachments based on the Great Depression seem lacking in relevance to the problems of the late twentieth century. Beginning with the racial issue in the 1960s, proceeding to the social issue of the 1970s, and to the energy, environment, and inflation issues of today, the parties have been rent by internal dissension. Sometimes they failed to take stands, at other times they took the wrong ones from the standpoint of the rank and file, and at most times they have failed to solve the new problems in any genuine sense. Since 1965 the parties have done little or nothing to earn the loyalties of modern Americans.

Party in Government

If the organizational capabilities of the parties have weakened, and their psychological ties to the voters have loosened, one would expect predictable consequences for the party in government. In particular, one would expect to see an increasing degree of split party control within and across the levels of American government. The evidence on this point is overwhelming.

* * *

The increased fragmentation of the party in government makes it more difficult for government officeholders to work together than in times past (not that it has ever been terribly easy). Voters meanwhile have a more difficult time attributing responsibility for government performance, and this only further fragments party control. The result is lessened collective responsibility in the system.

What has taken up the slack left by the weakening of the traditional [party] determinants of congressional voting? It appears that a variety of personal and local influences now play a major role in citizen evaluations of their representatives. Along with the expansion of the federal presence in American life, the traditional role of the congressman as an all-purpose ombudsman has greatly expanded. Tens of millions of citizens now are directly affected by federal decisions. Myriad programs provide opportunities to profit from government largesse, and myriad regulations impose costs and/or constraints on citizen activities. And, whether seeking to gain profit or avoid costs, citizens seek the aid of their congressmen. When a court imposes a desegregation plan on an urban school board, the congressional offices immediately are contacted for aid in safeguarding existing sources of funding and in determining eligibility for new ones. When a major employer announces plans to quit an area, the congressional offices immediately are contacted to explore possibilities for using federal programs to persuade the employer to reconsider. Contractors appreciate a good congressional word with DOD [Department of Defense] procurement officers. Local artistic groups cannot survive without NEA [National Endowment for the Arts] funding. And, of course, there are the major individual programs such as social security and veterans' benefits that create a steady demand for congressional information and aid services. Such activities are nonpartisan, nonideological, and, most important, noncontroversial. Moreover, the contribution of the congressman in the realm of district service appears considerably greater than the impact of his or her single vote on major national issues. Constituents respond rationally to this modern state of affairs by weighing nonprogrammatic constituency service heavily when casting their congressional votes. And this emphasis on the part of constituents provides the means for incumbents to solidify their hold on the office. Even if elected by a narrow margin, diligent service activities enable a congressman to neutralize or even convert a portion of those who would otherwise oppose him on policy or ideological grounds. Emphasis on local, nonpartisan factors in congressional voting enables the modern congressman to withstand national swings, whereas yesteryear's uninsulated congressmen were more dependent on preventing the occurrence of the swings.

* * *

[*The result is the insulation of the modern congressional member from national forces altogether.*] The withering away of the party organizations and the weakening of party in the electorate have begun to show up as disarray in the party in government. As the electoral fates of congressmen and the president have diverged, their incentives to cooperate have diverged as well. Congressmen have little personal incentive to bear any risk [on] their president's behalf, since they no longer expect to gain much from his successes or suffer much from his failures. Only those who personally agree with the president's program and/or those who find that program well suited for their particular district support the president. And there are not enough of these to construct the coalitions necessary for action on the major issues now facing the country. By holding only the president responsible for national conditions, the electorate enables officialdom as a whole to escape responsibility. This situation lies at the root of many of the problems that now plague American public life.

Some Consequences of the Decline of Collective Responsibility

The weakening of party has contributed directly to the severity of several of the important problems the nation faces. For some of these, such as the government's inability to deal with inflation and energy, the connections are obvious. But for other problems, such as the growing importance of single-issue politics and the growing alienation of the American citizenry, the connections are more subtle.

Immobilism

As the electoral interdependence of the party in government declines, its ability to act also declines. If responsibility can be shifted to another level or to another officeholder, there is less incentive to stick one's neck out in an attempt to solve a given problem. Leadership becomes more difficult, the ever-present bias toward the short-term solution becomes more pronounced, and the possibility of solving any given problem lessens.

* * * Political inability to take actions that entail short-run costs ordinarily will result in much higher costs in the long run—we cannot continually depend on the technological fix. So the present American immobilism cannot be dismissed lightly. The sad thing is that the American people

appear to understand the depth of our present problems and, at least in principle, appear prepared to sacrifice in furtherance of the long-run good. But they will not have an opportunity to choose between two or more such long-term plans. Although both parties promise tough, equitable policies, in the present state of our politics, neither can deliver.

Single-Issue Politics

In recent years both political analysts and politicians have decried the increased importance of single-issue groups in American politics. Some in fact would claim that the present immobilism in our politics owes more to the rise of single-issue groups than to the decline of party. A little thought, however, should reveal that the two trends are connected. Is single-issue politics a recent phenomenon? The contention is doubtful; such groups have always been active participants in American politics. The gun lobby already was a classic example at the time of President Kennedy's assassination. And however impressive the antiabortionists appear today, remember the temperance movement, which succeeded in getting its constitutional amendment. American history contains numerous forerunners of today's groups, from anti-Masons to abolitionists to the Klan—singularity of purpose is by no means a modern phenomenon. Why, then, do we hear all the contemporary hoopla about single-issue groups? Probably because politicians fear them now more than before and thus allow them to play a larger role in our politics. Why should this be so? Simply because the parties are too weak to protect their members and thus to contain single-issue politics.

In earlier times single-issue groups were under greater pressures to reach accommodations with the parties. After all, the parties nominated candidates, financed candidates, worked for candidates, and, perhaps most important, party voting protected candidates. When a contemporary single-issue group threatens to "get" an officeholder, the threat must be taken seriously.

* * *

Not only did the party organization have greater ability to resist single-issue pressures at the electoral level, but the party in government had greater ability to control the agenda, and thereby contain single-issue pressures at the policy-making level. Today we seem condemned to go through an annual agony over federal abortion funding. There is little doubt that politicians on both sides would prefer to reach some reasonable compromise at the committee level and settle the issue. But in today's decentralized Congress there is no way to put the lid on. In contrast, historians tell us that in the late nineteenth century a large portion of the Republican constituency was far less interested in the tariff and other questions of national economic development than in whether German immigrants should be permitted to teach their native language in their local schools, and whether Catholics and "liturgical Protestants" should be permitted to consume alcohol. Interestingly, however, the national agenda of the period is devoid of such issues. And when they do show up on the state level, the exceptions prove the rule; they produce party splits and striking defeats for the party that allowed them to surface.

In sum, a strong party that is held accountable for the government of a nation-state has both the ability and the incentive to contain particularistic pressures. It controls nominations, elections, and the agenda, and it collectively realizes that small minorities are small minorities no matter how intense they are. But as the parties decline they lose control over nominations and campaigns, they lose the loyalty of the voters, and they lose control of the agenda. Party officeholders cease to be held collectively accountable for party performance, but they become individually exposed to the political pressure of myriad interest groups. The decline of party permits interest groups to wield greater influence, their success encourages the formation of still more interest groups, politics becomes increasingly fragmented, and collective responsibility becomes still more elusive.

Popular Alienation from Government

For at least a decade political analysts have pondered the significance of survey data indicative of a steady increase in the alienation of the American public from the political process. * * * The American public is in a nasty mood, a cynical, distrusting, and resentful mood. The question is, Why?

If the same national problems not only persist but worsen while ever-greater amounts of revenue are directed at them, why shouldn't the typical citizen conclude that most of the money must be wasted by incompetent officials? If narrowly based interest groups increasingly affect our politics, why shouldn't citizens increasingly conclude that the interests run the government? For fifteen years the citizenry has listened to a steady stream of promises but has seen very little in the way of follow-through. An increasing proportion of the electorate does not believe that elections make a difference, a fact that largely explains the much-discussed post-1960 decline in voting turnout.

Continued public disillusionment with the political process poses several real dangers. For one thing, disillusionment begets further disillusionment. Leadership becomes more difficult if citizens do not trust their leaders and will not give them the benefit of a doubt. Policy failure becomes more likely if citizens expect the policy to fail. Waste increases and government competence decreases as citizens' disrespect for politics encourages a lesser breed of person to make careers in government. And "government by a few big interests" becomes more than a cliché if citizens increasingly decide the cliché is true and cease participating for that reason.

Finally, there is the real danger that continued disappointment with particular government officials ultimately metamorphoses into disillusionment with government per se. Increasing numbers of citizens believe that government is not simply overextended but perhaps incapable of any further bettering of the world. Yes, government is overextended, inefficiency is pervasive, and ineffectiveness is all too common. But government is one of the few instruments of collective action we have, and even those committed to selective pruning of government programs cannot blithely allow the concept of an activist government to fall into disrepute.

Of late, however, some political commentators have begun to wonder whether contemporary thought places sufficient emphasis on government *for* the people. In stressing participation have we lost sight of *accountability*? Surely, we should be as concerned with what government produces as with how many participate. What good is participation if the citizenry is unable to determine who merits their support?

Participation and responsibility are not logically incompatible, but there is a degree of tension between the two, and the quest for either may be carried to extremes. Participation maximizers find themselves involved with quotas and virtual representation schemes, while responsibility maximizers can find themselves with a closed shop under boss rule. Moreover, both qualities can weaken the democracy they supposedly underpin. Unfettered participation produces Hyde Amendments* and immobilism. Responsible parties can use agenda power to thwart democratic decision— for more than a century the Democratic party used what power it had to suppress the racial issue. Neither participation nor responsibility should be pursued at the expense of all other values, but that is what has happened with participation over the course of the past two decades, and we now reap the consequences in our politics.

DISCUSSION QUESTIONS

1. How do political parties provide "collective responsibility" and improve the quality of democracy? Do you believe the complaints raised by Fiorina decades ago remain persuasive?

2. Are strong parties in the interest of individual politicians? What might be some reasons that members of Congress would agree to strong parties? What would make them distance themselves from their party's leadership?

3. Donald Trump won the Republican Party nomination in 2016 despite opposition from many party leaders and elected officials. Is his electoral success in 2016 a confirmation of Fiorina's concerns or a rejection of them?

---

*The Hyde Amendment, passed in 1976 (three years after *Roe v. Wade*), prohibited using Medicaid funds for abortion [Editors].

55

"A Theory of Political Parties: Groups, Policy Demands, and Nominations in American Politics"

KATHLEEN BAWN, MARTIN COHEN, DAVID KAROL,
SETH MASKET, HANS NOEL, AND JOHN ZALLER

What is the connection between political parties and interest groups? In the previous article, Morris P. Fiorina presented the narrow interests of interest groups as being particularly influential because of the weakness of political parties. In this article, political scientist Kathleen Bawn and her coauthors argue that rather than seeing the rising or falling influence of interest groups and political parties as having an inverse relationship, the connections between parties and groups should be seen as tight and fundamental. They suggest we should view interest groups and activists as the key actors in political parties rather than the election-oriented officeholders and candidates that other theories emphasize and who, presumably, must take public opinion into account when governing. Coalitions of groups develop agendas and then filter candidates for party nominations. Controlling nominations is key to their eventual policy success. Dominated by the preferences of interest groups and activists, parties are responsive to the preferences of these groups and are less responsive to voters. Indeed, parties frequently rely on voter inattention to politics to advance policies preferred by activists and interest groups.

Scholars routinely cite E.E. Schattschneider's remark that "modern democracy is unthinkable save in terms of parties." But what is a party?

Contemporary scholarship views a party as a team of politicians whose paramount goal is to win electoral office. These teams make promises about what they will do if elected, standing for re-election based on their records of implementing their programs.

It is easy to see how such parties might serve democracy. Voters can give more effective direction to government by supporting a team's program rather than an individual's. By holding entire parties rather than individual politicians accountable for what government does, voters create an incentive for responsible governance that might not otherwise exist.

We contest the view of party that supports this rosy assessment. We argue that parties in the United States are best understood as coalitions of interest groups and activists seeking to capture and use government for their particular goals, which range from material self-interest to high-minded idealism. The coalition of policy-demanding groups develops an agenda of mutually acceptable policies, insists on the nomination of candidates with a demonstrated commitment to its program, and works to elect these candidates to office. In this group-centric view of parties, candidates will, if the coalition has selected them well, have as their paramount goal the advancement of the party program.

Most studies of parties assume that voters can judge which party offers more of what they want, implying that parties must construct programs with a keen eye to voter satisfaction. We regard this assumption as unrealistic. In its place we theorize an "electoral blind spot" within which voters are unable to reliably ascertain policy positions or evaluate party performance. Recognizing the limits of voter acuity, our group-centric parties exploit the complexities of politics to disguise the actions they take on behalf of party agendas.

In our account, parties are no great friends of popular sovereignty. Electoral competition does constrain group-centric parties to be somewhat responsive to citizen preferences, but they cede as little policy to voters as possible. Parties mainly push their own agendas and aim to get voters to go along.

Despite basic differences between our theory and the standard view of parties, critical tests are hard to identify. Some telling evidence exists, but party nominations, central to our theory, are hard to study and poorly documented. Measuring party responsiveness to groups or to voters is difficult. Hence, we content ourselves here with developing our theory and demonstrating its plausibility.

*   *   *

Legislative-Centered Theories of Party

Textbooks on political parties in the mid-twentieth century assigned a central role to interest groups, then considered the "raw material of politics." Five decades later, the view is radically different. The discipline's most developed theories of party feature office holders, especially legislators, as the dominant actors.

This legislative focus emerged as studies of party outside the legislature reported weakening and decline. Party identification in the electorate began to decrease in the 1960s and remained below historical levels through the 1980s. The decline of traditional urban machines and other developments brought loss of party control over legislative nominations. The McGovern-Fraser reforms of the 1970s opened presidential nominations to mass participation in state primaries and caucuses; as party leaders lost their official role, many scholars concluded that parties had little impact on nominations.

During roughly this same time period, observers of Congress began to note increasing influence of majority party leadership, and much stronger evidence of partisan voting than had previously been recognized. Scholars seeking to understand how party mattered in Congress quite naturally—given the consensus about the weakness of parties in other domains—focused on forces internal to Congress itself.

*   *   *

The question then becomes, how does a party keep its coalition together? According to Gary Cox and Mathew McCubbins, party leaders control the legislative agenda, suppressing proposals that might split the party and promoting the party program. The policies thus enacted create a "brand name," valuable for winning elections.

* * * The desire of incumbent office-holders for re-election animates parties, and forms the basis of theories that measure their impact.

*   *   *

Recent empirical scholarship has documented anomalies for politician-centered theories. The reputations created by legislative parties have been shown to hurt rather than help the re-election chances of members of Congress. A study of presidential nominations has argued that party insiders have managed to reassert much of their lost influence. * * * Finally, several studies have found that reorganization of party coalitions on racial issues in the 1940s and 50s sprang from demands of interest groups and activists within the party coalitions.

*   *   *

An Alternative Theory

*   *   *

Why Nominations?

Groups of organized policy demanders are the basic units of our theory of parties. Consider a group that wants the support of an independent office holder with its policy demand. Alone or with a coalition, it can lobby the officeholder to take up its cause, providing facts and talking points. This strategy is unlikely to succeed, however, unless the demand either can be framed as uncontroversially beneficial for a large number of voters, or lines up with the office-holder's existing goals. Lobbying works reliably only for policy demands that officials already favor.

*   *   *

Another tack is to get a genuine friend nominated and elected to office. In seeking to control a nomination, interest groups and activists are in a stronger position. Multiple aspiring office-seekers, none secure in the office they covet, compete for contributions and other campaign resources. At minimum, interest and activist groups can require promises of policy support. Often they can hold out for candidates who have actually demonstrated their commitment through prior service. In the small worlds of local politics, leading individuals are well known to each other; by selecting nominees out of such pools, policy-demanding groups can be fairly confident of getting the politician they want.

* * *

The advantageous position of groups at the nomination stage is bolstered by lack of voter interest. Most citizens pay little attention to general elections and less to nominations. The few who vote in primaries lack the anchoring cue of candidate partisanship, rendering them open to persuasion. Media coverage of primaries is generally less heavy than in general elections, thereby increasing the impact of small amounts of paid advertising. The voters who pay closest attention in primaries often have ties to local interest groups and activists, further contributing to the capacity of policy demanders to control the outcome. Thus, the costs of providing selected politicians with what they need to win a primary election are often small.

For many reasons, then, nominations are a natural focus of interest groups and activists. But how do multiple groups, each with different policy demands, choose a sympathetic candidate? Our answer is by cooperating with other groups as a long coalition. The long coalition strives to nominate a candidate whom each group trusts to represent its interests in a manner acceptable to the coalition as a whole. As in legislative long coalitions, each group is expected to support the party's position in most nomination contests and to oppose it in few.

* * *

* * * The benefit to policy demanders of coalition membership is tremendous. Acting alone, a policy demanding group has little hope of electing a majority of its friends to the legislature. To secure new policy, it must build support for its measures bill by bill in the legislature. But acting as a member of a party coalition, it can nominate and elect a large number of legislators—possibly even a majority—committed in advance to a program that incorporates the group's goals.

* * *

What About Voters?

One might question whether policy demanders have anything to gain from nominating a friendly candidate. According to the Median Voter Theorem, electoral competition should force parties to choose candidates who advocate policies close to those of centrist voters, far from what policy-demanding groups prefer.

This argument, however, depends on the assumption that voters can judge the policy and ideological positions of candidates. Is this assumption tenable?

* * * About 38 percent of voters in the 2000 election did not know that George W. Bush was more conservative than Al Gore. Voter awareness is even lower for two concrete policy items at the heart of the current partisan divide—limits on abortion, and cuts in government spending. Only 47 percent knew which party controlled the House of Representatives.

How much should a party be expected to moderate its positions in deference to an electorate in which half the voters do not even know whether it or its opposition controls the government? Some, perhaps, but probably not very much.

*   *   *

* * * On the one hand voters can recognize and react against some kinds of extremism. On the other hand, many voters, especially swing voters, know dramatically little about politics. In the competitive world of elections, voter ignorance gives parties the opportunity to win with candidates more extreme than swing voters would like if they knew better. * * *

*   *   *

Other scholars have observed that parties may be uncertain about what exactly voters want, and that this uncertainty can lead them to adopt non-centrist positions. Our theoretical claim is different. Lack of voter attentiveness creates license for parties to take non-centrist positions, regardless of what voters may actually want. * * *

*   *   *

Broader Implications of a Group Theory of Parties

Parties and Political Science

The following loose syllogism lurks behind most contemporary studies of American parties: [t]o win election[s], politicians must do what voters want. Politicians want above all to win elections. Politicians create parties to help win elections. Parties are good for democracy.

We have challenged this syllogism at two points: [f]irst, voters do not pay so much attention to politics that politicians must faithfully execute their wishes to win election; within fairly broad limits, obfuscation and phony credit claiming work quite well. Second, interest groups and activists are the dominant players in political parties, insisting on the nomination of candidates who will exploit the limitations of voter monitoring to advance party programs.

The evidence for these challenges is obviously not definitive, but we believe it is strong enough to raise serious doubts about the reigning conception of parties and to establish the plausibility of our own. Our empirical claims are as follows:

- Policy demanders outside of government form new party coalitions and force change in established ones. In this way, policy demanders rather than office holders determine the broad agendas of political conflict.
- Centrist members of Congress are more likely to win re-election than extremists, but the former are rare and the latter common in the House. The unnecessary risk borne by most office holders is consistent with our basic notion that policy-demanding groups rather than politicians are the dominant players in parties.
- When congressional districts and media markets align to conduce more informed electorates, extreme House members are at much greater risk for defeat. This finding suggests that the extremity of most members of Congress is not due to voter preferences, but to limitations in the ability of most voters to hold representatives accountable.
- In some cases, interest groups or activists can be shown to determine the particular individuals nominated for office. But more often, ideological conformity is imposed on party nominees through routine operation of the nomination process.

We have not claimed here that policy-demanding groups always succeed in controlling parties by controlling nominations. But they always have the incentive to try, and evidence shows they often succeed. Forming coalitions to control nominations is an effective way for policy-demanders to get what they want out of government.

* * *

Parties and Democracy

* * *

* * * To posit that American politics is mainly organized by election-minded politicians, as the textbook view of American politics does, is to miss its essence. Organized combat among groups that aim to control policy-making is closer to the heart of the matter.

* * *

These observations, though speculative, amount to another reason for taking a reserved attitude toward the value of parties to democracy. We do not assert, however, that democratic accountability is worse with parties than without. Perhaps in a society in which politics is complicated and most citizens are too busy with their lives to pay much attention, group-centric parties are the best that can be realistically hoped for. Perhaps then giving society's most intense policy demanders a semi-institutionalized position at the heart of government is a better way of insuring that all points of view are heard than relying on the insipid discourse of mass politics for this purpose. Not everyone is represented, but many are. Perhaps the solution to the problem of parties and democracy would be more group involvement rather than less, so that all segments of society have representation in the system. We are not sure. We are, however, sure that the answers to these questions will not come from continuing to underplay the role of interest groups and activists in the party system.

DISCUSSION QUESTIONS

1. Assume that Bawn et al. are correct in their analysis of political parties. How should voters go about choosing which party's candidates to vote for if the authors' analysis is correct? What about a voter who wants to believe, "I vote for the person, not the party"?

2. What are the main disadvantages to politicians paying more attention to interest groups than to voters? Are there any advantages?

56

"The Parties in Our Heads: Misperceptions about Party Composition and Their Consequences"

Douglas J. Ahler and Gaurav Sood

How accurate are Americans' perceptions about the supporters of the two major political parties? Not very, as it turns out, according to Douglas J. Ahler and Gaurav Sood. They find that Americans tend to greatly overestimate the proportion of a party's adherents who are members of stereotypical groups supporting that party. For example, the public greatly overestimates the percentage of union members among Democratic voters and the percentage of people earning over $250,000 among Republican supporters. Partisans have these mistaken perceptions of their own party but do even worse assessing the composition of the other party (the "out-party"). These misperceptions affect how people feel about the other party and how extreme they believe that party is while shoring up their allegiance to their own party. Ahler and Sood provide some evidence that when informed about the actual composition of the out-party, people will view that party as less extreme and less socially different from themselves.

Partisanship is arguably the most fundamental identity in American political life. Not only does it strongly influence vote choice, it also colors how partisans process politically relevant information. Partisanship also fuels animus and distrust across party lines, with roughly a third of partisans describing the other side as "a threat to the nation's well-being" and nearly as many aghast at the idea of an out-party supporter marrying into their family.

What explains the power of partisanship? A long line of research suggests that people tend to think about parties in terms of other, longer-standing groups. According to this account, people's feelings toward the groups that constitute the parties or parties' sociopolitical brands drive their feelings toward the parties, and ultimately their partisan attachments.

However, most supporting evidence for the theory is circumstantial—for example, aggregate stability in party affiliation in the face of changing economic conditions or economically consequential policy shifts by parties. We still largely lack direct evidence that the parties' social composition drives partisanship. The group account of partisanship is also at odds with the fact that the parties do not look very different. Majorities of both parties' supporters are white, middle class, and heterosexual, and both parties' modal supporters are middle aged, nonevangelical Christians. Given these similarities, how can differences in party composition explain the heft of partisanship?

The answer, as we discover, lies not in the actual composition of the parties, but in how people perceive the parties to be composed. People make large, systematic errors when judging party composition, considerably overestimating the extent to which partisans belong to party-stereotypical groups. For instance, Americans believe that 32% of Democrats are gay, lesbian, or bisexual (only 6.3% are in reality), and that 38% of Republicans earn over $250,000 per year (just 2.2% do in reality). These misperceptions are also consequential: they affect partisans' beliefs about and feelings toward the parties. Across multiple experiments, partisans who received information about the actual share of party-stereotypical groups in their out-party rated its supporters as less extreme and reported warmer feelings toward them.

Parties as Sociopolitical Brands

People tend to think about parties in terms of other, longer-standing groups. When evaluating political parties, Americans are thought to ask: "What kinds of social groups come to mind as I think about Democrats, Republicans, and independents?"

The groups that come to mind when people think about the parties tend to be shared, with Democrats, independents, and Republicans often associating the same groups with the parties. Group-party associations also tend to endure. For example, associations between the working class and Democrats and the wealthy and Republicans have endured for nearly a century.

* * *

Perceptions of Party Composition

In March 2015, we surveyed 1,000 Americans through You-Gov. * * * For both parties, respondents estimated the percentage of supporters belonging to four party-stereotypical groups.

We turned to existing research to identify stereotypically Democratic and Republican groups. The most enduring images of the parties are from the New Deal: the association of the rich with Republicans and the working class with Democrats. And, for a long time, Republicans have been seen as the party of older Americans. Over time, however, additional social cleavages have become aligned with partisanship. Most notably, as a consequence of partisan racial sorting in the mid-twentieth century, African Americans have come to be seen as prototypically Democratic. Events half a century ago also precipitated the end of the long-standing association between the South and the Democrats, replacing it with a new linkage between the region and the GOP. Separately, the rise of the evangelical movement in the 1980s led evangelical Christians to become more closely linked to Republicans, and the secular to Democrats. Given the recent politicization of gay rights, and the longer-standing linkage between minority groups and Democrats, we added gays, lesbians, and bisexuals to the list of groups associated with Democrats. * * *

In all, we asked respondents to estimate the percentage of Democrats who are black, atheist or agnostic, union members, and gay, lesbian, or bisexual, and the percentage of Republicans who are evangelical, 65 or older, Southern, and earn over $250,000 per year. Respondents typed their estimate, required to be between 0 and 100, in a box next to each group. The order of Democratic and Republican batteries was randomized, as was the order of items within the batteries. We compared respondents' reported perceptions to the actual shares of these groups in the parties, estimated from Pew's 2012 Religion and Public Life Project (for the two religious party-group dyads) and the 2012 American National Election Study.

People Overestimate the Share of Party-Stereotypical Groups in the Parties

People's perceptions of party composition contain large, systematic errors. In particular, people overestimate the share of party-stereotypical groups in the parties. On average, respondents overestimated these groups' prevalence by 342%. Not only are misperceptions large, they are also widespread. * * *

Looking separately at individual groups, little distinguishes misperceptions about old and new social cleavages. Respondents thought that 39.3% of Democrats belonged to a labor union—only 10.5% do. Even more egregiously, they estimated that 38.2% of Republicans earned over $250,000 per year when just 2.2% of GOP supporters do. But misperceptions were equally common on more recent cleavages. For instance, respondents thought that the share of Democrats who are gay, lesbian, or bisexual was roughly five times greater than it actually is (31.7% vs. 6.3%). Similarly, though by a considerably less dramatic margin—a bit more than 20%—respondents overestimated the share of evangelicals among Republicans.

While most people overestimate the share of party-stereotypical groups in the parties, the extent to which they overestimate varies by partisanship. Republicans' perceptions of Democratic composition exhibit significantly more bias than Democrats'. (Independents' perceptions about party composition are roughly as accurate as in-party estimates.) For example, while Democrats overestimate the percentage of copartisans belonging to a union by 25.2 percentage points, Republicans overestimate by an additional 8.3 percentage points. Similarly, Democrats' perceptions of Republicans tend to be more error prone. * * *

To formally test for differences between in- and out-party perceptions, we compare mean bias in perceptions by partisanship. Democrats overstate the share of party-stereotypical groups in the Democratic Party by 214%, while Republicans do so by 306%, a 92-point difference. Similarly, Democrats err about the degree to which the Republican Party is composed of prototypical supporters by 515%—134 percentage points worse than Republicans. In line with our hypothesis, the data suggest that out-party perceptions are more biased. But consistent with the notion that people rely on commonly shared, impersonal information to arrive at these judgments, people are not especially accurate when thinking about their own party; they are just more biased when thinking about the main opposing party.

Finally, the data suggest a potential source of these misperceptions. We asked respondents how interested they were in politics. Political knowledge generally increases with interest in politics, but in this case, perceptual bias about party composition increases with political interest. * * * Those who report following the news most closely also hold the most prototype-biased beliefs about party composition. * * * To restate the obvious, correlation is not causation. But along with existing theory and evidence on mass media's role in shaping perceptions of collectives, these results provide further reason to investigate the effect of media depictions of the parties on people's beliefs about party composition.

* * *

Consequences of Misperceptions about Party Composition

The evidence thus far suggests that people believe that party-stereotypical groups are far more common in the parties than they actually are, that partisans hold especially distorted perceptions of the composition of the out-party, and that these misperceptions are particular to the parties. We now assess the consequences of these misperceptions. Variation in perceptions of parties' composition and widespread bias in those perceptions provide leverage for doing so.

First, we examine the extent to which beliefs about party composition drive inferences about partisans' policy views. * * *

Second, we examine the extent to which beliefs about composition affect how people feel about out-party supporters. * * *

Believing that opposing partisans hold more extreme policy preferences, and feeling more socially distant from them, are both liable to cause citizens to become less receptive to out-party communications and less likely to consider voting for that party. This may happen because people come to see opposing partisans as working on behalf of the interests of a few groups (at the expense of other groups or even the national interest), or because they think that the opposing party supports more extreme policies that it does, or potentially even because they distrust elites representing disliked groups.

Discussion

Across five studies, we find that people overestimate the degree to which partisans belong to party-stereotypical groups, often vastly so. Even in cases where these groups comprise just a sliver of the population, people report that these groups constitute upward of 40% of the party they "fit." And when people are given information about these groups' shares in the population, the bias in their estimates does not decline, suggesting that people rely on representativeness when making judgments about party composition.

Republicans, Democrats, and independents all overestimate the share of party-stereotypical groups in both the major parties. Partisan differences, although statistically significant, are relatively small compared to the overall magnitude of these misperceptions. Strikingly, those most interested in politics hold the most skewed perceptions of party composition. One plausible explanation for both of these results is that mediated, impersonal information drives these misperceptions. However, all the evidence we have presented on this point is descriptive. Additional research is needed to assess the extent to which media shape these perceptions.

These misperceptions are also consequential. Experimental evidence suggests that beliefs about out-party composition affect perceptions of where opposing-party supporters stand on the issues. These findings provide a potential explanation for why people tend to overestimate the extremity of opposing partisans. * * * Misperceptions about out-party composition also lead partisans to feel more socially distant from the opposing party. Building on work by Hetherington and Weiler and Mason and Davis, who find that partisan animus is related to party composition, we experimentally show that people's beliefs about party composition affect their feelings toward the opposing party.

Beyond beliefs about extremity, we suspect that perceptions about party composition affect people's beliefs about the parties' priorities. For instance, believing that a third of Democrats are atheist or agnostic, or that half of Republicans are evangelical, may lead one to believe that cultural issues like school prayer are far more important to the parties than they actually are. More generally, we suspect that people associate a narrow set of policy demands with each party-stereotypical group and think these groups have sway over the party's agenda. This is liable to fuel more resentment and cynicism about the motivations of party elites.

More broadly, the data shed faint light on the nature of partisanship. A long-standing debate pits cognitive conceptions of partisanship against claims that partisan attachments are largely affective and stem from other group identities. The experimental findings support the notion that orientations toward constituent social groups affect how people feel toward the parties, among other things. However, they also show that beliefs about shares of various groups in the parties matter. Thus, while the group identity account makes a compelling case that partisanship is a relatively stable, affective attachment, work in this tradition must grapple more thoroughly with the social cognitions (and cognitive biases) that are relevant to how people reason about politics.

This is especially the case because partisans overestimate the share of party-stereotypical groups in their own party. For instance, many lower- and middle-class Republicans think that their party contains far more rich people than it actually does. This suggests that many partisans like their own parties to the extent they do—average ratings exceed 70 on the thermometer scale—despite believing that the party has a larger share of groups to which they do not belong than it actually does. Green et al. suggest that partisans choose parties based on "which assemblage of groups" looks like them. While this may still be true, the data suggest that people identify with parties based on which groups they like.

*   *   *

DISCUSSION QUESTIONS

1. Prior to reading Ahler and Sood's analysis, did you share some of the misperceptions about party composition that they report? Why do you think these misperceptions form? Can you imagine realistic ways to prevent them?

2. Considering the analysis in the Bawn et al. reading in this chapter, what are the advantages and disadvantages for interest groups and activists that arise from the public's misperceptions of the coalitions supporting the parties? Overall, would you expect that the misperceptions benefit, diminish, or have no major impact on the influence and control of the groups and activists?

Debating the Issues: Which Way Forward for the Parties?

It is commonly observed that American politics is deeply polarized, with each major party and its supporters taking increasingly harsh stances toward the other major party and its supporters. The idea that there are "two Americas"—Red America and Blue America, with stark divides between rural and urban areas and many other manifestations of a bifurcated population—is frequently noted. Amid this polarization, American political outcomes have also seesawed back and forth between Republican and Democratic control of the presidency, House, and Senate, with some similar patterns in the states.

These close-fought elections and frequent shifts in the balance of power have elevated tensions between and within the parties. After an election loss in this close environment or a worse-than-expected performance, party infighting often intensifies. Lines of division deepen between those who believe the party needs to become more strongly ideological in its policy stances to energize its supporters—more progressive for the Democrats and more conservative or populist for the Republicans—and those who believe the party needs to "move to the middle" to capture the votes of those turned off by political extremes. Both of these internally warring factions in each party believe they are doing what's in the best interest of the party's electoral success for the short and long term.

Ronald Brownstein reports on a major study of the 2020 electorate and concludes that the country should "brace for more years of grueling trench warfare" featuring two parties that are about evenly matched. He reports on a variety of findings from the study, including the shrinking size but deep loyalty of key Republican support groups, the increasing support for Republicans at lower socioeconomic levels and for Democrats at upper levels, some potentially shifting dynamics among Hispanic voters, the strong support for Democrats among younger voters, and the geographical distribution of the parties' support bases. Brownstein's report is followed by a look into each party. Elaine Godfrey examines the internal split in the Democratic Party about how to interpret the 2020 election results and the degree to which being perceived as being "extreme" or "radical" contributed to the defeats of Democratic incumbents or candidates running in districts that are relatively closely balanced in party support. Morgan Marietta and David C. Barker, examining the situation in the Republican Party, see the way forward as following the kinds of policies supported by Donald Trump without adopting some of the harsher edges of the former president's style. Populist policies that challenge entrenched institutions of power, including within the Republican Party, Marietta and Barker argue, are the path to success.

57

"The Most Complete Picture Yet of America's Changing Electorate"

Ronald Brownstein

Can big data explain the passion and vitriol of American politics? Like almost everything else in modern life, the choices are multiplying for analysts looking to understand how the key groups in American society divide in presidential elections.

Once, researchers and political operatives had only a few options: some postelection academic surveys (particularly the University of Michigan's American National Election Studies), precinct-level analyses, and, above all, the mainstay of Election Day television broadcasts—exit polls.

Now the choices for understanding the electorate's behavior have proliferated. The ANES poll has been joined by the Cooperative Election Study (CES), a consortium of academic researchers from some 50 institutions that surveys a huge sample of more than 60,000 voters. Catalist, a Democratic targeting firm, produces its own estimates of voting behavior, based on sophisticated modeling and polling it does with its database tracking virtually all actual voters. The Associated Press and Fox News teamed up with the venerable NORC at the University of Chicago this year to produce a competitor to the traditional exit polls called VoteCast.

* * * The Pew Research Center released its eagerly awaited Validated Voters survey. Pew builds its findings by surveying adults it can identify as definitely having voted in November [2020] based on voting records, a methodology many analysts favor. (The CES will soon issue revised results based on a similar process of matching poll respondents to voting records.)

Each of these methods has its fans: Catalist, for instance, has emerged as the data source most trusted by Democratic political professionals, while other politicos and academics swear by Pew or CES. "It is part art and part science," says the UCLA political scientist Lynn Vavreck, who helped launch the massive Nationscape polling project, which will eventually release its own assessment of 2020 in an upcoming book.

But with [the] release of the Pew results, one thing is now clear: [t]he principal data sources about 2020 have converged to a striking degree in their account of what happened. "As I've been looking at our data and comparing it to some of those other sources, I've actually been struck by how similar

[they] are," says the Tufts University political scientist Brian Schaffner, a co-director of the CES study. "You get a pretty consistent picture."

That consistent picture offers both parties reason for optimism and concern in roughly equal measure. The cumulative message from these studies is that we should brace for more years of grueling trench warfare between two coalitions that are becoming more and more inimical in both their demographic composition and vision of America. And to top it off? They appear to be about evenly matched. (While the Democratic coalition is clearly numerically larger—having won the popular vote in an unprecedented seven of the past eight presidential elections—Republicans have some offsetting advantages, some structural, others manufactured, that could allow them to control Washington nonetheless.)

Here are some other big conclusions from the studies:

GOP Constituencies Are Shrinking, but the Party's Hold over Them Is Tightening

A consistent message in these data sources is that the GOP's core groups—particularly white people without a college degree—are declining as a share of the electorate as the nation grows more diverse, better educated, and more secular.

The major election studies differ on the share of the vote they believe was cast by white people without a college degree, from a high of 44 percent in the Catalist data, to 42 percent in the new Pew results, to just under 40 percent in the recent registration and turnout study from the Census Bureau (the first time the group has fallen below that threshold in census data).

But whatever *absolute* level of the vote the studies attribute to those noncollege white people, Catalist, Pew, and the Census Bureau each found the same *relative* movement, with the share of the vote cast by them in 2020 dropping two percentage points from 2016. That continues a long-term pattern: [w]orking-class white people have declined as a share of the vote between two to three percentage points in each election during this century. That may not sound like much, but it adds up: [i]n census data, they were still a 51.5 percent majority of voters as recently as 2004, before falling just below half in 2008 (almost certainly for the first time in American history) and continuing down to their current level.

Other groups important to the GOP are also shrinking. According to Pew, white Christians fell to 49 percent of total voters in 2020, down from exactly 50 percent in 2016; that's also likely the first time in American history those voters didn't constitute at least half of the electorate. Rural communities are also contracting as a share of the total vote (and population) in most states.

The countertrend is that the GOP last year continued to amass commanding margins with all of these voters. Even Joe Biden, a 78-year-old white Catholic who touts his working-class background in blue-collar

Scranton, Pennsylvania, achieved only grudging gains among white voters without a college degree: Pew found that he won 33 percent of them, just slightly better than the meager 28 percent Hillary Clinton captured in Pew's 2016 survey. (The exit polls and Catalist, which also put Biden's share with noncollege white voters at about one-third, recorded similarly small gains.) Likewise, while Pew found that Biden narrowed Clinton's deficits among both white Catholics and white mainline Protestants, Donald Trump still carried both groups by roughly 15 percentage-point margins. All of the major data sources found that Trump also carried about four-fifths of white evangelical Christians. Similarly, Pew and Catalist both found that Biden remained stuck at the modest one-third of the vote Clinton won in rural areas.

These findings underline the trade that Trump has imposed on the GOP: [h]e's bequeathed Republicans a political strategy based on squeezing bigger margins out of shrinking groups. Many GOP strategists believe that's an utterly untenable long-term proposition. "That's not a formula for winning majorities and winning most of the time," says the longtime GOP pollster Glen Bolger, who notes that Trump lost the popular vote twice and "got beyond lucky" to win the Electoral College in 2016. But that doesn't preclude the GOP from continuing to win power in the near term with that approach—given that the Electoral College and Senate magnify the influence of states where those shrinking groups remain more plentiful (more on that below), and the determination of red-state Republicans, through their wave of restrictive voting laws, to suppress the influence of the rising groups that generally favor Democrats.

Class Inversion Is Here to Stay

The new Pew data, like the earlier 2020 assessments, underscore the durability of what I've called "the class inversion" in each party's base. In the ANES studies, the longest-running of these sources, every Democratic presidential nominee from Adlai Stevenson through Jimmy Carter ran better among white voters without a college degree than among white voters with one. But as cultural issues supplant economic concerns as the principal dividing line between the parties, every Democratic nominee since Al Gore in 2000 has run better among white voters with a degree than among those without one.

The class inversion hit a new peak in 2016, with Hillary Clinton running at least 15 points better among college than noncollege white voters in most of the major data sources (including a breathtaking 27 points better in Pew's assessment). In 2020, Catalist and the exit polls showed the gap widening, while Pew found it slightly narrowing, but the class inversion remained enormous in all three; each study also found Biden winning a majority of college-educated white voters. (Those gains were central to his strong showing in white-collar suburbs around major cities.) He was especially strong among college-educated white women: "[w]e have the ability to make [them] a base group," says Celinda Lake, who served as one of Biden's lead campaign pollsters. But ominously for the GOP, all three sources also showed Biden gaining significantly over Clinton in 2016 among college-educated white men, who historically have been a much more reliable Republican constituency. And while white people without a college degree have been steadily shrinking as a share of the vote, these college-educated white people have slightly grown since 2004 (from about 28 percent to 31 percent of the electorate, per the census). Especially valuable for Democrats: [t]hey are highly reliable midterm voters.

Voters of Color May Be Diverging

Pew's study found that Biden won 92 percent of Black voters last year, and the other major data sources gave him only slightly smaller shares. Democrats may need to keep an eye on Black men, among whom Trump performed slightly better in 2020 than in 2016, but their support among Black women—which reaches as high as 95 percent in some of these analyses—provides an immovable obstacle to broad GOP gains.

Asian Americans, the fastest-growing nonwhite community, also look solid for Democrats. Although Republicans have strong beachheads in some Asian communities sensitive to arguments against Democratic "socialism" (such as Vietnamese Americans and some Chinese groups), the major data sources agree that Biden still won about two-thirds or more of Asian American votes last year, even as their turnout soared.

Hispanics, though, could be emerging as a wild card. Pew put Biden's vote among Hispanics at only 59 percent; that's lower than any of the other major sources, but they all agree that Biden fell off measurably from Clinton (and Barack Obama before her). The decline was most visible among Central and South Americans in South Florida and rural Mexican Americans in South Texas, but it extended far beyond that, Catalist and others found. Trump may have raised the party floor with Hispanics by attracting more of the culturally conservative among them; the yellow light on that prediction, as I've written, is that almost every incumbent president ran better, as Trump did, with Hispanics in their reelection campaign than in their first race. The clearest conclusion is that both parties view Hispanics as more of a contested community after 2020 than they did before—and will spend their campaign dollars accordingly.

The Generational Cavalry Is Arriving for Democrats

Both Pew and Catalist found that the racially diverse, well-educated, and highly secular Millennials (born from 1981 through 1996) and Generation Z (born from 1997 through 2014) cast almost 30 percent of the votes last year, up substantially from 23 percent in 2016. Both sources also found Democrats winning about three-fifths of the votes from those two generations combined. If Democrats can defend their lead with that group, it will pay compounding dividends: [t]he nonpartisan States of Change project forecasts that the two generations combined will cast 37 percent of the vote in 2024 and 43 percent in 2028. "You add those two [generations] together and you are talking about permanent structural change," Lake says. Because these generations are the most racially diverse in American history, this current of new, young voters has been key in increasing people of color from about one-fifth of the electorate in 2004 to nearly three-tenths last year, according to census data. They are also swelling the numbers of Americans unaffiliated with any religious tradition, and Pew found Biden winning more than 70 percent of such "seculars" (even as they cast one-fourth of all votes).

Conversely, the preponderantly white Baby Boomer generation, which has aged from its 1960s roots into a Republican-leaning cohort, is receding: [w]hile Catalist and Pew agree that Boomers outvoted Millennials and Gen Z in 2020, States of Change projects that the younger groups to outvote them for the first time in 2024. (Generation X is projected to remain constant through the 2020s, at about one-fourth of the electorate.)

Two factors might dilute this potential Democratic advantage. One, Schaffner notes, is if the turnout of these two younger generations, which spiked to historic levels in 2018 and 2020, slackens with Trump off the ballot in 2022 and potentially 2024 as well. The other, cited by Vavreck, is that these generations might become more receptive to GOP arguments on issues such as taxes and crime as they move further into middle age, with families and mortgages.

But Lake, like many Democrats, is optimistic that the GOP focus on stoking their base through endless cultural conflict (on everything from undocumented immigration to critical race theory) will leave Republicans very limited opportunity for gains among the younger generations. "Young people are very turned off by the racism, by the climate deniers," she says. "So everything they are doing to solidify their base, and everything they are doing to try to win 2022, is digging them into a deeper hole for 2024 with young voters."

Place Matters

A big challenge for Democrats is that the broad demographic changes favoring them—growing racial diversity, rising education levels, increasing numbers of secular adults not affiliated with organized religion—are unevenly distributed throughout the country. Adding to that challenge: [t]he two-senators-per-state rule and Electoral College magnify the political influence of smaller interior states least affected by these trends (particularly the

increase in racial diversity). Red-state Republicans are moving to systemi-
cally reinforce those advantages with the most aggressive wave of laws
restricting access to the ballot since before the Voting Rights Act in 1965,
and they are gearing up for equally aggressive gerrymanders of state legislative and congressional districts in states they control.

As I've written, the unequal distribution of racial and cultural change
leaves Democrats facing something of a conundrum. The minority population is growing fastest across the Sun Belt, but the party generally doesn't
win as large a share of the vote among white people in those states as they
do in the Rust Belt states, where minority growth has been much slower.
Until Democrats can consistently win Senate seats and Electoral College
votes in the diversifying Sun Belt states, that means they still need to win
some of the Rust Belt states (particularly Wisconsin, Michigan, and Pennsylvania) where noncollege white people compose a much larger share of
the vote than they do nationally. Democrats lately have made progress in
the Sun Belt: Biden won both Georgia and Arizona, and the party now
holds all four of their Senate seats. But Democrats' Sun Belt gains aren't yet
expansive or secure enough to eliminate their need to hold the key Rust
Belt battlegrounds—and for that they need to win a competitive share of
working-class white voters.

The Grooves Are Deeply Cut

The major data sources do show some noteworthy shifts in voter preferences from 2016, such as Trump's gains with Hispanics and Biden's with
college-educated white voters. But given all that happened during Trump's
tumultuous presidency, including a deadly pandemic, most analysts are
struck by the extraordinary similarity in how voters behaved across the
two elections. "Continuity is the big story, consistency," says Alan
Abramowitz, an Emory University political scientist. Not only did the 2020
result "highly correlate" with the 2016 outcome both demographically and
geographically, he notes, but presidential preferences also predicted how
people voted in House and Senate races more closely than ever before.

Biden and his advisers clearly have a vision of how to break this stalemate: [t]hey hope that by delivering kitchen-table benefits, such as stimulus checks, infrastructure jobs, and expanded child-tax-credit payments,
while muting his personal engagement with hot-button cultural issues,
they can improve his standing among working-class voters of all races,
including white voters. But that strategy faces unstinting GOP efforts to
highlight the cultural issues that alienate those voters (especially white voters but also some Hispanics and Black men) from the Democrats. Ruy
Teixeira, a veteran Democratic analyst, argues that even if Biden delivers
material benefits for blue-collar families, downplaying cultural issues such
as crime and immigration won't be enough. "You are going to have to draw

the line a little bit more sharply against parts of the party and policies that are anathema to these voters," Teixeira says.

Still, almost all of the analysts I spoke with believe that however the parties position themselves through 2024, change in these durable voter alignments is likely to come only around the margins.

Big outside events could shatter that assumption, of course, but the striking message from all the data sources studying 2020 is that America remains deeply but closely divided. Wide partisan fissures by race, generation, education, and religion are combining to produce two coalitions that are matched almost equally, with a Democratic edge in overall numbers offset by a geographic advantage (potentially reinforced by restrictive voting laws) for Republicans. "It is going to be super, super close again in 2024, I can tell you this right now," Vavreck said firmly. "And I don't even need to know who the candidates are going to be."

58

"The Democrats Are Already Losing the Next Election"

ELAINE GODFREY

Debbie Mucarsel-Powell knew that winning reelection in her swingy Florida district would be difficult. But it wasn't until one night in February last year that the 50-year-old Democratic representative started to worry. That was the evening when then-presidential-candidate Bernie Sanders, in a *60 Minutes* interview, showered praise on Cuba's literacy programs under the Castro regime. "Is that a bad thing? Even though Fidel Castro did it?" the senator asked Anderson Cooper. Watching at home, Mucarsel-Powell was aghast. "How ignorant can you be?" she remembers thinking. "It was a complete insult to the Cuban diaspora that had fled that country." Right away, she condemned Sanders's remarks, but in her South Florida district, which is home to thousands of Cuban and other Latin American immigrants, the damage had been done. Republicans used Sanders's comments to raise money for her opponent, Carlos Gimenez, and to paint Mucarsel-Powell as an ally of the "Castro-loving socialist." She lost her reelection bid by three points.

Mucarsel-Powell was one of 13 House Democrats who were unseated in the 2020 election—many more than the party had anticipated—and most were moderates like her who had first been elected in the blue wave of 2018. Other centrists, such as Representative Abigail Spanberger of Virginia, barely held on to their seat. She and some other Democrats blamed their struggles on a voter backlash to leftist ideas. In a caucus call, Spanberger complained that the slogan "Defund the police" had been fodder for GOP attack ads, and Representative Conor Lamb of Pennsylvania argued in a *New York Times* interview that progressives had pushed ideas that were unpopular in purple districts. New York's Alexandria Ocasio-Cortez dismissed those criticisms, arguing that moderates had simply run weak campaigns.

Eight months later, the Democrats are still fighting over who's to blame. A new report from Third Way, the Collective PAC, and Latino Victory seems to support Lamb's original thesis: [a]lthough the party succeeded at demonizing Donald Trump, Republicans were successful at demonizing Democrats. "Republican attempts to brand Democrats as 'radicals' worked, including among voters of color," the analysis concludes. It is one of several comprehensive examinations of the 2020 election released recently by a range of liberal groups that include the Congressional Progressive Caucus, the Democratic Congressional Campaign Committee, and the left-wing donor network Way to Win. Each offers a distinct conclusion about 2020 and a different lesson about how to proceed—evidence that the fierce intra-party debate, which consumed Democrats in November, remains unsettled 16 months before the party heads into an already unfavorable midterm election.

The authors of the Third Way and co. report, Marlon Marshall and Lynda Tran, present a few linked findings. First, Democrats lost support among Latino and Black voters because the party didn't give them something to vote for. Part of the report's explanation was that Democrats were so busy attacking Trump that they failed to offer a consistent vision for rebuilding the economy. In the absence of a powerful message, Republicans had ample space to label Democrats "radicals" who endorsed a socialist agenda and violence in the streets, the report said. According to Marshall and Tran, districts where Republicans emphasized "law and order" and "socialism" also saw a higher share of Latino, Asian, and Black voters supporting the GOP. The report's prescription might sound familiar: [t]he party needs to start talking to voters—especially voters of color—earlier and to offer a focused message about jobs, wages, and economic prosperity.

Just as important as having a message is sticking to it. Democrats need to "fall in line" during campaign season, says Quentin James, the leader of the Collective PAC, which recruits and supports Black candidates for political office. "We have to be real about our ability to win elections and not just promote certain grassroots slogans," James says, alluding to the unpopularity of the movement to defund the police. "Running in deep-blue districts is super cool. But if you want to have a majority to legislate, then you need to help those candidates in more moderate districts. Shooting off the mouth on things that don't poll well is not helping the cause."

Mucarsel-Powell is not the only one who blames "shooting off the mouth" for her defeat. "[Voters] said to me directly, 'We support you, we know your positions, but we're worried about the direction of the national Democratic Party,'" Ben McAdams, who lost his reelection bid in his deep-red Utah district by fewer than 4,000 votes, told me. McAdams was one of the Democrats who voted most often against his own party. But "there were ads after ads saying I support a radical socialist agenda, and many of our loudest voices were saying things that reinforced that message." Other losing moderates, such as Xochitl Torres Small in New Mexico and Gil Cisneros in California, who'd flipped districts in 2018, were pelted with accusations of extremism and tied to progressive policy positions that they didn't endorse.

Democrats need to respond to these accusations directly, Lanae Erickson, a senior vice president at Third Way, told me. When now-Senator Ben Ray Luján's opponent in New Mexico accused him of wanting to defund the police, for example, Luján refuted the characterization in an ad touting his support for law enforcement. He won the race. "People are afraid to do that, because they're worried about the blowback" from left-wing activists, Erickson said. But providing a rebuttal gives voters "something to cling to on the other side, rather than letting it fester."

Attacks linking lawmakers with the fringiest elements of their base are not new in politics, but American politics is more national now than it used to be. "Everyone in the Democratic Party, for the first time in history, really, is sharing one common brand," David Shor, the head of data science at the progressive nonprofit OpenLabs, told me. "It becomes a share-of-voice question: Who are the people getting the most media coverage? If you tally it up, it means you have folks like [Joe] Biden [getting attention], but also the Squad." Message management is a particular challenge for the Democratic Party, whose members adhere to a wide range of ideological positions. Unlike the present-day GOP, Democrats have to contend with a majority that hinges on the success of their most moderate members.

Progressives offer a different diagnosis of 2020. The report sponsored by the Congressional Progressive Caucus PAC also concludes that voters don't seem to have a firm idea of what Democrats stand for. However, it argues that swing voters were not influenced by GOP messages attacking Democrats on socialism, open borders, and defunding the police. "We got very, very different results from our focus groups," Pramila Jayapal, the Progressive Caucus chair, told me. She believes that Democrats in different districts can campaign on different messages and still win if they embrace "bold, populist" ideas like raising the minimum wage and fighting climate change—"whether or not we agree on the details."

An analysis from Way to Win examined 2020 campaign ads and found that whereas Republicans spent millions of dollars casting Democrats as extremists, Democrats instead emphasized bipartisanship. That was a mistake, the report argues. Rather than spending valuable resources refuting outrageous accusations, Democrats need to turn the tables, leftists say, and campaign on the idea that Republicans, who encouraged the storming of the U.S. Capitol and pushed back against the expansion of voting rights, are the real extremists. "The message from the Dems was that Trump was a unique threat to democracy and that Joe Biden could work with the more normal Republicans, so the party has created a permission structure for people to vote for Republicans," the progressive pollster Sean McElwee told me.

Postmortems like these are a common ritual for parties that are disappointed after elections—a way to learn and grow from loss, to reform and redefine. But the process also offers an opportunity for factions within a political coalition to jockey for dominance. More than anything, these reports expose the fault lines in a party that has grown more and more progressive even as it relies on moderates to maintain power and pass legislation. The status of the pandemic, the economy, and Biden's popularity will undoubtedly be crucial to the outcome of next year's elections. But how Democrats resolve their disagreement about how to win—and who takes the blame for defeats—will matter.

59

"A Less Trumpy Version of Trumpism Might Be the Future of the Republican Party"

Morgan Marietta and David C. Barker

Donald Trump lost the 2020 election, but his populist ideas may continue to animate the Republican Party.

As scholars of American beliefs and elections, we can envision a less Trumpy version of Trumpism holding sway over the party in coming years. We call it "polished populism."

Populism is folk-politics based on the premise that ordinary citizens are wiser and more virtuous than supposedly corrupt and self-serving elites. Populist rhetoric is often expressed in cruder, coarser language than ordinary political speech—less like a politician on a stage and more like a guy in a bar.

Trump, a prime practitioner of populist rhetoric, took this to an extreme with the shorthand of Twitter and the insults of the locker room.

Polished populists take a different approach, arguing for the same policies that Trump did—limiting immigration, redistributing wealth toward the working class rather than just the poor, opposing the woke policies of social justice movements, promoting "America First" foreign and trade policies—but without his overtly antagonistic language.

Some Republicans are now arguing for a rejection of populism and a return to traditional conservatism. Those long-standing GOP priorities include limited government, strong national defense of American interests abroad, religious values and, perhaps most importantly, ordinary political personalities.

For two reasons—the GOP's narrow electoral defeat in 2020 and the changing demographics of the Republican Party—we believe that populist policies, if not rhetoric, will continue to be a dominant theme of the Republican Party.

Populism versus Traditional Conservatism

The contemporary conservatism associated with Ronald Reagan in the 1980s and George W. Bush in the 2000s has several facets and factions, but it can be summed up in the phrase, "You keep what you earn, it's a dangerous world, and God is good."

The economic, national defense, and social conservatives of previous decades tended to agree that human nature is untrustworthy and society is fragile, so the [United States] needs to defend against external enemies and internal decline.

Populist conservatism accepts those views but adds something different: the interests and perceptions of "ordinary" people against "elites." So populism rejects the notion of a natural aristocracy of wealth and education, replacing it with the idea that people it considers elites, including career politicians, bureaucrats, journalists, and academics, have been promoting their own interests at the expense of regular folk.

The Identity Divide

The recent rise of populism in America has been driven in part by a clear economic reality: [t]he expansion of wealth over the last 40 years has gone almost entirely to the upper reaches of society. At the same time, the middle has stagnated or declined economically.

The populist interpretation is that elites benefited from the globalization and technological advancements they encouraged, while the advantages of those trends bypassed ordinary working people. Calls for trade protections and national borders appeal to Americans who feel left behind.

Populism also has a cultural aspect: rejection of the perceived condescension and smugness of the "highly educated elite."

In that sense, populism is driven by identity (who someone believes they are like, and perhaps more importantly, who they are not like). For populists, the like-minded are ordinary folk—middle income, middle-brow educations at public high schools and state universities, often middle-of-the-country—and the dissimilar are the products of expensive educations and urban lifestyles.

While traditional conservatism has not vanished from the GOP, populist perceptions dominate the new working-class foundations of the party. And those reflect the emerging divide in education.

The base of the Republican Party has shifted from more wealthy and educated Americans to voters without college degrees. In the 1990s, whites who did not attend college tended to back Democrat Bill Clinton, but in 2016 they supported Republican Trump over Democrat Hillary Clinton by 39 percentage points. In 2020, it was roughly the same for Trump over Biden.

The 2020 Outcome and the GOP Future

We believe the Republican Party will be slow to move away from this new identity.

Even after a pandemic, a recession, an impeachment, four years of anti-immigration sentiment, and the Black Lives Matter protests, Trump still received more votes than any presidential candidate in history not named Joe Biden.

Biden's overall victory was by a margin of 7 million votes. But his victory in the Electoral College relied on a total of 45,000 votes in three states. This was similar to Trump's narrow 2016 Electoral College margin of 77,000 votes, also in three states. A strong Republican candidate, a foreign policy problem for the incumbent Democrat or a small piece of luck could shift the presidency back to the other party.

Support for Republicans even grew somewhat among traditionally Democratic African American and Hispanic voters, despite the GOP's anti-Black Lives Matter and anti-immigrant rhetoric.

Clearly, Trumpism was not repudiated by voters in the way that Democrats had hoped. It is entirely possible that if the pandemic had not occurred—which was a major source of the decline in his support—Donald Trump would still be in the White House.

The GOP could conclude that its loss was only due to an outside event and not a fundamental rejection of policy. That would give the party little incentive to change course, aside from changing the face on the poster.

Over the next four years we believe the GOP will solidify the transition to a populist base, though not without resistance from traditional conservatives.

Republican victory in a future presidential election would likely require an alliance between traditional and populist conservatives, with both groups turning out to vote. The question is which one will lead the coalition.

The competition for the 2024 Republican nomination will likely also be a contest between these two party bases and ideologies, with the emerging winner defining the post-Trump GOP.

The 2024 Standard Bearers

The Republican contenders for the 2024 nomination and the new leadership of the GOP include a broad range of populists versus traditional conservatives.

Perhaps a leading indicator of the move toward polished populism is the shift in the rhetoric employed by Marco Rubio.

The senator from Florida was once a traditional conservative, but has shifted toward populism after his trouncing by Trump in the 2016 Republican presidential primary. Recently he argued that "the future of the party is based on a multiethnic, multiracial, working-class coalition," defined as "normal, everyday people who don't want to live in a city where there is no police department, where people rampage through the streets every time they are upset about something."

The opposing trend toward rejecting Trumpist populism is exemplified by the shift in the arguments made by Nikki Haley. Haley, the U.N. ambassador under the Trump administration and former South Carolina governor, has rejected Trump's leadership, now arguing that "we shouldn't have followed him."

These two Republicans and several others see a potential president in the mirror. Which one mirrors the current GOP will depend on the realignment or retrenchment between the populists and the traditionalists.

Polished populism—Trump's policies without his personality—may be the future of the GOP's identity.

Discussion Questions

1. Considering the findings presented by Brownstein, what would you argue are the three most significant challenges faced by each major party as it develops its future electoral strategy?

2. Based on the different interpretations presented by Godfrey, do you think either side of the argument has a clearly stronger case? If so, which side? Why? If not, what additional information would you want to know in order to decide which interpretation is more convincing?

3. Donald Trump lost his re-election, but Republicans did better in 2020 than expected in the House of Representatives and nearly maintained control of the U.S. Senate, surprising many election observers. What would you want to know about these outcomes in order to assess Marietta and Barker's recommendations for the party? Should the data in the Brownstein reading encourage or discourage Marietta and Barker's points?

CHAPTER 12

Groups and Interests

60

"Group Politics and Representative Democracy" from *The Governmental Process*

DAVID B. TRUMAN

At various times in U.S. history, the public has become especially concerned with the power of interest groups in politics and has sought to limit their activities. One political scientist refers to this as the "ideals vs. institutions" gap—there are times when "what is" is so different from what Americans believe "should be," that pressure mounts to reform lobbying laws, campaign regulations, business practices, and so on. Going back to James Madison in his famous Federalist 10, *however, the argument that competition between interests should be encouraged has also been powerful in American political thought. The claim in this school of thought, known as pluralist theory, is that the competition among groups in society for political power produces the best approximation of the overall public good. In the following excerpt from* The Governmental Process, *David B. Truman argues that such groups have been a common and inevitable feature of American politics. Groups form to give individuals a means of self-expression and to help them find security in an uncertain world. In fact, the uncertainty of the social environment, and the resulting threat to one's interests, is a chief motivation for groups to form, and "taming" this environment is a central concern for group members. Rather than leading to a system rigidly ruled by a few dominant powers, Truman, writing in the 1950s, suggests that the reality is more dynamic. What critics of group influence fail to recognize is the fact that people have "multiple or overlapping membership" in groups so that "no tolerably normal person is totally absorbed in any group in which he participates." There is balance, in other words, to the views any one member brings to the organization and ultimately to the political process. Further, the potential for a group to form is always present, and "[s]ometimes it may be this possibility of organization that alone gives the potential group a minimum of influence in the political process." These features of the interest-group system push toward compromise and balance in public policy.*

Most accounts of American legislative sessions—national, state, or local—are full of references to the maneuverings and iniquities of various organized groups. Newspaper stories report that a legislative proposal is being promoted by groups of business men or school teachers or farmers or consumers or labor unions or other aggregations of citizens. Cartoonists picture the legislature as completely under the control of sinister, portly, cigar-smoking individuals labeled "special interests," while a diminutive John Q. Public is pushed aside to sulk in futile anger and pathetic frustrations. A member of the legislature rises in righteous anger on the floor of the house or in a press conference to declare that the bill under discussion is being forced through by the "interests," by the most unscrupulous high-pressure "lobby" he has seen in all his years of public life. An investigating committee denounces the activities of a group as deceptive, immoral, and destructive of our constitutional methods and ideals. A chief executive attacks a "lobby" or "pressure group" as the agency responsible for obstructing or emasculating a piece of legislation that he has recommended "in the public interest."

* * *

Such events are familiar even to the casual student of day-to-day politics, if only because they make diverting reading and appear to give the citizen the "low-down" on his government. He tends, along with many of his more sophisticated fellow citizens, to take these things more or less for granted, possibly because they merely confirm his conviction that "as everybody knows, politics is a dirty business." Yet at the same time he is likely to regard the activities of organized groups in political life as somehow outside the proper and normal processes of government, as the lapses of his weak contemporaries whose moral fiber is insufficient to prevent their defaulting on the great traditions of the Founding Fathers. These events appear to be a modern pathology.

Group Pressure and the Founding Fathers

Group pressures, whatever we may wish to call them, are not new in America. One of the earliest pieces of testimony to this effect is essay number 10 of *The Federalist*, which contains James Madison's classic statement of the impact of divergent groups upon government and the reasons for their development. He was arguing the virtues of the proposed Union as a means to "break and control the violence of faction," having in mind, no doubt, the groups involved in such actions of the debtor or propertyless segment of the population as Shays's Rebellion. He defined faction in broader terms, however, as "a number of citizens, whether amounting to a majority or minority of the whole, who are united and actuated by some common impulse of passion, or of interest. . . ."

* * *

[Madison's] analysis is not just the brilliant generalization of an armchair philosopher or pamphleteer; it represents as well the distillation from Madison's years of acquaintance with contemporary politics as a member of the Virginia Assembly and of [the Continental] Congress. Using the words "party" and "faction" almost interchangeably, since the political party as we know it had not yet developed, he saw the struggles of such groups as the essence of the political process. One need not concur in all his judgments to agree that the process he described had strong similarities to that of our own day.

The entire effort of which *The Federalist* was a part was one of the most skillful and important examples of pressure group activity in American history. The State ratifying conventions were handled by the Federalists with a skill that might well be the envy of a modern lobbyist. It is easy to overlook the fact that "unless the Federalists had been shrewd in manipulation as they were sound in theory, their arguments could not have prevailed."

* * *

Alexis de Tocqueville, perhaps the keenest foreign student ever to write on American institutions, noted as one of the most striking characteristics of the nation the penchant for promoting a bewildering array of projects through organized societies, among them those using political means. "In no country in the world," he observed, "has the principle of association been more successfully used or applied to a greater multitude of objects than in America." Tocqueville was impressed by the organization of such groups and by their tendency to operate sometimes upon and sometimes parallel to the formal institutions of government. Speaking of the similarity between the representatives of such groups and the members of legislatures, he stated: "[i]t is true that they [delegates of these societies] have not the right, like the others, of making the laws; but they have the power of attacking those which are in force and of drawing up beforehand those which ought to be enacted."

Since the modern political party was, in the Jackson period, just taking the form that we would recognize today, Tocqueville does not always distinguish sharply between it and other types of political interest groups. In his discussion of "political associations," however, he gives an account of the antitariff convention held in Philadelphia in October of 1831, the form of which might well have come from the proceedings of a group meeting in an American city today:

> Its debates were public, and they at once assumed a legislative character; the extent of the powers of Congress, the theories of free trade, and the different provisions of the tariff were discussed. At the end of ten days the Convention

broke up, having drawn up an address to the American people in which it declared: (1) that Congress had not the right of making a tariff, and that the existing tariff was unconstitutional; (2) that the prohibition of free trade was prejudicial to the interests of any nation, and to those of the American people especially.

Additional evidence might be cited from many quarters to illustrate the long history of group politics in this country. Organized pressures supporting or attacking the charter of the Bank of the United States in Jackson's administration, the peculations surrounding Pendleton's "Palace of Fortune" in the pre–Civil War period, the operations of the railroads and other interests in both national and state legislatures in the latter half of the last century, the political activities of farm groups such as the Grange in the same period—these and others indicate that at no time have the activities of organized political interests not been a part of American politics. Whether they indicate pathology or not, they are certainly not new.

* * *

The political interest group is neither a fleeting, transitory newcomer to the political arena nor a localized phenomenon peculiar to one member of the family of nations. The persistence and the dispersion of such organizations indicate rather that we are dealing with a characteristic aspect of our society. That such groups are receiving an increasing measure of popular and technical attention suggests the hypothesis that they are appreciably more significant in the complex and interdependent society of our own day than they were in the simpler, less highly developed community for which our constitutional arrangements were originally designed.

Many people are quite willing to acknowledge the accuracy of these propositions about political groups, but they are worried nevertheless. They are still concerned over the meaning of what they see and read of the activities of such organizations. They observe, for example, that certain farm groups apparently can induce the Government to spend hundreds of millions of dollars to maintain the price of food and to take "surplus" agricultural produce off the market while any urban residents are encountering painful difficulty in stretching their food budgets to provide adequately for their families. They observe that various labor organizations seem to be able to prevent the introduction of cheaper methods into building codes, although the cost of new housing is already beyond the reach of many. Real estate and contractors' trade associations apparently have the power to obstruct various governmental projects for slum clearance and low-cost housing. Veterans' organizations seem able to secure and protect increases in pensions and other benefits almost at will. A church apparently can prevent the appropriation of Federal funds to public schools unless such funds are also given to the schools it operates in competition with the public systems. The Government has declared that stable and friendly European governments cannot be maintained unless Americans buy more goods and services abroad. Yet American shipowners and seamen's unions can secure a statutory requirement that a large proportion of the goods purchased by European countries under the Marshall Plan* must be carried in American ships. Other industries and trade associations can prevent the revision of tariff rates and customs regulations that restrict imports from abroad.

In all these situations the fairly observant citizen sees various groups slugging it out with one another in pursuit of advantages from the Government. Or he sees some of them co-operating with one another to their mutual benefit. He reads of "swarms" of lobbyists "putting pressure on" congressmen and administrators. He has the impression that any group can get what it wants in Washington by deluging officials with mail and telegrams. He may then begin to wonder whether a governmental system like this can survive, whether it can carry its responsibilities in the world and meet the challenges presented by a ruthless dictatorship. He wants to see these external threats effectively met. The sentimental nonsense of the commercial advertisements aside, he values free speech, free elections, representative government, and all that these imply. He fears and resents practices and privileges that seem to place these values in jeopardy.

A common reaction to revelations concerning the more lurid activities of political groups is one of righteous indignation. Such indignation is entirely natural. It is likely, however, to be more comforting than constructive. What we seek are correctives, protections, or controls that will strengthen the practices essential in what we call democracy and that will weaken or eliminate those that really threaten that system. Uncritical anger may do little to achieve that objective, largely because it is likely to be based upon a picture of the governmental process that is a composite of myth and fiction as well as of fact. We shall not begin to achieve control until we have arrived at a conception of politics that adequately accounts for the operations of political groups. We need to know what regular patterns are shown by group politics before we can predict its consequences and prescribe for its lapses. We need to re-examine our notions of how representative government operates in the United States before we can be confident of our statements about the effects of group activities upon it. Just as we should not know how to protect a farm house from lightning unless we knew something of the behavior of electricity, so we cannot hope to protect a governmental system from the results of group organization unless we have an adequate understanding of the political process of which these groups are a part.

* * *

There are two elements in this conception of the political process in the United States that are of crucial significance and that require special emphasis. These are, first, the notion of multiple or overlapping membership and, second, the function of unorganized interests, or potential interest groups.

---

*The Marshall Plan was the U.S. European Recovery Plan after World War II [Editors].

The idea of overlapping membership stems from the conception of a group as a standardized pattern of interactions rather than as a collection of human units. Although the former may appear to be a rather misty abstraction, it is actually far closer to complex reality than the latter notion. The view of a group as an aggregation of individuals abstracts from the observable fact that in any society, and especially a complex one, no single group affiliation accounts for all of the attitudes or interests of any individual except a fanatic or a compulsive neurotic. No tolerably normal person is totally absorbed in any group in which he participates. The diversity of an individual's activities and his attendant interests involve him in a variety of actual and potential groups. Moreover, the fact that the genetic experiences of no two individuals are identical and the consequent fact that the spectra of their attitudes are in varying degrees dissimilar means that the members of a single group will perceive the group's claims in terms of a diversity of frames of reference. Such heterogeneity may be of little significance until such time as these multiple memberships conflict. Then the cohesion and influence of the affected group depend upon the incorporation or accommodation of the conflicting loyalties of any significant segment of the group, an accommodation that may result in altering the original claims. Thus the leaders of a Parent-Teacher Association must take some account of the fact that their proposals must be acceptable to members who also belong to the local taxpayers' league, to the local chamber of commerce, and to the Catholic Church.

*   *   *

We cannot account of an established American political system without the second crucial element in our conception of the political process, the concept of the unorganized interest, or potential interest group. Despite the tremendous number of interest groups existing in the United States, not all interests are organized. If we recall the definition of an interest as a shared attitude, it becomes obvious that continuing interaction resulting in claims upon other groups does not take place on the basis of all such attitudes. One of the commonest interest groups forms, the association, emerges out of severe or prolonged disturbances in the expected relationships of individuals in similar institutionalized groups. An association continues to function as long as it succeeds in ordering these disturbed relationships, as a labor union orders the relationships between management and workers. Not all such expected relationships are simultaneously or in a given short period sufficiently disturbed to produce organization. Therefore only a portion of the interests or attitudes involved in such expectations are represented by organized groups. Similarly, many organized groups—families, businesses, or churches, for example—do not operate continuously as interest groups or as political interest groups.

Any mutual interest, however, any shared attitude, is a potential group. A disturbance in established relationships and expectations anywhere in the society may produce new patterns of interaction aimed at restricting or eliminating the disturbance. Sometimes it may be this possibility of organization that alone gives the potential group a minimum of influence in the political process. Thus * * * the Delta planters in Mississippi "must speak for their Negroes in such programs as health and education," although the latter are virtually unorganized and are denied the means of active political participation.*

* * *

Obstacles to the development of organized groups from potential ones may be presented by inertia or by the activities of opposed groups, but the possibility that severe disturbances will be created if these submerged, potential interests should organize necessitates some recognition of the existence of these interests and gives them at least a minimum of influence.

More important for present purposes than the potential groups representing separate minority elements are those interests or expectations that are so widely held in the society and are so reflected in the behavior of almost all citizens that they are, so to speak, taken for granted. Such "majority" interests are significant not only because they may become the basis for organized interest groups [but also because the "membership" of such potential groups] overlaps extensively the memberships of the various organized interest groups. The resolution of conflicts between the claims of such unorganized interests and those of organized interest groups must grant recognition to the former not only because affected individuals may feel strongly attached to them but even more certainly because these interests are widely shared and are a part of many established patterns of behavior the disturbance of which would be difficult and painful. They are likely to be highly valued.

* * *

It is thus multiple memberships in potential groups based on widely held and accepted interests that serve as a balance wheel in a going political system like that of the United States. To some people this observation may appear to be a truism and to others a somewhat mystical notion. It is neither. In the first place, neglect of this function of multiple memberships in most discussions of organized interest groups indicates that the observation is not altogether commonplace. Secondly, the statement has no mystical quality; the effective operation of these widely held interests is to be inferred directly from verbal and other behavior in the political sphere. Without the notion of multiple memberships in potential groups it is literally impossible to account for the existence of a viable polity such as that in the United States or to develop a coherent conception of the political process. The strength of these widely held but largely unorganized interests

*Until the 1960s, most southern Black people were denied the right to vote [Editors].

explains the vigor with which propagandists for organized groups attempt to change other attitudes by invoking such interests. Their importance is further evidenced in the recognized function of the means of mass communication, notably the press, in reinforcing widely accepted norms of "public morality."

* * *

Thus it is only as the effects of overlapping memberships and the functions of unorganized interests and potential groups are included in the equation that it is accurate to speak of governmental activity as the product or resultant of interest group activity. As [political scientist Arthur F.] Bentley has put it:

> There are limits to the technique of the struggle, this involving also limits to the group demands, all of which is solely a matter of empirical observation. . . . Or, in other words, when the struggle proceeds too harshly at any point there will become insistent in the society a group more powerful than either of those involved which tends to suppress the extreme and annoying methods of the groups in the primary struggle. It is within the embrace of these great lines of activity that the smaller struggles proceed, and the very word struggle has meaning only with reference to its limitations.

To assert that the organization and activity of powerful interest groups constitutes a threat to representative government without measuring their relation to and effects upon the widespread potential groups is to generalize from insufficient data and upon an incomplete conception of the political process. Such an analysis would be as faulty as one that ignoring differences in national systems, predicted identical responses to a given technological change in the United States, Japan, and the Soviet Union.

DISCUSSION QUESTIONS

1. Even if you are not a member of an organized interest group, can you think of any such groups that speak for you? What would it take for you to become a member of or involved in the group?

2. Is Truman right that new organizations emerge in important policy debates, leaving most views well represented? Can you think of instances in which, counter to Truman's viewpoint, a new organization did not emerge, leaving a group unrepresented?

3. Among the many forms of interest-group activity, campaign contributions seem to provoke some of the harshest criticisms. Is this reasonable? Is there any reason to be more concerned about campaign contributions than about lobbying, lawsuits, funding research, or any other activities that groups employ to pursue their cause? How would Truman answer this question?

61

"The Logic of Collective Action," from *Rise and Decline of Nations*

MANCUR OLSON

Americans organize at a tremendous rate to pursue common interests in the political arena. Yet not all groups are created equal, and some types of political organizations are much more common than others. In particular, it is far easier to organize groups around narrow economic interests than it is to organize around broad "public goods" interests. Why do some groups organize while others do not?

The nature of collective goods, according to the economist Mancur Olson, explains this phenomenon. When a collective good is provided to a group, no member of the group can be denied the benefits of the good. For example, if Congress passes a law that offers subsidies for student loan repayments, anyone paying a student loan will benefit from the subsidy. The catch is that all individuals in repayment status will benefit even if they did not participate in the collective effort to win the subsidy. Olson argues that "the larger the number of individuals or firms that would benefit from a collective good, the smaller the share of the gains . . . that will accrue to the individual or firm." Hence, the less likely any one member of the group will join the collective effort to secure the collective benefit. For smaller groups, any one member's share of the collective good is larger and more meaningful. Thus, it is more likely any one member of the group will be willing to make an individual sacrifice to provide a benefit shared by the entire group. An additional distinction is that in a large group, there is often a tendency to assume someone else will take care of the problem—this is known as the "free rider" problem, or, as Olson puts it, "[L]et George do it." This is less likely to happen in smaller groups.

The logic helps to explain the greater difficulty so-called "public interest groups" have in organizing and staying organized to pursue such collective goods as environmental protection and consumer product safety. These goods benefit large numbers of people, but the benefit to any one person, Olson would argue, is not sufficient to sacrifice time or money for the effort to succeed, especially if individuals believe that they will benefit from the collective good even if they do not contribute. Olson identifies "selective incentives" as one way in which these larger groups are able to overcome the incentive for individuals to free ride.

The argument of this book begins with a paradox in the behavior of groups. It has often been taken for granted that if everyone in a group of individuals or firms had some interest in common, then there would be a tendency for the group to seek to further this interest. Thus many students of politics in the United States for a long time supposed that citizens with a common political interest would organize and lobby to serve that interest. Each individual in the population would be in one or more groups and the vector of pressures of these competing groups explained the outcomes of the political process. Similarly, it was often supposed that if workers, farmers, or consumers faced monopolies harmful to their interests, they would eventually attain countervailing power through organizations such as labor unions or farm organizations that obtained market power and protective government action. On a larger scale, huge social classes are often expected to act in the interest of their members; the unalloyed form of this belief is, of course, the Marxian contention that in capitalist societies the bourgeois class runs the government to serve its own interests, and that once the exploitation of the proletariat goes far enough and "false consciousness" has disappeared, the working class will in its own interest revolt and establish a dictatorship of the proletariat. In general, if the individuals in some category or class had a sufficient degree of self-interest and if they all agreed on some common interest, then the group would to some extent also act in a self-interested or group-interested manner.

If we ponder the logic of the familiar assumption described in the preceding paragraph, we can see that it is fundamentally and indisputably faulty. Consider those consumers who agree that they pay higher prices for a product because of some objectionable monopoly or tariff, or those workers who agree that their skill deserves a higher wage. Let us now ask what would be the expedient course of action for an individual consumer who would like to see a boycott to combat a monopoly or a lobby to repeal the tariff, or for an individual worker who would like a strike threat or a minimum wage law that could bring higher wages. If the consumer or worker contributes a few days and a few dollars to organize a boycott or a union or to lobby for favorable legislation, he or she will have sacrificed time and money. What will this sacrifice obtain? The individual will at best succeed in advancing the cause to a small (often imperceptible) degree. In any case he will get only a minute share of the gain from his action. The very fact that the objective or interest is common to or shared by the group entails that the gain from any sacrifice an individual makes to serve this common purpose is shared with everyone in the group. The successful boycott or strike or lobbying action will bring the better price or wage for everyone in the relevant category, so the individual in any large group with a common interest will reap only a minute share of the gains from whatever sacrifices the individual makes to achieve this common interest. Since any gain goes to everyone in the group, those who contribute nothing to the effort will get just as much as those who made a contribution. It pays to "let George do it," but George has little or no incentive to do anything in the group interest either, so (in the absence of factors that are completely left out of the conceptions mentioned in the first paragraph) there will be little, if any, group action. The paradox, then, is that (in the absence of special arrangements or circumstances to which we shall turn later) large groups, at least if they are composed of rational individuals, will *not* act in their group interest.

This paradox is elaborated and set out in a way that lets the reader check every step of the logic in a book I wrote entitled *The Logic of Collective Action*.

* * *

Organizations that provide collective goods to their client groups through political or market action * * * are * * * not supported because of the collective goods they provide, but rather because they have been fortunate enough to find what I have called *selective incentives*. A selective incentive is one that applies selectively to the individuals depending on whether they do or do not contribute to the provision of the collective good.

A selective incentive can be either negative or positive; it can, for example, be a loss or punishment imposed only on those who do *not* help provide the collective good. Tax payments are, of course, obtained with the help of negative selective incentives, since those who are found not to have paid their taxes must then suffer both taxes and penalties. The best-known type of organized interest group in modern democratic societies, the labor union, is also usually supported, in part, through negative selective incentives. Most of the dues in strong unions are obtained through union shop, closed shop, or agency shop arrangements which make dues paying more or less compulsory and automatic. There are often also informal arrangements with the same effect; David McDonald, former president of the United Steel Workers of America, describes one of these arrangements used in the early history of that union. It was, he writes, a technique

> which we called . . . visual education, which was a high-sounding label for a practice much more accurately described as dues picketing. It worked very simply. A group of dues-paying members, selected by the district director (usually more for their size than their tact) would stand at the plant gate with pick handles or baseball bats in hand and confront each worker as he arrived for his shift.

As McDonald's "dues picketing" analogy suggests, picketing during strikes is another negative selective incentive that unions sometimes need; although picketing in industries with established and stable unions is usually peaceful, this is because the union's capacity to close down an enterprise against which it has called a strike is clear to all; the early phase of unionization often involves a great deal of violence on the part of both unions and anti-union employers and scabs.

* * *

Positive selective incentives, although easily overlooked, are also commonplace, as diverse examples in *The Logic* demonstrate. American farm organizations offer prototypical examples. Many of the members of the stronger American farm organizations are members because their dues payments are automatically deducted from the "patronage dividends" of farm cooperatives or are included in the insurance premiums paid to mutual insurance companies associated with the farm organizations. Any number of organizations with urban clients also provide similar positive selective incentives in the form of insurance policies, publications, group air fares, and other private goods made available only to members. The grievance procedures of labor unions usually also offer selective incentives, since the grievances of active members often get most of the attention. The symbiosis between the political power of a lobbying organization and the business institutions associated with it often yields tax or other advantages for the business institution, and the publicity and other information flowing out of the political arm of a movement often generates patterns of preference or trust that make the business activities of the movement more remunerative. The surpluses obtained in such ways in turn provide positive selective incentives that recruit participants for the lobbying efforts.

Small groups, or occasionally large "federal" groups that are made up of many small groups of socially interactive members, have an additional source of both negative and positive selective incentives. Clearly most people value the companionship and respect of those with whom they interact. In modern societies solitary confinement is, apart from the rare death penalty, the harshest legal punishment. The censure or even ostracism of those who fail to bear a share of the burdens of collective action can sometimes be an important selective incentive. An extreme example of this occurs when British unionists refuse to speak to uncooperative colleagues, that is, "send them to Coventry." Similarly, those in a socially interactive group seeking a collective good can give special respect or honor to those who distinguish themselves by their sacrifices in the interest of the group and thereby offer them a positive selective incentive. Since most people apparently prefer relatively like-minded or agreeable and respectable company, and often prefer to associate with those whom they especially admire, they may find it costless to shun those who shirk the collective action and to favor those who over-subscribe.

Social selective incentives can be powerful and inexpensive, but they are available only in certain situations. As I have already indicated, they have little applicability to large groups, except in those cases in which the large groups can be federations of small groups that are capable of social interaction. It also is not possible to organize most large groups in need of a collective good into small, socially interactive subgroups, since most individuals do not have the time needed to maintain a huge number of friends and acquaintances.

The availability of social selective incentives is also limited by the social heterogeneity of some of the groups or categories that would benefit from a collective good. Everyday observation reveals that most socially interactive groups are fairly homogeneous and that many people resist extensive social interaction with those they deem to have lower status or greatly different tastes. Even Bohemian or other nonconformist groups often are made up of individuals who are similar to one another, however much they differ from the rest of society. Since some of the categories of individuals who would benefit from a collective good are socially heterogeneous, the social interaction needed for selective incentives sometimes cannot be arranged even when the number of individuals involved is small.

* * *

In short, the political entrepreneurs who attempt to organize collective action will accordingly be more likely to succeed if they strive to organize relatively homogeneous groups. The political managers whose task it is to maintain organized or collusive action similarly will be motivated to use indoctrination and selective recruitment to increase the homogeneity of their client groups. This is true in part because social selective incentives are more likely to be available to the more nearly homogeneous groups, and in part because homogeneity will help achieve consensus.

Information and calculation about a collective good is often itself a collective good. Consider a typical member of a large organization who is deciding how much time to devote to studying the policies or leadership of the organization. The more time the member devotes to this matter, the greater the likelihood that his or her voting and advocacy will favor effective policies and leadership for the organization. This typical member will, however, get only a small share of the gain from the more effective policies and leadership: in the aggregate, the other members will get almost all the gains, so that the individual member does not have an incentive to devote nearly as much time to fact-finding and thinking about the organization as would be in the group interest. Each of the members of the group would be better off if they all could be coerced into spending more time finding out how to vote to make the organization best further their interests. This is dramatically evident in the case of the typical voter in a national election in a large country. The gain to such a voter from studying issues and candidates until it is clear what vote is truly in his or her interest is given by the difference in the value to the individual of the "right" election outcome as compared with the "wrong" outcome, *multiplied by the probability a change in the individual's vote will alter the outcome of the election.* Since the probability that a typical voter will change the outcome of the election is vanishingly small, the typical citizen is usually "rationally ignorant" about public affairs. Often, information about public affairs is so interesting or entertaining that it pays to acquire it for these reasons alone—this appears to be the single most important source of exceptions to the generalization that *typical* citizens are rationally ignorant about public affairs.

Individuals in a few special vocations can receive considerable rewards in private goods if they acquire exceptional knowledge of public goods. Politicians, lobbyists, journalists, and social scientists, for example, may earn more money, power, or prestige from knowledge of this or that public business. Occasionally, exceptional knowledge of public policy can generate exceptional profits in stock exchanges or other markets. Withal, the typical citizen will find that his or her income and life chances will not be improved by zealous study of public affairs, or even of any single collective good.

The limited knowledge of public affairs is in turn necessary to explain the effectiveness of lobbying. If all citizens had obtained and digested all pertinent information, they could not then be swayed by advertising or other persuasion. With perfectly informed citizens, elected officials would not be subject to the blandishments of lobbyists, since the constituents would then know if their interests were betrayed and defeat the unfaithful representative at the next election. Just as lobbies provide collective goods to special-interest groups, so their effectiveness is explained by the imperfect knowledge of citizens, and this in turn is due mainly to the fact that information and calculation about collective goods is also a collective good.

*   *   *

The fact that the typical individual does not have an incentive to spend much time studying many of his choices concerning collective goods also helps to explain some otherwise inexplicable individual contributions toward the provision of collective goods. The logic of collective action that has been described in this chapter is not immediately apparent to those who have never studied it; if it were, there would be nothing paradoxical in the argument with which this chapter opened, and students to whom the argument is explained would not react with initial skepticism. No doubt the practical implications of this logic for the individual's own choices were often discerned before the logic was ever set out in print, but this does not mean that they were always understood even at the intuitive and practical level. In particular, when the costs of individual contributions to collective action are very small, the individual has little incentive to investigate whether or not to make a contribution or even to exercise intuition. If the individual knows the costs of a contribution to collective action in the interest of a group of which he is a part are trivially small, he may rationally not take the trouble to consider whether the gains are smaller still. This is particularly the case since the size of these gains and the policies that would maximize them are matters about which it is usually not rational for him to investigate.

This consideration of the costs and benefits of calculation about public goods leads to the testable prediction that voluntary contributions toward the provision of collective goods for large groups without selective incentives will often occur when the costs of the individual contributions are negligible, but that they will *not* often occur when the costs of the individual contributions are considerable. In other words, when the costs of individual action to help to obtain a desired collective good are small enough, the result is indeterminate and sometimes goes one way and sometimes the other, but when the costs get larger this indeterminacy disappears. We should accordingly find that more than a few people are willing to take the moment of time needed to sign petitions for causes they support, or to express their opinions in the course of discussion, or to vote for the candidate or party they prefer. Similarly, if the argument here is correct, we should not find many instances where individuals voluntarily contribute substantial sums of resources year after year for the purpose of obtaining some collective good for some large group of which they are a part. Before parting with a large amount of money or time, and particularly before doing so repeatedly, the rational individual will reflect on what this considerable sacrifice will accomplish. If the individual is a typical individual in a large group that would benefit from a collective good, his contribution will not make a perceptible difference in the amount that is provided. The theory here predicts that such contributions become less likely the larger the contribution at issue.

Even when contributions are costly enough to elicit rational calculation, there is still one set of circumstances in which collective action can occur without selective incentives. This set of circumstances becomes evident the moment we think of situations in which there are only a few individuals or firms that would benefit from collective action. Suppose there are two firms of equal size in an industry and no other firms can enter the industry. It still will be the case that a higher price for the industry's product will benefit both firms and that legislation favorable to the industry will help both firms. The higher price and the favorable legislation are then collective goods to this "oligopolistic" industry, even though there are only two in the group that benefit from the collective goods. Obviously, each of the oligopolists is in a situation in which if it restricts output to raise the industry price, or lobbies for favorable legislation for the industry, it will tend to get half of the benefit. And the cost-benefit ratio of action in the common interest easily could be so favorable that, even though a firm bears the whole cost of its action and gets only half the benefit of this action, it could still profit from acting in the common interest. Thus if the group that would benefit from collective action is sufficiently small and the cost-benefit ratio of collective action for the group sufficiently favorable, there may well be calculated action in the collective interest even without selective incentives.

* * *

Untypical as my example of equal-sized firms may be, it makes the general point intuitively obvious: other things being equal, *the larger the number of individuals or firms that would benefit from a collective good, the smaller the share of the gains from action in the group interest that will accrue to the individual or firm that undertakes the action. Thus, in the absence of selective incentives, the incentive for group action diminishes as group size increases, so that large groups are less able to act in their common interest than small ones.* If an additional individual or firm that would value the collective good enters the scene, then the share of the gains from group-oriented action that anyone already in the group might take must diminish. This holds true whatever the relative sizes or valuations of the collective good in the group.

* * *

The significance of the logic that has just been set out can best be seen by comparing groups that would have the same net gain from collective action, if they could engage in it, but that vary in size. Suppose there are a million individuals who would gain a thousand dollars each, or a billion in the aggregate, if they were to organize effectively and engage in collective action that had a total cost of a hundred million. If the logic set out above is right, they could not organize or engage in effective collective action without selective incentives. Now suppose that, although the total gain of a billion dollars from collective action and the aggregate cost of a hundred million remain the same, the group is composed instead of five big corporations or five organized municipalities, each of which would gain two hundred million. Collective action is not an absolute certainty even in this case, since each of the five could conceivably expect others to put up the hundred million and hope to gain the collective good worth two hundred million at no cost at all. Yet collective action, perhaps after some delays due to bargaining, seems very likely indeed. In this case any one of the five would gain a hundred million from providing the collective good even if it had to pay the whole cost itself; and the costs of bargaining among five would not be great, so they would sooner or later probably work out an agreement providing for the collective action. The numbers in this example are arbitrary, but roughly similar situations occur often in reality, and the contrast between "small" and "large" groups could be illustrated with an infinite number of diverse examples.

The significance of this argument shows up in a second way if one compares the operations of lobbies or cartels within jurisdictions of vastly different scale, such as a modest municipality on the one hand and a big country on the other. Within the town, the mayor or city council may be influenced by, say, a score of petitioners or a lobbying budget of a thousand dollars. A particular line of business may be in the hands of only a few firms, and if the town is distant enough from other markets only these few would need to agree to create a cartel. In a big country, the resources needed to influence the national government are likely to be much more substantial, and unless the firms are (as they sometimes are) gigantic, many of them would have to cooperate to create an effective cartel. Now suppose that the million individuals in our large group in the previous paragraph were spread out over a hundred thousand towns or jurisdictions, so that each jurisdiction had ten of them, along with the same proportion of citizens in other categories as before. Suppose also that the cost-benefit ratios remained the same, so that there was still a billion dollars to gain across all jurisdictions or ten thousand in each, and that it would still cost a hundred million dollars across all jurisdictions or a thousand in each. It no longer seems out of the question that in many jurisdictions the groups of ten, or subsets of them, would put up the thousand-dollar total needed to get the thousand for each individual. Thus we see that, if all else were equal, small jurisdictions would have more collective action per capita than large ones.

Differences in intensities of preference generate a third type of illustration of the logic at issue. A small number of zealots anxious for a particular collective good are more likely to act collectively to obtain that good than a larger number with the same aggregate willingness to pay. Suppose there are twenty-five individuals, each of whom finds a given collective good worth a thousand dollars in one case, whereas in another there are five thousand, each of whom finds the collective good worth five dollars. Obviously, the argument indicates that there would be a greater likelihood of collective action in the former case than in the latter, even though the aggregate demand for the collective good is the same in both. The great historical significance of small groups of fanatics no doubt owes something to this consideration.

The argument in this chapter predicts that those groups that have access to selective incentives will be more likely to act collectively to obtain collective goods than those that do not, and that smaller groups will have a greater likelihood of engaging in collective action than larger ones. The empirical portions of *The Logic* show that this prediction has been correct for the United States.

* * *

DISCUSSION QUESTIONS

1. Besides the size of a group, what other considerations do you think would play a role in people's decision to join a collective endeavor? Are you convinced that the size of a group is as important as Olson argues?

2. Think of your own decisions to join or not join a group. Have you ever been a "free rider"? For example, have there been protests against tuition increases at your school that you supported but did not participate in? If so, what would it have taken to get you to join?

3. If Olson is right, would Truman's view in the previous reading about the positive benefits of groups need to be modified? Or can both Olson and Truman be correct?

62

"Organizations and the Democratic Representation of Interests: What Does It Mean When Those Organizations Have No Members?"

KAY LEHMAN SCHLOZMAN, PHILIP EDWARD JONES,
HYE YOUNG YOU, TRACI BURCH, SIDNEY VERBA,
AND HENRY E. BRADY

Usually, when you think about organized interests, you most likely think about large membership groups like the National Abortion Rights Action League or the National Right to Life. Or you might think about organizations that have many organizations as their members, such as the Chamber of Commerce with its corporate and business members. But that's not the only way that interests make their voices heard in politics. Political scientist Kay Lehman Schlozman and her coauthors focus our attention on a different kind of organized interest: one with no members. Organizations like corporations or hospitals are heavily involved in political matters, and they have specific policy interests for which they advocate, but they do not have members in the way the other groups mentioned earlier do. Looking at change over a 30-year period, the authors find that by 2011 only about one-quarter of the organizations active in Washington, D.C., were membership organizations. Most politically active organized interests were memberless, and most were corporations. If organized interest politics is a prime way to influence public policy in America's political system, is it a problem when three-quarters of the organized interests aren't representing members and the views of members? The authors note that scholars have argued that the standard interest-group universe already creates challenges for representational democracy. They state that these concerns are exacerbated when an organized interest is representing only its own views and not those of a large number of members. Even in the universe of membership associations, scholars have argued that business interests are disproportionately represented. This representational advantage grows significantly when looking at memberless organizations engaged in the political world. For example, scholars have argued that the leaders of membership groups often lead without much real accountability from members. This problem would be even more acute in a memberless organization. A company, university, or hospital involved in policy making might say it represents workers or students or patients, but these individuals join these organizations for other reasons and would be unlikely to have any direct influence over the organization's policy stances in the way that members in a membership association theoretically would.

Organized interests play a significant role in the systems of representation in modern democracies. Indeed, democracy on a national scale almost surely requires a robust community of free organizations mediating between citizens and the state. However, studies of interest groups in the United States demonstrate consistently that they perform this representative function in ways that leave many, especially those who lack political resources, with diminished political voice: barriers to entry imply that not all of those with a stake in policy outcomes are represented by groups, interest groups do not represent all their members equally, and rank-and-file group members may not be able to hold accountable the leaders who presume to act on their behalf.

These concerns about political representation by organizations emerge from studies of traditional interest groups, that is, voluntary associations of individuals. Interest group scholarship overlooks the fact that, as we demonstrate, an increasing majority of organizations active in Washington politics have no members in the ordinary sense in which the Service Employees International Union and the National Rifle Association have individual members. We focus on such memberless organizations—for example, universities, hospitals and, especially, corporations—not because they behave differently from associations with individual members when they get involved in politics. On the contrary, membership associations and memberless organizations mobilize the same kinds of techniques in the pursuit of policy influence. For example, although they focus on different policy issues and different institutional targets within Congress and the executive branch, two perennially heavy-hitting organizations, the American Medical Association, a membership association composed of physicians, and Lockheed Martin Corporation, the nation's largest defense contractor, use a similar mix of traditional lobbying supplemented by targeted election donations. In 2014, the AMA spent $19.65 million on lobbying and was responsible for $2.08 million in campaign contributions. The analogous figures for Lockheed were $14.6 million and $4.13 million.

Our reason for focusing on memberless organizations in pressure politics is, instead, that each of the representational inequalities characteristic of membership associations of individuals is exacerbated when politically active organizations are organizations without members. Compared to membership associations of individuals, organizations without members tend to represent the interests of the advantaged, especially business. Even when organizations without members purport to represent less powerful interests in politics, problems of agency and inequality arise. Organizations without members frequently fail to represent stakeholders equally. When that happens, dissatisfied stakeholders may have difficulty calling organization executives to account. These considerations regarding the representational consequences of the growing dominance in pressure politics of organizations without members gain greater resonance when viewed in the context of other trends in contemporary American politics that facilitate the exercise of political voice by those with significant market resources.

In the following pages, we explore the presence of organizations without members in politics by drawing on an extensive data archive containing information about the organizations listed in the *Washington Representatives* directory as having a presence in national politics—either by maintaining an office in the capital or by hiring Washington-based consultants or counsel to manage their government relations activities. We show that organizations without members are the predominant organizational form with respect to both numbers and spending and that they raise in an even more profound way questions of inequality and accountability in political representation.

* * *

Finding Memberless Organizations: The Washington Representatives Study

In order to investigate these matters, we draw on an extensive data archive containing information about the organizations listed in the *Washington Representatives* directory as having a presence in national politics—either by maintaining an office in the capital or by hiring Washington-based consultants or counsel to manage their government relations activities. The Washington Representatives Study contains data for 1981, 1991, 2001, 2006, and 2011 and includes profiles of more than 33,000 organizations that are or have been active in national politics.

For each of these organizations, we coded what we call "organizational membership status": that is whether it is an association composed of individual members, an organization without members, an association of organizations without members, a mixture of types, or something else.

The Dominance of Memberless Groups in Organized Interest Politics

A generation ago, Robert Salisbury pointed out that the predominant organizational advocate in Washington is not an "interest group" or a "pressure group" or any kind of group at all. Rather, it is an organization without members in any traditional sense—for example, a corporation, university, or hospital. In addition, organizations composed of such memberless groups, most notably the trade associations that bring together companies in a single industry, are more numerous than organizations composed of individual members.

Despite the attention given to organizations of individuals in studies of interest group politics, these groups are a small minority of those active in Washington. * * * Just 11.3 percent of the more than 14,000 organizations active in 2011 were membership associations of individuals—less than memberless organizations (56.5 percent), associations of memberless organizations (13.9 percent), or sub-national governments or consortia of governments (14.3 percent).

Not only are there more memberless organizations than membership associations in the Washington pressure community, their share has grown over the past two decades. * * * Put another way, in 1991 there were 2.94 memberless organizations for every membership association of individuals in pressure politics. Twenty years later that ratio had grown to 5.00.

The memberless organizations that are so numerous command significant political resources. With regard to manpower, all of the organizations listed in the *Washington Representatives* directory hire professionals to represent their interests in national politics. They may open an office in Washington and rely on in-house staff or they may hire outside law, public relations, or consulting firms to handle their government affairs matters or both. Membership associations like the American Peanut Council, the American Nurses Association, or the Association of Home Appliance Manufacturers have more flexibility in locating their headquarters than Boeing, the Metropolitan Museum of Art, or the State of Nevada. Therefore, it is not surprising that * * * memberless organizations and also governments are less likely to have an office in Washington with government affairs professionals on staff than are associations with either individuals or institutions as members. In contrast, nearly all the organizations without members hire outside firms to handle their Washington representation. It is worth noting that the minority of memberless organizations that do have lobbyists on staff hire, on average, more of them than do their counterparts among associations. The result * * * is that organizations without members account for 43 percent of the in-house lobbyists and 62 percent of the outside firms hired by organizations in Washington to handle their government affairs needs.

When it comes to the amount of lobbying spending, organizations without members leave membership associations of individuals in the dust. * * * By 2010–2011, memberless organizations were responsible for fully 63 percent of the lobbying spending and the share attributable to voluntary associations of individuals—mostly unions, occupational associations, and citizen groups—had shrunk to 9 percent. Put another way * * * the ratio of lobbying spending by groups without members to lobbying spending by groups with individuals as members rose from 4.4-to-1 to 6.7-to-1 between 2001 and 2011, an even sharper slope than for the increase in the number of memberless groups.

Memberless Organizations and Democratic Representation

* * * Although organizations serve as critical links between citizens and policymakers, the membership associations of individuals that have absorbed the attention of scholars perform the function of democratic representation only very imperfectly: many with a presumable stake in

policy outcomes, in particular the resource-poor, lack organized political voice; members of interest groups are not necessarily represented on an equal basis; and they are not necessarily able to hold accountable the leaders who presume to act for them. Not only are the often-neglected memberless organizations dominant in pressure politics in terms of both their numbers and their spending, but each of these democratic deficits is more pronounced when the organizational representative has no members.

Memberless Organizations: Giving Voice to the Affluent

Organized interest politics is well known as a domain that overrepresents the economically privileged, a tendency that is exaggerated when it comes to organizations without members. Taken together, the organizations in the pressure community skew strongly in the direction of interests with substantial resources, especially business, at the expense of advocacy for broad public interests and those with limited resources.* * *

Systematic data demonstrate how little representation the interests of broad publics and the less affluent receive from organizations without members. * * * Virtually all the organizations that represent the less privileged, identity groups, or broad public interests are voluntary associations with individuals as members. In contrast, both memberless organizations and associations of those organizations tilt overwhelmingly in the direction of representing business: 70 percent of the memberless organizations, most of which are corporations, and 79 percent of associations composed of organizations without members, the vast majority of which are trade and business associations, represent the interests of business. In sum, while the pressure community as a whole tilts strongly in the direction of narrow interests and the affluent, memberless organizations and associations of them exacerbate that tendency substantially.

Memberless Organizations: Representing Stakeholders Unequally

A second problem of democratic representation, that leaders of organizations are more likely to represent some group members than others, becomes much more complicated when the organizations in question have no members. Although they have no individual members, memberless organizations do have multiple sets of stakeholders—who can be defined as "any group or individual who is affected by or can affect the achievement of an organization's objectives." The interests and preferences of various stakeholders—for example, the patients, physicians, nurses, other medical staff, nonmedical staff, administrators, board, third-party payers, suppliers, or neighbors of a hospital—are sometimes coincident and sometimes in conflict. * * *

* * *

With the sole exception of corporate political activity, the puzzle of which stakeholders are represented when memberless organizations get involved in politics has been largely neglected. Academic studies of corporate behavior in politics highlight the potential divergence between the interests of corporate shareholders on the one hand, and executives and directors on the other. However, they reach no definite conclusions as to whether boards and executives are able to act autonomously in politics and find no clear patterns for the circumstances under which either management or shareholders will benefit from political activity. Still, the concerns and preferences of other potential stakeholders—suppliers, customers, the communities in which firms are located and, especially, employees—are strikingly absent from the discussions.

Memberless Organizations: The Barriers to Accountability

A final concern about democratic representation through memberless organizations is that, compared to individual members of a voluntary association, stakeholders of a memberless organization have diminished prospects for democratic control. With regard to authorization, the executives or boards who run memberless organizations—whether a foundation, museum, university, or corporation—are more likely to be in a position to exercise autonomy in choosing whether and how to get involved in politics without having to consult with broader sets of stakeholders.

With respect to accountability, the extent to which membership associations have formal or informal mechanisms for enforcing accountability varies. However, many of those who seek to lead, or to continue to lead, membership associations confront the prospect of having to face the rank-and-file in periodic elections. Those who run organizations without members may, indeed, be held accountable by a board and, in the case of corporate CEOs, may on rare occasions be called to account by a shareholder revolt. Nevertheless, the stakeholders who are invested in such organizations have, on average, much less leverage and fewer democratic rights in holding their leaders accountable than do members of associations. * * *

* * * We have shown that the pressure system is dominated by organizations that have no members—universities, hospitals, museums, think tanks, foundations and, especially, corporations. By 2011, memberless organizations constituted 57 percent of the organizations active in Washington and 63 percent of all government-relations spending by organizations. In comparison, associations with individuals as members accounted for a mere 11 percent of the organizations active in politics and 9 percent of the lobbying expenditures.

All the concerns about democratic representation that emerge from studies of voluntary associations of individuals appear in exaggerated form when the organizational advocates have no members. Memberless organizations lean sharply in the direction of representing business interests and provide almost no representation for the less privileged or for broad public interests. Because they have stakeholders rather than members, it is difficult to know whom they represent through their political action. However, when corporations are involved in politics, some stakeholders—in particular, employees and the communities in which corporate facilities are located—seem to take a back seat to shareholders or management. Finally, compared to leaders of membership associations, leaders of memberless groups are less likely to be subject to democratic control when they pursue political influence: they are able to exercise greater freedom in initiating political action without authorization and have less reason to fear being rendered accountable.

Our findings about the dominance of organizations without members dovetail with a set of concerns that have been raised recently about various aspects of representation in American democracy. Scholars point to the ease with which economic inequalities are translated into political equalities. For one thing, through the political activity of individuals, public officials hear much more from the affluent than from the economically disadvantaged. Moreover, in electoral politics, skyrocketing campaign costs, coupled with a series of judicial decisions lifting the lid off the limits on campaign donations, have created an environment of enhanced possibilities for political voice and influence among those with very deep pockets. Campaign dollars increasingly derive from a narrow slice of the very affluent, and candidates, who must raise staggering sums, spend more and more time in the company of the very rich. And, long before the courts ruled that money is a form of speech when it comes to campaign donations, direct communications to policymakers by organizations enjoyed First Amendment protection from regulation. Finally, in making policy, legislators are disproportionately likely to respond to their affluent constituents and to business and professional associations rather than to mass-based interest groups.

Organized interest advocacy, which has traditionally been hospitable to the conversion of market resources into political resources, is an integral part of this configuration of representational mechanisms. That organizations without members figure so importantly in pressure politics only exacerbates the circumstance such that economic and political inequalities reinforce one another.

Discussion Questions

1. Is it persuasive for a memberless organized interest to say that it represents the interests of a stakeholder group? If so, why? If not, what might the memberless interest do to make the claim more persuasive?

2. Does the involvement of memberless organized interests in politics enrich pluralism, as described by Truman, or endanger pluralism? Explain why.

Debating the Issues: Should Interest Groups Be Required to Report the Names of Donors?

The First Amendment of the U.S. Constitution says that "Congress shall make no law . . . abridging the freedom of speech." The Supreme Court must define the boundaries of what that broad prohibition means. Does it apply to pornography? Commercial speech? Speech that advocates the overthrow of the government or incites violence? Contributions to nonprofit groups, including those engaged in campaign activity, similarly generate a difficult set of questions. In its rulings, the Court has equated the use of money as donations as a form of speech. In other words, money facilitates the making and spreading of messages. Supporting a group with a contribution is making a statement, and is thus speech, and the money itself helps the group speak through advertisements, publications, and other means. Where to draw the line between activity that is permissible and that which is prohibited has been a controversial issue.

In its January 2010 decision in *Citizens United v. Federal Election Commission*, the Supreme Court decided that the First Amendment protects the right of nonprofit and for-profit corporations and labor unions to spend directly to run ads calling for the election or defeat of a candidate in political campaigns. The Court decision said that corporations and unions could spend directly from their treasuries to speak on matters of interest to their organizations, including who they believe would be preferable candidates to elect. The decision also provided support for requiring disclosure of donor names so long as a regulation advanced a "'sufficiently important' governmental interest." *Citizens United* prompted passionate opposition and strong support for the Court's ruling, a debate that continues to this day.

In the years since the decision, debate has flared over the more general question of private donations to interest groups and private organizations. Should interest groups be required to disclose their donors? Proponents of disclosure note that although much funding must be disclosed, the amount that is undisclosed is also significant. For example, an individual can give to a group or entity whose donations need not be disclosed (call it Group A), and then Group A can give to another organization (call it Group B) for political messages and related purposes. Group B will report Group A as a donor, but it will not disclose the individuals who made the initial donation to Group A. Proponents of disclosure often refer to these donated funds as "dark money." Their chief argument is that the public has a right to know who is speaking through these funds, especially when the groups are engaged in advocacy around public policy and elections. Proponents of anonymous speech, who believe anonymous (undisclosed) speech should be protected, say the issue is simple: we should care more about the message than who is delivering it. Moreover, they say it can sometimes be risky if an individual's support for a particular cause is revealed, and they point to "cancel culture" examples where people lost their employment for contributing to a group or toward a cause. Supporters of anonymous speech say that because government officials take actions and make decisions that affect the livelihood of organizations and individuals, these organizations and individuals must be able to receive contributions and spend funds without fear of reprisal.

The authors in this debate respond to the Supreme Court's 2021 decision striking down a California law that required the disclosure of large donors to registered nonprofits. Ian Millhiser is not a fan of the *Citizens United* decision, but the bright spot for him was that the 2010 ruling provided support for donor disclosure. With the Court's 2021 ruling in *Americans for Prosperity v. Bonta*, Millhiser notes that the ruling added the requirement that a disclosure law or regulation be "narrowly tailored," meaning that the law or regulation will "typically be struck down if the government could have advanced its goal in some other way." He argues that with this change, the Court effectively made it nearly impossible to uphold disclosure requirements. Stephen L. Carter looks more sympathetically on the Court's decision. The U.S. Constitution protects the right to free association, he argues, but disclosing the individuals who choose to freely associate in a group can chill their willingness to join. He also notes that although the social situation is not nearly as dire as the one prompting the Court's 1958 ruling that the NAACP did not need to disclose its members' names (*NAACP v. Alabama ex rel. Patterson*), Carter views that people today are being significantly condemned and punished for the causes they support, thereby deterring them from freely associating with like-minded individuals through their donations. For that reason as well, he argues, it is reasonable to put limits on donor disclosure.

63

"The Supreme Court Just Made *Citizens United* Even Worse"

Ian Millhiser

In its infamous decision in *Citizens United v. FEC* (2010), the Supreme Court tossed a bone to lawmakers seeking to regulate money in politics. With a few exceptions, *Citizens United* stripped the government of its power to limit the amount of spending on elections, especially by corporations. But the decision also gave the Court's blessing to nearly all laws requiring campaigns and political organizations to disclose their donors.

They've now stripped most of the lingering meat off that bone.

On Thursday, the Court handed down a 6–3 decision in *Americans for Prosperity Foundation v. Bonta*, which flips *Citizens United*'s approach to disclosure laws on its head.

Before Thursday, the Court treated most disclosure laws as valid, and it typically only allowed plaintiffs who objected to such a law to seek an exemption from it—not to seek a court order striking down the law altogether. After *Americans for Prosperity*, there is now a presumption that all such laws are unconstitutional—although this presumption might be rebuttable in some cases.

As Justice Sonia Sotomayor writes in a dissenting opinion, "[T]oday's analysis marks reporting and disclosure requirements with a bull's-eye." The upshot is that wealthy donors now have far more ability to shape American politics in secret—and that ability is only likely to grow as judges rely on the decision in *Americans for Prosperity* to strike down other donor disclosure laws.

Americans for Prosperity was brought by two conservative organizations—the Americans for Prosperity Foundation, a conservative advocacy group closely associated with the billionaire Koch brothers; and the Thomas More Law Center, a conservative law firm that claims it was formed to promote "America's Judeo-Christian heritage"—against a California regulation requiring charities that wish to raise tax-deductible funds in California to disclose their largest contributors to the state attorney general's office. So the actual law at issue in this case is fairly far afield from actual campaigns for political office.

But Chief Justice John Roberts's opinion for himself and his fellow conservative justices has broad implications for all donor disclosure laws. It writes a new legal standard that will allow many future challenges to those laws to succeed, and that also will likely lead to sweeping victories for many of the plaintiffs in such suits.

Americans for Prosperity *Destroys a Consensus That Used to Exist between Liberal and Conservative Justices*

Not that long ago, there was broad consensus that disclosure laws aren't just permissible but essential in a democracy. As Justice Antonin Scalia wrote in a 2010 opinion:

> Requiring people to stand up in public for their political acts fosters civic courage, without which democracy is doomed. For my part, I do not look forward to a society which, thanks to the Supreme Court, campaigns anonymously . . . and even exercises the direct democracy of initiative and referendum hidden from public scrutiny and protected from the accountability of criticism. This does not resemble the Home of the Brave.

That consensus is now dead. Much of the Court's right flank spent the oral argument in *Americans for Prosperity* rejecting Scalia's "civic courage" in favor of a kind of paranoia over cancel culture. Justice Neil Gorsuch warned that the government could demand to see your "Christmas card lists" or to disclose your "dating history" to state regulators. Justice Samuel Alito spoke of "vandalism, death threats, physical violence, economic reprisals, [and] harassment in the workplace" directed against donors to an anti-LGBTQ campaign.

Under the previous consensus—the one announced in *Citizens United*—disclosure laws would be upheld so long as there is "a 'substantial relation' between the disclosure requirement and a 'sufficiently important' governmental interest." Moreover, while some disclosure laws might be vulnerable to challenge, the Court typically only permitted "as applied" challenges, meaning that the plaintiff could seek an exemption from a particular disclosure law, but the law would still apply to other individuals or organizations. In other words, most disclosure laws were valid, and the onus was on the donors who wanted secrecy to prove they individually deserved it.

The Court's previous decisions, moreover, suggested that the bar for bringing such an as-applied challenge is fairly high. The seminal decision establishing that some organizations must be exempted from disclosure laws is *NAACP v. Alabama ex rel. Patterson* (1958), which was an attempt by the state of Alabama to force the NAACP—then the nation's preeminent civil rights organization—to disclose its membership.

Had the NAACP done so, Alabama could have turned those names over to the Ku Klux Klan, among other things.

The plaintiffs in *Americans for Prosperity* do allege that they were the victims of death threats and other sorts of inexcusable activity—Roberts points [to] a statement from someone working in the same building as the AFP Foundation, who said that he could "easily walk into [the CEO's] office and slit his throat"—but nothing that even approaches the constant threat of terroristic violence that civil rights activists faced in the Jim Crow South.

In any event, as Sotomayor writes in her dissent, she "would be sympathetic" to a decision that "simply granted as-applied relief" to these plaintiffs, because of the threats they've faced. But the Court goes much further, striking down California's disclosure rules on their face—meaning that they are now invalid for everyone.

The Court Rewrites the Legal Standard Governing Disclosure Laws

As mentioned above, *Citizens United* held that disclosure laws would be upheld so long as there is "a 'substantial relation' between the disclosure requirement and a 'sufficiently important' governmental interest." Roberts's opinion abandons that standard, holding that disclosure laws must be "narrowly tailored" to advance the government's interest in requiring disclosure.

Most first-year law students will immediately recognize the significance of these two words, "narrowly tailored," as it is part of the test the Supreme Court applies when it wishes to impose a very high presumption that certain laws are unconstitutional. The Court, for example, imposes a narrow tailoring requirement on laws that discriminate on the basis of race.

Though *Americans for Prosperity* does not go quite as far as it could have—it does not apply a test known as "strict scrutiny," the most skeptical test the Court applies in constitutional challenges—it comes pretty damn close.

When the Court applies a narrow tailoring requirement, it signals that a law will typically be struck down if the government could have advanced its goal in some other way. The practical impact of *Americans for Prosperity* is that all disclosure laws, including campaign disclosure laws, are now vulnerable if a plaintiff can think of some other hypothetical way that the government might have fostered the goal of transparency.

Roberts justified such a result because he claims that "disclosure requirements can chill association '[e]ven if there [is] no disclosure to the general public.'" He fears, in other words, a world in which donors will choose not to donate to groups like the Americans for Prosperity Foundation, out of fear that their names will be disclosed.

And then, of course, there is the shift from as-applied to facial challenges. Rather than simply doling out exemptions to disclosure laws, courts are now much more likely to strike them down in their entirety.

The decision is, simply put, a disaster for anyone hoping to know how wealthy donors influence American politics.

64

"Anonymous Donors Should Stay That Way"

STEPHEN L. CARTER

The Supreme Court's decision to strike down California's law requiring disclosure of large donors to registered charities is bound to be controversial but seems to me, on balance, correct. Part of the reason is libertarian: [i]t's no business of mine where my neighbors choose to give money, and it's no business of theirs where I do. The rest of the reason . . . well, I'll get to that.

In *Americans for Prosperity Foundation v. Bonta*—popularly known as AFP—two conservative-leaning groups challenged the California requirement as violating their rights under the First Amendment. In a 6-3 opinion by Chief Justice John Roberts, the court largely agreed. The disclosure rule, according to the majority, burdens the right to free association, which is closely tied to the right to associate privately. To justify the burden, there must be "a substantial relation between the disclosure requirement and a sufficiently important governmental interest"—and, in addition, the disclosure must "be narrowly tailored to the interest it promotes." A generalized interest in preventing wrongdoing does not justify so broad a demand.

The source case for this analysis is the 1958 decision in *NAACP v. Alabama ex rel. Patterson,* where the court on similar grounds struck down an Alabama law requiring disclosure of the NAACP's membership list. The justices were rightly worried that, in the heart of Jim Crow country, members of the organization would face intimidation or worse. Thus keeping their names private was crucial to the ability to associate.

Justice Sonia Sotomayor's powerful dissent in AFP mocks the majority's notion that *NAACP v. Alabama* is a controlling case, pointing out that the court there was concerned about the "reprisals and violence" against civil rights activists that were all too common in the 1950s. Here, she writes, there's no serious prospect that well-shod donors to conservative activist groups will face "threats, harassment, or reprisals."

Sotomayor is largely correct—and probably as tired as I am of seeing important civil rights victories hijacked by the right. Yet the majority also has a point. *NAACP v. Alabama* did arise in the unique circumstance of the civil rights movement, but the justices rested the opinion on the First Amendment's right of free association. The language was categorical: "[i]nviolability of privacy in group association may in many circumstances be indispensable to preservation of freedom of association, particularly where a group espouses dissident beliefs." The court added that intimidation resulted from "private community pressures" rather than state action.

This sort of holding is hard to write around.

Things might be different if this were a world in which people were sufficiently reasonable to accept that the other side often has a case. But it isn't. For a long time, the American right made a specialty of tearing people down because of the causes they gave to. Nowadays a lot of the tearing down is done by the left. Whoever's doing it, our democracy isn't terribly good at helping us respect each other across our deep differences.

Which brings me to my second reason for agreeing, reluctantly, with the majority. *NAACP v. Alabama* arose under special circumstances, but the problem is more general. This is not a world in which civil rights protesters are routinely fired from jobs, have their houses torched, and dragged into the woods and murdered. It is in a world in which people try to punish each other for espousing controversial views. Not just criticize—punish. That the punishments are far smaller than those that led to *NAACP v. Alabama* doesn't mean they're not punishments.

In this sense, the close link between the right of public association and the right to associate privately may be viewed as a prophylactic approach to protecting constitutional rights. If the names of donors must be disclosed, there are people who won't give. If this weren't true, there would be no reason for the plaintiffs to litigate the case.

What about downstream effects? At oral argument, Justice Stephen Breyer worried that a ruling for the plaintiffs might eviscerate campaign-finance laws, which rest centrally on disclosure of contributions. But this needn't be so. For one thing, as my colleagues Bruce Ackerman and Ian Ayres have persuasively shown, it's possible to protect against corruption without disclosure, through the device of a "secret donation booth"—a mandate that all campaign contributions remain secret, even from the candidate. For another, campaign giving can be distinguished from other forms of associational activity, and the majority is careful to do just that.

Perhaps the decision in AFP is as dangerous as its critics will say. If so, I hope they will join me in resisting efforts to condemn others for the causes they give to. Otherwise, the majority will turn out to be right.

DISCUSSION QUESTIONS

1. As the readings note, supporters of anonymous speech worry about reprisals from government officials or from others who might oppose the political views of a donor. How heavily do you weigh this concern in deciding whether, or to what degree, to require disclosure of donations to nonprofits?

2. Imagine you hear an organization's message that you fully agree with, but you then find that the major donors to the organization support many causes that you strongly oppose. Would you be more likely to dismiss the message or to reevaluate your view of the donor? Does your answer affect your views on the value of disclosure?

3. The articles reference the distinction between disclosing donor names that would only be seen by a government entity gathering the information and disclosing donor names that would be available to the public. Considering the issues at play in the debate over donor disclosure, is this a meaningful distinction in your view?

4. If you believe donations to interest groups should always or almost always be disclosed, what do you find as the most challenging argument to rebut from those who disagree with your view? Likewise, if you always or nearly always oppose mandatory disclosure, what is the strongest argument taking the opposing view?

PART IV

Public Policy

CHAPTER 13

Government and the Economy

65

"Call for Federal Responsibility"

FRANKLIN ROOSEVELT

The national government has always played a role in the economy. Since the late 1700s, the government has provided property for private development, enforced contracts and prohibited the theft of private property, provided subsidies to encourage the growth of particular industries, developed the infrastructure of the growing country, and regulated trade. The question that commands the attention of political leaders and citizens alike today is what the limits of government involvement in the economy ought to be. To what extent should the free market make most economic decisions to maximize efficiency and productivity? Should the government regulate markets in the pursuit of other goals, such as equality, and to address market failures, such as monopolies and public goods that are underprovided by the market (such as education and environmental protection)?

This debate reached a peak during the Great Depression, as the nation struggled to define the government's role in reviving the economy, and played a critical role in the 1932 presidential election between the Democratic candidate, Franklin Roosevelt (FDR), and the Republican president, Herbert Hoover. In the campaign speech printed here, FDR argued that the federal government should play a role in unemployment insurance, housing for the poor, and public-works programs to compensate for the hardship of the Great Depression. Hoover, on the other hand, was very much opposed to altering the relationship between government and the private sector, which was "builded up by 150 years of toil of our fathers." It was the extension of freedom and the exercise of individual initiative, Hoover claimed, that made the American economic system strong and that would gradually bring about economic recovery. Roosevelt prevailed, and the resulting New Deal changed the face of government. Although the federal government adopted a much more active role in regulating the economy and providing social safety, the central issues discussed by Roosevelt and Hoover are still being debated today.

The first principle I would lay down is that the primary duty rests on the community, through local government and private agencies, to take care of the relief of unemployment. But we then come to a situation where there are so many people out of work that local funds are insufficient.

It seems clear to me that the organized society known as the State comes into the picture at this point. In other words, the obligation of government is extended to the next higher unit.

I [practice] what I preach. In 1930 the state of New York greatly increased its employment service and kept in close touch with the ability of localities to take care of their own unemployed. But by the summer of 1931 it became apparent to me that actual state funds and a state-supervised system were imperative.

I called a special session of the legislature, and they appropriated a fund of $20 million for unemployment relief, this fund to be reimbursed to the state through the doubling of our income taxes. Thus the state of New York became the first among all the states to accept the definite obligation of supplementing local funds where these local funds were insufficient.

The administration of this great work has become a model for the rest of the country. Without setting up any complex machinery or any large overhead, the state of New York is working successfully through local agencies, and, in spite of the fact that over a million people are out of work and in need of aid in this one state alone, we have so far met at least the bare necessities of the case.

This past spring the legislature appropriated another $5 million, and on November 8 the voters will pass on a $30-million bond issue to tide us over this winter and at least up to next summer.

* * *

I am very certain that the obligation extends beyond the states and to the federal government itself, if and when it becomes apparent that states and communities are unable to take care of the necessary relief work.

It may interest you to have me read a short quotation from my message to the legislature in 1931:

> What is the State? It is the duly constituted representative of an organized society of human beings, created by them for their mutual protection and well-being. One of the duties of the State is that of caring for those of its citizens who find themselves the victims of such adverse circumstances as make them unable to obtain even the necessities of mere existence without the aid of others.
>
> In broad terms, I assert that modern society, acting through its government, owes the definite obligation to prevent the starvation or the dire want of any of its fellowmen and women who try to maintain themselves but cannot. To these unfortunate citizens aid must be extended by the government, not as a matter of charity but as a matter of social duty.

That principle which I laid down in 1931, I reaffirm. I not only reaffirm it, I go a step further and say that where the State itself is unable successfully to fulfill this obligation which lies upon it, it then becomes the positive duty of the federal government to step in to help.

In the words of our Democratic national platform, the federal government has a "continuous responsibility for human welfare, especially for the protection of children." That duty and responsibility the federal government should carry out promptly, fearlessly, and generously.

It took the present Republican administration in Washington almost three years to recognize this principle. I have recounted to you in other speeches, and it is a matter of general information, that for at least two years after the crash, the only efforts made by the national administration to cope with the distress of unemployment were to deny its existence.

When, finally, this year, after attempts at concealment and minimizing had failed, it was at last forced to recognize the fact of suffering among millions of unemployed, appropriations of federal funds for assistance to states were finally made.

I think it is fair to point out that a complete program of unemployment relief was on my recommendation actually under way in the state of New York over a year ago; and that in Washington relief funds in any large volume were not provided until this summer, and at that they were pushed through at the demand of Congress rather than through the leadership of the President of the United States.

At the same time, I have constantly reiterated my conviction that the expenditures of cities, states, and the federal government must be reduced in the interest of the nation as a whole. I believe that there are many ways in which such reduction of expenditures can take place, but I am utterly unwilling that economy should be practised at the expense of starving people.

We must economize in other ways, but it shall never be said that the American people have refused to provide the necessities of life for those who, through no fault of their own, are unable to feed, clothe, and house themselves. The first obligation of government is the protection of the welfare and well-being, indeed the very existence, of its citizens.

* * *

The next question asks my attitude toward appropriations for public works as an aid to unemployment. I am perfectly clear as to the principles involved in this case also.

From the long-range point of view it would be advisable for governments of all kinds to set up in times of prosperity what might be called a nest egg to be used for public works in times of depression. That is a policy which we should initiate when we get back to good times.

But there is the immediate possibility of helping the emergency through appropriations for public works. One question, however, must be answered first because of the simple fact that these public works cost money.

We all know that government treasuries, whether local or state or federal, are hard put to it to keep their budgets balanced; and, in the case of the federal Treasury, thoroughly unsound financial policies have made its situation not exactly desperate but at least threatening to future stability if the policies of the present administration are continued.

All public works, including federal, must be considered from the point of view of the ability of the government Treasury to pay for them. There are two ways of paying for public works. One is by the sale of bonds. In principle, such bonds should be issued only to pay for self-sustaining projects or for structures which will without question have a useful life over a long period of years. The other method of payment is from current revenues, which in these days means in most cases added taxes. We all know that there is a very definite limit to the increase of taxes above the present level.

From this point, therefore, I can go on and say that, if funds can be properly provided by the federal government for increased appropriations for public works, we must examine the character of these public works. I have already spoken of that type which is self-sustaining. These should be greatly encouraged. The other type is that of public works which are honestly essential to the community. Each case must rest on its own merits.

It is impossible, for example, to say that all parks or all playgrounds are essential. One may be and another may not be. If a school, for instance, has no playground, it is obvious that the furnishing of a playground is a necessity to the community. But if the school already has a playground and some people seek merely to enlarge it, there may be a very definite question as to how necessary that enlargement is.

Let me cite another example. I am much interested in providing better housing accommodations for the poor in our great cities. If a slum area can be torn down and new modern buildings put up, I should call that almost a human necessity; but, on the other hand, the mere erection of new buildings in some other part of the city while allowing the slums to remain raises at once a question of necessity. I am confident that the federal government working in cooperation with states and cities can do much to carry on increased public works and along lines which are sound from the economic and financial point of view.

Now I come to another question. I am asked whether I favor a system of unemployment insurance reserves made compulsory by the states, supplemented by a system of federally coordinated state employment offices to facilitate the reemployment of jobless workers.

The first part of the question is directly answered by the Democratic platform which advocates unemployment insurance under state laws.

This is no new policy for me. I have advocated unemployment insurance in my own state for some time, and, indeed, last year six Eastern governors were my guests at a conference which resulted in the drawing up of what might be called an idea plan of unemployment insurance.

This type of insurance is not a cure-all but it provides at least a cushion to mitigate unemployment in times of depression. It is sound if, after starting it, we stick to the principle of sound insurance financing. It is only where governments, as in some European countries, have failed to live up to these sound principles that unemployment insurance has been an economic failure.

As to the coordinated employment offices, I can only tell you that I was for the bills sponsored by Senator Wagner of my own state and passed by the Congress. They created a nationally coordinated system of employment offices operated by the individual states with the advisory cooperation of joint boards of employers and employees.

To my very great regret this measure was vetoed by the President of the United States. I am certain that the federal government can, by furnishing leadership, stimulate the various states to set up and coordinate practical, useful systems.

DISCUSSION QUESTIONS

1. Franklin Roosevelt's call for a New Deal and the importance of government investment in "public works" as a way of helping the economy get out of the Great Depression and get people back to work sounds very similar to President Biden's plan for more investment in the nation's infrastructure. What is the proper role of the government in helping people get jobs? Should this be left to the private sector, or should the national government invest more in building highways, bridges, and airports to get more people back to work?

2. FDR's famous line from this speech is, "The first obligation of every government is the protection of the welfare and well-being, indeed the very existence, of its citizens." Do you agree? If so, how do you define the limits of that obligation?

66

"Against the Proposed New Deal"

Herbert Hoover

This campaign is more than a contest between two men. It is more than a contest between two parties. It is a contest between two philosophies of government.

We are told by the opposition that we must have a change, that we must have a new deal. It is not the change that comes from normal development of national life to which I object but the proposal to alter the whole foundations of our national life which have been builded through generations of testing and struggle, and of the principles upon which we have builded the nation. The expressions our opponents use must refer to important changes in our economic and social system and our system of government, otherwise they are nothing but vacuous words. And I realize that in this time of distress many of our people are asking whether our social and economic system is incapable of that great primary function of providing security and comfort of life to all of the firesides of our 25 million homes in America, whether our social system provides for the fundamental development and progress of our people, whether our form of government is capable of originating and sustaining that security and progress.

This question is the basis upon which our opponents are appealing to the people in their fears and distress. They are proposing changes and so-called new deals which would destroy the very foundations of our American system.

Our people should consider the primary facts before they come to the judgment—not merely through political agitation, the glitter of promise, and the discouragement of temporary hardships—whether they will support changes which radically affect the whole system which has been builded up by 150 years of the toil of our fathers. They should not approach the question in the despair with which our opponents would clothe it.

Our economic system has received abnormal shocks during the past three years, which temporarily dislocated its normal functioning. These shocks have in a large sense come from without our borders, but I say to you that our system of government has enabled us to take such strong action as to prevent the disaster which would otherwise have come to our nation. It has enabled us further to develop measures and programs which are now demonstrating their ability to bring about restoration and progress.

We must go deeper than platitudes and emotional appeals of the public platform in the campaign if we will penetrate to the full significance of the changes which our opponents are attempting to float upon the wave of distress and discontent from the difficulties we are passing through. We can find what our opponents would do after searching the record of their appeals to discontent, group and sectional interest. We must search for them in the legislative acts which they sponsored and passed in the Democratic-controlled House of Representatives in the last session of Congress. We must look into measures for which they voted and which were defeated. We must inquire whether or not the presidential and vice-presidential candidates have disavowed these acts. If they have not, we must conclude that they form a portion and are a substantial indication of the profound changes proposed.

And we must look still further than this as to what revolutionary changes have been proposed by the candidates themselves.

We must look into the type of leaders who are campaigning for the Democratic ticket, whose philosophies have been well known all their lives, whose demands for a change in the American system are frank and forceful. I can respect the sincerity of these men in their desire to change our form of government and our social and economic system, though I shall do my best tonight to prove they are wrong. I refer particularly to Senator Norris, Senator La Follette, Senator Cutting, Senator Huey Long, Senator Wheeler, William R. Hearst and other exponents of a social philosophy different from the traditional American one. Unless these men feel assurance of support to their ideas, they certainly would not be supporting these candidates and the Democratic Party. The seal of these men indicates that they have sure confidence that they will have voice in the administration of our government.

I may say at once that the changes proposed from all these Democratic principals and allies are of the most profound and penetrating character. If they are brought about, this will not be the America which we have known in the past.

Let us pause for a moment and examine the American system of government, of social and economic life, which it is now proposed that we should alter. Our system is the product of our race and of our experience in building a nation to heights unparalleled in the whole history of the world. It is a system peculiar to the American people. It differs essentially from all others in the world. It is an American system.

It is founded on the conception that only through ordered liberty, through freedom to the individual, and equal opportunity to the individual will his initiative and enterprise be summoned to spur the march of progress.

It is by the maintenance of equality of opportunity and therefore of a society absolutely fluid in freedom of the movement of its human particles that our individualism departs from the individualism of Europe. We resent class distinction because there can be no rise for the individual through the frozen strata of classes, and no stratification of classes can take place in a mass livened by the free rise of its particles. Thus in our ideals the able and ambitious are able to rise constantly from the bottom to leadership in the community.

This freedom of the individual creates of itself the necessity and the cheerful willingness of men to act cooperatively in a thousand ways and for every purpose as occasion arises; and it permits such voluntary cooperations to be dissolved as soon as they have served their purpose, to be replaced by new voluntary associations for new purposes.

There has thus grown within us, to gigantic importance, a new conception. That is, this voluntary cooperation within the community. Cooperation to perfect the social organization; cooperation for the care of those in distress; cooperation for the advancement of knowledge, of scientific research, of education; for cooperative action in the advancement of many phases of economic life. This is self-government by the people outside of government; it is the most powerful development of individual freedom and equal opportunity that has taken place in the century and a half since our fundamental institutions were founded.

It is in the further development of this cooperation and a sense of its responsibility that we should find solution for many of our complex problems, and not by the extension of government into our economic and social life. The greatest function of government is to build up that cooperation, and its most resolute action should be to deny the extension of bureaucracy. We have developed great agencies of cooperation by the assistance of the government which promote and protect the interests of individuals and the smaller units of business. The Federal Reserve System, in its strengthening and support of the smaller banks; the Farm Board, in its strengthening and support of the farm cooperatives; the Home Loan Banks, in the mobilizing of building and loan associations and savings banks; the Federal Land Banks, in giving independence and strength to land mortgage associations; the great mobilization of relief to distress, the mobilization of business and industry in measures of recovery, and a score of other activities are not socialism—they are the essence of protection to the development of free men.

The primary conception of this whole American system is not the regimentation of men but the cooperation of free men. It is founded upon the conception of responsibility of the individual to the community, of the responsibility of local government to the state, of the state to the national government.

It is founded on a peculiar conception of self-government designed to maintain this equal opportunity to the individual, and through decentralization it brings about and maintains these responsibilities. The centralization of government will undermine responsibilities and will destroy the system.

Our government differs from all previous conceptions, not only in this decentralization but also in the separation of functions between the legislative, executive, and judicial arms of government, in which the independence of the judicial arm is the keystone of the whole structure.

It is founded on a conception that in times of emergency, when forces are running beyond control of individuals or other cooperative action, beyond the control of local communities and of states, then the great reserve powers of the federal government shall be brought into action to protect the community. But when these forces have ceased, there must be a return of state, local, and individual responsibility.

The implacable march of scientific discovery with its train of new inventions presents every year new problems to government and new problems to the social order. Questions often arise whether, in the face of the growth of these new and gigantic tools, democracy can remain master in its own house, can preserve the fundamentals of our American system. I contend that it can; and I contend that this American system of ours has demonstrated its validity and superiority over any other system yet invented by human mind.

It has demonstrated it in the face of the greatest test of our history—that is the emergency which we have faced in the past three years.

When the political and economic weakness of many nations of Europe, the result of the World War and its aftermath, finally culminated in collapse of their institutions, the delicate adjustment of our economic and social life received a shock unparalleled in our history. No one knows that better than you of New York. No one knows its causes better than you. That the crisis was so great that many of the leading banks sought directly or indirectly to convert their assets into gold or its equivalent with the result that they practically ceased to function as credit institutions; that many of our citizens sought flight for their capital to other countries; that many of them attempted to hoard gold in large amounts. These were but indications of the flight of confidence and of the belief that our government could not overcome these forces.

Yet these forces were overcome—perhaps by narrow margins—and this action demonstrates what the courage of a nation can accomplish under the resolute leadership in the Republican Party. And I say the Republican Party, because our opponents before and during the crisis, proposed no constructive program; though some of their members patriotically supported ours. Later on the Democratic House of Representatives did develop the real thought and ideas of the Democratic Party, but it was so destructive that it had to be defeated, for it would have destroyed, not healed.

In spite of all these obstructions, we did succeed. Our form of government did prove itself equal to the task. We saved this nation from a quarter of a century of chaos and degeneration, and we preserved the savings, the insurance policies, gave a fighting chance to men to hold their homes. We saved the integrity of our government and the honesty of the American dollar. And we installed measures which today are bringing back recovery. Employment, agriculture, business—all of these show the steady, if slow, healing of our enormous wound.

I therefore contend that the problem of today is to continue these measures and policies to restore this American system to its normal functioning, to repair the wounds it has received, to correct the weaknesses and evils which would defeat that system. To enter upon a series of deep changes, to embark upon this inchoate new deal which has been propounded in this campaign, would be to undermine and destroy our American system.

Discussion Questions

1. State governments have always played a role in regulating the economy, from consumer protection to using tax breaks as a way to attract business investment within a state's borders. What kind of economic activities are best regulated at the state level? When should the federal government play a role?

2. Which of the activities that the government performs do you consider essential? Why?

3. Hoover's arguments against government bureaucracy and in favor of individual and community responsibility resonate today with the Freedom Caucus in Congress and other conservative Republicans. What similarities do you see between Hoover's arguments and the current opponents of big government?

67

"'Socialism' Isn't a Dirty Word Anymore"

Sarah Jones

Democrats and Republicans have debated about the proper role of the government in the national economy since at least Franklin Roosevelt's New Deal in the 1930s. However, the central role of the free market and our capitalist economy was never questioned by even liberal Democrats. However, in recent years, with the rise of income inequality, the concentration of wealth in the top 1 percent and the power of large international corporations have led more Americans to question the capitalist system and support redistributive policies. For example, polls show a majority of Americans support a wealth tax to address the fact that the 745 billionaires in the United States have a combined wealth of about $5 trillion, which is significantly more than the $3.42 trillion owned by the bottom half of American households (about 161 million people). Sarah Jones cites a broad range of public-opinion polls showing that while Americans still generally support capitalism, socialism is viewed more favorably today than in recent years. A majority of younger and Black Americans, and 45 percent of women, have a favorable view of socialism. Jones argues that "voters are eager for something new," and socialism may be part of the new appeal.

Most Americans still think positively of capitalism, but that's beginning to change among young adults, a new poll suggests. According to an Axios/Momentive survey released on Friday, adults ages 18 to 34 "are almost evenly split between those who view capitalism positively and those who view it negatively." Those numbers have changed significantly over the last two years, when 20 percentage points separated those who viewed capitalism positively from those who did not. Among adults aged 18 to 24, capitalism is in even deeper trouble: 42 percent say they have a positive view of it, and 54 percent do not.

If capitalism has begun to lose its shine, what solutions do people prefer? Socialism, for one. While positive views of socialism have slipped slightly among adults under 35 over the last two years, falling from 55 to 51 percent, it's picked up some support from older adults and especially people of color. Axios reports that 60 percent of Black Americans view socialism positively, as do 45 percent of women, and even 33 percent of non-white Republicans. "Those numbers have grown over the past two years from 53 percent, 41 percent, and 27 percent respectively," Felix Salmon writes. Capitalism is still more popular than socialism nationally, but there's not much evidence that Americans categorically despise the anti-capitalist ideology any more.

The Axios/Momentive poll didn't measure attitudes toward common socialist ideas though. Asking the public about the wealth gap is not quite the same as asking them if they support redistribution of wealth to close it. Nevertheless, the poll did indicate some broad support for a form of social democracy. 66 percent said the federal government "should pursue policies that try to reduce the gap between the wealthy and the less well-off in America," which tracks with earlier, similar polls. In January 2020, the Pew Research Center found that most Americans believed there was too much economic inequality in the [United States], though only 42 percent said it should be a top priority for the federal government. The same poll, however, did show high rates of support for another form of government intervention: 72 percent said its top priority should be making health care more affordable for the public.

Support for other, broadly progressive policy solutions remain high. In an April Hill-HarrisX poll, 56 percent of registered voters "said billionaires paying a wealth tax is part of the solution to wealth inequality," a figure consistent with previous poll results. Another March Morning Consult/Politico poll found that around seven in ten voters support a public health insurance option, and 55 percent support Medicare for All. Considered together, these numbers tell a political story. As the pandemic reordered American life and the economy along with it, Americans have become more critical of the dominant economic order. That creates an opening for Democrats—if they're savvy enough to take advantage of it.

Most Democratic electeds remain eager to differentiate themselves from their socialist colleagues, who are themselves a small faction of the party's presence in Congress. Should public opinion hold, however, that faction is likely to grow with time. That doesn't spell doom for the party's overall electoral chances, either. Democrats should ask themselves which is the more damaging possibility: A failure to condemn socialism, or a failure to critique capitalism? Given the numbers, the answer is clearly the latter, at least among the demographic groups Democrats need to inspire in order to keep winning elections.

Of course, Republicans will conflate milquetoast versions of liberalism with socialism as they successfully did during the last election in Florida among Latino voters. As a result, Democrats should have learned there's no effective way to dodge a smear campaign except to counter it with a more effective message. Perhaps they could even make inroads with non-white Republicans. Party moderates may dislike it, but socialism has a growing constituency: [i]n Buffalo, voters just elected socialist nurse India Walton in an upset over the Democratic incumbent, Byron Brown.*

---

*After this article was written, Walton lost to Brown in the general election when he ran as a write-in candidate [Editors].

Should Democrats mount a cohesive critique of capitalism, they'll meet many Americans where they are. That's sensible politics, the key to a winning strategy. For the last year, Americans have lost jobs, stability, and in many cases, hope. A crisis as dramatic as COVID-19 should expand the party's definition of what's possible. Voters are eager for something new. Someone will provide it. That person could be a socialist or social democrat, or they could be a Republican cunning enough to wrap conservative politics in a populist-sounding message. Democrats will have to conquer their hostility to the former in order to prepare for the latter. There is a vanishing constituency for the status quo.

DISCUSSION QUESTIONS

1. Jones points out that socialism is becoming more popular with some segments of the population. Do you think embracing socialism is a winning strategy for liberal Democrats?

2. Are some voters more likely to support progressive policies, such as a wealth tax, but still reject the label of a socialist? If so, does that influence your answer to the first question?

3. If you were a left-leaning Democrat running for office in a competitive district, would you call yourself a socialist or a social Democrat?

Debating the Issues: Should the Government Pick Winners and Losers in Business, or Leave It to the Free Market?

Since Alexander Hamilton wrote the "Report on the Subject of Manufactures" in 1791, the U.S. government has expressed interest in industrial policy, defined as "government support for particular industries that are deemed strategically important." Along with redistributive policies, countercyclical fiscal and monetary policy, and regulatory and trade policies, industrial policy is one of the important ways the government tries to influence economic outcomes. As with each of these policies, opposing views argue for an active role for the government versus leaving more decisions up to the free market economy.

Scott Lincicome has not been swayed by such patriotic and nationalist appeals and remains committed to a pro–free market, anti-interventionist approach when it comes to industrial policy. He argues that the market is better at picking winners and losers in the economy than the government. He runs through a long list of failed government interventions and argues that even in industries that are undeniably important for the economy and national security, such as computer chips, the government does not have a strong track record. Furthermore, he says that China's record is not always stellar, either: despite massive government subsidies of its chip industry, China is not dominant in this critical area. Lincicome bases his analysis of industrial policy on the insights of "public choice theory," which states that politicians are self-interested actors who try to maximize their chances for re-election by pushing localized benefits to their constituents (pork-barrel politics). Thus, if politicians are in charge of creating industrial policy, we are doomed to have an inefficient allocation of resources and would be better off leaving those decisions up to the free market.

Anshu Siripurapu provides a balanced account of industrial policy in the United States, discussing the pros and cons of the government's promotion of certain sectors of the economy. He points out that the United States has had periods of stronger industrial policy, as with various New Deal policies in the 1930s and the massive war economy during World War II. But in general, the United States has been more reluctant to back favored industries than many of our competitors, especially China. Today, there is renewed interest in a revived industrial policy on both the Left, with calls for a "Green New Deal," and the Right, with a Trump-inspired "America first" position on trade and its support for industries such as steel and aluminum. The latter has been a significant pivot in terms of the partisan politics of this issue because the Republican Party had always been strongly free-trade and against government intervention in the economy.

68

"The 'Endless Frontier' and American Industrial Policy"

Scott Lincicome

For the last week or so, the U.S. Senate has been considering one of the largest "industrial policy" packages in recent history. In particular, the United States Innovation and Competition Act of 2021 (formerly known as the "Endless Frontier Act" or EFA) is intended to boost federal funding for applied industrial research and development by tens of billions of dollars. Well, at least it *was*. The bill has morphed considerably since it was first delivered to the Senate Commerce Committee for markup under "regular order." Today, the 1,400-plus page bill is as much—if not more—about *other stuff* than it is about subsidizing "key technology focus areas" like artificial intelligence, advanced semiconductors, and quantum computing. And even the policies targeting those key areas have been watered down and changed.

All of this has shocked and exasperated many industrial policy advocates who saw the EFA as an essential part of future U.S. industrial competitiveness. I, as you can imagine, tend not to agree with their plans or their sense of urgency (and the data tend to support me—see this week's links), but that's beside the point, at least for today. Instead, the whole episode provides us with a golden opportunity to dig into a field of economics—public choice theory—that helps to explain a lot of what goes on in Washington and one of the main reasons why designing and implementing good industrial policy in the United States is so darn difficult.

What Is 'Public Choice Theory'?

I briefly addressed public choice in February when discussing the Jones Act but never provided the basics, so let's start there.

Public choice theory is a branch of economics developed by economists James Buchanan and Gordon Tullock and elucidated in their 1962 book *The Calculus of Consent*. Public choice hit the big time in 1986 when Buchanan won the Nobel Memorial Prize in economics for his work in the field. In general, public choice takes the same principles that economists use to analyze people's actions in the private market and applies them to people's actions in the public sphere. Thus, political actors are presumed to act not in the "public interest" but in their own rational self-interest and thus to use the political systems in which they operate to make themselves, not the general public or nation as a whole, better off. In this context, elected officials' primary goal is reelection, whereas bureaucrats strive to advance (or protect) their own careers. Surely, political actors have motivations other than self-interest, but the general public choice framework assumes the latter until proven otherwise. As Buchanan put it, the theory "replaces . . . romantic and illusory . . . notions about the workings of governments [with] . . . notions that embody more skepticism."

Today many of us may take such skepticism for granted, but questioning the image of the altruistic "public servant" was pretty radical when Buchanan, Tullock, and other public choice scholars first started doing it. Nevertheless, once you're aware of public choice theory's basic tenets, you see it everywhere in public policy—especially in both the design *and* implementation of American industrial policy. On the former, elected officials frequently advance legislative policies that confer concentrated benefits upon small, homogenous, often local interest groups and impose diffuse (but larger) costs upon the general public, because only the small groups have sufficient motivation to follow the issues closely and apply political pressure (lobbying, campaign contributions, and votes) based thereon. Because the public is "rationally ignorant" about these policies (and thus does not tie their votes or contributions to them), elected officials act rationally in supporting them, even when the policies are known to produce net losses for the country.

This "collective action" problem not only generates "pork barrel" projects (often through "logrolling" bargains, in which legislators trade votes on each other's pet project), but also makes reform or elimination of these programs exceedingly difficult, regardless of their efficacy.

Implementation of industrial policies can also fall victim to politics, even in systems designed to be insulated from elected officials. Research shows, for example, that government agencies' agendas often mirror those of the members of the congressional committees that primarily oversee them—members that often actively seek out these committee assignments in order to affect the regulatory agencies beneath them. Thus, the same political pressures that distort elected officials' creation of and support for a certain industrial policy can similarly distort the federal bureaucracy's work to effectuate it. Similarly, numerous studies show that agencies can become "captured" by motivated special interest groups (or their elected benefactors) who use the agency to further their own narrow interests at the broader public's expense. Even where political pressure is limited (often by design), capture can occur where bureaucrats lack the same level of specialized knowledge as the entities they're regulating and thus grow to rely on those entities for both information and manpower (aka "the revolving door").

The U.S. political system amplifies the public choice hurdles facing industrial policies (and others) for two big reasons. First, large segments of Congress are replaced (or threatened with replacement) every two years and the president every four. This dynamic not only injects "short-termism" and uncertainty into the decisionmaking process, but also makes elected officials more risk-averse and focused on reelection instead of the long-term national interest. Second, the [United States] has a well-developed lobbying and interest group system, which would inevitably affect (and likely deteriorate) the design and implementation of any significant industrial policy. Economist Mancur Olson explained how these two dynamics undermined U.S. industrial policies back in 1986, and both are almost certainly more intense today.

How Public Choice Confounds U.S. Industrial Policy

Past U.S. industrial policy efforts show how public choice issues can thwart planners' intentions, especially in the high-tech space. For example, in critiquing the Endless Frontier Act's structure back in 2020, technology experts Patrick Windham, Christopher T. Hill, [and] David Cheney noted that "U.S. efforts in the 1990s to identify 'critical technologies' did not succeed, partly because it is hard to predict which technologies will be most valuable in the future [*note: this "Knowledge Problem" is another common industrial policy hurdle*] and partly because decisions about R&D funding priorities inevitably become political, as groups and leaders vie to have their favorites supported."

Once legislation is passed, moreover, politics can still intervene. In the 1991 book, *The Technology Pork Barrel*, for example, the authors—sympathetic to industrial policy—examined six federal programs from the 1960s and 1970s intended to develop commercial technologies for the private sector. They found that *none* were truly successful, while four were "almost unqualified failures," costing billions, crowding out more meritorious R&D projects, yet enduring long after fiscal, technological, and commercial failure was established—a survival owed to political pressure (especially financial benefits accruing to numerous congressional districts) and captured regulators.

To block a potential National Science Foundation purchase of a super-computer made by Cray's Japanese rival NEC in the 1990s, for example, the House of Representatives "passed legislation sponsored by Rep. David R. Obey (D-Wis.), whose district includes a Cray facility, that would virtually ensure the contract goes to Cray," and the captured Commerce Department imposed record-setting anti-dumping duties of 454 percent on Japanese supercomputer imports in 1997. (Members of Congress routinely influence U.S. agencies' anti-dumping determinations—either by informal pressure or by changing the governing statutes—in order to enrich their corporate or union constituents.) For other examples of tech industry capture and corporatism during the last heyday of U.S. industrial policy (the '80s and '90s), check out *High Tech Protectionism* by AEI's Claude Barfield.

More recently, studies have shown that various Department of Energy projects funded by the 2009 American Recovery and Reinvestment Act

(ARRA) had significant political, not scientific, motivations—with project funding often linked to lobbying expenditures or campaign contributions. Solyndra got the headlines, but there were plenty of other messes (see, for example, "clean coal" calamities in Illinois and Mississippi). DoE loan guarantee programs from the same period also suffered from other political problems, such as non-economic objectives like job protection and local sourcing ("Buy American") rules. Other recent research finds that politically connected firms (as measured by contributions to home state elections) were "64 percent more likely to secure an ARRA grant and receive 10 percent larger grants" than other, less-connected companies.

And then there's the whole Emergent Biosolutions fiasco: a "longtime government contractor" that invested heavily in lobbying; had effectively "captured" the government agency (the Biomedical Advanced Research and Development Authority) authorized to disburse and monitor pandemic-related contracts; and, despite repeated failures, was rewarded with a $628-million contract to manufacture COVID-19 vaccines.

Surely, not every U.S. industrial policy effort has become a public choice poster child, but the theory has proven remarkably prescient overall. As *The Technology Pork Barrel* authors put it, numerous U.S. industrial policy experiences "justify skepticism about the wisdom of government programs that seek to bring new technologies to commercial practice." (If only!)

So What Happened to the Endless Frontier?

The Endless Frontier Act (EFA) obviously hasn't been implemented yet, but its Senate consideration is consistent with the aforementioned theory and practice. For starters, the actual innovation section of the bill has changed dramatically in terms of scope and operation: instead of $100 billion going to the National Science Foundation, "[w]hat we have now are single-digit percentage boosts to the NSF's funding, some money out of left field for the Department of Energy, and a plus-up for National Labs like Los Alamos (thanks to the National Labs Caucus which, perhaps unsurprisingly, seems more focused on pushing money to their states' arguably duplicative labs than addressing domestic innovation challenges)."

Maybe, as Yuval Levin argues, the National Labs changes are a good thing, but a press release issued by the National Labs Caucus senators makes clear that their motivation wasn't the "public interest" but simply bringing home the bacon for the labs in their states. It also appears that the NSF itself was involved in lowering the price tag, "given worries that the EFA would give the Technology Directorate too much autonomy and detract from the agency's traditional focus on inquiry-oriented science in favor of applied research and technology."

But that's just the EFA sections. Senators have also added all sorts of other provisions that are mostly (or entirely) unrelated to the original EFA, including:

- $52 billion in new subsidies for the domestic semiconductor industry, $39 billion of which is for commercial (non-defense) manufacturing facilities and workers, not bleeding-edge R&D. We've already gone over how most of these subsidies are dubious at best (Intel agrees!), but Sen. Chuck Schumer's latest press release touting the benefits for New York chip companies is a useful addition. * * * New to the semiconductor subsidy package, however, is $2 billion for "legacy chips" (read: old, low-tech stuff) that U.S. automakers need—an amendment helpfully offered by Michigan Sen. Gary Peters because it "would boost the U.S. auto industry in his home state of Michigan." And, just for the record, it's not only libertarians opposed to this obvious corporate welfare. Sen. Bernie Sanders tweeted, "Yes. Congress should work to expand U.S. microchip production. No. As part of the Endless Frontiers bill we should not be handing out $53 billion in corporate welfare to some of the largest and most profitable corporations in the country with no strings attached."
- Peters' other amendment, applying "Davis-Bacon" wage and work requirements (which labor unions love) to the aforementioned semiconductor subsidies—reportedly violating a deal with Senate Republicans on that very issue.
- Washington Democratic Sen. Maria Cantwell's amendment adding $10 billion to NASA's budget "to give Blue Origin a shot at winning the lunar landing contract NASA has already awarded to SpaceX at a fraction of the cost, all while requiring NASA to continue developing an unnecessary launch system that Boeing just happens to have the contract for." Blue Origin was founded by Cantwell constituent Jeff Bezos.
- New, protectionist country of origin labeling requirements for online retailers (unlike brick-and-mortar shops), but excepting cooked king crab and tanner crab to win the vote of Alaska's Dan Sullivan.
- More restrictive—and thus more destructive—"Buy American" rules for federal construction projects (which the steel industry, of course, cheered) and new rules for federal procurement of domestic PPE (which the textile industry, of course, cheered).
- A new ban on U.S. sales of shark fin. (I got nothin'.)

I'm confident that there's more nonsense in there, but the bill is more than 1,400 pages long, so it's almost impossible to sort through all of it. And more amendments are on the way.

Industrial policy advocates have expressed shock and dismay at the various Senate Committees' "logrolling" efforts, but their surprise is unwarranted. Indeed, this kind of behavior is *exactly what the literal dictionary definition of public choice tells us will happen.*

The logic of collective action explains why farmers have secured government subsidies at the expense of millions of unorganized consumers, who pay higher prices for food, and why textile manufacturers have benefited significantly from trade barriers at the expense of clothing buyers. Voted on separately, neither of those legislatively enacted special-interest measures would pass. But by means of logrolling bargains, in which the representatives of farm states agree to trade their votes on behalf of trade protectionism in exchange for pledges of support for agricultural subsidies from the representatives of textile-manufacturing states, both bills can secure a majority. Alternatively, numerous programs of this sort can be packaged in omnibus bills that most legislators will support in order to get their individual pet projects enacted. The legislative pork barrel is facilitated by rational-voter ignorance about the adverse effects of legislative decisions on their personal well-being. It also is facilitated by electoral advantages that make it difficult for challengers to unseat incumbents, who, accordingly, can take positions that work against their constituents' interests with little fear of reprisal.

And we've known for months now that every industry group and lobbyist in town was gearing up for this moment. Throw in the fact that this is (supposedly) must-pass, bipartisan "China legislation," and it'd be shocking if all the logrolling and pork *didn't* happen.

At this point, advocates are left to hope that this is all cleaned up by the House. (Good luck, as they say, with all *that*.)

Summing It All Up

So U.S. industrial policy has a long history of struggling to overcome political pressures, just as public choice predicts, and the EFA is no different. None of this means that all legislating is bad, or that politicians don't at least occasionally vote in the national interest. Instead, the public choice framework simply adds another hurdle—along with things like the "knowledge problem," seen and unseen costs, and misaligned incentives—to designing and implementing commercial policies specifically intended to beat the admittedly messy and imperfect situation that the market generates. It's imperative that we understand these risks before supporting policies that, while they might look good on paper, could easily morph into a counterproductive boondoggle—one we've seen countless times with respect to U.S. industrial policy. Buchanan's "skepticism" is most definitely warranted.

We tolerate these risks and costs when there's a real crisis or when the subject is national defense, where government involvement is both necessary and inevitable (because it's the sole consumer of defense-related goods) and public support is more widespread and enduring. (We also tend to get better results in that case.) But there's little excuse to do so for industrial policy—*especially* when there's plenty of evidence that America's urgent manufacturing or investment problems are neither as urgent nor as problematic as advocates claim.

69

"Is Industrial Policy Making a Comeback?"

Anshu Siripurapu

As the United States confronts a series of challenges—the COVID-19 pandemic, growing income inequality, climate change, and the rise of China foremost among them—there is renewed debate about the role of industrial policy, or government support for particular industries that are deemed strategically important.

To its supporters, a new U.S. industrial policy is essential to respond to China's state-led development, secure a supply of critical materials and products, and develop technologies that could preserve the planet. They point to the use of industrial policy not only in China, but also in countries such as Germany, Japan, and South Korea, as well as its historical use in the United States. To critics, such a policy inevitably distorts the free market and rewards companies not for the quality of their products and services but for their skill at lobbying lawmakers.

After President Donald J. Trump upended the Republican Party's traditional stance on trade and economic policy, the debate over the need for an American industrial policy intensified. President Joe Biden has made clear his desire to transform an economy upended by the pandemic.

What Is Industrial Policy?

Industrial policy generally refers to efforts to promote specific industries that the government has identified as critical for national security or economic competitiveness. The Roosevelt Institute's Todd Tucker has defined industrial policy as: "any government policy that encourages resources to shift from one industry or sector into another, by changing input costs, output prices, or other regulatory treatment."

Industries often included are those with heavy manufacturing or that have military applications, such as aerospace, steel, and shipbuilding. Policy measures could be protective tariffs or other trade restrictions, direct subsidies or tax credits, public spending on research and development (R&D), or government procurement (goods and services, such as military equipment, that the government buys). "It's about the government putting a thumb on the scale, rather than just assuming that market outcomes are going to produce the maximum benefit," says CFR's Edward Alden.

Alexander Hamilton is widely considered to be the first major proponent of industrial policy in the United States. In his famous 1791 "Report on the Subject of Manufactures," the nation's first treasury secretary advocated supporting the fledgling U.S. manufacturing sector through a combination of tariffs and subsidies.

This Hamiltonian tradition has been expressed in various forms throughout U.S history, such as Henry Clay's vision of an "American System"—a combination of tariffs, a national bank, and infrastructure development—in the early nineteenth century, writes Ganesh Sitaraman of Vanderbilt University. Sitaraman ascribes several other traditions of U.S. industrial policy to early American leaders, including a "Franklinian" tradition focused on promoting research and infrastructure, rather than particular industries, and a "Madisonian" tradition centered on creating a competitive market through the use of antitrust and other regulations.

However, among advanced economies, the United States has historically been "the most averse to using industrial policies in any kind of consistent fashion," says CFR's Alden. Washington has typically embraced it only in response to a perceived external threat, he says.

Experts cite many of President Franklin D. Roosevelt's (FDR) New Deal programs of the 1930s as early examples. These include the National Recovery Administration, which sought to regulate wages and prices across a slew of industries. The massive, government-directed World War II mobilization that followed was also an extreme case.

After the war, U.S. industrial policy was largely driven by competition with the Soviet Union, including the space race. The Pentagon's Defense Advanced Research Projects Agency (DARPA)—conceived in response to the Soviet Union's launch of Sputnik, the first artificial satellite—has been credited with paving the way for the modern internet and the Global Positioning System (GPS), among other breakthroughs. Massive government purchases of semiconductors spurred the growth of that U.S. industry. But competition with Japan in the semiconductor industry in the 1980s stoked fears of a U.S. decline. This led to the creation of Sematech, a government-backed consortium of fourteen U.S. companies aimed at strengthening the industry by coordinating R&D spending and setting common standards.

More recent examples include ARPA-Energy, the Department of Energy's own version of DARPA, which focuses on developing new energy technologies. President Barack Obama's Manufacturing USA initiative, started in 2016, established more than a dozen public-private research institutes focused on promoting advanced manufacturing.

What about Other Countries?

Many countries, including Germany, Japan, South Korea, and most Latin American countries, have implemented industrial policies with varying degrees of success.

Europe. Industrial policy has a long tradition in Europe, including in France, Germany, and the United Kingdom. The economist Ha-Joon Chang has detailed, for example, how England fostered the development of wool manufacturing as early as the fourteenth century using tariffs, export restrictions, and other measures. Germany's nineteenth-century Chancellor Otto von Bismarck, who created a unified German state, introduced tariffs to protect both agriculture and industry, known as the "marriage of iron and rye." Chang explains that state-owned enterprises have played an important role in several European economies. The French government today is still a major shareholder of the automaker Renault, while the aerospace giant Airbus is the result of a collaborative effort by the British, French, Spanish, and German governments to challenge American companies such as Boeing.

The 1980s saw a turn against heavy state involvement, with the UK's Margaret Thatcher and other leaders privatizing nationalized industries such as steel and airlines. More recently, however, UK Prime Minister Boris Johnson announced plans for a "green industrial revolution," pledging investments in renewable energies and electric vehicles to help make the country carbon-neutral by 2050. In Germany today, research is supported by a network of public-private institutes, and manufacturing is aided by an apprenticeship program. Berlin has also developed an "Industry 4.0" plan to boost high-tech manufacturing through research subsidies and other initiatives.

The European Union, meanwhile, has recently adopted a climate-focused industrial policy, which includes the European Battery Alliance, a network to coordinate research and subsidize battery manufacturing across the continent. The bloc is also looking to increase its share of the global semiconductor market and lead the way in quantum computing.

Asia. Many experts argue that industrial policy stoked the "East Asian miracle," the rapid post–World War II economic development of countries in the region, including Japan and South Korea. The Japanese government fostered the development of industries such as steel and semiconductors using a combination of trade and investment restrictions, subsidies, and other policies. By the 1980s, Japan had transformed into an economic powerhouse rivaling the United States. Yet, some experts argue that the effects of industrial policy on Japan's economic growth are overstated, and that other factors, such as entrepreneurship and the country's high savings rate, played bigger roles. After more than thirty years of rapid growth, Japan suffered what some have called a lost decade in the 1990s, and it has since struggled with low growth and deflation.

South Korea also sought to rapidly modernize its economy in the 1960s and 1970s, including by developing its steel, shipbuilding, electronics, and automobile manufacturing sectors. This led to the creation of the chaebol, massive conglomerates such as Samsung and LG that dominate South Korea's economy. Seoul also heavily subsidized its semiconductor industry, helping it become one of the world's largest. In Taiwan, meanwhile, the government played a crucial role in developing its semiconductor industry—also a global leader—by funding research and recruiting U.S.-trained engineers. However, economist Arvind Panagariya has argued that South Korea's and Taiwan's success is the result of their embrace of trade, not industrial policy.

China, under Communist Party leadership since 1949, has long had a state-directed economy despite some market-oriented reforms beginning in the late 1970s. In recent years, Beijing has embraced an aggressive industrial policy in the form of its Made in China 2025 strategy, which outlines Beijing's ambition to achieve global dominance in ten high-tech industries, including electric vehicles, advanced rail and shipbuilding, and artificial intelligence; the government has poured subsidies into the development of these industries.

Latin America. Many countries in the postwar era, worried that they were too dependent on low-value-added commodities in sectors such as agriculture and mining, experimented with import substitution industrialization (ISI). This approach sought to promote domestic industries by discouraging the importation of manufactured goods through tariffs and other trade restrictions. Experts say the results were mixed: some new industries and successful companies were formed, but it also resulted in corruption, inefficiency, and unsustainable government budgets.

Why Is It Controversial?

The debate over industrial policy is heated because it gets to the heart of a deeper, long-standing controversy over the role of free markets and the role of the government in the economy.

Proponents argue that the government has both the ability and the duty to structure the economy in the national interest, since the free market may fail to do so. For example, the manufacturing industry provides broad societal benefits, such as stable, well-paid employment, that are not factored into an individual company's decision-making, argues Oren Cass, executive director of the think tank American Compass. Harvard Business School professors Gary Pisano and Willy Shih have long argued that offshoring production hinders the United States' ability to innovate, as manufacturing know-how is lost.

What's more, a country could determine that it needs to domestically produce critical goods, such as medical supplies or military equipment, for national security reasons. Supporters also argue that the government should fund R&D because the societal benefits go far beyond what companies will invest in.

A smart industrial policy should focus on high-value industries that compete internationally, have civilian and military applications, and are difficult to revive once lost, says Robert D. Atkinson of the Information

Technology and Innovation Foundation. Atkinson cites semiconductor manufacturing as one example.

Critics counter that the government is worse at identifying successful firms than the free market, and that intervention inevitably leads to crony capitalism, where politically well-connected companies benefit at the expense of their competitors. The Cato Institute's Scott Lincicome has documented what he describes as a series of security-motivated industrial policy failures, including U.S. government efforts to support the semiconductor industry in the 1980s that he argues did little to help, and perhaps even harmed, it. Some experts on the left, such as Matt Stoller of the anti-monopoly American Economic Liberties Project, have warned that industrial policy could lead to an even greater concentration of corporate power that he argues would stifle innovation and harm national security.

What Is the Current U.S. Debate About?

Industrial policy fell out of favor in the 1980s and 1990s with the development of the Washington Consensus, by which mainstream economists saw economic development as the result of free-market policies such as the privatization of state enterprises and promotion of free trade. But there is renewed interest among policymakers on both sides of the aisle due primarily to the rise of China, increasing economic inequality, the threat of climate change, and supply-chain vulnerabilities revealed by the COVID-19 pandemic.

Some Democrats have put forward bold proposals that intentionally hearken back to FDR–era interventionism. During the 2020 presidential campaign, Senator Elizabeth Warren (D-MA) proposed a sweeping "economic patriotism" plan to reorient the federal government to protect American jobs and industries. Progressive lawmakers have also proposed a Green New Deal, which envisions a broad, climate-centered industrial policy focused on clean energy, infrastructure, and manufacturing. Senate Majority Leader Chuck Schumer (D-NY) is pushing legislation, known as the Endless Frontier Act, that would invest $100 billion in research in many of the same industries in China's Made in China 2025 plan.

On the right, President Trump broke with long-standing Republican economic orthodoxy with the stated goal of bringing back American jobs, particularly in manufacturing. He imposed tariffs on imported steel and aluminum products, washing machines, and solar panels; he took aggressive action against China, slapping additional tariffs on hundreds of billions of dollars worth of Chinese goods and blocking several high-profile Chinese acquisitions of U.S. tech firms. But many experts criticized Trump's tariffs as ineffective, saying they generated few jobs at a huge cost to consumers and other industries.

Some other Republicans have followed suit. "The market will always reach the most efficient economic outcome, but sometimes the most efficient outcome is at odds with the common good," Senator Marco Rubio (R-FL) said in a December 2019 speech advocating for a new U.S. industrial policy to counter China and bring back "dignified work." His plan includes increasing federal R&D spending, encouraging investment in "strategically important industries" such as aerospace and rail, and incentivizing businesses to invest more in factories and machinery.

Cato's Lincicome warns against overstating the success of China's state capitalism, noting that Chinese semiconductor companies have failed to become global leaders despite billions of dollars in subsidies. Moreover, he says, "the United States should lean in to what makes the United States great": increasing high-skilled immigration, cutting taxes and regulations, and securing new trade agreements with allies. Lincicome further argues that industrial-policy proponents paint a picture of U.S. decline that is far bleaker than reality. Though employment has declined, the value of manufacturing output has risen over the past two decades, and the sector's declining share of the economy is consistent with those of other advanced economies as service industries expand.

What Could Biden Do?

President Biden campaigned on a pledge to "Build Back Better," a plan that would put hundreds of billions of dollars toward improving U.S. economic competitiveness and promises a foreign policy "for the middle class." As the full extent of the disruptions wrought by the COVID-19 pandemic become clearer, Biden is reportedly eyeing a broad transformation of the U.S. economy.

One of Biden's first actions in office was an executive order aimed at strengthening so-called Buy American laws, which require the federal government to purchase goods and services from U.S. companies. In another executive order, he began the process of replacing the federal government's massive fleet of vehicles with clean-energy models made in the United States, a potential boon to the domestic electric vehicle industry. Amid a global shortage of semiconductors and concerns over insufficient stocks of basic medical supplies during the pandemic, Biden also ordered a review of U.S. supply chain vulnerabilities.

However, CFR's Shannon K. O'Neil warns that the push to return supply chains to the United States could make them less resilient by concentrating production among a few U.S. manufacturers. A better approach, she writes, would be to coordinate with allies such as Canada and Mexico to create joint supply chains and strategic stockpiles to respond to future crises. "An industrial policy that tries to preserve the past through protectionism and isolation will only weigh down the United States," O'Neil writes in *Foreign Affairs*.

Discussion Questions

1. Do you think that the United States should have a more aggressive industrial policy to be able to better compete with other countries who support their favored industries? Or should we leave these decisions up to the free market?

2. Many observers have pointed out that Bernie Sanders and Donald Trump had very similar positions on trade. How have partisan politics changed on this issue in recent years?

3. If you took the free market position in answering the first question, would you support a larger role for the federal government in supporting basic research and development, and then leave the commercialization of that research up to the private sector?

CHAPTER 14

Government and Society

70

"American Business, Public Policy, Case Studies, and Political Theory"

Theodore J. Lowi

Before Theodore J. Lowi's article appeared in 1964, many social scientists analyzed public policy through case studies that focused on one particular policy and its implementation. Lowi argued that what the social sciences lacked was a means to cumulate, compare, and contrast the diverse findings of these studies. We needed, in other words, a typology of policy making. In the article below, Lowi argues that different types of public policies produce different patterns of participation. Public policies can be classified as distributive, regulatory, or redistributive, each with its own distinctive "arena of power." For example, public policies that provide benefits to a single congressional district, group, or company can be classified as distributive. In the distributive arena of power, policy beneficiaries are active in seeking to expand or extend their benefits, but there is no real opposition. Rather, legislators build coalitions premised upon "mutual noninterference" interests, and their representatives seek particular benefits, such as a research and development contract, a new highway, or a farm subsidy, but they do not oppose the similar requests of others. The regulatory and redistributive policy arenas also display distinctive dynamics and roles that participants in the process play. Lowi's work was important not only for providing a classification scheme by which social scientists could think more systematically about different public policies, but for proposing that we study "politics" as a consequence of different types of public policy. Traditionally, social scientists have studied politics to see what kinds of policies are produced.

What is needed is a basis for cumulating, comparing, and contrasting diverse findings. Such a framework or interpretative scheme would bring the diverse cases and findings into a more consistent relation to each other and would begin to suggest generalizations sufficiently close to the data to be relevant and sufficiently abstract to be subject to more broadly theoretical treatment.

* * *

The scheme is based upon the following argument: (1) The types of relationships to be found among people are determined by their expectations—by what they hope to achieve or get from relating to others. (2) In politics, expectations are determined by governmental outputs or policies. (3) Therefore, a political relationship is determined by the type of policy at stake, so that for every type of policy there is likely to be a distinctive type of political relationship. If power is defined as a share in the making of policy, or authoritative allocations, then the political relationship in question is a power relationship or, over time, a power structure.

* * *

There are three major categories of public policies in the scheme: distribution, regulation, and redistribution. These types are historically as well as functionally distinct, distribution being almost the exclusive type of national domestic policy from 1789 until virtually 1890. Agitation for regulatory and redistributive policies began at about the same time, but regulation had become an established fact before any headway at all was made in redistribution.

These categories are not mere contrivances for purposes of simplification. They are meant to correspond to real phenomena—so much so that the major hypotheses of the scheme follow directly from the categories and their definitions. Thus, *these areas of policy or government activity constitute real arenas of power.* Each arena tends to develop its own characteristic political structure, political process, elites, and group relations. What remains is to identify these arenas, to formulate hypotheses about the attributes of each, and to test the scheme by how many empirical relationships it can anticipate and explain.

Areas of Policy Defined

(1) In the long run, all governmental policies may be considered redistributive, because in the long run some people pay in taxes more than they receive in services. Or, all may be thought regulatory because, in the long run, a governmental decision on the use of resources can only displace a private decision about the same resource or at least reduce private alternatives about the resource. But politics works in the short run, and in the short run certain kinds of government decisions can be made without regard to limited resources. Policies of this kind are called "distributive," a term first coined for nineteenth-century land policies, but easily extended to include most contemporary public land and resource policies; rivers and harbors

("pork barrel") programs; defense procurement and R & D [research and development]; labor, business, and agricultural "clientele" services; and the traditional tariff. Distributive policies are characterized by the ease with which they can be disaggregated and dispensed unit by small unit, each unit more or less in isolation from other units and from any general rule. "Patronage" in the fullest meaning of the word can be taken as a synonym for "distributive." These are policies that are virtually not policies at all but are highly individualized decisions that only by accumulation can be called a policy. They are policies in which the indulged and the deprived, the loser and the recipient, need never come into direct confrontation. Indeed, in many instances of distributive policy, the deprived cannot as a class be identified, because the most influential among them can be accommodated by further disaggregation of the stakes.

(2) Regulatory policies are also specific and individual in their impact, but they are not capable of the almost infinite amount of disaggregation typical of distributive policies. Although the laws are stated in general terms ("Arrange the transportation system artistically." "Thou shalt not show favoritism in pricing."), the impact of regulatory decisions is clearly one of directly raising costs and/or reducing or expanding the alternatives of private individuals ("Get off the grass!" "Produce kosher if you advertise kosher!"). Regulatory policies are distinguishable from distributive in that in the short run the regulatory decision involves a direct choice as to who will be indulged and who deprived. Not all applicants for a single television channel or an overseas air route can be propitiated. Enforcement of an unfair labor practice on the part of management weakens management in its dealings with labor. So, while implementation is firm by firm and case by case, policies cannot be disaggregated to the level of the individual or the single firm (as in distribution), because individual decisions must be made by application of a general rule and therefore become interrelated within the broader standards of law. Decisions cumulate among all individuals affected by the law in roughly the same way. Since the most stable lines of perceived common impact are the basic sectors of the economy, regulatory decisions are cumulative largely along sectoral lines; regulatory policies are usually disaggregable only down to the sector level.

(3) Redistributive policies are like regulatory policies in the sense that relations among broad categories of private individuals are involved and, hence, individual decisions must be interrelated. But on all other counts there are great differences in the nature of impact. The categories of impact are much broader, approaching social classes. They are, crudely speaking, haves and have-nots, bigness and smallness, bourgeoisie and proletariat. The aim involved is not use of property but property itself, not equal treatment but equal possession, not behavior but being. The fact that our income tax is in reality only mildly redistributive does not alter the fact of the aims and the stakes involved in income tax policies. The same goes for our various "welfare state" programs, which are redistributive only for those who

entered retirement or unemployment rolls without having contributed at all. The nature of a redistributive issue is not determined by the outcome of a battle over how redistributive a policy is going to be. Expectations about what it *can* be, what it threatens to be, are determinative.

Arenas of Power

Once one posits the general tendency of these areas of policy or governmental activity to develop characteristic political structures, a number of hypotheses become compelling. And when the various hypotheses are accumulated, the general contours of each of the three arenas begin quickly to resemble, respectively, the three "general" theories of political process identified earlier. The arena that develops around distributive policies is best characterized in the terms of [E. E.] Schattschneider's findings. The regulatory arena corresponds to the pluralist school, and the school's general notions are found to be limited pretty much to this one arena. The redistributive arena most closely approximates, with some adaptation, an elitist view of the political process.

(1) The distributive arena can be identified in considerable detail from Schattschneider's case study alone. What he and his pluralist successors did not see was that the traditional structure of tariff politics is also in largest part the structure of politics of all those diverse policies identified earlier as distributive. The arena is "pluralistic" only in the sense that a large number of small, intensely organized interests are operating. In fact, there is even greater multiplicity of participants here than the pressure-group model can account for, because essentially it is a politics of every man for himself. The single person and the single firm are the major activists.

* * *

When a billion-dollar issue can be disaggregated into many millions of nickel-dime items and each item can be dealt with without regard to the others, multiplication of interests and of access is inevitable, and so is reduction of conflict. All of this has the greatest of bearing on the relations among participants and, therefore, the "power structure." Indeed, coalitions must be built to pass legislation and "make policy," but what of the nature and basis of the coalitions? In the distributive arena, political relationships approximate what Schattschneider called "mutual non-interference"—"a mutuality under which it is proper for each to seek duties [indulgences] for himself but improper and unfair to oppose duties [indulgences] sought by others." In the area of rivers and harbors, references are made to "pork barrel" and "log-rolling," but these colloquialisms have not been taken sufficiently seriously. A log-rolling coalition is not one forged of conflict, compromise, and tangential interest but, on the contrary, one composed of members who have absolutely nothing in common; and this is possible because the "pork barrel" is a container for unrelated items. This is the typical form of relationship in the distributive arena.

The structure of these log-rolling relationships leads typically, though not always, to Congress; and the structure is relatively stable because all who have access of any sort usually support whoever are the leaders. And there tend to be "elites" of a peculiar sort in the Congressional committees whose jurisdictions include the subject matter in question. Until recently, for instance, on tariff matters the House Ways and Means Committee was virtually the government. Much the same can be said for Public Works on rivers and harbors. It is a broker leadership, but "policy" is best understood as cooptation rather than conflict and compromise.

* * *

(2) The regulatory arena could hardly be better identified than in the thousands of pages written for the whole polity by the pluralists. But, unfortunately, some translation is necessary to accommodate pluralism to its more limited universe. The regulatory arena appears to be composed of a multiplicity of groups organized around tangential relations. * * * Within this narrower context of regulatory decisions, one can even go so far as to accept the most extreme pluralist statement that policy tends to be a residue of the interplay of group conflict. This statement can be severely criticized only by use of examples drawn from non-regulatory decisions.

As I argued before, there is no way for regulatory policies to be disaggregated into very large numbers of unrelated items. Because individual regulatory decisions involve direct confrontations of indulged and deprived, the typical political coalition is born of conflict and compromise among tangential interests that usually involve a total sector of the economy. Thus, while the typical basis for coalition in distributive politics is uncommon interests (log-rolling), an entirely different basis is typical in regulatory politics. The pluralist went wrong only in assuming the regulatory type of coalition is *the* coalition.

* * *

What this suggests is that the typical power structure in regulatory politics is far less stable than that in the distributive arena. Since coalitions form around shared interests, the coalitions will shift as the interests change or as conflicts of interest emerge. With such group-based and shifting patterns of conflict built into every regulatory issue, it is in most cases impossible for a Congressional committee, an administrative agency, a peak association governing board, or a social elite to contain all the participants long enough to establish a stable power elite. Policy outcomes seem inevitably to be the residue remaining after all the reductions of demands by all participants have been made in order to extend support to majority size. But a majority-sized coalition of shared interests on one issue could not possibly be entirely appropriate for some other issue. In regulatory decision-making, relationships among group leadership elements and between them on any one or more points of governmental access are too unstable to form a single policy-making elite. As a consequence, decision-making tends to pass from administrative agencies and Congressional committees to Congress, the place where uncertainties in the policy process have always been settled. Congress as an institution is the last resort for breakdowns in bargaining over policy, just as in the case of parties the primary is a last resort for breakdowns in bargaining over nominations. No one leadership group can contain the conflict by an almost infinite subdivision and distribution of the stakes. In the regulatory political process, Congress and the "balance of power" seem to play the classic role attributed to them by the pluralists.

* * *

(3) Issues that involve redistribution cut closer than any others along class lines and activate interests in what are roughly class terms. If there is ever any cohesion within the peak associations, it occurs on redistributive issues, and their rhetoric suggests that they occupy themselves most of the time with these. In a ten-year period just before and after, but not including, the war years [World War II], the Manufacturers' Association of Connecticut, for example, expressed itself overwhelmingly more often on redistributive than on any other types of issues.

* * *

Where the peak associations, led by elements of Mr. Mills's power elite,* have reality, their resources and access are bound to affect power relations. Owing to their stability and the impasse (or equilibrium) in relations among broad classes of the entire society, the political structure of the redistributive arena seems to be highly stabilized, virtually institutionalized. Its stability, unlike that of the distributive arena, derives from shared interests. But in contrast to the regulatory arena, these shared interests are sufficiently stable and clear and consistent to provide the foundation for ideologies.

* * *

Finally, just as the nature of redistributive policies influences politics towards the centralization and stabilization of conflict, so does it further influence the removal of decision-making from Congress. A decentralized and bargaining Congress can cumulate but it cannot balance, and redistributive policies require complex balancing on a very large scale. What [William] Riker has said of budget-making applies here: "legislative governments cannot endure a budget. Its finances must be totted up by party leaders in the legislature itself. In a complex fiscal system, however,

---

*According to C. Wright Mills, a small network of individuals, which he called the "power elite," controls the economy, the political system, and the military [Editors].

haphazard legislative judgments cannot bring revenue into even rough alignment with supply. So budgeting is introduced—which transfers financial control to the budget maker. . . ." Congress can provide exceptions to principles and it can implement those principles with elaborate standards of implementation as a condition for the concessions that money-providers will make. But the makers of principles of redistribution seem to be the holders of the "command posts."

None of this suggests a power elite such as Mills would have had us believe existed, but it does suggest a type of stable and continual conflict that can only be understood in class terms. The foundation upon which the social-stratification and power-elite school rested, especially when dealing with national power, was so conceptually weak and empirically unsupported that its critics were led to err in the opposite direction by denying the direct relevance of social and institutional positions and the probability of stable decision-making elites. But the relevance of that approach becomes stronger as the scope of its application is reduced and as the standards for identifying the scope are clarified. But this is equally true of the pluralist school and of those approaches based on a "politics of this-or-that policy."

* * *

Discussion Questions

1. Provide examples of each type of policy that Lowi discusses (distributive, regulatory, and redistributive).

2. If you were a member of Congress, which type of policy would you try to emphasize if your main interest was in getting re-elected?

3. Are there any types of policies that do not seem to fit Lowi's framework? Do some policies fit more than one category?

71

"The Time Is Now for Action on Social Security"

Jeffrey R. Brown and Mark Duggan

With so much attention devoted to COVID-19 response and President Biden's infrastructure plan (which will spend roughly $100 billion a year for the next decade), it was easy to lose sight of the continuing issue with Social Security: the size of the working population will not be sufficient to support everyone receiving Social Security benefits. Because Social Security is a "pay as you go" program, the benefits are paid for by the payroll taxes collected each year. Policy makers have known this for decades, and, since 1983, payroll taxes have exceeded benefits, with the surplus put in a "trust fund" that, once taxes can no longer cover benefits, will be drawn down to sustain benefit levels. This has always been a controversial solution—in part because the trust fund consists of legal obligations rather than an "account" with actual funds that can be paid out. But there is now a new problem, which is that the program will go into the red earlier than expected (partly because people have left the workforce or retired because of COVID-19). The trust fund, moreover, will be depleted years before it was projected to, which means that Congress will have to make some changes—raising taxes, reducing benefits, implementing means tests, or raising eligibility ages.

Social Security is such a popular program that proposing changes can be dangerous to elected officials' careers. The 1983 reforms—which raised taxes and gradually increased the retirement age over a 40-year period—emerged from a bipartisan effort, and any potential backlash could not be targeted at one party.

Jeffrey R. Brown and Mark Duggan argue that we are once again at this point: a failure to act will mean abrupt changes to Social Security, possibly hurting millions of retirees or soon-to-retire workers who have been counting on the promised benefits. Alternatively, current workers might see their payroll taxes increase substantially, forcing them to take an income hit.

While policymakers in Washington, D.C., are focused on increases in infrastructure spending and changes to corporate and capital gains taxes, an arguably even more important issue is receiving absolutely no attention.

Social Security is America's largest government program and is the most important source of income for most elderly Americans, along with millions of others: individuals with disabilities, widows and children of deceased workers. But if policymakers do not make changes to this program soon, benefits for tens of millions of Americans will be at risk.

The nonpartisan Congressional Budget Office (CBO) recently forecast that Social Security will, for the first time in 40 years, run a deficit this year. And 40 years ago this month, President Reagan sent a letter to Congress asking them to "launch a bipartisan effort to save Social Security."

He quickly established the bipartisan National Commission on Social Security Reform to address the looming financial crisis facing our nation's public retirement system. The Commission's recommendations became the basis for bipartisan legislation that passed two years later.

The 1983 reforms were necessary because Social Security's "pay-as-you-go" design, in which the payroll taxes paid by current workers were used to provide benefits to current retirees, had run headlong into demographic changes. Longer lives and lower birth rates meant that the ratio of workers paying into the system to those receiving benefits had been steadily declining. As a result, there was a fiscal mismatch that required a rebalancing of taxes and benefits.

Those reforms were substantial, expanding coverage to millions of new workers, raising social security's payroll tax rate (to its current 12.4 percent), and cutting future benefits by gradually phasing in increases in the age at which retirees could claim full benefits. The program has since built up a trust fund, with total assets of $2.9 trillion (roughly equal to the combined value of Facebook, Google, and Tesla).

Those fixes were not enough. Four decades later, we urgently need that same bipartisan cooperation. The ratio of workers to beneficiaries continues to decline and will do so beyond the next decade. That will leave increasing deficits and a rapid decline in Social Security's trust fund.

CBO projects a Social Security deficit of $120 billion this year that will steadily grow to $384 billion by 2030. Two years later, the trust fund will be fully depleted. If we do not act soon, the Social Security Administration will not have the resources or authority to pay full benefits, leading to an immediate 25 percent benefit cut. Such an outcome would be a crisis for most of the 80 million Americans who will be receiving Social Security in that year.

This information is disturbing, but not surprising. Had we heeded earlier calls by Presidents Clinton, Bush, and Obama, we could have phased in tax and benefit changes gradually to minimize the disruption to people's lives. Instead, Social Security became increasingly polarized and both parties became less honest about the implications. Too many Republicans pinned their hopes on an ill-conceived plan to convert Social Security into a nationwide 401(k) style system. Democrats have been content to minimize the scope of the problem, even calling for benefit increases despite not having a plan to pay for those benefits already promised.

In a world of combatting narratives and alternative facts, it is worth remembering that mathematics does not distort or lie. And the mathematics of Social Security are clear: benefits are at risk. And the longer we wait to face this, the more disruptive those changes will be.

If we wait until the trust fund runs dry, then we will be faced with a mix of ugly choices. We could immediately cut benefits for 80 million recipients by 25 percent. We could raise payroll tax rates for 180 million workers from 12.4 percent to about 16.4 percent. In either case, further spending cuts or tax increases would be required going forward. Neither of these options or the others that could close the funding gap are economically attractive, let alone politically palatable.

If we act soon, we can phase in changes in a much less disruptive way, while making improvements to the program's structure and incentives. As two economists who previously served in Republican (Brown) and Democratic (Duggan) administrations, we believe all proposals should be on the table. This includes, but is not limited to, raising the payroll tax rate, increasing the maximum annual earnings upon which those taxes are levied (currently $142,800 annually), enacting further increases in Social Security's retirement age, and reducing the generosity of benefits for those with higher incomes.

Will these changes be politically or economically pleasant? No. But as economist Herb Stein once quipped, "[I]f something cannot go on forever, it will stop." And the rapidly increasing Social Security deficits that are on the horizon cannot go on forever.

So, the questions for policymakers are: Will it stop abruptly, creating economic hardship for tens of millions of vulnerable Americans? Or will you find the courage to work together to fix it?

As President Reagan said 40 years ago, "[F]or generations of Americans, the future literally rests upon our actions." And as dysfunctional and fiscally undisciplined as politics in Washington, D.C., may be today, at least we have history on our side to show that action is possible.

DISCUSSION QUESTIONS

1. Politics is much more polarized and divisive now than it was in 1983. Do you think a bipartisan agreement—in which legislators from both parties agree to take unpopular but necessary action—is likely? Is action on Social Security possible without that agreement?

2. One reason Social Security is so popular is that it is universal: nearly everyone receives benefits (almost 90 percent of people 65 or older). Would implementing means tests—limiting or eliminating benefits for higher-income retirees—change Social Security's popularity?

3. Brown and Duggan identify the main reform proposals: raising payroll taxes, removing the maximum taxable earnings ceiling (which was $147,000 in 2022; no income above this level is subject to the payroll tax), raising the age at which retirees become eligible for benefits, and reducing benefits for high-income retirees. Which of these do you support? Are there other possible reforms?

DEBATING THE ISSUES: WILL COVID-19 MAKE LARGE SOCIAL WELFARE PROGRAMS PERMANENT?

The COVID-19 pandemic upended economic and social relationships when it tore through the world starting in the spring of 2020. Within nine months of the first cases in the United States, 200,000 Americans had died of COVID-19; 21 million people had lost their jobs; schools and universities had shut down; health care facilities were overwhelmed; and GDP shrank at an annual rate not seen since the Great Depression.

The economic and societal effects, as catastrophic as they were, would have been far worse without huge amounts of federal government assistance and activity. Since March 2020, the federal government has spent over $5 trillion on pandemic-related programs and economic aid. The amounts would be almost unimaginable in other circumstances: $1.5 trillion in loans and grants to businesses; $1.8 billion in payments to individuals through stimulus checks, expanded unemployment benefits, and social welfare programs; $300 billion in aid to schools; $600 billion in tax credits; and $700 billion in health care spending. Most of this money was spent in a two-year period, although some spending will continue as late as 2030.

The government response has been critical in the country's recovery from the COVID-19 recession (the fastest return to prerecession levels of economic activity ever). By the beginning of 2022, the economy had regained almost all of the ground that was lost in 2020.

What impact will this response have on social policy and public attitudes toward government intervention in the economy? The readings offer two perspectives. Julia Lynch argues that COVID-19 exposed the weaknesses of U.S. social policy, particularly with respect to the lack of support for families, the precariousness of employer-provided health insurance, declining investment in education, and inequitable health outcomes. More robust investments, she argues, will lead to better outcomes for everyone and will also increase social cohesion as people see the benefit of social protection.

Ronald Bailey and his coauthors would agree with Lynch that COVID-19 exposed weaknesses in American governance but for the opposite reason: they argue that the federal government made the COVID-19 pandemic *worse* by interfering with private-sector activities, introducing excessive regulation, getting in the way of private companies and philanthropies, and supporting "crony capitalism," in which government benefits (trillions of dollars, in this instance) go to well-placed and politically powerful interests. In particular, the authors further caution against accepting restrictions on liberty, which they argue can become permanent.

72

"Health Equity, Social Policy, and Promoting Recovery from COVID-19"

Julia Lynch

The COVID-19 pandemic has revealed starkly and publicly the close interconnections between social and economic equality, health equity, and population health. Social epidemiologists and health policy experts have long understood that social policies can contribute to health equity by reducing inequalities in the distribution of the social determinants of health (SDOH). The pandemic has made it more obvious to the public and to policy makers that well-designed social policies are essential to good population health. To better understand what social policies would best promote population health, health equity, and preparedness for future pandemics, we must look both upstream and abroad for inspiration.

What Do We Currently Know (and Not Know) about the Link
between COVID-19, Social Policy, and Health Equity?

Social policies that reduce inequalities in the distribution of a variety of SDOH, from access to medical care to transportation networks to workplace safety to income security, shape health inequalities across a wide variety of health outcomes. Unequal health outcomes for groups defined by socioeconomic status, race or ethnicity, and gender, among others, result when these groups have different endowments (on average) of both downstream social determinants and upstream or fundamental causes. This is because social determinants pattern both exposure to risks or protective factors and the effects of these exposures on health. COVID-19 is no exception.

Particularly in the early phases of the pandemic, protective factors such as access to accurate information about the importance of hand washing and social distancing and the ability to stay home from work or order groceries for delivery were stratified by income and education. Exposure to risks has also been socially patterned throughout the pandemic. Exposure to the virus that causes COVID-19 is much higher among people working in "essential" jobs. While some of these jobs, such as physicians and nurses, are well-paid and occupied by relatively high-status individuals, far more are not: hospital orderlies and cafeteria workers, nursing home aides, city bus drivers, sanitation workers, grocery store clerks, and meat packers are among the lowest-paid workers in our society, are disproportionately women and members of racial/ethnic minority groups, and not only must go to work but also are less likely than their higher-status managers and coworkers to have access to personal protective equipment on the job. Unsurprisingly, infection and death rates are particularly high among these groups of workers.

Past social policies shape socioeconomic stratification, which in turn not only patterns exposure to protective and risk factors but also affects whether and how exposure is translated into health outcomes. For example, high levels of air pollution, which are disproportionately found in lower-income and predominantly minority communities, appear to cause higher mortality from COVID-19. Similarly, people with preexisting conditions such as diabetes, cardiovascular disease, and asthma are more likely to become seriously ill or die from COVID-19, but these conditions are not distributed at random in society. The strong social gradient and intersecting racial/ethnic disparities in these kinds of chronic conditions means that minority and low-income people have been over-represented in the COVID-19 infection and death counts so far.

The best available data on infection and death rates from COVID-19 suggest that there is substantial variation in the impact of the disease not only within countries, states/regions, and localities but also between them. It is tempting to use these data as evidence to explain how public policy—different government responses to the pandemic itself as well as prior policy patterns, including social policy—affects population health and health equity. The problem is that the best available data right now are not very good. Lack of widespread testing in many localities, highly variable criteria for counting deaths as resulting from COVID-19, and a failure on the part of many governments to collect systematic information on the race/ethnicity and socioeconomic status of affected people means that current information about the impact of the pandemic is radically incomplete and noncomparable across political units.

This means we ought to be careful about claiming causal connections between variation in social policies and variations in infection or death rates, especially given the likelihood of unobserved heterogeneity across units that may be associated with both the character of social policies and the (reported) incidence of COVID-19. Nevertheless, it is worth keeping in mind that there *may* be a causal link between robust, equalizing social policies in the past and how countries, subnational regions, and/or localities are experiencing the pandemic today. It is even more important to use what we know about the links between social policy, health equity, and population health to mitigate the effects of the pandemic in the short term, encourage an equitable exit from the pandemic in the medium term, and prepare for future pandemics.

Social Policies to Contain the Epidemic and Minimize Inequality

In the short term, social policies are needed to help us contain the epidemic effectively, prevent recurrent waves of infection, and minimize mortality. Some of these policies are obvious and have already been extensively discussed or even (partially) implemented: [p]aid sick leave and some form of income replacement for missed hours are needed to allow workers who are ill to stay home and avoid infecting coworkers and the public. (I will address in the next section what I think the most helpful forms of income replacement would be.) Universal access to affordable health care is a must if people who become ill are to seek timely care for both COVID-19 and other emergent or preexisting conditions, control underlying conditions that would worsen prognosis in the event of a COVID-19 infection, and avoid spreading illness in their families and communities. The millions of American workers who have lost employer-sponsored health care along with their jobs, or who are unable to purchase insurance due to loss of income, must be offered in a timely manner and for as long as the pandemic continues an affordable, comprehensive form of insurance for the medical bills they would incur if they were to seek care. Effective mental health care coverage (including but not limited to actual parity in coverage of mental health treatment among those lucky enough to be insured) is also needed to prevent loss of (quality of) life due to the psychological stress of pandemic-related social and economic disruption. Finally, income and nutrition supports are needed to prevent the poorest members of our society from suffering physical harm from exposure or hunger at a time when earnings are reduced and savings depleted. Thirty percent of American adults reported reducing their spending on food in the early weeks of the pandemic, and one quarter experienced food insecurity. Conditions are likely to worsen, especially if school-based nutrition programs remain disrupted.

Social Policies for an Equitable Exit from the Pandemic

Within the next year to eighteen months, one hopes, we will move beyond the immediate need to contain the spread of infection and sustain life in pandemic conditions, and into a phase of recovery. As we exit from the pandemic, creating the conditions for a healthy and equitable recovery will require us to deploy social policies that shape the upstream social determinants of health. Because economic recovery is necessary to sustain such social policies over the long term, it is worth considering not only what we can do to promote population health and equity but also which social policies are likely to support a sustainable economic recovery.

Promoting Population Health via Social Policy

Many of the same policies that are needed to protect health during a pandemic are also needed to ensure population health and health equity over the longer term. Universal access to affordable, timely, and appropriate health care that is not conditional on employment; real behavioral and mental health parity; and paid sick leave for all workers are critical reforms that are needed well beyond the current crisis situation. The precise effects of the pandemic on the politics of health care reform are difficult to predict. However, it seems likely that some major reforms are likely to occur, including the possible expansion of Medicare and Medicaid to new groups of beneficiaries, and/or introduction of some form of "public option." As reforms to the health care system are undertaken, expanded behavioral and mental health care surveillance and treatment should be prioritized to counteract the likely long-term consequences of mass trauma stemming from extended confinement and loss of life and livelihood during the pandemic. Finally, the United States must introduce a more robust form of sickness benefit, that is, insurance against short-term income losses sustained due to illness, disease, or injury. The current system of disability insurance plus workers' compensation is inadequate and results in unnecessary hardship, reduced productivity, and the spread of infection when workers cannot afford to stay home when they are sick or injured.

While health care and other protections for people who are already sick are important, still greater benefits for population health and health equity can be gained by considering social policies that act on more distal social determinants of health. For example, direct government provision of housing, zoning policies, rental subsidies, and regulation of consumer credit could all be deployed to ensure access to safe, affordable housing, which is a major social determinant of health. Similarly, more stringent regulation of environmental hazards could help to reduce the overall burden of disease in the primarily poor and minority communities that are exposed to them.

But perhaps most critical for the United States context are social and labor market policies aimed at reducing our very high levels of poverty and inequality, and with them the morbidity and mortality associated with both absolute and relative low socioeconomic status. Universal Basic Income (UBI) programs have received growing attention on both the left and the right in U.S. politics. If set at a high enough level to support even the neediest households, UBI holds some promise as a tool for reducing poverty and making social policy more efficient. Universalism is a desirable feature in social policy design, as it prevents stigmatization of recipients, reduces administrative burden on both individuals and the state, and generates higher levels of political support than targeted programs do. However, it seems very unlikely that in the U.S. context there would be political support for UBI payments that are high enough to meet the multiple needs of poor individuals.

Precisely because poverty is so often comorbid with multiple other adverse conditions (e.g., disability, single-parenthood, divorce, poor labor market conditions, insecure housing), a broader scope of support is needed than the $500 to $1000 per month proposed by many domestic advocates of UBI. Fortunately, many other kinds of policies are effective in alleviating poverty—as is amply evidenced by the fact that other rich democracies have rates of poverty among children and working-age adults much lower than ours. From job guarantees, living wage ordinances, and advanced maintenance (child support) directives to protections for organizing and broadening the tax base, there are many things we could do to reduce poverty. And any of these would help promote population health and health equity, since resource poverty is a key upstream social determinant of health.

Large gains in population health overall are also likely to come from policies that reduce income inequality. Despite high rates of poverty, the bulk of the U.S. population falls in the middle of the income distribution rather than at the very low end, and health status rises across the full social gradient, not only when one goes from being poor to not poor. This means that policies that reduce inequality, and not just poverty, have an important role to play in ensuring that our emergence from the pandemic is equitable and healthy. Fair taxation of capital gains and wealth and raising the level of income on which social insurance contributions are levied would generate revenue and so reduce the need for austerity in social spending, and would allow us to shift the burden of taxation away from those with incomes near the middle of the income distribution and toward those with the highest earnings and wealth. Along with greater public support for health care and education, this would free up resources for middle-class people and allow them to live less-stressed, healthier lives.

Policies That Are Good for Health Equity Are Also Good for Promoting Economic Recovery

Any set of postpandemic social policies that hopes to promote population health and health equity must also contribute to economic growth, as a thriving economy is necessary to generate employment, income, and tax revenues—all of which are necessary to ensure individual and societal well-being. High levels of social protection are generally compatible with economic performance, but certain types of social policies are particularly valuable for promoting economic dynamism. I will focus here on four aspects of social policy—income protection policies, support for families, investment in public education, and administrative systems reform—in which the United States lags significantly behind our OECD (Organization for Economic Cooperation and Development) peers, and that have significant implications for both economic performance and health.

The COVID-19 pandemic has revealed stark deficiencies in our policies for protecting both workers and firms during crises in which there is major disruption to employment. Recovery from the pandemic is likely to continue to be characterized by significant disruptions to employment across multiple sectors of the economy. Yet our unemployment insurance system, which is significantly less generous than in most other rich democracies, is administratively cumbersome and difficult to access, delivers benefits that are often inadequate to maintaining household consumption during prolonged periods of unemployment, and does not protect all workers. Unemployment benefits are critical "social shock absorbers" because they allow households to have adequate income to consume, without which consumption-based economies falter. However, other forms of wage protection, such as the wage insurance or *kurzarbeit* systems used in Germany and Denmark, may be even more valuable during the recovery from COVID-19. Such programs protect not only workers' ability to consume but also employers' ability to rehire quickly and without loss of firm-specific skills. Emergency support for small businesses to retain salaried workers during the pandemic has been a welcome relief to many firms and workers, and should be regularized and expanded to support economic recovery.

Another area in which the United States currently lags and that will be needed to promote economic recovery is support for families with young children. The United States is unique among rich democracies, and nearly unique in the world, in lacking paid leave policies to support mothers after the birth of a child. Paid maternal leave protects the health of very young children and their mothers, and, if structured correctly, also facilitates the reentry of mothers into the workforce. Most rich democracies also now have leave policies that support fathers in taking time off to care for young children, which encourages mothers' reemployment and fathers' engagement with children, both of which promote longer-term gains for household earnings and child well-being. Affordable, high-quality childcare and early childhood education are also critical for parents' ability to return to work after the birth of a child as well as for child development and subsequent earning potential. The United States performs remarkably poorly in international comparisons of the availability and quality of affordable childcare. Making society work better for parents with young children can help boost the employment and earnings of both caregivers and parents, which are necessary for economic recovery in the medium term, and is an important long-term investment in the health and productivity of our future workforce.

Wise investment in public education at all levels will also help foster the productivity gains and high employment levels that are necessary for a complete recovery from the pandemic. U.S. educational outcomes for K–12 students lag behind those in other rich democracies, with poor results driven by the very large disparities in achievement between high- and low-performing students. Current spending by states and localities on primary and secondary education has remained fairly steady since the mid-1990s, but the distribution of funding across districts within many states has become markedly less progressive during this period. Student achievement is exceptionally strongly correlated with socioeconomic status in the United States, with the result that the educational opportunities that are critical for ensuring both health and economic prosperity will be limited unless states and localities commit to more equitable funding of primary and secondary education.

Since its peak in the late 1970s, and accelerating since the mid-2000s, both federal and state spending on upper-secondary (vocational and technical) and tertiary education has declined as a share of GDP. Robust vocational education and training programs are regarded by many scholars and European policy makers as engines of both economic growth and social inclusion, while strong public investment in mass tertiary education facilitates the emergence of economies characterized by relatively low earnings inequality and a larger role for high-productivity manufacturing. The COVID-19 pandemic has disrupted higher education. Faculty and staff employed at public institutions have been furloughed, and private colleges and universities already struggling with declining enrollments before the crisis are likely to lay off teaching staff permanently. Without public investment in upper secondary and tertiary education, our nation's capacity to educate productive workers will suffer, with consequences for both economic recovery and health equity.

A final area of desperately needed interventions in U.S. social policy concerns our antiquated informational and benefits delivery infrastructure. Well before the pandemic, lax government regulation of commercial systems resulted in excessive administrative costs and substandard care in the health sector, where electronic medical records lack interoperability. Government systems that do not speak to one another impose further administrative burdens on individuals, who must repeatedly prove their eligibility for means-tested programs and often forego benefits as a result. The troubled rollout of state health insurance exchanges under the Affordable Care Act a decade ago illustrated vividly how difficult it is to introduce policy innovations when separate government systems for recording data about income, benefits eligibility, and enrollment are housed on obsolete computer systems with limited connectivity across government departments and U.S. states. During the COVID-19 pandemic, fragile records systems have delayed processing of claims for unemployment insurance payments, resulting in severe hardship. Without substantial reforms to government records systems, it will be extraordinarily difficult to launch and maintain the robust system of immunization, testing, and contact tracing needed to ensure safe restarting of economic activity.

Social Policy, Health Equity, and Preparing for the Next Pandemic

Global climate change and mass movement of populations means that the current novel pandemic is unlikely to be the last one we face. If we get the social policy response to COVID-19 right, however, the very same policies we use now to promote health equity and a robust economic recovery will also help prepare us for the next pandemic. Universal access to health care, paid sick leave, and insurance against lost wages will help slow the spread of novel illnesses. Better administrative systems will help us track and respond more effectively to new challenges. Perhaps most importantly, the enhanced sense of social solidarity and trust that stems from strong systems of social protection also protects our health.

At both the individual and societal level, higher levels of social trust are associated with better health outcomes. Generous public social programs in turn are associated with higher levels of social and political trust, with some research demonstrating a causal relationship flowing from welfare states to trust. In pandemic situations, individuals are more likely to cooperate with rules issued by trusted leaders. Investing in social welfare systems that promote social cohesion and trust in government are thus not only good for population health, equity, and economic recovery but also essential for our survival.

73

"America Wasn't Ready for Coronavirus"

Ronald Bailey, Damon Root, Nick Gillespie, Elizabeth Nolan Brown, and Scott Shackford

Red Tape Stymied Testing and Made the Coronavirus Pandemic Worse

The United States is home to the most innovative biotech companies and university research laboratories in the world. That should have provided us with a huge advantage with respect to detecting and monitoring emerging cases of COVID-19 caused by the coronavirus pandemic. Public health officials had the opportunity to slow, if not contain, the outbreak: [b]y tracing the contacts of diagnosed people and quarantining those who in turn tested positive, they could have severed the person-to-person chains of disease transmission.

South Korea demonstrates that such a campaign can work. While both countries detected their first cases of COVID-19 on January 20, [2020], the trajectories in the United States and South Korea have since sharply diverged. By the beginning of March, South Korea had "flattened the curve"—that is, substantially reduced the number of people being diagnosed each day with coronavirus infections—whereas the United States was still struggling to do so when this article went to press six weeks later.

South Korean health officials met on January 27 with private biomedical companies, urging them to develop coronavirus diagnostic tests and assuring them of speedy regulatory approval. The first commercial test was approved in that country a week later. South Korea's now-famous drive-through testing sites were soon testing tens of thousands for the virus. By the first week in March, the country had tested more than 150,000 people, compared to just 2,150 in the United States. Testing and contact tracing helped daily diagnosed cases in South Korea peak at 909 on February 29.

In stark contrast, officials at the U.S. Food and Drug Administration (FDA) and the Centers for Disease Control and Prevention (CDC) stymied private and academic development of diagnostic tests. Much to the contrary, the CDC required that public health officials use only a diagnostic test designed by the agency. That test—released on February 5—turned out to be contaminated by a reagent that made it impossible for outside labs to tell if the virus was present in a sample or not. The CDC's insistence on top-down centralized testing meant there were no available alternatives, which greatly slowed down disease detection just as the infection rate was accelerating.

This massive bureaucratic failure is a big part of why a larger proportion of Americans than of South Koreans will suffer and die from the viral illness.

On February 29, the FDA finally moved to allow academic labs and private companies to develop and deploy their own diagnostic tests. But in the meantime, the Trump administration had begun lying about the availability of tests. On March 2, FDA Commissioner Stephen Hahn declared that "by the end of this week, close to 1 million tests will be able to be performed." During a tour of CDC headquarters on March 6, President Donald Trump asserted that "anyone who wants a test can get a test." In fact, it took until the end of March for 1 million tests to be administered in the United States.

Once the FDA got out of the way, diagnostics companies LabCorp and Quest rolled out tests almost immediately. Many academic labs followed suit. Unfortunately, pent-up demand led to significant delays in reporting results.

By the end of March, companies such as Abbott Laboratories had introduced tests that report results in less than 15 minutes. But after four start-ups began offering at-home testing, promising to further improve access, an obstinate FDA shut them down.

The FDA has finally managed to smooth the way for private companies to begin introducing blood tests for antibodies to the virus produced by people's immune systems. General population screening using these tests will reveal undetected cases, providing a better idea of the actual extent of the pandemic. The tests will also identify people who have recovered and probably can go safely back to their lives beyond quarantine.

In the absence of effective treatments for COVID-19, testing and contact tracing on a massive scale will be vital to restoring economic activity—

assuming the epidemic is beaten back, in the meantime, by social distancing. But due to red tape, the coronavirus outbreak in the United States has turned out to be far more deadly than it could, and should, have been.

Beware "Temporary" Emergency Restrictions on Liberty

State and local officials have taken sweeping emergency actions to combat the spread of COVID-19, including shelter-in-place orders, bans on large gatherings, and widespread business closures. Such measures may well fall under the traditional police powers of the states to regulate actions on behalf of public health, safety, and welfare. But even the most necessary of emergency actions may still pose a significant risk to liberty.

The U.S. experience during World War I offers a cautionary tale about how government restrictions passed in the heat of a national emergency can linger for years afterward—a lesson that must be quickly learned if we are to avoid repeating some grave mistakes in 2020.

When President Woodrow Wilson took the nation to war against Germany in 1917, he did so in the name of making the world safe for democracy. But the president also targeted certain enemies much closer to home. "There are citizens of the United States, I blush to admit," Wilson said at the time, "who have poured the poison of disloyalty into the very arteries of our national life. . . . The hand of our power should close over them at once."

At Wilson's urging, Congress passed the Espionage Act of 1917, a notorious law that effectively criminalized most forms of anti-war speech. Among those snared in its net was the left-wing leader Eugene Debs, who was arrested in 1918 and sentenced to 10 years in federal prison. His crime had been to exercise his First Amendment rights by giving a mildly anti-war speech at an afternoon picnic. In 1919, the same year that the U.S. government signed the peace treaty that formally ended World War I, the U.S. Supreme Court upheld Debs' conviction for speaking out against the war. Debs would rot in federal prison until he was pardoned by President Warren G. Harding in 1921. As for the Espionage Act, while it has been amended several times over the years, it remains on the books.

State governments imposed various restrictions of their own. Nebraska's legislature responded to America's entry into the Great War by cracking down on the civil liberties of its German immigrant communities. Most notably, the state banned both public and private school teachers from instructing children in a foreign language. That law was aimed directly at the state's extensive system of Lutheran parochial schools, where teachers and students commonly spoke German.

Robert Meyer, who taught the Bible in German at the Zion Evangelical Lutheran Parochial School, sued the state for violating his constitutional rights. But the Nebraska Supreme Court waved his objections away. "The salutary purpose of the statute is clear," that court said. "The legislature had seen the baleful effects of permitting foreigners, who had taken residence in this country, to rear and educate their children in the language of their native land."

The U.S. Supreme Court reversed that ruling in 1923. Thankfully, the rights of Meyer and others were ultimately restored. But the offending restriction was not eliminated until well after the war was over.

We should all be on guard to make sure that temporary COVID-19 restrictions—as necessary as they may be—remain temporary.

*   *   *

COVID-19 Makes the Case for Deregulation Everywhere You Look

It didn't take long after the coronavirus crisis began for the smart set to write off small-government types in articles with such snarky headlines as "There Are No Libertarians in a Pandemic." By now, it seems more correct to believe there are only libertarians in a pandemic, including many public officials, who suddenly find themselves willing and able to waive all sorts of ostensibly important rules and procedures in the name of helping people out.

How else to explain the decision by the much-loathed and irrelevant-to-safety Transportation Security Administration (TSA) to allow family-sized jugs of hand sanitizer onto planes? The TSA isn't going full Milton Friedman—it's reminding visitors to its website "that all other liquids, gels and aerosols brought to a checkpoint continue to be allowed at the limit of 3.4 ounces or 100 milliliters carried in a one quart-size bag." But it's a start.

Something similar is going on in Massachusetts, a state well known for high levels of regulation, including in the medical sector. Expecting a crush in health care needs due the coronavirus, Republican Gov. Charlie Baker has seen the light and agreed to streamline the Bay State's recognition of "nurses and other medical professionals" who are registered in other parts of the United States, something that 34 states do on a regular basis.

As Walter Olson of the Cato Institute observes, that move "should help get medical professionals to where they are most needed, and it is one of many good ideas that should be kept on as policy after the pandemic emergency passes. After Super-storm Sandy in 2012, by contrast, when storm-ravaged ocean-side homeowners badly needed skilled labor to restore their premises to usable condition, local laws in places like Long Island forbade them to bring in skilled electricians even from other counties of New York, let alone other states."

The group Americans for Tax Reform has published a list of more than 170 regulations that have been suspended in response to the current crisis: Secretary of Health and Human Services Alex Azar has waived certain laws in order to facilitate "telehealth," or the use of videoconferencing and other technologies to allow doctors to see patients remotely; the Department of Education is making it easier for colleges and universities to move their classes online; cities are doing away with open-container restrictions and allowing home delivery of beer, wine, and spirits in places where it was previously prohibited; the Federal Emergency Management Agency belatedly permitted Puerto Rico and other U.S. territories to acquire personal protective equipment from sources outside the country; and on and on.

You can probably see where this is headed: [i]f the policies above are worth tossing out in an emergency, maybe they ought to be sidelined during normal times too.

Situations like the 9/11 terrorist attacks and the coronavirus outbreak often open the door to naked power grabs whose terrible consequences stick around long after the events that inspired them. Governments rarely return power once they've amassed it. But if you listen carefully, you can hear them telling us which restrictions they realize can be safely tossed.

When the infection rates come down and life begins to get back to normal, it may be tempting just to go back to the way we were. Resist the temptation: [m]any of the rules we put up with every day are worth re-evaluating. And not only during an emergency.

The Coronavirus Stimulus Is a Crony Capitalist Dream

Crony capitalism triumphed as members of Congress voted in March on a massive COVID-19 response bill. The $2.3 trillion package was unanimously approved in the Senate before clearing the U.S. House of Representatives 419 to 6.

Getting the most attention in the new Coronavirus Aid, Relief, and Economic Security (CARES) Act is a stipulation that many Americans will be getting $1,200 apiece from Uncle Sam. People making less than $75,000 individually or $150,000 as a couple will receive the full amount, with pro-rated amounts available to single earners making up to $99,0000 and couples up to $198,000. Families with kids will get an additional $500 for every child 16 and under.

But the 880-page bill is also brimming with handouts for government-favored industries.

For airlines, the CARES Act includes a $25-billion grant plus $29 billion in loans and loan guarantees. Grant money is also available for agricultural companies, to the tune of $33.5 billion.

Government institutions—including some far removed from direct COVID-19 relief efforts—will also be getting cash infusions. For instance, the legislation includes $150 million for the National Endowment for the Arts and the National Endowment for the Humanities. The CARES Act also inexplicably provides $10.5 billion for the Department of Defense, though only $1.5 billion of that is directed at coronavirus-related National Guard deployment, and just $415 million is for vaccine and antiviral medicine research and development by the agency.

Rep. Justin Amash (I-Mich.), one of the few in Congress to vote against the CARES Act, rightly called it "corporate welfare" that "reflects government conceit. Only consumers, not politicians, can appropriately determine which companies deserve to succeed."

Amash supports payments to individual Americans in this time of crisis but opposes the carve-outs for favored industries. If the federal government is going to spend $2 trillion, "then the best way to do it, by far, is a direct cash transfer that otherwise keeps government out of the way," Amash tweeted.

The bill has been celebrated by many Democrats and Republicans as a measure to help working Americans and ordinary people in the face of the new coronavirus. But the corporatist bent means that ordinary people will be paying more in the long run for this "help."

The total cost of the measure leaves every American "on the hook for over $6,000 in debt for these 'investments,'" commented Libertarian Party Chairman Nicholas Sarwark on Twitter, "but it's the businesses that will receive the rewards." He called the measure a "socialist" bailout for "corporate cronies."

Rep. Thomas Massie (R-Ky.) strikes a similar theme. "When we were attacked at Pearl Harbor, did we come up with a $2 trillion stimulus package, or did we declare a war on our enemies?" he asked. "We declared war on our enemies. Why have we not declared war on this virus? Why is our first instinct to make sure that the rich people get to keep all their riches?"

While Government Dithered, Private Companies and
Philanthropists Swung into Action

Microsoft founder and philanthropist Bill Gates saw the pandemic coming. In a February 28 *New England Journal of Medicine* article, he warned that "COVID-19 has started behaving a lot like the once-in-a-century pathogen we've been worried about." He called for public health agencies across the board to take steps to slow the virus's spread. He argued for the importance of accelerating work on treatments and vaccines.

At the same time, the U.S. Food and Drug Administration (FDA) was slowly—so very slowly—swinging into action. On February 4, the agency formally acknowledged the public emergency and agreed that the situation called for a quicker-than-usual response to entities seeking emergency approval for new COVID-19 diagnostic tests. Nevertheless, it took the FDA almost a whole month to provide guidance on exactly *how* laboratories and commercial companies could accelerate that process.

By then, private-sector leaders were already putting plans in motion. The first confirmed case of COVID-19 in the United States was in January in Washington state, where Gates' philanthropic organization, the Bill and Melinda Gates Foundation, is based. On March 10, the Gates Foundation announced a partnership with MasterCard and Wellcome, a U.K.-based research charity, to commit $125 million to a "COVID-19 Therapeutics Accelerator" that hoped to speed up the response by "identifying, assessing, developing, and scaling-up treatments." The private response would turn out to be critical. A group of Seattle doctors had already had to defy the U.S. Centers for Disease Control and Prevention in order to implement the tests that caught the virus's arrival in America.

On the same day of the Gates Foundation announcement, the Kaiser Family Foundation, a nonprofit health policy think tank, put together a tracker showing how much private philanthropy was going into the worldwide response. The group calculated that at least $725 million had then been committed by private nonprofits, businesses, and foundations to aid in international relief efforts. Candid, a foundation that helps nonprofits and foundations connect to donors, calculated that $4.3 billion in grants had been funded by early April for coronavirus responses around the world.

Early on, much of the assistance was directed toward China. But as COVID-19 spread everywhere, so did private philanthropy and innovation. As hospitals and health providers ran out of face masks (thanks in part, again, to FDA regulations that made it hard to ramp up production in response to demand), businesses donated their unused stockpiles. Soon, the private sector was iterating novel solutions as well. Across the world, companies and crafters with access to 3D printers and sewing machines began designing and producing masks of their own.

The number of breathing devices at hospitals became one of the more dangerous chokepoints in the COVID-19 response, leading to rationing and difficult medical choices in areas with high concentrations of infections. Again, innovators went to work. In Italy, for example, volunteers reverse-engineered a respirator valve that was in short supply, began manufacturing it with a 3D printer, and donated a stock to local hospitals.

As the spread of COVID-19 shut down auto manufacturing in the United States, companies such as GM and Tesla stepped up to suggest repurposing some unused spaces in their plants to help produce more ventilators. While President Donald Trump was a big fan of this response, both logistical and bureaucratic barriers got in the way. Yet again, the FDA's slow response was a problem. It wasn't until March 23, when the FDA announced it was relaxing some guidelines that strictly regulated where, how, and with what materials ventilators could be manufactured, that this problem could even begin to be solved.

Meanwhile, the worldwide collapse of tourism due to the spread of COVID-19 left hotels and short-term rental services such as Airbnb bereft of customers. Some hotels near medical centers were converted into clinics. Others, like the Four Seasons Hotel in New York City, announced plans to let medical personnel responding to the pandemic stay there free of charge. Airbnb offered to waive its fees if its hosts would likewise volunteer to house medical personnel and aid workers responding to the crisis. The company claims to have gotten 20,000 such offers by the end of March.

Beyond the philanthropic response, the ability of citizens to abide by shelter-in-place or stay-at-home recommendations and continue to thrive is entirely due to private-sector responses. While some small restaurants have had to shut their doors, many others are surviving thanks to delivery services such as Grubhub, DoorDash, and Postmates. Mass runs on grocery stores cleared shelves of staples, but within a week America's truck drivers and warehouse workers had gone into overdrive to get things back to a certain level of normalcy. There continued to be shortages of some goods, but even amid a deadly pandemic, almost no one had to worry about starving. For those stuck without companionship, Pornhub even offered one-month premium subscriptions for free.

The colossal response from the private sector most certainly helped make it possible for greater numbers of people to work from home, spend less time interacting with others, and "flatten the curve" to reduce the spread of COVID-19. While the government was still trying to figure out its messaging and untangle its bureaucracy, countless individuals, businesses, and community groups were quickly adapting to solve problems on the ground.

Discussion Questions

1. Is it plausible to think that private entities—whether corporations, charities, philanthropies, or religious organizations—could have mobilized activity on the scope of what the federal government did in 2020 and 2021 (with over $5 trillion in COVID-19 aid)? Can there be a balanced allocation between public (government) and private action during a pandemic?

2. Many pandemic-related policies—mask mandates and vaccine requirements, for example—exist at the heart of striking a balance between individual autonomy and the public good. What should that balance look like?

CHAPTER 15

Foreign Policy and World Politics

74

"The Age of Open Society"

GEORGE SOROS

"Globalization" refers, generally speaking, to the diffusion of interests and ideologies across national borders. Proponents of globalization argue that it will encourage global economic development and foster universal human rights that are not dependent on where someone happens to live. Critics fall into two camps. One consists of those who fear that globalization will undermine national sovereignty and lead to a "one world" government that leaves everyone at the mercy of distant bureaucrats and officials. The other camp consists of those who see globalization as a smoke screen for corporate hegemony, where multinational corporations exploit workers in countries with low wages, few job protections, and lax environmental regulation, all in the name of higher profits. George Soros, a philanthropist who promotes democracy, believes that economic globalization and political globalization are out of sync: although capital and markets move freely across national boundaries, political institutions do not. A global "open society" would, in his view, ensure that the political and social needs of all countries (not simply the needs of industrialized nations, whose interests tend to dominate international markets) are met and would foster the development of stable political and financial institutions. This would require a broad international organization, either as part of the United Nations or as an independent institution. It would have to be based on the idea that certain interests transcend questions of national sovereignty.

Global politics and global economics are dangerously out of sync. Although we live in a global economy characterized by free trade and the free movement of capital, our politics are still based on the sovereignty of the state. International institutions exist, but their powers are limited by how much authority states are willing to confer on them. At the same time, the powers of the state are limited by the freedom of capital to escape taxation and regulation by moving elsewhere. This is particularly true of the countries at the periphery of the global capitalist system, whose economic destiny depends on what happens at the center.

This state of affairs would be sustainable if the market mechanism could be trusted to satisfy social needs. But that is not the case.

We need to find international political arrangements that can meet the requirements of an increasingly interdependent world. These arrangements ought to be built on the principles of open society. A perfect society is beyond our reach. We must content ourselves with the next best thing: a society that holds itself open to improvement. We need institutions that allow people of different views, interests, and backgrounds to live together in peace. These institutions should assure the greatest degree of freedom compatible with the common interest. Many mature democracies come close to qualifying as open societies. But they refuse to accept openness as a universal principle.

How could this principle of openness be translated into practice? By the open societies of the world forming an alliance for this purpose. The alliance would have two distinct but interrelated goals: to foster the development of open society within individual countries; and to establish international laws, rules of conduct, and institutions to implement these norms.

It is contrary to the principles of open society to dictate from the outside how a society should govern itself. Yet the matter cannot be left entirely to the state, either. The state can be an instrument of oppression. To the extent possible, outside help should take the form of incentives; the evolution of open society requires aid for economic and institutional development. Punitive measures, though sometimes unavoidable, tend to be counterproductive.

Unfortunately, positive intervention is out of favor because of an excessive faith in the magic of the marketplace. There is an alliance of democratic countries, NATO, capable of military intervention, but there is no similar alliance to engage in constructive intervention. This open-society alliance ought to have a much broader membership than NATO, and it must include nongovernmental members as well as heads of state. As former U.S. Secretary of State Henry Kissinger points out, states have interests but no principles; we cannot rely on them to implement the principle of openness.

Democratic governments are, however, responsive to the wishes of their electorates. Therefore, the impulse for the alliance has to come from the people, not from their leaders. Citizens living in open societies must recognize a global open society as something worth sacrifice. This responsibility rests in particular with the United States, the sole surviving superpower and the dominant force in the global capitalist system. There can be no global open society without its leadership. But the United States has become carried away by its success and fails to see why it should sub-ordinate its self-interest to some nebulous common principle. The United States jealously guards its sovereignty and behaves as if it ought to be the sole arbiter of right and wrong. Washington will have to undergo a sig-nificant change of heart before it is ready to lead an open-society alliance.

The alliance, if it comes to pass, must not lose sight of its own fallibility. Foreign aid, though very valuable, is notoriously inefficient. Rule-based incentives are more promising. The international financial architecture needs to be redesigned to help give underdeveloped countries a leg up. Incentives would be conditional on each country's success in establishing open political and financial institutions.

The alliance could act within the United Nations, or it could go it alone. But a commitment to such an alliance would offer an opportunity to reform the United Nations. The noble intentions enunciated in the preamble of the U.N. Charter can never be attained as long as the United Nations remains a rigid association of sovereign states. But there is ample room for improve-ment, and an open-society alliance would be a start. Perhaps one day, then, historians will look back at these years to come as the Age of Open Society.

Discussion Questions

1. Is Soros's suggestion about an open society practical? Do you think there are circumstances under which nations would agree to such a proposal?

2. How, if at all, will globalization change notions about national iden-tity? Do you think that, 25 or 50 years from now, being a U.S. citizen—or a citizen of any other country—will have the same meaning as it does now?

75

"Globalization Is Good for You"

Ronald Bailey

International trade, according to economic theory, should lead to net benefits because of efficiencies and competition. In practice, though, it can cause economic disruption because domestic products (and jobs) are replaced by imports from other countries with lower wages, looser environmental standards, and less regulation. The result is economic dislocation in regions that see massive job losses, and the overall economic benefits are of little comfort to these workers and communities who see their livelihoods disappear. Yet free trade has been a centerpiece of global economic policy for decades, and supporters argue that efforts to protect domestic producers through trade barriers—chiefly tariffs, which are taxes paid when a good is imported—wind up increasing the costs of goods, creating inefficiencies, and reducing overall wealth. In this selection, Ronald Bailey summarizes recent research on the overall effects of the increasingly free movement of goods, capital, and even people across borders. In just about every dimension one can think of—individual income, overall wealth, economic growth, life expectancy, gender equality, child labor, environmental protection, and even the likelihood of military conflict—free trade and globalization have positive effects. "All of this open movement of people and stuff across borders pays off in many measurable ways," argues Bailey, "some obvious, some more surprising."

How important is the open exchange of goods to the spreading of prosperity? This important: [s]ince 1950, world trade in goods has expanded from $600 billion (in 2015 dollars) to $18.9 trillion in 2013. That's a more than 30-fold increase, during a period in which global population grew less than threefold.

This massive increase in trade was kicked off in 1948 by the General Agreement on Tariffs and Trade, which began the liberalization process of lowering tariff and non-tariff barriers. As a result, autarkic national economies became more integrated and intertwined with one another. The World Bank reports that openness to trade—the ratio of a country's trade (exports plus imports) to its gross domestic product (GDP)—has more than doubled on average since 1950.

Immigration has also contributed significantly to economic growth and higher wages. Today some 200 million people, about 3 percent of the world's population, live outside their countries of birth. According to the Partnership for a New American Economy, 28 percent of all U.S. companies started in 2011 had immigrant founders—despite immigrants comprising roughly 13 percent of the population. In addition, some 40 percent of Fortune 500 firms were founded by immigrants or their children.

All of this open movement of people and stuff across borders pays off in many measurable ways, some obvious, some more surprising.

Longer, Healthier Lives

A 2010 study in *World Development*, titled "Good For Living? On the Relationship between Globalization and Life Expectancy," looked at data from 92 countries and found that economic globalization significantly boosts life expectancy, especially in developing countries. The two Swedish economists behind the study, Andreas Bergh and Therese Nilsson, noted that as Uganda's economic globalization index rose from 22 to 46 points (almost two standard deviations) over the 1970–2005 period, average life expectancy increased by two to three years.

Similarly, a 2014 conference paper titled "The long-run relationship between trade and population health: evidence from five decades," by Helmut Schmidt University economist Dierk Herzer, concluded, after examining the relationship between economic openness and population health for 74 countries between 1960 and 2010, that "international trade in general has a robust positive long-run effect on health, as measured by life expectancy and infant mortality."

Women's Liberation

A 2012 working paper by University of Konstantz economist Heinrich Ursprung and University of Munich economist Niklas Potrafke analyzed how women fare by comparing globalization trends with changes in the Social Institutions and Gender Index (SIGI), which was developed by the Organisation for Economic Co-operation and Development (OECD). SIGI takes several aspects of gender relations into account, including family law codes, civil liberties, physical integrity, son preference, and ownership rights. It's an index of deprivation that captures causes of gender inequality rather than measuring outcomes.

"Observing the progress of globalization for almost one hundred developing countries at ten-year intervals starting in 1970," Ursprung and Potrafke concluded, "we find that economic and social globalization exert a decidedly positive influence on the social institutions that reduce female subjugation and promote gender equality." They further noted that since globalization tends to liberate women from traditional social and political orders, "social globalization is demonized, by the established local ruling class, and by western apologists who, for reasons of ideological objections to markets, join in opposing globalization."

Less Child Labor

A 2005 *World Development* study, "Trade Openness, Foreign Direct Investment and Child Labor," by Eric Neumayer of the London School of Economics and Indra de Soysa of the Norwegian University of Science and Technology, looked at the effects of trade openness and globalization on child labor in poor countries. Their analysis refuted the claims made by anti-globalization proponents that free trade induces a "race to the bottom," encouraging the exploitation of children as cheap laborers. Instead the researchers found that the more open a country is to international trade and foreign investment, the lower the incidence of exploitation. "Globalization is associated with less, not more, child labor," they concluded.

Faster Economic Growth

A 2008 World Bank study, "Trade Liberalization and Growth: New Evidence," by the Stanford University economists Romain Wacziarg and Karen Horn Welch, found that trade openness and liberalization significantly boost a country's rate of economic growth.

The authors noted that in 1960, just 22 percent of countries representing 21 percent of the global population had open trade policies. This rose to 73 percent of countries representing 46 percent of world population by the year 2000. The study compared growth rates of countries before and after trade liberalization, finding that "over the 1950–98 period, countries that liberalized their trade regimes experienced average annual growth rates that were about 1.5 percentage points higher than before liberalization" and that "investment rates by rose 1.5–2.0 percentage points."

Higher Incomes

Trade openness boosts economic growth, but how does it affect per-capita incomes? A 2009 Rutgers University-Newark working paper, "Trade Openness and Income—A Re-examination," by economists Vlad Manole and Mariana Spatareanu, calculated the trade restrictiveness indices for 131 developed and developing countries between 1990 and 2004. Its conclusion: [a] "lower level of trade protection is associated with higher per-capita income."

Less Poverty

A 2011 Research Institute of Industrial Economics working paper— "Globalization and Absolute Poverty—A Panel Data Study," by the Swedish economists Bergh and Nilsson—analyzed the effects of globalization and trade openness on levels of absolute poverty (defined as incomes of less than $1 per day) in 100 developing countries. The authors found "a robust negative correlation between globalization and poverty."

Interestingly, most of the reduction in absolute poverty results from better information flows—e.g., access to cellphones—that improve the functioning of markets and lead to the liberalization of trade. For example, the globalization index score for Bangladesh increased from 8 points in 1980 to 30 points in 2000, which yielded a reduction in absolute poverty of 12 percentage points.

More Trees

A number of studies have found that trade openness tends to improve environmental quality in rich countries while increasing pollution and deforestation in poor countries. For example, a 2009 *Journal of Environmental Economics and Management* study by three Japanese researchers, titled "Does Trade Openness Improve Environmental Quality?", found that air and water pollution decline among rich-country members of the OECD, whereas it increases in poor countries as they liberalize and embark on the process of economic development.

But as poor countries become rich, they flip from getting dirtier to becoming cleaner. A 2012 *Canadian Journal of Agricultural Economics* study, "Deforestation and the Environmental Kuznets Curve in Developing Countries: A Panel Smooth Transition Regression Approach," explored the relationship between deforestation and real income for 52 developing countries during the 1972–2003 period. The study found that deforestation reverses when average incomes reach a bit more than $3,000 per year.

These studies basically confirm the Environmental Kuznets Curve hypothesis, in which various indicators of environmental degradation tend to get worse during the early stages of economic growth, but when average income reaches a certain point, subsequent economic growth leads to environmental improvement. Since trade openness and globalization boost economic growth and incomes, this suggests that opposing them slows down eventual environmental improvement in poor countries.

Peace

In 1943, Otto T. Mallery wrote, "If soldiers are not to cross international boundaries, goods must do so. Unless the shackles can be dropped from trade, bombs will be dropped from the sky." This insight was bolstered by a 2011 working paper, "Does Trade Integration Contribute to Peace?" by the University of California, Davis researcher Ju Hyun Pyun and the Korea University researcher Jong-Wha Lee. The two evaluated the effects of bilateral trade and global openness on the probability of conflict between countries from 1950 to 2000, and concluded that "an increase in bilateral trade interdependence significantly promotes peace." They added, "More importantly, we find that not only bilateral trade but global trade openness also significantly promotes peace."

More Productive Workers

The economic gains from unfettered immigration are vastly more enormous than those that would result from the elimination of remaining trade restrictions. Total factor productivity (TFP) is the portion of output not explained by the amount of inputs used in production. Its level is determined by how efficiently and intensely the inputs are utilized in production. In other words, it is all those factors—technology, honest government, a stable currency, etc.—that enable people to work "smarter" and not just harder.

A 2012 working paper titled "Open Borders," by the University of Wisconsin economist John Kennan, found that if all workers moved immediately to places with higher total factor productivity, it would produce the equivalent of doubling the world's supply of laborers. Using U.S. TFP as a benchmark, the world's workers right now are the equivalent of 750 million Americans, but allowing migration to high TFP regions would boost that to the equivalent of 1.5 billion American workers.

Think of it this way: [a] worker in Somalia can produce only one-tenth the economic value of a worker in the United States. But as soon as she trades the hellhole of Mogadishu for the comparative paradise of Minneapolis, she can immediately take advantage of the higher American TFP to produce vastly more. Multiply that by the hundreds of millions still stuck in low-productivity countries.

Assuming everybody moved immediately, Kennan calculated that it would temporarily depress the average wages of the host countries' natives by 20 percent. If emigration were more gradual, there would be essentially no effects on native-born wages.

In a 2011 working paper for the Center for Global Development, "Economics and Emigration: Trillion Dollar Bills on the Sidewalk?", Michael Clemens reviewed the literature on the relationship between economic growth and migration. He concluded that removing mobility barriers could plausibly produce overall gains of 20–60 percent of global GDP. Since world GDP is about $78 trillion now, that suggests that opening borders alone could boost global GDP to between $94 and $125 trillion.

Better Job Prospects

A 2013 University of Munich working paper on immigration and economic growth by the University of Auvergne economist Ekrame Boubtane and her colleagues analyzed data from 22 OECD countries between 1987 and 2009. It found that "migration inflows contribute to host country economic prosperity (positive impact on GDP per capita and total unemployment rate)." The authors concluded that "immigration flows do not harm the employment prospects of residents, native- or foreign-born. Hence, OECD countries may adjust immigration policies to labor market needs, and can receive more migrants, without worrying about a potential negative impact on growth and employment."

In a 2009 National Bureau of Economic Research study, "The Effect of Immigration on Productivity: Evidence from U.S. States," the University of California, Davis economist Giovanni Peri looked at the effects of differential rates of immigration to various American states in the 1990s and 2000s. Peri found that "an increase in employment in a U.S. state of 1 percent due to immigrants produced an increase in income per worker of 0.5 percent in that state." In other words, more immigrants meant higher average wages for all workers.

Discussion Questions

1. The positive effects of free trade are of little comfort to factory workers who lose their jobs because their employer moved production to a country with lower labor costs. How do you make the case for free trade to those who bear the brunt of the costs? What happens when the "rising tide" of economic growth doesn't lift all boats?

2. Many critics of globalization argue that allowing goods and capital to move freely across borders only moves jobs to countries with the cheapest and most exploitable labor forces, where job protections are minimal (or nonexistent). Supporters respond that these jobs, even though they might not pay much by Western standards, still provide much better opportunities for people in developing nations than would otherwise be the case. Who do you think has the better case?

3. What is the alternative to globalization? What costs are associated with, for example, trying to protect domestic jobs from being exported? What are the benefits of such efforts?

Debating the Issues: What Is the United States' Role in the International Order?

Throughout the Cold War—the period from 1945 to 1991—the United States was the dominant global superpower, leading global alliances to counter the influence of the Soviet Union. The collapse and dissolution of the Soviet Union in 1991 shifted the global balance, prompting questions about how active the United States should be in international affairs.

Two recent events have prompted another round of reassessment. The first was the collapse of the Afghan government and the withdrawal of all U.S. military personnel in August 2021. It ended the longest war in U.S. history (2001–21) and served as a reminder of the limits of both nation building and the reach of U.S. military power. It seemed to presage an era of reduced U.S. influence in the world.

The second was Russia's invasion of Ukraine on February 24, 2022, beginning the largest military conflict in Europe since World War II. In response, the United States, the European Union, and other allies have imposed economic sanctions on Russia and its oligarchs and provided advanced weapons to Ukraine. As of this writing in June 2022, the war continues, and Russian president Vladimir Putin threatened to expand the scope of the conflict by considering military assistance to Ukraine an act of war.

The two readings here grapple with the meaning of these two events. Jessica T. Mathews, writing in the fall of 2021 after the U.S. withdrawal from Afghanistan, advocates for a rethinking of the core of U.S. foreign policy—particularly the "hegemony to which the United States has been clinging," which involves less willingness to rely on the use of force as "the only meaningful form of U.S. engagement abroad." What is required, she argues, is a recognition that the United States is not the only international power, a realization that militarily imposed regime change rarely works, and a return to truly cooperative international diplomacy.

Has Russia's invasion of Ukraine changed that calculation? Damien Cave, writing in the *New York Times*, argues that the invasion seems to have reinvigorated the notion that international coalitions can respond to and act collectively to counter security threats. "The demise of the global postwar rules–based order may not be inevitable," he writes, and he notes that leaders around the world "almost universally" see Ukraine as a test for the idea that liberal democracy is the best path to global peace.

It is likely that the events of 2021–22 will reshape the nature of international politics and the United States' role in that system.

"American Power after Afghanistan"

Jessica T. Mathews

For 30 years, since the end of the Cold War, the United States has searched unsuccessfully for a purpose for its now unrivaled global power. No other country (or combination of countries in the European Union) equals its combined military, economic, and political strength. Yet the United States has used this rare moment in history poorly, trying and discarding various rationales for a global role after experience has revealed their inutility or unpopularity. It first tried the all-encompassing role of "indispensable nation," then the role of shaper and main pillar of a liberal world order, principal prosecutor of a global "war on terror," protector and promoter of democratic governments (including regime change by force), and, finally, leader of the democratic side in a global contest between democratic and authoritarian governments. Throughout, Washington grew more and more reliant on the use of military power and, through lack of use, lost confidence in concerted diplomacy as a means of dealing with adversaries.

The existential threat of the Cold War has masked deep disagreements about the United States' appropriate global posture. Ever since, debate has veered inconclusively between those who believe that U.S. interests are global and demand aggressive, often unilateral, leadership on most issues and those who argue for a narrower conception of the national interest and a more collaborative approach in pursuing it. The harder question of what constitute the core interests vital to national security also remains unanswered. Despite these divisions, Congress largely abandoned a serious voice on foreign policy, even on its constitutional responsibility to declare war. Other than on trade, the Senate managed to ratify only a single multilateral treaty in the last 25 years, rejecting many that were the United States' own initiatives (such as the Comprehensive Nuclear Test Ban Treaty) or that embody U.S. values (the Protocol on Torture), aims (the Kyoto Protocol on climate), and even domestic legislation (restricting international trade in tobacco).

There is now, perhaps, an opportunity to begin to end this impasse. Once attention shifts from tactical errors made in the closing weeks of the U.S. withdrawal from Afghanistan to the drifting purpose and self-delusion of the preceding 20 years, the shock of failure in America's longest war may provide an open moment to reexamine the lengthy list of earlier interventions and to reconsider U.S. foreign policy in the post–Cold War era more broadly.

Doomed from the Start

A first step toward such a reappraisal would be to recognize that what happened in Afghanistan matched past experience. In 2003, the political scientist Minxin Pei examined the record of U.S. military interventions made for the purpose of regime change. His measure of success was whether democracy existed ten years after the departure of U.S. forces. Out of 16 such efforts, he identified just four successes: Germany and Japan after World War II, highly developed countries that had surrendered after total war, and tiny Grenada and Panama, where the United States made quick interventions of less than a year.

The success stories shared several characteristics, including a strong national identity, high state capacity, a high degree of ethnic homogeneity, relative socioeconomic equality, and previous experience—however short—with effective rule of law. Deep ethnic and religious divisions were fatal, as was alignment with an unpopular ruling elite, especially if it was highly corrupt.

Pei published his study just as the United States was declaring the end of "major combat" in Afghanistan and the transition to "stabilization and reconstruction." Just 8,000 U.S. soldiers were in Afghanistan at the time. What is clear now—and should have been even then—is that Afghanistan had none of the qualities that predicted success and all of those that presaged failure. Setting aside the special cases of Germany and Japan, and assuming that Afghanistan will not be a democracy ten years from now, the U.S. failure rate is 86 percent.

Among the many lessons that should be drawn from this experience, three are overriding. First, among colonial and postcolonial intervenors, the United States is particularly bad about ignoring the history, culture, and values of the countries in which it intrudes. This is not a result of ignorance. The individuals with the relevant knowledge are simply usually not in the room when top-level policy is made. Routinely, history and culture are treated as background or context rather than as critical factors that will determine success or failure—as they unmistakably did in Afghanistan.

Second, what happened in Afghanistan was not caused by the lack of good intelligence. Throughout history, the commonest form of intelligence failure has been the failure of civilian and military leaders to listen to what they don't want to hear. At the outset of his presidency, Barack Obama commissioned a 60-day study to shape U.S. strategy in Afghanistan. In his memoir, he writes that the report "made one thing clear. Unless Pakistan stopped sheltering the Taliban, our efforts at long-term stability in

Afghanistan were bound to fail." U.S. intelligence agencies knew that the connections between Pakistan and the Taliban were deep and long-standing and that Pakistan was providing a safe haven for Taliban fighters and leadership. The conclusion should have been that the United States must somehow break that bond or cut its losses in nation building in Afghanistan. Instead, policymakers noted the problem, tried unsuccessfully to ameliorate it, and went ahead anyway.

The third lesson is one of process: U.S. policymakers cannot rely on the military to conclude that a mission is unachievable. The military's core value is executing whatever mission it has been assigned. Its spirit is "can do." Generals can identify difficulties in advance, but once a mission is underway, they will insist that things are getting better or that they will improve given more money, time, weaponry, and troops. The military will not question the validity of the mission. This means that a president who recognizes that the country has undertaken something it cannot achieve will at some point have to "reject the advice of his generals." Americans should recognize and reward the rare moral courage President Joe Biden exercised in doing so—something three presidents before him failed to summon.

It is also worth noting that the United States has a habit of wildly exaggerating the consequences of its failures. In the last few weeks, there has been talk of "the end of empire," a "return to isolationism," and huge gains accruing to Russia and China (which may instead be saddled with the fallout from a continuing civil war in Afghanistan, growing opium production, and rising Islamic extremism). Similar talk, with far greater reason, greeted the end of the Vietnam War. Yet 15 years later, the United States won the Cold War and dominated the world.

Lessons Learned

Setting aside such grim predictions, then, what might a different U.S. approach to foreign policy entail? A first step should be a hard look at the notion of American exceptionalism. Domestically, high income inequality, flat or declining intergenerational mobility, deeply polarized politics, racial division, rampant embrace of conspiracy theories, diminished civic duty, and even a question mark beside the sine qua non of democracy—the peaceful transition of power through elections—together make the "power of our example," to use Biden's phrase, dubious at best.

The U.S. record of international leadership is questionable as well. Since the mid-1990s, when the United States began to withhold its legally obligated dues to the United Nations and then to other international agencies, its foreign policies have, on balance, arguably weakened the world's capacity to solve global problems. Among the agreements the United States has rejected since the end of the Cold War, in addition to examples cited above, are the Law of the Sea Treaty, the Anti-Personnel Mine Ban

Convention, and the International Criminal Court. Most of the rest of the world approved them. It has also refused to ratify treaties protecting genetic resources, restricting trade in conventional arms, banning persistent organic pollutants and cluster bombs, and protecting persons with disabilities. In the first two years of Donald Trump's presidency alone, it rejected the Trans-Pacific Partnership trade agreement, withdrew from (and then renegotiated) the North American Free Trade Agreement, the Intermediate-Range Nuclear Forces Treaty, the UN Human Rights Council, the UN Educational, Scientific and Cultural Organization, the Paris climate accord, and the Iran nuclear deal. Major international agreements such as the latter two must now be designed to avoid formal treaty confirmation since the world knows the United States cannot deliver Senate ratification. If this is exceptionalism, a globalized, interdependent world needs less of it.

To that end, the United States should reconsider several long-standing practices. One is the belief that shunning another country—refusing to formally recognize it or talk to its representatives—is a useful form of leadership. To the contrary, there is clear evidence—from Cuba, Iran, Afghanistan, and elsewhere—that this practice mostly harms the United States, crippling diplomacy where it is needed most, draining the modicum of trust required for bridging differences, and necessitating that the most difficult and delicate negotiations be turned over to a middleman. Overreliance on sanctions, especially unilateral sanctions, is similarly unhelpful and should be drastically cut back.

Washington also needs to recognize the degree to which its own policies, spending, and rhetoric have fostered the belief that the only meaningful form of U.S. engagement abroad is a military commitment. Twenty-five years of near-constant U.S. military operations has conditioned the world to expect American interventions, to measure U.S. seriousness by them, and, among friends and allies, to underspend on their own defense. During both Democratic and Republican administrations, members of Congress have lavished funding on the Pentagon, tolerating enormous waste in return for dollars spent in their states and districts. At the same time, Congress has chronically underfunded the State Department and other nondefense foreign operations. As the defense budget has swelled, the gap has become grotesque. In the fiscal years 2019 and 2020, Trump's budget proposals sought increases in defense spending that were larger than the entire State Department and foreign operations budget—which it still sought to reduce.

This funding disparity translates into a huge disparity in human capital and operational strength—one that is compounded by a political patronage system that routinely puts ambassadorial posts into the hands of completely unqualified donors. Often, the lack of resources elsewhere forces the Pentagon to undertake humanitarian and governance duties for which it is ill suited and generally the most expensive option.

Finally, Washington's policies on democracy promotion need a thorough reappraisal. Far too often, the United States acts as though democracy is, in the words of former U.S. Ambassador Chas Freeman, the "default political system." To the contrary, it is the most demanding of political systems, requiring a literate, relatively cohesive population and a bedrock of institutions that can take a century or more to build. Laying a foundation for it can require a commitment of many decades, as the United Kingdom made in India and the United States made in South Korea. But countries that would welcome a lengthy foreign occupation are extremely rare in today's world, if they exist at all. And domestic U.S. support for such commitments will only be sustained where the country's core strategic interests are unmistakable. Criticizing the decision to end the war in Afghanistan for its lack of "strategic patience" misses the point that the American public had long grasped: there was no strategic interest in the war Washington was prosecuting. It should not be necessary to add that democracy cannot be delivered by force—although the United States keeps trying.

The belief, evidently held by the Biden administration, that democracy is under generalized attack from authoritarianism also needs to be rethought. Dividing the world along this line greatly reduces the chance that the major global problems—nonproliferation, climate change, global health, cybercrime, and financial stability—can be successfully tackled. There are simply too many authoritarian states whose active cooperation will be necessary. It is also vital that Washington be able to distinguish self-interest in another country from an ideological crusade, particularly with regard to U.S. policy toward China. Mistaking the Chinese Communist Party's determination to strengthen its position at home and in its region for a global ambition to destroy democracy could prove truly disastrous, raising the likelihood of a war over Taiwan that would be catastrophic for all.

These changes do not add up to a new foreign policy doctrine. Given the pace and scope of recent global change and the depth of American political polarization, it is doubtful whether such an advance is currently possible. Moreover, some of the needed shifts are not within the power of the United States to make. It will be some time, for example, before other countries see an American choice not to intervene abroad or to draw down a foreign troop presence as something other than disengagement or retreat.

Still, these shifts would amount to a dramatic alteration in U.S. practice since the end of the Cold War. America would no longer see itself as "the cop walking a global beat," as neoconservatives would have it, nor would it shrink its core interests to defense against threats from China and Russia, as some realists have proposed. These changes would lead to a policy rebalanced between military and nonmilitary instruments; more restrained in the launching of military interventions and wiser in their execution; more cognizant of the need for and the potential of multilateral instruments; less prone to unilateral—often self-defeating—actions; and more sensible in its attitude toward democracy elsewhere. They would mean, in short, an end to the tatters of hegemony to which the United States has been clinging.

77

"The War in Ukraine Holds a Warning for the World Order"

DAMIEN CAVE

The liberal world order has been on life support for a while. President Biden, in his inaugural address, called democracy "fragile." President Vladimir V. Putin of Russia said two years ago that "the liberal idea" had "outlived its purpose," while China's leader, Xi Jinping, has extolled the strength of an all-powerful state and, as he put it last March, "self-confidence in our system."

The multinational response to Russia's invasion of Ukraine has shown that the demise of the global postwar rules-based order may not be inevitable. A month ago, no one predicted that Germany would reverse decades of military hesitancy and pour 100 billion euros into its defense budget, or that Switzerland would freeze the assets of Russian oligarchs, or that YouTube, World Cup soccer, and global energy companies would all cut ties to Russia.

But the reappearance of war in Europe is also an omen. With toddlers sheltering in subway tunnels, and nuclear power plants under threat, it is a global air raid siren—a warning that the American-led system of internationalism needs to get itself back into gear, for the war at hand and for the struggle against authoritarianism to come. "The global system was built in the 1950s, and if you think of it as a car from those years, it is battered, out of date in some ways, and could use a good tuneup," said James Stavridis, a retired U.S. Navy admiral and former NATO commander in Europe. "But it is still on the road, rolling along, and, ironically enough, Vladimir Putin has done more in a week to energize it than anything I can remember."

Almost universally, from leaders in Europe and Asia to current and former American officials, Ukraine is being viewed as a test for the survival of a 75-year-old idea: that liberal democracy, American military might, and free trade can create the conditions for peace and global prosperity.

Because the founder of that concept, the United States, continues to struggle—with partisanship, COVID-19, and failure in distant war zones—

many foreign policy leaders already see Ukraine in dire terms, as marking an official end of the American era and the start of a more contested, multipolar moment.

For at least a decade, liberal democracies have been disappearing. Their numbers peaked in 2012 with 42 countries, and now there are just 34, home to only 13 percent of the world population, according to V-Dem, a nonprofit that studies governments. In many of those, including the United States, "toxic polarization" is on the rise.

For Ukraine and its democratically elected leaders, the prospects for survival look especially dim. Sanctions, the preferred weapon for the anti-Putin coalition, have a long history of failing to alter the behavior of rogue states or leaders. And for all the talk of defending freedom, Mr. Biden has repeatedly promised that no American soldiers will fight for Ukraine's right to exist, even as a million refugees have already fled and Mr. Putin seems intent on taking the entire country.

Ukraine may also be just the first of several tests for the old order. Mr. Xi, the Chinese leader, said a few months ago that "reunification" with Taiwan—another democracy living in the shadow of an authoritarian neighbor—"must be fulfilled."

Mr. Biden, in his State of the Union address on Tuesday, spoke bluntly of the future risk, saying, "When dictators do not pay a price for their aggression, they cause more chaos." He insisted that the free world was holding Mr. Putin accountable.

And even some skeptics do see signs of a liberal revival. Ryan C. Crocker, a retired former U.S. ambassador to Iraq and Afghanistan, said that after the disastrous American withdrawal from Kabul, the Biden administration had proved that the United States could still lead and gather together a strong global response.

Robert Kagan, a historian whose latest book, *The Jungle Grows Back: America and Our Imperiled World*, has been widely cited during the Ukraine conflict, said he too had been pleasantly surprised by how quickly the liberal order had "snapped back into place."

"There has been a significant reconfirmation of a lot of the old lessons we learned a long time ago and forgot about," he said.

One lesson seems to be that alliances matter. But for many, the most important lesson echoes what Franklin D. Roosevelt and Harry S. Truman concluded about World War II: America cannot retreat into isolationism; its own prosperity depends on actively trying to keep the world's major powers at peace.

"We have become increasingly indifferent—that's why the Putin example has been so striking," said Mr. Kagan, who served in the U.S. State Department from 1984 to 1988. "A lot of people had a comforting and benign view of what a post-American world would look like—it would just be adjusting to other people having different opinions—so for the consequence to be war, it's shocking to people."

"It should make them rethink their earlier assumptions about what America should be doing," he added.

Any attempt to rebuild a model of intervention, however, must deal with fraught recent history. The costly "war on terror" that followed the attacks of Sept. 11, 2001, shifted the country's focus and undermined the world's confidence in American intentions and competence.

Invading Iraq despite global protests, seeing wars drag on for decades without much progress—it was all too much for the American public, Vanda Felbab-Brown, a senior fellow at the Brookings Institution, said in an interview from the Libya-Tunisia border.

"You have this exhaustion of dying for nothing," she said. "For the Taliban to come back to power, and with corrupt Iraqi politics run by Iran."

The American way of the world took another hit with the 2008 global financial crisis. Wall Street and Washington, not Moscow or Beijing, created economic havoc without addressing a surge of inequality tied to globalization. Then came President Donald J. Trump, who turned all the frustration into an inward-looking campaign of grievance.

In his view, the United States had become a victim rather than a beneficiary of the "rules-based order." European nations, for Mr. Trump, were not allies but hangers-on. And while Mr. Biden has since argued that "America is back," most of the world is still asking: For how long?

Polls have consistently shown declining interest in international affairs among Americans and declining faith in the ability of democracy to deliver. Political divisions have reached levels high enough for comparisons with the Civil War.

"The biggest challenge to the system is the domestic basis of American power," said Ivo Daalder, the president of the Chicago Council on Global Affairs and an ambassador to the North Atlantic Treaty Organization under President Barack Obama. "It's still the only global military power, it's still the largest economy, and it's the only power that brings other countries together. The question is: Does domestic politics allow America to play that leadership role?"

After four years of "America First," "there are," Mr. Daalder said, "justifiable doubts."

Like Mr. Putin, Mr. Xi has more than just doubts.

Ian Storey, a senior fellow at the ISEAS-Yusof Ishak Institute in Singapore, said that what's happening in Ukraine "will not change Xi's ideological beliefs one iota." While the resistance to the invasion may inform his calculations on Taiwan, China's most powerful leader in decades ultimately believes that "the U.S.–led Western world is fading and authoritarianism is the future," Mr. Storey said. "While the liberal order has rallied to Ukraine's defense, he will see this as a blip."

To be more than that, many argue, American politics needs to heal—fast. The country's leaders have to explain the value of engagement, as Roosevelt did before World War II, historians note, and reinvigorate both American democracy and the institutions of the international order, which have yet to significantly change or expand their capacity to deal with the challenges of China and Russia.

At the same time, other democracies must also take on more of the international burden, with money, defense, and convening allies.

Mr. Daalder envisions a system in which the world's 12 or 13 largest democracies share leadership, "where the [United States] is maybe first among equals but still one among equals."

Michael Fullilove, the executive director of the Lowy Institute in Sydney and the author of a book about Roosevelt, described such a grouping as an ensemble in which countries like Germany and Australia step forward for larger roles.

"The beneficiaries of the liberal international order have realized they must serve in its bodyguard," he said.

Mr. Crocker was one of many who laid out the stakes in the starkest of terms.

"If we emerge from Ukraine with the narrative being that a united NATO, a united Europe, were able to face down Putin," he said, then "we move forward to deal with the inevitable challenges ahead from a position of unity and American leadership."

If Russia takes over most or all of Ukraine and Mr. Putin is still in charge of a largely stable Russian economy, he added, "welcome to the new world of disorder."

Discussion Questions

1. Is the United States' role in international affairs threatened by domestic political problems, such as polarization?

2. How might the U.S. response differ under the traditional rule that "politics stops at the water's edge" (meaning that domestic political disagreements are suspended in the face of international threats)?

3. How has Russia's invasion of Ukraine changed the U.S. role in the international system?

Appendix

The Declaration of Independence

In Congress, July 4, 1776

When in the course of human events, it becomes necessary for one people to dissolve the political bands which have connected them with another, and to assume among the Powers of the earth, the separate and equal station to which the Laws of Nature and of Nature's God entitle them, a decent respect to the opinions of mankind requires that they should declare the causes which impel them to the separation.

We hold these truths to be self-evident, that all men are created equal, that they are endowed by their Creator with certain unalienable rights, that among these are Life, Liberty and the pursuit of Happiness. That to secure these rights, Governments are instituted among Men, deriving their just powers from the consent of the governed. That whenever any Form of Government becomes destructive of these ends, it is the Right of the People to alter or to abolish it, and to institute new Government, laying its foundation on such principles and organizing its powers in such form, as to them shall seem most likely to effect their Safety and Happiness. Prudence, indeed, will dictate that Governments long established should not be changed for light and transient causes; and accordingly all experience hath shown, that mankind are more disposed to suffer, while evils are sufferable, than to right themselves by abolishing the forms to which they are accustomed. But when a long train of abuses and usurpations, pursuing invariably the same Object evinces a design to reduce them under absolute Despotism, it is their right, it is their duty, to throw off such Government, and to provide new Guards for their future security.—Such has been the patient sufferance of these Colonies; and such is now the necessity which constrains them to alter their former Systems of Government. The history of the present King of Great Britain is a history of repeated injuries and usurpations, all having in direct object the establishment of an absolute Tyranny over these States. To prove this, let Facts be submitted to a candid world.

He has refused his Assent to Laws, the most wholesome and necessary for the public good.

He has forbidden his Governors to pass Laws of immediate and pressing importance, unless suspended in their operation till his Assent should be obtained; and when so suspended, he has utterly neglected to attend to them.

He has refused to pass other Laws for the accommodation of large districts of people, unless those people would relinquish the right of Representation in the Legislature, a right inestimable to them and formidable to tyrants only.

He has called together legislative bodies at places unusual, uncomfortable, and distant from the depository of their public Records, for the sole purpose of fatiguing them into compliance with his measures.

He has dissolved Representative Houses repeatedly, for opposing with manly firmness his invasions on the rights of the people.

He has refused for a long time, after such dissolutions, to cause others to be elected; whereby the Legislative powers, incapable of Annihilation, have returned to the People at large for their exercise; the State remaining in the mean time exposed to all the dangers of invasion from without, and convulsions within.

He has endeavoured to prevent the population of these States; for that purpose obstructing the Laws for Naturalization of Foreigners; refusing to pass others to encourage their migrations hither, and raising the conditions of new Appropriations of Lands.

He has obstructed the Administration of Justice, by refusing his Assent to Laws for establishing Judiciary Powers.

He has made Judges dependent on his Will alone, for the tenure of their offices, and the amount and payment of their salaries.

He has erected a multitude of New Offices, and sent hither swarms of Officers to harrass our People, and eat out their substance.

He has kept among us, in times of peace, Standing Armies without the Consent of our legislature.

He has affected to render the Military independent of and superior to the Civil Power.

He has combined with others to subject us to a jurisdiction foreign to our constitution, and unacknowledged by our laws; giving his Assent to their Acts of pretended Legislation:

For quartering large bodies of armed troops among us:

For protecting them, by a mock Trial, from Punishment for any Murders which they should commit on the Inhabitants of these States:

For cutting off our Trade with all parts of the world:

For imposing Taxes on us without our Consent:

For depriving us in many cases, of the benefits of Trial by jury:

For transporting us beyond Seas to be tried for pretended offences:

For abolishing the free System of English Laws in a neighbouring Province, establishing therein an Arbitrary government, and enlarging its

Boundaries so as to render it at once an example and fit instrument for introducing the same absolute rule into these Colonies:

For taking away our Charters, abolishing our most valuable Laws, and altering fundamentally the Forms of our Governments:

For suspending our own Legislatures, and declaring themselves invested with Power to legislate for us in all cases whatsoever.

He has abdicated Government here, by declaring us out of his Protection and waging War against us.

He has plundered our seas, ravaged our Coasts, burnt our towns, and destroyed the lives of our people.

He is at this time transporting large armies of foreign mercenaries to compleat the works of death, desolation and tyranny, already begun with circumstances of Cruelty & perfidy scarcely paralleled in the most barbarous ages, and totally unworthy the Head of a civilized nation.

He has constrained our fellow Citizens taken Captive on the high Seas to bear Arms against their Country, to become the executioners of their friends and Brethren, or to fall themselves by their Hands.

He has excited domestic insurrections amongst us, and has endeavored to bring on the inhabitants of our frontiers, the merciless Indian Savages, whose known rule of warfare, is an undistinguished destruction of all ages, sexes, and conditions.

In every stage of these Oppressions we have Petitioned for Redress in the most humble terms: Our repeated Petitions have been answered only by repeated injury. A Prince, whose character is thus marked by every act which may define a Tyrant, is unfit to be the ruler of a free people.

Nor have we been wanting in attention to our British brethren. We have warned them from time to time of attempts by their legislature to extend an unwarrantable jurisdiction over us. We have reminded them of the circumstances of our emigration and settlement here. We have appealed to their native justice and magnanimity, and we have conjured them by the ties of our common kindred to disavow these usurpations, which, would inevitably interrupt our connections and correspondence. They too must have been deaf to the voice of justice and of consanguinity. We must, therefore, acquiesce in the necessity, which denounces our Separation, and hold them, as we hold the rest of mankind, Enemies in War, in Peace Friends.

WE, THEREFORE, the Representatives of the UNITED STATES OF AMERICA, in General Congress, Assembled, appealing to the Supreme Judge of the world for the rectitude of our intentions, do, in the Name, and by Authority of the good People of these Colonies, solemnly publish and declare, That these United Colonies are, and of Right ought to be FREE AND INDEPENDENT STATES; that they are Absolved from all Allegiance to the British Crown, and that all political connection between them and the State of Great Britain, is and ought to be totally dissolved; and that as Free and Independent States, they have full Power to levy War, conclude Peace, contract Alliances, establish Commerce, and to do all other Acts and Things which Independent States may of right do. And for the support of this Declaration, with a firm reliance on the protection of Divine Providence, we mutually pledge to each other our Lives, our Fortunes and our sacred Honor.

The foregoing Declaration was, by order of Congress, engrossed, and signed by the following members:

John Hancock

NEW HAMPSHIRE
Josiah Bartlett
William Whipple
Matthew Thornton

MASSACHUSETTS BAY
Samuel Adams
John Adams
Robert Treat Paine
Elbridge Gerry

RHODE ISLAND
Stephen Hopkins
William Ellery

CONNECTICUT
Roger Sherman
Samuel Huntington
William Williams
Oliver Wolcott

NEW YORK
William Floyd
Philip Livingston
Francis Lewis
Lewis Morris

NEW JERSEY
Richard Stockton
John Witherspoon
Francis Hopkinson
John Hart
Abraham Clark

PENNSYLVANIA
Robert Morris
Benjamin Rush
Benjamin Franklin
John Morton
George Clymer
James Smith
George Taylor
James Wilson
George Ross

DELAWARE
Caesar Rodney
George Read
Thomas M'Kean

MARYLAND
Samuel Chase
William Paca

Thomas Stone
Charles Carroll,
  of Carrollton

VIRGINIA
George Wythe
Richard Henry Lee
Thomas Jefferson
Benjamin Harrison
Thomas Nelson, Jr.
Francis Lightfoot Lee
Carter Braxton

NORTH CAROLINA
William Hooper
Joseph Hewes
John Penn

SOUTH CAROLINA
Edward Rutledge
Thomas Heyward, Jr.
Thomas Lynch, Jr.
Arthur Middleton

GEORGIA
Button Gwinnett
Lyman Hall
George Walton

Resolved, That copies of the Declaration be sent to the several assemblies, conventions, and committees, or councils of safety, and to the several commanding officers of the continental troops; that it be proclaimed in each of the United States, at the head of the army.

The Constitution of the United States of America

Annotated with references to The Federalist Papers;
bracketed material is by the editors of this volume.

Federalist
Paper
Number
and Author

[PREAMBLE]

84
(Hamilton)
We the People of the United States, in Order to form a more perfect Union, establish Justice, insure domestic Tranquility, provide
for the common defence, promote the general Welfare, and secure
the Blessings of Liberty to ourselves and our Posterity, do ordain
and establish this Constitution for the United States of America.

ARTICLE I

Section 1

[LEGISLATURE POWERS]

10, 45
(Madison)
All legislative Powers herein granted shall be vested in a Con-
gress of the United States, which shall consist of a Senate and
House of Representatives.

Section 2

[HOUSE OF REPRESENTATIVES, HOW
CONSTITUTED, POWER OF IMPEACHMENT]

39
(Madison)
45
(Madison)
52–53, 57
(Madison)
The House of Representatives shall be composed of Members
chosen every second Year by the People of the several States, and
the Electors in each State shall have the Qualifications requisite
for Electors of the most numerous Branch of the State Legislature.

52
(Madison),
60
(Hamilton)
No Person shall be a Representative who shall not have attained
to the Age of twenty five Years, and been seven Years a Citizen of
the United States, and who shall not, when elected, be an Inhabitant of that State in which he shall be chosen.

54
(Madison)
Representatives and *direct Taxes** shall be apportioned among
the several States which may be included within this Union,

*[Modified by the Sixteenth Amendment.]

according to their respective Numbers, *which shall be determined by adding to the whole Number of free Persons, including those bound to*
54
(Madison) *Service for a Term of Years,* and excluding Indians not taxed, *three-fifths of all other Persons.** The actual Enumeration shall be made
58 within three Years after the first Meeting of the Congress of the
(Madison) United States, and within every subsequent Term of ten Years, in such Manner as they shall by Law direct. The Number of Repre-
55–56 sentatives shall not exceed one for every thirty Thousand, but
(Madison) each State shall have at Least one Representative; *and until such enumeration shall be made, the State of New Hampshire shall be entitled to chuse three, Massachusetts eight, Rhode Island and Providence Plantations one, Connecticut five, New-York six, New Jersey four, Pennsylvania eight, Delaware one, Maryland six, Virginia ten, North Carolina five, South Carolina five and Georgia three.†*

When vacancies happen in the Representation from any State, the Executive Authority thereof shall issue Writs of Election to fill such Vacancies.

79 The House of Representatives shall chuse their Speaker and
(Hamilton) other Officers; and shall have the sole Power of Impeachment.

Section 3

[THE SENATE, HOW CONSTITUTED, IMPEACHMENT TRIALS]

39, 45 The Senate of the United States shall be composed of two Sena-
(Madison),
60 tors from each State, *chosen by the Legislature thereof,‡* for six Years;
(Hamilton), and each Senator shall have one Vote.
62–63 Immediately after they shall be assembled in Consequence of
(Madison)
59 the first Election, they shall be divided as equally as may be into
(Hamilton) three Classes. The Seats of the Senators of the first Class shall be vacated at the Expiration of the second Year, of the second Class at the Expiration of the fourth Year, and of the third Class at the Expiration of the sixth Year, so that one third may be chosen every
68 Expiration of the sixth Year, so that one third may be chosen every
(Hamilton) second Year: *and if Vacancies happen by Resignation, or otherwise, during the Recess of the Legislature of any State, the Executive thereof may make temporary Appointments until the next Meeting of the Legislature, which shall then fill such Vacancies.§*
62 No person shall be a Senator who shall not have attained to the
(Madison),
64 (Jay) Age of thirty Years, and been nine Years a Citizen of the United States, and who shall not, when elected, be an Inhabitant of that State for which he shall be chosen.

*[Modified by the Fourteenth Amendment.]
†[Temporary provision.]
‡[Modified by the Seventeenth Amendment.]
§[Modified by the Seventeenth Amendment.]

The Vice-President of the United States shall be President of the Senate, but shall have no Vote, unless they be equally divided.

39
(Madison),
65–67, 79
(Hamilton)
65
(Hamilton)
84
(Hamilton)

The Senate shall chuse their other Officers, and also a President pro tempore, in the Absence of the Vice-President, or when he shall exercise the Office of President of the United States.

The Senate shall have the sole Power to try all Impeachments. When sitting for that Purpose, they shall be on Oath or Affirmation. When the President of the United States is tried, the Chief Justice shall preside: And no Person shall be convicted without the Concurrence of two thirds of the Members present.

Judgment in Cases of Impeachment shall not extend further than to removal from Office, and disqualification to hold and enjoy any Office of honor, Trust or Profit under the United States: but the Party convicted shall nevertheless be liable and subject to Indictment, Trial, Judgment and Punishment, according to Law.

Section 4

[ELECTION OF SENATORS AND REPRESENTATIVES]

59–61
(Hamilton)

The Times, Places and Manner of holding Elections for Senators and Representatives, shall be prescribed in each State by the Legislature thereof; but the Congress may at any time by Law make or alter such Regulations, except as to the Place of Chusing Senators.

*The Congress shall assemble at least once in every Year, and such Meeting shall be on the first Monday in December, unless they shall by Law appoint a different Day.**

Section 5

[QUORUM, JOURNALS, MEETINGS, ADJOURNMENTS]

Each House shall be the Judge of the Elections, Returns and Qualifications of its own Members, and a Majority of each shall constitute a Quorum to do Business; but a smaller Number may adjourn from day to day, and may be authorized to compel the Attendance of absent Members, in such Manner, and under such Penalties as each House may provide.

Each House may determine the Rules of its Proceedings, punish its Members for disorderly Behavior, and, with the Concurrence of two-thirds, expel a Member.

Each House shall keep a Journal of its Proceedings, and from time to time publish the same, excepting such Parts as may in their Judgment require Secrecy; and the Yeas and Nays of the

*[Modified by the Twentieth Amendment.]

Members of either House on any question shall, at the Desire of one-fifth of those Present, be entered on the Journal.

Neither House, during the Session of Congress, shall, without the Consent of the other, adjourn for more than three days, nor to any other Place than that in which the two Houses shall be sitting.

Section 6

[COMPENSATION, PRIVILEGES, DISABILITIES]

The Senators and Representatives shall receive a Compensation for their Services, to be ascertained by Law, and paid out of the Treasury of the United States. They shall in all Cases, except Treason, Felony and Breach of the Peace, be privileged from Arrest during their Attendance at the Session of their respective Houses, and in going to and returning from the same; and for any Speech or Debate in either House, they shall not be questioned in any other Place.

55
(Madison),
76
(Hamilton)

No Senator or Representative shall, during the Time for which he was elected, be appointed to any civil Office under the authority of the United States, which shall have been created, or the Emoluments whereof shall have been increased during such time; and no Person holding any Office under the United States, shall be a Member of either House during his Continuance in Office.

Section 7

[PROCEDURE IN PASSING BILLS AND RESOLUTIONS]

66
(Hamilton)

All bills for raising Revenue shall originate in the House of Representatives; but the Senate may propose or concur with Amendments as on other Bills.

69, 73
(Hamilton)

Every Bill which shall have passed the House of Representatives and the Senate, shall, before it become a Law, be presented to the President of the United States; If he approve he shall sign it, but if not he shall return it, with his Objections to that House in which it shall have originated, who shall enter the Objections at large on their Journal, and proceed to reconsider it. If after such Reconsideration two-thirds of that House shall agree to pass the Bill, it shall be sent, together with the Objections, to the other House, by which it shall likewise be reconsidered, and if approved by two-thirds of that House it shall become a Law. But in all such Cases the Votes of both Houses shall be determined by Yeas and Nays, and the Names of the Persons voting for and against the Bill shall be entered on the Journal of each House respectively. If any Bill shall not be returned by the President within ten Days (Sundays excepted) after it shall have been presented to him, the Same shall be a Law, in like Manner as if he had signed it, unless the Congress by their Adjournment prevent its Return, in which Case it shall not be a Law.

69, 73 (Hamilton)

Every Order, Resolution, or Vote to which the Concurrence of the Senate and House of Representatives may be necessary (except on a question of Adjournment) shall be presented to the President of the United States; and before the Same shall take Effect, shall be approved by him, or being disapproved by him, shall be repassed by two-thirds of the Senate and House of Representatives, according to the Rules and Limitations prescribed in the Case of a Bill.

Section 8

[POWERS OF CONGRESS]

The Congress shall have Power

30–36 (Hamilton), 41 (Madison)

To lay and collect Taxes, Duties, Imposts and Excises, to pay the Debts and provide for the common Defence and general Welfare of the United States; but all Duties, Imposts and Excises shall be uniform throughout the United States;

56 (Madison)

To borrow money on the Credit of the United States;

42, 45, 56 (Madison)

To regulate Commerce with foreign Nations, and among the several States, and with the Indian Tribes;

32 (Hamilton),

To establish an uniform Rule of Naturalization, and uniform Laws on the subject of Bankruptcies throughout the United States;

42 (Madison)

To coin Money, regulate the Value thereof, and of foreign Coin, and fix the Standard of Weights and Measures;

42 (Madison)

To provide for the Punishment of counterfeiting the Securities and current Coin of the United States;

42 (Madison)

To establish Post Offices and Post Roads;

42 (Madison) 43 (Madison)

To promote the Progress of Science and useful Arts, by securing for limited Times to Authors and Inventors the exclusive Right to their respective Writings and Discoveries;

81 (Hamilton)

To constitute Tribunals inferior to the supreme Court;

42 (Madison)

To define and Punish Piracies and Felonies committed on the high Seas, and Offenses against the Law of Nations;

41 (Madison)

To declare War, grant Letters of Marque and Reprisal, and make Rules concerning Captures on Land and Water;

23, 24, 26 (Hamilton),

To raise and support Armies, but no Appropriation of Money to that Use shall be for a longer Term than two Years;

41 (Madison)

To provide and maintain a Navy;

To make Rules for the Government and Regulation of the land and naval forces;

29
(Hamilton) To provide for calling forth the Militia to execute the Laws of the Union, suppress Insurrections and repel Invasions;

29
(Hamilton),
56
(Madison) To provide for organizing, arming, and disciplining the Militia, and for governing such Part of them as may be employed in the Service of the United States, reserving to the States respectively, the Appointment of the Officers, and the Authority of training the Militia according to the discipline prescribed by Congress;

32
(Hamilton),
43
(Madison) To exercise exclusive Legislation in all Cases whatsoever, over such District (not exceeding ten Miles square) as may, by Cession of particular States, and the Acceptance of Congress, become the Seat of the Government of the United States, and to exercise

43
(Madison) like Authority over all Places purchased by the Consent of the Legislature of the State in which the Same shall be, for the Erection of Forts, Magazines, Arsenals, dock-Yards, and other needful Buildings;—And

29, 33
(Hamilton)
44
(Madison) To make all Laws which shall be necessary and proper for carrying into Execution the foregoing Powers, and all other Powers vested by this Constitution in the Government of the United States, or in any Department or Officer thereof.

Section 9

[SOME RESTRICTIONS ON FEDERAL POWER]

42
(Madison) *The Migration or Importation of such Persons as any of the States now existing shall think proper to admit, shall not be prohibited by the Congress prior to the Year one thousand eight hundred and eight, but a tax or duty may be imposed on such Importation, not exceeding ten dollars for each Person.**

83, 84
(Hamilton) The privilege of the Writ of *Habeas Corpus* shall not be suspended, unless when in Cases of Rebellion or Invasion the public Safety may require it.

84
(Hamilton) No Bill of Attainder or ex post facto Law shall be passed.

No Capitation, or other direct, Tax shall be laid, unless in Proportion to the Census or Enumeration herein before directed to be taken.†

No Tax or Duty shall be laid on Articles exported from any State.

32
(Hamilton) No Preference shall be given by any Regulation of Commerce or Revenue to the Ports of one State over those of another: nor shall Vessels bound to, or from, one State, be obliged to enter, clear, or pay Duties in another.

No Money shall be drawn from the Treasury, but in Consequence of Appropriations made by Law; and a regular Statement

*[Temporary provision.]
†[Modified by the Sixteenth Amendment.]

and Account of the Receipts and Expenditures of all public Money shall be published from time to time.

39
(Madison),
84
(Hamilton)

No Title of Nobility shall be granted by the United States: And no Person holding any Office of Profit or Trust under them, shall, without the Consent of the Congress, accept of any present, Emolument, Office, or Title, of any kind whatever, from any King, Prince or foreign State.

Section 10

[RESTRICTIONS UPON POWERS OF STATES]

33
(Hamilton),
44
(Madison)

No State shall enter into any Treaty, Alliance, or Confederation; grant Letters of Marque and Reprisal; coin Money; emit Bills of Credit; make any Thing but gold and silver Coin a Tender in Payment of Debts; pass any Bill of Attainder, ex post facto Law, or Law impairing the Obligation of Contracts, or grant any Title of Nobility.

32
(Hamilton),
44
(Madison)

No State shall, without the Consent of the Congress, lay any Imposts or Duties on Imports or Exports, except what may be absolutely necessary for executing its inspection Laws: and the net Produce of all Duties and Imposts, laid by any State on Imports or Exports, shall be for the Use of the Treasury of the United States; and all such Laws shall be subject to the Revision and Controul of the Congress.

No State shall, without the Consent of Congress, lay any duty of Tonnage, keep Troops, or Ships of War in time of Peace, enter into any Agreement or Compact with another State, or with a foreign Power, or engage in War, unless actually invaded, or in such imminent Danger as will not admit of Delay.

ARTICLE II

Section 1

[EXECUTIVE POWER, ELECTION, QUALIFICATIONS OF THE PRESIDENT]

39
(Madison),
70, 71, 84
(Hamilton)

The executive Power shall be vested in a President of the United States of America. *He shall hold his Office during the Term of four years, and, together with the Vice-President, chosen for the same Term, be elected, as follows:**

69, 71
(Hamilton)

39, 45
(Madison),

Each State shall appoint, in such Manner as the Legislature thereof may direct, a Number of Electors, equal to the whole Number of Senators and Representatives to which the State may be entitled in the Congress: but no Senator or Representative, or

---

*[Number of terms limited to two by the Twenty-Second Amendment.]

Person holding an Office of Trust or Profit under the United
States, shall be appointed an Elector.

68, 77
(Hamilton)

*The electors shall meet in their respective States, and vote by ballot
for two Persons, of whom one at least shall not be an Inhabitant of the
same State with themselves. And they shall make a List of all the Persons
voted for, and of the Number of Votes for each; which List they shall sign
and certify, and transmit sealed to the Seat of the Government of the
United States, directed to the President of the Senate. The President of
the Senate shall, in the Presence of the Senate and House of Representatives, open all the Certificates, and the Votes shall then be counted. The
Person having the greatest Number of Votes shall be the President, if
such Number be a Majority of the whole Number of Electors appointed;
and if there be more than one who have such Majority, and have an
equal Number of Votes, then the House of Representatives shall immediately chuse by Ballot one of them for President; and if no Person have a
Majority, then from the five highest on the List the said House shall in
like Manner chuse the President. But in chusing the President, the Votes
shall be taken by States, the Representation from each State having one
Vote; a quorum for this Purpose shall consist of a Member or Members
from two-thirds of the States, and a Majority of all the States shall be
necessary to a Choice. In every Case, after the Choice of the President, the
Person having the greatest Number of Votes of the Electors shall be the
Vice-President. But if there should remain two or more who have equal
Votes, the Senate shall chuse from them by Ballot the Vice-President.**

66
(Hamilton)

The Congress may determine the Time of chusing the Electors,
and the Day on which they shall give their Votes; which Day shall
be the same throughout the United States.

No Person except a natural born Citizen, or a Citizen of the
United States, at the time of the Adoption of this Constitution,
shall be eligible to the Office of President; neither shall any Person
be eligible to that Office who shall not have attained to the Age of
thirty-five Years, and been fourteen Years a Resident within the
United States.

64 (Jay)

In Case of the Removal of the President from Office, or his
Death, Resignation, or Inability to discharge the Powers and Duties
of the said Office, the same shall devolve on the Vice-President,
and the Congress may by Law provide for the Case of Removal,
Death, Resignation or Inability, both of the President and Vice-
President, declaring what Officer shall then act as President, and
such Officer shall act accordingly, until the Disability be removed,
or a President shall be elected.

The President shall, at stated Times, receive for his Services, a
Compensation, which shall neither be encreased nor diminished

73, 79
(Hamilton)

*[Modified by the Twelfth and Twentieth Amendment.]

during the Period for which he shall have been elected, and he shall not receive within that Period any other Emolument from the United States, or any of them.

Before he enter on the Execution of his Office, he shall take the following Oath or Affirmation:—"I do solemnly swear (or affirm) that I will faithfully execute the Office of President of the United States, and will to the best of my Ability, preserve, protect and defend the Constitution of the United States."

Section 2

[POWERS OF THE PRESIDENT]

69, 74
(Hamilton)

The President shall be Commander in Chief of the Army and Navy of the United States, and of the Militia of the several States, when called into the actual Service of the United States; he may require the Opinion, in writing, of the principal Officer in each of the executive Departments, upon any Subject relating to the Duties of their respective Offices, and he shall have Power to Grant Reprieves and Pardons for Offenses against the United States, except in Cases of Impeachment.

74
(Hamilton)
69
(Hamilton)
74
(Hamilton)
42
(Madison)
64 (Jay),
66
(Hamilton)

He shall have Power, by and with the Advice and Consent of the Senate, to make Treaties, provided two thirds of the Senators present concur; and he shall nominate, and by and with the Advice and Consent of the Senate, shall appoint Ambassadors, other public Ministers and Consuls, Judges of the Supreme Court, and all other Officers of the United States, whose Appointments are not herein otherwise provided for, and which shall be established by Law: but the Congress may by Law vest the Appointment of such inferior Officers, as they think proper, in the President alone, in the Courts of Law, or in the Heads of Departments.

42
(Madison),

66, 69,
76, 77
(Hamilton)

67, 76
(Hamilton)

The President shall have Power to fill up all Vacancies that may happen during the Recess of the Senate, by granting Commissions which shall expire at the End of their next Session.

Section 3

[POWERS AND DUTIES OF THE PRESIDENT]

77
(Hamilton)
69, 77
(Hamilton)

He shall from time to time give to the Congress Information of the State of the Union, and recommend to their Consideration such Measures as he shall judge necessary and expedient; he may, on extraordinary Occasions, convene both Houses, or either of them, and in Case of Disagreement between them, with Respect to the Time of Adjournment, he may adjourn them to such Time as he shall think proper; he shall receive Ambassadors and other public Ministers; he shall take Care that the Laws be faithfully

77
(Hamilton)
69, 77
(Hamilton)
42
(Madison),
69, 77
(Hamilton)

78
(Hamilton)
executed, and shall Commission all the Officers of the United States.

Section 4

[IMPEACHMENT]

39
(Madison),
69
(Hamilton)
The President, Vice-President and all civil Officers of the United States, shall be removed from Office on Impeachment for, and Conviction of, Treason, Bribery, or other high Crimes and Misdemeanors.

ARTICLE III

Section 1

[JUDICIAL POWER, TENURE OR OFFICE]

81, 82
(Hamilton)
65
(Hamilton)
78, 79
(Hamilton)
The judicial Power of the United States, shall be vested in one Supreme Court, and in such inferior Courts as the Congress may from time to time ordain and establish. The Judges, both of the supreme and inferior Courts, shall hold their Offices during good Behavior, and shall, at stated Times, receive for their Services a Compensation, which shall not be diminished during their Continuance in Office.

Section 2

[JURISDICTION]

80
(Hamilton)
The judicial Power shall extend to all Cases, in Law and Equity, arising under this Constitution, the Laws of the United States, and Treaties made, or which shall be made, under their Authority;—to all Cases affecting Ambassadors, other public Ministers and Consuls;—to all Cases of admiralty and maritime Jurisdiction;—to Controversies to which the United States shall be a party;—to Controversies between two or more States;—*between a State and Citizens of another State;*—between Citizens of different States,—between Citizens of the same State claiming Lands under Grants of different States, *and between a State*, or the Citizens thereof, *and foreign States, Citizens or Subjects.**

81
(Hamilton)
In all Cases affecting Ambassadors, other public Ministers and Consuls, and those in which a State shall be Party, the supreme Court shall have original Jurisdiction. In all the other Cases before mentioned, the Supreme Court shall have appellate Jurisdiction, both as to Law and Fact, with such Exceptions, and under such Regulations as the Congress shall make.

*[Modified by the Eleventh Amendment.]

83, 84
(Hamilton)
    The Trial of all Crimes, except in Cases of Impeachment, shall be by Jury; and such Trial shall be held in the State where the said Crimes shall have been committed; but when not committed within any State, the Trial shall be at such Place or Places as the Congress may by Law have directed.

Section 3

[TREASON, PROOF, AND PUNISHMENT]

43
(Madison),
98
(Hamilton)
    Treason against the United States, shall consist only in levying War against them, or in adhering to their Enemies, giving them Aid and Comfort. No Person shall be convicted of Treason unless on the Testimony of two Witnesses to the same overt Act, or on Confession in open Court.

43
(Madison),
84
(Hamilton)
    The Congress shall have Power to declare the Punishment of Treason, but no Attainder of Treason shall work Corruption of Blood, or Forfeiture except during the Life of the Person attained.

ARTICLE IV

Section 1

[FAITH AND CREDIT AMONG STATES]

42
(Madison)
    Full Faith and Credit shall be given in each State to the public Acts, Records, and judicial Proceedings of every other State. And the Congress may by general Laws prescribe the Manner in which such Acts, Records and Proceedings shall be proved, and the Effect thereof.

Section 2

[PRIVILEGES AND IMMUNITIES, FUGITIVES]

80
(Hamilton)
    The Citizens of each State shall be entitled to all Privileges and Immunities of Citizens in the several States.

    A Person charged in any State with Treason, Felony, or other Crime, who shall flee from Justice, and be found in another State, shall on demand of the executive Authority of the State from which he fled, be delivered up, to be removed to the State having Jurisdiction of the Crime.

    *No Person held to Service or Labour in one State, under the Laws thereof, escaping into another, shall, in Consequence of any Law or Regulation therein, be discharged from such Service or Labour, but shall be delivered up on Claim of the Party to whom such Service or Labour may be due.**

---

*[Repealed by the Thirteenth Amendment.]

Section 3

[ADMISSION OF NEW STATES]

43
(Madison) New States may be admitted by the Congress into this Union; but no new States shall be formed or erected within the Jurisdiction of any other State; nor any State be formed by the Junction of two or more States, or Parts of States, without the Consent of the Legislatures of the States concerned as well as of the Congress.

43
(Madison) The Congress shall have Power to dispose of and make all needful Rules and Regulations respecting the Territory or other Property belonging to the United States; and nothing in this Constitution shall be so construed as to Prejudice any Claims of the United States, or of any particular State.

Section 4

[GUARANTEE OF REPUBLICAN GOVERNMENT]

39, 43
(Madison) The United States shall guarantee to every State in this Union a Republican Form of Government, and shall protect each of them against Invasion; and on Application of the Legislature, or of the Executive (when the Legislature cannot be convened) against domestic Violence.

ARTICLE V

[AMENDMENT OF THE CONSTITUTION]

39, 43
(Madison)
85
(Hamilton) The Congress, whenever two-thirds of both Houses shall deem it necessary, shall propose Amendments to this Constitution, or, on the Application of the Legislatures of two-thirds of the several States, shall call a Convention for proposing Amendments, which, in either Case, shall be valid to all Intents and Purposes, as Part of this Constitution, when ratified by the Legislatures of three-fourths of the several States, or by Conventions in three-fourths thereof, as the one or the other Mode of Ratification may be proposed by the Congress; *Provided that no Amendment which may be made prior to the Year One thousand eight hundred and eight shall in any Manner affect the first and fourth Clauses in the Ninth Section of the first Article;* and that no State,

43
(Madison) without its Consent, shall be deprived of its equal Suffrage in the Senate.

*[Temporary provision.]

ARTICLE VI

[DEBTS, SUPREMACY, OATH]

43
(Madison)

All Debts contracted and Engagements entered into, before the Adoption of this Constitution, shall be as valid against the United States under this Constitution, as under the Confederation.

27, 33
(Hamilton),
39, 44
(Madison)

This Constitution, and the Laws of the United States which shall be made in Pursuance thereof; and all Treaties made, or which shall be made, under the Authority of the United States, shall be the supreme Law of the Land; and the Judges in every State shall be bound thereby, any Thing in the Constitution or Laws of any State to the Contrary notwithstanding.

27
(Hamilton),
44
(Madison)

The Senators and Representatives before mentioned, and the Members of the several State Legislatures, and all executive and judicial Officers, both of the United States and of the several States, shall be bound by Oath or Affirmation, to support this Constitution; but no religious Test shall ever be required as a Qualification to any Office or public Trust under the United States.

ARTICLE VII

[RATIFICATION AND ESTABLISHMENT]

39, 40, 43
(Madison)

The Ratification of the Conventions of nine States, shall be sufficient for the Establishment of this Constitution between the States so ratifying the Same.*

Done in Convention by the Unanimous Consent of the States present the Seventeenth Day of September in the Year of our Lord one thousand seven hundred and Eighty seven and of the Independence of the United States of America the Twelfth. *In Witness* whereof We have hereunto subscribed our Names,

G:⁰ WASHINGTON—
Presidt, and Deputy
from Virginia

---

*[The Constitution was submitted on September 17, 1787, by the Constitutional Convention, was ratified by the conventions of several states at various dates up to May 29, 1790, and became effective on March 4, 1789.]

New Hampshire	JOHN LANGDON NICHOLAS GILMAN	Delaware	GEO READ GUNNING BEDFOR JUN JOHN DICKINSON
Massachusetts	NATHANIEL GORHAM RUFUS KING		RICHARD BASSETT JACO: BROOM
Connecticut	WM SAML JOHNSON ROGER SHERMAN	Maryland	JAMES MCHENRY DAN OF ST THOS. JENIFER
New York	ALEXANDER HAMILTON		DANL CARROLL
New Jersey	WIL: LIVINGSTON DAVID BREARLEY	Virginia	JOHN BLAIR— JAMES MADISON JR.
	WM PATERSON JONA: DAYTON	North Carolina	WM BLOUNT RICHD DOBBS SPAIGHT
Pennsylvania	B FRANKLIN		HU WILLIAMSON
	THOMAS MIFFLIN ROBT MORRIS	South Carolina	J. RUTLEDGE
	GEO. CLYMER THOS. FITZSIMONS		CHARLES COTESWORTH PINCKNEY CHARLES PINCKNEY
	JARED INGERSOLL		PIERCE BUTLER
	JAMES WILSON GOUV MORRIS	Georgia	WILLIAM FEW ABR BALDWIN

Amendments to the Constitution

Proposed by Congress and Ratified
by the Legislatures of the Several States,
Pursuant to Article V of the Original Constitution.

Amendments I–X, known as the Bill of Rights, were proposed by Congress on September 25, 1789, and ratified on December 15, 1791. The Federalist Papers comments, mainly in opposition to a Bill of Rights, can be found in No. 84 (Hamilton).

AMENDMENT I

[FREEDOM OF RELIGION, OF SPEECH, AND OF THE PRESS]
   Congress shall make no law respecting an establishment of religion, or prohibiting the free exercise thereof; or abridging the freedom of speech, or of the press; or the right of the people peaceably to assemble, and to petition the Government for a redress of grievances.

AMENDMENT II

[RIGHT TO KEEP AND BEAR ARMS]
   A well regulated Militia, being necessary to the security of a free State, the right of the people to keep and bear Arms, shall not be infringed.

AMENDMENT III

[QUARTERING OF SOLDIERS]
   No Soldier shall, in time of peace be quartered in any house, without the consent of the Owner, nor in time of war, but in a manner to be prescribed by law.

AMENDMENT IV

[SECURITY FROM UNWARRANTABLE SEARCH AND
SEIZURE]

The right of the people to be secure in their persons, houses, papers, and effects, against unreasonable searches and seizures, shall not be violated, and no Warrants shall issue, but upon probable cause, supported by Oath or affirmation, and particularly describing the place to be searched, and the persons or things to be seized.

AMENDMENT V

[RIGHTS OF ACCUSED PERSONS IN CRIMINAL
PROCEEDINGS]

No person shall be held to answer for a capital, or otherwise infamous crime, unless on a presentment or indictment of a Grand Jury, except in cases arising in the land or naval forces, or in the Militia, when in actual service in time of War or public danger; nor shall any person be subject for the same offence to be twice put in jeopardy of life or limb; nor shall be compelled in any Criminal Case to be a witness against himself, nor be deprived of life, liberty, or property, without due process of law; nor shall private property be taken for public use, without just compensation.

AMENDMENT VI

[RIGHT TO SPEEDY TRIAL, WITNESSES, ETC.]

In all criminal prosecutions, the accused shall enjoy the right to a speedy and public trial, by an impartial jury of the State and district wherein the crime shall have been committed, which district shall have been previously ascertained by law, and to be informed of the nature and cause of the accusation; to be confronted with the witnesses against him; to have compulsory process for obtaining Witnesses in his favor, and to have the Assistance of Counsel for his defence.

AMENDMENT VII

[TRIAL BY JURY IN CIVIL CASES]

In suits at common law, where the value in controversy shall exceed twenty dollars, the right of trial by jury shall be preserved, and no fact tried by a jury shall be otherwise re-examined in any Court of the United States, than according to the rules of the common law.

Amendment VIII

[bails, fines, punishments]
Excessive bail shall not be required, nor excessive fines imposed, nor cruel and unusual punishments inflicted.

Amendment IX

[reservation of rights of people]
The enumeration in the Constitution, of certain rights, shall not be construed to deny or disparage others retained by the people.

Amendment X

[powers reserved to states or people]
The powers not delegated to the United States by the Constitution, nor prohibited by it to the States, are reserved to the States respectively, or to the people.

Amendment XI

[Proposed by Congress on March 4, 1794; declared ratified on January 8, 1798.]
[restriction of judicial power]
The Judicial power of the United States shall not be construed to extend to any suit in law or equity, commenced or prosecuted against one of the United States by Citizens of another State, or by Citizens or Subjects of any foreign State.

Amendment XII

[Proposed by Congress on December 9, 1803; declared ratified on September 25, 1804.]
[election of president and vice-president]
The Electors shall meet in their respective states, and vote by ballot for President and Vice-President, one of whom, at least, shall not be an inhabitant of the same state with themselves; they shall name in their ballots

the person voted for as President, and in distinct ballots the person voted for as Vice-President, and they shall make distinct lists of all persons voted for as President, and of all persons voted for as Vice-President, and of the number of votes for each, which lists they shall sign and certify, and transmit sealed to the seat of the government of the United States, directed to the President of the Senate;—The President of the Senate shall, in presence of the Senate and House of Representatives, open all the certificates and the votes shall then be counted;—The person having the greatest number of votes for President, shall be the President, if such number be a majority of the whole number of Electors appointed; and if no person have such majority, then from the persons having the highest numbers not exceeding three on the list of those voted for as President, the House of Representatives shall choose immediately, by ballot, the President. But in choosing the President, the votes shall be taken by states, the representation from each state having one vote; a quorum for this purpose shall consist of a member or members from two-thirds of the states, and a majority of all the states shall be necessary to a choice. And if the House of Representatives shall not choose a President whenever the right of choice shall devolve upon them, before the fourth day of March next following, then the Vice-President shall act as President, as in the case of the death or other constitutional disability of the President. The person having the greatest number of votes as Vice-President, shall be the Vice-President, if such number be a majority of the whole number of Electors appointed, and if no person have a majority, then from the two highest numbers on the list, the Senate shall choose the Vice-President; a quorum for the purpose shall consist of two-thirds of the whole number of Senators, and a majority of the whole number shall be necessary to a choice. But no person constitutionally ineligible to the office of President shall be eligible to that of Vice-President of the United States.

AMENDMENT XIII

[Proposed by Congress on January 31, 1865; declared ratified on December 18, 1865.]

Section 1

[ABOLITION OF SLAVERY]

Neither slavery nor involuntary servitude, except as a punishment for crime whereof the party shall have been duly convicted, shall exist within the United States, or any place subject to their jurisdiction.

Section 2

[POWER TO ENFORCE THIS ARTICLE]

Congress shall have power to enforce this article by appropriate legislation.

AMENDMENT XIV

[Proposed by Congress on June 13, 1866; declared ratified on July 28, 1868.]

Section 1

[CITIZENSHIP RIGHTS NOT TO BE ABRIDGED BY STATES]

All persons born or naturalized in the United States, and subject to the jurisdiction thereof, are citizens of the United States and of the State wherein they reside. No state shall make or enforce any law which shall abridge the privileges or immunities of citizens of the United States; nor shall any State deprive any person of life, liberty, or property, without due process of law; nor deny to any person within its jurisdiction the equal protection of the laws.

Section 2

[APPORTIONMENT OF REPRESENTATIVES IN CONGRESS]

Representatives shall be apportioned among the several States according to their respective numbers, counting the whole number of persons in each State, excluding Indians not taxed. But when the right to vote at any election for the choice of electors for President and Vice-President of the United States, Representatives in Congress, the Executive and Judicial officers of a State, or the members of the Legislature thereof, is denied to any of the male inhabitants of such State, being twenty-one years of age, and citizens of the United States, or in any way abridged, except for participation in rebellion, or other crime, the basis of representation therein shall be reduced in the proportion which the number of such male citizens shall bear to the whole number of male citizens twenty-one years of age in such State.

Section 3

[PERSONS DISQUALIFIED FROM HOLDING OFFICE]

No person shall be a Senator or Representative in Congress, or elector of President and Vice-President, or hold any office, civil or military, under the United States, or under any State, who, having previously taken an oath, as a member of Congress, or as an officer of the United States, or as a member of any State legislature, or as an executive or judicial officer of any State, to support the Constitution of the United States, shall have engaged in insurrection or rebellion against the same, or given aid or comfort to the enemies thereof. But Congress may by a vote of two-thirds of each House, remove such disability.

Section 4

[WHAT PUBLIC DEBTS ARE VALID]

The validity of the public debt of the United States, authorized by law, including debts incurred for payment of pensions and bounties for services in suppressing insurrection or rebellion, shall not be questioned. But neither the United States nor any State shall assume or pay any debt or obligation incurred in aid of insurrection or rebellion against the United States, or any claim for the loss or emancipation of any slave; but all such debts, obligations and claims shall be held illegal and void.

Section 5

[POWER TO ENFORCE THIS ARTICLE]

The Congress shall have power to enforce, by appropriate legislation, the provisions of this article.

AMENDMENT XV

[Proposed by Congress on February 26, 1869; declared ratified on March 30, 1870.]

Section 1

[BLACK SUFFRAGE]

The right of citizens of the United States to vote shall not be denied or abridged by the United States or by any State on account of race, color, or previous condition of servitude.

Section 2

[POWER TO ENFORCE THIS ARTICLE]

The Congress shall have power to enforce this article by appropriate legislation.

AMENDMENT XVI

[Proposed by Congress on July 12, 1909; declared ratified on February 25, 1913.]

[AUTHORIZING INCOME TAXES]

The Congress shall have power to lay and collect taxes on incomes, from whatever source derived, without apportionment among the several States, and without regard to any census or enumeration.

AMENDMENT XVII

[Proposed by Congress on May 13, 1912; declared ratified on May 31, 1913.]

[POPULAR ELECTION OF SENATORS]

The Senate of the United States shall be composed of two Senators from each State, elected by the people thereof, for six years; and each Senator shall have one vote. The electors in each State shall have the qualifications requisite for electors of the most numerous branch of the State Legislature.

When vacancies happen in the representation of any State in the Senate, the executive authority of such State shall issue writs of election to fill such vacancies: Provided, That the Legislature of any State may empower the executive thereof to make temporary appointments until the people fill the vacancies by election as the Legislature may direct.

This amendment shall not be so construed as to affect the election or term of any Senator chosen before it becomes valid as part of the Constitution.

AMENDMENT XVIII

[Proposed by Congress on December 18, 1917; declared ratified on January 29, 1919.]

Section 1

[NATIONAL LIQUOR PROHIBITION]

After one year from the ratification of this article, the manufacture, sale, or transportation of intoxicating liquors within, the importation thereof into, or the exportation thereof from the United States and all territory subject to the jurisdiction thereof for beverage purposes is hereby prohibited.

Section 2

[POWER TO ENFORCE THIS ARTICLE]
Congress and the several states shall have concurrent power to enforce this article by appropriate legislation.

Section 3

[RATIFICATION WITHIN SEVEN YEARS]
This article shall be inoperative unless it shall have been ratified as an amendment to the Constitution by the legislatures of the several states, as provided in the Constitution, within seven years from the date of the submission hereof to the states by Congress.*

AMENDMENT XIX

[Proposed by Congress on June 4, 1919; declared ratified on August 26, 1920.]

[FEMALE SUFFRAGE]
The right of the citizens of the United States to vote shall not be denied or abridged by the United States or by any state on account of sex.

Congress shall have power, by appropriate legislation, to enforce this article by appropriate legislation.

AMENDMENT XX

[Proposed by Congress on March 2, 1932; declared ratified on February 6, 1933.]

Section 1

[TERMS OF OFFICE]
The terms of the President and Vice-President shall end at noon on the 20th day of January, and the terms of Senators and Representatives at noon on the 3rd day of January, of the years in which such terms would have ended if this article had not been ratified; and the terms of their successors shall then begin.

*[Repealed by the Twenty-First Amendment.]

Section 2

[TIME OF CONVENING CONGRESS]

The Congress shall assemble at least once in every year, and such meeting shall begin at noon on the 3rd day of January, unless they shall by law appoint a different day.

Section 3

[DEATH OF PRESIDENT-ELECT]

If, at the time fixed for the beginning of the term of the President, the President-elect shall have died, the Vice-President-elect shall become President. If a President shall not have been chosen before the time fixed for the beginning of his term, or if the President-elect shall have failed to qualify, then the Vice-President-elect shall act as President until a President shall have qualified; and the Congress may by law provide for the case wherein neither a President-elect nor a Vice-President-elect shall have qualified, declaring who shall then act as President, or the manner in which one who is to act shall be selected, and such person shall act accordingly until a President or Vice-President shall have qualified.

Section 4

[ELECTION OF THE PRESIDENT]

The Congress may by law provide for the case of the death of any of the persons from whom the House of Representatives may choose a President whenever the right of choice shall have devolved upon them, and for the case of the death of any of the persons from whom the Senate may choose a Vice-President whenever the right of choice shall have devolved upon them.

Section 5

[AMENDMENT TAKES EFFECT]

Sections 1 and 2 shall take effect on the 15th day of October following ratification of this article.

Section 6

[RATIFICATION WITHIN SEVEN YEARS]

This article shall be inoperative unless it shall have been ratified as an amendment to the Constitution by the legislatures of three-fourths of the several States within seven years from the date of its submission.

Amendment XXI

[Proposed by Congress on February 20, 1933; declared ratified on December 5, 1933.]

Section 1

[NATIONAL LIQUOR PROHIBITION REPEALED]

The eighteenth article of amendment to the Constitution of the United States is hereby repealed.

Section 2

[TRANSPORTATION OF LIQUOR INTO "DRY" STATES]

The transportation or importation into any State, Territory, or Possession of the United States for delivery or use therein of intoxicating liquors, in violation of the laws thereof, is hereby prohibited.

Section 3

[RATIFICATION WITHIN SEVEN YEARS]

The article shall be inoperative unless it shall have been ratified as an amendment to the Constitution by conventions in the several States, as provided in the Constitution, within seven years from the date of the submission hereof to the States by the Congress.

Amendment XXII

[Proposed by Congress on March 21, 1947; declared ratified on February 26, 1951.]

Section 1

[TENURE OF PRESIDENT LIMITED]

No person shall be elected to the office of the President more than twice, and no person who has held the office of President or acted as President for more than two years of a term to which some other person was elected President shall be elected to the Office of the President more than once. But this Article shall not apply to any person holding the office of President when this Article was proposed by the Congress, and shall not prevent any person who may be holding the office of President, or acting as President, during the term within which this Article becomes operative from holding the office of President or acting as President during the remainder of such term.

Section 2
[RATIFICATION WITHIN SEVEN YEARS]
This Article shall be inoperative unless it shall have been ratified as an amendment to the Constitution by the legislatures of three-fourths of the several states within seven years from the date of its submission to the States by the Congress.

AMENDMENT XXIII

[Proposed by Congress on June 21, 1960; declared ratified on March 29, 1961.]

Section 1
[ELECTORAL COLLEGE VOTES FOR THE DISTRICT OF COLUMBIA]
The District constituting the seat of Government of the United States shall appoint in such manner as the Congress may direct:

A number of electors of President and Vice-President equal to the whole number of Senators and Representatives in Congress to which the District would be entitled if it were a State, but in no event more than the least populous State; they shall be in addition to those appointed by the States, but they shall be considered, for the purposes of the election of President and Vice-President, to be electors appointed by a State; and they shall meet in the District and perform such duties as provided by the twelfth article of amendment.

Section 2
[POWER TO ENFORCE THIS ARTICLE]
The Congress shall have power to enforce this article by appropriate legislation.

AMENDMENT XXIV

[Proposed by Congress on August 27, 1963; declared ratified on January 23, 1964.]

Section 1

[ANTI-POLL TAX]

The right of citizens of the United States to vote in any primary or other election for President or Vice-President, for electors for President or Vice-President, or for Senator or Representative in Congress, shall not be denied or abridged by the United States or any State by reason of failure to pay any poll tax or other tax.

Section 2

[POWER TO ENFORCE THIS ARTICLE]

The Congress shall have power to enforce this article by appropriate legislation.

AMENDMENT XXV

[Proposed by Congress on July 7, 1965; declared ratified on February 10, 1967.]

Section 1

[VICE-PRESIDENT TO BECOME PRESIDENT]

In case of the removal of the President from office or his death or resignation, the Vice-President shall become President.

Section 2

[CHOICE OF A NEW VICE-PRESIDENT]

Whenever there is a vacancy in the office of the Vice-President, the President shall nominate a Vice-President who shall take office upon confirmation by a majority vote of both houses of Congress.

Section 3

[PRESIDENT MAY DECLARE OWN DISABILITY]

Whenever the President transmits to the President pro tempore of the Senate and the Speaker of the House of Representatives his written declaration that he is unable to discharge the powers and duties of his office, and until he transmits to them a written declaration to the contrary, such powers and duties shall be discharged by the Vice-President as Acting President.

Section 4

[ALTERNATE PROCEDURES TO DECLARE AND TO END
PRESIDENTIAL DISABILITY]

Whenever the Vice-President and a majority of either the principal officers of the executive departments or of such other body as Congress may
by law provide, transmit to the President pro tempore of the Senate
and the Speaker of the House of Representatives their written declaration
that the President is unable to discharge the powers and duties of his
office, the Vice-President shall immediately assume the powers and duties
of the office as Acting President.

Thereafter, when the President transmits to the President pro tempore
of the Senate and the Speaker of the House of Representatives his written
declaration that no inability exists, he shall resume the powers and duties
of his office unless the Vice-President and a majority of either the principal officers of the executive department or of such other body as Congress
may by law provide, transmit within four days to the President pro tempore of the Senate and the Speaker of the House of Representatives their
written declaration that the President is unable to discharge the powers
and duties of his office. Thereupon Congress shall decide the issue, assem-
bling within 48 hours for that purpose if not in session. If the Congress,
within 21 days after receipt of the latter written declaration, or, if Congress is not in session, within 21 days after Congress is required to assemble, determines by two-thirds vote of both houses that the President is
unable to discharge the powers and duties of his office, the Vice-President
shall continue to discharge the same as Acting President; otherwise, the
President shall resume the powers and duties of his office.

Amendment XXVI

[Proposed by Congress on March 23, 1971; declared ratified on June 30, 1971.]

Section 1

[EIGHTEEN-YEAR-OLD SUFFRAGE]

The right of citizens of the United States, who are eighteen years of age
or older, to vote shall not be denied or abridged by the United States or by
any State on account of age.

Section 2

[POWER TO ENFORCE THIS ARTICLE]

The Congress shall have power to enforce this article by appropriate legislation.

AMENDMENT XXVII

[Proposed by Congress on September 25, 1789; declared ratified on May 7, 1992.]

[LIMITING CONGRESSIONAL PAY CHANGES]

No law varying the compensation for the services of the Senators and Representatives shall take effect until an election of Representatives shall have intervened.

Acknowledgments

Greg Abbott: "Restoring the Rule of Law with States Leading the Way," by Governor Greg Abbott. Office of the Governor Press Release, January 8, 2016. Reprinted by permission of the Office of the Governor, State of Texas.

Christopher Achen and Larry Bartels: Excerpts from "Democratic Ideals and Realities," *Democracy for Realists: Why Elections Do Not Produce Responsive Government*. Copyright © 2016 by Princeton University Press. Reprinted by permission of Princeton University Press.

Douglas J. Ahler and Gaurav Sood: "The Parties in Our Heads: Misperceptions about Party Composition and Their Consequences," *The Journal of Politics*, Vol. 80, No. 3 (April 2018). Copyright © 2018 by the Southern Political Science Association. Reprinted by permission of the University of Chicago Press.

Ronald Bailey: "Globalization Is Good for You," *Reason Magazine* and Reason.com, June 2015. Reprinted by permission of the Reason Foundation.

Ronald Bailey, Damon Root, Nick Gillespie, Elizabeth Nolan Brown, and Scott Shackford: "America Wasn't Ready for Coronavirus," by Ronald Bailey, Damon Root, Eric Boehm, Nick Gillespie, Elizabeth Nolan Brown, and Scott Shackford. *Reason Magazine*, June 2020. Reprinted by permission of the Reason Foundation and Reason Magazine.

Bob Bauer and Jack Goldsmith: Excerpt from Chapter 1, "Reconstructing the Presidency," *After Trump: Reconstructing the Presidency* (Washington, DC: Lawfare Press, 2020), pp. 1–6. Reprinted by permission.

Kathleen Bawn, Martin Cohen, David Karol, Seth Masket, Hans Noel, and John Zaller: "A Theory of Political Parties: Groups, Policy Demands, and Nominations in American Politics," *Perspectives on Politics*, Vol. 10, No. 3 (September 2012). Copyright © 2012 American Political Science Association. Reprinted with the permission of Cambridge University Press.

Charles A. Beard: From *An Economic Interpretation of the Constitution of the United States* by Charles A. Beard. Copyright © 1913 and 1935 by Macmillan Publishing Co. Copyright renewed © 1941 by Charles A. Beard. Copyright renewed © 1963 by William Beard and Miriam B. Vagts. Reprinted with the permission of Free Press, a division of Simon & Schuster, Inc. All rights reserved.

Susan J. Brison: "Free Speech Skepticism," *Kennedy Institute of Ethics Journal*, Vol. 31, No. 2 (2021), pp. 101–32. Copyright © 2021 Johns Hopkins University Press. Reprinted with permission of Johns Hopkins University Press.

Jeffrey R. Brown and Mark Duggan: "The Time Is Now for Action on Social Security," *The Hill*, May 29, 2021. Reprinted by permission of Featurewell.

Ronald Brownstein: "The Most Complete Picture Yet of America's Changing Electorate," *The Atlantic*, July 1, 2021. Courtesy of Atlantic Media.

Rick Hills: "Will Federalism (and Conflicts of Law Doctrine) Deregulate Abortion?" by Rick Hills. Originally published on PrawfsBlawg, December 5, 2021. Reprinted by permission of the author.

Jonathan Holloway: "To Unite a Divided America, Make People Work for It," *The New York Times*, July 2, 2021. From The New York Times. Copyright © 2021 The New York Times Company. All rights reserved. Used under license. www .nytimes.com.

Rebecca Ingber: "Bureaucratic Resistance and the Deep State Myth," by Rebecca Ingber. *Just Security*, October 18, 2019. Reprinted by permission.

Jihii Jolly: "How Algorithms Decide the News You See." This article by Jihii Jolly originally appeared online in the *Columbia Journalism Review*, May 20, 2014, as part of a series on News Literacy. Reprinted by permission of the author.

Sarah Jones: "'Socialism' Isn't a Dirty Word Anymore." Originally published by *Intelligencer*, June 25, 2021. https://nymag.com/intelligencer/2021/06/socialism -isnt-a-dirty-word-anymore.html. Copyright © Vox Media, LLC. Reprinted with permission.

Mark Jurkowitz, Amy Mitchell, Elisa Shearer, and Mason Walker: Excerpts from "U.S. Media Polarization and the 2020 Election: A Nation Divided," Pew Research Center, Washington, DC (January 24, 2020). https://www.pewresearch.org /journalism/2020/01/24/u-s-media-polarization-and-the-2020-election-a-nation -divided/.

Michael Kammen: "Introduction" from *The Origins of the American Constitution: A Documentary History*, edited by Michael Kammen. Copyright © 1986 by Michael Kammen. Used by permission of Viking Books, an imprint of Penguin Publishing Group, a division of Penguin Random House LLC. All rights reserved.

V. O. Key, Jr.: "The Voice of the People: An Echo," from *The Responsible Electorate: Rationality in Presidential Voting, 1936–1960* by V. O. Key, Jr., with the assistance of Milton C. Cummings, Jr. (Cambridge, Mass.: The Belknap Press of Harvard University Press). Copyright © 1966 by the President and Fellows of Harvard College. Used by permission. All rights reserved.

John Kincaid and J. Wesley Leckrone: "Partisan Fractures in U.S. Federalism's COVID-19 Policy Responses," *State and Local Government Review*, Vol. 52, No. 4 (December 2020): pp. 298–308. https://doi.org/10.1177/0160323X20986842. Copyright © 2021 The Authors. Reprinted by permission of SAGE Publications, Inc.

Jennifer L. Lawless and Richard L. Fox: Excerpts from "Girls Just Wanna Not Run: The Gender Gap in Young Americans' Political Ambition," Jennifer L. Lawless and Richard L. Fox., American University, Women & Politics Institute. Reprinted by permission.

Frances E. Lee and James M. Curry: "What's Really Holding the Democrats Back: It's Not the Filibuster," *The Atlantic*, April 23, 2021. Courtesy of Atlantic Media.

Sanford Levinson: Chapter 1, "The Ratification Referendum," from *Our Undemocratic Constitution: Where the Constitution Goes Wrong (And How We the People Can Correct It)* by Sanford Levinson, pp. 11–24. Copyright © 2006 by Oxford University Press, Inc. Reprinted with permission of Oxford University Press.

Scott Lincicome: "The 'Endless Frontier' and American Industrial Policy." First published in *The Dispatch*, May 26, 2021. Reprinted by permission of the author.

Christina Villegas: "Electing the People's President: The Popular Origins of the Electoral College," *Perspectives on Political Science*, Vol. 47, No. 4 (2018), pp. 201–9. DOI: 10.1080/10457097.2016.1254492. Reprinted by permission of Taylor & Francis Ltd. http://www.tandfonline.com.

David Von Drehle: "The Religious Freedom Bomb May Be About to Detonate," *The Washington Post*, June 18, 2021. From The Washington Post. Copyright © 2021 The Washington Post. All rights reserved. Used under license. www.washingtonpost .com.

Travis Waldron: "A Radical Right-Wing Dream to Rewrite the Constitution Is Close to Coming True," *HuffPost*, April 27, 2021. From HuffPost. Copyright © 2021 BuzzFeed. All rights reserved. Used under license. www.huffpost.com.

Darrell M. West: "It's Time to Abolish the Electoral College," by Darrell M. West. Brookings Policy 2020, October 15, 2019. Reprinted by permission.

James Q. Wilson: Excerpts from *Bureaucracy: What Government Agencies Do and Why They Do It*. Copyright © 1989 James Q. Wilson. Reprinted by permission of Hachette Books Group.